The Age of Civil War and Reconstruction, 1830–1900
A Book of Interpretative Essays

THE DORSEY SERIES IN HISTORY
Editor GENE A. BRUCKER
University of California at Berkeley

The Age of Civil War and Reconstruction, 1830-1900

A Book of Interpretative Essays

Edited, with Introductions and
Bibliographical Essays by
CHARLES CROWE
University of Georgia

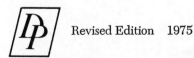 Revised Edition   1975

The Dorsey Press   *Homewood, Illinois   60430*
Irwin-Dorsey International   London, England   WC2H 9NJ
Irwin-Dorsey Limited   Georgetown, Ontario   L7G 4B3

Revised Edition

First Printing, February 1975

ISBN 0-256-01528-7
Library of Congress Catalog Card No. 74–18711

Printed in the United States of America

To Joyce, Lisa, and Thad

Preface

THE REMOTENESS of textbooks from contemporary scholarship and their failure to present history as a complex, evolving discipline, rich in intellectual demands and rewards, suggest very strongly the need for specific teaching remedies. As early as the 1930s scholars who recognized these difficulties began to publish "problem" and "crisis" anthologies. Unfortunately and perhaps unavoidably the anthology editors, with an air of total impartiality, often assumed the existence of an impossible freedom from value judgments and limited the utility of their books by reducing the most complex historical situations to simple "either/or" categories. While the discipline could not exist without explanations, they need not be slogan-like formulas and implausibly over-simplified categories which obscure or falsify the richness of collective human experiences of the past. Nor does the need for the scholar to follow the standard rules on evidence, and to be on guard against some of the more arbitrary moralizations and subjective statements, invalidate the fact that history is always written by individuals from within a particular cultural context. The historian, who is himself in history, views the past from a constantly moving vantage point. From time to time old lines of inquiry become irrelevant, conventional solutions fade into implausibility, and modern sensibilities interacting with changing events reveal new patterns of research and bring to the foreground insights unavailable to earlier generations. It is also possible that the discipline itself progresses as scholars find new approaches and better uses for old ones.

I wish to make available to students the best scholarship of present times in a way that will reveal the most probable conclusions as well as the plastic context from which they emerge. It seems self-defeating for those who wish to depart from the narrow vistas of the textbook world to assign students, without adequate explanation and as if the scholarship of the various generations existed on the same plane of meaning, the more precise, relevant, and thoughtful work of leading contemporary scholars side by side with essays by James Ford Rhodes, William A. Dunning, and Ulrich B. Phillips from the high era of racism and imperalism of fifty years ago. Such a procedure is unhistorical; just as it misses the point that the historian is in history, so it fails to grasp the fact that historical writing becomes in time a part of intellectual history. The scholar who assumes a democracy of authorities and sources tells us something about his mind and culture, but he does not provide a valid scholarly technique. Will anyone argue that Phillips' book of 1918 on slavery, immersed as it was in conceptions we know to be false and assumptions we can no longer accept, is somehow "equal" in authority during the 1970s to the best of modern scholarship?

Undoubtedly historians of our times fall into transgressions which future generations will be quick to pounce upon. Such a statement can be taken for granted in a discipline which seems to be moving toward a greater awareness of complexity, paradox, ambiguity, and irony. Fully aware of the probability of our own errors, we look back across the past half a century with a certain wryness at all the banners of "scientific" history waving from the fortresses of doubtful, false, and malicious values, assumptions, double standards of judgment, sympathies, hostilities, and interpretative myths. Yet it would be unwise to dismiss all explanations as "myths," and the man who insists that all explanations are equal simply ceases to function as a historian. That history bears some resemblance to philosophy, where questions can disappear before they are dismissed and conclusions be abandoned before they are disproved, we can readily admit without surrendering the historical quest. A consciousness of these conditions may both improve the discipline and enable the historian to bury his own dead past. To suggest today as a topic for scholarly inquiry, whether or not slavery was a totally benevolent institution, would be an implausible notion, a bogus act of inquiry. Thus, we might try to abandon implausible inquiries and to seek plausible ones.

Yet the question has been greatly complicated by the frequent display in historical works of "American values," by the scholarship forged in ideological rebellion, and by the general fact of differing motives and intentions, values and perceptions, and all the various ideological, cultural, social, economic, political, personal and professional lenses through which historians view the world. For example, just when the pervasive malignancy of slavery seemed one of the most foregone of conclusions, Robert W. Fogel and Stanley L. Engerman (*Time on the Cross*, 1974), in the name of presumably liberal intentions and with the most avant-garde quantitative methods, revived some of the hoariest conclusions of the proslavery argument by insisting that the material conditions of bondage were vastly better than nearly all other scholars had supposed. Naturally, conservative historians found the least to be troubled about in *Time on the Cross* while liberal, left-liberal and radical scholars expressed hostility roughly in proportion to the extent of ideological departure from the values actually sustained by Fogel and Engerman. Controversies in the 1970s over books such as *Time on the Cross* and Robert Manson Myers' editorial paean to the slavocracy in *Children of Pride* (1972) not only expressed the zeitgeist of an era enamored of the status quo but also pointed to the traditional function of much scholarship in the service of power as expressions of an enduringly conservative "national consensus."

My goal has been to briefly identify the major problems in historical interpretation, to present modern scholarship as it emerged from its own antecedents and precedents, and to provide key interpretative and explanatory essays from both senior and junior scholars on the grand issues of the age of Civil War and Reconstruction. Like many of my contemporaries I have been much impressed by a sense of *déjà vu*, by the interplay of present sensibilities and past events, and by the fundamental value judgments that all historians make. Few professors will agree with the choice of every single essay, but I hope that the collection in general will be useful to historians. In several areas of study such as racism the large number of superior monographs and articles made the dilemma of choice particularly difficult. On the other hand, much impressive scholarship has been done on Indians in recent years but little of it relates directly to the grand issues of Civil War and Reconstruction. Chapters 5, 10, and 11 contain fewer selections than I had planned because I could not obtain several reprint permissions. I regret very much the need to delete in this edition some fine essays by Thomas P. Govan, Ralph E. Morrow, Kenneth W. Porter, Cushing Strout, Thomas C. Cochran, John A. Carpenter, and others which graced the first edition.

I am indebted to my graduate students, and particularly to James B. Stewart, Thomas G. Dyer, Stephan Engerrand, Gaye Hewitt, Anderson Williams, Theda Perdue, Lewis N. Wynn, Lynn Tatum, Pat Brewer, and Clarence Mohr for many interesting and useful seminar sessions, reports and discussions on historiography. In earlier years I benefitted substantially from dialogues on the nature of the historical craft with Jack P. Greene of Johns-Hopkins University. As so often in the past my wife, Joyce Slocumb Crowe, put aside her splendid photography to give generously and intelligently long hours of editing and proofreading. Finally a brief note of thanks is in order to Lisa Crowe and Thad Crowe for being the autonomous and satisfying children who sustained rather than hampered their father's work.

January 1975   CHARLES CROWE

Contents

15. The Retreat from Reconstruction............................ 408

chapter 1

Explaining the South

EVEN BEFORE THE BIRTH of the nation in 1776 distinctive Southern economic and social interests gave rise to sectional conflict. The authors of the Declaration of Independence and the Constitution concentrated on the process of creating a new nation but not to the extent of abandoning sectional disputes. Regional hostilities affected the party battles of the Jeffersonian era and gave rise to so fiery a controversy over the admission of Missouri as a slave state in 1819 that Thomas Jefferson was reminded of "a fire bell in the night" tolling the death knell of the Union. If conflict slumbered for a decade, the abolitionists broke that sleep in the 1830s with an uncompromising campaign against "the peculiar institution" which stimulated both troubled intrasectional disputes and still more agonizing sectional conflicts. The great debate over newly acquired territories in the 1840s fed the springs of sectional hostility, which increased steadily until the outbreak of the Civil War in 1861. Not even Northern military victory and Confederate defeat destroyed the pattern of conflict, and at times during the postwar era Reconstruction yielded more bitter recriminations than the war itself. Sectional disputes, which receded after 1900 without ever completely disappearing, came to the center of the political stage during the civil rights controversies and black freedom struggles of the 1950s and 1960s.

Although antebellum opinion makers in the South tended to define sectional differences in terms of one or several aspects of racial slavery, several generations of postwar Dixie apologists preferred to speak of tariffs, states rights, the weather, "agrarianism," and "the Southern way of life." In 1928 Ulrich B. Phillips, a Georgian at Yale and one of the leading historians of his generation, dismissed all of these explanations as "central themes" in order to trace the touchstone of Southern identity to "the indomitable resolve" expressed in "the patrician's quietude" as well as "the frenzy of the demagogue" to preserve the region as "a white man's country." Despite the forcefulness of Phillips' analysis and the

1

substantial influence of so large a stream of widely read monographs and essays, his devotion to white supremacy values offended liberal scholars and his candor embarrassed genteel twentieth century Dixie apologists who preferred to dwell in a highly romanticized plantation world remote from "sordid" social realities.

After liberal orientations on race (some would say liberal versions of racism) came to dominance in the post-World War II era Phillips' works collected dust on the library shelves, but the task of attempting to explain the peculiarities of Southern history with one or several central themes continued. At the time of James W. Silver's courageous presentation to the Southern Historical Association in 1963 of his address on "Mississippi: The Closed Society" (Selection 1), recent murders of civil rights workers, pervasive political terrorism, church burnings, and the need to use 20,000 Federal troops to place the first black student in "Ole Miss," all made the South appear to many Americans as virtually a foreign country.

Yet the three dramatic years from 1965 to 1968 with their urban ghetto uprisings from New York to Los Angeles, their student rebellions in universities such as Columbia and Berkeley, and their wave of angry black protest against racism as a national affliction, suggested to many observers that the South might not be so different after all. As early as 1964 Howard Zinn, (Selection 2), a Northern white scholar teaching in a Southern black college, rejected "the Southern mystique" of "the mysterious and terrible South soaked in blood and history" and racial hatreds violent almost beyond Northern comprehension. The South was indeed "racist, violent, hypocritically pious, xenophobic, false in its elevations of women, nationalistic, conservative," and harbored "extreme poverty in the midst of ostentatious wealth," but "the United States as a civilization embodies all of these same qualities" and the South merely provided a mirror for the Republic which reflected national images more sharply and vividly.

Zinn's analysis did not persuade C. Vann Woodward, a Southern white scholar at Yale, and the author of notable essays on Southern identity and uniqueness. Woodward argued that Southerners as men and women baptized in social evil by slavery and shaped in the bitter historical experience of defeat and poverty might have something to say to other Americans whose outlook had been formed by affluence, the gospel of progress, and the comforting faith of presumably innocent and virtuous souls that every evil had a cure and every social problem a solution. The contrast between the romantic rhetoric of plantation apologists and the terrible realities of slavery, between secessionist visions of a golden age and the galling taste of Confederate defeat, provided an old set of ironic incongruities from which modern cold war America tempted toward antidemocratic directions at home and abroad in the name of democracy might well profit. By 1965 Woodward's contemplations on Southern uniqueness (Selection 3) had made him more conscious of the black experience and of the cutting edge of white racism but he still clung to the notion of the "exceptional" South and to the impossibility of breaking with the past as sharply as Howard Zinn proposed to do.

Another important interpretative work, David Bertelson's *The Lazy South* (Selection 4), seemed on the surface to be far from the conflicting theories of Woodward and Zinn and from the spirit of the racially torn 1960s. Nevertheless Bertelson's analysis had its grim aspects and still another version of Southern uniqueness. Unlike both Woodward and Zinn, he brushed aside all past notions of anticapitalist agrarians to reveal a dominant elite with the attitudes of Manchester capitalists, economic egotists so devoted to the single-minded pursuit of private gain as to leave the region naked of the sense of community which could have given meaning and social context to both work and leisure. Reversing the usual analogy, Bertelson contrasted a disorganized, dispersed and fragmented Southern society with the North (especially New England and Quaker Pennsylvania) which had the social responsibility and concern for communal needs most nearly resembling the traditional European society of civilized order and community consciousness. Bertelson made his point forcefully but a substantial number of observers in the mid 1970s could still believe that Howard Zinn had provided the best key to understanding the South as a mirror to the nation which reflected in exaggerated fashion national characteristics.

BIBLIOGRAPHY

Works Discussed in This Chapter

Bertelson, David, *The Lazy South* (1967).
Phillips, Ulrich B., "The Central Theme of Southern History," *American Historical Review* (1928).
Silver, James W., *Mississippi: The Closed Society* (1964).
Woodward, C. Vann, "Southern Mythology," *Commentary* (1965).
Zinn, Howard, *The Southern Mystique* (1964).

Suggested Readings

For *general works* see the useful brief volume edited by Monroe L. Billington on *The South: A Central Theme?* (1968). While many scholars will reject some aspects of C. Vann Woodward's work, no other historian of the South since Ulrich B. Phillips has been so influential. For this chapter see especially *The Burden of Southern History* (1960, enlarged edition 1968) and *American Counterpoint: Slavery and Racism in the North-South Dialogue* (1971). For the eloquent conception of quite a different South (dismissed by Woodward as "the hillbilly South") which has influenced many scholars despite a number of racist opinions and passages, see W. J. Cash, *The Mind of the South* (1940). For some interesting cultural fantasies and some characteristic racist assertions of the 1930s by the Nashville Agrarians read Donald Davidson, et al., *I'll Take My Stand* (1930).

Among *black perspectives* some observers with particularly rewarding perceptions are Carl Rowan who drew national attention to Southern caste with *South of Freedom* (1952), the brilliant novelist Ralph Ellison, *The Invisible Man* (1947), and the Southern black novelist John O. Killens whose several novels evoke a white violence difficult for conservative Southern whites to come to terms with. For sensitive portraits of both blacks and whites in the South see psychologist Robert Coles' *Children of Crisis* (1968). For some curious speculations about the antebellum South by a black historian see Earl E. Thorpe, *The Old South: A Psychohistory* (1972).

For the *perspectives of civil rights rebels* read Howard Zinn, *SNCC: The New Abolitionists* (1964) and Louis Lomax, *The Negro Revolt* (1962). Black Power rhetoric tended to address itself to the nation generally, but see Stokely Carmichael, "What We Want," *New York Review of Books* (Sept. 22, 1966) and Floyd Barbour, ed., *The Black Power Revolt* (1968). Valuable perceptions on the South can be gained from books by participants such as James Peck (Northern white), Sally Belfrage (Northern white) and Anne Moody (Southern black).

Among *white perspectives* the work of Willie Morris, an editor with a Mississippi background, is interesting on sectional and racial sensibilities. See his anthology *The South Today* (1965) and his autobiographical writings. For the efforts of an accomplished journalist to pick up the pieces after a decade of white debacles see Pat Watters, *The South and the Nation* (1969). For insights about Southern white writers see F. Gavin Davenport, Jr., *The Myth of Southern History: Historical Consciousness in Twentieth Century Southern Literature* (1970).

For *definitions of the South* see journalist Harry S. Ashmore's *Epitaph for Dixie* (1958). Ashmore thought that with the decline of the segregation and rural life which defined the South regional distinctiveness would die. Thomas P. Govan, "Agrarian and Agrarianism: A Study in the Use and Abuse of Words," *Journal of Southern History* (1964) demonstrated persuasively ways in which the term "agrarian" had been often used in contradictory fashion in conventional explanations about the South. David M. Potter defined the South as a "folk culture" with "a more direct and primal relation of people to land" in "The Enigma of the South," *Yale Review* (1961) and in *The South and the Sectional Image* (1968). For a thoroughly improbable and inappropriate explanation, see Sheldon Hackney, "The South as a Counter-Culture," *American Scholar* (1971). David L. Smiley provided a limited summary of "the central theme" since Phillips in "The Quest for a Central Theme in Southern History," *South Atlantic Quarterly* (1972). Dewey Grantham offered an interesting but not entirely persuasive explanation in *The Democratic South* (1963). Thomas P. Govan gave a general summary of the debate on Southern uniqueness in "Was the Old South Different?" *Journal of Southern History* (1955); Carl N. Degler discussed the same question in "There Was Another South," in *American Heritage* (1960); and David M. Potter a few years later in "On Understanding the South," *Journal of Southern History* (1964). Much discussion on the uniqueness of the South has sprung from accounts of modern Southern literature.

For *definitions from literature, sociology and religion* see Louis Rubin, "The South and the Faraway Country," *Virginia Quarterly Review* (1962) and Cleanth Brooks, "Regionalism in American Literature," *Journal of Southern History* (1960). On sociological definitions see Rupert B. Vance, "The Sociological Implications of Southern Regionalism," *Journal of Southern History* (1960). For a general discussion of all aspects of the question see George B. Tindall, "The Status and Future of Regionalism—A Symposium," *Journal of Southern History* (1960). On the point of religious distinctiveness in the modern South see Kenneth Bailey, *Southern White Protestantism in the Twentieth Century* (1964). The modern South was analyzed by Thomas D. Clark in *The Emerging South* (1961) and Robert B. Highsaw (ed.), *The Deep South in Transformation* (1964). A distinctively oppressive South emerged from the study of the sociologist John Dollard on *Caste and Class in a Southern Town* (1937).

On the early South one scholar argued cogently that the South as a distinctive region dates back to the 1770s. See John R. Alden, *The First South* (1961) and for the argument that this "first South" was not characterized by declining slavery and Jeffersonian liberals, see Robert McColley, *Slavery and Jeffersonian Virginia* (1964). E. James Ferguson traced some economic origins of sectionalism in "Public Finance and the Origins of Southern Sectionalism," *Journal of Southern History* (1962). Margaret K. Latimer argued that the flush of "nationalism" that hit South Carolina was based on a cotton boom in "South Carolina, a Protagonist of the War of 1812," *American Historical Review* (1956).

For a *Marxist view* of "the central theme" see Herbert Aptheker, *Toward Negro Freedom* (1956). On the exaggerations and confusions of *agrarianism*, see Anne Ward Amacher, "Myths and Consequences: Calhoun and Some Nashville Agrarians," *South Atlantic Quarterly* (1960); Edward M. Moore, "The Agrarians of the 1930's," *Sewanee Review* (1963); and I. A. Newby, "The Southern Agrarians: A View After Thirty Years," *Agricultural History* (1963).

On *class differences* among Southern whites as affected by slavery see Wilbert E. Moore, "Slave Law and the Social Structure," *Journal of Negro History* (1941); Wilbert E. Moore and Robin W. Williams, "Stratification in the Ante-Bellum South," *American Sociological Review* (1942); Rudolf Heberle, "The Changing Social Stratification of the South," *Social Forces* (1959); Nancy C. Roberson, "Social Mobility in Ante-Bellum Alabama," *Alabama Review* (1960); and George R. Woolfolk, "Taxes and Slavery in the Ante-Bellum South," *Journal of Southern History* (1960).

Among *other definitions of the South* Frank E. Vandiver analyzed the more absurd popular myths about the Confederacy in "The Confederate Myth," *Southern Review* (1961) and "The Confederacy and the American Tradition," *Journal of Southern History* (1962). See also Vandiver's discussion of Southern "extremism" in *The Idea of the South* (1964). George B. Tindall wrote an interesting account of myths in "The Benighted South: Origins of a Modern Image," *Virginia Quarterly Review* (1964), but one fears that all "reality" has been dissolved in "myth" and that all "myths" are created equal. Also stimulating is Burl Noggle, "Variety and Ambiguity: The Recent Approach to Southern History," *Mississippi Quarterly* (1963–64). Still the scholar who surrenders completely to "Variety and Ambiguity" may cease to function. Wilma Dykeman once again followed the central theme of Southern history to race in "The Southern Demagogue," *Virginia Quarterly Review* (1957). Dewey Grantham provided a resume of the debate to 1964 in "Interpreters of the Modern South," *South Atlantic Quarterly* (1964).

For recent trends in *Southern and Negro history* see Charles Crowe, "Historians and 'Benign Neglect': Conservative Trends in Southern History and Black Studies," *Reviews in American History* (1974).

Mississippi: A Closed Society from the 1850s to the 1960s*

James W. Silver

The striking parallel between people and events of the 1850s and the 1950s reminds us that Mississippi has been on the defensive against inevitable social change for more than a century, and that for some years before the Civil War it had developed a closed society with an orthodoxy accepted by nearly everybody in the state. The all-pervading doctrine then and now has been white supremacy—whether achieved through slavery or segregation—rationalized by a professed adherence to state rights and bolstered by religious fundamentalism. In such a society a never ceasing propagation of the "true faith" must and has gone on relentlessly with a constantly reiterated demand for loyalty to the united front demanding that nonconformists be hushed, silenced with a vengeance, or in crisis situations driven from the community. Violence and the threat of violence have reinforced the presumption of unanimity.

By 1861 Mississippians had been thoroughly prepared for secession by their short-sighted politicians, their chauvinistic press, their political preachers, and their blind philosophers, all operating within the authoritarian society. Even to the present generation the people have been paying for and *eulogizing* their most unwise decision of all time. In fact the romanticism associated with the Old South, the glorification of the Confederacy, and the bitter remembrances of Reconstruction have played their witless and powerful role in preserving a social order based on neither fact nor reason. According to Citizens Council literature, Mississippi is now the innocent victim of a second vicious Reconstruction from which its stalwart citizenry, demonstrating ancestral courage, will emerge triumphant as it did in 1875.

One of today's little sophistries asserts that equality must be earned, can never be achieved by force or law. The forgotten truth is that between 1875 and 1890 *inequality* was effected by force and regularized by law. By the end of the century Negroes had long since learned that Mississippi freedom included neither political nor any other kind of equality. The caste system had once and apparently for all [time] been substituted for slavery, the Negro was in his place, and the society was once more closed and sacrosanct. . . .

No meaningful challenge to the caste system was possible in Missis-

* James W. Silver, "Mississippi: The Closed Society," *Journal of Southern History* (1964). An expanded version of the presidential address delivered at the annual meeting of the Southern Historical Association at Asheville, North Carolina, November 7, 1963. Copyright 1963 by James W. Silver.

sippi in the first half of the twentieth century. In public life no white man, demagogue or patrician, proposed to do anything constructive about the Negro. Preferring corrupt and inefficient government to participation by the black man, the whites got a one-party system without competition between recognizable groups. . . . .

Today the totalitarian society of Mississippi imposes on all its people an obedience to an official orthodoxy almost identical with the proslavery philosophy—this in the teeth of the nearly universal dissipation of whatever intellectual sanction white supremacy had among the enlightened at the turn of this century. Every Mississippi politician not only denies the validity of the Fourteenth Amendment but in his heart hungers for the negative days of the Articles of Confederation. Governor Ross Barnett, whose personal constitution stops with the Tenth Amendment, is conveniently ignorant of the incompatibility of state rights and modern industrialization. . . .

The state retains a good deal of the frontier recklessness toward human life found by William Howard Russell who noted that casual Mississippi conversations had "a smack of manslaughter about them." In the year after the Brown decision, four Negroes were openly slain, with no conviction for any crime; it would almost seem that when these atrocities had served their purpose, murder as an instrument of policy was then put in cold storage for a time.

On March 31, 1963, the Voter Education Project of the Southern Regional Council released a chronological list of 64 acts of violence and intimidation against Negroes since January 1961. The 30-page indictment of man's inhumanity to man, with its accusations of whippings, shootings, murder, and outrageous debasement of the courts, admittedly came from an interested party, but it is characterized by understatement. . . .

The Mississippi Advisory Committee to the United States Commission on Civil Rights made, in January 1963, a report on the administration of justice within the state. In a period of 14 months it had held six open meetings in which a hundred or so Mississippians had testified, though "actively opposed by agents and instrumentalities of the State Government." The legislature in 1960 "passed an act," the committee stated, "to intimidate persons who might wish to assert their rights as citizens by altering the requirement of proof for prosecution of perjury solely in cases where the defendant has testified before this Committee."

In its published findings, the committee declared that

> in all important areas of citizenship, a Negro in Mississippi receives substantially less than his due consideration as an American and as a Mississippian. . . . [They found that] a pattern exists in our State that leads to the denial of Constitutional rights and, in some instances, to brutality and terror. From the moment a Negro adult is hailed as 'boy' or 'girl' by a police officer, through his arrest, detention, trial—during which his Negro lawyer is treated with contemptuous familiarity by the judge and other officers of the court—and eventual imprisonment, he is treated with a pernicious difference. This difference is incompatible with Christian ideals about the dignity of man and with principles of Anglo-Saxon criminal law.

[Declaring that]. . . .

> justice under law is not guaranteed for the Negro in Mississippi in the way that it is for the white man . . . [the committee reported that] 42.3% of the citizens of this State must either accept an inferior station in life and an attitude of servility or endanger themselves and their families by protesting. We find that terror hangs over the Negro in Mississippi and is an expectancy for those who refuse to accept their color as a badge of inferiority; and terrorism has no proper place in the American form of government. . . . [The committee found that] in general the press is failing to meet its obligation to our society. The people of Mississippi are largely unaware of the extent of illegal official violence and the press is partly to blame. . . . When a State disregards a large segment of its population, the Federal Government is compelled to intervene in behalf of the victims.

Although there have been moments of enlightenment, the spiritual secession of Mississippi from history has never ended. For more than a century Mississippians have refused to be bound by the national will. Perhaps this recalcitrance could be borne with in the past, as have been many other excesses of democracy. But with the sanctuary provided by the oceans gone, the national interest, the instinct for survival, demand discipline. They demand also that attitudes or "principles" growing out of racial situations not be allowed to intrude themselves into the country's policy making decisions. Since Reconstruction Mississippians have had no real reason to believe that they were not free to handle the race question as they wished, without meaningful interference from the federal government; and, when they now discover that all their bluster and subterfuge and intransigence will avail them nothing, they have little to fall back on except blind rage and fierce hatred.

In committing itself to the defense of the biracial system, Mississippi has erected a totalitarian society. . . . For the foreseeable future the people of Mississippi will plod along the troubled road of resistance, violence, anguish, and injustice, moving slowly until engulfed in the predictable cataclysm.

And yet, in spite of all that has been presented in this paper, it seems inescapable that Mississippians one day will drop the mockery of the late Confederacy and resume their obligations as Americans. It is just that there is small reason to believe that they will somehow develop the capability to do it themselves, to do it, as William Faulkner said, in time. If not, the closed society will become the open society with the massive aid of the country as a whole, backed by the power and authority of the federal government. . . .

Dissolving the Southern Mystique*

Howard Zinn

. . . Because the South embarrasses us, we try to disown it, apologize for it, hold it at a distance, pretend it is an abnormal growth on the national body. Once, however, we face the truth—that the South crystallizes the defects of the nation—there may be some value in the acknowledgment. In this part, I shall examine a number of these traits alleged to be peculiarly Southern. Then I shall suggest how candid self-recognition by the nation can be an occasion not for shame, but for insight, and how the South, miserable and rejected, may yet turn out to be the savior of the American dream.

We start, of course, with racism. The ugliest bastions of racist thought and action are in the South: that is undisputed. But when the white Southerner tries to lighten the burden of his guilt by pointing to prejudice and discrimination in the North, the equalitarians, while continuing to denounce the South, become uneasy, for they know how much truth is in the accusation. Although the symptoms show mostly in the South, the entire mind and body of the American nation are afflicted. And it may be important, exactly at this moment in our history, when the South is going through the early stages of a kind of shock therapy, for the rest of the nation to understand that it stands by not as an administering doctor but as the next patient in line. The South turned out to be a convenient place—a kind of Fort Knox of prejudice—where the nation has always stored the bulk of its bigotry, while the rest has circulated—though sometimes stealthily—all over the country.

Slavery, because of favorable agricultural conditions, was concentrated in the American South, but it existed everywhere in the American colonies for over a hundred years. . . . New York law in the eighteenth century provided that any slave caught traveling 40 miles above Albany would be executed upon the oath of two credible witnesses. In 1712, a slave uprising took place in New York, when a group of armed Negro slaves killed nine white men. Awaiting capture by the militia, four cut their own throats and one shot his wife and then himself. Twenty-one were executed. A woman was hanged; one man was broken on the wheel and quartered; some were burned to death.

New York again became the scene of race terror in 1741 when a series of fires led to wild rumors of insurrection and to a hysterical trial. . . . Eighteen Negroes were hanged. Thirteen other Negroes were burned alive. One account reads: "At the rate of two every week, one hanged,

---

* Reprinted by permission of Alfred A. Knopf, Inc. from *The Southern Mystique* by Howard Zinn. Copyright, 1959, 1960, 1963, 1964 by Howard Zinn.

and one burned alive, the victims were executed amid prayers, impreca-
tions, and shrieks of agony."

New Jersey, 24 years after the Declaration of Independence, had 1,000
slaves; in 1741 the state burned two Negroes at the stake for setting fire
to seven barns in Hackensack. Pennsylvania, the Quaker State, famed
for its tolerance of Negroes, had 3,700 slaves in 1790. Negroes were
tried by special courts in that state, and were not allowed to assemble
in groups of more than four.

In New England, the source of so much abolitionist agitation, slavery
was well-established in the first generation of colonization. Those celebrating the heritage of Puritan New England speak fondly of the "Body
of Liberties" adopted in Massachusetts in 1641. This prohibited slavery
"unless it be lawful captives taken in just wars, and such strangers as
willingly sell themselves or are sold to us." In other words, the enslavement of people was obnoxious—except through war or commerce. It is
as clear an example of Puritan hypocrisy as we have, and a striking
example of the emptiness of Northern moralizing.

When Southerners, stung by Northern posturing, retorted that their
slaves had been brought to them by Yankee traders, they were telling the
truth. It was an accident of geography and economics, rather than a different attitude of mind or a different capacity to tolerate evil, that kept
the number of slaves relatively low in the North. It was the immediate
situation—particularly the spur of profit—rather than any persistent
difference in regional history or psychology, that determined the extent
of enslavement.

The state-by-state abolition of slavery in the North after the Revolution did not signify the abolition of racism; it merely ended one special
form of it. For the key factor which ended slavery in the North was not
a significant breaking down of racial attitudes, but a set of circumstances
which made slavery unprofitable and inconvenient. That these circumstances were heightened by some of the ideological ferment of the Declaration of Independence and the Revolution I would not deny, but ideology played, I believe, only a marginal role. Certainly, moral considerations
may tip the scales of social decision, but their weight is usually so slight
that they can do this only when the scales are already closely balanced
by harder considerations of self-interest. Specifically, it was in the interest of winning the war that the Continental Army enlisted 5,000 Negroes,
promising freedom to many after victory over England.

Differences existed between the sections. Abolitionists could not operate at all in the South after the 1830s. In the North they could speak and
print—but at the risk of their lives. Garrison was mobbed in Boston,
Phillips was stoned throughout the North, and Lovejoy was murdered in
Illinois. . . .

[Thus, the differences between the sections are differences of degrees
whether they relate to violence, racism, or fundamentalism.] There is
more Baptist emotionalism in the preaching that goes on in the South,
more religious revivalism, more faith healing, more Bible quoting, more
downright religious hypocrisy. But this is only an intense form of what
has gone on for so long in the whole nation; in the North it has managed

to duck below the level of absurdity just often enough to steer the chuckles and jibes of the rationalists toward the harassed South. . . .

Xenophobia is widespread in the South, as anyone who moves into the region, or travels through it, soon recognizes. It is one of the curious paradoxes of Southern life that suspicion of strangers, of outsiders, goes along with what is called "Southern hospitality." The answer to the paradox is that there is a line of demarcation which separates the accepted person from the unaccepted. Within that line, the warmth is almost overwhelming. But outside it, the coolness can become hostility to the point of violence. The foreign-born is almost always outside that line in the South, as is, of course, the Negro. So Southern hospitality exists, but within rigidly defined limits.

But isn't this true, though to a lesser extent, of the nation? Americans are considered generally to be warm and friendly people, unlike, let us say, the English. If other peoples criticize us, it is rather for being overbearingly friendly rather than withdrawn. We welcomed, let us recall, tens of millions of people from other countries to our shores, with virtually no restriction, for most of our history. But we too laid down our lines, and once laid down, those outside them were treated as coldly, as suspiciously, as any Yankee traveler in the Southern hills.

We began in 1882, with the Chinese, whom we had eagerly sought right after the Civil War as cheap labor to work on the railroads and in the mines, but who later were wanted neither by the industrialists nor the labor unions. The result was the Chinese Exclusion Act of that year. That inaugurated a period of 70 years during which we said very plainly to Asians, in the stiff words of a legislative enactment, that we wanted none of their kind in this country. Our national attitude toward Orientals was one reason for increasing irritation in our relations with Japan all through the early twentieth century up to Pearl Harbor. And our policy toward the immigration of Orientals today, as expressed in the McCarran-Walter Act of 1952, is hardly more friendly: we will admit a hundred Japanese a year, a hundred Chinese, a hundred Indonesians, as compared to tens of thousands for each major country in Western Europe. The message reads clearly to them: in the United States Asians are not wanted.

Our quotas are higher for Europeans, but still there are quotas. Nativism as a private action goes back to the early nineteenth-century resentment of the Irish immigrant; as a public policy it was first written into the law in the 1920s, and it remains on our national statute books in the quota system of the McCarran-Walter Act. The line remains drawn against most foreigners, though the placement of the line varies, depending on where the stranger comes from. Hospitality—in the law—goes first to the English, Irish, and Germans. The Italians, Greeks, and Eastern Europeans are definitely secondhand recipients of welcome. Africans and Asians are last. . . .

. . . A 1950 study by Hyman and Sheatsley concluded:

> The majority of Americans appear to deny still another traditional feature of democracy, that of offering political asylum and refuge to home-

less and oppressed peoples. Faced with the simple proposition of whether or not to admit a certain number of displaced persons from Europe, less than one person in four approved.

The same study found that most Americans who were given a list of seventeen nationalities found only five of these "as good as we are in all important respects." These were: the Canadians, English, Dutch, Scandinavians, and Irish. The rest were judged "not quite as good" or "definitely inferior."

Nativism not only keeps people out: it affects our relationship with those who have come in. And from the Alien Acts of 1798 to the Alien Registration Act of 1940 and the McCarran-Walter Act of 1952, our national policy has been to look with suspicion on the non-citizen.

Aliens must register every year with the government. An alien, in American judicial doctrine, is not entitled to the same constitutional rights accorded a citizen. An alien, for instance, can be deported for an act which has been made a crime ex post facto, though the Constitution bars ex post facto laws to punish Americans. Because aliens are tied in with foreign policy, an area where the national government has almost unlimited powers, Congress has broad legislative authority over them to an extent not true of citizens.

Even a person who has already become a citizen through naturalization is not looked upon by our government as an equal with all other United States citizens. According to the McCarran-Walter Act of 1952, if a naturalized citizen is convicted of contempt of Congress for refusing, within ten years of his naturalization, to testify before a congressional committee on his "subversive" activities, he may be deported. In other words, the Fifth Amendment provision against self-incrimination, and the First Amendment (which in some cases protects against political interrogation), cannot protect the naturalized citizen in any event, so long as the law remains what it is.

Until our national policies—on immigration, on aliens, on naturalization—are changed, until our national attitudes get closer to our oratorical claims, it ill becomes us to let the South bear the burden of the charge of nativism or xenophobia.

The deification of Southern womanhood, more a subject for bemused wonder than for intellectual analysis, has brought both admiration and ridicule. Cash calls it "downright gyneolatry." He says:

> She was the South's Palladium, this Southern woman—the shield-bearing Athena gleaming whitely in the clouds, the standard for its rallying, the mystic symbol of its nationality in face of the foe. She was the lily-pure maid of Astolat and the hunting goddess of the Boeotian hill. And—she was the pitiful Mother of God. Merely to mention her was to send strong men into tears—or shouts. There was hardly a sermon that did not begin and end with tributes in her honor, hardly a brave speech that did not open and close with the clashing of shields and the flourishing of swords for her glory. At the last, I verily believe, the ranks of the Confederacy went rolling into battle in the misty conviction that it was wholly for her that they fought. . . .

But now that we've paid obeisance to the tradition of glorification, we need to bring the analysis somewhat closer to the truth, both for the South and the nation. There were several crucial limitations to the Southern attitude. Remember, the phrase is really "Southern *white* womanhood." And *rich* white womanhood, too—for the poor white wife was hardly an object of worship in the South, then or now, bred in poverty, . . . [with] much of her time spent in labor bearing children, and the rest of her time in labor between childbirths, is a thousand times more numerous than Scarlett O'Hara.

And even the white aristocratic woman, back in slavery days—how genuine was the veneration, how deep the reverence, when the man of the house rushed as often as he could into sexual union with brown and black women? The existence of millions of tan and fair Negroes in America belies the image of the glorified Southern white woman. What more damning reminder is there of the emptiness of that claim that the white woman was the "center and circumference . . ." of affection than the fact that so often she waited at the periphery while her man was having sexual relations with a darker woman? The hurtful fact about the woman on the pedestal is that she is quite alone.

For the nation, as for the South, the fuss about womanhood has always been somewhat dishonest. The Southern veneration was circumscribed with modifications—whiteness, aristocratic birth, wealth, idleness; so was this true in the United States as a whole. In the country at large, to be considered superior a woman must have certain qualifications: beauty or talent, foremost. Brains alone, however, are not enough for a woman to gain genuine recognition. Mental agility, superior intelligence, bring tolerance and respect, but nothing like idolization; that is reserved for Venus or Diana, not for the lady Ph.D.

The difference in accent, North and South, the soft consonant and prolonged vowels of the Southern woman, conceal the essential similarity of the position of women in the nation, regardless of geographic section. The haughty Daughter of the Confederacy with the big hat at the garden club in Charleston, South Carolina, can hardly be distinguished, except in speech, from the equally haughty, equally big-hatted Daughter of the American Revolution at a lawn party in Newport, Rhode Island. Women in the textile mills, North and South, wear the same slacks, the same bandannas, and the same look of alienation from life.

Cash speaks of the "suppression of class feeling" in the South, both before the Civil War and after Reconstruction. He attributes this "social solidity" to the existence of the Negro as a drain for the ego of the Southern white, drawing off what might have been a natural hostility to the rich, Southern white man. And true, it was only *before* the cotton gin magnified and solidified slavery in the nineteenth century that occasional violent class explosions shook the South.

Bacon's Rebellion of 1676 was only one of many signs of sharp hostility between the frontier farmers and the seaboard aristocracy in Virginia and Maryland. And a century later, the Regulator Movement in the Carolinas expressed, by force of arms, resentments of the poor against the wealthy. In that hundred years between, many clashes of a class nature took place in the Southern colonies. What was said by a contemporary of Bacon was true of much of the South during that period: "Indigent People as had no benefits from the Taxes groaned under our being thus overborn."

No doubt the Negro, as slave before the Civil War and as semi-slave after the War, formed some sort of a block between the downtrodden white and the Southern aristocracy and diverted attention from obvious differences in wealth. Up North, in the same years when Nat Turner's insurrection was fresh in Virginia minds, working men were organizing in the cities of New York and Philadelphia. And the year 1877, which for the South meant preoccupation with the restoration of white supremacy, was the year when gunfire sounded along the railroad lines of the Northeast, and railway workers fought bloody battles against employers over wages and working conditions.

I am trying, in these paragraphs, to do justice to the real difference between North and South in the matter of class conflict and class consciousness, before I move to what I think is the larger truth and the more significant one for our national history: that such differences between North and South have been matters of degree, based on time and circumstance. In the longer perspective, both sections—Americans as a whole—despite periods of sporadic conflict, have moved into a semi-happy narcosis in which consciousness of class has been dulled.

That the South is perfectly capable of *class* violence is shown by the revolts referred to above in the colonial period and by isolated situations, like the Gastonia textile strike of the 1920s, as bitter in its own way as was the Lawrence, Massachusetts textile strike of a decade earlier. That the South is also capable of subordinating race to class is shown in that brief interlude of the Populist period in the South, when there was some evidence that white and black farmers could be drawn together by common grievances against "the interests." And we get a glimmer of the possible in the South's embrace of Franklin D. Roosevelt during the depression.

True, the North between 1877 and 1940 (such a short span in our history, really!) was the scene of our most intense labor struggles, but this can be laid to the circumstances that brought industrial growth to that area first. And it is in the first agony of such growth (almost as peasants revolted against the Soviet collectivization of the thirties before settling down to live with it) that rebellion occurs. But there is nothing in "the Southern mind," no mystical quality of the Southern temper, which prevents the Southerner from feeling class hostility. As racism erodes and industrialization develops in the South, that chance may come.

True, our national class grievances are nowhere near as sharp as they might be; the distribution of wealth in Latin America, in the Middle East, is unspeakably more uneven. Yet we do have our poor. A substantial part of the nation has to battle every day to keep the family fed, clothed, sheltered, and alive. But the hurt is not so keen, apparently, that it cannot be suppressed by an injection of nationalism; this has always been the salve for internal discomfort, and it has never been available in such gross quantities as now.

Nationalism, manifested extremely in patriotism and superpatriotism, has often been seen as a distinctive Southern trait—oddly juxtaposed with the South's own jealous sectionalism. Aside from those few years around the Civil War, the South has been recognized as the most jingoistic of the sections, the most loudly reverent of the country, flag, national honor. After all, the Daughters of the American Revolution go further back than the Daughters of the Confederacy and are especially strong in the South. A formidable quintet of Virginians—Washington, Jefferson, Madison, Monroe, John Marshall—founded our nation and dominated those early patriotic years.

Southern estrangement from the nation during the Civil War soon ended, and when we fought Spanish armies in Cuba, the Gray stood alongside the Blue. After Appomattox, as before Bull Run, Southern men were especially prominent in the national military establishment. So the emphasis has continued to this day on the idea of a particularly "militant South."

And it is true. Yet, to dwell on that obscures another truth, perhaps more necessary to sober us in today's world; that militant nationalism has been a persistent United States tradition.

Today, sprawled comfortably across the continent from ocean to ocean, our eyes on the galaxies, we are bemused and irritated at what seems a petulant nationalism in the new nations of Africa and Asia. But we were quite feverish in those first decades after the Revolution—eyeing Canada and Florida, snapping at England, France, and Spain, finally devouring half of Mexico in a burst of indignation. Tocqueville had written, in Jackson's time: "Nothing is more embarrassing in the ordinary intercourse of life than this irritable patriotism of the Americans."

Still, nationalism was contained within the continent through most of the nineteenth century; we left Europe and Asia alone. Even after the Spanish-American War, perhaps because we were full of moralistic protestations, perhaps because the European powers were dividing up the world, we still had a look of innocence. This was not easy to maintain, because now we were firmly planted, not only in the Caribbean, but on the other side of the Pacific Ocean.

When we did enter European affairs in World Wars I and II, it was with grand pronouncements. We fought to make the world safe for democracy the first time, to save the world from Hitlerism the second time; the idea that national interest—imagined in the first instance and real in the second—lay behind it all, was kept obscure. The $16 billion we gave through the Marshall Plan after the war was seen, not as a power move sweetened with good intention, but as nothing more than a sincere effort on our part to help the fallen world. That Asia, Africa, and Eastern Europe were more fallen but less politically susceptible was overlooked.

In the 1960s, if it was not clear before, it is now: Americans as a whole are hot for patriotism, armed and challenging and as self-glorifying as any Southern orator ever was.

Edmund Wilson, in *Patriotic Gore*, points out that the South, in the

Civil War, always had its "Great Alibi" for retrogression and that the North has had its "Treasury of Virtue," which "has enabled us to carry along into all our subsequent wars . . . the insufferable moral attitudes that appeared to us first to be justified by our victory over the Confederacy in 1865."

The same goes for conservatism. It was the South that always talked of defending its "way of life." The nation was young, vigorous, forward-looking, the legend goes, and the South was recalcitrant, hugging its traditions, fearful of progress. Supporting this is the fact of our revolutionary tradition. Did not Tocqueville have to explain our rash radicalism, our equalitarianism, our upstart ideas, to the conservatives of Metternichean Europe? The reality of that revolutionary spirit is gone, but its aura remains, with which we find it convenient to belabor the "conservative South."

Today, however, it is the United States that talks of defending "its way of life" against revolutionary threats all over the world. We are now the conservative nation, trying to maintain the *status quo* against what appears to be a torrent of change threatening Western civilization. I am not attempting to assess the quality of our revolutionary ideals of the past as against the quality of the present upsurge, but only to assert that we stand fast, guarding the present, with as much nervous fear as any Southern politician has who holds on to what he is sure of, against the uncertainties of transformation.

The South is poor. Franklin D. Roosevelt called it the "Number One economic problem" of the United States. In 1959, when the median income for the United States was $5,600, in Mississippi it was $2,800, exactly half. While in that year 13 percent of the nation's families earned under $2,000, the percentage for Alabama was 26 percent, for Georgia 22 percent, for Mississippi 37 percent. Poverty marks the South today as clearly as cotton once did.

I do not want to challenge the fact that the South is poorer than the rest of the nation. But I do want to point to something which has been often overlooked (though in the year 1963, notice began to be taken): that there are large and numerous pockets of poverty in the United States as shocking as that one which is the South; that the idea of a rich North and a poor South is demolished by the statistics and the stories of human despair which come out of the cities of the North, out of the run-down little towns of New England and the Midwest. The divisions of rich and poor in this country do not run along sectional lines but exist, to different degrees, in every section of the country.

We reject poverty as a national problem when we relegate it to the South, with the implication that this is a startling divergence from the general United States picture of prosperity. A more accurate image is of a land where thin threads of wealth run through all the sections, along with broad shaded areas representing middle-class, mortgaged affluence, and of millions of people *everywhere,* fighting to meet the basic requirements of life for themselves and their children.

The realities of life are obscured under meaningless statistics when we measure the wealth of people in huge aggregates, pushing all people into one section or taking a national average. To say that the national average income is $5,600 is impressive in giving a picture of a quite well-off nation, but it doesn't do justice to the distinctions by group. When we move slightly closer to piecemeal examination, more light is shed on the subject of income distribution: in 1960, the lowest fifth of the United States population averaged about $1,500 a year in income and the highest fifth averaged about $15,000. And this is only the beginning of the process of making distinctions within the national average, only the first step toward a truly human appraisal of the extent of poverty in the United States. The details themselves have been well told in Michael Harrington's *The Other America* and Leon Keyserling's *Poverty and Deprivation in the U.S.*

Let me go back over my argument. The South is everything its revilers have charged, and more than its defenders have claimed. It is racist, violent, hypocritically pious, xenophobic, false in its elevation of women, nationalistic, conservative, and it harbors extreme poverty in the midst of ostentatious wealth. The only point I have to add is that the United States, as a civilization, embodies all of those same qualities. That the South possesses them with more intensity simply makes it easier for the nation to pass off its characteristics to the South, leaving itself innocent and righteous.

In any truth which is knotted and complex, we can choose what strand we want to grasp. To pick out the South has the advantage of focusing attention on what is worst; but it has the disadvantage of glossing over the faults of the nation. It is particularly appropriate in this time, when the power of the United States gives it enormous responsibility, to focus our critical faculties on those qualities which mark—or disfigure—our nation. With this approach, the South becomes not damnable, but marvelously useful, as a mirror in which the nation can see its blemishes magnified, so that it will hurry to correct them. In effective psychotherapy, the patient is at first disturbed by self-recognition, then grateful for the disclosure. It is the first step toward transformation, and in the 1960s, this nation, with its huge potential for good, needs to take another look in the mirror. We owe this to ourselves, and to our children.

BIBLIOGRAPHICAL NOTES

. . . [In an earlier section] "Is the Southern White Unfathomable?" what started as a germ of an idea based on observation and experience became strengthened as I began to read the literature of post-Freudian psychology and certain works of sociology and history. Stanley Elkins's *Slavery* (University of Chicago Press, 1959), besides providing provocative insights, helped me to find a direction for my own thoughts. . . . Melvin Tumin, in *Desegregation: Resistance and Readiness* (Princeton University Press, 1958), gives solid support, it seems to me, to the importance of distinguishing between idea and *action* in the attitudes and behavior of white Southerners. Sociologist Arnold M. Rose, in his article "The Influence of Legislation on Prejudice" in *Common Ground* (1949), showed early the value of firm authority in changing social practices. Among the social psychologists, there is, first, Harry Stack Sullivan, who, in *The Interpersonal Theory of Psychiatry* (Norton, 1953), buttresses optimism about the capacity of the white Southerner (and the white Northerner) to change his behavior swiftly. Kurt Lewin, in *Field Theory in Social Science* (Harper, 1951), goes into great detail to describe the effects of the *present* field on human behavior. Dorwin Cartwright continued Lewin's experimentation and reports on some of this in his article "Achieving Change in People," *Human Relations* (1951). I found particularly stimulating Gardner Murphy's *Personality*, and its discussion of "situationism" and "role." A good survey of the whole subject is in J. A. C. Brown's *Freud and the Post-Freudians* (Penguin Books, 1961). In Herbert Marcuse's *Eros and Civilization* (Beacon Press, 1955) and Norman O. Brown's *Life Against Death* (Wesleyan University Press, 1959), we have two brilliant arguments against what Marcuse calls "neo-Freudian revisionism." The social psychologist who has applied "situationist" theories most closely to the present race problem in America is Thomas Pettigrew, as in his article "Social Psychology and Desegregation Research," in *American Psychologist* (1961). A strong influence along the same lines is Gordon Allport, *The Nature of Prejudice* (Beacon Press, 1954). For a fresh view of race relations in the postbellum South, I drew upon C. Vann Woodward, *The Strange Career of Jim Crow* (Oxford University Press, 1957). Also a new Southern view is that of Dewey Grantham, *The Democratic South* (University of Georgia Press, 1963). . . .

[In a later section] "The South as a Mirror," my starting point was Wilbur J. Cash's *The Mind of the South* (Knopf, 1946), a beautifully written book which captures so much of the South, past and present, and yet which also may have a narcotic effect on one's will for change. For the early history of the Negro in America, I have depended on John Hope Franklin, *From Slavery to Freedom* (Knopf, 1956). Valuable for the nineteenth century is Fanny Kemble's *Journal* (Carey, Lea, and Blanchard, 1835). Some of the material on abolitionism and on revivalism is drawn from Alice Felt Tyler's *Freedom's Ferment* (University of Minnesota, 1944). The reference to Richard Hofstadter's comment on the Emancipation Proclamation comes from one of the great books written by this generation of historians, his *The American Political Tradition* (Knopf, 1948). Material on anti-Negro attitudes in Michigan during Reconstruction came from an unpublished work by Ida Meltzer, *The Negro in Michigan 1865–70.* The brief comments on the social gospel movement are based on Stow Persons's *American Minds* (Holt, 1958).

Southern History Is Still Unique*

C. Vann Woodward

The making of Southern mythology has not been an exclusively regional enterprise. No doubt Southerners themselves have been the most
prolific contributors, but they have had too much assistance from outside to claim exclusive authorship. Northern contributions derive in part
from felt needs and deprivations of Yankee culture that have sought fulfillment in compensatory fantasy. . . .

Southern contributions to the myth grow out of more conventional
needs for defense, self-flattery, and intersectional polemics. And on a
more serious level they are part of the unending struggle to make the
collective experience intelligible and meaningful. Whatever differences
may exist between Northern and Southern sources and their respective
handiwork, on one point there is general agreement—that the South is
"different." . . .

Throughout the confrontation between North and South over school
desegregation, civil rights, and voter registration there has been a mounting impatience among friends of the Negro movement with the uses to
which the national mythology about the South have too frequently been
put. The myth of a mysterious distinctiveness beyond the reach of reason
and impervious to change has been employed as a fog to hide realities,
an excuse for inaction, evasion, and postponement. It has helped to slow
Deliberate Speed to a halt, to rationalize tokenism, and to justify defeatism. It is common to the thinking of liberals and moderates as well as
conservatives and reactionaries. It is a mainstay of Southern defiance
and a salve for Northern conscience.

Under these circumstances it is not surprising that a recent Northern
work on Southern mythology should take the form of iconoclasm. This
is a book by Howard Zinn that he chooses to call *The Southern Mystique.* . . .

The avowed purpose of the book is "to dispose of the myth of Southern
exceptionalism," to do it in, the whole thing, once and for all. Mystery
in any department is anathema and must be banished. Mr. Zinn's method
is not to deny the South the formidable array of characteristics traditionally attributed to it but to concede them and at the same time to claim
them all as American characteristics. The South is simply America exaggerated, "the essence of the nation." . . .

In the long roster of its revilers the South has rarely had so genial and
disarming a critic. What has poisoned the North-South colloquy for a

* C. Vann Woodward "Southern Mythology," reprinted from *Commentary* (May
1965), by permission; copyright 1965 by the American Jewish Committee.

century and half has been the standing indictment of self-righteousness and hypocrisy. The classic riposte of the South under attack is *tu quoque:* you're another—what about Harlem? Mr. Zinn's strategy is to smother the question with concessions. Harlem is "as terrible as any colored section of a Deep South city." Racism afflicts "the entire mind and body of the American nation" and forms a "basic community of interest of all sections of the United States, reaching back to our earliest history." He obligingly documents these concessions with chapter and verse. New Jersey burned two Negroes at the stake for setting fire to barns in 1711, and in the same year New York hanged eighteen and burned thirteen alive —two a week, one hanged, one burned. And so on through the appalling record of the two centuries that followed, including the shameful timidity, vacillation, and compromise of the Civil War and Reconstruction, and the betrayal, desertion, and oppression of the years since. The conclusion is that "there is no part of the United States where Negroes as a group have ever stood equal with whites." The South remains, however, the main bastion of racism, "a kind of Fort Knox of prejudice—where the nation has always stored the bulk of its bigotry, while the rest has circulated—though sometimes stealthily—all over the country." The failure of national policy against racial discrimination and injustice is, nevertheless, attributed to "national weakness rather than to Dixie strength."

Having thus disposed of the myth of racist exceptionalism in the South, Mr. Zinn turns to other alleged Southern peculiarities in the same spirit of iconoclasm. These include such themes as violence, fundamentalism, xenophobia, nativism, chauvinism, absence of class feeling, prevalence of poverty, and what W. J. Cash called "downright gyneolatry," the cult of Southern womanhood. Like racism these are all conceded to be Southern traits, but at the same time the South is denied exclusiveness in their possession. They, too, are American. . . . .

One conspicuous omission among Mr. Zinn's targets of Southern exceptionalism is the historical experience of the region. This is not an oversight. With the best will in the world for sharing guilt, paranoia, and tragedy, the doctrine of anti-exceptionalism cannot be stretched to endow the North with the South's past. Other Americans are fortunate enough not to share two-and-a-half centuries of chattel slavery, a wild and disastrous adventure in secession and independence ending in crushing defeat, and another century begun with an abortive reconstruction and ending in a second one still in progress. Yet this is the only authentic basis of the South's claim to a distinctive heritage. That heritage can be, often has been, abused, but its distinctiveness cannot be denied.

Mr. Zinn, a historian, does not deny it. He dismisses it. His conviction is that we have an "overly heavy sense of history," and that "we are too much impressed with the power of the past. . . .

Along with the past, Mr. Zinn would cast off the burden of Freudian psychology, which he considers as much of an incubus upon the individual as history is upon society. Like history, this school of psychology, with its stress on the long arm of the past, especially the determinants of early childhood experience upon lifelong behavior, has "led to a pervasive pessimism about man and society." He embraces instead the "situational psychology" of men like Gardner Murphy, who hold that "the present situation may be far more important than any past experience" in determining behavior and personality. . . .

As test and proof of his hypotheses regarding history and psychology, Mr. Zinn offers testimony of his personal experiences in the Southern race crisis. No summer soldier in the Southern campaigns, he taught for seven years at a Negro college (Spelman) in Atlanta and took active part in sit-in and desegregation demonstrations there and at Albany, Georgia, and observed the movement in other states. As late as 1958 Atlanta was a tightly segregated city with an apparently solid white support behind the slogan, "Never." The change that followed was striking:

> By 1963: the busses had desegregated; so had the public libraries, the rail and bus terminals, a number of theaters and restaurants downtown, the department store cafeterias, the opera, the municipal auditorium, the legitimate theater, the public schools, the colleges (public and private), several hotels, the plainclothes squad of the Police Department, the Fire Department, the baseball team, the tennis courts, the parks, the golf courses, the public swimming pools, the Chamber of Commerce, several professional organizations, the county committee of the Democratic party and even the Senate of the Georgia General Assembly!

This was all done without violence in a city with 350,000 white people, the overwhelming majority of whom preferred a segregated society, who could have prevented most of the change "if they had cared enough." The point is they did not care enough when it came to a showdown. They would have readily responded to yes-and-no questions of a public opinion pollster with a percentage of "no's" that would have made change appear hopeless. But a real-life situation is quite different from an abstract situation such as an opinion poll. In real life there were multiple choices, none of them perfect: riding an integrated bus or walking, and so with restaurants, parks, schools, etc. . . .

Our social engineer will take advantage of a number of human failings, now known as behavioral principles. One, already mentioned, is that "the public has a poor memory." Another is the individual's "need to conform to society at large." A third is "the need to meet the approval of a few people whose influence—consciously or unconsciously felt—is potent and continuous." A fourth is Mr. Zinn's own contribution growing out of personal experience, a doctrine heavily stressed and often repeated, that "the universal detergent for race prejudice is *contact*—massive, prolonged, equal, and intimate contact" between races.

. . . The plain and demonstrable fact is that in the last few years, in response to judicial decision and legislative enactments, the South has changed. It has changed deeply, widely, and rapidly. It has not changed as much as many would like or as much as it must to comply with the law or to live up to its own standards of justice. But it has changed. Southern whites and Southern Negroes and the relations between them have changed, and the changes are acknowledged and understood by both.

The analysis and theory of change and the technique of engineering it proposed by Mr. Zinn, however, are open to considerably more question. If change is to be accomplished at the cost of some sort of prefrontal lobotomy on society that blocks off the past irretrievably from the present, the cure may be worse than the malady. If change is only accomplished in contrived circumstances of the "immediate situation," upon individuals whose personality alters automatically with temporarily assigned "roles," the stability of the new order is in some doubt. . . .

The panacea of massive contact as "the universal detergent for race prejudice" also leaves something to be desired. In the first place, the hypothesis is embarrassed for want of illustrative examples. The one illustration Mr. Zinn offers was shortly to prove singularly unfortunate —"Harlem, or Bedford-Stuyvesant, at the fringes of all-Negro neighborhoods, where whites and Negroes live as cordial neighbors.". . .

Little comfort is to be derived from the alleged success of the great twentieth-century experiments in obliterating the past that have been conducted in Russia, Germany, and China. . . .

It is difficult to imagine where the civil rights movement and the Negro Revolution would be, or how they could be at all, without the past and without constant reference to the past. The white man is not the only Southerner with a history. The Negro is another American minority with a distinctive, un-American experience of history. And that experience has informed and colored every phase of the present movement and endowed it with its basic philosophy. Nonviolence is not an invention of white intellectuals, or whites of any sort, nor was it borrowed from India. It was born out of the anguish of an encounter with the white man through the centuries of his greatest power and arrogance. It saw the Negro through slavery, Civil War, and Reconstruction, in all of which he rejected the bloody tactics urged by well-wishers. And his steadfast adherence to the wisdom of his historic experience explains in large part why he, and not the red Indian, is the center of attention today.

But there is more of the past in the present than philosophy. There are also the music and the rhythm and the words, the songs the people sing and the way they sing them and the meaning behind them, the unfathomable simplicity and the sly pun, the inexhaustible patience and the unflagging purpose, songs of King Jesus and the weary blues, the imagery and rhetoric of the speeches and the shouted response of the audience. To hear Mahalia Jackson sing, or Fannie Lou Hamer speak, or Martin Luther King preach is to be overwhelmed with the elemental impact of the past on the present. Cut these people off from the past and they would be struck mute.

There are, of course, other potent reminders of the past, the sort of past without which the savagery and brutality of Oxford and Birmingham and Selma are unimaginable. That is the Southern white past according to the historiography of Professor Mink Snopes and his patron, Ross Barnett. If that is accepted as the authentic reading of Southern history we really had better turn it all over to the sanitation department of the social engineers. Fortunately there are rival readings of Southern history that do not square with the Snopes version. They expose its sham, its hypocrisy, and its self-deception. The Southerner will find liberation instead of bondage in his true history. He will find in it persuasive evidence of the futility of erecting blockades against new ideas and attempting to stop the clock of history. He will recognize what obscene caricatures some of his present spokesmen have made of the best in his tradition. And he can gain some degree of immunity from the American myths of success and affluence and innocence and invincibility, which have little foundation in his own heritage.

There is no more use trying to persuade the white Southerner that he is a black man with a white skin than there is trying to persuade the Negro that he is a white man with a black skin—or trying to persuade both of them that they are undifferentiated and indistinguishable Americans with a slight accent. They are the oldest, the largest, and the most incorrigible of the hyphenate American minorities. "Negroes and white Southerners do, in fact, want to be Americans," as Robert Penn Warren remarks, "but by and large, they want to be themselves too; and the fact that both belong to minorities means that both may cling defensively to what they are, or what they take themselves to be. They may refuse to be totally devalued, gutted and scraped before being flung into the melting pot." There is, of course, a Southern counterpart of the transplanted Yankee who seeks to outdo the natives in being Southern—just as there is a white counterpart of the Negro who tries abjectly to be a white man. But none of these performances, however expert, really commands respect or encourages self-respect. And none of them rings true psychologically as a solution to problems of identity—racial, regional, or national. In each of them there is a large ingredient of self-hatred. And self-hatred is hardly the healthiest foundation for identity or the soundest foundation for the new order that is now struggling to be born in the South.

The Uncommunal South*

David Bertelson

. . . This is what leisure as an ideal has essentially always meant in the South—taking life easy. And this is why before the Civil War it was so intimately linked in men's minds with other aspects of the Southern way. Whether it was considered an element in a general pattern of laziness or as something good depended upon whether one's point of view was social or personal. When Southerners glorify leisure as a basis for characteriz-

* From *The Lazy South* by David Bertelson. Copyright © 1967 by Oxford University Press, Inc. Reprinted by permission.

ing the South as a society, they are attempting to make a private activity grounds for uniting a society in the same way that attractionists once sought to make the personal pursuit of gain an argument for social unity.

What has traditionally been associated with the ideal of leisure and is often taken as evidence of a sense of community—courtesy, hospitality, graciousness—is simply a series of devices for minimizing friction at the most intimate and personal level. David M. Potter, nevertheless, sees the characteristically Southern emphasis upon personalism as part of an authentic folk culture, which "survived in the South long after it succumbed to the onslaught of urban-industrial culture elsewhere." Thus he asks if the nostalgia for the Southern past "persists was it because even the inequality and wrong were parts of a life that still had a relatedness and meaning which our more bountiful life in the mass culture seems to lack?"[1] Doubtless at times in the past or in certain limited areas of the South people's lives did attain relatedness and meaning. But for the region as a whole the persistently disorienting effects of economic conditions, outside criticism, and geographical and even social mobility have been too common to permit personal relationships to impart the kind of stability which one usually associates with folk cultures.

It may in fact be argued that the way in which the stress upon the personal has operated in the South has in many respects militated against a real sense of belonging. Among strangers the social graces function only to create the appearance of intimacy or affection, and the element of formality often governs even the closest personal relations. Contacts between the races are highly formalized, and whites tend to view Negroes mainly in terms of stereotypes. Thus emphasis upon personal relationships seems essentially to focus on appearances rather than on human emotions. At best, many Southerners must have been left unsatisfied by this tendency to ignore how people really feel. At worst, in the area of race relations, it has meant misunderstanding and insult. Viewing contemporary Mississippi society, Walker Percy deplores the absence of any really private and public spheres of life—the result of the fact that everyone is forced to live as if he were a member of one great family. "It is this hypertrophy of pleasant familial space at the expense of a truly public sector which accounts for the extraordinary apposition in Mississippi of kindliness and unspeakable violence," Percy notes.[2] This society, one feels, differs from the rest of the South past and present only in the unrelieved intensity with which the personal emphasis operates to undercut both social values and individual rights.

The persistent metaphor of the frontier seems especially appropriate, for it suggests a people living in a state of nature without ever really having formulated a social compact among themselves. Yet from the arguments of allurement to the celebrations of leisure and personal relationships, Southerners have been searching for a definition of how a society is

---

[1] David M. Potter, "The Enigma of the South," *Yale Review* (Autumn 1961), 150, 151.

[2] Walker Percy, "Mississippi: The Fallen Paradise," *Harper's Magazine* (April 1965), 171.

united, how men are bound together to fulfill through labor the purposes of organized social life. In sociological terms, they have been seeking their own definition of social integration. In his study *The Integration of American Society*, Robert Cooley Angell argues that if American society were very small, it might be integrated on the basis of intimate personal relationships because "affection and friendship are the chief cementing forces in small groups." But no society can cohere on these terms. It must be integrated, if at all, by ties which do not necessitate intimacy of acquaintance. Over long periods of time "societies are chiefly knit together by a common attachment of their members to systems of value like those of a religion or of democracy, systems that define the character of the collective life."[3] Angell further notes that "an integrated society . . . is in some respects a moral community. Its members have at least a few ultimate values in common."[4] While his study is aimed at testing the degree to which modern American society is successfully integrated, it is possible to apply his definitions specifically to the society of the South considered separately and historically. Neither the celebrations of allurement nor those of leisure and its associated characteristics are values which define collective life—however descriptive they may be of certain widely held assumptions.

The geographical conditions of the South permitted a form of society consisting of nearly isolated individuals, who depended almost exclusively upon traders, merchants, and financiers from the outside to perform many essential social services for them. But geography did not create the South. As Richard Shryock has pointed out, Pennsylvania, with a soil as well adapted to tobacco as that of Virginia and Maryland and an excellent river system for ready marketing, could just as easily have become a staple-producing area as its neighbors.[5] The difference lay not in the land but in the people, and that difference was ultimately due to the different attitudes and assumptions which they brought with them and their descendants perpetuated. Both the Quakers and to an even greater degree the Puritans in New England founded societies based on communities of consent and common goals. Imbued with a sense of community and social purposefulness, these people were truly able to build cities in the wilderness.

The doctrine of allurement can be viewed as a very early expression of the idea of *laissez-faire*, a point which is further supported by the views of George Fitzhugh. In England the social implications of this philosophy were limited by the fact that it was, after all, preached in an old and fully elaborated society. Only in the South (and the sugar islands) were attempts made to form whole societies in accordance with this notion. And these attempts worked—after a fashion. Only the jeremiads remained to testify to disappointed expectations. Always in the background lay the example first of New England and later of the North in general.

---

3 Robert Cooley Angell, *The Integration of American Society: A Study of Groups and Institutions* (New York and London, 1941), pp. 14–15.

4 Ibid., p. 19.

5 Richard H. Shryock, "British versus German Traditions in Colonial Agriculture," *Mississippi Valley Historical Review*, 26 (1939–40), 39–54.

Southerners were urged to repent and become like those whose way of life best seemed to approximate what men expected. In fact Northern society only imperfectly exemplified a sense of community, for the American experience as a whole has involved the weakening of institutions and the ascendency of the individual. The South represents the logical extreme of this tendency. To the degree that America has meant economic opportunity without social obligations or limitations, Southerners are Americans and Americans Southerners. Yet America has also been a nation of men professing a common allegiance and social values which have operated to check unlimited self-aggrandizement and its effects. In this sense the jeremiads were not really mistaken in noting differences North and South.

When the formation of a united nation made the issue of national cohesion explicit, the question of the distinctiveness of the South became important in a way it had not been earlier. What the jeremiads have always implied and what the Civil War proved is that Southern distinctiveness has never meant a cohesive and separate identity. It is not really accurate to equate the persistent feeling of distinctiveness with Southerners' sense of sectionalism. The latter is of relatively recent origin and is ironically the creation of outside forces—first the anti-slavery agitation, then the Civil War, and finally Reconstruction—which have not changed the essential pattern of distinctiveness. Recently C. Vann Woodward has defined the unique quality of the Southern experience in terms of a tradition of poverty, failure, and guilt—in a nation which values abundance, success, and innocence. Also Southerners are aware of the weight of the past as Northerners are not.[6] One can, however, argue that the South as a whole does not exhibit a style of politics or social behavior which in any way reflects these elements of difference. Quite the contrary, poverty and failure have never discouraged Southerners from pursuing opportunity and success, and protestations of purity are more common than affirmations of guilt. Uniqueness, as Woodward employs it, serves essentially as a frame of reference by means of which Americans and Southerners in particular can understand and gain a perspective upon the national experience and contemporary society. This makes the South not a social reality, but rather a concept existing only in the realm of values.

The sense of distinctiveness has never defined a real society, and yet it persists. If it keeps alive the old interest in a changed South, it also encourages a special loyalty to what makes the South Southern. And so when Southerners begin to celebrate their own distinctiveness too loudly, a Jeremiah usually appears to remind them that they know better.

---

[6] C. Vann Woodward, *The Burden of Southern History* (Baton Rouge, 1960), chaps. 1, 2, 8.

chapter 2

The Antebellum South

BY 1900 MOST AMERICANS HAD LONG CEASED to think of the South as the house of racial bondage or even as a serious impediment to the nation's progress. Southern attitudes conquered the American mind. Northerners and Westerners, who looked upon their small black populace with scorn and gladly left the care of the black majority to Southern caste, enthusiastically embraced popular and learned historical presentations of the antebellum South as a civilized and graceful land of plenty populated by aristocratic and paternalistic planters and their faithful black retainers. For many decades white Southerners responded by basking in the general celebration of their legends and by displaying a keen sense of national sanction for their modern system of white supremacy. During the 1930s and 1940s, however, this sectional and racial settlement began to show signs of instability.

Hitler's lunatic racial policies and his total defeat followed by the rise of "colored" nations tended to discredit ideological racism throughout the world. In the United States the wartime immigration of blacks from the rural South to the industrial centers created a new force in the labor movement and a voting bloc large enough to demand the attention of some politicians and institutional power brokers. The collapse of the old European empires and the rise of the Russian-American "Cold War" competition for support from the new Afro-Asian Third World countries established a set of conditions which made Southern caste appear to many Americans to be both obsolete and harmful to national interests. The Supreme Court's Brown decision against school segregation in 1954 marked the recognition of this feeling and signaled the beginning of a series of racial changes in the United States.

When white Southerners in the 1950s responded to school desegregation and the emergence of a civil rights movement with defiance, hatred, and violence, they set the stage for a reconsideration of Southern history. The annual September Saturnalia of violence around the public schools, the open brutality of police against black demonstrators, the midnight assassinations, the church bombings and the often uncontrolled rage of mobs, all did much to undermine belief in the existence of a Southern heritage of chivalrous "Cavaliers" and of a history of paternalistic race relations dominated by the rules of noblesse oblige. As a result, the perceptions of the 1950s made possible the rise of more realistic and critical scholarly approaches to the antebellum South. In 1964 the Kentucky historian Clement Eaton summarized many years of research in concluding that the Old South knew "little of liberalism" and had been dominated by "extreme conservatism, a spirit of intolerance, a powerful religious orthodoxy, an intense attachment to . . . local community, and a powerful race feeling." In the same year another veteran scholar of Southern history James W. Silver portrayed Mississippi as a "closed society" organized along totalitarian lines for the defence of slavery and white supremacy and capable of limitless quantities of self-deception.

By the 1960s John Hope Franklin's pioneer study of 1956 on Southern belligerence (Selection 1) had become a modern classic and a great many historians had incorporated into their own teaching and writing his findings on the ways in which slavery had helped to create the surfeit of militarism, the violent play of unbridled and aggressive egos, and the frequent willingness to settle disputes by gun and Bowie knife rather than by due process. William R. Taylor took a different approach in his monograph on "Cavaliers and Yankees" (Selection 2), but his work also tended to corrode the old stereotypes about antebellum life. Taylor demonstrated that Southern fiction during the first four decades of the nineteenth century tended to be a means of self-admonition and sectional reconciliation rather than the militant advocacy of a Southern cause against all comers. In the 1840s and 1850s writers from all parts of the country devised Cavalier myths to fill the common need for codes and creeds not bound to the bustling, acquisitive materialism of nineteenth century American society. However, mythology served a special function in the South by sustaining the power of the planter elite who embraced the cavalier "less because they believed in him than because they badly needed him." In the crisis of 1859–61 the "fire-eaters" manipulated the Cavalier legend to help bring about the Civil War.

If critical perceptions of Southern caste during the 1950s led to a more realistic assessment of the Old South, the discovery that the North and the West had a racist history made more revisionism inevitable. When historians began to write about racism as a national affliction, the Southern scholar could then suggest that the habit of using a Southern "scapegoat" for the sins of the country concealed the fact that the South had shared nearly every portion of the national experience. As early as 1960 Charles G. Sellers (Selection 3), who described the Southerner as an American with both democratic and reactionary aspects, insisted that the encounter with slavery produced a guilt-ridden and tragic inner civil war rather than simply a monolithic "closed society."

The black struggles and riots of the mid and late 1960s which pointed to the existence of racism in all parts of the country, seemed to give the nineteenth century North less to boast about and the antebellum South less to feel guilty about. In this changing pattern of sensibilities Eugene D. Genovese (Selection 4) won a hearing for a singular revisionism which revived some of the old, romantic images of the antebellum slaveowner. Genovese's curious "Marxist" interpretation (with some reservations) made racism "an aspect of the class question" and described the planters as the high-minded and socially responsible masters of a "pre-industrial . . . seigneurial . . . paternalistic and patriarchical" society at war with an ultra-racist and more harshly exploitative Northern capitalism. He rejected the concept of a tragically divided Southern mind and dismissed W. J. Cash, Charles Sellers, Kenneth M. Stampp and other scholars and writers as victims of "the currently fashionable disease of guiltomania." Genovese personally could think of no reasons for the slavemasters to feel guilty and found nothing in historical records to sustain Sellers and Cash.

Although an increasingly conservative climate of opinion during the late 1960s and early 1970s diminished hostile images of the slave-holding South, Genovese represented too wide a swing of the pendulum to gain general acceptance. Like other scholars Ronald T. Takaki (Selection 5) objected to Genovese's approach, dismissed the "legend of the old South" as "more fiction than fact" and portrayed the successful cotton planter as an aggressive capitalist entrepreneur. As Takaki demonstrated, the campaign to reopen the African slave trade promised to keep the road to riches open to small planters and men of the middle class thwarted in their ambitions by the soaring prices of American slaves. Moreover, the movement's leadership displayed "an anxious concern" for the professed morality of a slave society and a passion to alleviate seldom acknowledged but very real guilt feelings. The leaders insisted that the generally accepted ethics of domestic slavery made the African trade moral and that laws which properly tended to define slaves as property must be cleansed of the ambigious legal clauses which sometimes dealt with mere chattel as people. By this strategy the "reformers" would still all inner doubts and launch an effective counter-attack against the abolitionist charges of immorality and inhumanity. Thus Takaki reaffirmed the ideas of Cash, Sellers, and Stampp in holding the Southerner to be an American with a mind tragically divided and guilt-ridden on the issues of race and slavery.

BIBLIOGRAPHY

Works Discussed in This Chapter

Eaton, Clement, *Freedom of Thought in the Old South* (1964).
Franklin, John Hope, *The Militant South* (1956).
Genovese, Eugene D., *The World the Slaveholders Made* (1969).
Sellers, Charles G., ed., *The Southerner as American* (1960).
Stampp, Kenneth M., *The Peculiar Institution* (1956).
Takaki, Ronald T., *A Pro-Slavery Crusade* (1971).
Taylor, William R., *Cavalier and Yankee: The Old South and American National Character* (1961).

Suggested Readings

Most of the titles in the bibliography for Chapter 1 also relate to this chapter. Chapter 2 contains only basic titles on *general explanations of the antebellum South*. Richard N. Current's *John C. Calhoun* (1966) is good not only for correcting the inflated estimates of earlier Calhoun biographers but also on the antebellum Southern mind. See also William Y. Thompson, *Robert Toombs of Georgia* (1966). Worth noting but rather short on useful and substantial conclusions (like many recent quantitative studies) is Ralph A. Wooster's *The People in Power: Courthouse and Statehouse in the Lower South, 1850–1860* (1969). David M. Potter suggested that the reason for the South's disproportionate power in national affairs until recently could be traced to Dixie power among Congressional Democrats. See Potter's *The South and the Concurrent Majority* (1972). Potter continued his long record of conservative reflections on Southern history in *The South and the Sectional Image* (1968). Donald L. Robinson explored early Southern sectionalism in *Slavery in the Structure of American Politics 1765–1820* (1971). A quantitative study which is useful but contains very little economic data is Chalmers G. Davidson, *The Last Foray, The South Carolina Planters of 1860: A Sociological Study* (1971). Fletcher M. Green continued to open new areas of study in *The Role of the Yankee in the Old South* (1972) and *Democracy in the Old South and Other Essays* (1969), as Clement Eaton did in *The Waning of the Old South Civilization, 1860–1880* (1968). The numerous earlier works of Green and Eaton should be consulted. D. Clayton James deals with the social irresponsibility of both the plantation elite and the town merchants and professionals in *Ante Bellum Natchez* (1968). Roland has attempted the impossible task of trying to modernize Simkins by deleting a few ultra-racist adjectives and phrases. See Francis B. Simkins and Charles P. Roland, *A History of the South* (4th ed., 1972). A characteristic Nixon era piece of conservatism was the "Gone With the Wind" conceptions of Robert Manson Myers' editorial work on the vast collection of Jones family letters. See Myers, ed., *Children of Pride: A True Story of Georgia and the Civil War* (1972). The same comment might be made about David Donald's "The Pro-Slavery Argument Reconsidered," *Journal of Southern History* (1971). Three interpretive articles of note are Joseph L. Morrison, "The Obsessive Mind of W. J. Cash," *Virginia Quarterly Review* (1965); Robert C. Shalhope, "Race, Class, Slavery and the Ante-Bellum Mind," *Journal of Southern History* (1971); and Jane H. Pease, "A Note on Patterns of Conspicuous Consumption Among Seaboard Planters, 1820–1860," *Journal of Southern History* (1969). All of Eugene D. Genovese's controversial works should be noted including *The Political Economy of Slavery* (1965); *The World the Slaveholders Made* (1969); *In Red and Black: Marxian Explorations in Southern and Afro-American History* (1971); and *Roll, Jordan, Roll* (1974). A recent work on the 1850s and secession is William Barney's *The Road to Secession: A New Perspective on the Old South* (1972).

See also Robert E. May, *The Southern Dream of a Caribbean Empire, 1854–1861* (1973). Three articles by F. N. Boney well worth noting are, "Thomas Stevens, Ante-Bellum Georgian," *South Atlantic Quarterly* (1973); "Look Away, Look Away, A Distant View of Dixie," *Georgia Review* (1969); and "Nathaniel Francis, Representative Antebellum Southerner," *Proceedings of the American Philosophical Society* (1974).

The Militant Southerner*
John Hope Franklin

. . . By 1860 the South claimed to be the fountainhead of martial spirit in the United States. It argued that it had turned the tide of battle in the nation's wars and had been the training ground for the soldiers of the country. America's soldiers had even been schooled in the art and science of war by treatises written by Southerners. . . .

. . . Many [Southerners] were hotheaded and high-tempered, and, in personal relations, conducted themselves as though each were a one-man army exercising and defending its sovereignty. Duels were as "plenty as blackberries." . . .

When there was not dueling, there was fighting. The public walks were arenas for sport among the rustics, most of whom carried weapons and "counted on the chance of getting into difficulty."[1] This violence was described with a mixture of jest and disgust by an Alabama editor:

> The Summer Sports of the South, as Major Noah calls them, have already commenced in Huntsville. On Monday last, in the Court Square, and during the session of Court, too, a man by the name of Taylor stabbed another by the name of Ware in such a shocking manner that his life is despaired of . . . this stabbing and dirking business has become so common and fashionable, that it has lost all the horror and detestation among . . . our population. . . .[2]

[Moreover,] the fighting spirit was no respecter of class or race, and the willingness of Negroes to resort to violence shows the extent to which such conduct pervaded the entire community. . . .

The prevalence of violence was due, in part at least, to the section's peculiar social and economic institutions and to the imperfect state of its political organization. The passions that developed in the intercourse of superiors and inferiors showed themselves in the intercourse with equals, for, observed Stirling, "the hand of the violent man is turned against itself."[3] Far from loathing violence, the man of the South was the product of his experiences as a frontiersman, Indian fighter, slaveholder, self-sufficient yeoman, poor white, and Negro. He gladly fought, even if only to preserve his reputation as a fighter. . . .

[The Northern boy] went into law or politics; and could enjoy travel, the excitement of urban life in the North or abroad, or select the best

---

* Reprinted by permission of the publishers from John Hope Franklin, *The Militant South* (Cambridge, Mass.: Harvard University Press. Copyright 1956 by the President and Fellows of Harvard College).

1 Ingraham, *The Southwest*, 1, 208.

2 *Southern Literary Messenger*, 21 (January 1855), 2.

3 Stirling, *Letters from the Slave States*, p. 271.

that the South had to offer as diversion. But few Southerners had such opportunities, and few of the alternatives in a sluggish social and economic order were very attractive. As boys, even the average could hunt; as men they could join some local military outfit and seek the glory attached to successful forays against the Indians. . . . From this frontier atmosphere, a combination of monotony and conflict, emerged a tense, sensitive fighting man. . . .

It was easy for such . . . [attitudes] to ripen into contempt for control and to render the further development of law and government even more difficult. While this attitude never succeeded in completely destroying government, it did make for distrust of all authority beyond the barest minimum essential to the maintenance of the political and social organism. . . .

While the concept of honor was an intangible thing, it was no less real to the Southerner than the most mundane commodity that he possessed. It was something inviolable and precious to the ego, to be protected at every cost. . . . It sanctioned prompt demand for the redress of grievance, because of the imputation of guilt that might follow a less precipitate policy. It countenanced great recklessness of life, because of the imputation of cowardice that might follow forgiveness of injuries. The honor of the Southerner caused him to defend with his life the slightest suggestion of irregularity in his honesty or integrity; and he was fiercely sensitive to any imputation that might cast a shadow on the character of the women of his family. To him nothing was more important than honor. Indeed, he placed it above wealth, art, learning. . . .

This Southern concept of honor discouraged the growth of strong law enforcement agencies. (The individual insisted on the right to defend his own honor.) To him it was a peculiarly personal thing in which the rest of the community could have little more than a casual interest. And his peers upheld him, realizing that they might play a similar role. The community, going beyond mere acceptance of vigorous defense of honor, regarded such action with hearty approval. The man who killed his adversary in a personal quarrel (while showing some regard for the amenities), need not fear public disgrace. The chances were excellent that his conduct would be judged as self-defense. . . .

The idea of honor contained certain elements that encouraged its excessive application. Whenever a difficulty arose in which there was a *possibility* that honor was involved, it was usually decided—just to be on the safe side—that it *was* involved. Alexander Mackay saw this phenomenon among the people of Richmond and was shocked at its consequences. "Their code of honour," he remarked, "is so exceedingly strict that it requires the greatest circumspection to escape its violation. . . ." It has been suggested, with some reason, that these excesses in violence, growing out of the code of honor, actually created a "cult of murder" in the South from which sprang feuds between families as well as between individuals.[4]

---

[4] Thomas Cooper DeLeon, *Belles, Beaux, and Brains of the 60's* (New York, 1909), pp. 11–12; and William O. Stevens, *Pistols at Ten Paces; The Story of the Code of Honor in America* (Boston, 1940), p. 108.

The feeling of personal responsibility in defending himself, together with the deep appreciation for the idea of honor, created in each Southerner a sense of "personal sovereignty." Ruler of his own destiny, defender of his own person and honor, keeper and breaker of the peace, he approached a personal imperiousness that few modern men have achieved. Not since the days of the medieval barons, perhaps, had there been such individual sovereignty as was found in the antebellum South. Whenever a Southerner fought another, he was, in a very real sense, engaged in war. The honor and dignity at stake were no less important to the individual than they would be to an embattled nation.

No single class had a monopoly on these sentiments and attitudes. . . . The sense of personal insecurity in the absence of law and order was an important factor in the lives of *all* Southern whites, and violence was to be found at every level of the social scale. . . .

The reckless disregard for life and the consequent violence in evidence throughout the South and Southwest greatly alarmed Harriet Martineau, who called it the most savage in the world. Where else, in the nineteenth century, she asked, were there such practices as "burning alive, cutting the heart out, and sticking it on the point of a stick, and other such diabolical deeds?"[5] The countryside and the towns vied in their production of violent incidents. Violence could be predicted whenever there was any considerable assemblage of persons for a militia muster, protracted meeting, or a similar gathering. On such occasions there were numerous fights, some to avenge an alleged wrong, others merely for sport. It was hardly possible to distinguish by observation between the sport and the "blood fight." Even if it began in good humor as a display of physical prowess, there was a good chance that it would end on a more serious and, sometimes, deadly note.

In some communities there were men who, by their own appointment or by popular consensus, were the champion fighters of their respective bailiwicks. Such champions "strutted, bragged, and issued challenges" that were frequently accepted.[6] These local heroes provided diversion for spectators and anxious moments for their opponents who felt compelled to defend not only their manhood but their lives. Bishop Whipple[7] was disgusted to find that in Florida in 1843, people were witnessing public fights in which "those who ought to be gentlemen descend to the common bully." . . .

While the duel was not an outgrowth of slavery, it was the most convenient and proper way for a slaveholder to settle a dispute involving honor. Accustomed to the use of firearms and the exercise of almost unlimited power over his dependents, "he could not endure contradiction, he would not brook opposition. When one lord ran against another in controversy, if the feelings were deeply engaged the final argument was the pistol."[8] . . .

---

[5] Harriet Martineau, *Society in America*, 2, 329.

[6] Everett Dick, *Dixie Frontier* (New York, 1948), p. 140.

[7] Whipple, *Southern Diary*, pp. 26–27.

[8] James Ford Rhodes, *History of the United States* (New York, 1928), 1, 362; see also Osterweis, *Romanticism and Nationalism*, 97.

[Southern politicians sometimes] set out to chastise their critics by caning, pistol-whipping, or some other form of corporal punishment. In the contest over the House speakership in the winter of 1855–56, Horace Greeley went to Washington to support the candidacy of Nathaniel P. Banks. He criticized and probably helped to defeat a House resolution presented by Albert Rust of Arkansas calling for all candidates to withdraw. At their next encounter Rust and Greeley exchanged a few words, and Rust began to strike Greeley on the head with his cane. They were separated, but a few minutes later Rust met Greeley again and resumed the lashing. Once more they were separated by bystanders.[9]

In general, the South approved the summary chastisement of those who offended it or censured its leaders. When, in 1856, Representative Preston Brooks of South Carolina beat Charles Sumner into insensibility with a cane because of Sumner's severe strictures against South Carolina in his "Crime Against Kansas" speech, the South was delighted. Even the next day Brooks could write his brother that the "fragments of the stick are begged for as *sacred relics*."[10] Southern newspapers lavishly praised Brook's deed and numerous groups, among them the student body of the University of Virginia, passed resolutions endorsing it.[11] A leading Richmond paper rejoiced that a Southern gentleman had the courage to register his objections to Sumner's "insults" and to "cow-hide bad manners *out* of him, or good manners into him."[12]. . . When Brooks resigned and returned to South Carolina—to be triumphantly reelected—he was given a hero's welcome. In Columbia an enormous crowd greeted him, and the mayor presented him a silver pitcher, a goblet, and a "fine hickory cane," with a handsome gold head. In Charleston the citizens presented him a cane with the inscription, "Hit Him Again," while his constituents in the Fourth District gave him one that was inscribed, "Use Knock-Down Arguments."[13]

No class of Southerner, perhaps, went to the field of honor more frequently than newspaper editors.[14] . . . The written word by which he was compelled to stand made him especially vulnerable; and the occasions on which he was called to defend, by pistol or sword, his words are so

---

[9] *New York Times*, January 30, 31, 1856, and Glyndon G. Van Deusen, *Horace Greeley, Nineteenth Century Crusader* (Philadelphia, 1953), pp. 201 ff. During these years there were numerous altercations of a similar nature, both in and out of the Congress. For an engaging account of several of them see Benjamin Perley Poore, *Perley's Reminiscences of Sixty Years in the National Metropolis* (Philadelphia, n.d.) 1, 466, 532 ff.

[10] Preston Brooks to J. H. Brooks, May 23, 1856, in Robert Meriwether (ed.), "Preston Brooks on the Caning of Charles Sumner," *South Carolina Historical and Genealogical Magazine*, 52 (January 1951), 3.

[11] *Daily Richmond Enquirer*, June 14, 1856. These students presented Brooks with a goblet.

[12] Ibid., May 29, 1856; June 3, 1856.

[13] Columbia Citizens, *Reception and Speech* (n.p., n.d.), pp. 4–5; and James E. Campbell, "Sumner—Brooks—Burlingame," *Ohio Archaeological and Historical Quarterly*, 34 (October 1925), 453 ff. . . .

[14] For a comprehensive discussion of the duels of Southern editors, see Frederic Hudson, *Journalism in the United States from 1690 to 1872* (New York, 1873), pp. 761–68.

numerous that it is not possible to make more than a brief reference to some of them. . . .

Fanny Kemble, after marrying a Southern planter, was greatly disturbed by what her oldest child's superior position was doing. With dismay, she saw how the little girl's "swarthy worshiper . . . sprang to obey her little gestures of command. She said something about a swing, and in less than five minutes head man Frank had erected it for her, and a dozen young slaves were ready to swing little 'missus'—think of learning to rule despotically your fellow-creatures before the first lesson of self-government has been well spelt over!" Miss Kemble said that the habit of command, developed so early among Southerners, seemed to give them a certain self-possession and ease. This, she believed, was rather superficial, and upon closer observation the vices of the social system became apparent. The "haughty, overbearing irritability, effeminate indolence, reckless extravagance, and a union of profligacy and cruelty" of the slaveholders were the immediate result of their "irresponsible power over their dependents." These traits became apparent upon intimate acquaintance with Southern character, she asserted.[15]

That slavery tended to create tyranny in the South was not merely abolitionist prattle. For years it had been the considered judgment of some responsible white Southerners that a powerful socio-political absolutism was a significant consequence of the institution of slavery. In the debate on the question of the importation of slaves, Colonel George Mason of Virginia told the Federal Convention in 1787 that slaves produced "a most pernicious effect on manners" and that every master was a "born petty tyrant."[16] Ulrich B. Phillips said that the actual regime "was one of government not by laws but by men." In fact, he continued, each slave was under a paternalistic despotism, "a despotism in the majority of cases benevolent but in some cases harsh and oppressive, a despotism resented and resisted by some . . . but borne with light-heartedness, submission and affection by a huge number of blacks."[17]

The amount of benevolence, if any, in the despotism depended on the individual's relationship with his slaves. The system provided the despot with extensive prerogatives and ample opportunities for their abuse. The master had almost unlimited personal authority over his slaves as long as they were guilty of no flagrant violations of the rights of whites or of the feebly enforced state laws. For all practical purposes he was the source of law on the plantation; and, in the rare instances when he resorted to the law of the state to invoke his right over his human property, its interpretation and enforcement were in his control. If the government of the plantation was not by laws but by men, its stability rested on force or the threat of force. Believing that slavery could be sustained by force and violence exercised against the slave, or against the challenges of free men, owners had no qualms about resorting to force and violence.

---

15 Fanny Kemble, *Residence on a Georgia Plantation*, pp. 57–58, 305.

16 Max Farrand, *Records of the Federal Convention* (New Haven, 1927), 2, 370.

17 Ulrich B. Phillips, *Race Problems, Adjustments and Disturbances in the Ante-Bellum South* (Richmond, 1909), p. 200.

The planter regarded arms as a necessary adjunct to the machinery of control. The lash was used generously or sparingly, depending on the temperament of the master and the tractability of the slave. If the slave resisted the "mild" discipline of the lash or undertook to return blow for blow, how else could the master maintain his complete authority except through the use of, or the threat to use, more deadly weapons whose possession was forever denied the slave? Arming themselves with knives and guns became habitual with some masters and overseers. In moments of anger, they sometimes turned their weapons against each other. This was to be expected among an aggregation of armed lords having no superimposed discipline. The rule of tyranny by which they lived fostered independence and self-sufficiency—almost an individual sovereignty— that occasionally burst out in their quarrels.

The relationship between master and slave was that of superior and subordinate, despot and subject, or victor and vanquished. A spirit approaching the martial pervaded the entire plantation atmosphere. The conduct of the master toward the slave was determined by rules and considerations not unlike those of the military. Slaves enjoyed no well-defined rights: infractions brought summary punishment from which there was no appeal. A vigorous antislavery tract pointed out that the plantation was "the seat of a little camp, which over-awes and keeps in subjection the surrounding peasantry." The master could claim and exercise over his slaves all the rights of a victorious warrior over a vanquished foe.[18]

The connection between slavery and the martial spirit was almost universally recognized. If the observer were an implacable foe like Charles Sumner, he could see only its bad effects; to him the result was a criminal distortion of the values and notions regarding the fighting spirit. In the South, the swagger of the bully was called chivalry, a swiftness to quarrel was regarded as courage. The bludgeon was adopted as a substitute for argument; and assassination was lifted to a fine art.[19] If the observer were an apologetic friend, he could be proud of the fact that Southerners had been bred under the influences of an institution "which, with its admitted evils, was calculated to foster the martial spirit and give force of character."[20]

The slave was never so completely subjugated as to allay all fears that he would make a desperate, bloody attempt to destroy the institution which bound him. Slaveholders could never be quite certain that they had established unquestioned control; fear and apprehension were always present. Judgment insisted on the strictest vigilance with no relaxation—the only policy consistent with the maintenance of the institution. . . .

---

18 Richard Hildreth, *Despotism in America* . . . (Boston, 1840), p. 37.

19 Charles Sumner, "The Barbarism of Slavery," speech delivered in the U.S. Senate, June 4, 1860 (Washington, 1860), p. 13.

20 H. S. Fulkerson, *Random Recollections of Early Days in Mississippi* (Vicksburg, 1885), p. 143. See also the account of the planter who was seriously considering putting his slaves in uniform and providing drill music for them. MS fragment, Nov. 8, 1853, in the Mary Eliza Fleming Papers, Duke University Library.

The Frailty of the Aristocratic Idea*
William R. Taylor

By the summer of 1861 the subdued, candid and reasonable exchange of views which had taken place between Jefferson and John Adams some 45 years before seemed to belong to another, faraway age.[1] Early that year, as every schoolboy knows, a separate Southern government had been organized in Montgomery, Alabama. Fort Sumter had fallen in April, a peace conference in Washington had collapsed and by July the United States were at war with themselves. Historians agree that the vast majority of people in the North and South had not wanted secession, to say nothing of war, but events swept them up in a whirlwind of excitement and precipitant action over which no one, finally, could exercise control.

In the South the move to separate had at first received massive support. Of those who hung back, some, perhaps most, were genuinely undecided, others confused or indifferent, and still others afraid to acknowledge their secret convictions. Little recourse was left open for moderation. The choice, to use the language of the time, lay between "secession" and "submission." . . .

Neither Jefferson nor Adams, furthermore, had thought of the natural aristocrat—their choice for the republican leader—as possessing any particular regional traits. Neither, certainly, would have localized either lower-class villainy or aristocratic honor and virture in any North or South which they knew. Adams, with his alertness to the danger of a false aristocracy in New England and with his keen sense of fallibility, saw evil and ambition lurking in every man's heart. He probably would have found the fully developed idea of the Yankee laughable and yet a little appealing, but he scarcely would have looked for better human materials south of the Potomac. Jefferson would have looked upon the full-blown Cavalier ideal with something like loathing and seen in its currency the undoing of much that he had worked to accomplish. Yet some three decades were sufficient to bring about these changes and to usher in a whole new set of assumptions concerning the history, cultural background, and racial composition of the two regions from which these two men had sprung—and for which they had made themselves the spokesmen. The nature of these changes is implicit in the preceding chapters,

---

[1] [For an interesting letter on secession] See Representative David Clopton of Alabama to Senator Clement C. Clay, Dec. 13, 1860, in Clement Eaton, *A History of the Southern Confederacy* (New York, 1954), p. 12.

but the pattern of change is a somewhat complicated one and perhaps deserves brief reiteration.

THE SOUTHERN CAVALIER REDIVIVUS

The first quarter of the nineteenth century had not passed before a significant number of Americans in both the North and the South had begun to express decided reservations about the direction progress was taking and about the kind of aggressive, mercenary, self-made man who was rapidly making his way in their society. In everyone's eyes this type of parvenu came to express a worrisome facet of the national character, to symbolize, in fact, both the restless mobility and the strident materialism of new world society. In the face of the threat which seemed to be posed by this new man, Americans—genteel and would-be genteel—began to develop pronounced longings for some form of aristocracy. They longed for a class of men immune to acquisitiveness, indifferent to social ambition and hostile to commercial life, cities, and secular progress. They sought, they would frankly have conceded, for something a little old-fashioned.

Writers like Cooper, Sarah Hale, and Paulding, themselves representative spokesmen of a much larger group, were particularly attracted by the idea of a conservative country gentry such as England possessed—or, at least, had possessed—only purer and better. The equalitarian character of life in the North provided an unsuitable terrain in which to locate, even in fantasy, an aristocracy of this kind. By the 1830s the legendary Southern planter, despite reservations of one kind or another, began to seem almost perfectly suited to fill the need. His ample estates, his spacious style of life, his Cavalier ancestry and his reputed obliviousness to money matters gained him favor in the eyes of those in search of a native American aristocracy. More and more, he came to be looked upon as *the* characteristic expression of life in the South. Meanwhile, the acquisitive man, the man on the make, became inseparably associated with the North and especially with New England. In the end, the Yankee —for so he became known—was thought to be as much the product of the North as the planter-Cavalier of the South. By 1850 these two types —the Cavalier and the Yankee—expressed in the popular imagination the basic cultural conflict which people felt had grown up between a decorous, agrarian South and the rootless, shifting, money-minded North.

No such absolute division, of course, ever really existed between the North and the South. Southerners engaged in business, speculated on real estate, sought profits, lived in towns and cities, voted for the same national parties and subscribed to many of the same ideals and values as other Americans. What differences they developed, as over the issue of Negro slavery, did not lead many of them to formulate a totally different set of social objectives; these differences simply complicated their response to objectives which they already in large measure had accepted. Thus, in crying out against the Yankee North, Southerners who did so were, in a sense, striking out at part of themselves. By 1860 they had become self-divided, frustrated in their hopes and wishes, increasingly unrealistic in their social aspirations and ripe for some kind of bloody showdown.

The problem for the self-conscious South finally lay in the need which it felt to isolate—to quarantine—itself from the contaminating influence of the Yankee North, which it both feared and envied—and which, finally, was so much a part of itself. The result was the creation of an exclusively Southern historical, and even racial, heritage. Outvoted or overruled in national affairs, outgrown in population, outproduced and, as many Southerners at least secretly felt, outraged on the justice of slavery, the South in 1860 sought some kind of redemption in separateness, only to set up a Confederate government which was not essentially different, even in its constitutional details, from the federal republic from which it had just seceded.

The "Southern" problem was, then, for these men a condition of paralysis brought on by conflicting loyalties—they finally could not believe in either their own regional ideals or those of the country as a whole. Belief in the one conflicted with belief in the other; the result was confusion, indecision, and a kind of gnawing dispiritedness. By the 1850s, certainly, they no longer believed wholeheartedly in the effectiveness of the Cavalier gentleman, since they, too, came to measure achievement by financial success and the gentleman planter was, almost by definition, born to fail. But neither could they worship success, since it was measured in dollars and cents rather than in honor and cultural elevation. The improvident, generous-hearted gentleman planter for them became increasingly a symbol of a Lost Cause—an insurgent, a dueler, a fighter against overwhelming odds—in short, a figment of a utopian social world which was doomed to be submerged under a tide of middle-class materialism.

Without quite acknowledging it, many Southerners during these years had been waging a kind of war with themselves. Increasingly their ideal of a stable social order came into conflict with the social and political realities with which they were confronted. The lowly, whether white or black, gave clear evidence that they did not wish to remain lowly and feudally dependent upon the planter's goodwill. Even women were beginning to speak out in their own names, and some of the things they said represented a distinct challenge to the patriarchal role which the planter had assumed for himself and to many of the values which he thought of himself as embodying. Meanwhile, in the larger sphere of political events, the planter class in the Southern states, divested of the support of the West and challenged at home by its own yeomanry, found its power threatened both in Washington and in state legislatures. And what was an aristocrat who did not possess the power to order his own home, to say nothing of ruling over the national councils, especially when he was beginning to question some of the sanctions upon which his power had been based?

The Alabaman Daniel Hundley,[2] for example, expressed his ambivalent attitude toward the force of the Cavalier ideal in his *Social Relations*

---

[2] Hundley is discussed at greater length in another section.

in our Southern States, the book which he published on the eve of the war. In it he drew an ominous picture of the aristocrat in the South surrounded by predatory, or at least more forceful, social types, who seemed destined to overthrow his cultural and political domination. His book contained chapters devoted to the Southern Yankee, the Southern bully, the poor white, and the enterprising and forward-looking representative of the new middle class. While he argued for the aristocratic ethos of the Southern gentleman, his confidence in his effectiveness clearly wavered before the vision of a rising Southern bourgeoisie.

Few figures in Southern history exemplify better than Edmund Ruffin the tensions and frustrations felt by those who had long battled for the Lost Cause. Ruffin, for years one of the South's leading agricultural scientists and an advocate of a diversified farm economy, was never reconciled to the defeat of the Cavalier ideal. Toward the end of his life, weary and partly deaf, he became obsessed by the idea of an independent, uncontaminated South and fought every inroad of what he regarded as Yankeeism. Dressed—rather conspicuously—in coarse Southern homespun; or, in 1859, at the age of 63, attending John Brown's hanging clad in the uniform of a VMI cadet; or, as a volunteer in the Palmetto Guards, pulling the lanyard that sent one of the first shells toward Fort Sumter, he became a kind of Lanny Budd of the Old South, his every act a symbolic representation of Southern intransigeance before the Yankee North.

Few men more keenly sensed or more deeply resented the obstacles with which true Southernism was confronted within the South itself; no one, certainly, lashed out at the Yankee with greater bitterness or, finally, expressed his feelings of frustration and self-defeat more melodramatically. As an agitator he repeatedly faced indifferent Southern audiences and, poor speaker that he was, he constantly reproached himself for his failure to bring the South to a boil. Virginia he early abandoned as reprobate; he was appalled to find the large planters in Kentucky holding strong Unionist views; and even South Carolina constantly disappointed him by her unwillingness, as in 1850, to take deliberate action. On a visit to White Sulphur Springs in August, 1859, he was astonished to find himself virtually alone among some 1600 Southern guests in calling for secession. For a time after John Brown's raid he hoped "the sluggish blood of the South" would be stirred,[3] and he personally sent pikes with which Brown had intended to arm the slaves to the governors of all the Southern states; but once again he was disappointed in his expectations. Even when confronted with the virtual certainty of Lincoln's election, no state except South Carolina expressed a willingness to take the initiative in seceding. The election of 1860, in which the more moderate Bell triumphed over Breckinridge within the South by a majority of 136,875, only confirmed his fear that the South would never act.

Then, as Southern states began to pass ordinances of secession, his hopes soared one final time. After a lifetime of ceaseless struggle, his dream of an independent South seemed about to become a reality. Once

---

[3] Avery Craven, *Edmund Ruffin Southerner: A Study in Secession* (New York, 1932), p. 171.

the exciting days of Fort Sumter were over, even these hopes were dashed as Jefferson Davis neglected former secessionists and formed a government dominated by moderates and men Ruffin regarded as would-be reunionists. Davis himself, furthermore, seemed slow to move and indecisive, and left Southern extremists generally dissatisfied with his leadership. But for Ruffin—as for most Southerners—the most crushing blow, one which destroyed for all time the myth of Southern invincibility, was the military defeat of the South by the Northern armies that swarmed across his beloved Virginia, destroying his plantation "Beechwood" and leaving obscene graffiti scrawled on the walls of his house. His plantation a shambles, deserted by his slaves, his hearing gone, and the alien North on his very doorstep, he had little left to him that he valued save his sense of honor, his bitterness, and his pride, to which he regularly gave expression in a diary kept through these trying years.

On June 17, 1865, after he had digested the news from Appomattox, he made this entry in the diary:

> I here declare my unmitigated hatred to Yankee rule—to all political, social and business connections with the Yankees and to the Yankee race. Would that I could impress these sentiments, in their full force, on every living Southerner and bequeath them to every one yet to be born! May such sentiments be held universally in the outraged and downtrodden South, though in silence and stillness, until the now far-distant day shall arrive for just retribution for Yankee usurpation, oppression and atrocious outrages, and for deliverance and vengeance for the now ruined, subjugated and enslaved Southern States! . . . And now with my latest writing and utterance, and with what will be near my latest breath, I here repeat and would willingly proclaim my unmitigated hatred to Yankee rule—to all political, social and business connections with Yankees, and the perfidious, malignant and vile Yankee race.[4]

Almost before the ink of this entry had dried the old man performed his most symbolic act. Seating himself erectly in his chair, he propped the butt of his silver-mounted gun against a trunk at his feet, placed the muzzle in his mouth and, as his son reported in a letter to members of the family, "pulled the trigger with a forked stick."[5]

CODA

With Edmund Ruffin's suicide and the collapse of the Confederacy which it symbolized, the Old South as a concrete entity passed beyond history and into legend. One prolonged attempt to establish and sustain an aristocratic ideal in the face of obstacles of the kind invariably thrown up by American circumstances had ended. It was not the first such attempt, as colonial historians have shown,[6] nor was it to be the last, as

---

4 Ibid., p. 259. The information about Ruffin, except for the details of his death, derives entirely from Professor Craven's biography.

5 Edmund Ruffin, Jr., to his sons, June 20, 1865, in "Death of Edmund Ruffin," *Tyler's Quarterly Historical and Genealogical Magazine*, 5 (January 1924), 193.

6 Bernard Bailyn, "Politics and Social Structure in Virginia," *Seventeenth-Century America: Essays in Colonial History* (ed.), James Morton Smith (Chapel Hill, 1959), pp. 90–115.

those familiar with elitist groups at the end of the century can testify;[7] but perhaps, because of its bearing on the course of American history before 1861 and because of its more general consequences for the development of our cultural self-awareness, it has been the most important.

The Cavalier ideal was predestined to fail, as some of its earliest proponents secretly knew. The men who originated it were not aristocrats in any sense which Europeans would have recognized. Often they themselves were self-made men, provincial in their outlook and historically naïve, who possessed no sure sense of any cultural tradition. I have spoken, principally as a matter of convenience, of "the South" and "the planter class" in assigning a specific locus to the kind of thinking which I have been describing; but at no time, I suspect, was the Cavalier ideal as it was defined by Beverley Tucker, for example, widely understood or embraced by Southern planters in general, to say nothing of other people living within the South. Such an ideal was significant because it exemplified an important American cultural problem and because it defined a tendency in Southern thought which ultimately affected political events.

As it moved toward implementation, of course, the ideal was repeatedly and necessarily compromised. The constitution of no Southern state, not even that of South Carolina, provided for anything more than a kind of modified planter oligarchy; most of the older states within the South yielded to democratic pressures before the war; and the newer states of the Southwest were no more exclusive in their political arrangements than comparable states in the North. The Confederate constitution, finally, despite its explicit recognition of slavery, was in no sense meant to set up an aristocracy, and in certain ways it provided more assurance of popular government than the federal Constitution.

The legacy left behind by the Cavalier ideal is a little difficult to define; a careful consideration of it would require a study in itself. The close of the war did not mean, certainly, that some kind of aristocratic ideal ceased to form a part of Southern thinking, nor did it mean, once Reconstruction was over, that some kind of planter class ceased to dominate Southern politics. Quite the contrary. The century had virtually ended before the old dominant groups in the South and their new business allies received any substantial challenge from the majority of Southerners, whose affairs they had historically directed. After the war, as everyone knows, the legend, far from dying away, was given a new lease on life and, in the North, probably enjoyed greater popularity and evoked more interest than at any other time. Its vitality, it seems apparent enough, has not yet exhausted itself today after more than a century of discussion and dramatic reembodiment. The nostalgia felt by Americans for the antebellum South and for the drama of the Civil War is a phenomenon which continues to startle those unfamiliar with our culture, with our collective anxieties about the kind of civilization we have created, and with our reservations concerning the kind of social conformity

---

[7] Barbara Miller Solomon, *Ancestors and Immigrants: A Changing New England Tradition* (Cambridge, Mass.; 1956); Arthur Mann, *Yankee Reformers in The Urban Age* (Cambridge, Mass., 1954).

which, it appears, it has been our destiny to exemplify before the world. Some of our greatest writers—Henry Adams and Henry James within the nineteenth century—have employed the Cavalier legend as a means of defining and measuring the failures and limitations of our culture at large. It seems scarcely necessary to add that this same concern has characteristically engaged the imagination of William Faulkner. But for the great mass of Americans, even those who take their impression exclusively from popular novels, television plays, and Civil War centennials, the Old South has also become an enduring part of our sense of the past. At odd moments probably even the most skeptical of us allow our thoughts to play over this lingering social image, and to concede with mingled pride and wonderment: "Once it was *different* down there."

The Tragic Southerner*

Charles G. Sellers, Jr.

The American experience knows no greater tragedy than the Old South's twistings and turnings on the rack of slavery. Others suffered more from the "peculiar institution," but only the suffering of white Southerners fits the classic formula for tragedy. Like no other Americans before or since, the white men of the antebellum South drove toward catastrophe by doing conscious violence to their truest selves. No picture of the Old South as a section confident and united in its dedication to a neofeudal social order, and no explanation of the Civil War as a conflict between "two civilizations," can encompass the complexity and pathos of the antebellum reality. No analysis that misses the inner turmoil of the antebellum Southerner can do justice to the central tragedy of the southern experience.†

The key to the tragedy of southern history is the paradox of the slaveholding South's devotion to "liberty." Whenever and wherever Southerners sought to invoke their highest social values—in schoolboy declamations, histories, Fourth of July orations, toasts, or newspaper editorials —"liberty" was the incantation that sprang most frequently and most fervently from their lips and pens. "The love of liberty had taken deep

* Reprinted from Charles G. Sellers, Jr., *The Southerner as American* (Chapel Hill, N.C.: University of North Carolina Press, 1960).

† My interpretation of the Old South draws heavily on the brilliant insights of Wilbur J. Cash in *The Mind of the South* (New York, 1941), and also on Clement Eaton's *Freedom of Thought in the Old South* (Durham, 1940).

root in the minds of carolinians [sic] long before the revolution," explained South Carolina's historian David Ramsay in 1809. The "similarity of state and condition" produced by the early settlers' struggle to subdue the wilderness had "inculcated the equality of rights" and "taught them the rights of man."[1]

The Revolutionary struggle made this implicit colonial liberalism explicit and tied it to patriotic pride in the new American Union. From this time on, for Southerners as for other Americans, liberty was the end for which the Union existed, while the Union was the instrument by which liberty was to be extended to all mankind. . . .

If the Southerner had been embarrassed by his devotion to liberty and Union alone, he would have had less trouble easing his mind on the subject of slavery. But as a Virginia legislator exclaimed in 1832, "This, sir, is a Christian community." Southerners "read in their Bibles, *Do unto all men as you would have them do unto you*; and this golden rule and slavery are hard to reconcile."[2] During those early decades of the nineteenth century, when the South was confessing the evils of slavery, it had been swept by a wave of evangelical orthodoxy. Though the wave crested about the time some Southerners, including some clergymen, began speaking of slavery as a positive good, it does not follow that the evangelical reaction against the eighteenth century's religious ideas contributed significantly to the reaction against the eighteenth century's liberalism with regard to slavery.

On the contrary, the evangelical denominations had strong antislavery tendencies. Methodists, Quakers, and Baptists nurtured an extensive abolitionist movement in the upper South during the twenties, when the rest of the country was largely indifferent to the slavery question; and the Presbyterians were still denouncing slavery in Kentucky a decade later. It would be closer to the truth to suggest that as Southerners wrestled with their consciences over slavery, they may have gained a firsthand experience with the concepts of sin and evil that made them peculiarly susceptible to Christian orthodoxy. At any rate, as late as 1849, a proslavery professor at the University of Alabama complained to Calhoun that no one had yet published a satisfactory defense of slavery in the light of New Testament teachings. The "many religious people at the South who have strong misgivings on this head," he warned, constituted a greater threat to the peculiar institution than the northern abolitionists.[3] . . .

It is essential to understand that the public declarations of Southerners never revealed the full impact of all these antislavery influences on the southern mind. Fear of provoking slave insurrections had restrained free discussion of slavery even in the Revolutionary South, and an un-

---

[1] David Ramsay, *The History of South Carolina, from Its First Settlement in 1670, to the Year 1808* (2 vols.; Charleston, 1809), 2, 384. Fletcher M. Green, "Listen to the Eagle Scream: One Hundred Years of the Fourth of July in North Carolina (1776–1876)," *North Carolina Historical Review*, 31 (July & October 1954), 36, 534.

[2] Goodloe, *Southern Platform*, 49.

[3] E. Mitchell to John C. Calhoun, February 5, 1849, John C. Calhoun Papers (Clemson College Library).

easy society exerted steadily mounting pressure against antislavery utterances thereafter. Only when Nat Turner's bloody uprising of 1831
shocked Southerners into open debate over the peculiar institution did
the curtain of restraint part sufficiently to reveal the intensity of their
misgivings. Thomas Ritchie's influential Richmond *Enquirer* caught the
mood of that historic moment when it quoted a South Carolinian as
exclaiming,

> We may shut our eyes and avert our faces, if we please, but there it
> is, the dark and growing evil at our doors; and meet the question we must,
> at no distant day. . . . What is to be done? Oh! my God, I do not know, but
> something must be done.[4] . . .

The nub of the Southerner's ambivalent attitude toward slavery was
his inability to regard the slave consistently as either person or property.
Slaves "were a species of property that differed from all others," James
K. Polk declared as a freshman congressman, "they were rational; they
were human beings."[5] The slave's indeterminate status was writ large in
the ambiguity of the whole structure of southern society. A sociologist
has analyzed the institutional features of slavery as lying along a "ra-
tionality-traditionalism range," whose polar points were mutually contradictory. At one pole lay the economic view. Since slavery was a labor
system employed in a highly competitive market economy, a minimum
of rational efficiency was necessarily prescribed for economic survival.
This called for a "sheerly economic" view of slavery, one which regarded
the slave as property, which gave the master unlimited control over the
slave's person, which evaluated the treatment of slaves wholly in terms
of economic efficiency, which structured the slave's situation so that his
self-interest in escaping the lash became his sole motivation to obedience, which sanctioned the domestic slave trade and demanded resumption of the foreign slave trade as essential mechanisms for supplying
and redistributing labor, and which dismissed moral considerations as
both destructive of the labor supply and irrelevant. Though the plantation system tended during the latter part of the slavery period to approach
the ideal type of a purely commercial economic organization, especially
with the geographical shift to the new lands of the Southwest, few if any
Southerners ever fully accepted this "sheerly economic" view of slavery.

At the other pole lay a "traditional" or "familial" view, which regarded
the slave more as person than property and idealized "the patriarchal
organization of plantation life and the maintenance of the family estate
and family slaves at all costs." Both the "sheerly economic" and the
"familial" views of slavery were sanctioned by southern society; economics and logic drove Southerners toward the former, while sentiment, liberalism, and Christianity dragged them in the other direction.[6] . . .

---

4 Joseph C. Robert, *The Road from Monticello: A Study of the Virginia Slavery
Debate of 1832* (Durham, 1941), 17–18, and *passim*.

5 *Register of Debates*, 19th Cong., 1st Sess., 1649.

6 Wilbert E. Moore, "Slavery, Abolition, and the Ethical Valuation of the Individual: A Study of the Relations between Ideas and Institutions" (Ph.D. dissertation,
Harvard University, 1940), 193–212.

Nowhere, in fact, was the South's painful inner conflict over slavery more evident than in the elaborate body of theory by which it tried to prove (mainly to itself) the beneficence of its peculiar social system. "It has not been more than . . . thirty years since the abolition of slavery was seriously debated in the legislature of Virginia," observed the *Southern Literary Messenger* on the eve of the Civil War. "Now, on the contrary . . . the whole Southern mind with an unparalleled unanimity regards the institution of slavery as righteous and just, ordained of God, and to be perpetuated by Man." Yet the stridency with which southern unanimity was ceaselessly proclaimed stands in suggestive contrast to the private views of many Southerners. "To expect men to agree that Slavery is a blessing, social, moral, and political," wrote a North Carolina congressman to his wife, "when many of those who have all their lives been accustomed to it . . . believe exactly the reverse, is absurd." Even the fireeaters confessed privately that outside South Carolina most slaveholders were "mere negro-drivers believing themselves wrong and only holding on to their negroes as something to make money out of." South Carolinians themselves had "retrograded," wrote Robert W. Barnwell in 1844, "and must soon fall into the same category."[7]

Close examination of the superficially impressive proslavery philosophy reveals, as Louis Hartz has brilliantly demonstrated, a "mass of agonies and contradictions in the dream world of southern thought." The peculiar institution could be squared theoretically with either the slave's humanity or democratic liberalism for whites, but not with both. Thus the necessity for justifying slavery, coupled with the white South's inability to escape its inherited liberalism or to deny the common humanity it shared with its Negro slaves, inspired "a mixture of pain and wild hyperbole."[8]

Recognizing that the religious argument by itself was a threat to the peculiar institution, one school of proslavery philosophers sought to preserve both slavery and the slave's humanity by sacrificing democratic liberalism and falling back to a neofeudal insistence on the necessity of subordination and inequality in society. "Subordination rules supreme in heaven and must rule supreme on earth," asserted Bishop Elliott, and he did not attempt to disguise the repudiation of democratic liberalism that followed from this principle. Carried away by Revolutionary fervor, Southerners along with other Americans had "declared war against all authority and against all form"; they had pronounced all men equal and man capable of self-government. "Two greater falsehoods could not have been announced," Elliott insisted, "because the one struck at the whole

---

[7] Jay B. Hubbell, "Literary Nationalism in the Old South," in David K. Jackson (ed.), *American Studies in Honor of William Kenneth Boyd* (Durham, 1940), 183n.; David Outlaw to Mrs. David Outlaw, July [28], 1848, David Outlaw Papers (Southern Historical Collection, University of North Carolina); Robert W. Barnwell to Robert Barnwell Rhett, November 1, 1844, Robert Barnwell Rhett Papers (Southern Historical Collection, University of North Carolina).

[8] Louis Hartz, *The Liberal Tradition in America: An Interpretation of American Political Thought since the Revolution* (New York, 1955), 145–200.

constitution of civil society as it had ever existed, and because the other denied the fall and corruption of man."[9]

George Fitzhugh, the most logical and impressive of the proslavery philosophers and the leading exponent of southern neo-feudalism, would have preserved the humanity of the Negroes but denied freedom to the white masses by making both subject to the same serf-like subordination. Only thus could men be saved from the frightful corruption and turbulence of "free society." But southern planters were too much bourgeois capitalists and southern farmers were too much Jacksonian democrats to entertain the neo-feudalists' vituperation at "free society." "Soon counties, neighborhoods, or even individuals will be setting up castles," commented a sarcastic Alabamian.[10] Fitzhugh and his fellow intellectuals might talk all they pleased about reducing the masses, white and black, to serfdom, but practical politicians and publicists knew better than to fly so directly in the face of the South's liberal bias.

At the hands of men like James H. Hammond, therefore, neo-feudalism became a racial "mud-sill" theory, which divided society along the color line, relegating Negroes to bondage and reserving democratic liberalism for white men only. . . .

The debate between the religionists and feudalists, on the one hand, and the racists, on the other, defined the old South's central dilemma. The first two championed personalism and the familial view of the peculiar institution. The religionists were willing to question the beneficence and permanence of slavery in order to assert the slave's humanity; and the feudalists were willing to surrender democratic liberalism in order to retain a personalized system of servitude. The racists, on the other hand, denied the slave's full human status in order to reconcile slavery with democratic liberalism for whites. The South's ingrained liberalism and Christianity, in short, were continually thwarting the logic-impelled effort to develop a fully rationalized, sheerly economic conception of slavery, warranted by the racist argument.

It was this inner conflict which produced the South's belligerent dogmatism in the recurrent crises of the fifties. The whole massive proslavery polemic had the unreal ring of logic pushed far beyond conviction. "I assure you, Sir," Fitzhugh confessed in a private letter, "I see great evils in Slavery, but in a controversial work I ought not to admit them."[11] If the South's best minds resolutely quashed their doubts, it is small wonder that crisis-tossed editors and politicians took refuge in positive and extreme positions.

The final open collision between the two contradictory tendencies in the South's thinking about slavery came on the very eve of the Civil War, when some Southerners relentlessly pursued the logic of slavery's beneficence to the conclusion that the foreign slave trade should be reopened.

---

9 Jenkins, *Pro-Slavery Thought*, 239–40.

10 Ollinger Crenshaw, *The Slave States in the Presidential Election of 1860* (Baltimore, 1945), 253.

11 Wish, *Fitzhugh*, 111.

"I would sweep from the statute-book every interference with slavery," shouted a fire-eating South Carolina congressman. "I would repeal the law declaring the slave trade piracy; I would withdraw our slave squadron from the coast of Africa; and I would leave slavery unintervened against, wherever the power of the country stretches."[12]

Despite the lip service paid to the "positive good" doctrine, majority southern opinion was deeply shocked by its logical extension to sanction the foreign slave trade. Few Southerners were willing "to roll back the tide of civilization and Christianity of the nineteenth century, and restore the barbarism of the dark ages," declared a Georgia newspaper, and churchmen denounced the proposal with special vehemence. Even one of its original advocates turned against it when he witnessed the suffering of the Negroes aboard a captured slave ship. This "practical, fair evidence of its effects has cured me forever," confessed D. H. Hamilton. "I wish that everyone in South Carolina, who is in favor of re-opening of the Slave-trade, could have seen what I have been compelled to witness. . . . It seems to me that I can never forget it."[13] This was the agony of the proslavery South under the shadow of Civil War.

How, then, did the fundamentally liberal, Christian, American South ever become an "aggressive slavocracy"?[14] How did it bring itself to flaunt an aristocratic social philosophy? To break up the American Union? To wage war for the purpose of holding four million human beings in a bondage that violated their humanity? The answer is that Southerners did not and could not rationally and deliberately choose slavery and its fruits over the values it warred against. Rather it was the very conflict of values, rendered intolerable by constant criticism premised on values Southerners shared, which drove them to seek a violent resolution.

Social psychologists observe that such value conflicts—especially when they give rise to the kind of institutional instability revealed by the ambiguities of southern slavery—make a society "suggestible," or ready to follow the advocates of irrational and aggressive action.[15] Thus it was fateful that the Old South developed an unusually able minority of fire-eating sectionalists, who labored zealously, from the 1830s on, to unite the South behind radical measures in defense of slavery. Though a majority of Southerners remained profoundly distrustful of these extremists throughout the antebellum period, their unceasing agitation steadily aggravated the South's tensions and heightened its underlying suggestibility. By egging the South on to ever more extreme demands, the Calhouns, Rhetts, and Yanceys provoked violent northern reactions, which could then be used to whip the South's passions still higher. At length, in 1860, capitalizing on intrigues for the Democratic presidential

---

12 Harold S. Schultz, *Nationalism and Sectionalism in South Carolina, 1852–1860: A Study of the Movement for Southern Independence* (Durham, 1950), 182.

13 Stampp, *Peculiar Institution*, 278; Schultz, *Nationalism and Sectionalism*, 158–59.

14 The viewpoint of the present essay is not to be confused with the interpretation of the Civil War in terms of a "slave power conspiracy." . . .

15 Hadley Cantril, *The Psychology of Social Movements* (New York, 1941), 61–64. . . .

nomination, the fire-eaters managed to split the Democratic party, thus insuring the election of a Republican President and paving the way for secession.

Inflammatory agitation and revolutionary tactics succeeded only because Southerners had finally passed the point of rational self-control. The almost pathological violence of their reactions to northern criticism indicated that their misgivings about their moral position on slavery had become literally intolerable under the mounting abolitionist attack. "The South has been moved to resistance chiefly . . . by the popular dogma in the free states that slavery is a crime in the sight of GOD," said a New Orleans editor in the secession crisis. "The South, in the eyes of the North, is degraded and unworthy, because of the institution of servitude."[16]

Superimposed on this fundamental moral anxiety was another potent emotion, fear. John Brown's raid in October, 1859, created the most intense terror of slave insurrection that the South had ever experienced; and in this atmosphere of dread the final crisis of 1860–61 occurred. The press warned that the South was "slumbering over a volcano, whose smoldering fires, may at any quiet starry midnight, blacken the social sky with the smoke of desolation and death." Southerners believed their land to be overrun by abolitionist emissaries, who were "tampering with our slaves, and furnishing them with arms and poisons to accomplish their hellish designs." Lynch law was proclaimed, and vigilance committees sprang up to deal with anyone suspected of abolitionist sentiments. A Mississippian reported the hanging of 23 such suspects in three weeks, while the British consul at Charleston described the situation as "a reign of terror."[17]

Under these circumstances a large part of the southern white population approached the crisis of the Union in a state of near-hysteria. One man thought that "the minds of the people are aroused to a pitch of excitement probably unparalleled in the history of our country." "The desire of some for change," reported a despairing Virginian, "the greed of many for excitement, and the longing of more for anarchy and confusion, seems to have unthroned the reason of men, and left them at the mercy of passion and madness."[18]

Just as important as the hysteria which affected some Southerners was the paralysis of will, the despair, the sense of helplessness, which the excitement created in their more conservative fellows. Denying that the southern people really wanted to dissolve the Union, a Georgia editor saw them as being "dragged on, blindfolded, to consummation of the horrid act." A "moral pestilence" had "swept over the South," said a prominent North Carolinian, "dethroning reason, & paralyzing the ef-

16 Dwight L. Dumond (ed.), *Southern Editorials on Secession* (New York, 1931), 315–16.

17 Crenshaw, *Slave States*, 100, 103, 106; Laura A. White, "The South in the 1850's as Seen by British Consuls," *Journal of Southern History*, 1 (February 1935), 44.

18 Crenshaw, *Slave States*, 111; Robert C. Gunderson, "William C. Rives and the 'Old Gentlemen's Convention,'" *Journal of Southern History*, 22 (November 1956), 460.

forts of the best Union men of the country." But even some who decried the hysteria felt that "no community can exist & prosper when this sense of insecurity prevails," and concluded that almost any alternative was preferable to the strain of these recurrent crises. It was this conviction, more than anything else, which caused moderate men to give way to the bold and confident radicals.[19]

From the circumstances of the secession elections—the small turn-outs, the revolutionary tactics of the fire-eaters, the disproportionate weighting of the results in favor of plantation areas, the coercive conditions under which the upper South voted, and the hysteria that prevailed everywhere—it can hardly be said that a majority of the South's white people deliberately chose to dissolve the Union in 1861. A member of South Carolina's secession convention frankly admitted that "the common people" did not understand what was at stake. "But whoever waited for the common people when a great movement was to be made?" he asked. "We must make the move and force them to follow. That is the way of all revolutions and all great achievements."[20]

The leaders made the move, and the people followed, but with what underlying misgivings the sequel only too plainly demonstrated. The first flush of enthusiasm was rapidly supplanted by an apathy and a growing disaffection which historians have identified as major factors in the Confederacy's failure. During the dark winter of 1864–65, North Carolina's Governor Zebulon Vance commented on the supineness with which the southern population received the invading Sherman. It was evidence, said Vance, of what he had "always believed, that *the great popular heart* is not now, and never has been in this war! It was a revolution of the *Politicians,* not the *People.*"[21]

And when the cause was lost, Southerners abandoned it with an alacrity which underscored the reluctance of their original commitment. It was left for a leading ex-fire-eater to explain why they returned to the Union of their fathers with so little hesitation. Standing before the Joint Congressional Committee on Reconstruction in 1866, James D. B. De Bow attested in all sincerity the South's willingness to fight once again for the flag of the Union. "The southern people," he said "are Americans, republicans."[22]

Yet it is idle to wonder whether secession represented the deliberate choice of a majority of white Southerners, or to speculate about the outcome of a hypothetical referendum, free from ambiguity, coercion, and hysteria. Decisions like the one that faced the South in 1860–61 are never reached in any such ideal way. And even had the South decided for the Union, its and the nation's problem would have remained unsolved, and a violent resolution would only have been postponed. Slavery was doomed

---

[19] Crenshaw, *Slave States,* 111n., 237; Klingberg, *Southern Claims Commission,* 13. Cf. Cantril, *Psychology of Social Movements,* 61.

[20] White, *Rhett,* 177n.

[21] Klingberg, *Southern Claims Commission,* 138.

[22] *Report of the Joint Committee on Reconstruction, at the First Session, Thirty-Ninth Congress* (Washington, 1866), 133.

by the march of history and by the nature of Southerners themselves, but so deeply had it involved them in its contradictions that they could neither deal with it rationally nor longer endure the tensions and anxieties it generated. Under these circumstances the Civil War or something very like it was unavoidable. It was also salutary, for only the transaction at Appomattox could have freed the South's people—both Negro and white—to move again toward the realization of their essential natures as Southerners, liberals, Christians, and Americans.

The Slavemaster's World-View*

Eugene D. Genovese

The Old South offers us the greatest paradox in a subject overflowing with paradox. Here was a regime as clearly capitalist in its origins as any other, but which came closest to perfecting slavery as a distinct mode of production. . . .

The foundation of a patriarchal and paternalistic ethos ultimately proved to be not the European institutional inheritance, which did play a role, but the plantation regime itself. The confrontation of master and slave, white and black, on a plantation presided over by a resident planter for whom the plantation was a home and the entire population part of his extended family generated that ethos, although where it advanced in harmony with the past, with inherited values, and with received institutions, it had a much easier time. . . .

. . . The colonization of the New World re-created archaic regimes shaped by the patriarchal plantation, the dominant tendency of which was paternalism. All slave regimes exhibited this tendency, for it was inherent in the master-slave relationship. The strength of this tendency depended primarily on the nature of its particular slaveholding class, which grew up on the spot but was also deeply influenced by its own historic past and relationship to a seigneurial or bourgeois society abroad. Each such class therefore simultaneously displayed general characteristics and yet was unique. Side by side with this process of internal archaic development there continued the far more powerful and ultimately triumphant process of world capitalist expansion—a process that absorbed the independent, internal process within itself and distorted it in decisive ways. The great revolt of the slaveholders of the Old South rep-

* By permission of the author from *The World the Slaveholders Made* (New York: Random House, Inc., 1969). Copyright by Eugene D. Genovese.

resented, in this sense, a dramatic reactionary movement to reverse the fundamental thrust of world history. . . .

. . . [After the Civil War] the remnants of the old aristocracy professed to deplore the demagogy and gangsterism of the Tillmans and Varda-mans, but they quietly capitulated and sometimes set the pace for racist vituperation. That capitulation is a long and bitter story in itself; for our immediate purposes it is enough that it occurred after a headlong fall from power and reflected defeat, despair, and a frantic attempt to sur-vive in a new and dangerous world. In this sense, too, the triumph of the bourgeoisie in a society that had been originally shaped by slavery spelled the triumph of racist extremism. . . .

The history of the Southern slaveholders had . . . [several] decisive turning points. . . . The first was the American Revolution, which, what-ever its significance in the North, constituted a reactionary slaveholders' rebellion in the South. If separation from England liberated a national capitalist regime in the North, it simultaneously liberated a plantation slave regime in the South. With the threat of British interference re-moved and a relatively weak central government to contend with, the road to regional power lay open before the slaveholders, who constituted the only class capable of treading it. . . .

The second decisive turning point was the formulation of the positive-good proslavery argument, which signaled the maturation of the ruling class and its achievement of self-consciousness. Far from being mere apologetics or rationalization, it represented the formulation of a world view that authentically reflected the position, aspirations, and ethos of the slaveholders as a class. . . . [Masters tried to live by class ethics.] In the Old South, most slaves probably did have the possibility of marital stability because their masters provided it. They provided it for two com-plementary reasons: they could more easily control married slaves with families, and their Christian consciences demanded it. . . .

John Berkeley Grimball of the aristocratic South Carolina low coun-try and Francis Terry Leak of the Mississippi Black Belt come to us as very different men: the one an urbane Charlestonian with that poise and charm to which men must generally be raised from birth; the other a rustic resident planter with that certain awkwardness which betrayed his simple origins and limited horizons. Yet, they had much in common. It was not, after all, Grimball's elegant tastes or the scale of his entertain-ing that stamped him as a Southern gentleman, nor even the delicacy and deceptive formality of his relationship with the gracious lady who adorned his estate. Grimball was a man of affairs, a public-spirited mem-ber of a self-conscious ruling class, and above all, a conscientious and dutiful master of the human beings in his charge. But no more so than was Francis Terry Leak.

When Leak brought his slaves together for the marriage of Moses and Pol in the winter of 1857, he performed the ceremony, as he always did, with a simple dignity and a seriousness worthy of the occasion. The whole plantation family, white and black, attended; the barbecue lived up to its advance notice; and the dancing carried on well into the early hours of the morning. Slave marriages had no status in law in the South as they had in the Catholic slaveholding countries; the marriage relation between Moses and Pol existed on Leak's sufferance. It was no less secure for so doing. . . .

The values of the plantation, its ways of thought and feeling, were antithetical to those of the bourgeois world. The relationship of master to slave, in itself an extension of the relationship of father to perpetual child, could be reconciled to the cash nexus only imperfectly. . . .

The South had a market economy; it did not have an essentially market society, and the whole point of the defense of slavery in the abstract was to ensure that it did not develop one. The relationship of master to slave was an organic, not a market, relationship. As a slave society, the South had a market in slaves, but master faced master in that market; the relationship to labor existed in another sphere. . . .

The world view of the slaveholders contained contradictions, as every world view must, but properly understood, it demonstrated adequate coherence and integrity. Like all class ideologies, it infuriated many of those who held it. Slaveholders, like the rest of us, rarely wanted to face the implications of each notion, prejudice, or ingrained commitment. They wished their ideology to be careless, pragmatic, inarticulate, disorganized, lazy; only political fanatics, philosophers, and lunatics can live any other way. How easy, therefore, for us to judge them as cynics who rationalized a system of exploitation or as rustic windbags who talked nonsense, or as thoughtless reactionaries of no account. They were all of these, but none. No matter how guilty they hay have been on each count, they did nonetheless stand for a world different from our own that is worthy of our sympathetic attention. The questions they asked are still with us; the inhumanity they condemned must still be condemned; and the values for which they fought still have something to offer. . . .

We cannot, I fear, ignore the currently fashionable disease, guiltomania, which threatens to reach epidemic proportions among historians. A strange malady, it induces fits of masochistic fantasy and a strong tendency toward self-destruction. All historical problems explain themselves away under its ravages, and if it continues its relentless advance, it will soon render historians obsolete. Nietzsche observed, in *Ecce Homo*, that were a god to come down to earth, he would do nothing but wrong: "To take upon oneself guilt and not punishment, that alone would be godlike." Some of our infected historians manifest this godlike trait. When they project it onto the slaveholders, however, they take account of the ungodlike and human frailty appropriate to the plantation and mete out fearful punishment at Appomattox. These remarks may well be received with indignation by those who could justly argue that they are *ad hominem* and show rank discourtesy toward colleagues whose views ought to be considered on their merits. Normally, decency would require that we discuss the thesis, not probe the motives behind it. The principle dictated by decency is a fine one, but it entails responsibilities. The slaveholders of Virginia, South Carolina, and Mississippi were and are entitled to the same courtesy, and the sensibilities of living historians call for no greater consideration than that which they extend to their dead subjects. The popular practice is to treat the proslavery advocates and the slaveholders generally as men whose ideas deserve only patronizing dismissal and who are of historical interest only as subjects for amateur psychological analysis. . . .

Did substantial numbers of slaveholders feel guilty about holding slaves? There is no evidence that they did, especially during the nineteenth century, and it is difficult to see why they should have. . . . We are, in short, back with the ideological struggle between two world views and systems of morality, which have to be examined as products of social confrontations and conflicts. The guilt-complex thesis is not necessarily wrong. It is irrelevant. . . .

Southern Guilt and the African Slave Trade Agitation*

Ronald T. Takaki

. . . The legend of the Old South is just that—a legend. It is more fiction than fact. What particularly concerns us here is the legend's description of the planter class as an established aristocracy. No doubt a number of the Virginia and Charleston planter aristocrats belonged to a long line of wealthy planters. But the planter of the Old South was usually a one-generation planter aristocrat—a rough and highly competitive entrepreneur who overcame the frontier and made a huge fortune. He was Wilbur J. Cash's young Irishman. He began as a lowly yeoman farmer in the Carolina upcountry around 1800. One winter he drifted down the river and found the people at the halfway station of Columbia greatly excited about a new invention—the cotton gin. When he returned home, he bought 40 acres of land, and worked hard to clear the land and cultivate the cotton. Eventually he bought a slave, then more slaves and more land, and built a large and impressive house with white columns. When he died years later, he was the owner of 114 slaves, and was remembered as "a gentleman of the old school."[1] Cash's story about the Irishman graphically illustrates the reality of slaveholding social mobility in the Old South. Yet, as even Cash himself recognized but did not fully appreciate, this slaveholding social mobility had begun to freeze before the Civil War. More importantly, many Southerners *thought* it had. The traditional Southern optimism rooted in the yeoman-to-planter mobility was splinter-

---

* Ronald T. Takaki, *A Pro-Slavery Crusade: The Agitation to Reopen the African Slave Trade* (New York: The Free Press, 1971). By permission of the publisher.

1 Wilbur J. Cash, *The Mind of the South* (New York: Knopf, 1941), pp. 14–17.

ing in the 1850s. This raises highly important and fascinating questions: what happened in the white society of the Old South when the chief basis of economic mobility and the symbol of social status—slaves— were being closed to the white majority? To what extent did the fear of the monopolization of slaves contribute to class conflicts between non-slaveholders and slaveholders below the Mason-Dixon line? How was the agitation to reopen the African slave trade a response to these internal social tensions?

While many Southerners worried about a threatening class upheaval within Southern society, they also felt an anxious concern for a Southern disquietude about the morality of their peculiar institution. As Kenneth M. Stampp, David Brion Davis, and Winthrop D. Jordan have pointed out, the institution of slavery involved a fundamental ambivalence.[2] Slaveholders regarded the slave as property, as a thing. Yet they also regarded the slave as a person, and in certain circumstances the master-slave relationship took place at a human level. While we are not primarily interested here in the ambivalence itself, we are immensely concerned about how this contradiction bothered and gnawed at the Southern conscience, how Southern pro-slavery radicalism was a response to this Southern moral turmoil, and how the new aggressive pro-slavery ideology of the 1850s—the pro-African slave trade argument—had a psychological function for troubled and uneasy white Southerners. Thus, as we shall see, Eugene Genovese crucially misinterprets the Southern defense of slavery when he states: "Slavery may have been immoral to the world at large, but to these men [slaveholders], *notwithstanding their doubts and inner conflicts*, it increasingly came to be seen as the very foundation of a proper social order and therefore as the essence of morality in human relationships."[3] The controversy over slavery was undoubtedly a conflict of world views between the South and the outside world. But Genovese fails to appreciate the importance of the struggle of these very world views within Southern white society and in the minds of many white Southerners, and the relationship between this Southern turmoil and Southern militancy against the anti-slavery values of western civilization. Actually, to an important extent, slaveholders became increasingly committed to slavery as a moral institution *because of* "their doubts and inner conflicts." They were desperately trying to free themselves from the chains of moral anxiousness based on their ambivalence towards the slave.

Historians have traditionally tended to analyze the Southern pro-slavery movement within the context of the conflict between the North and the South. Obviously we cannot ignore the reality of the sectional crisis. Yet, as Charles G. Sellers and William Freehling have shown in their studies of the Southern defense of slavery, we must also give more

---

[2] Kenneth M. Stampp, *The Peculiar Institution: Slavery in the Ante-Bellum South* (New York: Random House, 1956), pp. 192–236; David Brion Davis, *The Problem of Slavery in Western Culture* (Ithaca: Cornell University Press, 1966), pp. 58–61; Winthrop D. Jordan, *White Over Black: American Attitudes Toward the Negro, 1550–1812* (Chapel Hill: University of North Carolina Press, 1968), pp. 104, 322–23.

[3] Eugene Genovese, *The Political Economy of Slavery: Studies in the Economy and Society of the Slave South* (New York: Random House, 1966), p. 8. Italics added.

serious attention to the inner tensions and problems of Southern society. We must not label this view "guiltomania" and dismiss it as "irrelevant."[4] We must try to deepen our understanding of the Southern predicament and the irony so pervasive in Southern history. This is especially true if we wish to appreciate fully the significance of pro-slavery aggressiveness during the decade before the Civil War.

Thus, in this study of the pro-slavery mind of the South, we shall focus on the agitation to reopen the African slave trade in order to probe a crucial question about the Southern defense of the peculiar institution: how was Southern pro-slavery radicalism of the 1850s not only a reaction to Northern abolitionism, but also a response to the *internal crisis* of the Old South—a crisis based chiefly on the distressing awareness that slaveholding social mobility was tightening, and on the disturbing recognition that white Southerners themselves doubted the rightness of slavery? . . .

Thus, in their ideological attack on the North, these Southern fire-eaters were also aiming at Southerners. They were advancing a radical pro-slavery ideology to discipline the abolitionist helpers and the distrusted nonslaveholders of the South. While they could not persuade Congress to repeal the federal laws and actually import large numbers of African slaves to restore slaveholding social mobility and thereby reinforce the security of the institution in the South, they sought to wield the pro-African slave-trade argument to intimidate Southern nonslaveholders. They also sought to use their ideological weapon to discipline perplexed and guilt-tortured slaveholders. Advocates of the African slave trade like Spratt and Yancey were defining the norms for Southerners, for themselves.[5] They were trying to give Southerners a new and a consistent pro-slavery identity. They were telling Southerners who they were, or should be—Southerners were *both* slaveholders *and* righteous men. They were leading a Southern crusade to ferret out "unsoundness" on slavery within the South. Support for the African slave trade was a test of Southern loyalty to the peculiar institution.

Their aggressive and insistent affirmation of slavery as the essence of morality could help some of the African slave-trade advocates overcome their private moral qualms about the institution. Public declarations of confidence in slavery sometimes concealed inner misgivings. Even leading pro-slavery theoretician George Fitzhugh confessed privately that he saw "great evils in Slavery, but in a controversial work I ought not to admit them." Possibly even Edmund Ruffin had not completely conquered his early feelings about slavery as an evil to be abolished someday.[6] In

---

4 Charles G. Sellers, "The Travail of Slavery," in Sellers (ed.), *The Southerner as American* (Chapel Hill: University of North Carolina Press, 1960); William Freehling, *Prelude to Civil War: The Nullification Controversy in South Carolina* (New York: Harper and Row, 1966); Eugene Genovese, *The World the Slaveholders Made* (New York: Random House, 1969), pp. 143, 150.

5 For a suggestive study of norms and deviancy, see Kai T. Erikson, *Wayward Puritans: A Study in the Sociology of Deviance* (New York: John Wiley, 1966).

6 Fitzhugh to Holmes, April 11, 1855, Holmes Letter Book, quoted in Wish, *Fitzhugh*, p. 111; Craven, *Ruffin*, p. 108.

their assault on Southerners who might have been unsound on slavery, some of the advocates were actually trying to convince themselves as well as others that slavery was not a sin.

The African slave-trade agitation's press for a proslavery conformity was related to the thrust for Southern independence. Secession could give the South much more than political independence from the North: it could provide a framework for the reconstruction of values in the South on a sound pro-slavery basis. A Southern Confederacy could reopen the African slave trade, widen the social base of slaveholding, and buttress the commitment to the institution. The presence of numerous blacks in Southern society would compel whites, anxious about their survival, to support slavery, an institution of race control, and condemn the Helper schemes for abolition and colonialization as ridiculous. If the African slave trade could be used to provide labor support for Southern industrialization, then even the industrial society of a Confederacy would be committed to slavery. But even if African slaves were not imported into a Confederate South, the defiance of secession and the violence of war in defense of slavery would surely help to confirm the rightness of slavery in the minds of Southerners. In short, the agitation for the reopening of the African slave trade was designed not only to repel the moral crusade of William Lloyd Garrison but also to help Southerners get right with slavery! . . .

. . . The African slave trade would transport unfortunate, degraded, and barbarous Africans from a depraved continent; and Southern slavery would elevate them to a condition of usefulness, well-being, and morality. In the American South, the African would be transformed from a cannibal to a "submissive," "docile," "patient," and "happy" slave—a Sambo. Slavery would teach the wild African how to work in the cotton fields, "to speak English, to say the Lord's prayer, to trample his fetish, and to loathe raw frogs and redworms, roasted lizards and parched wasps, beetles, bumble-bees and grasshoppers." The African slave trade was a "commerce of mercy," and slavery a missionizing institution.[7] . . .

. . . Southerners must launch their own crusade, advance their own principles, and challenge the anti-slavery sentiments of the Western world. To accomplish this, the advocates asserted, the South must give to slavery "the moral strength of an aggressive attitude—a position in which there could be no admission of a wrong—no implication of a sense of

---

[7] George S. Sawyer, *Southern Institutes; or an Inquiry into the Origins and Early Prevalence of Slavery and the Slave-trade . . . with Notes and Comments in Defense of the Southern Institutions* (Philadelphia: J. B. Lippincott, 1859), p. 204; Augusta *Dispatch*, in Galveston *Weekly News*, May 3, 1859. For additional evidence, see Charleston *Standard*, in Boston *Liberator*, December 12, 1856; Clayton Banner, in Charleston *Mercury*, March 3, 1857; Galveston *News*, December 6, 1856; E. Ruffin, Diary, Ruffin Papers, Library of Congress; Richmond *Whig*, September 3, 1859; Edward B. Bryan, *Letters to the Southern People Concerning the Acts of Congress and Treaties with Great Britain, in Relation to the African Slave Trade* (Charleston: Walker, Evans & Co., 1858), p. 17; Presentment of the Grand Jury of Williamsburg, in Consul Bunch to the Earl of Clarendon, December 28, 1854, *British and Foreign State Papers, 1854–1855*, p. 1156; Jackson *Semi-Weekly Mississippian*, September 17, 1858; New Orleans *Crescent*, in Savannah *Morning News*, May 5, 1859; "Southern," in Richmond *Enquirer*, July 28, 1857.

shame in its condition."[8] Thus in this war of opinion they proposed to plant their standard in the very faces of their adversaries and to declare boldly the renewal of the African slave trade as the leading principle of the South.[9]

Contemporary observers recognized this new aggressiveness. . . . But, while these unhappy observers correctly described the African slave-trade agitation as a revolt against the antislavery values of western culture, they did not understand that much of the new Southern aggression against the outside western world was actually being directed inward against the uncertain South.

In the supreme expression of Southern pro-slavery defiance, Mississippi State Senator Henry Hughes caustically proposed an identification system for newly imported Africans.

> The identification of our negroes [from Africa] will not be difficult. Public officers . . . may be ordained and sworned to identify. If necessary bloody letters may by State authority, be branded on the negroes' cheeks or chins. Or if rampant, free-labor philanthropy, fattening on its own abuses but sickening at ours, shall still fall into foaming convulsions at the horrors of our labor system, then, let us in healthy, cool and laughing defiance, identify by other means, the negroes and their children. Let us in hard and staunch protest against what is philanthropy in design but misanthropy indeed; let us in humorous contempt, in delightful and deliberate detestation of sanctimonious meddlers; let us if expedient to identify our new negroes, mark them like hogs and brand them like beeves; let us slit their nostrils; let us pinch in their bleeding ears, crosscuts and underbits, or with hot and salted irons, fry on their brows and breasts, lasting letters. . . . Then let freedom shriek till her face is red, and her voice is cracked as her skull.[10]

Hughes's extreme protest can help us understand an anxiety at the heart of the internal crisis of the Old South. In his scornful call for the branding of slaves "like beeves," Hughes was trying to make it unmistakably clear to Southerners as well as Northerners what the slave should be: the slave should not be both person and property, but only property. If the slave were nothing more than property, nothing more than "hogs" and "beeves," how could the slaveholder be condemned as sinful and inhuman? Yet the shrillness of his arrogant and desperate scream suggests that Senator Hughes himself knew the slave, despite the bloody letters fried on his brows and breasts, was still nothing but a man.

---

8 Spratt, in De Bow's Review, 27 (June 1859), p. 208.

9 E. Bryan, in Charleston Mercury, August 28, 1857; Charleston Standard, in New York Weekly Tribune, November 8, 1856. For additional evidence, see Fitzhugh, "Southern Thought," De Bow's Review, 23 (October 1857), p. 339; New Orleans Delta, in Charleston Mercury, January 16, 1856; J. D. McRae, in De Bow's Review, 27 (1859), pp. 362–363; New Orleans Crescent, in Charleston Mercury, August 30, 1859; J. G. M. Ramsey to Spratt, April 29, 1858; Ramsey Papers, University of North Carolina Library; Presentments of the Grand Juries of Williamsburg and Richland, in Consul Bunch to the Earl of Clarendon, December 28, 1854, British and Foreign State Papers, 1854–1855, p. 1156.

10 Letter signed "St. Henry," in Jackson Semi-Weekly Mississippian, October 4, 1859. "St. Henry" was Henry Hughes's pen name. See Henry Hughes's scrapbook and diary, Hughes Papers, Mississippi State Archives.

chapter 3

Modern Interpretations
of Slavery

FEW WORKS ON SLAVERY before Kenneth M. Stampp's study of 1956 (Selection 1) escaped the crippling consequences of the racial myths prevalent for so long among scholars and scientists as well as ordinary people. Until a generation ago the Western world in general and Americans in particular regarded Africans as barbarians and based their belief in inherent and enduring black inferiority on the idea that personality, individual conduct, and group behavior sprang from fixed racial traits. Anthropologist Franz Boas on the eve of World War I initiated the movement to disassociate culture and race, and his junior colleague Melville Herskovits produced pioneer studies in the 1920s and 30s which revealed the diversity and the creativity of African peoples, but the old ideas on inherited inferiority, African "savagery," and "Caucasian civilization" continued to dominate American thought until after the second World War.

Among the social scientists who challenged the dominant myths in the 1930s and 40s were John Dollard and Allison Davis and among the historians Frederick Bancroft, Herbert Aptheker, and Richard Hofstadter. Dollard and Davis described an oppressive Southern caste system and discussed "the children of bondage" in ways which made highly improbable the historical myths about contented slaves. Historian Frederick Bancroft meticulously documented the participation without social stigma of upper class Southerners in a large scale domestic slave trade which sustained the economy of the Southeast and brutalized and disorganized black life across the entire South. Herbert Aptheker portrayed a slave South seething with discontent and rebelliousness and Richard Hofstadter became the first white scholar to provide an effective critique of some of U. B. Phillips' most basic assumptions and assertions. Hofstadter granted that Phillips had thoroughly and carefully used many sources (in 1962 Reuben F. Kugler accused him of the willing and frequent distortion of sources), but argued that the Georgia scholar had relied on the records of large plantations rather than on materials relating to smaller and more representative land holdings. After establishing the probability that another scholar with the same evidence and different presuppositions would reach far different conclusions, Hofstadter called for quite another approach oriented toward the slave himself and written by a scholar with both a knowledge of modern cultural anthropology and a comprehensive grasp of the concepts and procedures of modern social psychology.

The book which met these requirements and added the most exhaustive study of the documents in the history of slavery studies appeared in 1956 under the authorship of Kenneth M. Stampp. Although Stampp left himself open to criticism by drawing a black-red comparison hostile to Indians and by making the quickly challenged assertion that "innately Negroes *are,* after all, only white men with black skins, nothing more, nothing less," his book generally was a compendium of the best scholarly thought and research of the 50s. Very deftly and convincingly Stampp laid to rest many myths about the alleged natures of blacks and whites, plantation society, and the peculiar institution itself. After perusing *The Peculiar Institution* open-minded scholars *had* to reject the idea that slavery represented the movement from "savagery" to "civilization" and accept the conclusion that Southern bondage represented an oppressive social institution for economic exploitation which tore captives from organic positions in viable societies and placed them painfully "between two cultures."

Stampp routed Phillips so completely and established a new interpretation so persuasively that for years to come few scholars presumed to take public issue with him on the basic issues. It seemed unlikely that any other historian could do a better job with the same materials or would in the near future uncover any very large quantity of manuscripts unknown to Stampp, but as Stanley Elkins (Selection 2) demonstrated in 1959 a scholar might still make a worthwhile contribution by taking a new approach to old themes and materials. Elkins drew upon social psychology, anthropology, and comparative history in an effort to demonstrate that by contrast with the milder slave systems of the quasi-medieval Spanish and Portuguese colonies, the "unregulated agricultural capitalism" of the colonial American plantation owners developed a uniquely exploitative and oppressive form of slavery.

Alternate approaches to Elkins and Stampp in breaking new ground could be found by exploring aspects of slavery not carefully considered by scholars at an earlier time. Richard C. Wade (Selection 3), one of the major urban historians in America, wrote the first study of bondage in the cities and discovered that the urban slavery, which resembled that of the plantation countryside in 1820, had by 1860 moved rapidly toward disintegration. In an urban environment "the old system no longer really controlled, the wall no longer really confined; the chains no longer really held." A few years later Robert S. Starobin (Selection 4) examined the 5 percent of the slave labor force employed in factories and the extraction of natural resources and explained industrial slavery in the context of the drive for Southern self-sufficiency. Many powerful Southerners wanted the slave-operated factories badly enough but they wanted them firmly in the hands of the slaveowning elite.

Just as Wade and Starobin learned from urban studies and Elkins and Stampp borrowed insights from sociology, anthropology and social psychology, so another scholarly approach of the 1960s and 1970s proposed to make use of econometrics and other tools of the "'new economics." Twentieth century analytical comment on the economics of slavery began with Ulrich B. Phillips who argued in a framework of racist assumption that on the eve of the Civil War planters maintained a generally unprofitable system of labor from noblesse oblige and from a desire to uphold white supremacy. During the 1930s several scholars such as Louis C. Gray and Robert R. Russell took dissenting positions on the profitability of slavery and in 1942 Thomas P. Govan used modern bookkeeping and accounting methods to demonstrate that planters made substantial profits, but Phillips continued to prevail until Stampp collected and advanced the critical scholarship on the economic issues in a very cogent presentation showing substantial capital returns from slavery.

An article of 1958 on profitability (expanded into a book six years later) by Alfred H. Conrad and John R. Meyer seemed at first only to confirm the position which Stampp and others had made most probable. However, the essay also marked an important turning point in slavery studies by abandoning accounting and bookkeeping methods for modern economic thought and procedures, particularly a Keynesian capital-value formulae, in an effort to provide as final an answer as possible to the question of profitability. Conrad and Meyer demonstrated the existence of handsome profits in a "two commodity, two region system" based on the production of staples in the Southwest and some Eastern areas and on "the use of slaves to produce other slaves as intermediate goods" (i.e. slavebreeding) in the Southeast. In the years since 1958 books, articles, and panel presentations challenged several aspects of Conrad's and Meyer's presentation but in the mid-70s the basic position which they, Stampp, and other scholars held still seemed sound.

The controversy raised other questions such as "profitable to whom?" and "was it profitable in *the long run?*" A small plantation elite might make windfall profits while wantonly destroying the lives of vast numbers of black bondsmen, impoverishing the white masses, and condemning the entire society to live in economic want and stagnation during later years. The economic aspects of Southern slavery had some relevance to a modern world in which vast population blocs lived in poverty-ridden, "underdeveloped" economies with histories of production based on forced labor. In this context Douglas F. Dowd (Selection 5) raised his critique against much of the new economics and discussed the ways in which slavery (like imperialism) had simultaneously made large profits for ruling elites and played havoc with the true developmental interests of entire societies.

In 1974 two "cliometrical" experts in the new marriage of history and mathematics, Robert W. Fogel and Stanley L. Engerman, published an extremely provocative monograph on slavery. Some of the conclusions did not arouse so much controversy. Portions of the book supported the belief of John Blassingame and other scholars that the slave family and community had greater strength than earlier scholarship had supposed, and other sections in the volume sustained the fairly common notion that slavery was definitely *not* a moribund institution, unprofitable to the masters, responsible for general economic retardation or stagnation, and destined to expire soon. However, many of Fogel's and Engerman's conclusions, by confirming the most arrogant assertions of slaveholding ultras, aroused stormy objections and prompted the *New York Review of Books* to brush aside the liberal protestations of the authors about psychological oppression and their sympathetic book title *Time on the Cross* to describe the monograph with the cover headline "In Defense of Slavery" and with the inside caption "The Jolly Institution."

In the cliometrical hands of Fogel and Engerman slaves were transformed from the oppressed victims of inhuman material conditions to people with better food, shelter, and medical care than Northern whites and a longer lifespan than urban workers. The lash counted for much less than various bonuses and other incentives in a labor system with few brutal and sadistic masters and a very large number of reasonable and competent entrepreneurs who generally left administration and supervision to the slaves themselves, assigned one black in five to a "preferred occupational position," and allowed the bondsman to keep 90 percent of the value of his labor. The slave family turned out to be a strong, stable, nuclear family headed by a dominant male, largely because the masters on plantations moved 98 percent of the slaves taken West in family groups, fathered no more than 1 to 2 percent of slave children, sold a slave only once in 22 years, and presided over a system which allowed slave women to have the first child at 22½ years of age and to experience a lower death rate in childbirth than Southern white women. The system worked so well economically that plantation agriculture produced 35 percent more than free farming and the slave 53 percent more than the Northern worker. Postwar developments rather than slavery held back the blacks. Nor did the white masses suffer greatly from a regional society with an income distribution equal to the North, a per capita income greater than the Midwest and all European countries except England, and a per capita income growth 30 percent greater than the North.

No scholar had ever dared to claim so much for the peculiar institution. Despite the great skill in methodology and techniques displayed by Fogel and Engerman, some of their conclusions seemed to lack basic credibility and several assertions quickly came under fire from fellow cliometricians. Certainly *Time on the Cross* contains rich materials for many angry debates in the second half of the 70s. In the controversies to come historians would do well to remember how often in the past the most capable natural and social scientists have served as intellectual handmaidens of bondage and racism.

BIBLIOGRAPHY

Works Consulted in This Chapter

Aptheker, Herbert, *American Negro Slave Revolts* (1943).
Bancroft, Frederick, *Slave Trading in the Old South* (1931).

Boas, Franz, *The Mind of Primitive Man* (1911).

Conrad, Alfred H., and Meyer, John R., "The Economics of Slavery in the Ante-Bellum South," *Journal of Political Economy* (1954) and *The Economics of Slavery* (1964).

Davis, Allison, and Dollard, John, *Children of Bondage* (1940).

Dollard, John, *Caste and Class in a Southern Town* (1937).

Dowd, Douglas F., "Slavery as an Obstacle to Economic Growth in the U.S.: A Comment," *Journal of Economic History* (1967).

Elkins, Stanley M., *Slavery, A Problem in American Institutional and Intellectual Life* (1959).

Fogel, Robert William, and Engerman, Stanley L., *Time on the Cross: The Economics of American Negro Slavery* (1974).

————, *Time on the Cross: Evidence and Methods—A Supplement* (1974).

Gray, Lewis C., *History of Agriculture in the Southern U.S. to 1860* (2 vols., 1933, 1941).

Herskovits, Melville, *The American Negro* (1928), *The Myth of the Negro Past* (1941) and other books and articles.

Hofstadter, Richard, "U. B. Phillips and the Plantation Legend," *Journal of Negro History* (1944).

Kugler, Rueben F., "U. B. Phillips' Use of Sources," *Journal of Negro History* (1962).

Russell, Robert R., "The General Effects of Slavery Upon Southern Economic Progress," *Journal of Southern History* (1938).

Stampp, Kenneth M., *The Peculiar Institution: Slavery in the Ante-Bellum South* (1956).

Starobin, Robert S., *Industrial Slavery in the Old South* (1970).

Wade, Richard C., *Slavery in the Cities: The South, 1820–1860* (1964).

Suggested Readings

Among *general works* Stampp's book continues to be the best general account and Allen Weinstein and Frank Otto Gattell, eds., *American Negro Slavery* (2nd ed., 1972) is the most useful anthology. See also Robert S. Starobin, ed., *Blacks in Bondage, Letters of American Slaves* (1974). Important works on slave resistance and community and on comparative slave studies are listed in the bibliographies to chapters 4 and 5.

Among the studies on *Southern states* only Robert McColley's excellent study on *Slavery and Jeffersonian Virginia* (1964) is satisfactory and many books in this category, particularly the older works, are heavy with the burden of racist assumption, but for some of the better studies see Roger W. Shugg, *Origins of Class Struggle in Louisiana 1840–1875* (1939); Joe Gray Taylor, *Negro Slavery in Louisiana* (1963); Chase C. Mooney, *Slavery in Tennessee* (1957); Joseph K. Menn, *The Large Slaveowners of Louisiana, 1860* (1964); James B. Sellers, *Slavery in Alabama* (1950); Charles S. Sydnor, *Slavery in Mississippi* (1933); and Robert C. Reinders, "Slavery in New Orleans in the Decade Before the Civil War," *Mid-America* (1962). The last item is informative on urban slavery.

On *slavery in the North* see Edgar J. McManus' fine monographs, *A History of Negro Slavery in New York* (1966) and *Black Bondage in the North* (1972); the first few chapters of Arthur Zilversmit in *The First Emancipation, The Abolition of Slavery in the North* (1967); David M. Katzman, "Black Slavery in Michigan," *Midcontinent American Studies Journal* (1971); and Robert C. Twombly and Richard H. Moore, "Black Puritan: The Negro in Seventeenth Century Massachusetts," *William and Mary Quarterly* (1967).

On the *slave trade* see Basil Davidson's dramatic *Black Mother: The Years of the African Slave Trade* (1961); Malcolm Cowley and Daniel Mannix, *Black Cargoes* (1963); James Pope-Hennessy, *Sins of the Fathers, A Study of the Atlantic Slave Traders, 1441–1807* (1968); and Phillip D. Curtin, *The Atlantic Slave Trade: A Census* (1969).

On the *domestic slave trade* Eugene D. Genovese in *The World the Slave-holders Made* (1969) regarded the internal trade as small but provided no substantial evidence. William Calderhead provides enough supporting evidence to at least reopen the question in "How Extensive was the Border State Slave Trade: A New Look," *Civil War History* (1972).

On the *origins of slavery* see Alden T. Vaughn, "Blacks in Virginia: A Note on the First Decade;" *William and Mary Quarterly* (1972); Edmund S. Morgan, "Slavery and Freedom, The American Paradox," *Journal of American History* (1972); and Winthrop D. Jordan's brilliant study, *White Over Black: American Attitudes Toward the Negro, 1550–1812* (1968) which discusses all the earlier literature on origins. See also two unusually fine studies, Thad W. Tate, *The Negro in Eighteenth Century Williamsburg* (1965) and Wesley Frank Craven, *White, Red and Black: The Seventeenth Century Virginian* (1971). The reader should also consult the bibliography on racism in this volume.

Historical literature on the *economics of slavery* flourished in the 1960s. The structure of scholarly debate was effectively perceived and presented in Hugh G. J. Aitken, ed., *Did Slavery Pay?* (1971); Harold D. Woodman, ed., *Slavery and the Southern Economy* (1966); and William N. Parker, ed., *The Structure of the Cotton Economy* (1970). The *Journal of Economic History and Agricultural History* devoted issues to the theme in 1967 and 1970. Other important journals with essays on the theme are *Explorations in Entrepreneurial History*, the *Business History Review*, and the *Journal of Political Economy*. For a good summary, see Part 7 in Robert W. Fogel and Stanley L. Engerman, eds., *The Reinterpretation of American Economic History* (1968). Some of the more important interpretive essays of the early 1970s are Otto H. Olson, "Historians and the Extent of Slave Ownership in the South," *Civil War History* (1972); William N. Parker, "Slavery and Southern Economic Development: An Hypothesis and Some Evidence," *Agricultural History* (1970); Stanley L. Engerman, "The Slave Trade and British Capital Formation," *Business History Review* (1972); Gavin Wright, "New and Old Views on the Economics of Slavery," *Journal of Economic History* (1973); Peter Passell and Gavin Wright, "The Effects of Pre-Civil War Territorial Expansion on the Price of Slavery," *Journal of Political Economy* (1973); and Gerlad Gunderson, "Southern Ante-Bellum Income Remembered," *Explorations in Economic History* (1973). For an interesting local study see Clarence L. Mohr, "Slavery in Oglethorpe County, Georgia, 1773–1865," *Phylon* (1974).

The Travail of Slavery*

Kenneth M. Stampp

. . . A wise master did not take seriously the belief that Negroes were natural-born slaves. He knew better. He knew that Negroes freshly imported from Africa had to be broken in to bondage; that each succeeding generation had to be carefully trained. This was no easy task, for the bondsman rarely submitted willingly. Moreover, he rarely submitted completely. In most cases there was no end to the need for control—at least not until old age reduced the slave to a condition of helplessness. . . .

. . . The first step, advised those who wrote discourses on the management of slaves, was to establish and maintain strict discipline. An Arkansas master suggested the adoption of the "Army Regulations as to the discipline in Forts." "They must obey at all times, and under all circumstances, cheerfully and with alacrity," affirmed a Virginia slaveholder. "It greatly impairs the happiness of a negro, to be allowed to cultivate an insubordinate temper. Unconditional submission is the only footing upon which slavery should be placed. . . ."

The second step was to implant in the bondsmen themselves a consciousness of personal inferiority. They had "to know and keep their places," to "feel the difference between master and slave," to understand that bondage was their natural status. They had to feel that African ancestry tainted them, that their color was a badge of degradation. In the country they were to show respect for even their master's nonslaveholding neighbors; in the towns they were to give way on the streets to the most wretched white man. The line between the races must never be crossed, for familiarity caused slaves to forget their lowly station and to become "impudent."

Frederick Douglass explained that a slave might commit the offense of impudence in various ways: "in the tone of an answer; in answering at all; in not answering; in the expression of countenance; in the motion of the head; in the gait, manner and bearing of the slave." Any of these acts, in some subtle way, might indicate the absence of proper subordination.[1] . . .

The third step in the training of slaves was to awe them with a sense of their master's enormous power. The only principle upon which slavery could be maintained, reported a group of Charlestonians, was the "principle of fear."[2] . . .

* Reprinted by permission of Alfred A. Knopf, Inc. from *The Peculiar Institution* by Kenneth Stampp. Copyright, 1956 by Kenneth Stampp.

[1] *Southern Planter*, 12 (1852), pp. 376–79; *Southern Cultivator*, 8 (1850), p. 163; *Farmers' Register*, 1 (1834), pp. 564–65; Douglass, *My Bondage*, p. 92.

[2] *DeBow's Review*, 7 (1849), p. 498.

In this the slaveholders had considerable success. Frederick Douglass believed that most slaves stood "in awe" of white men; few could free themselves altogether from the notion that their masters were "invested with a sort of sacredness." Olmsted saw a small white girl stop a slave on the road and boldly order him to return to his plantation. The slave fearfully obeyed her command. A visitor in Mississippi claimed that a master, armed only with a whip or cane, could throw himself among a score of bondsmen and cause them to "flee in terror." He accomplished this by the "peculiar tone of authority" with which he spoke. "Fear, awe, and obedience . . . are interwoven into the very nature of the slave."[3]

The fourth step was to persuade the bondsmen to take an interest in the master's enterprise and to accept his standards of good conduct. . . . Though slaveholders induced only a few chattels to respond to this appeal, these few were useful examples for others.

The final step was to impress Negroes with their helplessness, to create in them "a habit of perfect dependence" upon their masters.[4] Many believed it dangerous to train slaves to be skilled artisans in the towns, because they tended to become self-reliant. Some thought it equally dangerous to hire them to factory owners. In the Richmond tobacco factories they were alarmingly independent and "insolent." A Virginian was dismayed to find that his bondsmen, while working at an iron furnace, "got a habit of roaming about and *taking care of themselves*." Permitting them to hire their own time produced even worse results.[5] . . .

A spirit of independence was less likely to develop among slaves kept on the land, where most of them became accustomed to having their master provide their basic needs, and where they might be taught that they were unfit to look out for themselves. . . .

Here, then, was the way to produce the perfect slave: accustom him to rigid discipline, demand from him unconditional submission, impress upon him his innate inferiority, develop in him a paralyzing fear of white men, train him to adopt the master's code of good behavior, and instill in him a sense of complete dependence. This, at least, was the goal.

But the goal was seldom reached. Every master knew that the average slave was only an imperfect copy of the model. He knew that some bondsmen yielded only to superior power—and yielded reluctantly. This complicated his problem of control. . . .

Although cruelty was endemic in all slaveholding communities, it was always most common in newly settled regions. Along the rough southern frontier thousands of ambitious men were trying swiftly to make their fortunes. They operated in a frantically competitive society which provided few rewards for the virtues of gentility and almost put a premium upon ruthlessness. . . .

. . . No master denied the propriety of giving a moderate whipping to a disobedient bondsman. During the seventeenth and eighteenth cen-

---

3 Douglass, *My Bondage*, pp. 250–51; Olmsted, *Back Country*, pp. 444–45; [Ingraham], *South-West*, 2, pp. 260–61.

4 *Southern Cultivator*, 4 (1846), p. 44.

5 *Southern Planter*, 12 (1852), pp. 376–79; Olmsted, *Seaboard*, pp. 58–59.

turies the lash was used to punish free men as well as slaves. By mid-nineteenth century, however, it was seldom used upon any but slaves, because public opinion now considered it to be cruel. Why it was less cruel to whip a bondsman was a problem that troubled many sensitive masters. That they often had no choice as long as they owned slaves made their problem no easier to resolve.

Bennet H. Barrow, a Louisiana planter, kept an unusually full record of punishments—a record which illustrates the difficulty of distinguishing between cruelty and reasonable "correction." A substantial and respected man in his community, Barrow inherited lands and slaves from his father; he was in no sense a crude parvenu. Yet he flogged his chattels freely, sometimes severely. On various occasions he had a "general whipping frollick," whipped "every hand in the field . . . commencing with the driver," or gave "a number of them a good flogging." He broke his sword cane on the head of one offending slave, "beat" another "very much" and "cut him with a club in 3 places verry bad." Barrow was one of the few large planters who refused to employ overseers, because of their bad reputation.[6]

If it was cruel to flog slaves so frequently and severely that their backs were permanently scarred, southern newspapers provided evidence of an abundance of this variety of inhumanity. The following illustrations are from antebellum fugitive-slave advertisements and from sheriffs' committal notices: Charles, "an old sinner" who escaped from a Louisiana plantation, had "many stripes of the lash"; a Mississippi slave had "large raised scars or whelks in the small of his back and on his abdomen nearly as large as a person's finger"; Nancy, a Georgia slave, was "considerably marked by the whip"; Esther, an Alabama slave, was "marked about the shoulders from whipping"; a Missouri fugitive had "many scars on his back"; Gid, according to his North Carolina master, had a "remarkably bad temper" and had in consequence "marks of the lash upon his back"; Tom, who was held by the jailer of Augusta County, Virginia, had "the appearance of frequent and severe flogging"; Anaca, who escaped from her Kentucky master, had "a large scar immediately on her chest from the cut of a whip." . . .

Beyond this were cases of pure brutality—cases of flogging that resulted in the crippling, maiming, or killing of slaves. An early nineteenth-century Charleston grand jury presented "as a serious evil the many instances of Negro Homicide" and condemned those who indulged their passions "in the barbarous treatment of slaves."[7] "Salting—washing the cuts received from the whip with brine—was a harsh punishment inflicted upon the most obstinate bondsmen. Though all but a few deplored such brutality, slaveholders found themselves in a dilemma when nothing else could subdue a rebel.

If a master was too squeamish to undertake the rugged task of humbling a refractory bondsman, he might send him to a more calloused neighbor, or to a professional "slave breaker." . . .

---

6 Davis (ed.), *Diary of Bennet H. Barrow*, passim.

7 Henry, *Police Control*, pp. 67–68.

The branding of slaves was a widespread custom in colonial days; it was less common in the nineteenth century. But as late as 1838, a North Carolinian advertised that Betty, a fugitive, was recently "burnt . . . with a hot iron on the left side of her face; I tried to make the letter M." In 1848, a Kentuckian identified his runaway Jane by a brand mark "on the breast something like L blotched."[8] Mutilation as a form of punishment also declined without disappearing entirely. A Louisiana jailer, in 1831, gave notice that he had a runaway in his custody: "He has been lately gelded, and is not yet well." Another Louisianian recorded his disgust for a neighbor who had "castrated 3 men of his."[9]

Some masters who were otherwise as humane as the peculiar institution would permit tolerated almost anything that might "cure" habitual runaways. Andrew Jackson once offered fifty dollars reward for the capture of a fugitive, "and ten dollars extra for every hundred lashes any person will give him to the amount of three hundred." A Georgian punished his runaways by pulling out one of their toenails with a pair of pincers. Others hunted them with shotguns. A North Carolinian advertised for an escaped slave who had "some marks of shot about his hips, thighs, neck and face." Bennet H. Barrow caught Jerry "in the Bayou behind the Quarter, [and] shot him in the thigh"; when Jerry absconded again, Barrow vowed he would this time "shoot to kill." A Mississippian, apparently wishing to give his slaves a stern warning, promised to compensate whoever captured his fugitive "dead or alive."[10]

The tracking of runaways with dogs was no figment of abolitionist imaginations; it was a common practice in all slave states, defended and justified in the courts. Groups of slaveholders sometimes rode through the swamps with their dogs and made the search for fugitives a sport comparable to fox hunting. Others preferred to hire professional slave catchers who provided their own "Negro dogs." . . .

The angry mobs who dealt extra-legal justice to slaves accused of serious crimes committed barbarities seldom matched by the most brutal masters. "They call it Lintch's Law," wrote a frightened Louisiana plantation mistress during a local insurrection panic. "If they continue hanging, as they have done for some time past, we should be careful of the children, otherwise the World might be left without people."[11] Fear turned groups of decent white men into ferocious mobs—fear and the knowledge that the law was not strong enough to touch them.

After the Nat Turner rebellion a Richmond newspaper declared that the reprisals of the whites were "hardly inferior in barbarity to the atrocities of the insurgents." During the insurrection panic of 1856, a Texas editor affirmed that at such a time "the popular vengeance may be meted

---

8 Johnson, *Ante-Bellum North Carolina*, pp. 493–94; Coleman, *Slavery Times in Kentucky*, pp. 248–49.

9 Taylor, "Slavery in Louisiana," p. 236; Davis (ed.), *Diary of Bennet H. Barrow*, pp. 173–74.

10 Phillips (ed.), *Plantation and Frontier*, 2, pp. 85–88; Olmsted, *Texas*, pp. 104–5; Davis (ed.), *Diary of Bennet H. Barrow*, pp. 239, 242; Jackson *Mississippian*, July 11, 1834.

11 Rachel O'Conner to Frances S. Weeks, September 7, 1835, Weeks Collection.

out to the criminal with as much necessity as we would strike down an enemy in self-defence, or shoot a mad dog in our path." A Mississippian was ready for the "fagot and the flame" and to "let every tree in the country bend with Negro meat."[12] . . .

Mobs all too frequently dealt with slaves accused of murder or rape. They conducted their own trials or broke into jails or court rooms to seize prisoners for summary execution. Their more fortunate victims were hanged; the others were burned to death, sometimes in the presence of hundreds of bondsmen who were forced to attend the ceremony. Thus, wrote a Mississippian after one such incident, "justice was satisfied; the law of retaliation was inflicted . . . while the example made of this wretch had, no doubt, a salutary effect upon the two thousand slaves who witnessed his execution." An Alabama editor justified the burning of a slave at the stake by the "law of self-protection, which abrogates all other law. . . ."[13]

In Africa the Negroes had been accustomed to a strictly regulated family life and a rigidly enforced moral code. But in America the disintegration of their social organization removed the traditional sanctions which had encouraged them to respect their old customs. . . .

. . . Because the slaves failed to conform to the white pattern, the master class found the explanation, as usual, in the Negro's innate racial traits. Actually, the differences resulted from the fact that slavery inevitably made much of the white caste's family pattern meaningless and unintelligible—and in some ways impossible—for the average bondsman. Here, as at so many other points, the slaves had lost their native culture without being able to find a workable substitute and therefore lived in a kind of cultural chaos. . . .

. . . In every state white marriages were recognized as civil contracts which imposed obligations on both parties and provided penalties for their violation. Slave marriages had no such recognition in the state codes; instead, they were regulated by whatever laws the owners saw fit to enforce. . . .

After a marriage many masters ignored the behavior of the couple so long as neither husband nor wife caused any loud or violent disturbances. Others insisted that they not only live together but respect their obligations to each other. . . .

Divorce, like marriage, was within the master's jurisdiction. He might permit his slaves to change spouses as often and whenever they wished, or he might establish more or less severe rules. A Louisiana master granted a divorce only after a month's notice and prohibited remarriage unless a divorcee agreed to receive 25 lashes. James H. Hammond inflicted 100 lashes upon partners who dissolved their marriage and forced them to live singly for three years. . . . While one master might enforce divorce laws as rigid as these, his neighbor might tolerate a veritable

12 Richmond *Whig*, quoted in Alexandria (Va.) *Phenix Gazette*, September 1, 1831; Austin *Texas State Gazette*, November 15, 1856; Jackson *Mississippian*, December 19, 1856.

13 Vicksburg *Weekly Sentinel*, June 13, 1855; Huntsville *Democrat*, quoted in Sellers, *Slavery in Alabama*, pp. 262–63.

regime of free love—of casual alliances and easy separation. Inevitably the rules on a given estate affected the family life of its slaves.

Not only did the slave family lack the protection and the external pressure of state law, it also lacked most of the centripetal forces that gave the white family cohesiveness. In the life of the slave, the family had nothing like the social significance that it had in the life of the white man. The slave woman was first a full-time worker for her owner, and only incidentally a wife, mother, and homemaker. She spent a small fraction of her time in the house; she often did no cooking or clothes making; and she was not usually nurse to her husband or children during illness. Parents frequently had little to do with the raising of their children; and children soon learned that their parents were neither the fount of wisdom nor the seat of authority. Thus a child on a Louisiana farm saw his mother receive 25 lashes for countermanding an order his mistress had given him.[14] Lacking autonomy, the slave family could not offer the child shelter or security from the frightening creatures in the outside world.

The family had no greater importance as an economic unit. Parents and children might spend some spare hours together in their garden plots, but, unlike rural whites, slaves labored most of the time for their masters in groups that had no relationship to the family. The husband was not the director of an agricultural enterprise; he was not the head of the family, the holder of property, the provider, or the protector. If his wife or child was disrobed and whipped by master or overseer, he stood by in helpless humiliation. In an age of patriarchal families, the male slave's only crucial function within the family was that of siring offspring.

Indeed, the typical slave family was matriarchal in form, for the mother's role was far more important than the father's. Insofar as the family did have significance it involved responsibilities which traditionally belonged to women, such as cleaning house, preparing food, making clothes, and raising children. The husband was at most his wife's assistant, her companion, and her sex partner. He was often thought of as her possession ("Mary's Tom"), as was the cabin in which they lived.[15] It was common for a mother to raise her children to be considered a family without reference to the father.

Given these conditions—the absence of legal marriages, the family's minor social and economic significance, and the father's limited role—it is hardly surprising to find that slave families were highly unstable. Lacking both outer pressures and inner pulls, they were also exposed to the threat of forced separations through sales. . . . Thus every slave family had about it an air of impermanence, for no master could promise that his debts would not force sales, or guarantee that his death would not cause divisions. . . .

The general instability of slave families had certain logical consequences. One was the casual attitude of many bondsmen toward marriage; another was the failure of any deep and enduring affection to

---

14 Marston Diary, entry for June 12, 1829.

15 Johnson, *Sea Islands*, pp. 135, 137–38; *id., Ante-Bellum North Carolina*, p. 535.

develop between some husbands and wives. The South abounded in stories of slaves who elected to migrate with kind masters even when it meant separation from their spouses. . . .

Still another consequence was the indifference with which most fathers and even some mothers regarded their children. An angry Virginian attributed the death of a slave infant to "the unnatural neglect of his infamous mother"; he charged that another infant was "murdered right out by his mother's neglect and barbarous cruelty." Fanny Kemble observed the stolid reaction of slave parents to the death of their children. "I've lost a many; they all goes so," was the only comment of one mother when another child died; and the father, "without word or comment, went out to his enforced labor."[16] Many slaveholders complained that mothers could not be trusted to nurse their sick children, that some showed no affection for them and treated them cruelly. This, of course, was not a manifestation of Negro "character" as masters seemed to think. How these calloused mothers could have produced the affectionate slave "mammies" of tradition was never explained. But one master spoke volumes when he advocated separating children from their parents, because it was "far more humane not to cherish domestic ties among slaves."[17]

The final consequence of family instability was widespread sexual promiscuity among both men and women. . . . A Virginia planter kept a record of the fathers of his slave children when he knew who the fathers were, but often he could only guess—and sometimes he suggested that the child was sired "by the Commonwealth," or "by the Universe," or "God knows who by." Overseers were generally even less concerned; as one overseer explained, the morals of the slaves were "no business of his, and he did not care what they did. Nor was the law concerned. In Mississippi, when a male slave was indicted for the rape of a female slave; the state Supreme Court dismissed the case on the ground that this was not an offense known to common or statute law.[18]

If most slaves regarded the white man's moral code as unduly severe, many whites did too. Indeed, the number of bastardy cases in southern court records seems to confirm the conclusion that women of the poor-white class "carried about the same reputation for easy virtue as their sable sisters."[19] . . .

That numerous slaves did manage somehow to surmount the corrupting influences everywhere about them, their masters themselves freely admitted. A South Carolinian admired the slave mother's "natural and often ardent and endearing affection for her offspring"; and another declared that "sound policy" as well as humanity required that everything be done "to reconcile these unhappy beings to their lot, by keeping moth-

---

[16] Massie Slave Book; Kemble, *Journal*, p. 95.

[17] Lyell, *Travels*, 1, p. 184.

[18] Brown, *Narrative*, p. 13; *De Bow's Review*, 10 (1851), p. 623; Olmsted, *Back Country*, pp. 89, 113, 154; Massie Slave Book; Catterall (ed.), *Judicial Cases*, 2, pp. 544–45; 3, p. 363.

[19] Avery O. Craven, "Poor Whites and Negroes in the Ante-Bellum South," *Journal of Negro History*, 15 (1930) 17–18.

ers and children together." The majority of slave women were devoted to their children, regardless of whether they had been sired by one or several fathers. Nor was sexual promiscuity a universal trait of southern Negroes even in bondage. Many slave couples, affirmed a Georgian, displayed toward each other a high degree of "faithfulness, fidelity, and affection."[20]

Seldom, when slave families were broken to satisfy creditors or settle estates, was a distinction made between those who were indifferent to the matter and those who suffered deeply as a consequence. . . . Sometimes the "derangement" or sudden rebelliousness of a slave mother was attributed to "grief at being separated from her children." Often mothers fought desperately to prevent traders from carrying off their children, and often husbands and wives struggled against separation when they were torn apart.[21]

But the most eloquent evidence of the affection and devotion that bound many slave families together appeared in the advertisements for fugitives. A Virginian sought a runaway whose wife had been transported to Mississippi, "and I understand from some of my servants, that he had been speaking of following her." A Maryland master was convinced that a female fugitive would attempt to get back to Georgia "where she came from, and left her husband and two children." Even when fugitives hoped to reach the free states, husbands often took their wives and parents, their children, though this obviously lessened their chance of a successful escape. Clearly, to many bondsmen the fellowship of the family, in spite of its instability, was exceedingly important. . . .

. . . A poignant example was the scene that transpired when an overseer tied and whipped a slave mother in the presence of her children. The frightened children pelted the overseer with stones, and one of them ran up and bit him in the leg. During the ruction the cries of the mother were mingled with the screams of the children, *"Let my mammy go—let my mammy go."*[22] . . .

Other slaves exhibited toward whites no strong emotion either of affection or hatred, but rather an attitude of deep suspicion. Many contemporaries commented upon their "habitual distrust of the white race" and noted that they were "always suspicious." When this was the Negro's basic attitude, the resulting relationship was an amoral one which resembled an unending civil war; the slave then seemed to think that he was entitled to use every tactic of deception and chicanery he could devise. Many ex-slaves who spoke of their former masters without bitterness still recalled with particular pleasure the times when they had outwitted or beguiled them ("'cause us had to lie").[23]

---

20 *De Bow's Review*, 17 (1854) 425–26; Abbeville District, South Carolina, Judge of Probate Decree Book, 1839–1858, May term, 1841; Catterall (ed.), *Judicial Cases*, 2, p. 314.

21 Henson, *Story*, pp. 10–11; Ingraham (ed.), *Sunny South*, p. 439; Catterall (ed.), *Judicial Cases*, 1, p. 298; 3, p. 632; 5, pp. 229–30; Loguen *Narrative*, pp. 112–20; Andrews, *Slavery and the Domestic Slave Trade*, pp. 128–33.

22 Douglass, *My Bondage*, pp. 92–95.

23 Olmsted, *Back Country*, p. 114; Bremer, *Homes of the New World*, 1, p. 292; Botkin, *Lay My Burden Down, passim*.

To a few slaves this civil war was an intense and serious business, because they felt for their masters (sometimes for all whites) an abiding animosity. In speaking of the whites, such bondsmen used "the language of hatred and revenge"; on one plantation the slaves in their private conversations contemptuously called their master "Old Hogjaw." Externally these slaves wore an air of sullenness. . . . Fieldhands often gave no sign of pleasure when their master approached; some made clumsy bows, but others ignored him entirely.[24]

The poor whites were the one group in the superior caste for whom the slaves dared openly express their contempt, and the slaves did so in picturesque terms. Masters often tolerated this and were even amused by it. However, it is likely that some slaves were thereby expressing their opinion of the whole white race. A transparent example of the malice that a portion of the slaves bore the whites occurred in St. Louis when a mob tarred and feathered a white man. "One feature of the scene I could not help remarking," wrote a witness: "the negroes all appeared in high glee, and many of them actually danced with joy."[25]

But the predominant and overpowering emotion that whites aroused in the majority of slaves was neither love nor hate but fear. "We were always uneasy," an ex-slave recalled; when "a white man spoke to me, I would feel frightened," another confessed. In Alabama, a visitor who lost his pocketbook noted that the slave who found it "was afraid of being whipped for theft and had given it to the first white man he saw, and at first was afraid to pick it up." A fugitive who was taken into the home of an Ohio Quaker found it impossible to overcome his timidity and apprehension. "I had never had a white man to treat me as an equal, and the idea of a white lady waiting on me at the table was still worse! . . . I thought if I could only be allowed the privilege of eating in the kitchen, I should be more than satisfied."[26]

The masters themselves provided the most vivid evidence of the frightening image that white men assumed in the minds of many slaves. When they advertised for runaways, the owners frequently revealed a distressing relationship between the two races, a relationship that must have been for these slaves an emotional nightmare. In their advertisements no descriptive phrases were more common than these: "stutters very much when spoken to"; "speaks softly and has a downcast look"; "has an uneasy appearance when spoken to"; "speaks quickly, and with an anxious expression of countenance"; "a very down look, and easily confused when spoken to"; "stammers very much so as to be scarcely understood."

"I feel lighter—the dread is gone," affirmed a Negro woman who had escaped to Canada. "It is a great heaviness on a person's mind to be a slave."[27] . . .

---

[24] Northup, *Twelve Years a Slave*, pp. 62–63, 197; Russell, *Diary*, pp. 133, 146–47, 258, 262; Stirling, *Letters*, p. 49; Buckingham, *Slave States*, 1, pp. 62–63.

[25] Drew, *The Refugee*, pp. 156–57; Benwell, *Travels*, p. 99.

[26] Drew, *The Refugee*, pp. 30, 86; Watson Diary, entry for January 1, 1831; Brown, *Narrative*, pp. 102–3.

[27] Drew, *The Refugee*, p. 179.

Critics of slavery, certain white men think, err, when they assume that Negroes suffered as much in bondage as white men would have suffered. One must remember, argue the critics of the critics, that to the Negroes slavery seemed natural; knowing no other life, they accepted it without giving the matter much thought. Not that slavery was a good thing, mind you—but, still, it probably hurt the Negro less than it did the whites. Indeed, the whites were really more enslaved by Negro slavery than were the Negro slaves. This postslavery argument, like the antebellum proslavery argument, is based upon some obscure and baffling logic. It is not unlike James H. Hammond's confident assertion that "our slaves are the happiest . . . human beings on whom the sun shines"; or his complaint that "into their Eden is coming Satan in the guise of an abolitionist."[28]

A former slave once pronounced a simple and chastening truth for those who would try to understand the meaning of bondage: "Tisn't he who has stood and looked on, that can tell you what slavery is—'tis he who has endured." "I was black," he added, "but I had the feelings of a man as well as any man."[29] One can feel compassion for the antebellum Southern white man; one can understand the moral dilemma in which he was trapped. But one must remember that the Negro, not the white man, was the slave, and the Negro gained the most from emancipation. When freedom came—even the quasi-freedom of "second-class citizenship"—the Negro, in literal truth, lost nothing but his chains.

Slavery as a Product of Unregulated Agricultural Capitalism*

Stanley M. Elkins

. . . Here, even in its embryonic stages, it is possible to see the process whereby capitalism would emerge as the principal dynamic force in American society. The New World had been discovered and exploited by a European civilization which had always, in contrast with other world cultures, placed a particularly high premium on personal achievement, and it was to be the special genius of Englishmen, from Elizabeth's time

---

[28] *De Bow's Review*, 8 (1850), p. 123.

[29] Drew, *The Refugee*, pp. 201–2.

* Stanley M. Elkins, *Slavery: A Problem in American Institutional and Intellectual History* (Chicago: University of Chicago Press, 1959). By permission of the publisher.

onward, to transform this career concept from its earlier chivalric form into one of economic fulfilment—from "glory" to "success." Virginia was settled during the very key period in which the English middle class forcibly reduced, by revolution, the power of those standing institutions—the church and the crown—which most directly symbolized society's traditional limitations upon personal success and mobility. What the return of the crown betokened in 1660 was not so much "reaction" as the fact that all society had by then somehow made terms with the Puritan Revolution. Virginia had proven a uniquely appropriate theater for the acting-out of this narrower, essentially modern ideal of personal, of *economic*, success. Land in the early days was cheap and plentiful; a ready market for tobacco existed; even the yeoman farmer could rise rapidly if he could make the transition to staple production; and above all there was a quick recognition of accomplishment, by a standard which was not available in England but which was the only one available in Virginia: success in creating a plantation.[1] . . .

It was . . . in a period of relatively hard times that it became clear, if the colony of Virginia were to prosper, that capitalism would be the dynamic force in its economic life. "Success" could no longer be visualized as a rise from small beginnings, as it once could, but must now be conceived as a matter of substantial initial investments in land, equipment, and labor, plus the ability to undertake large annual commitments on credit. With the fall in tobacco prices, and with the tiny margin of profit that remained, the yeoman farmer found it difficult enough to eke out a bare living, let alone think of competing with the large planter or of purchasing slaves' or servants' indentures. Success was still possible, but now its terms were clearer, and those who achieved it would be fewer in numbers. The man who managed it would be the man with the large holdings —the man who could command a substantial force of laborers, white or black—who could afford a sizable yearly investment in the handling of his crop: in short, the capitalist planter.

The period beginning in the 1680s and ending about 1710 marked still a new phase. It saw, now under conditions of comparative prosperity, the full emergence of the plantation as the basic unit of capitalist agriculture. By about 1680 the market for Virginia and Maryland tobacco had been restored, though it is important to note that this was accompanied by no great rise in prices. It was rather a matter of having recaptured the European market by flooding it with cheap tobacco and underselling competitors. Returning prosperity, therefore, meant something far more concrete to the man with resources, who could produce tobacco in large enough amounts to make a slim profit margin worthwhile, than to the one whose productivity was limited by the acreage which he and his family could work. These years also witnessed the initial exploitation of the Carolinas, a process which moved much more directly toward large

---

[1] Despite the relative mobility of English society since Tudor times, personal achievement and status still inhered in any number of preferable alternatives to trade and production. But the openness of Virginia lay in the fact that purely capitalistic incentives were being used to get people to come there. No nobles, with their retinues of peasants, migrated to the colony. . . .

agricultural units than had been the case in Virginia.[2] The acceleration of this development toward clarifying the terms of commercial production—large plantations and substantial investments—had a direct connection with the widening of the market for slaves during this same period. Hand in hand with large holdings went slaves—an assumption which was now being taken more or less for granted. "A rational man," wrote a South Carolina colonist in 1682, "will certainly inquire, 'when I have Land, what shall I doe with it? What commoditys shall I be able to produce, that will yield me money in other countrys, that I may be inabled to buy Negro-slaves, (without which a planter can never doe any great matter)?"[3] The point had clearly passed when white servants could realistically, on any long-term appraisal, be considered preferable to Negro slaves. Such appraisals were now being made in terms of capitalized earning power, a concept appropriate to large operations rather than small, to long-term rather than short-term planning.

It was, of course, only the man of means who could afford to think in this way. But then he is the one who most concerns us—the man responsible for Negro slavery. Determined in the sixties and seventies to make money despite hard times and low prices, and willing to undertake the investments which that required, he could now in the eighties reap the fruits of his foresight. His slaves were more valuable than ever—a monument to his patience and planning. What had made them so? For one thing he, unlike the yeoman farmer, had a large establishment for training them and was not pressed by the need, as he would have been with white servants on limited indenture, to exploit their *immediate* labor. The labor was his permanently. And for another thing, the system was by now just old enough to make clear for the first time the full meaning of a second generation of native-born American Negroes. These were the dividends: slaves born to the work and using English as their native tongue. By the 1690s the demand for slaves in the British colonies had become so great, and the Royal African Company so inefficient in supplying them, that in 1698 Parliament revoked the company's monopoly on the African coast and threw open the traffic to independent merchants and traders. The stream of incoming slaves, already of some consequence, now became enormous, and at the same time the annual flow of white servants to Virginia and the Carolinas dropped sharply. By 1710 it had become virtually negligible.[4]

What meaning might all this have had for the legal status of the Negro? The connection was intimate and direct; with the full development

---

2 The Carolina proprietors had a far clearer notion of the terms on which money was to be made from their colony than had been true of the London Company of sixty years before with regard to Virginia. They appear at the very outset to have fostered the establishment of large estates, and a number of such estates set up in the 1670s and 1680s were organized by Barbados men with first-hand plantation experience. See Gray, *History of Agriculture*, 1, 324–25; also J. P. Thomas, "Barbadians in Early South Carolina," *South Carolina Historical Magazine*, 31 (April 1930), 89....

3 Quoted in Gray, *History of Agriculture*, 1, 352.

4 Greene and Harrington, *American Population*, pp. 136–37; Gray, *History of Agriculture*, 1, 349–50.

of the plantation there was nothing, so far as his interests were concerned; to prevent unmitigated capitalism from becoming unmitigated slavery. The planter was now engaged in capitalistic agriculture with a labor force entirely under his control. The personal relationship between master and slave—in any case less likely to exist on large agricultural units than on smaller ones—now became far less important than the economic necessities which had forced the slave into this "unnatural" organization in the first place. For the plantation to operate efficiently and profitably, and with a force of laborers not all of whom may have been fully broken to plantation discipline, the necessity of training them to work long hours and to give unquestioning obedience to their masters and overseers superseded every other consideration. The master must have absolute power over the slave's body, and the law was developing in such a way as to give it to him at every crucial point. . . .

. . . That very strength and bulwark of American society, capitalism, unimpeded by prior arrangements and institutions, had stamped the status of slave upon the black with a clarity which elsewhere could never have been so profound, and had further defined the institution of slavery with such nicety that the slave *was*, in fact, degraded. That the black, as a species, was thus contemptible seemed to follow by observation. This assumption took on a life of its own in the attitudes of the people, and the very thought of such a creature existing outside the pale of their so aptly devised system filled the most reasonable of Southerners with fear and loathing. Quite apart from the demands of the system itself, this may account for many of the subsidiary social taboos—the increasing severity of the laws against manumission, the horror of miscegenation, the depressed condition of the free Negro and his peculiar place in Southern society: all signs of how difficult it was to conceive a non-slave colored class. Nothing in their experience had prepared them for it; such a class was unnatural, logically awry, a blemish on the body politic, an anomaly for which there was no intellectual category. . . .

The basic fact was, of course, that the slave himself was property. He and his fellow bondsmen had long since become "chattels personal . . . to all intents, constructions and purposes whatsoever."

In the slave system of the United States—so finely circumscribed and so cleanly self-contained—virtually all avenues of recourse for the slave, all lines of communication to society at large, originated and ended with the master. The system was unique, *sui generis*. . . .

Urban Slavery*
Richard C. Wade

By 1860 slavery was disintegrating in Southern cities. Forty years earlier, the institution had seemed as stable and vigorous in town as in
country. Slaves comprised at least 20 percent of the population of the
major cities. In most places the proportion was much higher, and in
Charleston blacks outnumbered whites. Slaves handled the bulk of domestic drudgery; worked in shops and factories; built the streets, bridges,
and municipal installations; some even acquired mechanical skills.
Within four decades, however, the picture had changed dramatically. In
the border cities the institution had nearly disappeared altogether; farther south it had diminished in extent and vitality. Everywhere propor-
tionately, and in many places absolutely, the number of town slaves declined. In the countryside slavery still appeared stable and successful, but
wherever it touched urban conditions it was in deep trouble. . . .

But what became clear in 1860 was not apparent forty years earlier.
In 1820, slavery was as much a part of life in the city as on farm and
plantation. In fact, some municipal officials expressed anxiety over the
rapid increase in colored townspeople. And surely no one questioned the
adaptability of slavery to the urban milieu. Yet experience ultimately
proved this assumption mistaken. For, as the cities grew, they produced
conditions which first strained, then undermined, the regime of bondage
in the South's metropolises. . . .

. . . Shifting statistics suggest that in the cities slavery was never a
static institution. In fact, nearly every critical aspect of the system
changed constantly in the ante-bellum years. The Negro population, the
number of slaveowners, the incidence and size of slaveholding, and the
sex differentials all varied considerably in each decade. Furthermore,
the towns themselves also changed, altering the conditions in which
bondage functioned and forcing institutional adjustments to meet new
situations. This flux was less conspicuous on the countryside. There the
rural setting promoted a stability seldom found in towns. Indeed, a recent historian has asserted that by the 1830s "slavery had crystallized;
its form was fixed. In 1860 the peculiar institution was almost precisely
what it had been thirty years before." Hence, he continues, it is possible
"to examine it institutionally with only slight regard for chronology."[1]

These generalizations were perhaps too sweeping even for slavery on
the plantations, but they are clearly inappropriate for the cities. In fact,

* From *Slavery in the Cities: The South 1820–1860* by Richard C. Wade. Copyright © 1964 by Oxford University Press, Inc. Reprinted by permission.
[1] Kenneth M. Stampp, *The Peculiar Institution* (1956), 28.

urban slavery developed through two distinct phases in the ante-bellum years. It is hard to find a single dividing point that would fit all places because of the variations in the speed and the extent of growth of Southern towns. Yet a rough watershed can be established between 1835 and 1845. Before that period slavery was an integral part of urban life. As the cities grew, so did slavery. But at some moment the system began to lose ground in the metropolis, and though still present it played an increasingly less important role. That "moment" usually came in the late thirties or early forties. But whether earlier or later its appearance was common in all Dixie's cities.

In the earlier period urban slavery resembled the plantation system. The incidence of ownership was high, the size of the holdings often substantial, and the presumption of permanence widespread. While slavery encountered difficulties in the city, no one predicted, much less advocated, its abandonment. And the statistical indices in 1820 and 1830 apparently pointed to further steady and substantial growth.

Yet within a decade or two there were many indications of change. The number of urban Negroes declined, fewer whites owned any, and the size of holdings dwindled. In addition, the sale of young bondsmen to the countryside produced an increasing surplus of female slaves remaining in the towns. New people meanwhile swelled Dixie's cities, which further reduced the importance of the blacks. Clearly the vitality was gone from the system in the urban centers, and each year witnessed a further waning. The transformation was never uniform, but every city experienced it.

No such development occurred in the rural South. "If anything," writes Kenneth Stampp in *The Peculiar Institution*, "the chains of bondage were strengthened, not weakened, in this ante-bellum period."[2] It may be, as some contemporaries and historians have contended, that slavery contained a residual weakness and its vigor in 1860 was largely illusory. Yet, as a Virginian put it, it was "a fixed fact" in that year, and few indices suggested an early collapse. And certainly few Southerners were of a mind to overturn it themselves.

The contrast, then, between urban and rural slavery was marked. Whether the comparison be made of the proportion of slaves to the general population, the distribution of bondsmen among whites, the size of the holdings, or the sex ratio among the blacks, the statistical differences are striking. These figures, however, merely outline a deeper antithesis. Behind the census returns, tax ledgers, and official reports lies a sharper cleavage between ways of living. The city had created its own kind of world, with a pace, sophistication, and environment that separated it from rural modes. In the process it transformed Negro no less than white, slave no less than free man. Hence it is not surprising that slavery as an urban institution differed greatly from its rural counterpart, and that the city slave was often quite unlike his country brother. . . .

The rising incidence of segregation was another index of the increasing weakness of slavery in the cities. Rooted in the white's need for dis-

---

[2] Ibid., 28.

cipline and deference, it developed to take up the slack in the loosening system. It provided public control to replace dwindling private supervision of the master over his slave. To do this, the difference between free and enslaved Negroes had to be narrowed, depriving free blacks of part of their freedom even while permitting a wider latitude to bondsmen. To most whites, however, there seemed no alternative. The old system no longer really controlled; the walls no longer really confined; the chains no longer really held.

The decline of slavery in the cities was the central fact of race relations in the South's cities in the ante-bellum decades. It was also a fact that conditioned Negro life in subsequent generations, for it meant that, when emancipation finally did come, most of the colored population would be in the countryside rather than in cities. Accustomed only to routine tasks, imbruted by the severe limitations of plantation existence, and unused to managing their own affairs, they became free under the most difficult of circumstances.

If the Negro population in the cities had grown in the same proportion as the whites, there would have been present an invaluable pool of potential leadership, for there many blacks, even under slavery, had begun to develop the most important tools of citizenship. There they acquired some skills and learned the rudiments of reading and writing. There, too, many had commenced to manage their own affairs, and in churches they developed a capacity for organization. In short, the metropolis nourished the literacy and self-reliance needed in a free system.

Observers generally agreed on the other hand that rural blacks plainly bore the mark of their servitude. "The field-hand negro is, on the average, a very poor and bad creature," Olmsted wrote sadly, "much worse than I supposed before I had seen him and grown familiar with his stupidity, indolence, duplicity, and sensuality. He seems to be but an imperfect man, incapable of taking care of himself in a civilized manner."[3] . . .

Olmsted found quite the opposite in the cities. "Slaves can never be brought together in denser communities but their intelligence will be increased to a degree dangerous to those who enjoy the benefit of their labor," he observed. "Hundreds of slaves in New Orleans must be constantly reflecting and saying to one another, 'I am as capable of taking care of myself as this Irish hod-carrier, or this German market-gardner.'" . . .

Olmsted saw this distinction more clearly than most.[4] But visitors from the North, travelers from abroad, in fact, masters and slaves, also understood the difference. It was an uncomfortable fact for the whites. To them it presaged a wider freedom for the Negro, with all the uncertainties and perhaps chaos that would follow. Hence the response of owners and officials was to tighten rather than adjust, to expel rather than emancipate, to segregate rather than liberate. At the end the "free

---

3 Olmsted, *Back Country*, 432.
4 Olmsted, *Seaboard Slave States*, 591.

air of the city" was being increasingly denied to a higher and higher proportion of blacks.

The full significance of the de-urbanization of the Negro under slavery was apparent only much later. Emancipation found him located primarily in the least dynamic area of American life. Capable of simple tasks, familiar only with rural routine, largely illiterate, and unused to managing his own affairs, he faced a long road to full freedom. Ultimately that road carried him to the city. Though confronted by both discrimination and segregation, he could find there the numbers and leadership which could one day spring him loose from the confinements of an earlier bondage.

The recovery of the metropolis began before the First World War. The depression slowed the pace somewhat, but a second global conflict produced an irresistible urban undertow. Colored families had abandoned the land by now or were pushed off it by machines and new techniques. By the thousands each day they flocked to the cities both North and South. There, often amid squalor and deprivation, they began the dramatic rally of forces that would dissolve the walls which for three centuries had kept them outside the promised land of equal rights.

Significantly, among the datelines which reported the new phase of the story were New Orleans, Mobile, Savannah, Charleston, Richmond, Louisville, and St. Louis. A new generation of Negroes pushed aside older leadership and took to the lunchrooms and streets as well as the courts in a drive to desegregate the public life of the South. Though Dixie resisted everywhere, the first breakthrough appeared in the urban areas. Parks, buses, public facilities, and a few schools opened first; commercial enterprises, restaurants, and hotels grudgingly followed. Moreover, the rise of Negro voting in the major cities gradually provided a stable base for further successes.

The characteristic focus of the movement was the churches. Like their ante-bellum predecessors, they were more than religious centers, encompassing in a unique way the whole range of organized Negro life in the city. Their ministers spoke not merely for their own congregations but for the colored community as a whole. And standing in a long Christian and Southern tradition, they commanded respect among important white groups in the city. In the churches the people gathered, heard speeches, and bolstered their morale. Boycotts were planned, discipline established, even demonstrations started from the same sanctuaries. Ironically now, the pattern of social organization born in slavery became the vanguard of a new freedom.

Industrial Slavery*

Robert S. Starobin

Between the American Revolution and the Civil War, industrial slavery was often a significant political issue in the South. During these years, Southerners attempted to develop their own industries and periodically debated whether slaves were the best industrial force. Important on both local and regional levels, there were three more or less distinct political campaigns for slave-based industries. The first campaign ran roughly from 1790 to 1815; the second occurred in the late 1820s; the third lasted from about 1845 to 1861. The first two campaigns for slave-based industries were stymied by changes in southern society. The final political thrust was intimately related to the sectional strife of the 1850s, and contributed in part to the secession of the slave states in 1861.[1] Industrial slavery thus assumed an important role in the politics of antebellum America.

After secession, many slaveowning manufacturers who had only reluctantly acceded to disunion became active supporters of the Confederacy—indicating further the link between industrial slavery and southern nationalism. Rufus Barringer, the prominent North Carolina manufacturer became a famous rebel army general. The Bell-Yeatman family, which controlled one of the largest slaveowning iron works in middle Tennessee, became a staunch backer of southern nationhood. More than a score of other industrialists served in the Confederate Congress. Governor Francis W. Pickens, however, perhaps best summed up the sentiments of the secessionists in his November, 1861, message to the South Carolina Assembly. "True war is a great calamity," he wrote, "but if this war shall end, as there is every prospect that it will do, by

---

* From *Industrial Slavery in the Old South* by Robert S. Starobin. Copyright © 1970 by Oxford University Press, Inc. Reprinted by permission.

[1] Previous discussions of the debate over and the campaign for industrial slavery have suffered from several shortcomings. Opinion on the use of slave labor in industries has generally been confused with actual employment. The "boosterism" which permeated many magazines, such as *De Bow's Review*, has not been adequately accounted for. The debate was not confined simply to the question of textile manufacturing, but embraced the industrialization process as a whole. The controversy began in the 1790s and continued in the 1820s, long before the most intensive period of debate in the 1840s and 1850s. See, for example, P. G. Davidson, "Industrialism in the Ante-Bellum South," *SAQ*, 27 (1938), 405–25; J. G. Van Deusen, *The Economic Bases of Disunion in South Carolina* (New York, 1928); C. S. Boucher, "The Ante-Bellum Attitude of South Carolina towards Manufacturing and Agriculture," *Washington University Studies*, 3 (St. Louis, 1916); F. Linden, "Repercussions of Manufacturing in the Ante-Bellum South," *NCHR*, 18 (1940), 313–31; N. W. Preyer, "The Historian, The Slave, and The Ante-Bellum Textile Industry," *JNH*, 46 (April 1961), 67–83; H. Collins, "The Southern Industrial Gospel before 1860," *JSH*, 12 (1946), 386–402. Cf. E. D. Genovese, *The Political Economy of Slavery* (New York, 1965), chapters 8, 9.

making us not only independent of our most deadly enemies, but commercially independent also, and at the same time, shall develop our own artisan skill and mechanical labor, so as to place us entirely beyond their subsidy hereafter, then, indeed, will it prove, in the end, a public blessing."[2]

By the time of secession in 1861, the use of slave labor to industrialize the South had become accepted in theory and practice. This movement —to "bring the cotton mills to the cotton fields," so to speak—did not begin suddenly in the 1840s or even in the 1880s, as some historians have suggested. Industries emerged at least as early as the 1790s, and the campaigns for industry became most intense when Southerners felt least secure within the Union. The greatest interest in slave-based industries thus occurred from the late 1820s to the early 1830s, when southern agriculture was in difficulty, the tariff controversy raged, and when the South was coming under intense moral criticism. Interest also developed during the late 1840s and 1850s, when anti-slavery parties emerged and the sectional conflict was most bitter.

By the time of the Civil War, the struggle for southern self-sufficiency had reached a climax. Slaveowning agriculturists were now vigorously campaigning for slave-based industrialization and they were investing some of their surplus capital in southern industries. Such men, who included many influential Southerners, had overcome their traditional agrarianism and whatever backward-looking tendencies they may have had. They were seeking to create a balanced economy in which the South's great natural potential for agriculture would be complemented by its opportunities for extracting, processing, manufacturing, and transporting its resources and staples. Indeed, one reason why they wanted to expand slavery into the territories, and if possible to reopen the African slave trade, was to accelerate the development of southern industries.

Slaveowners were determined to industrialize the South under their own auspices exclusively, however, so that existing class and caste relationships would remain unchanged. They therefore opposed the creation not only of a slaveless industrial bourgeoisie independent of planter control, but also of a free industrial labor force. Had either of these two groups come into being, it might have challenged the slaveowners' domination of southern society. Unless slaveowners directed industries themselves, their ultimate security as a class was in jeopardy.

To maintain their hegemony, slaveowners insisted that slaves continue to be the chief labor force in southern industries. Long experience had demonstrated that bondsmen were more tractable, efficient, and profitable than alternative labor forces. The proslavery ideology also dictated that slaves were less troublesome than whites and better suited to work in tropical climates. Slaveowners also stymied the challenges of poor whites and free artisans by permitting the former to work in some textile mills and the latter to compete with some slave craftsmen. Fi-

---

[2] South Carolina *Journal of the House of Representatives*, called session, November, 1861, p. 36; cf. Message of Governor John Letcher, Virginia *Journal of the Senate,* regular session, 1861–62, p. 19.

nally, slaveowning agriculturists insisted that they themselves, or their allies, should continue to control southern industries, in order to prevent the emergence of independent entrepreneurial groups. Industrialists hoped that by these arrangements caste conflicts would continue to subsume class conflicts and that slaveowners would remain the dominant class.[3]

Industrially minded Southerners also came into conflict with their northern counterparts for various reasons. Since southern industries lagged behind those of the North and trading patterns seemed unfair, slave employers had great difficulty competing in market places. The use of slave labor in industries helped reduce these disadvantages, but it could not overcome lost time entirely. The political power of slaveowners within the Union also seemed threatened by outsiders, as the North's population increased, as the Abolitionist attack became more shrill, as more and more free states entered the Union, and especially as the Republican Party—dedicated at least to the containment of slavery in the states—gained ground.

As a result, by the 1850s, many Southerners felt frustrated so long as they remained within a hostile Union. They believed that economic self-sufficiency, territorial expansion, the continuance of slavery, and their political survival depended on southern independence and could only be achieved by disunion. Slave-based industrialization and slave-state nationalism had, by 1861, entwined in a bloody struggle for southern sovereignty. Industrial slavery had, in this sense, directly contributed to the coming of the Civil War.

---

[3] Genovese, *Political Economy of Slavery*, 206–207, suggests that some Southerners considered "a Prussian road to industrial capitalism, paved with authoritarianism [and] benevolent despotism." For an excellent discussion of industrial "revolution from above"—something which southern secessionists contemplated—in Germany and Japan in the late nineteenth century, see B. Moore, Jr., *Social Origins of Dictatorship and Democracy* (Boston, 1966), chaps. 5, 7, 8, and 9.

Slavery as an Obstacle to Economic Growth*

Douglas F. Dowd*
(Introductory Note by Hugh G. J. Aitken)

Revised interpretations of the course of economic development in the South called for revised interpretations of the economic significance of slavery. But did they require abandonment of the view that a society based on slavery was incapable of sustained economic development? By no means, claimed Douglas Dowd. Economic development means more than maintaining a certain rate of growth of income per head; it implies qualitative as well as quantitative change—change, that is to say, in the structure of the economy and, at one remove, in the values and structure of the society. A society whose whole efforts were compulsively devoted to maintaining, justifying, and defending domination of the black man by the white was not capable of this kind of development. To prove the contrary surely required more than a demonstration that prewar growth rates had attained a certain height, reinforced by references to war destruction and East Indian cotton. Readjustment after the Civil War to a legally emancipated labor force and to foreign competition in cotton called for structural changes in Southern society, and these were not forthcoming. The economic effects of slavery were evident not in the high growth rates of the prewar years—easily explained in terms of the economic circumstances of the period—but in the inability of the South to restructure its economy and society after the war. And why this inability? Because in essence, despite emancipation, Civil War, and Reconstruction, social, political, and economic power in the South was still held by the group that had created slavery and fought to maintain it. If such a society is to develop, says Dowd, the distribution of power has to be changed; that is to say, the possessors of power have to be changed.

. . . It is clear that he intended his remarks to be as applicable to the problems of our world today as to the interpretation of Southern history. . . .

Whether in the slavery or the new economic history controversies of the past decade, one moves to a feeling that the participants are often

* From *The Journal of Economic History*, 27, Number 4 (December 1967), pp. 531–38. Copyright © 1967 by The Economic History Association. Reprinted by permission of the author and the Business Manager. Comments from Hugh G. J. Aitken's introductory notes, pp. 287–88 in Aitken, ed., *Did Slavery Pay?*, Houghton Mifflin Co., 1971.

talking past one another, talking to themselves and to what may loosely be thought of as their respective adherents. The new economic historians, it may be said, put one in mind of rather light-hearted evangelists; while those who dissent from their innovations seem, by comparison, stuffy, old-fashioned, fearful of the new truths, perhaps of truth itself. . . .

. . . The slavery controversy provides a useful basis for an exploration of this question, not least because it came as the opening gun of the new economic history, a decade ago, when Messrs. Conrad and Meyer presented their twin papers on methodology and on slavery to the joint EHA-NBER meetings and I served as a critic.

Then, as still today, I puzzled over what Conrad and Meyer were trying to show. If they were attempting to demonstrate that Ulrich B. Phillips (in his *American Negro Slavery, inter alia*) was wrong, there was much more than profitability of slavery on which to focus, for by the time they wrote Phillips had been quite thoroughly discredited on both narrow and broad questions, perhaps most completely by Kenneth Stampp (in his *Peculiar Institution*). . . . And was it not generally accepted by students of the South that writers like Phillips took the position that slavery was unprofitable because to do otherwise would muddy the more fundamental justifications for the system?

. . . It is of course reasonably obvious that in any functioning social system, slave or otherwise, there will be incomes that are high at the top and decrease as one moves to the bottom of the social scale; and that power will be roughly proportionate to income and wealth. What is less obvious are the costs of a given system—costs in terms of alternatives foregone, as well as the social and human costs of the existent reality.

For the American South, it surely was good business sense that led planters to emphasize cotton cultivation, slaveholding, and slavebreeding; and good business sense was also good economic sense, if the short run and the interests of those in power are taken as guiding criteria. But when we speak of economic development it is not business sense or economic sense for the short run as viewed by those in power that are, or should be, taken as the appropriate referents for judgment; for then we are speaking not only of structural realities and changes in the economy, but also of far-reaching social and political structures and changes.

As I said a decade ago, one cannot evaluate the meaning of slavery as though it were merely one kind of a labor force rather than another, *ceteris paribus*. Slavery normally implies and requires, and especially in the United States implied and required, a slavery-dominated society as much as a society dominating slaves. In turn, this meant that whatever business considerations might support the continuation of the slave-cum-cotton system, these were immeasurably reinforced by the social and political imperatives—ever more on the defensive in the ante-bellum South—of maintaining a slave society. Is this not made more evident when we examine the post-Civil War development of the South?

I should have thought it would be unnecessary to raise these questions once more, except that . . . [we have Robert Fogel[1] saying that]

---

[1] Robert W. Fogel, "The New Economic History: Its Findings and Methods," *Economic History Review*, 29 (December 1966), 642–56.

The retarded development of the South during the last third of the nine-teenth century and the first half of the twentieth was due not to stagna-tion during the slave era, but to the devastation caused by the Civil War. As Stanley Engerman points out, if *ante-bellum* growth-rates had con-tinued through the war decade, southern *per capita* income would have been twice the level that actually prevailed in 1870. So disruptive was the war that it took the South some thirty years to regain the *per capita* in-come of 1860 and another sixty years to reach the same relative position in national *per capita* income that it enjoyed at the close of the *ante-bellum* era. The case for the abolition of slavery thus appears to turn on issues of morality and equity rather than on the inability of a slave sys-tem to yield a high rate of economic growth (p. 647). . . .

[I say that the slave economy explains later economic stagnation.]

It was of utmost significance that slavery in the United States could not be maintained without vitally affecting "all other things," whether that slavery was profitable or not. As Stanley M. Elkins has so capably shown in his *Slavery*,[2] American Negro slavery was the very "worst" the world had known, in its nature and in its consequences, whether it be compared with ancient or contemporaneous slavery (in, for example, Brazil or the Caribbean). What does "worst" signify in this context, and why should it have been so? Slaves have always and everywhere been cruelly treated (and always with exceptions), and black slaves especially. Even so, their treatment, their rights (or total lack of rights), their "family" lives, the depths to which racism sank, the manner in which the present and long-distant future of black slaves (even, as we know, their past) was distorted and doomed—in social, psychological, political, and of course economic terms—in the United States reached the lowest of depths. Why should this be so, in the land of the free and the home of the brave? Was not economic individualism adhered to in the South? It surely was, extending to trafficking in human beings as commodities. Did not the Enlightenment, did not Christianity, extend into the American South? Most assuredly, but as with economic individualsm, certain exotic notions had to be grafted onto otherwise healthy plants. To achieve such exoticism took a mighty effort, an effort that became obsessive, compul-sive, and sickening not just to those who lived under the system, but also to those who lived from it and with it and for it.

Which brings me to the postwar period, if a bit abruptly, with Mr. Engerman's contributions in mind. Without asking how *ante-bellum* growth rates could have continued indefinitely; without asking, that is, how the South could have maintained its power in the nation while it also maintained slavery (with or without westward expansion); without ask-ing whether or not there was some determining relationship between the Civil War and the socioeconomic system of the South and its power struggle with the North; without asking any of these questions, let us point to some questions that relate growth to development, and war destruction to growth and development.

Keeping in mind the well-recognized distinctions between growth and development, between quantitative and qualitative change (and

---

[2] Stanley M. Elkins, *Slavery* (New York: Grosset and Dunlap, 1963).

keeping in mind, too, their connections), let us examine the notion of "*ante-bellum* growth rates continuing through the war decade" and even more, beyond that time. By 1860, the South showed few significant signs of moving away from its dependence on slaves and cotton. The signs that such a concentration might be something less than promising had begun to appear already during the Civil War; but what were then mere whispers turned into a roar in the years after 1870. Were the falling cotton prices (among other prices) in the last quarter of the century a function largely, if at all, of the Civil War? Is there any reasonable basis to assume either (1) that slave-breeding would have maintained the supply of slaves within economically viable magnitudes, or (2) that political realities would have allowed the reopening of the external trade? Has anyone specified how the maintenance of slavery (and the power of those who would so maintain it) in the United States in the late nineteenth century might be made compatible with economic development? Or how its forceful abolition (apart from the Civil War) would have been accomplished? Or its peaceful abolition, by those squarely dependent upon it? Is there any ground for believing that the kinds of structural (economic, political, social) changes that are implied by economic development would have ensued in a South whose economy could no longer "thrive" on the basis of agriculture (for the majority of either its white or its black population)? And, given that the slaves were in fact (legally) emancipated, how does one explain the persistence of all the essential qualities of *ante-bellum* southern society in *post-bellum* southern society, down to the very recent past? Civil war damage? But is it not difficult to believe that for eighty years the southern economy was retarded by war destruction, in the light of what we have seen of so many other war-damaged economies in our own lives? Can the answers to any of these questions be turned to the advantage of the relevant conclusions of the new economic history? Or to its procedures? Can we learn nothing about our own economic development from our studies of the complex interrelationships of development (or its lack) in the contemporary underdeveloped world?

Furthermore, and in a different vein: What is the point of the analyses that have occupied these studies? "The case for the abolition of slavery" *of course* "turns on issues of morality and equity rather than on the inability of a slave system to yield a high rate of economic growth." To state otherwise would be to say, one presumes, that an economically viable slave system is to be recommended to . . . whom? The underdeveloped countries? Of course not, and the sneers of the new economic historians to such a query are appropriate. But then what is the point? If students of the South had earlier believed the system was profitable, what then, besides elegance, was the point of going on? Or did we have to be told, once more, that the Civil War was terribly destructive? Are we going back to Ranke, "simply" recording the facts, with technical trimmings? Or are there more vital tasks facing social scientists today; more vital, more demanding, more promising?

Of course slavery was profitable. And of course imperialism has been profitable. And of course the status quo in today's underdeveloped countries is profitable. Profitable, in all cases, to investors, whose definitions of profit do not go beyond the balance sheet and the income statement, and whose definitions of propriety are quite identical with their definitions of property. And of course slavery damaged both whites and blacks in the long run (and most, also, in the short run). And imperialism damages most citizens of both metropolis and colony, in the long run; and similarly with underdevelopment. Nor is it difficult to show that the damage that accrues from such systems is not solely, or mostly, economic; it is social, psychological, political, cultural. As it is also true that economic development both requires and brings about social, political, psychological, and cultural changes.

We are concerned in these meetings with obstacles to economic development, a focus that requires us to look at reality. That is a considerable improvement over the earlier inclinations of economists to develop and to use abstract models that, if they had any application at all, were relevant only to highly industrialized, politically stable societies, operating within basically capitalist institutions. But improvements do not constitute sufficiencies; and especially they do not if their effect is to fragmentize an area of inquiry that requires broadening, deepening, and an enhanced sense of relevance.

Because in practice the meaning of economic development extends out and down so broadly and deeply, the analysis of development, not to say its implementation, must be as broad and as deep. This is to say that "experts" in economic development must take on the staggering task of attempting to understand the functioning of *societies*, and the manner in which *social* change takes place. One of my criticisms of the new economic history, and not only in its manifestations as regards the South, is that its methods, its thrust, are in exactly the opposite direction from that so desperately needed in the field today. Market relationships (for capital, commodities, labor) are indeed central to the functioning of an economy, as the heart is to the body. But the heart functions in relationship with a nervous system, and a circulatory system, and, among other things, in an environment. If the problem is a heart murmur, perhaps—no more than perhaps—total concentration on the heart itself will do. But those who will understand a cardiac condition, and prescribe for it, require themselves to understand the body in all its essential functions and characteristics. The lack of economic development is a problem in today's world that does not fall within the purview of the man who thinks in terms of heart murmurs. And the South had a cardiac condition in the nineteenth century.

To say that slavery was profitable and yet it inhibited economic development is not to say that slavery but that slave society in the United States in the nineteenth century, during and after its existence, inhibited economic development. But this is to say something else. Both before and after emancipation, social, economic, and political power in the South was held by those who had helped to create, and fought to maintain, slavery; nor was there a lack of interested parties in the North either before or after the War. For the South to develop economically, it was essential—and it is essential—either for a social upheaval within the South to take place, and/or for steady pressures, positive and negative, to be introduced from "outside." Power—its sources and its uses—has to be changed; that is, its possessors have to be changed.

What is true for the South is true for other societies that would develop. To detail such changes, let alone to understand, advocate, and support them, on a country-by-country basis is not only to move out from partial equilibrium analysis, but to move into the swirl and turbulence that characterize the world. And that suggests the stance of the committed and concerned social scientist—distasteful though such an idea is to our profession—more than that of the cheerful and comfortable economist.

Slavery and the "Cliometric Revolution"*

Robert W. Fogel and Stanley L. Engerman

The years of black enslavement and the Civil War in which they terminated were our nation's time on the cross. Certainly if any aspect of the American past evokes a sense of shame, it is the system of slavery. And no war in our history, including World Wars I and II, took more American lives, was more devastating to our economy, or more threatening to our national survival, than the Civil War. The desire of scholars to lay bare the economic, political, and social forces which produced the tensions of the antebellum era and exploded into the worst holocaust of our history is not difficult to appreciate.

A vast literature has accumulated on the operation of the slave economy. Hundreds of historians have examined virtually every aspect of the institution. While scholars have disagreed on many points, a broad consensus has gradually emerged. By the midpoint of the twentieth century the consensus had been repeated so often that it had earned the status of a traditional interpretation. This interpretation is taught in most high school and college classes across the nation. It is the view that has been accepted by most of the readers of this book.

What is not generally known is that the traditional interpretation of slavery has been under intensive critical review for almost a decade

---

* Robert W. Fogel and Stanley L. Engerman, *Time on the Cross: The Economics of American Negro Slavery* (Boston: Little, Brown and Company, 1974). By permission of the publisher.

Editor's Note: "Cliometrics" refers to the exploration of historical problems with mathematical, quantitative, computerized procedures.

and a half by historians and economists who are trained in the application of quantitative methods to historical problems. This review involves the processing of large quantities of numerical data. Although these data have been available for some time, the techniques required to analyze and interpret them systematically were not perfected until after the close of World War II. Then a series of rapid advances in economics, statistics, and applied mathematics, together with the availability of high-speed computers, put information long locked in obscure archives at the disposal of a new generation of scholars.

The review based on these new techniques and hitherto neglected sources has contradicted many of the most important propositions in the traditional portrayal of the slave system. As significant as the correction of past errors is the new information brought to light on the conditions of black bondage. Though the investigations are still in progress, enough have been completed so that the main features of the actual operation of the slave economy are now clear. The reconstruction which has emerged is so much at variance with common beliefs, and its implications are so central to the understanding of contemporary issues, that we believe the new findings should no longer be restricted to the pages of esoteric scholarly journals.

The following are some of the principal corrections of the traditional characterization of the slave economy:

1. Slavery was not a system irrationally kept in existence by plantation owners who failed to perceive or were indifferent to their best economic interests. The purchase of a slave was generally a highly profitable investment which yielded rates of return that compared favorably with the most outstanding investment opportunities in manufacturing.

2. The slave system was not economically moribund on the eve of the Civil War. There is no evidence that economic forces alone would have soon brought slavery to an end without the necessity of a war or some other form of political intervention. Quite the contrary; as the Civil War approached, slavery as an economic system was never stronger and the trend was toward even further entrenchment.

3. Slaveowners were not becoming pessimistic about the future of their system during the decade that preceded the Civil War. The rise of the secessionist movement coincided with a wave of optimism. On the eve of the Civil War, slaveholders anticipated an era of unprecedented prosperity.

4. Slave agriculture was not inefficient compared with free agriculture. Economies of large-scale operation, effective management, and intensive utilization of labor and capital made southern slave agriculture 35 percent more efficient than the northern system of family farming.

5. The typical slave field hand was not lazy, inept, and unproductive. On average he was harder-working and more efficient than his white counterpart.

6. The course of slavery in the cities does not prove that slavery was incompatible with an industrial system or that slaves were unable to cope with an industrial regimen. Slaves employed in industry compared favorably with free workers in diligence and efficiency. Far from declining, the demand for slaves was actually increasing more rapidly in urban areas than in the countryside.

7. The belief that slave-breeding, sexual exploitation, and promiscuity destroyed the black family is a myth. The family was the basic unit of social organization under slavery. It was to the economic interest of planters to encourage the stability of slave families and most of them did so. Most slave sales were either of whole families or of individuals who were at an age when it would have been normal for them to have left the family.

8. The material (not psychological) conditions of the lives of slaves compared favorably with those of free industrial workers. This is not to say that they were good by modern standards. It merely emphasizes the hard lot of all workers, free or slave, during the first half of the nineteenth century.

9. Slaves were exploited in the sense that part of the income which they produced was expropriated by their owners. However, the rate of expropriation was much lower than has generally been presumed. Over the course of his lifetime, the typical slave field hand received about 90 percent of the income he produced.

10. Far from stagnating, the economy of the antebellum South grew quite rapidly. Between 1840 and 1860, per capita income increased more rapidly in the South than in the rest of the nation. By 1860 the South attained a level per capita income which was high by the standards of the time. Indeed, a country as advanced as Italy did not achieve the same level of per capita income until the eve of World War II. . . .

chapter 4

Slavery and Racism in a Comparative Context

In 1947 the Latin-Americanist Frank Tannenbaum (Selection 1) compared the largely peaceful relations of modern times among the various color groups in Latin countries with white and black conflict in a Yankee colossus still afflicted with lynchings, white mobs, and a pervasive Jim Crow system which extended from rural Mississippi to the U.S. Army. Tannenbaum concluded that a less oppressive system of race relations in Central and South America could be attributed to a different kind of historical experience with slavery in which church and state staved off trends toward a permanent and totally degraded racial bondage by making manumission easy and by dealing with slaves as unfortunates whose enslavement through history and chance did not deprive them of limited but very real human rights. Although Tannenbaum had little influence for a decade, his position won some support during the late 1950s and early 60s because of a minor vogue among U.S. historians for Gilberto Freyre's contentions that Brazilian slavery had been very patriarchal and that the Portuguese at home and abroad displayed little or no racial prejudice. (Both Freyre and Tannenbaum failed to account for bloody Brazilian slave revolts and completely ignored the even more violent and successful Caribbean rebellions.)

Stanley Elkins (Selection 2) in 1959 joined his ideas with those of Tannenbaum to extend and strengthen the comparison in one of the most influential books ever written on slavery. Eight years later the Elkins-Tannenbaum thesis gained more advocates when Herbert S. Klein seemingly demonstrated the greater harshness of colonial Virginian slavery in contrast to Cuban bondage during the same time span. Finally Elkins' contentions gained probability in the eyes of some scholars from Winthrop D. Jordan's modern classic of 1969 on the intensity and pervasiveness of white hostility and racial slavery in British North America and the United States.

In the status and treatment of slaves Elkins saw a world of difference between "the liberal, Protestant, secularized, capitalist culture of the North" and "the conservative, paternalistic, Catholic, and quasi-medieval culture of Spain and Portugal." While color constituted only one factor among many in the elaborate status hierarchy of the "quasi-medieval" South, the ruthless and absolute Northern dichotomy of black *or* white, slave *or* free, sprang from a uniquely oppressive slave system and "the most implacable race consciousness ever studied" in the otherwise more progressive and middle class English colonies. Concerned Iberian monarchs, a militant counter-reformation Catholic church and ancient legal codes with long established limits on the power of masters, all combined to give the slave easier access to baptism, marriage, property, emancipation, and to provide better prospects for the freedman. To the North, however, little stood between the master and totalitarian power.

Elkins' book probably would not have gained so large a following if U.S. scholars had been aware of the work done in the late 50s and early 60s in English, Portuguese, and Spanish by Latin-American historians and by anthropologists. As early as 1944 the West Indian scholar Eric Williams in an important but largely neglected volume presented North and South American slave systems as much the same, refused to ascribe bondage to racism, and traced the fate of blacks to "three words . . . sugar . . . tobacco and cotton" in an economic explanation which regarded "the cheapness of labor" as fundamental rather than "the color of the laborer." Also virtually unknown to U.S. historians was anthropologist Stanley Stein's study of 1957 which revealed the harsh exploitation and the pervasive brutality of 19th century coffee planters in the Vassouras district of Brazil. Six years later Latin Americanist C. R. Boxer discussed colonial Brazil as "a hell for blacks" and in 1964 anthropologist Marvin Harris (Selection 3) insisted that patterns in race relations were determined by differences in agricultural production and in labor systems rather than by the political and cultural factors stressed by Elkins and Tannenbaum. Throughout the 60s and the early 70s scholars continued to publish studies on Brazil, Cuba and other countries which revealed the existence of racism and very oppressive slave conditions. In 1972 Gwendolyn Hall produced an extremely interesting comparison between two similar societies, Cuba and St. Dominique, at different times but during the same stage of economic development. Apparently Herbert S. Klein's mistake had been to contrast the slavery of Virginia tobacco plantations with Cuban bondage before the advent of the sugar era, and Hall attempted to avoid the same error by selecting two countries at the peak of their sugar plantation booms. While church and crown *may* have mitigated slavery in earlier times and allowed some shreds of status for free colored people, the sugar barons of nineteenth century Cuba repressed mulattoes and brooked no interference with their harsh and repressive use of forced labor in the quest for soaring profits.

Most historians in the United States got their information on the findings of the anthropologists and the Latin-Americanists from the erudite scholarship of David B. Davis (Selection 4) and Carl N. Degler (Selection 5). In 1966 and 1968 Davis asserted that English and Latin slave systems did not differ greatly and explained the apparent differences by noting that in daily life Northern masters and institutions tempered harsh legal codes while oppressive Latin masters often evaded their relatively lenient statutes. Davis found color hostility among the masters in South *and* North America as well as in medieval Italy and stressed the fact that Egyptians, Babylonians, Greeks, and Romans preceded Americans in holding bondsmen as chattels. According to Davis, all slave systems bore large resemblances to each other because they all involved the contradictions inherent in the effort to treat men as things. Thus North American slavery could not be uniquely oppressive, and differing patterns of race relations could not be traced to radical differences in slave systems.

Carl Degler could find few basic differences between Latin and English slavery beyond the lack of a full-blown ideological defense of racial bondage and the presence of more lenient emancipation policies in the Southern nations. With slavery excluded as a cause Degler traced disparities in twentieth century racial conditions to the traditional Brazilian "mulatto escape hatch" which allowed upward social mobility to mulattoes as persons "neither black nor white" in contrast to the rigid black-or-white color system of the North with its fanatical insistence on assigning people with the smallest degree of known African ancestry to the despised black category. Mulatto gains sprang from two historical circumstances: first, the paucity of white women in Brazilian colonial history which led to a higher place for black concubines as well as a special status for children of mixed ancestry, and second, the small numbers and lack of a work ethic among the white minority which made it necessary to defend the country and to accomplish other nonservile tasks with the aid of blacks.

These two fine works of scholarship merit great praise but they also require criticism because Degler stresses cultural factors over economic forces and Davis tends to "homogenize" large and very different slices of human history. While Davis displays excellent analytical skills and an impressive scholarship, he seems to have inherited several basic habits of thought from the consensus historians of the 1950s and consequently tends to blur distinctions by paying too little attention to the specific economic, social, and cultural context in which a particular slave system existed. Degler almost persuades completely until one remembers that like Elkins and Tannenbaum he may have relied too much on cultural and social explanations and not enough on "three words, sugar, cotton and tobacco." One has to conclude, however, by noting that both men demonstrate the rich possibilities of comparative history and suggest that in this approach the 70s will build substantially on the solid foundation of the 50s and 60s.

BIBLIOGRAPHY

Works Discussed in This Chapter

Boxer, C. R., *Race Relations in the Portuguese Colonial Empire, 1415–1825* (1963).

Davis, David B., *The Problem of Slavery in Western Culture* (1966), and

"Slavery" in C. Vann Woodward, ed., *The Comparative Approach to American History* (1968).

Degler, Carl N., *Neither Black Nor White: Slavery and Race Relations in Brazil and the United States* (1971).

Elkins, Stanley M., *Slavery, A Problem in American Institutional and Intellectual Life* (1959).

Freyre, Gilberto, *The Masters and the Slaves: A Study in the Development of Brazilian Civilization* (1946).

Hall, Gwendolyn M., *Social Control in Slave Plantation Societies: A Comparison of St. Dominique and Cuba* (1972).

Harris, Marvin, *Patterns of Race in the Americas* (1964).

Jordan, Winthrop D., *White Over Black: American Attitudes Toward the Negro* (1969).

Klein, Herbert S., *Slavery in the Americas: A Comparative Study of Cuba and Virginia* (1967).

Stein, Stanley J., *Vassouras: A Brazilian Coffee County, 1850–1900* (1957).

Tannenbaum, Frank, *Slave and Citizen: The Negro in the Americas* (1947).

Williams, Eric, *Capitalism and Slavery* (1944).

Suggested Readings

Among *general works* for an excellent anthology with a useful bibliography to about 1968 see Laura Foner and Eugene D. Genovese, eds., *Slavery in the New World: A Reader in Comparative History* (1969). See also Robin Winks, ed., *Slavery, A Comparative Perspective* (1972). Two anthropologists who agree with Marvin Harris in opposing the Elkins-Tannenbaum thesis and in stressing economic over cultural factors are Sydney W. Mintz and Arnold A. Sio. See Mintz's review of Elkins in the *American Anthropologist* (1961); Mintz "The House and the Yard Among Three Caribbean Peasantries," *Extrait des actes du VIᵉ Congrès International des Sciences Anthropologiques et Ethnologiques,* Tome II, Vol. I (1960); and Sio, "Interpretations of Slavery: The Slave Status in the Americas," *Comparative Studies in Society and History* (1965).

On *American slavery* many U.S. specialists commented on Elkins in a comparative context. See Ann J. Lane, ed., *Slavery and Personality: The Elkins Thesis and Its Critics* (1969); the several works of Eugene D. Genovese listed in the Chapter 2 bibliography; and the David B. Davis works listed earlier in this chapter. For Elkins' response see the added essay in *Slavery* (2nd ed., 1968); his essay in the Ann Lane book; and his review essay on Degler's last book in *The Journal of Negro History* (1973). Sio's review essay on Degler's book in *Civil War History* (1972) is also worth reading. Genovese provided little evidence to support his contention that U.S. slavery was substantially less harsh than most slave systems, but A. E. Keir Nash produced enough evidence in a dissertation and several articles to at least reopen the question. See Nash, "Fairness and Formalism in the Trials of Blacks in the State Supreme Courts of the old South," *Virginia Law Review* (1970); "A More Equitable Past?" *North Carolina Law Review* (1970); and "The Texas Supreme Court and Trial Rights of Blacks, 1845–1860." *Journal of American History* (1971). The English historian J. H. Plumb related slavery and racism to an extreme hostility and repression of the poor and the dispossessed by the English in "Slavery, Race and the Poor," *The Light of History* (1972).

On *West Indian servitude* a comparative essay and a book which stressed the triumph of slavery and racial hostility in harsh plantation settings were

Sydney W. Mintz's "Labor and Sugar in Puerto Rico and in Jamaica," *Comparative Studies in Society and History* (1959) and the Dutch scholar Harry Hoetink's *Two Variants in Caribbean Race Relations* (1967). Alan H. Adamson suggested that the plantation was more important than slavery in *Sugar Without Slaves: The Political Economy of British Guiana, 1834–1904* (1972). Franklin W. Knight opposed Klein's basic contention and demonstrated the oppressive triumph of sugar plantation slavery even more effectively than Gwendolyn M. Hall in the study on *Slave Society In Cuba During the Nineteenth Century* (1970). Richard S. Dunn vividly traced the transformation of a society of small landowners into a harsh plantation system in Barbados and other islands in *The Rise of the Planter Class in the English West Indies 1624–1713* (1972). For an excellent study on codes and laws relating to slavery and color status and for an examination of the importance of the ratios of white to black and slave to nonslave blacks, see Elsa V. Goveia *Slave Society in the British Leeward Islands at the End of the 18th Century* (1965). Winthrop D. Jordan examined laws of different English colonies on color and status in "American Chiaroscuro: The Status and Definition of Mulattoes in the British Colonies" *William and Mary Quarterly* (1962). For a comparative essay on the origins of New World bondage, see Richard B. Sheridan, "Africa and the Caribbean in the Atlantic Slave Trade," *American Historical Review* (1972). For a criticism of Davis' failure to see slave systems adequately in context, see Moses I. Finley's review essay in the *New York Review of Books* (#1, 1967). Other comparative studies on slavery and racism of special distinction by French, Dutch, and Swedish scholars are Roger Bastide, *Les Amériques noires: Les Civilisations africaines dans le nouveau monde* (1967); Pierre L. van den Berghe, *Race and Racism. A Comparative Perspective* (1967); W. Kloosterboer, *Involuntary Labor Since the Abolition of Slavery* (1960); and Magnus Morner, *Race Mixture in the History of Latin America* (1967).

On *slavery in other times and cultures* the best work is M. I. Finley, ed., *Slavery in Classical Antiquity: Views and Controversies* (1960). Also informative are F. M. Snowden, *Blacks in Antiquity* (1970); William L. Westermann, *The Slave Systems of Greek and Roman Antiquity* (1955); Isaac Mendelsohn, *Slavery in the Ancient Near East* (1949); Charles Verlinden, *L'Esclavage dans l'Europe médiévale* (1955); Dev Raj Chanana, *Slavery in Ancient India* (1960); Melville J. Herskovits, *Dahomey: An Ancient West African Kingdom* (1938); and C. Martin Wilbur, *Slavery in China During the Former Han Dynasty* (1945).

For *slavery in Africa* see A. Norman Klein, "West African Unfree Labor Before and After the Rise of the Slave Trade" in Foner and Genovese, eds., *Slavery in the New World: A Reader in Comparative History* (1969).

Other works of note on *Brazil* are Robert Conrad, *The Destruction of Brazilian Slavery, 1850–1880* (1972); Roger Bastide, *Religions africaines au Brésil* (1960); C. R. Boxer, *The Golden Age of Brazil, 1695–1750: Growing Pains of a Colonial Society* (1964); Boxer, *Four Centuries of Portuguese Expansion, 1415–1825: A Succinct Survey* (1965); Florestan Fernandes, *A Integracao de negro à sociedade de classes* (1965); Gilberto Freyre, *The Mansions and the Shanties: The Making of Modern Brazil* (1963); Octavio Ianni *As Metamorfoses do escrevo: Apogeu e crise da escravatura no Brasil meriodional* (1962); and Caio Prado Junior, *The Colonial Background of Modern Brazil* (1967).

On *Cuba* see Phillip S. Foner, *A History of Cuba and Its Relations with the U.S.*, 2 vols. (1962–1963); Ramiro Guerra y Sanchez, *Sugar and Society in the Caribbean* (1964); and Fernando Ortiz, *Hampa afro-cubana: Los Negros esclavos* (1916); and Ortiz, *Cuban Counterpoint* (1947).

On *other Spanish Countries* see Gonzalo Aguirre Beltran, *La Población negra de Mexico, 1519–1810* (1946); John V. Lombardi, *The Decline and Abolition of Negro Slavery in Venezuela, 1820–1854* (1971); Rolando Mellafe, *La Esclavitud en Hispano-America* (1964); J. H. Parry, *The Spanish Seaborne Empire* (1966); and Frederick P. Bowser, *The African Slave in Colonial Peru, 1524–1650* (1974).

On *French, English, Dutch and Danish areas* see C. L. R. James, *The Black Jacobins: Toussaint L'Ouverture and the San Domingo Revolution* (2d ed., 1963); James G. Leyburn, *The Haitian People* (2d ed., 1966); Marcel Trudel, *L'Esclavage au Canada française* (1960); Phillip Curtain, *Two Jamaicas* (1955); C. R. Boxer, *The Dutch Seaborne Empire, 1600–1800* (1965); and Waldemar Westergaard, *The Danish West Indies under Company Rule* (1917).

Latin Slavery Less Oppressive*

Frank Tannenbaum

. . . The Negro slave, brought into the Iberian peninsula as early as 1442, fitted into a society where slavery was still in existence. As a result of the many centuries of warfare with the Moors, if not for other reasons, Spanish society accepted slavery as normal, while it had long since died out in Western Europe. At the time the Negro was brought to Spain, there were Moorish slaves, Jewish slaves, and even some native Spaniards were slaves. Captured prisoners could be held for ransom or could be held as slaves, and the laws allowed other reasons for slavery. But the important point is that there was a slave law, an elaborate code, embodied as part of the *Siete Partidas* going back to Alfonso the Wise (1252–84), which endowed the slave with a legal personality, with duties, and with rights. The slave was known to the law as a human being; he could marry, he could buy his freedom, he could change his master if he found one to purchase him, and he could under certain conditions testify in court even against his master. If a slave became a priest, he had to give his master one slave, but if he became a bishop, he had to give him two slaves.

The Negro brought over from Africa became the beneficiary of this body of law. He was not merely a slave—a chattel, as he was under West Indian and American colonial codes—but also a human being with rights enforceable in the king's court. The Negro in Iberia was also converted to

---

* Frank Tannenbaum, "Toward an Appreciation of Latin America," in *The United States and Latin America*, Herbert L. Matthews, Ed., 2d ed. © 1963 by The American Assembly, Columbia University, pp. 47–48. Reprinted by permission of Prentice-Hall, Inc., Englewood Cliffs, New Jersey.

the Catholic faith, and the master had to see to it that he came to church. While Catholic doctrine did not oppose slavery as such, it asserted that master and slave were equal in the sight of God, that what mattered was the moral and religious character of man, and that the master must treat his slaves as moral beings, as brothers in Christ. It also emphasized the merits of manumission. Negroes in Spanish and Portuguese colonies were the inheritors of this legal and religious tradition. It is not suggested that slavery was not cruel, nor that in Brazil, Cuba, Venezuela, or Peru abominable and inhuman acts were not committed against Negro slaves. But cruelty was against the law, and unusual punishment could be brought to the attention of the court by a recognized legal protector of the slave. The killing of a slave was treated as murder. The entire atmosphere was different, and manumission was so frequent that there were often more freed Negroes than there were slaves.

The fact that the slave had both a legal personality and a moral status made manumission natural and the abolition of slavery no great shock. The question of the slave's fitness for freedom never arose, and the freed Negro was a free man, not a freedman. He was legally the equal of all other free men. And when slavery was abolished in Brazil, the crowd in the galleries threw flowers upon the members of the Congress, and the people danced in the streets of Rio de Janeiro throughout the night. The question of segregation, so agonizing and so disturbing in our own South, could never have arisen anywhere in Latin America—neither with the Negro nor with the Indian. . . .

North American Slavery Uniquely Oppressive*

Stanley M. Elkins

. . . Tannenbaum's book, in its format and proportions, was an excessively modest and unpretentious affair. There was no room, for instance, in the compendious Stampp work (eight years later) for taking any notice of it—not even in a footnote. But what would happen if the sort of thinking which Tannenbaum represents were simply moved out of the center of the stage? The technique of *Slave and Citizen* is one which has remained practically unexploited in the work done in American history—the tech-

---

* Stanley M. Elkins, *Slavery, A Problem in American Institutional and Intellectual Life* (Chicago: University of Chicago Press, 1959). By permission of the publisher.

nique of comparison—and there are conceivably problems in which one judicious and intelligent comparative statement can be worth an entire attic full of plantation records. Such a statement seems to have been made here. What Tannenbaum compares is the institution of slavery in two very distinct types of culture. Slavery as an evil is simply taken for granted; what interested the author were the resources of two cultures, Hispano-Portuguese and British-American, for sustaining and dealing with evil in their midst. He finds staggering contrasts and leaves us with a problem: the problem of *why*. Here is something that seems well worth picking up. . . .

An examination of American slavery, checked at certain critical points against a very different slave system, that of Latin America, reveals that a major key to many of the contrasts between them was an institutional key: The presence or absence of other powerful institutions in society made an immense difference in the character of slavery itself. In Latin America, the very tension and balance among three kinds of organizational concerns—church, crown, and plantation agriculture—prevented slavery from being carried by the planting class to its ultimate logic. For the slave, in terms of the space thus allowed for the development of men and women as moral beings the result was an "open system": a system of contacts with free society through which ultimate absorption into that society could and did occur with great frequency. The rights of personality implicit in the ancient traditions of slavery and in the church's most venerable assumptions on the nature of the human soul were thus in a vital sense conserved, whereas to a staggering extent the very opposite was true in North American slavery. The latter system had developed virtually unchecked by institutions having anything like the power of their Latin counterparts; the legal structure which supported it, shaped only by the demands of a staple-raising capitalism, had defined with such nicety the slave's character as chattel that his character as a moral individual was left in the vaguest of legal obscurity. In this sense American slavery operated as a "closed" system. . . .

. . . [In the U.S.] that most ancient and intimate of institutional arrangements, marriage and the family, had long since been destroyed by the law, and the law never showed any inclination to rehabilitate it. . . .

The rights of property, and all other civil and legal "rights," were everywhere denied the slave with a clarity that left no doubt of his utter dependency upon his master. "A slave is in absolute bondage; he has no civil right, and can hold no property, except at the will and pleasure of his master. He could neither give nor receive gifts; he could make no will, nor could he, by will, inherit anything. He could not hire himself out or make contracts for any purpose—even including, as we have seen, that of matrimony—and thus neither his word nor his bond had any standing in law. He could buy or sell nothing at all, except as his master's agent, could keep no cattle, horses, hogs, or sheep and, in Mississippi at least, could raise no cotton. Even masters who permitted such transactions, except under express arrangement, were uniformly liable to fines. It was obvious, then, that the case of a slave who should presume to buy his own freedom—he being unable to possess money—would involve a legal absurdity. "Slaves have no legal right in things, real or personal; but whatever they may acquire, belongs, in point of law, to their masters."[1] . . .

Such proscriptions were extended not only over all civil rights but even to the civic privileges of education and worship. Every Southern state except Maryland and Kentucky had stringent laws forbidding anyone to teach slaves reading and writing, and in some states the penalties applied to the educating of free Negroes and mulattoes as well. It was thought that "teaching slaves to read and write tends to dissatisfaction in their minds, and to produce insurrection and rebellion",[2] in North Carolina it was a crime to distribute among them any pamphlet or book, not excluding the Bible. The same apprehensions applied to instruction in religion. Southern society was not disposed to withhold the consolations of divine worship from its slaves, but the conditions would have to be laid down not by the church as an institution, not even by the planters as laity, but by planters simply as masters. . . .

. . . [The South developed] the most implacable race-consciousness yet observed in virtually any society. It was evolved in the Southern mind, one might say, as a simple syllogism, the precision of whose terms paralleled the precision of the system itself. All slaves are black; slaves are degraded and contemptible; therefore all blacks are degraded and contemptible and should be kept in a state of slavery. How had the simple syllogism come into being? That very strength and bulwark of American society, capitalism, unimpeded by prior arrangements and institutions, had stamped the status of slave upon the black with a clarity which elsewhere could never have been so profound, and had further defined the institution of slavery with such nicety that the slave *was*, in fact, degraded. That the black, as a species, was thus contemptible seemed to follow by observation. This assumption took on a life of its own in the attitudes of the people, and the very thought of such a creature existing outside the pale of their so aptly devised system filled the most reasonable of Southerners with fear and loathing. Quite apart from the demands of the system itself, this may account for many of the subsidiary social taboos—the increasing severity of the laws against manumission, the horror of miscegenation, the depressed condition of the free Negro and his peculiar place in Southern society: all signs of how difficult it was to conceive a non-slave colored class. Nothing in their experience had prepared them for it; such a class was unnatural, logically awry, a blemish on the body politic, an anomaly for which there was no intellectual category. . . .

The basic fact was, of course, that the slave himself was property. He and his fellow bondsmen had long since become "chattels personal . . . to all intents, constructions and purposes whatsoever."[3]

In the slave system of the United States—so finely circumscribed and

---

[1] Goodell, *American Slave Code*, p. 88. A substantial number of Negroes did in fact buy their freedom in the ante-bellum South but this required the full co-operation of their masters. Legally the slave had no claim to the money he may have collected for his own purchase. . . .

[2] Goodell, *American Slave Code*, p. 321.

[3] Hurd, *Law of Freedom and Bondage*, 1, 303.

so cleanly self-contained—virtually all avenues of recourse for the slave, all lines of communication to society at large, originated and ended with the master. The system was unique, *sui generis*. The closest parallel to it at that time was to be found in the Latin-American colonies of Spain and Portugal. But the differences between the two systems are so much more striking than the similarities that we may with profit use them not as parallels but as contrasts. In the Spanish and Portuguese colonies, we are immediately impressed by the comparative lack of precision and logic governing the institution of slavery there; we find an exasperating dimness of line between the slave and free portions of society, a multiplicity of points of contact between the two, a confusing promiscuity of color, such as would never have been thinkable in our own country.[4]. . .

. . . For all the cruelty and bigotry of this quasi-medieval society, the balance between property rights and human rights stood in a vastly different ratio—much to the advantage of human rights—from that seen in the American South.

In the colonies of Latin America we are thus able to think of the church, the civil authority, and the property concerns of the planter-adventurer as constituting distinct and not always harmonious interests in society. The introduction of slaves into the colonies brought much discomfort to the royal conscience; when the trade in Negroes became of consequence, the monarchs gave it their growing concern, and it never occurred to them not to retain over it a heavy measure of royal control. . . .

The other item in this equation was the presence of a powerful church with needs of its own. A considerable measure of its power as an institution naturally depended upon its position of leadership in matters touching the morals of society. The maintenance of that leadership required the church as a matter of course to insist on a dominant role in the formulation of all policy which might bear on the morality of the slave system and have consequences for the Faith. . . . As an eighteenth-century prelate, Cardinal Gerdil categorically stated, "Slavery is not to be understood as conferring on one man the same power over another that men have over cattle. . . . For slavery does not abolish the natural equality of man. . . ."[5]

. . . The Jesuits would labor excessively in places such as Brazil to mitigate the evils of slavery; the papacy itself would denounce it in various ways in 1462, 1537, 1639, 1741, 1815, and 1839. . . .

It would be misleading to imply that slavery in the colonies drew its total character from the powerful influence of the church. But it may be asserted that the church, functioning in its capacity as guardian of morals, was responsible for whatever human rights were conserved for

---

4 Four works upon which I have drawn heavily for my material on Latin-American slavery are Frank Tannenbaum's *Slave and Citizen* (New York: Knopf, 1947), Fr. Dieudonné Rinchon's *La traite et l'esclavage des Congolais par les Européens* (Wetteren, Belgium, 1929), Sir Harry Johnston's *The Negro in the New World* (London: Methuen, 1910), and Fernando Ortiz, *Los Negros esclavos* (Havana: Revista bimestra cubana, 1916).

5 James J. Fox, "Ethical Aspect of Slavery," in Charles G. Hebermann and others (eds.), *The Catholic Encyclopedia* (New York: Encyclopedia Press, 1913), 14, 40.

the slave within the grim system. What it came to was that three formidable interests—the crown, the planter, and the church—were deeply concerned with the system, that these concerns were in certain ways competing, and that the product of this balance of power left its profound impress on the actual legal and customary sanctions governing the status and treatment of slaves. These sanctions were by no means what they would have been had it been left to the planting class alone to develop them systematically with reference only to the requirements of a labor system. . . .

Neither in Brazil nor in Spanish America did slavery carry with it such precise and irrevocable categories of perpetual servitude, *"durante vita"* and "for all generations," as in the United States. The presumption in these countries, should the status of a colored person be in doubt, was that he was free rather than a slave.[6] There were in fact innumerable ways whereby a slave's servitude could be brought to an end. The chief of these was the very considerable fact that he might buy his own freedom. The Negro in Cuba or Mexico had the right to have his price declared and could, if he wished, purchase himself in instalments. Slaves escaping to Cuba to embrace Catholicism were protected by a special royal order of 1733 which was twice reissued. . . . Indeed, in Cuba and Brazil such freedom might be purchased for a nominal sum at the baptismal font. All such manumissions had the strong approval of both church and state and were registered gratis by the government.

In extending its moral authority over men of every condition, the church naturally insisted on bringing slave unions under the holy sacraments. Slaves were married in church and the banns published; marriage was a sacred rite and its sanctity protected in law. . . .

The master's disciplinary authority never had the completeness that it had in the United States, and nowhere did he enjoy powers of life and death over the slave's body. Under the Spanish code of 1789 slaves might be punished for failure to perform their duties, with prison, chains, or lashes, "which last must not exceed the number of twenty-five, and those must be given them in such manner as not to cause any contusion or effusion of blood: which punishments cannot be imposed on slaves but by their masters or the stewards."[7] For actual crimes a slave was to be tried in an ordinary court of justice like any free person,[8] and, conversely, the murder of a slave was to be prosecuted just as that of a free man would be.[9] Excessive punishments of slaves—causing "contusion, effusion of blood, or mutilation of members" . . . were themselves punishable.

As was implied in his right to purchase his own freedom, the slave in

---

6 "In the Cuban market freedom was the only commodity which could be bought untaxed; every negro against whom no one had proved a claim of servitude was deemed free. . . ." William Law Mathieson, *British Slavery and Its Abolition* (London: Longmans, Green, 1926), pp. 37–38.

7 Johnston, *Negro in the New World*, p. 45.

8 The sentence, however, was apparently to be executed by the master. Ibid., p. 45.

9 Ibid., pp. 45–46. The code does not make it clear whether the penalty would be the same against the slave's master as against another person. But in any case the murderer, master or other, was liable to prosecution.

the Spanish and Portuguese colonies had the right to acquire and hold property. This meant something specific; in Brazil a master was obliged by law to give liberty to his slaves on all Sundays and holidays—which totaled eighty-five in the year—during which a slave might work for himself and accumulate money for his purchase price,[10] and the Spanish code of 1789 provided that slaves must be allowed two hours each day in which to be employed in "occupations for their own advantage."[11] In many places slaves were encouraged to hire themselves out regularly (there were skilled artisans among them as well as ordinary laborers), an arrangement which was to the advantage of both the master and the slave himself, since the latter was allowed to keep a percentage of the wage. Slaves even in rural areas might sell the produce of their gardens and retain the proceeds.[12] For all practical purposes slavery here had become, as Mr. Tannenbaum puts it, a contractual arrangement: it could be wiped out by a fixed purchase price and leave no taint. "There may have been no written contract between the two parties, but the state behaved, in effect, as if such a contract did exist, and used its powers to enforce it."[13] It was a contract in which the master owned a man's labor but not the man. . . .

The Spaniards and Portuguese had the widespread reputation by the eighteenth century—whatever may have been the reasons—for being among all nations the best masters of slaves. The standards for such a judgment cannot, of course, be made too simple. Were slaves "physically maltreated" in those countries? They could, conceivably, have been treated worse than in our own nineteenth-century South without altering the comparison, for even in cruelty the relationship was between man and man.[14] Was there "race prejudice"? No one could be more arrogantly proud of his racial purity than the Spaniard of Castile, and theoretically there were rigid caste lines, but the finest Creole families, the clergy, the army, the professions, were hopelessly "defiled" by Negro blood;[15] the taboos were that vague in practice. Was there squalor, filth, widespread depression of the masses? Much more so than with us—but there it was the class system and economic "underdevelopment," rather than the color barrier, that made the difference. In these countries the concept of "beyond the pale" applied primarily to beings outside the Christian fold rather than to those beyond the color line.[16]

---

[10] It was not even uncommon for ex-slaves who had thus acquired their freedom to become actual slaveholders on their own account. Johnston, *Negro in the New World*, p. 90.

[11] Ibid., p. 44.

[12] Tannenbaum, *Slave and Citizen*, pp. 58–61.

[13] Ibid., p. 55. . . .

[14] Most writers and students do seem to think that the system was "milder" in the Spanish colonies and in Brazil, but nobody has ever claimed that it was a life of ease and comfort. . . .

[15] Even the legendary corruption of the Spanish upper classes was apparently biracial in the New World. . . .

[16] "The thing that barred an immigrant in those days was heterodoxy; the blot of heresy upon the soul and not any racial brand upon the body." Freyre, *The Masters and the Slaves*, pp. 40–41.

We are not, then, dealing with a society steeped, like our own, in traditions of political and economic democracy. We are concerned only with a special and peculiar kind of fluidity—that of their slave systems—and in this alone lay a world of difference. It was a fluidity that permitted a transition from slavery to freedom that was smooth, organic, and continuing. Manumitting slaves, carrying as it did such high social approval, was done often, and the spectacle of large numbers of freedmen was familiar to the social scene. Such opportunities as were open to any member of the depressed classes who had talent and diligence were open as well to the ex-slave and his descendants. Thus color itself was no grave disability against taking one's place in free society; indeed, Anglo-Saxon travelers in nineteenth-century Brazil were amazed at the thoroughgoing mixture of races there. . . .

All such rights and opportunities existed *before* the abolition of slavery; and thus we may note it as no paradox that emancipation, when it finally did take place, was brought about in all these Latin-American countries "without violence, without bloodshed, and without civil war."[17]. . .

Brazil a Hell for Blacks[*]

Marvin Harris

. . . What the laws of the Spanish and Portuguese kings had to do with the attitudes and values of the Spanish and Portuguese planters, however, baffles one's imagination. The Crown could publish all the laws it wanted, but in the lowlands, sugar was king. If there were any Portuguese or Spanish planters who were aware of their legal obligations toward the slaves, it would require systematic misreading of colonialism, past and present, to suppose that these laws psychologically represented anything more than the flatus of a pack of ill-informed Colonel Blimps who didn't even know what a proper cane field looked like. Ortiz leaves no room for doubt in the case of Cuba. Yes, the slave had legal rights, "But these rights were not viable . . . if they contrast with the barbaric laws of the French and above all, of the English colonies, it was no less certain that all of these rights were illusory, especially in earlier times. . . ." Sanctity of the family? "Man and wife were permanently separated, sold in sep-

17 Tannenbaum, *Slave and Citizen*, p. 106.

* Marvin Harris, *Patterns of Race in America* (New York: Walker and Company, 1964). By permission of Walker and Company, a division of Publications Development Corporation.

arate places, and separated from their children."¹ "How many times was a son sold by his father!" and "Pregnant or nursing slaves were sold with or without their actual or future offspring."² Protection of the law? "The sugar and coffee plantations were in fact feudal domains where the only authority recognized was that of the master. . . . Could the Negroes hope in these circumstances to change masters? The rawhide would quiet their voices. . . ." Rights to property? "From what I have said in relation to the work of the rural slave, to speak of his right to hold property and to buy freedom, is futile. . . ." "But I repeat, the plantation slave was treated like a beast, like a being to whom human character was denied. . . ."³

Tannenbaum makes much of the fact that there was no set of ancient slave laws to which the Anglo-Saxon planters or the slaves could turn for guidance. He prominently displays the meager penalties attached to murder of slaves as examples of their subhuman status in the eyes of the Anglo-Saxon colonists. But Ortiz informs us that "it was not until 1842 that there was any specific legal regulation of the form of punishment which a Cuban master could give his slave."⁴ Actually it turns out that "the state did not concern itself with the limitation of the arbitrary power of the master in relation to the punishment of his slave until after the abolition of slavery [1880]."⁵

In Brazil, as everywhere in the colonial world, law and reality bore an equally small resemblance to each other. Stanley Stein's recent historical study of slavery in the county of Vassouras during the last century yields a picture almost totally at variance with that drawn by Gilberto Freyre for the earlier plantations. The Vassouras planters went about their business, methodically buying, working, beating, and selling their slaves, in whatever fashion yielded the most coffee with the least expense. The master's will was supreme. "It was difficult to apply legal restraints to the planter's use of the lash."⁶

> Typical is an eyewitness account of a beating told by an ex-slave. On order from the master, two drivers bound and beat a slave while the slave folk stood in line, free folk watching from further back. The slave died that night and his corpse, dumped into a wicker basket, was borne by night to the slave cemetery of the plantation and dropped into a hastily dug grave. *"Slaves could not complain to the police, only another fazendeiro* [master] *could do that,"* explained the eyewitness.⁷ [Italics are mine.]

If Stein's picture of nineteenth-century Vassouras is accurate—it is the most carefully documented study of its kind in existence—then the fol-

---

¹ Fernando Ortiz, *Los negros esclaves* . . . (1916), pp. 303–4.

² Ibid., p. 173.

³ Ibid., pp. 303–4.

⁴ Ibid., p. 265.

⁵ Ibid., p. 267.

⁶ Stanley Stein, *Vassouras* (Cambridge, Mass.: Harvard University Press, 1957), p. 135.

⁷ Ibid., p. 136.

lowing recent pronouncement from Charles Boxer will have to be accepted minus the time restriction:

> The common belief that the Brazilian was an exceptionally kind master is applicable only to the nineteenth century under the Empire, and it is contradicted for the colonial period by the testimony of numerous reliable eyewitnesses from Vieira to Vilhena, to say nothing of the official correspondence between the colonial authorities and the Crown.[8]

Of special interest in Boxer's refutation of the myth of the friendly master is the evidence which shows that Brazilian planters and miners did not accept the legal decisions which awarded human souls and human personalities to the slaves. The Brazilian slave-owners were convinced that Negroes were descended from Cain, black and "therefore not people like ourselves." Making due allowance for exceptions and the special circumstances of household slaves, Boxer concludes that "it remains true that by and large colonial Brazil was indeed a 'hell for blacks.' "[9] . . .

The Similarity of Slave Systems*

David B. Davis

The status of slavery has always been surrounded with certain ambiguities that seem related to the institution's origins. To be enslaved as a result of capture in war or punishment for crime implied total subordination to coercive authority. Yet bondage for debt or as the result of self-sale suggested merely a reciprocal exchange of labor and obedience for sustenance and protection. When a bondwoman's offspring were claimed by her owner on the same basis as the natural increase of livestock, the status was assimilated to that of movable property. In societies where slaves have largely been recruited from the native poor and have performed no specialized economic function, as in ancient China, Egypt, and the Near East, the element of reciprocal rights and obligations has taken precedence over the elements of punishment and ownership. Nev-

---

8 Charles Boxer, *The Golden Age of Brazil* (Berkeley, Calif.: University of California Press, 1962), p. 173.

9 Charles Boxer, *Race Relations in the Portugese Colonial Empire, 1415–1825* (Oxford, Eng.: Clarendon Press, 1963), p. 114.

* David B. Davis, "The Similarity of Slave Systems" in C. Vann Woodward, ed., *A Comparative Approach to American History* (New York: Basic Books, 1968). By permission of the author.

ertheless, the slave was legally defined as a thing not only in the Southern United States but in ancient Egypt, Babylonia, Greece, and Rome. And the Roman conception of the slave as at once a person and a piece of movable property prevailed in medieval France, Italy, and Spain; it was extended to Latin America and was incorporated in the Code Noir for the French colonies; and it reappeared in the laws and judicial decisions of British North America. A Viriginia court merely affirmed the ancient Latin concept of chattel slavery when it ruled that "Slaves are not only property, but they are rational beings, and entitled to the humanity of the Court, when it can be exercised without invading the rights of property." And when an American master claimed the offspring of his female slaves or asserted his right to move, sell, trade, bequest, or give away his chattel property, he added nothing to a legal notion of slavery that had persisted in Europe for more than two thousand years.

The definition of the slave as chattel property implied a condition of rightlessness on the part of the slave. In neither Europe nor the Americas could a slave testify in court against a free person, institute a court action in his own behalf, make a legally binding will or contract, or own property. There were, to be sure, minor exceptions and variations. Slaves were sometimes allowed to testify in certain civil cases or give evidence against a master accused of treason. In North America at various times Negro bondsmen were permitted to plead benefit of clergy and to give evidence in capital cases involving other slaves. As in Rome and Latin America, they were accorded limited rights over personal property, including horses and cattle, and might act as a master's legal agent, though never with the freedom and complex prerogatives of the Roman slave. But what stands out above the exceptions and variations is the fact that from pre-Christian laws to the slave codes of the New World the bondsman had no civil capacities and was considered only as an extension of his master's legal personality. Even in Puritan Massachusetts slaves were, in the words of Cotton Mather, who was simply echoing Aristotle, "the *Animate, Separate, Active Instruments* of other men." . . .

. . . One of the paradoxes of American slavery was that the laws protecting the physical welfare of slaves were accompanied by the severest restrictions on manumission. This brings us to the most important distinction between the legal status of slaves in British and Latin America. It should be stressed that taxes and other restrictions on manumission were common in antiquity, particularly in Rome, and that freedom suffered from prejudice and legal disabilities even when the stigma of slavish origin was not associated with race. There were discriminatory freedmen's laws, for example, in medieval Spain and Italy, and in Latin America as well. But only in the Southern United States did legislators try to bar every route to emancipation and deprive masters of their traditional right to free individual slaves. It is true that thousands of American slaves were manumitted by their owners, many after buying their freedom in installments, as was far more common in Latin America. It is also true that in some areas of Latin America a slave had no more realistic chance of becoming free than did his brother in Mississippi. Nevertheless, one may conclude that slavery in North America was distinctive in its efforts to build ever higher barriers against manumission. And there is evidence that this had less to do with slavery as such than with social attitudes toward racial integration.

Although the questions are of compelling importance, we cannot begin to determine whether slavery was a source of racial prejudice or prejudice a source of slavery, nor can we explain why prejudice became more dominant in the United States than in other parts of the New World. One may briefly state the principal facts that are relevant to a comparative study of slavery. Without denying the significance of racial difference as an aggravation to American bondage, we may note that throughout history slaves have been said to be naturally inferior, lazy, cunning, thievish, lascivious, fawning, deceitful, and incapable of life's higher thoughts and emotions. When not differentiated by race, they have often been physically marked off by shaven heads, brands, tattoos, and collars. There is unmistakable evidence of racial prejudice in Italy and the Iberian Peninsula, where colored slaves generally suffered from various indignities and disabilities. In Latin America Negro bondsmen were long denied the privileges and protections of Indian workers. Nonetheless, while Latin America was by no means immune from racial prejudice, even against freedmen of mixed blood, there was a gradual acceptance of racial intermixture and a willingness to accept each stage of dilution as a step toward whiteness. In the British colonies, although the first Negroes had an ill-defined status and worked side by side with white servants, there was never any tolerance of racial blending. White fathers seldom acknowledged their colored offspring, and a mulatto or quadroon was still legally classed as a Negro. These differences may have been related to religion, sexual mores, social stratification, or the proportion of white women in a colonial population. But whatever the reason, prejudice against Negroes seems to have grown in the United States with the advance of popular democracy. It can be argued that this had less to do with slavery than with the status of the free Negro in an unusually mobile and unstratified white society. In other words, differences in slave systems may not account for the fact that while the Negro in the United States today has far more economic and educational opportunities than the Negro in Latin America, he also suffers from more overt discrimination from whites who feel superior but are unsure of their own status.

By focusing thus far on the legal status of slaves, we have given an oversimplified picture of institutional homogeneity. In actuality, of course, American slavery took a great variety of forms that were largely the result of economic pressures and such derivative factors as the nature of employment, the number of slaves owned by a typical master, and the proportion of slaves in a given society. Thus we correctly categorize North American slavery as plantation and staple-crop slavery, but tend to forget that in 1820 Negro bondsmen constituted 20 percent of the population of Southern cities and that in 1860 there were a half million slaves working in factories, on railroad construction, as stevedores, as lumberjacks, on steamboats, and in numerous other jobs unconnected with agriculture. As in ancient Athens and Rome, and as in Latin America, slaves in the Southern states were employed as valets, waiters, cooks, nurses, craftsmen, and prostitutes. In spite of these well-known facts, most comparisons of slavery in Britain and Latin America have assumed that the institutions were virtually monolithic. We still lack comparative studies of the domestic servant, the slave artisan, the rented worker, and the slave in manufacturing establishments.

It has been said that the latifundia of southern Italy and Sicily provided an ancient precedent for the gang labor, the rationalized system of production, and the absentee ownership of the Caribbean plantation. But one must be careful not to lump all plantation agriculture in an undifferentiated class. Since the production of sugar, for example, was a long and continuous process that could be ruined by a delay in cutting, milling, boiling, or curing, the rhythm of plantation life was probably much the same in parts of Brazil as in Jamaica and Louisiana. The cultivation of sugar and rice required heavy capital investment, and in the West Indies and South Carolina led to slave gangs of several hundred being divided for specialized tasks under constant surveillance. Slavery in colonial South Carolina, though less characterized by absentee ownership, had more in common with slavery in the West Indies than either had with the institution in Virginia and Maryland. By 1765 South Carolina's forty thousand whites were outnumbered by ninety thousand slaves; eight years later Jamaica's sixteen thousand whites kept uneasy watch over two hundred thousand slaves. In neither society could a field slave be in close or frequent contact with white men. In Virginia, on the other hand, the proportion of Negroes and whites was roughly equal, and the typical tobacco plantation employed less than twenty slaves. Unlike any of the previously mentioned staples, cotton did not require elaborate stages of preparation and processing, and could be profitably grown on small-scale farms. It was thus not uncommon for a cotton farmer to own less than ten slaves and even to work beside them in the field. Even by 1860, after a long period of rising slave prices, nearly one-half of the Southern slaveholders owned less than five Negroes apiece; 72 percent owned less than ten apiece and held approximately one-quarter of the entire number of American slaves.

Compared with the plantation agriculture of the West Indies and Brazil, the striking features of the American South were the wide dispersal of slave ownership and the relatively small units of production scattered over immense areas. This may have led to a greater variation and flexibility in the relationship between master and slaves, although we still lack comparative research on such vital questions as labor management, the social roles and subculture of Negroes, and the relation of plantation life to social structure. It seems plausible that if American Negroes sometimes benefited by a close relationship with white families, they were also denied the sense of massive solidarity that was probably essential for revolt. In the West Indies slaves not only had the opportunity to plan and organize revolts, but they were seldom tied by the close bonds of loyalty that led so many North American slaves to divulge plots before they were hardly formed.

This is not to suggest that North American slaves were less oppressed than those of other times and regions, but only that there were different forms of oppression. As comparative studies move ahead toward finer distinctions and a typology of slave systems, it is likely that less attention will be paid to legal status than to stages of economic development. It would be absurd to claim that all slave economies must pass through a pre-set cycle of boom and depression. Nevertheless, regardless of cultural differences and other variables, there are striking examples throughout the Americas of a pattern which began with an unmitigated drive for quick profit, a rapid expansion in slaves and land under cultivation, and a subsequent overproduction of staples. Whenever slaves were worked under boom conditions, as in the West Indies in the mid-eighteenth century and the Brazilian coffee plantations in the nineteenth, the institution was one of grinding attrition. A more relaxed paternalism tended to appear when prices had fallen, when there was little incentive to maximize production, and when planters in longer-settled regions looked to social and cultural distinctions to differentiate themselves from new generations of hard-driving speculators. Thus in the mid-nineteenth century there is evidence that in such states as Virginia and Maryland a more easy-going, paternalistic pattern of slavery was emerging, not unlike that of the depleted sugar plantations of Brazil. In Maryland and Delaware there was even a rapid decline in the proportion of slaves to freedmen, though this was partly a result of interstate migration. At the same time there was a heavy drain of slaves toward the expanding cotton areas of the Southwest, where the price of labor kept rising and slaves became more concentrated in the hands of a relatively few planters.

The question of stages of economic development is related to the much larger question of the place of slavery in the evolution of industrial capitalism. And here, though historians have long acknowledged the dependence of the world's cotton textile industry on the slave systems of North and South America, there is an astonishing lack of systematic and comparative analysis. The whole complex relationship between capitalism and slavery is still in the realm of suggestive speculation. Scholars still debate whether slavery was profitable and whether the forms it took in America can be termed capitalistic. We do not yet fully understand why so many areas where slavery flourished were stultified by soil depletion and a lack of capital formation, by an absence of internal markets, of urbanization, and of technological innovation. And finally, if we are really to comprehend the significance of slavery and the burdens it has entailed, comparative history must explain the great challenge posed to the institution by an emerging urban, bureaucratic, and capitalistic civilization, which led to a bitter conflict between England and her Caribbean colonies, to a sharp struggle between the Brazilian coastal cities and the interior valleys, and to an epic contest between the North and South in the United States.

[Editor's Note. Since nearly all the titles listed in Davis' brief bibliography are included in my chapter bibliography, I have deleted his list.]

The Latin Difference: The Mulatto Escape Hatch*

Carl N. Degler

. . . What may we conclude from this examination of slavery in Brazil and the United States? That there were in fact differences in the practices of slavery in the two countries there can be no doubt. That Brazil kept the foreign slave trade open longer than the United States was not only a difference, but a cause for several other differences, as we have seen. The two countries also differed markedly in their attitudes toward arming slaves and toward defending slavery on grounds of race. The explanations for these differences, however, are not to be found in differences in the laws of the two home governments nor in the attitudes and practices of the respective national religious persuasions. Neither the church nor the state in Brazil displayed any deep concern about the humanity of the slave and, in any event, neither used its authority to affect significantly the life of the slave. . . . Even when the Portuguese Crown sought to provide some protection for the Negro as a human being, it was not always obeyed by white masters in Brazil. Much more persuasive as explanations for the differences are the demographic and economic developments and geographic circumstances in the two countries, that is, the differences in their respective historical experiences.

At the same time, there is yet something else that might be gained from this comparison. For there is a pattern behind some of the differences that becomes clear only as the individual differences are viewed together. Behind several of the divergencies in practice and ideology is the clear implication that in Brazil the slave may have been feared, but the black man was not, whereas in the United States both the slave and the black were feared. Thus the willingness of Brazilians to manumit slaves much more freely than North Americans is a result of their not fearing free blacks in great numbers, regardless of the fears they may have entertained about slave uprisings. Thus Brazilians did not feel it necessary to restrict manumission as North Americans did. In the United States, slavery was always a means of controlling dangerous blacks as well as a way of organizing labor. That is why most plans for emancipation, prior to the great abolitionist crusade, looked to expatriation to Africa or some other place once the Negroes were freed. Winthrop Jordan, in *White Over Black,* points out that the "earliest American suggestion of colonization included an observation that it was not safe to have

* By permission of the author from *Neither Black Nor White: Slavery and Race Relations in Brazil and the United States* (New York: The Macmillan Company, 1971). Copyright by Carl N. Degler.

Negroes free in America." The "warning" was published in 1715.[1] As late as the Civil War, President Abraham Lincoln was still seriously considering the founding of a settlement in Central America for the blacks who would be freed by the war. Only the impracticality of resettling four million people caused him to give up the idea.[2]

United States fear of Negroes is also highlighted in the contrast between the willingness of Brazilian slaveholders to use blacks as slave catchers and overseers, whereas in the United States, few white men, much less slaveholders, were prepared to put Negroes in such positions of authority. Nor is it accidental that a racial defense of slavery was developed in the United States and largely absent from Brazil. Such a defense followed almost logically from the fear of blacks and was quite consonant with the refusal to permit free blacks to be overseers and slave catchers. Although when one looks at the United States experience alone the development of a racial defense of slavery seems quite natural, the Brazilian experience compels us to realize that the development of such a defense was not a simple function of slavery, but the result of a special attitude on the part of whites toward blacks—an attitude derived from a particular history. It would be difficult for Brazilians to develop a racial defense of slavery when they used these same blacks as overseers and slave catchers, that is, as defenders of the system.

Finally, the fear of Negroes on the part of North Americans emerges nowhere more forcefully than when one asks why the slave trade remained open in Brazil down to 1851, but was closed in most of the United States before the end of the eighteenth century. If one examines official explanations for the closing of the slave trade, the fear of being overwhelmed by blacks stands out as a significant, if not the chief motive.[3] . . .

In Brazil . . . the slave trade came to an end not only much later, but only after great pressure had been applied from outside the society. Although there were also some Brazilians in the nineteenth century who advocated the closing of the infamous traffic, the principal force came from the British government. In 1827, on pain of commercial restrictions, Britain compelled the Brazilian government to agree to the closing of the trade. But from the outset the Brazilians showed that they were not going to stop a traffic so important to them and especially when agreement to do so was exacted under duress. Thus for almost a quarter of a century thereafter the British navy harassed Brazilian shipping while the foreign office harassed the Imperial government in an effort to put teeth into the treaty of 1827. Success was meager. As we have

---

[1] Jordan, *White Over Black*, p. 561 n.

[2] For a full discussion of Lincoln's attitudes toward free Negroes and his plans for their future see Benjamin Quarles, *Lincoln and the Negro* (New York, 1962), especially pp. 108–23.

[3] See W. E. B. DuBois, *The Suppression of the African Slave Trade to the United States of America 1638–1870* (New York, 1896), pp. 215–29. Don B. Kates, Jr., "Abolition, Deportation, Integration: Attitudes Toward Slavery in the Early Republic," *Journal of Negro History*, 53 (January 1968), 33–47 contains many expressions by white Americans of their opposition to free Negroes' remaining in the United States.

seen already, it was during that twenty year period that several hundred thousand fresh slaves entered Brazil from Africa.

The trade was definitely ended in 1851 by Brazilian action. Behind that decision lay twenty years of British harassment and humiliating violation of Brazilian sovereignty. At times the Royal Navy, in its zealous suppression of the hated traffic, actually chased slavers through the harbors and inlets of Brazil. It was not fear of being inundated by blacks that wrote an end to the trade in Brazil, but the desire on the part of Brazilians to put a stop to British hectoring and to have their country take its place among those nations that refused to participate in a business no longer considered civilized.[4] Besides, in a country in which most of the people were black or brown, fear of being overwhelmed by colored people could hardly have been an important consideration.

The overall conclusion that emerges from this comparison of slave systems is that the differences are not fundamental to an explanation of differences in contemporary race relations. It is evident that differences in the practices of slavery in Brazil and the United States can be quite adequately accounted for by the accidents of geography, demography, and economy and the underlying differences in attitudes toward Negroes rather than by differences in the laws and practices of church and state regarding slavery. In short, the differences were a result of historical circumstances in the New World, not of inherited moral intent or law. As a part of the whole complex of interacting events and circumstances, to be sure, the practices of slavery certainly played a part. But as a causal factor in the shaping of race relations slavery was itself a consequence of deeper differences rather than a primary explanation. If we seek the basic origins of the diverging racial patterns of Brazil and the United States, clearly we must look behind the practices of slavery. . . .

The key that unlocks the puzzle of the differences in race relations in Brazil and the United States is the mulatto escape hatch. Complex and varied as the race relations in the two countries have been and are today, the presence of a separate place for the mulatto in Brazil and its absence in the United States nevertheless define remarkably well the heart of the difference. Let us look for a moment at some of the ways in which the mulatto escape hatch distinguishes race patterns in Brazil and the United States.

The existence of the mulatto, for example, makes most difficult, if not impossible, the kind of segregation patterns that have been so characteristic of the United States. With many shades of skin color, segregating people on the basis of color would incur both enormous expense and great inconvenience. Facilities, for instance, would have to be duplicated several times, beyond reason and financial feasibility. Furthermore, in a society in which distinctions are made among a variety of colors, rather than by race as in the United States, families would be split by the color

---

4 Richard Graham, "Causes for the Abolition of Negro Slavery in Brazil: An Interpretive Essay," *Hispanic American Historical Review*, 46 (May 1966), 129, lists the large literature on the preeminent role of the British in compelling Brazil to put a stop to the African trade. See especially Leslie Bethell, *The Abolition of the Brazilian Slave Trade* (Cambridge, 1970), Chapters 10–12.

line. Children of mulattoes, after all, vary noticeably in color. In view of the high value that western society places upon the nuclear family it would be neither practical nor likely that a system of segregation that would disrupt families would be permitted to develop. Moreover, in a society in which the mulatto has a special place, a racist defense of slavery or of Negro inferiority cannot easily develop, for how can one think consistently of a white "race" or a Negro "race" when the lines are blurred by the mulatto? The search for purity of race is thus frustrated before it begins. Similarly, the existence of the mulatto escape hatch helps to explain why relations between the races in Brazil have been less rigid and less prone to hostility than in the United States. The presence of the mulatto not only spreads people of color through the society, but it literally blurs and thereby softens the line between black and white. To seek out the origins of the mulatto as a socially accepted type in Brazil, then, is to be on the trail of the origins of significant differences in the race relations of Brazil and the United States.

The point should not be misunderstood. I am not contending that the mulatto escape hatch in itself "prevented" the development of racist thought, or segregation laws, or somehow "caused" a system of race relations in which it occurred to be milder than one in which it did not develop. Such an argument would reify a social abstraction and turn it falsely into a so-called historical "factor." It is men, after all, not abstractions, who act and thereby make history. Yet even that statement, true as it is, needs qualification. It should not be construed to mean that the mulatto escape hatch was the conscious or intentional act of men. It was not that either. It was the result of many men's actions, none of which was *intended* to create the mulatto escape hatch. As Karl Marx wrote, "Men make their own history, but they do not know that they are making it." It is the historian, looking at the events later who discerns, if he can, the pattern of actions that quite unconsciously resulted in the development of an institution like the mulatto escape hatch.

Put another way, I am contending that when a society develops a place for the mulatto, as occurred in Brazil, then certain other responses to the presence of black men in a white-dominated society, such as those that were worked out in the United States, for example, are foreclosed. The mulatto escape hatch serves as a symbol, actually a condensation of a range of relationships between blacks and whites and of attitudes toward one another. If we focus attention upon that symbol and seek to explain its historical development, then an explanation for the whole range of social attitudes and behavioral patterns for which that symbol stands is also accounted for.

It is in that sense that I call the mulatto escape hatch the key to the difference between race relations in the United States and Brazil. It does not encompass all that we want explained, but it is a crucial part of the answer. . . .

chapter 5

The Black Experience:
Slave Accommodation,
Resistance, and Rebellion

UNTIL LATE IN THE DECADE of the 1930s the task of combating the myth of the inferior and contented slave fell almost exclusively to a few radical white scholars and to the thin ranks of Carter G. Woodson and his fellow black historians. In 1937, however, Harvey Wish wrote an essay on slave disloyalty and four years later Henrietta Buckmaster published a book on the underground railroad which contained many useful profiles of black resistance. During the 1940s the *Journal of Negro History* gave space to several articles such as Raymond A. and Alice H. Bauer's essay "Day to Day Resistance to Slavery." Herbert Aptheker provided the most sweeping attack on the stereotype of black passiveness in a 1943 volume which portrayed the South as seething with unrest, conspiracies, and rebellions. Although most historians dismissed the study for its "exaggerations" and the author's Marxism, Aptheker actually wrote in an undogmatic way and needed to prove the authenticity of only a fraction of the incidents to establish his case.

Black protest and rebellion in the 1960s stimulated much interest in the slave insurrectionists and when the white novelist William Styron in 1967 shaped his Nat Turner after the traditions of twentieth century antiheroes he set off a furor which raged for several years on issues briefly summarized by Robert McColley (Selection 1). Although the controversy attracted the attention of most historians, a more central development for scholars was the publication of Stanley Elkin's study of slavery in 1959 and the long historical debate which the book inspired. In a dramatic comparison (Selection 2) between the collapse of adult personality into the infantilization of survivors in the Nazi death camp and the "Samboization" of the enslaved African, Elkins reasoned that the Nazi and the American slave systems made sustained and substantial resistance virtually impossible. Although the critics acknowledged that Elkins had effectively highlighted the oppressiveness of the peculiar institution, they objected that his analogy did not account for the some indisputable black resistance, for the competence of tens of thousands of black soldiers in the Civil War, and for the millions who survived bondage to function as rebels, sailors, cowboys, skilled workers, and masters of that most difficult art of human survival in a militantly hostile environment.

Several scholars who disliked Elkins' comparison searched for a more appropriate analogy. At roughly the same time in the 60s two white historians, George M. Frederickson and Christopher Lasch, and one black scholar, Roy Simon Bryce-Laporte, suggested that a better analogy for slavery could be found in other "total institutions" such as the prison and the asylum in which inmates displayed not one bundle of "Sambo" reactions but rather a variety of changing roles and responses from sporadic, open resistance and "intransigence" to "colonization" "conversion," and "situational withdrawal." Bryce-LaPorte (Selection 3), who stressed his belief that Elkins had confused a single role with "many roles played . . . and careers pursued," insisted on reaffirming the existence of slaves as men.

The consideration of slaves as men in an Afro-American cultural context provided another turning point for scholarship in the late 1960s. For nearly 20 years many historians had fought the old racist myths by stressing the oppressiveness of slavery but if the slave experience had produced nothing except oppressors and victims how could scholars account for the social strength displayed by blacks in later generations and for the rich and tenacious culture which developed in slavery times? Among the early efforts of recent times to suggest that the victims had wrung from oppression valuable expressions of culture was the essay of 1963 (Selection 4) in which Wayman G. McLaughlin reported the existence of profound symbolic and mystical insights rather than slave religion confined to the bleakness of servile catechism.

During the 1960s scholars, working from a growing consciousness of viable if hard pressed institutions and of a complex cultural context, continued to attack Elkins and to probe the question of rebellion and resistance in a black communal framework. Gerald W. Mullin (Selection 5) in a 1971 volume on late eighteenth century black Virginia portrayed both country masses responding to evangelical Christianity and a black leadership class "literate, skilled, mobile and working in a commercial environment." In the events leading to the Gabriel Prosser insurrection conspiracy of 1800 the leaders influenced the masses but failed to find means of rebellion comparable to "Nat Turner's magnificent Old Testament visions." Mullin, unlike other scholars who regarded rebellion as most likely in African tribal islands like the Hausa in Brazil, traced insurrection to largely acculturated Afro-Americans.

A year later in 1972 John W. Blassingame published an anti-Elkins study which contributed knowledge about both black institutions in slavery and the question of resistance. Indeed, the major instrument of resistance was the very existence of black culture based on a nurturing African heritage which made it possible for the bondsman to survive "without becoming abjectly docile, infantile or submissive." As a man with a sense of identity outside white frames of reference, the plantation black had ideals, values, norms and a life beyond the master's control, all of which "bolstered his self-esteem, courage, and confidence, and served as his defense against personal degradation." An essay by Charles B. Dew in 1974 gave new weight to the idea that the industrial slave in particular gained "some sense of personal dignity and individual initiative" from a system which functioned "more through mutual accommodation than outright oppression." While the new directions taken by Mullin, Blassingame and other scholars represented an important scholarly breakthrough, they also created the possibility that insights of the 1950s and 1960s about the masters would be lost in the positive exploration of the roots of Afro-American culture. During the late 60s Eugene D. Genovese used some of the new historical perceptions in a context which actually glorified the slavemasters, and we may now be on the eve of a kind of cultural bargain which will ignore white oppression while celebrating the vitality and strength of black people in bondage.

BIBLIOGRAPHY

Works Discussed in This Chapter

Aptheker, Herbert, *American Negro Slave Revolts* (1943).

Bauer, Raymond A., and Bauer, Alice, "Day to Day Resistance to Slavery," *Journal of Negro History* (1942).

Bryce-LaPorte, Roy Simon, "The Slave as Inmate," in Ann J. Lane, ed., *The Debate Over Slavery: Stanley Elkins and His Critics* (1971).

Buckmaster, Henrietta, *Let My People Go: The Story of the Underground Railroad and the Growth of the Abolition Movement* (1941).

Dew, Charles B., "Disciplining Slave Ironworkers in the Ante-Bellum South: Coercion, Conciliation and Accommodation," *American Historical Review* (1974).

Elkins, Stanley, *Slavery: A Problem in American Institutional and Intellectual Life* (1959).

Frederickson, George M., and Lasch, Christopher, "Resistance to Slavery," *Civil War History* (1967).

Genovese, Eugene D., *The World the Slaveholders Made* (1969).

McColley, Robert, review of William Styron's *The Confessions of Nat Turner* (1967) in *Civil War History* (1969).

McLaughlin, Wayman G., "Symbolism and Mysticism in the Spirituals," *Phylon* (1963).

Mullin, Gerald W., *Flight and Rebellion: Slave Resistance in Eighteenth Century Virginia* (1972).

Wish, Harvey, "American Slave Insurrections Before 1861," *Journal of Negro History* (1937).

Woodson, Carter G., *The Story of the Negro Retold* (4th ed., 1959) and other works.

Suggested Readings

For surprisingly independent slaves and for a practice which often marked a step toward more autonomy see John H. Moore, "Simon Gray, Riverman, A Slave Who Was Almost Free," *Mississippi Valley Historical Review* (1962) and Clement Eaton, "Slave Hiring in the Upper South," Ibid. (1960).

On the *roots of black culture* see Mina Davis Caulfield, "Slavery and the Origins of Black Culture," in Peter I. Rose, ed., *Americans From Africa* (Vol. I, 1970); Romeo B. Garrett, "African Survivals in American Culture," *Journal of Negro History* (1966); Robert F. Thompson, "African Influence on the Art of the United States," in Armstead L. Robinson, et al., eds., *Black Studies in the University* (1969); and Lorenzo D. Turner, "African Survivals in the New World with Special Emphasis on the Arts," in John A. Davis, *Africa Seen by American Negro Scholars* (1963). On the use of music folklore and religious forms to study black culture see Lyle Glazier, "The Uncle Remus Stories," *Hacettepe Bulletin of Social Sciences and Humanities* (1969); Guy B. Johnson, *Folk Culture on St. Helena Island* (1930); Howard Thurman *Deep River: Reflections on the Religious Insight of . . . the Negro Spirituals* (2nd ed. 1955); and Mary A. Twining, "An Anthropological Look at Afro-American Folk Narrative," *CLA Journal* (1970). Two of the best essays in this category are Sterling Stuckey, "Through the Prism of Folklore," *Massachusetts Review* (1968) and Lawrence W. Levine, "Slave Songs and Slave Consciousness An Exploration in Neglected Sources," in Tamara K. Hareven, ed., *Anonymous Americans: Explorations in Nineteenth Century Social History* (1971). Two older but still rewarding works on the slave songs are Mark Miles Fisher, *Negro Slave Songs in the U.S.* (1953) and Bernard Wolfe, "Uncle Remus and the Malevolent Rabbit" *Commentary* (1958). The two best essays on slave religion and black culture are Leroy Moore, Jr. "The Spiritual: Soul of Black Religion," *American Quarterly* (1971) and Vincent Harding, "Religion and Resistance Among Ante-Bellum Negroes, 1800–1869," in August Meier and Elliott Rudwick, eds., *The Making of Black America* (1969).

Frederick Douglass' *Autobiography* in the several versions has long been a classic in American letters, but the new interest in slave culture and in black resistance has led to the republication of many *slave narratives.* See particularly the narratives in Gilbert Osofsky, ed., *Puttin' On Ole Massa* (1969); George P. Rawick, ed., *The American Slave: A Composite Autobiography from Eighteen Volumes of W. P. A. Federal Writers' Projects* (1971); Arna Bontemps, ed., *Five Slave Narratives* (1968); and *Great Slave Narratives* (1968); and F. N. Boney, ed., *Slave Life in Georgia: A Narrative of the Life, Sufferings and Escape of John Brown, A Fugitive Slave* (1972). Works about the narratives which should be examined are Rawick, *From Sundown to Sunup: The Making of the Black Community* (1972); Charles H. Nichols, *Many Thousands Gone* (1963); and C. Vann Woodward, "History From Slave Sources," *American Historical Review* (1974).

A pair of useful modern anthologies on *black resistance* are William F. Cheek, ed. *Black Resistance Before the Civil War* (1970) and John H. Bracey, Jr., August Meier, and Elliot Rudwick, eds., *American Slavery: The Question of Resistance* (1971).

Just as Elkins for *social science background* relied upon Bruno Bettelheim, "Individual and Mass Behavior in Extreme Situations," *Journal of Abnormal Psychology* (1943), Frederickson, Lasch, and Byrce-Laporte took information for their essays on the slave as inmate from Gresham M. Sykes. *The Society of Captives: A Study of Maximum Security Prisons* (1958) and Erving Goffman, *Asylums: Essays on the Social Situations of Mental Patients and Other Inmates* (1961).

On *slave revolts* in other countries see for Jamaica, H. Orlando Patterson, *The Sociology of Slavery* (1967) and for Haiti, Brazil, etc., see C. L. R. James, *The Black Jacobins: Toussaint L'Ouverture and the San Domingo Revolution* (2d ed., 1962) and several essays in Laura Foner and Eugene D. Genovese, eds., *Slavery in the New World* (1969).

A dated and racist work on *American slave revolts* is Joseph Carroll, *Slave Insurrections in the United States, 1800–1865* (1938). Some more recent analyses are Herbert Aptheker, "Slave Guerrilla Warfare" in *To Be Free: Studies in American Negro History* (1948); Marion Kilson, "Toward Freedom: An Analysis of Slave Revolts in the U.S." *Phylon* (1964); Nicholas Halasz, *The Rattling Chains: Slave Unrest and Revolt in the Ante-Bellum South* (1966); Kenneth W. Porter, "Negroes and the Seminole War, 1835–1842," *Journal of Southern History* (1964); Herbert Aptheker, Eugene D. Genovese and others, "The Legacy of Slavery and Black Nationalism," in *Studies on the Left* (1966); and William C. Suttles, Jr. "African Religious Survivals as Factors in American Slave Revolts," *Journal of Negro History* (1971).

For accounts of *shipboard revolts* see Lorenzo J. Greene, "Mutiny on the Slave Ships," *Phylon* (1944) and Mary Cable, *Black Odyssey* (1971). On the Gabriel Prosser conspiracy see Gerald W. Mullin, cited earlier. John M. Lofton has a lengthy account of the Denmark Vesey plot in *Insurrection in South Carolina* (1964). Richard C. Wade rejects the existence of a plot but Robert S. Starobin, John O. Killens and Sterling Stuckey refute Wade. See Wade, "The Vesey Plot: A Reconsideration," *Journal of Southern History* (1964); Starobin, "Denmark Vesey's Slave Conspiracy of 1822: A Study in Rebellion and Repression," in Bracey, Meier, and Rudwick, *American Slavery: The Question of Resistance* (1970); Starobin, ed., *Denmark Vesey: The Slave Conspiracy of 1822* (1970); Killens, ed., *The Trial Record of Denmark Vesey* (1970); and Stuckey, "Remembering Denmark Vesey," *Negro Digest* (1966).

On the *Nat Turner Rebellion* see Herbert Aptheker, *Nat Turner's Slave Rebellion* (1966); the almost exhaustive account of Henry I. Tragle, *The Southampton Slave Revolt of 1831* (1971); and Stephen B. Oates, *Nat Turner* (1975). For some angry black reactions to Styron's fictional "meditation on history," see John Henrik Clarke, ed., *William Styron's Nat Turner: Ten Black Writers Respond* (1968). See also Aptheker and Styron "Truth and Nat Turner," *The Nation* (Apr. 22, 1968); Jervis Anderson, "Styron and His Black Critics," *Dissent* (1969); Seymour L. Gross and Eileen Binder, "History, Politics and Literature: The Myth of Nat Turner," *American Quarterly* (1971); and John B. Duff and Peter Mitchell, eds., *The Nat Turner Rebellion: The Historical Event and the Modern Controversy* (1971).

Nat Turner: The Historical Figure and the Modern Controversy*

Robert McColley

William Styron's *Confessions of Nat Turner* [1967] is the most widely read and discussed representation of American Negro slavery since *Uncle Tom's Cabin*. Like the classic by Mrs. Stowe, it gains favorable publicity

* Robert McColley, Review in *Civil War History*, 14 (1968), 346–48. By permission of the Kent State University Press.

even when it is attacked, and is now being seriously recommended to students of history as a generally valid description of slavery as it was in the southern United States.

Much of the debate over the novel has turned on the character of Nat Turner himself. Partisans of the revolutionary tradition and especially black militants see Turner as a folk hero, and are understandably offended that Styron portrays him as aloof and contemptuous toward most blacks, and affectionate only toward selected black boys and white girls. On the matter of his superior attitude toward fellow slaves, the best historical evidence that exists supports Styron, but aloofness is not always an expression of contempt, and the real Nat Turner may very well have felt more identification with and compassion for his fellow slaves than Styron allows. Most of the reasoning about Turner's personality must be inferential, and so must the reconstruction of his full intentions about his rebellion. It was surely something more than a rational stroke for political freedom. The slaughtering of even the most harmless and helpless whites is outstanding evidence that Turner and his followers had an apocalyptic vision of vengeance guiding them. But the real *Confessions* of 1831 and the other known facts of the rebellion suggest that Turner and his followers hoped for their rising to spread throughout the whole country. Styron's Turner, hoping only to cut a path to the Dismal Swamp and set up a permanent fortress there, is both less bloodthirsty and less dedicated to freeing his people than the record warrants.

In an introductory note, Styron says: "During the narrative that follows I have rarely departed from the *known* facts about Nat Turner and the revolt of which he was the leader." So far as the actual events of the revolt are concerned, that is true. But Styron by no means builds on the meager information supplied in the original *Confessions;* much of it he ignores. In the novel Turner's grandmother is brought from Africa to Virginia by a Yankee slaver in 1782. Distraught by her capture and passage, she dies shortly after giving birth to the girl who will eventually be Turner's mother. This is a good way to get the horrors of the slave trade into the story, but in fact most slaves were brought in by Englishmen, and Virginia firmly outlawed the trade in 1778. Worst of all, the real Nat Turner spoke of his grandmother "who was very religious, and to whom I was much attached." (Herbert Aptheker, *Nat Turner's Slave Rebellion,* New York, 1968, p. 133.)

The white Turners were also very religious, and often held prayer meetings in their home. They were clearly caught up in that evangelical religion which thrived quite as well in eastern rural America as on the frontier. Such people were often criticized in Jeffersonian Virginia for teaching their slaves to read and write, and for treating them in many ways as equal beings. Styron, however, has a large aristocratic household of white Turners, managed successively by the brothers Benjamin and Samuel. These characters are very like the good-natured but corrupted Messrs. Shelby and St. Clair in *Uncle Tom's Cabin,* being the descendants of fine and cultured families running rapidly downhill. Only two of the women of the household are truly religious, and they instruct Nat in a private and intimate way, not by taking him to prayer meetings.

Styron has Nat Turner influenced by his mother, a cook, to hold in contempt those blacks who labor in the fields, an attitude which grows stronger as he himself is selected for household chores, and acquires polished manners and literacy. His ability to read and to commit large sections of the Bible to memory make him a sort of pet of his owners, and cause him to be regarded as a kind of black preacher. This is one of the most curious features of the book. In antebellum America people were called preacher because they preached. But strangely there is neither an instance of Nat Turner leading a worship service nor anyone else doing so in the entire novel. Of course Negroes, slave and free, were prohibited from being regularly ordained ministers, but even so they often were lay preachers. By failing to develop scenes of Nat Turner praying to or with his fellow slaves Styron accentuates that aloofness of which his critics complain.

The real Nat Turner was explicit about another talent for leadership: "I was not addicted to stealing in my youth, nor have ever been—yet such was the confidence of the Negroes in the neighborhood, even at this early period of my life, in my superior judgment, that they would often carry me with them when they were going on any roguery, to plan for them." (Aptheker, *Nat Turner*, pp. 134–35.) Here was another invitation to the novelist to invent scenes of the young Nat Turner consorting with fellow slaves, but Styron made nothing of this.

Styron has been blamed by some of his critics for an overly traditional sketching of his Negro characters. Their speech is slurred, their manner comic or obsequious, their imagination dull. Others have rushed to the novelist's defense, reviving the abolitionist charge that the enormity of slavery was precisely that it brutalized human nature, and that of the master just as much as that of the slave. In fact, with very few exceptions, indeed, all the characters of the novel, white as well as black, are grotesque and degraded, and perhaps this accounts for the popularity of the novel and its reputation for "realism" among neo-abolitionist historians. These are not propitious times to defend the memory of those Virginians who once bought and sold human beings. But Styron's white Virginians are unpleasant in many other ways: they rave, they drink to excess, they fornicate in the garden, they lie, they cheat, they have foul breath and unsound digestions. The white clergy of the novel are its sorriest characters, and of the major denominations in Virginia, only the Methodists escape the novelist's libel. He gives us two representatives of the Episcopal bishop who are cynically attempting to reconcile their church to slavery. He gives us a Presbyterian parson who rejects with disgust the notion of helping a sick and aging—but penitent—sinner. And he gives us the Baptist Reverend Eppes whose face has a "skinny, bignosed, pentecostal, Christ-devoured, wintry look of laughterless misery about it." (p. 234.) This man swindles Nat Turner out of his promised freedom, works him incessantly, and even makes a half-hearted effort at seduction.

Professor Martin Duberman, of Princeton University, has written in the New York *Times* (Aug. 11, 1968) that William Styron's book is "seriously flawed as a novel," but "is, at the same time, superlative history." It must have occurred to Professor Duberman that he represents today's academic establishment and that praise of this kind is the highest the establishment can give. It is odd that he should have withheld praise for the literary quality of the work, while praising so unreservedly its historical veracity. What is best about the book is its evocation of the landscape, and whether or not the story is historically valid, it surely is exciting and compelling. But where are there grounds in the historical records of Jeffersonian Virginia for all those grotesque characters, white and black? And what warrant is there for the unrelenting use of excremental imagery and the sexual obsessions of so many of the characters?

In the June, 1968, issue of *Civil War History*, Leslie Fishel, Jr. took Herbert Aptheker to task for making an heroic freedom fighter out of Nat Turner. But even though Professor Aptheker is often willing to generalize broadly from his evidence, he does have and use evidence in a responsible way. He rightly points out that white Virginians were deeply committed to the spreading of free republicanism throughout America and Europe, and that it was impossible to keep that subject concealed from the omnipresent slaves. Nor could they keep out the doctrines of the abolitionists, which were being heard all over Virginia when Nat Turner was a child, and were still likely to be brought up, however guardedly, when he was prepared to launch his rebellion.

There are good historical grounds for seeing Nat Turner as a self-declared partisan of wronged black manhood, as a zealot for liberty, and as a religious fanatic in the style of John Brown. It is the curious achievement of William Styron that he has created a character who is really none of these things, and it is an even more curious feature of our times that so many people believe in his creation.

The Slave as Sambo: Nazi Camp Survival and Slavery Compared*

Stanley M. Elkins

. . . We may suppose that every African who became a slave underwent an experience whose crude psychic impact must have been staggering and whose consequences superseded anything that had ever previously happened to him. Some effort should therefore be made to picture the series of shocks which must have accompanied the principal events of that enslavement.

* Reprinted from *Slavery* by Stanley M. Elkins by permission of the University of Chicago Press. Copyright 1959 by University of Chicago Press.

The majority of slaves appear to have been taken in native wars,[1] which meant that no one—neither persons of high rank nor warriors of prowess—was guaranteed against capture and enslavement.[2] Great numbers were caught in surprise attacks upon their villages, and since the tribes acting as middlemen for the trade had come to depend on regular supplies of captives in order to maintain that function, the distinction between wars and raiding expeditions tended to be very dim.[3] The first shock, in an experience destined to endure many months and to leave its survivors irrevocably changed, was thus the shock of capture. It is an effort to remember that while enslavement occurred in Africa every day, to the individual it occurred just once.[4]

The second shock—the long march to the sea—drew out the nightmare for many weeks. Under the glaring sun, through the steaming jungle, they were driven along like beasts tied together by their necks; day after day, eight or more hours at a time, they would stagger barefoot over thorny underbrush, dried reeds, and stones. Hardship, thirst, brutalities, and near starvation penetrated the experience of each exhausted man and woman who reached the coast.[5] One traveler tells of seeing hundreds of bleaching skeletons strewn along one of the slave caravan routes.[6] But then the man who must interest us is the man who survived —he who underwent the entire experience, of which this was only the beginning.

The next shock, aside from the fresh physical torments which accompanied it, was the sale to the European slavers. After being crowded into pens near the trading stations and kept there overnight, sometimes for days, the slaves were brought out for examination. Those rejected would be abandoned to starvation; the remaining ones—those who had been bought—were branded, given numbers inscribed on leaden tags, and herded on shipboard.[7]

---

1 There were other pretexts, such as crime or debt, but war was probably the most frequent mode of procurement. Snelgrave, *New Account*, p. 158; "John Barbot's Description," in Donnan, *Documents*, 1, 284, 289, 294, 298; "Observations on the Slave Trade, 1789" [C. B. Wadström] in ibid., 2, 599; Matthews, *Voyage to Sierra-Leone*, pp. 145–46, 163. See also below, n. 34.

2 As to "character types," one might be tempted to suppose that as a rule it would be only the weaker and more submissive who allowed themselves to be taken into slavery. Yet it appears that a heavy proportion of the slaves were in fact drawn from among the most warlike. . . .

3 "The Wars which the inhabitants of the interior parts of the country, beyond Senegal, Gambia, and Sierra Leone, carry on with each other, are chiefly of a predatory nature, and owe their origin to the yearly number of slaves, which the Mandingoes, or the inland traders suppose will be wanted by the vessels that will arrive on the coast." "Observations" [Wadström], in Donnan, *Documents*, 2, 599.

4 A number of excerpts describing these raids are cited in Thomas Fowell Buxton, *Letter on the Slave Trade to the Lord Viscount Melbourne* (London, 1838), pp. 34–38.

5 Descriptions of the march may be found in Park, *Travels*, pp. 371 ff.; Buxton, *Letter*, pp. 41–44; Rinchon, *La traite et l'esclavage*, pp. 174–75; L. Degrandpré, *Voyage à la côte occidentale d'Afrique, fait dans les années 1786 et 1787* (Paris, 1801), 2, 48–50.

6 Buxton, *Letter*, p. 43.

7 Bosman, *New and Accurate Description*, p. 364. See also Degrandpré, *Voyage*, 2, 53–56; Buxton, *Letter*, pp. 47–49; Rinchon, *La traite et l'esclavage*, pp. 188–89; "John Barbot's Description," in Donnan, *Documents*, 1, 289, 295; Park, *Travels*, p. 360.

The episode that followed—almost too protracted and stupefying to be called mere "shock"—was the dread Middle Passage, brutalizing to any man, black or white, ever to be involved with it. The holds, packed with squirming and suffocating humanity, became stinking infernos of filth and pestilence. Stories of disease, death, and cruelty on the terrible two-month voyage abound in the testimony which did much toward ending the British slave trade forever.[8]

The final shock in the process of enslavement came with the Negro's introduction to the West Indies. Bryan Edwards, describing the arrival of a slave ship, writes of how in times of labor scarcity crowds of people would come scrambling aboard, manhandling the slaves and throwing them into panic. The Jamaica legislature eventually "corrected the enormity" by enacting that the sales had to be held on shore. Edwards felt a certain mortification at seeing the Negroes exposed naked in public, similar to that felt by the trader Degrandpré at seeing them examined back at the African factories.[9] Yet here they did not seem to care. "They display . . . very few signs of lamentation for their past or of apprehension for their future condition; but . . . commonly express great eagerness to be sold."[10] The "seasoning" process which followed completed the series of steps whereby the African Negro became a slave.

The mortality had been very high. One-third of the numbers first taken, out of a total of perhaps 15 million, had died on the march and at the trading stations; another third died during the Middle Passage and the seasoning.[11] Since a majority of the African-born slaves who came to the North American plantations did not come directly but were imported through the British West Indies, one may assume that the typical slave underwent an experience something like that just outlined. This was the man—one in three—who had come through it all and lived and was about to enter our "closed system." What would he be like if he survived and adjusted to that?

Actually, a great deal had happened to him already. Much of his past had been annihilated; nearly every prior connection had been severed. Not that he had really "forgotten" all these things—his family and kinship arrangements, his language, the tribal religion, the taboos, the name he had once borne, and so on—but none of it any longer carried much meaning. The old values, the sanctions, the standards, already unreal, could not longer furnish him guides for conduct, for adjusting to the

---

8 Descriptions of the Middle Passage may be found in *An Abstract of the Evidence Delivered before a Select Committee of the House of Commons in the Years 1790, and 1791; on the Part of the Petitioners for the Abolition of the Slave Trade* (London, 1791); Alexander Falconbridge, *An Account of the Slave Trade on the Coast of Africa* (London: J. Phillips, 1788); Rinchon, *La traite et l'esclavage*, pp. 196–209; Edwards, *History*, 2; Brantz Mayer, *Captain Canot* (New York: D. Appleton, 1854); Averil Mackenzie-Grieve, *The Last Years of the English Slave Trade, Liverpool 1750–1807* (London: Putnam, 1941).

9 Degrandpré, *Voyage* 2, 55–56.

10 Edwards, *History*, 2, 340. See also *Abstract of Evidence*, pp. 46–47, and Falconbridge, *Account*, pp. 33–36.

11 Tannenbaum, *Slave and Citizen*, p. 28. As for the total exports of slaves from Africa throughout the entire period of the trade, estimates run as high as 20 million. "Even a conservative estimate," notes Mr. Tannenbaum, "would hardly cut this figure in half." Ibid., p. 32.

expectations of a complete new life. Where then was he to look for new
standards, new cues—who would furnish them now? He could now look
to none but his master, the one man to whom the system had committed
his entire being: the man upon whose will depended his food, his shelter,
his sexual connections, whatever moral instruction he might be offered,
whatever "success" was possible within the system, his very security—
in short, everything. . . .

ADJUSTMENT TO ABSOLUTE POWER
IN THE CONCENTRATION CAMP

. . . The only mass experience that Western people have had within
recorded history comparable in any way with Negro slavery was under-
gone in the nether world of Nazism. The concentration camp was not
only a perverted slave system; it was also—what is less obvious but even
more to the point—a perverted patriarchy.

The system of the concentration camp was expressly devised in the
1930s by high officials of the German government to function as an instrument of terror. . . . Yet the basic technique was everywhere and at all
times the same: the deliberate infliction of various forms of torture upon
the incoming prisoners in such a way as to break their resistance and
make way for their degradation as individuals. These brutalities were not
merely "permitted" or "encouraged"; they were prescribed. . . .

The concentration camps and everything that took place in them were
veiled in the utmost isolation and secrecy. . . . The undenied existence of
the camps cast a shadow of nameless dread over the entire population;
on the other hand the *individual* who actually became a prisoner in one
of them was in most cases devastated with fright and utterly demoralized
to discover that what was happening to *him* was not less, but rather far
more terrible than anything he had imagined. . . .

The arrest was typically made at night, preferably late; this was
standing Gestapo policy, designed to heighten the element of shock,
terror, and unreality surrounding the arrest. After a day or so in the
police jail came the next major shock, that of being transported to the
camp itself. . . . [Initiation] involved a planned series of brutalities inflicted by guards making repeated rounds through the train over a 12-
to 36-hour period during which the prisoner was prevented from resting.
If transported in cattle cars instead of passenger cars, the prisoners were
sealed in under conditions not dissimilar to those of the Middle Passage.[12]
Upon their arrival—if the camp was one in which mass exterminations
were carried out—there might be sham ceremonies designed to reassure
temporarily the exhausted prisoners, which meant that the fresh terrors
in the offing would then strike them with redoubled impact. An SS officer

---

12 Bruno Bettelheim, "Individual and Mass Behavior in Extreme Situations,"
Journal of Abnormal Psychology, 38 (October 1943), 424. A description of such a
trip may be found in Olga Lengyel, *Five Chimneys: The Story of Auschwitz* (Chicago, 1947), pp. 7–10. See also Eugen Kogon, *The Theory and Practice of Hell* (New
York: Farrar, Straus, 1946), p. 67.

might deliver an address, or a band might be playing popular tunes, and it would be in such a setting that the initial "selection" was made. The newcomers would file past an SS doctor who indicated with a motion of the forefinger, whether they were to go to the left or to the right. To one side went those considered capable of heavy labor; to the other would go wide categories of "undesirables"; those in the latter groups were being condemned to the gas chambers.[13] Those who remained would undergo the formalities of "registration," full of indignities, which culminated in the marking of each prisoner with a number.[14]

There were certain physical and psychological strains of camp life, especially debilitating in the early stage, which should be classed with the introductory shock sequence. There was a state of chronic hunger whose pressures were usually effective in detaching prior scruples of all kinds; even the sexual instincts no longer functioned in the face of the drive for food.[15] The man who at his pleasure could bestow or withhold food thus wielded, for that reason alone, abnormal power. Another strain at first was the demand for absolute obedience, the slightest deviation from which brought savage punishments.[16] The prisoner had to ask permission—by no means granted as a matter of course—even to defecate.[17] The power of the SS guard, as the prisoner was hourly reminded, was that of life and death over his body. A more exquisite form of pressure lay in the fact that the prisoner had never a moment of solitude: he no longer had a private existence; it was no longer possible, in any imaginable sense, for him to be an "individual."[18]

Another factor having deep disintegrative effects upon the prisoner was the prospect of a limitless future in the camp. In the immediate sense this meant that he could no longer make plans for the future. But there would eventually be a subtler meaning: it made the break with the outside world a *real* break; in time the "real" life would become the life of the camp, the outside world an abstraction. Had it been a limited detention, whose end could be calculated, one's outside relationship—one's roles, one's very "personality"—might temporarily have been laid aside, to be reclaimed more or less intact at the end of the term. Here, however, the prisoner was faced with the apparent impossibility of his old roles or even his old personalality ever having any future at all; it became more

---

[13] Elie Cohen, *Human Behavior in the Concentration Camp* (New York: Norton, 1953), pp. 118–22; Kogon, *Theory and Practice*, pp. 66–76; Lengyel, *Five Chimneys*, pp. 12–22.

[14] One aspect of this registration ceremony involved a sham "inspection" of the body, whose effect on the women prisoners in particular was apparently very profound. See Lengyel, *Five Chimneys*, p. 19; Ella Lingens-Reiner, *Prisoners of Fear* (London: Victor Gollancz, 1948), p. 26. This may be compared with Degrandpré's description of a similar "inspection" on the African slave coast in the 1780s; see his *Voyage*, 2, 55–56. . . .

[15] Ibid., pp. 134–35, 140–43.

[16] These punishments are discussed most vividly in Kogon, *Theory and Practice*, pp. 102–8, 207–11.

[17] Bettelheim, "Individual and Mass Behavior," p. 445.

[18] The effects of never being alone are noted in Cohen, *Human Behavior*, pp. 130–31, and David Rousset, *The Other Kingdom* (New York: Reynal & Hitchcock, 1947), p. 133.

and more difficult to imagine himself resuming them.[19] It was this that underlay the "egalitarianism" of the camps; old statuses had lost their meaning. A final strain, which must have been particularly acute for the newcomer, was the omnipresent threat of death and the very unpredictable suddenness with which death might strike. Quite aside from the periodic gas-chamber selections, the guards in their sports and caprices were at liberty to kill any prisoner any time.[20] . . .

. . . "The prisoners' feelings," according to Mr. Bettelheim, "could be summed up by the following sentence: 'What I am doing here, or what is happening to me, does not count at all; here everything is permissible as long and insofar as it contributes to helping me survive in the camp.' "[21]

One part of the prisoner's being was thus, under sharp stress, brought to the crude realization that he must thenceforth be governed by an entirely new set of standards in order to live. Mr. Lingens-Reiner puts it bluntly: "Will you survive, or shall I? As soon as one sensed that this was at stake everyone turned egotist."[22] ". . . I think it of primary importance," writes Dr. Cohen, "to take into account that the superego acquired new values in a concentration camp, so much at variance with those which the prisoner bore with him into camp that the latter faded."[23] But then this acquisition of "new values" did not all take place immediately; it was not until some time after the most acute period of stress was over that the new, "unreal" self would become at last the "real" one. . . .

The most immediate aspect of the old inmates' behavior which struck these observers was its *childlike* quality. "The prisoners developed types of behavior which are characteristic of infancy or early youth. Some of these behaviors developed slowly, others were immediately imposed on the prisoners and developed only in intensity as time went on."[24] Such infantile behavior took innumerable forms. The inmates' sexual impotence brought about a disappearance of sexuality in their talk,[25] instead, excretory functions occupied them endlessly. They lost many of the

---

19 "When the author [Bettelheim] expressed to some of the old prisoners his astonishment that they seemed not interested in discussing their future life outside the camp, they frequently admitted that they could no longer visualize themselves living outside the camp, making free decisions, taking care of themselves and their families." Bettelheim, "Individual and Mass Behavior," p. 439.

20 M. Rousset tells of how, on one of the death marches, a prisoner came to him bringing a French compatriot and begging his protection for the wretched man. "He told me that he was a lawyer from Toulouse, and it was only with the greatest difficulty that I kept from laughing aloud. For this social designation, *lawyer,* no longer fitted the poor wretch in the slightest. The incongruity of the thought was irresistibly comic. And it was the same with all of us." Rousset, *Other Kingdom,* p. 77.

21 Bettelheim, "Individual and Mass Behavior," p. 432. "We camp prisoners," writes Mrs. Lingens-Reiner, "had only one yardstick: whatever helped our survival was good, and whatever threatened our survival was bad, and to be avoided." *Prisoners of Fear,* p. 142.

22 Lingens-Reiner, *Prisoners of Fear,* p. 23.

23 *Human Behavior,* p. 136. The "superego," Freud's term for the "conscience," is discussed below, pp. 116–18.

24 Bettelheim, "Individual and Mass Behavior," p. 141.

25 Says Dr. Cohen, "I am not asserting that sex was never discussed; it was, though not often. Frankl also states 'that in contrast to mass existence in other military communities . . . here (in the concentration camp) there is *no smut talk.'* " *Human Behavior,* p. 141.

customary inhibitions as to soiling their beds and their persons.[26] Their humor was shot with silliness and they giggled like children when one of them would expel wind. Their relationships were highly unstable. "Prisoners would, like early adolescents, fight one another tooth and nail . . . only to become close friends within a few minutes."[27] Dishonesty became chronic. . . .

. . . The old prisoners came to share the attitude of the SS toward the "unfit" prisoners; newcomers who behaved badly in the labor groups or who could not withstand the strain became a liability for the others, who were often instrumental in getting rid of them. Many old prisoners actually imitated the SS; they would sew and mend their uniforms in such a way as to make them look more like those of the SS—even though they risked punishment for it. "When asked why they did it, they admitted that they loved to look like . . . the guards." Some took great enjoyment in the fact that during roll call "they really had stood well at attention." There were cases of nonsensical rules, made by the guards, which the older prisoners would continue to observe and try to force on the others long after the SS had forgotten them.[28] Even the most abstract ideals of the SS, such as their intense German nationalism and anti-Semitism, were often absorbed by the old inmates—a phenomenon observed among the politically well educated and even among the Jews themselves.[29] . . .

To all these men, reduced to complete and childish dependence upon their masters, the SS had actually become a father symbol. "The SS man was all-powerful in the camp, he was the lord and master of the prisoner's life. As a cruel father he could, without fear of punishment, even kill the prisoner and as a gentle father he could scatter largesse and afford the prisoner his protection."[30] The result, admits Dr. Cohen, was that "for all of us the SS was a father image. . . ."[31] The closed system, in short, had become a kind of grotesque patriarchy. . . .

It is hoped that the very hideousness of a special example of slavery has not disqualified it as a test for certain features of a far milder and more benevolent form of slavery. . . .

Both were closed systems from which all standards based on prior connections had been effectively detached. A working adjustment to either system required a childlike conformity, a limited choice of "significant others." Cruelty per se cannot be considered the primary key to this;

---

[26] "With reference to this phenomenon Miss Bluhm has pointed out that it is not at all unusual that people in extraordinary circumstances, for example soldiers in wartime, 'are able to give up their habitual standards of cleanliness without deeper disturbance; yet only up to certain limits.' The rules of anal cleanliness, she adds, are not disregarded. 'Their neglect means return to instinctual behavior of childhood.'" Ibid., p. 175.

[27] Bettelheim, "Individual and Mass Behavior," p. 445.

[28] Ibid., pp. 448–50.

[29] Ibid. See also Cohen, *Human Behavior*, pp. 189–93, for a discussion of anti-Semitism among the Jews.

[30] Cohen, *Human Behavior*, pp. 176–77.

[31] Ibid., p. 179. On this and other points I must also acknowledge my indebtedness to Mr. Ies Spetter. . . .

of far greater importance was the simple "closedness" of the system, in which all lines of authority descended from the master and in which alternative social bases that might have supported alternative standards were systematically suppressed.[32] The individual, consequently, for his very psychic security, had to picture his master in some way as the "good father,"[33] even when, as in the concentration camp, it made no sense at all.[34] But why should it not have made sense for many a simple plantation Negro whose master did exhibit, in all the ways that could be expected, the features of the good father who was really "good"? If the concentration camp could produce in two or three years the results it did, one wonders how much more pervasive must have been those attitudes, expectations, and values which had, certainly, their benevolent side and which are accepted and transmitted over generations.

For the Negro child, in particular, the plantation offered no really satisfactory father image other than the master. The "real" father was virtually without authority over his child, since discipline, parental responsibility, and control of rewards and punishments all rested in other hands; the slave father could not even protect the mother of his children except by appealing directly to the master. . . .

From the master's viewpoint, slaves had been defined in law as property, and the master's power over his property must be absolute. But then this property was still human property. These slaves might never be quite as human as *he* was, but still there were certain standards that could be laid down for their behavior: obedience, fidelity, humility, docility, cheerfulness, and so on. Industry and diligence would of course be demanded, but a final element in the master's situation would undoubtedly qualify that expectation. Absolute power for him meant absolute dependency for the slave—the dependency not of the developing child but of the perpetual child. . . . Should the entire prediction prove accurate, the result would be something resembling "Sambo."

The social and psychological sanctions of role-playing may in the last analysis prove to be the most satisfactory of the several approaches to Sambo, for, without doubt, of all the roles in American life that of Sambo was by far the most pervasive. The outlines of the role might be sketched in by crude necessity, but what of the finer shades? The sanctions against overstepping it were bleak enough,[35] but the rewards—the sweet applause, as it were, for performing it with sincerity and feeling—were

---

[32] The experience of American prisoners taken by the Chinese during the Korean War seems to indicate that profound changes in behavior and values, if not in basic personality itself, can be effected without the use of physical torture or extreme deprivation. . . . See Edgar H. Schein, "Some Observations on Chinese Methods of Handling Prisoners of War," *Public Opinion Quarterly*, 20 (Spring 1956), 321–27.

[33] In a system as tightly closed as the plantation or the concentration camp, the slave's or prisoner's position of absolute dependency virtually compels him to see the authority figure as somehow really "good." . . .

[34] Bruno Bettelheim tells us of the fantastic efforts of the old prisoners to believe in the benevolence of the officers of the SS. . . . Bettelheim, "Individual and Mass Behavior," p. 451.

[35] Professor Stampp, in a chapter called "To Make Them Stand in Fear," describes the planter's resources for dealing with a recalcitrant slave. *Peculiar Institution*, pp. 141–91.

something to be appreciated on quite another level. The law, untuned to the deeper harmonies, could command the player to be present for the occasion, and the whip might even warn against his missing the grosser cues, but could those things really insure the performance that melted all hearts? Yet there was many and many a performance, and the audiences (whose standards were high) appear to have been for the most part well pleased. They were actually viewing their own masterpiece. Much labor had been lavished upon this chef d'oeuvre, the most genial resources of Southern society had been available for the work; touch after touch had been applied throughout the years, and the result—embodied not in the unfeeling law but in the richest layers of Southern lore —had been the product of an exquisitely rounded collective creativity. And indeed, in a sense that somehow transcended the merely ironic, it was a labor of love. "I love the simple and unadulterated slave, with his geniality, his mirth, his swagger, and his nonsense," wrote Edward Pollard. "I love to look upon his countenance shining with content and grease; I love to study his affectionate heart; I love to mark that peculiarity in him, which beneath all his buffoonery exhibits him as a creature of the tenderest sensibilities, mingling his joys and his sorrows with those of his master's home."[36] Love, even on those terms, was surely no inconsequential reward.

But what were the terms? The Negro was to be a child forever. "The Negro . . . in his true nature, is always a boy, let him be ever so old. . . ."[37] "He is . . . a dependent upon the white race; dependent for guidance and direction even to the procurement of his most indispensable necessaries. Apart from this protection he has the helplessness of a child—without foresight, without faculty of contrivance, without thrift of any kind."[38] . . .

The role, of course, must have been rather harder for the earliest generations of slaves to learn. "Accommodation," according to John Dollard, "involves the renunciation of protest or aggression against undesirable conditions of life and the organization of the character so that protest does not appear, but acceptance does. It may come to pass in the end that the unwelcome force is idealized, that one identifies with it and takes it into the personality; it sometimes even happens that what is at first resented and feared is finally loved."[39]

Might the process, on the other hand, be reversed? It is hard to imagine its being reversed overnight. The same role might still be played in the years after slavery—we are told that it was.[40] . . .

---

[36] Edward A. Pollard, *Black Diamonds Gathered in the Darkey Homes of the South* (New York: Pudney & Russel, 1859), p. 58.

[37] Ibid., p. viii.

[38] John Pendleton Kennedy, *Swallow Barn* (Philadelphia: Carey & Lea, 1832).

[39] John Dollard, *Caste and Class in a Southern Town* (2d ed.; New York: Harper, 1949), p. 255. . . .

[40] Even Negro officeholders during Reconstruction, according to Francis B. Simkins, "were known to observe carefully the etiquette of the Southern caste system." "New Viewpoints of Southern Reconstruction," *Journal of Southern History*, 5 (February 1939), 52.

Problems of Resistance: Slaves as Inmates, Slaves as Men[*]

Roy Simon Bryce-Laporte

. . . We concur that the duration of confinement, breadth of control, and extent of pervasiveness of the slave plantation must have had intense mortifying and dehumanizing impact on the slaves and their offspring. However, had slaves *fully* succumbed to those conditions they would have been all zombiefied or psychologically dead, and to have *fully* resisted they would have all been physically dead or absent by way of escape, exodus, or revolution. Slave literature indicates many cases which fell on both these extremes. Slave literature also illustrates and implies that many more fell somewhere between the two extremes.

It is our thesis that the impact of the slave plantation is more appropriately understood in terms of alternative and varied behavioral mechanisms used by slaves rather than prevalence of a fixed personality type derived from the contrived dichotomy of choices between killing or being killed. Even if every slave may at some time have engaged in submissive behavior it is unfair to suggest that inasmuch as he was not a "successful" revolutionary he was a Sambo. Situation variation and choice were characteristic of all levels of behavior within the contextual limitation of the slave plantation.

Most students of American slavery agree that large-scale, open, collective resistance by the slaves was unusual, those cases that occurred being largely unsuccessful. Even Aptheker,[1] who perhaps makes the claim for the largest number of such revolts by American slaves, does not deny their abortive nature and limited revolutionary success. On the other hand, rather than portraying zombiefied, emasculated Sambos or Toms, plantation scholars have described and presented the wide variety and unending efforts of slaves to engage in both individual defiance and more subtle collective protest against the system. Among the forms of protest most commonly referred to by plantation scholars were slowing down work, misuse of implements, resistance to acculturation, apologetic and fantasy folklore, religion and exorcism, malingering, running away, suicide, infanticide, stealing, poisoning, murder, and arson.[2] The observa-

---

[*] Roy Simon Bryce-Laporte, "Slaves as Inmates, Slaves as Men," in Ann J. Lane, ed., *The Debate Over Slavery: Stanley Elkins and His Critics* (Urbana: University of Illinois Press, 1971). By permission of the publisher.

[1] See Herbert Aptheker, *Negro Slave Revolts* (New York, 1943).

[2] Raymond Bauer and Alice Bauer, "Day to Day Resistance to Slavery," *Journal of Negro History*, 27 (October 1962), 388–419; Melville Herskovits, *Myth of the Negro Past* (New York, 1941).

tion can be made that these forms ranged from intro-punitive to extra-punitive measures, from elusive to openly defiant or resistive actions, and from individual to group behavior. They were largely subversive or expressively rebellious. That is, they were usually not directed to replacement or overthrowing of the estate, region, system, or society. Their effect was generally to create nuisances for the planter or estate, although in some cases they caused widespread fear. Some, the more subtle or intro-punitive, caused no great surprise to planters and Southern whites, inasmuch as many such acts were explainable within the ideology or stereotype that was entertained of the slaves. These actions were often viewed as symptoms of inbred illness, indolence, inferiority, and barbarism. Thus, as Genovese has suggested, when slaves stole (justified as they were) they were not taken seriously (even if punished). Their stealing merely reinforced the stereotype held by their masters about them.[3] Other forms of protest, even though extra-punitive, were individual or small-scale, i.e., murder, robbery, and rape, and were often considered criminal rather than rebellious.[4] Others, the extra-punitive but collective forms, caused great awe in the slaveholding population, particularly in the light of the successes of Caribbean and Latin American slave revolts and the increasing number of short-lived slave revolts and alleged mass slave crimes in the United States.

Elkins' suggestion that slavery in general and the large plantation system in particular demanded a submissive, dependent, childish, obedient performance of the slave and that it prohibited and punished aggressive independence or assertive resistance may be well taken. It is known that

---

[3] Eugene D. Genovese, "The Legacy of Slavery and the Roots of Black Nationalism," *Studies on the Left*, 6, No. 6 (1966), 7–8. Parenthetical phrases added by this writer. Even so, we must agree with Sterling Stuckey ("Through the Prism of Folklore") with regard to the inappropriate need of the notion of "nihilistic thrashing about" to which Genovese relegates the rebellious behavior of the slaves. Such a notion presupposes a break between the insinuations of the spirituals and folk tales and the heightening of awareness and discontent among the slaves and another break between the more simplistic gestures of defiance by individual slaves and the sophistication of the underground railroad. Genovese really does not speak from the world view of the slaves as *actors*, but from an *objective*-Marxist analytic stance. In fact, he seemingly disregards the *subjective*-Marxist analytic stance, where identification and consciousness rather than consequence become the issues of concern. He furthermore does not allow for the structural development of *organization* to take place before discrediting these early "black revolutionaries"—*slaves as they were*. See Genovese's essay "American Slaves and Their History," herein, for a modification of the *objective* stance.

Notwithstanding the distinction between rebellion and revolution as portrayed in Camus' *The Rebel* and in Harold Cruse's *Rebellion or Revolution* (New York, 1969), the Black movement is objectively revolutionary, inasmuch as its basic demand for equality cannot take place without serious institutional rearrangements of the social order. This is true even though the acts of slaves and their contemporary successors may often be acts of rebellion when seen "objectively." But from a "subjective" approach there is no difference between rebellious and revolutionary acts if the actors themselves do not distinguish the motives and purposes behind such acts. In this sense the Black Revolution is an old and real revolution with no reasons for apologies to be made for the "unsuccessful" slave revolutionaries. The Black Revolution is an unending political process of planned and unplanned activities and planned and unplanned consequences, as are all revolutions.

[4] Winthrop D. Jordan, *White over Black: American Attitudes toward the Negro, 1550–1812* (Chapel Hill, 1968), 112–13.

not all plantation slaves complied with the regulations of the plantations. And, it does not necessarily follow that the slaves who complied experienced an *internalization* of their compliant role as part of their selves, nor does it mean such personality traits were inherited by the latter-day Blacks.[5] Elkins himself voices his reluctance to see at neat separation of "mere acting" and "true self" but concedes at least the existence of a broad belt of "indeterminacy" between the two (pp. 227–29). However, he fails to pursue the point. By so doing he is unable to reconcile observations that the same slaves who were believed to be indolent and irresponsible in their plantation chores would perform competently and competitively in their own lots or when hired out on their own time. By so doing he also is unable to elucidate the variation in slaves, situation, and styles of elusion or escape, e.g., those who tried to escape or elude, those who helped or concealed the effort of others but did not do it themselves, those who entertained the thought but did not try it, those who betrayed, discouraged, or seriously hunted out the escapees or would-be escapees, and those who were ambivalent in these and other situations. . . .

Elkins' thesis fails to explain how some slaves made it then and how some blacks make it now—without being Toms, Jemimas, house slaves, or black bourgeoisie, geniuses or gifted. By his conclusion Elkins obscures or overlooks the kinds of *roles played* by slaves and the *careers pursued* by blacks in "making it." Slave literature identifies music, magic, arts, and religion as activities in which leading blacks were permitted to perform. These activities were permitted because they were perceived as either necessary, legitimate, or harmless. They were not usually perceived as dangerous to the regimen, or at least not seriously so. The fact is that they were all ambivalent and allegorical self- and group-asserting actions and thus subversive of the slave plantation system even if they were also partially legitimate.

Since Emancipation, and among the freedmen of antebellum times, the more conventional careers and roles among "leaders" and "successful" blacks have included these: musicians, minstrels, ministers, composers, comedians, con men, artists, actors, authors, poets, rhythmic, symbolic, and "fictional" prose writers. These roles are much the same as those of their ancestors but of wider range. Kiel has openly criticized the emasculating, ephemeral, and effeminate image of the black male as a misunderstanding and disservice to the race (notwithstanding the perhaps noble intentions behind such portrayals).[6] In the autobiographical novels such as Richard Wright's *Black Boy*, Claude Brown's *Manchild in the Promised Land*, Robert Peck's (Iceberg Slim) *Pimp, the Story of My*

---

[5] For historical treatments of Black culture which go beyond the unidimensional approach utilized by Elkins, see Roger Abrahams, *Positively Black* (Englewood Cliffs, 1970); Houston Baker, "Completely Well: One View of Black American Culture," in Nathan Huggins, Martin Kilson, and Daniel Fox (eds.), *Key Issues in the Afro-American Experience* (New York, 1971); Vincent Harding, "Religion and Resistance among Antebellum Negroes, 1800–1860," in August Meier and Elliott Rudwick (eds.), *The Making of Black America* (New York, 1969), 1, 179–97; Sterling Stuckey, "Through the Prism of Folklore: The Black Ethos in Slavery," herein; Okan Uya, "Everyday Life in Slavery," unpublished manuscript.

[6] Charles Kiel, *Urban Blues* (Chicago, 1966).

Life, and Henry Williamson's *The Hustler,* in the early parts of the *Auto-biography of Malcolm X,* and in the escapades and comments of Langston Hughes' "Mr. Semple" (that modern Brer' Rabbit), one sees the other side of the story: the cunning, creative black individual in his struggle against the cruel closed society and the wide repertoire of mechanisms and roles played by black people in their efforts to "make it," "beat the system," or "put on." The resources and styles differ for various classes of people and in various situations.

Other students of personality suggest wide variation in responses among contemporary victims of oppression and prejudice. Pettigrew points out that there are three kinds of reactions to oppression—moving toward, against, or away from the oppressor.[7] Allport views clowning as an intro-punitive and cunnning as an extra-punitive response, but both as pretensive or elusive measures which allow the victim to "escape" the system often unnoticed. The reason why the escape is unnoticed is be-cause such measures "fit" so well the prejudicial stereotypes entertained about the actor or his group. Thus while he escapes, he continues to re-inforce the stereotype and fulfill the prophecy. He thus does not fully escape nor destroy the system.[8]

We think, in fact, that Elkins' analysis falters because he inadvertently accepts the stereotype of the clown or Sambo as given. He then proceeds to explain it and use it to chastise the system, as well as to demand a change. As Allport points out: "If the master jokes, the slave laughs; if the master storms, the slave quails; if the master wants flattery, the slave gives it. And if the master wants to be amused, the slave sometimes obligingly plays the clown." Differentiation between meaning of category and meaning of conduct is manifested in the following statement by Fanon: "It is the white man who creates the Negro. But it is the Negro who creates Negritude."[9] Even though it be positive, Fanon avoids equivo-cating between Negro and Negritude. Even though it be innocent, Elkins equivocates between *being* and *playing* the clown. Elkins makes the same mistakes as some of the masters he condemns. Others knew better. As a supposedly "unbiased" intellectual he compounds the problems, and his treatise contributes weightedly to the verification of a stereotype which some antebellum white men merely entertained but others exploited for their own ends—a stereotype which is inaccurate about the past and harmful as a ploy for correcting the present.[10] Sadly we find it possible

---

[7] Thomas F. Pettigrew, *A Profile of the Negro American* (Princeton, 1964).

[8] Gordon Allport, *The Nature of Prejudice* (New York, 1958). See also Orlando Patterson, *The Sociology of Slavery* (London, 1967).

[9] Franz Fanon, *A Dying Colonialism* (New York, 1967).

[10] Glazer and Moynihan have made rather bold projective assertions about the persistence of Sambo among North American Blacks. Nathan Glazer Introduction to the 1962 paperback edition of *Slavery,* vii; Daniel Patrick Moynihan, *The Negro Family: The Case for National Action* (Washington, D.C., 1965), 15–16. Some black scholars have almost fallen into the trap of appearing to implicitly support Elkins' thesis in their efforts to explain Sambo. See James Comer, "Individual Development and Black Rebellion, Some Parallels," *Midway* (1968), 33–45; Grier and Cobbs, *Black Rage,* 60. For rejections of the notion of persistence using Reconstruction, see Amistead Robinson, "The Reconstruction in Memphis: A Test of the Elkins Thesis," unpublished senior essay in history, Yale University, 1969; Willie Lee Rose, *Rehearsal*

to quote Lerone Bennett's commentary on William Styron with reference to Elkins: "The fascination horror of a bigot may be more compelling than the fascination-anxiety of a white liberal."[11] But then Styron seemingly derived some of his notions or defense of *his* Nat Turner from Elkins' Sambo.

SLAVES AS MEN

Crucial in the understanding of slavery is the issue of the definition of man by other men, and of course the purposes underlying and the treatments and interactions accompanying such definitions.[12] Elkins' notion of *moral personality* stresses the presumably internalized psychological attributes of the individual, and accordingly presents the defeated slaves as deficient men. Tannenbaum, upon whom Elkins draws heavily, also concedes the lack of *moral personality* on the part of the North American slaves, but he defines personality in terms of the social denial of full-fledged and equal status to the ex-slaves by their former masters. Although there seems to be a controversy developing among historians on the nature of *slave personality*, [13] it is obvious that Elkins does not consider the possibility that slaves—as displaced or bicultural Africans with a past and folklore, and more so as a fairly stabilized status group in a persistently segregated society—would have retained or developed as a part of their "underlife" a notion of manhood distinct from or even complementary to that of their masters. Consequently, Elkins finds himself hard put . . . to demonstrate that the prevalence of Sambo was indeed an *empirical reality* rather than a *conceptual construct.* . . .

To put it succinctly, our criticisms of Elkins are directed not to his history but rather to his sociology—to its overly deterministic and prematurely comparative features. . . . The empirical, particularly the phenomenological study of human behavior requires the *accessible presence* of the *actors* themselves. However at one time most slaves were foreigners, at another time they were illiterate and restricted, and at this time they are dead and of a disant past. Notwithstanding the immense wealth of folklore available, there are few autobiographies and interviews of slaves

---

for *Reconstruction: The Port Royal Experiment* (New York, 1967); Herbert Gutman, *The Invisible Fact*, forthcoming; and Thomas Holt, "The Emergence of Black Political Leadership during Reconstruction, 1865–1890," proposal for a Ph.D. dissertation, Yale University.

11 Lerone Bennett, "Nat's Last White Man," in John Henrik Clarke (ed.), *William Styron's Nat Turner: Ten Black Writers Respond* (Boston, 1968).

12 Frank Tannenbaum, *Slave and Citizen* (New York, 1963), vii; Eric Williams, "Race Relations in Caribbean Society," in Vera Rubin (ed.), *Caribbean Studies: A Symposium* (Seattle, 1960), 54–59.

13 Mina Davis Caulfield, "Slavery and the Origins of Black Culture: Elkins Revisited," in Peter Rose (ed.), *Americans from Africa* (New York, 1969), 171–91; M. I. Finley, "Slavery," *International Encyclopedia of the Social Sciences* (New York, 1968); Mary Agnes Lewis, "Slavery and Personality," herein; David McClelland, *The Achieving Society* (Princeton, 1961); Richard Morse, "Comments on Degler's 'Slavery in the United States and Brazil: An Essay in Comparative History,' " unpublished; Rose, *Rehearsal for Reconstruction*; Arnold A. Sio, "Society, Slavery, and the Slave," *Social and Economic Studies*, 16 (1967); Earl E. Thorpe, "Chattel Slavery and Concentration Camps," herein.

whose authenticity and representativeness would allow fullest confidence for generalizing about slavery. At this moment in time the records of masters, witnesses, and historians, like some of the alleged autobiographies of slaves, are being viewed askance by serious scholars. Our concern then must be to get more adequate insights or impressions *as a first step,* rather than spuriously claim accuracy about slavery. Elkins' treatment of slavery brought us closer to such insights by his analogy of the slave plantation to the concentration camp, a like-situated system of captive men.[14] Elkins level of *understanding phenomenologically* the behavior of inmates or did not reach the slaves but his work took us to the threshold of analyzing the institutions to which such men were confined.

In this paper, we have approached Elkins' statements, especially regarding the *prevalence* of a Sambo personality, as *theses*—logical possibilities rather than empirical claims. After all, his study did not include field work nor primary research. It was largely an effort to reinterpret positions and synthesize the teachings of various relevant fields of study. We have criticized his effort on grounds of its naive deterministic exaggerations and we have magnified the extent and number of conclusions that would follow a more humanistic sociological approach. By so doing we have tried to lift the topic of American slavery out of the arena of ideological and historistic polemics. American slavery is not simply an historical or symbolic artifact. It is a period of human experience, the causes, contexts, and consequences of which are yet to be fully understood in behavioral terms. We have tried to present the case that the study of slavery can be carried out by studying like-situated men in like-situated institutions—some of which exist in our midst even today. By the same token a more systematic study of the slave plantation and its inmates as part of the *genre* of total institution should provide much more plausible and verifiable propositions about the relation between behavior of captive men and the institutional-ideological context of their captivity, without limitation to a single period, institution, people, or society. These propositions need not be present-time oriented nor confined to the U.S. black population.

Other critics have chosen to view Elkins' assertions as stated *findings.* But then some of these critics have proceeded to attempt to disprove these findings or to better explain them. In our opinion many such critics commit the same mistake that they attribute to Elkins of positing as a general, factual truth something that has not been and, perhaps, cannot quite yet be tested empirically.[15] The traditional methodological tools of history and the social sciences are inadequate for testing long-dead, illit-

---

14 Lasch and Fredrickson inadvertently extended the analogy even further as they used both Goffman's asylums and Sykes' maximum security penitentiary to challenge Elkins' conclusion. See Bryce-Laporte, "The Conceptualization of the American Slave Plantation," for other proposed analogies.

15 This criticism is directed less to those who view his statements as predictive, explanatory, or relational *hypotheses,* and are now *testing* them on different levels or by use of various creative empirical methods. See Joseph Boskin, "Black Humor and Black Militancy," forthcoming; Robert Marsh, "The Bearing of Comparative Analysis on Sociological Theory," *Social Forces,* 43, No. 2; or Norman Yetman, "Testing Elkins' 'Sambo' Thesis: Some Preliminary Problems," unpublished manuscript.

erate, subjugated men in sufficient numbers, depth, or variety to either support or disprove such alleged empirical claims. The logic of internal consistency so useful in winning debates may be necessary, but is not sufficient for verifying empirical relations. For these critics Elkins has served best as a straw man to give them audience on a topic worth airing. Hopefully they will begin to see him also as a scholar who boldly applied academic borrowing and new scholarship to a subject still worth studying: The slaves are dead but their successors and substitutes are living.

Yes (we) Black men are still living! And it is in our self interest, our ancestors' and our offsprings', that we strive to correct the vestiges of any image which can be injurious to our integrity and inaccurate of our being. We must search for another scholarly way to lay bare the cruelties of our conditions without further degrading our identity as men—proud, normal, and equal men. All God's chillun got soul! Moreover, there is need for us to discern the resilience and resourcefulness that we derived from and developed despite such conditions. What is needed then is new scholarly redirection so that such resilience and resourcefulness may be utilized to improve the lives—chances, social conditions, images, and being—of Black men, once captive, somewhat still captive men.

The Human Riches of Slave Religion*

Wayman B. McLaughlin

The concrete problem of the present paper is to explore some basic aspects of symbolism and mysticism in the spirituals.[1] The spirituals are sacred folk music born out of the aches, pains, and joys of existence. The soul-life of a people is here woven into a testament of mystery and holiness. Nymph-like, amid shadows and echoes, the singers of this music

---

* Wayman B. McLaughlin, "Symbolism and Mysticism in the Spirituals," *Phylon* (1963).

[1] Richard Wright, *White Man, Listen!* (New York, 1937), p. 128. Wright expresses the opposite point of view in the following words: "It was through the door of religion that the American Negro first walked into the house of Western culture, and it was through religious symbols that he has given voice to his most poignant yearnings. And yet, instead of his songs being mystical or metaphysical, they are simply and directly wish fulfillments, projections of his longings to escape his chains and blows." The view of this paper is that Wright's psychological factor is one among many others in the spirituals.

weaved out of the matrix of economic, social, and religious circumstances a web of being which was ultimate and personal. Thus, these songs reflect light and darkness in the heave and flow of a personal reality.

In pursuing this problem there is the need at the outset to define two terms: "symbolism" and "mysticism." Symbolism is simply the art of representing something by symbols. But what is a symbol? In general terms a symbol is an outward sign of an inward meaning. In the book, *The Forgotten Language*, Erich Fromm says this concerning the role of symbolical thinking in life:

> Symbolical thinking represents the very substance of the psychic life. . . . Symbolical language is language in which the world outside is a symbol of the world inside, a symbol for our souls and minds.[2]

If this statement of Fromm be true, perhaps one of the most fruitful ways of thinking about spirituals may be in terms of symbolical language and mystical meaning.[3]

. . . Mysticism may be defined as the experience of direct communion of the soul with God. Bergson's *The Two Sources of Morality and Religion* reveals the fragile beauty of the mystical criterion of truth in the following words:

> What a shock to the soul is the passing from the static to the dynamic, from the closed to the open, from everyday life to mystic life. When the darkest depths of the soul are stirred, what rises to the surface and attains consciousness takes on there an image or an emotion. . . . The image becomes symbolic of what is about to happen. . . . The soul ceases to revolve around itself. It feels an indefinable presence, or divines through a symbolic vision. Then comes an enthralling rapture. God is there, and the soul is God.[4] . . .

It is clear, in the light of the foregoing, that the spirituals represent predominantly personal mysticism of the Christian tradition. They personalize in the concrete the individual's "I-Thou" encounter with God. They have dramatic intensification, extemporaneous creations, and spontaneous dialogues between man and God. We are struck in these religious songs by the exceptional awareness of reality. . . .

The mystic insight begins with the view of the unveiling of a mystery. Closely related to this view is the emphasis upon revelation rather than reason. The soul appears in utter loneliness to bring forth out of its own depths a within that is beyond. Similarly, many of the spirituals issue out of a fourth dimension of personality, that is, the faith situation. Existentially, they whisper of hope, grief, affection, loneliness, regret, toil, struggle, death and faith. . . .

In the following spiritual the individual begins with the experience of cosmic exile from world and God that ends in an exclamatory faith:

---

[2] Erich Fromm, *The Forgotten Language* (New York, 1951), p. 12.

[3] Bertrand Russell, *Mysticism and Logic* (London, 1917), p. 3.

[4] Henri Bergson, *The Two Sources of Morality and Religion* (New York, 1954), p. 230.

> I feel like a motherless child;
> I feel like a motherless child;
> Glory Hallelujah!
> Sometimes my way is sad and lone,
> When far away and lost from home;
> Glory Hallelujah!

. . . The singer realizes for a luminous moment that he is at home within the Absolute. This moment of certainty is to be found in his joyous epithet, "Glory Hallelujah!" This spiritual has the same motif of Augustine's *Confessions:* "Thou has made us for Thyself, our heart is restless until it finds its rest in Thee."[5] . . . In the symbol-characters of Shadrack, Moses, Samson, and others, the slave singers found men of voices like their own. Daniel's experiences illustrate his lively faith in the reality of God in the world.

Or take this beautiful folk song; here the singer's firm certainty of fulfillment in God is demonstrated:

> I've just come from the fountain,
> I've just come from the fountain,
> Lord! I've just come from the fountain,
> His name's so sweet.

This spiritual is like the morning star, full of splendor, light, and joy. It is one of the noblest spirituals in terms of mystical intuition. Its soul-poet points out that he has been to the "All-Source" of life with the beauty of sensuousness, "His name's so sweet." Free imagination, warmth, freshness, abandonment, majectic flashes, and depth of spiritual insight are at work here. . . .

There is inherent within the mystical tradition the will to believe in a calling or task:

> O, I know the Lord,
> I know the Lord,
> I know the Lord laid his hands on me.
>
> Did you ever see the like before,
> I know the Lord laid his hands on me;
>
> King Jesus preaching to the poor,
> I know the Lord laid his hands on me.

The thought-symbol of this song is found in the scene of Christ beginning his ministry (Luke 4:17–19). Graphic description is given by the gifted singers of these songs to Jesus' concept of being called to preach to the poor. "Did ever you see the like before . . . King Jesus preaching to the poor.". . .

This certainty of life is not a closed, static, frozen belief, but open, moving, and alive. In fact, there is always the need of more of it:

> Did you ever see such a man as God?
> A little more faith in Jesus,

---

5 Augustine, *Confessions,* Book 1, p. 1.

> A preaching the Gospel to the poor,
> A little more faith in Jesus.

. . . The spirituals center around man's search for unity. The spiritual "Ezekiel Saw the Wheel" is a vision of beauty and the song of mankind. The words are:

> Ezekiel saw the wheel,
> Way up in the middle of the air,
> Ezekiel saw the wheel,
> Way up in the middle of the air.
>
> Ezekiel saw the wheel of time,
> Ev'ry spoke was of the humankind,
> A wheel in a wheel,
> Way in the middle of the air.
>
> O, the big wheel runs by faith
> And the little wheel runs by the grace of God,
> A wheel in a wheel,
> Way in the middle of the air.

Ezekiel's vision in the Old Testament is used to bring out the key symbols. "Ev'ry spoke was of the humankind." "The big wheel runs by faith," and "the little wheel runs by the grace of God." These symbols reveal that the real grandeur of mankind is seen as a moral elevation held by the grace of God. The strong, significant symbol, "Wheel in a wheel," expresses the universal harmony of the human family in God.

"He Has the Whole World in His Hands" has in it the echo of the world. It comes out of the heartsearch of experience, like Pushkin's poetry and Shakespeare's plays. Its symbols are concrete and universal. The charm and significance of this song lie in the intermingling of themes. It is enumerative of the universal in the particular. It starts with the "wind and rain." "He's got the wind and the rain in His hands, He's got the whole world in His hands." It states: "He's got the lying man," "He's got the gambling man," "He's got the crap shooting man in His hands." Then, it adds a tender touch, "He's got the little bits-a-baby in His hands." Next: "He's got you and me, sister, in His hands. He's got everybody in His hands. He's got the whole world in His hands.". . .

Another dominant factor of mysticism is the denial of temporal time. The trinity of clock time, past, present, and future, is an illusion. The true being of time is one-future oriented event. Accordingly, time is viewed in terms of its eternalism.

Again and again, the spirituals strike this eternal note of time. For instance:

> Soon I will be done with the
>   troubles of the world,
> Troubles of the world, troubles
>   of the world;
> Soon I will be done with the
>   troubles of the world
> Going home to live with God.

The view of time as being a future event of the "promised land" can be seen in the following:

> I am a po' pilgrim of sorrow,—
> I'm in this wide worl' alone.
> No hope in this worl' for to-morrow,
> I'm strivin'—for heav'n my home—
> Sometimes I'm both tossed and driven,
> Sometimes I know not where to roam
> I've heard of a city called heav'n
> I've started to make it my home.

In their eternal view of time there is the affirmation of life in terms of an ideal end. Time is telescoped into the symbol of heaven. "Heavenly shoes," "long white robes," "starry crowns," "golden slippers," "golden street," "golden harp" are not mystic-mild, but mystic-potent symbols. This eternal world for them is the true time. Heaven and the royal gifts of shoes are symbols of the fact that they are a part of the true world of goodness, truth, and beauty. These are the riches of the kingdom of ends. Here will be found the priceless treasure of worth and dignity.

Thus, these bards of the spiritual life sang of it in all its mystic beauty:

> I got shoes,
> You got shoes,
> All God's children got shoes.
> When we get to Heaven
> We're going to put on our shoes
> And shout all over God's Heaven.
> Heaven! Heaven!

According to John Lovell, "I Got Shoes" symbolizes that the slaves had latent abilities and talents that they could not realize in this world of man's time, but in the world of God's time their possibilities for good would be fulfilled. "Shout all over God's Heaven" implies that when the singers got a chance, they would make their influence felt in all areas of the heavenly community.[6]

In their Prometheus' struggle toward the light, the singers saw death as a necessary prerequisite in order to enter into the real world. Often the singers' symbol of death was a boat or ship crossing the river of Jordan. Here original symbols were preserved to denote death:

> Tis the old ship of Zion,
> Get on board, get on board.

However, a new concept was retained by a vital symbolism in the slave's everyday experience. Death was emphasized as the "same train." This train carried off his mother, father, sister, and brother. The continuation of this process of death can be seen in the repetition of the term "same train" three times. The train will be back tomorrow for him.

---

6 John Lovell, "The Social Implication of the Negro Spirituals," *Journal of Negro Education* (October 1939), 636–43. Lovell emphasizes the social aspect of the spirituals. It is the point of this paper that the social aspect is one among other factors. One of the main other factors is the mystical and religious insight.

> Same train, same train, same train
> Carry my mother,
> Same train be back to-morrer.

Death was not an end, but the means of entering into God's eternity. As heaven was the true home, eternity was the true time. . . .

Another striking mystical symbol used in the spirituals is that of a ladder. The Christian life is the passing from darkness into light, from partiality to completeness. Each "round" is a growth stage until the individual reaches his creative maker and destiny. With a note that has the ring of reality, the singers cry out:

> We are climbing Jacob's ladder
> We are climbing Jacob's ladder
> Soldier of the Cross.
>
> Every round goes higher and higher
> Every round goes higher and higher
> Soldier of the Cross.

Jacob's ladder is really of mystic import. It is a signification of the communion of the soul with the Ultimate Other. With vibrant insight this spiritual reveals the constant process of growth toward the reality of the Divine. . . .

Christ, in the spirituals, means God. As the slave singer saw it, Christ is a continuing consummation of the reality of God. There seemed to be, for them, no basic distinction between God and Christ. Although these slave bards used the basic symbols of the Old and New Testaments in their contemplation of the birth, life, and death of Christ, they gave fresh interpretation of these experiences by fusing them with their own experiences. In their songs an old issue was dealt with afresh.

As those on the mountain top first see the coming beams of the sun, the advent of Christ is symbolized in these words:

> Go tell it on de mountain
> Over the hills and everywhere,
> Go tell it on de mountain
> That Jesus Christ is born.
>
> When I was a seeker,
> I sought both night and day,
> I asked de Lord to help me,
> And he show'd me de way.

The universal significance of the birth of Jesus is symbolized in this statement, "Go tell it on de mountain/Over the hills and everywhere." However, there is also a clear personal symbol, "When I was a seeker." The word "seeker" must be understood in terms of the background of Quaker mysticism. It implies the searching for the inner light, finding the right path, and entering into a new truth. This spiritual connects the birth of Jesus with His coming into the life of the individual. . . .

The ontological solitude of Jesus, that is, the serenity of His spirit amid overwhelming odds, was seen by the slaves in the following words:

> They crucified my Lord, and He never said
>   a mumblin' word,
> Not a word, not a word.
> The blood came twinklin' down, but He
>   never said a mumblin' word,
> Not a word, not a word.

The soul singers meant to say "trinklin," implying that His blood was trickling down. But they said "twinklin." If this be a true image, it signalizes that like a sparkling, shimmering star, the blood of Jesus was bejeweled. Here, if anywhere, shines forth the poetic essence of these remarkable souls. Mystically, it is no wonder that songs poured from their hearts like rain from Shelley's "Cloud."

"He Arose" is an instance in which the singers saw in the resurrection of Jesus a new hope for man's creativity, progress, and renewal. In the woof and warp of experience they saw a rhyme and reason stronger than the back of the mythological Greek figure, Atlas, able to "bear my spirit on.". . .

The Slave Community and the Conditions of Rebellion*

Gerald W. Mullin

In the summer of 1800 a group of slave-artisans organized an attack on Richmond. Because their plan was essentially an expression of their class and its understanding of the values and norms of the American Revolutionary era, Gabriel's Rebellion was exceptionally political in character.[1]

[Slaveowner William Young's] . . . actions called in question the practices of other slaveowners, who on this count were as guilty as he was. This carelessness was indicative of the permissive, confused, and disordered state of slavery in the final years of the eighteenth century: careless and permissive because whites usually ignored such critical features of the slave code as the system of written passes for slaves who traveled, prohibitions against selling to slaves, and the supervision of their gatherings. Slavery was also in a confused and indecisive state, because in

---

* From *Flight and Rebellion: Slave Resistance in Eighteenth-Century Virginia* by Gerald W. Mullin. Copyright © 1972 by Oxford University Press, Inc. Reprinted by permission.

[1] Unless otherwise indicated, sources for this are the Executive Papers (September–December 1800) in the Virginia State Library, Richmond). . . .

this period of revolutionary and religious idealism reform ameliorated the slave's condition but seldom made him a free man. Such examples of "humanitarianism" as the liberalized manumission procedure, a restricted slave trade,[2] and the encouragement of the sale of slaves in families (mothers and their children only) did not placate some slaves.[3] Governor James Monroe's remarks to the Governor of South Carolina were representative of the slaveowners misconceptions about the effects of liberalizing slavery without abolishing it outright. . . .

Opportunities for recruiting men were numerous. Slaves late in the century had a rich fraternal and religious life; and recruiters were sufficiently free of any kind of meaningful supervision to travel extensively to meet slaves at barbecues, Sunday afternoon drinking sessions beneath well-known bridges, at meeting-houses, and outdoor "preachings."

The accounts of the recruitment procedure reveal what the conspiracy meant for most slaves, and indicate how the first group lost the initiative to Gabriel and his brothers, Martin, a preacher, and Solomon, a blacksmith. Recruitment usually followed a pattern. The organizer contacted one man in a small group of blacks, and in words such as these, asked: "was he willing to fight the white people for his freedom?" The enlistee often responded by declaring his hatred for whites and his willingness to kill them without compassion, by sharing his views of the insurrection's goals, and by requesting a command position. Sometimes the leader's questions were put in the context of the slave's manhood or toughness. Patrick was asked "if he was a Man?" . . .

More than any other organizer [Gabriel] sensed the narcotic and self-justifying effects of revolutionary rhetoric and organization. Because he was able to make decisions, delegate responsibilities, and pursue routine tasks to their completion in order to avert the strong possibility of disaster, the rebellion came to be his. And it bore his own quietly methodical, businesslike character. . . .

. . . But by the end of the century a significant change had taken place in the revolutionary awareness of men who had previously viewed slavery as an individual problem and resisted it as fugitives. These men and this change, in fact, are the key to the relationship between the social and personal dimensions of the conspiracy. Writing in 1801 about fugitives who became insurrectionists, St. George Tucker, aristocrat and lawyer, analyzed the conspiracy's preconditions for the state legislature. Comparing the slaves' reactions to Dunmore and Gabriel, he discussed their exceptionally rapid material and spiritual development in the "few short

---

2 *Hening*, 11, 24–25, 390–94. See also, Robert E. and B. Katherine Brown, *Virginia 1705–1786; Aristocracy or Democracy?* (East Lansing, Michigan, 1964), 285f; and Robert McColley, *Slavery and Jeffersonian Virginia* (Urbana, Ill., 1964), chapters 7–8.

3 The following plantation accounts and newspaper advertisements offering slaves for sale indicate that some Virginians in the last quarter of the century were reluctant to separate slave children from their mothers. *VaH & FA*, October 11, 1792 (subscriber, James Lewis); October 24, 1793 (John Minor, Jr.); July 25, 1793 (Burges Ball); November 14, 1793 (Charles Taylor), and October 30, 1794 (Robert Patton and John Mercer). See also the will of Young Short (September 4, 1795); the Hawkes and McGehee Family Papers; Thomas Jefferson to T. M. Randolph, Sr., October 22, 1790, Edgehill-Randolph Papers, UVA.

years" following the war. He attributed their new outlook to the growth of towns, trades, and a complementary increase in the extent of literacy among slaves. More opportunities for work in commercial areas brought about a "prodigious change" in the skilled slaves' outlook, a change Tucker characterized as the "love of freedom," and that "evolving spirit we fear." While only a few runaways, a "few solitary individuals," joined the British in 1775, the insurrectionists of 1800 organized extensively in order to "assert their claims, while rest[ing] their safety on success alone." The difference between the two rebellions, Tucker argued, was basically ideological: whereas in 1775 slaves "fought [for] freedom merely as a good; now they also claim it as a right."[4]

Thus in the closing years of the century, revolutionary conflict and ideology were resolved for most free men, but not for black men, especially if they were artisans. Between 1775 and 1800, a type of slave who was literate, skilled, mobile, and working in a commercial environment accepted the fact that regardless of his comparatively privileged position, and the whites' efforts to ameliorate slavery, the institution would survive and grow. Skilled slaves had become sufficiently marginal to believe that the values and "rights" of the Revolutionary era were theirs also and that they were sufficiently resourceful and strategically placed to do something about their situation with the aid of other men. Nonetheless, their expanded revolutionary consciousness was still focused by their traditional and relatively advantaged positions. So, to the extent that they were motivated by ideas, these ideas established definite boundaries of their revolutionary action.

The insurrectionists' goals were essentially political. While using the rhetoric of their generation to clearly distinguish between oppressors and victims, white as well as black, they displayed a keen sense of their own time and place. One man testified that he wanted "to fight for his Country," and another said they were to "subdue the whole of the Country where Slavery was permitted but no further." "As far as I understand all the whites were to be massacred, except the Quakers, the Methodists & Frenchmen," Woolfolk testified, and "they were to be spared on account as they conceived of their being friendly to liberty." Prosser's Ben, an 18-year-old who worked beside Gabriel in the blacksmith shop, mentioned that "whites were to [be] murdered & killed indiscriminately excepting French Men, none of whome were to be touched." And another said simply, they "intended to spare all poor white women who had no slaves." The continual discussions of who was to be spared or killed, as well as the occasionally cathartic posturing that characterized the recruitment process, seldom impaired the participant's expression of his clear understanding of the leading principles of the day.[5] . . .

The occupational and ideological values which separated organizers

---

4 [St. George Tucker], *Letter to a Member of the General Assembly of Virginia on the Subject of the Late Conspiracy of the Slaves, with a Proposal for their Colonization* (Richmond, 1801). VSL microfilm.

Imbued with the mood and themes of the Enlightenment and revolutionary idealism, Tucker's prescient analysis is worth citing at length; for it deals with nearly all of the major preconditions for insurrection. . . .

5 "Woolfolk's Confessions"; Prosser's Ben at Woolfolk's trial. . . .

from those they had to recruit were basically a function of their comparatively more thorough acculturation. The slaves' awareness of their profound cultural differences was sharpened by the dramatic quality of religious life at the end of the century.[6] The country people, reluctant and suspicious, came off the quarters and gathered at the large and exciting revival meetings of the Great Awakening. Seeking spiritual assistance, they were confronted by Gabriel and his men, who used the meetings to disguise both their real intentions and the structure of their organization, and to recruit men and discuss tactics. The high point of the revival was the exhortation which, if it had been used by Gabriel, could have been the catalyst for changing religious fervor and concern for the hereafter into revolutionary action in the here-and-now. But this never happened. The leaders and their potential followers were faithful in different ways. The conspiracy was composed of autonomous men confronting religious men. Because of the nature of its leader and the rational, political character of its goals, Gabriel's Rebellion never became a viable part of the great religious revivals.

Because religious and eschatological elements often generate the large-scale rebellions of pre-industrial folk, perhaps it was not merely coincidental that one leader looked beyond the country people's fundamentalism to an even more ancient heritage which leavened their Christianity. For some, like the leader George Smith, Africa was still a very meaningful part of their lives. Smith, who was closer to the soil and the harvest cycles than any other organizer, once proposed that he hire his own time, travel down-country to what he called the "pipeing tree," and enlist the "Outlandish people." For they were "supposed to deal with Witches and Wizards, and thus [would be] useful in Armies to tell when any calamity was about to befall them."[7] Whether or not Smith later talked about bullets turning to water is an intriguing conjecture, but he did announce to the gathering at Young's Spring that when he finished plowing his master's corn field, he would make as many crossbows "as he could," an equally fantastic proposition. Although there was no more said about wizards, crossbows, and Africa, Smith, in his own way, called attention to the one means—charisma—by which the slaves could have transcended their significant cultural and occupational differences. But his proposal (as well as Woolfolk's unfulfilled search for a Moses) calls attention to the relationship between acculturation levels and religious beliefs and practices, on the one hand, and styles of resistance, on the other. Here is the source of Gabriel's failure: at a time when revivalism was a vital force among plantation slaves, those who would lead couched their appeal in political and secular terms. Unlike Nat Turner's magnificent Old Testament visions, which transfigured him and sustained his movement, Gabriel's Rebellion, lacking a sacred dimension, was without a Moses, and thus without a following.[8]

---

[6] Robert McColley, *Slavery and Jeffersonian Virginia* (Urbana, Ill., 1964), chap. vii. Wesley M. Gewehr, *The Great Awakening in Virginia, 1740–90* (Durham, 1930), chap. vii.

[7] Woolfolk at the trial of George Smith.

[8] On the relationship between charismatic leaders, chiliasm, and the rebellious

Preliminary research indicates that an understanding of the acculturative experience, as a hitherto neglected dimension of slavery, may also enrich our studies of the other major insurrections about which the slaves have provided ample testimony. The cultural differences among slaves—so evident and divisive in the 1800 rebellion—were also manifested in the religious contexts of the insurrections of Denmark Vesey (Charleston, South Carolina, 1882) and Nat Turner (Southampton County, Virginia, 1831).

Religion and magic sustained Nat Turner's Rebellion.[9] Executed by plantation slaves in an economically backward area, this insurrection was not as politically coherent and extensive as Gabriel's. Turner, who was not a preacher in the conventional sense but a seer and a holy man, also politicized his men by means of dream interpretations and feats of fortune-telling and numerology. In this instance too, a celestial event (an eclipse of the sun) made a tremendous impact on the black country folk; but they were prepared to see it as a favorable sign. Denmark Vesey, the third great insurrectionist, stands midway between Gabriel and Turner. While he normally based his appeal on political grounds, he recognized the connection between religious sanctions and rebellion from below. On a few special occasions he used sermons based on the Bible; and he also delegated to Gullah Jack, a native African and "doctor," the responsibility of forming the rural blacks of the low country's sea islands into "African legions." But, like Gabriel, he failed, because his rebellion was urban-based and restricted to artisans, shopkeepers, and free Negroes. Only Nat Turner, who charged his plan with supernatural signs, and sacred, poetic language that inspired action, was able to transcend the worlds of the plantation and the city. Only Turner led a "sustained" insurrection.

But Gabriel's men were ensnared in an earlier and a different era. Although these artisans, by 1800, had become so much more numerous, strategically placed, and imbued with an ideology supporting collective action, they were still isolated—cut off not only from their own people, but from the new economic realities of the ante-bellum period. There was in this conspiracy, then, a note of cultural despair. . . . Since the South after the introduction of Eli Whitney's gin was again moving away from manufactures and economic diversification, the occupational strata and milieu productive of this type of slave was rapidly becoming anachronistic. Hence from this threat to their way of life came this group's despair. Isaac declared "if the [insurrection] was not soon he would run off, as he was determined not to serve a white man [for] another year," and Martin said "he could no longer bear what he had borne." To a third, the transformation from slave to free man was forthrightly expressed: "I will kill or be killed." And Solomon, one of the few mulattoes

---

activities of pre-industrial folk, see E. J. Hobsbawm, *Primitive Rebels* (New York, 1959); George M. Fredrickson and Christopher Lasch, "Resistance to Slavery," *Civil War History*, 13 (December 1967), 317–18; 317 n–18 n.

[9] From data collected for an extended study on the role of cultural change and slave insurrections tentatively entitled: "Religion, Acculturation, and American Negro Slave Rebellions."

in the conspiracy, joined and died even though he was to be legally free at age thirty-one.[10]

But where were the other slaves? The reality of slavery in post-war Virginia was radically different for leaders and followers. An elite initiated, planned, and dominated Gabriel's Rebellion. In the four months before the insurrection they lived and were sustained by it; they knew one another well. Living with death, they accepted it. Slowly and profoundly freedom, revolution, and death came to be a large part of their lives. Meanwhile, the rank and file simply raised their hands at meetings; a few personalized their commitment by volunteering for specific responsibilities and acquiring weapons. Enlisting in the most inauthentic manner, they did not share the leaders' distinctive revolutionary awareness. Thus their commitment was fragile at best; and in the end, Gabriel and his men stood alone.

Slavery in eighteenth-century Virginia was remarkably flexible and unstructured, in part because the society itself was unsettled, rapidly growing, and insecure. Central to this openness was the planters' overwhelming need for self-sufficiency. Although they were politically and economically subservient to Great Britain, and absolutely dependent on African slaves, patriarchs wished to be "independent on every one but Providence."

In their quest for this goal, slaveowners esteemed highly those Africans who began to change their ways and were then capable, in their masters' eyes, of becoming skilled and of forming the very basis for the planters' vaunted autonomy. Paradoxically, acculturation—the changes by which the African's customs fell away as he acquired English and occupational specialization—ultimately created slaves who were able to challenge the security of the society itself.

Viewing acculturation as another dimension of slave behavior in the colonial period not only clarifies our understanding of adjustments to slavery, but calls attention to the most important ways in which slavery changed as it developed from the colonial to the ante-bellum period. Acculturation and work were the most important variables determining a slave's adjustment. As a new arrival, the African initially reacted to the strange and hostile society on the basis of his communal upbringing. For him, procurement was a brutal but not a brutalizing experience; the "outlandish" African remained a man, and for a time, a highly distinctive slave. In fact, until his prior cultural sanctions proved unworkable, such measurable evidence of acculturation as speaking English did not occur.

Nearly all Africans soon became "new Negroes"—field hands on the up-country quarters. For these men, as well as the field laborers and house servants on the home plantation, resistance was an inward-directed endeavor. Plantation slaves turned their limited rebelliousness back toward the plantation setting itself; their reactions were usually

---

[10] Prosser's Ben at the trial of James Allen's Isaac; Ben at the trial of William Burton's Isaac; "Information" of William Young's Gilbert given to John Foster (September 23).

easily contained; they brought a direct, punitive response, and seldom improved the slave's status. But some of this resistance was cooperative, and it was especially effective because the plantation was so vulnerable to acts of sabotage.

A few Africans and many of their American-born children learned proficient English, acquired an intelligent demeanor, advanced in the work hierarchy, and so became relatively assimilated. These men were self-reliant, individualistic, and less cooperative. This is what the colonists desired; slaves who were more like themselves were slaves they could better understand. But these men, in jobs where they learned to function resourcefully in the colonial society outside the plantation, came to understand that they still had little control over their lives. When they resisted, then, it was, for three-quarters of the century, directed away from the plantations; as resourceful fugitives, the skilled slaves went to towns, passed as free men, and found work. They were still unable to escape slavery completely, however; they still contributed their labor to the society, although more on their own terms than previously.

As the assimilateds replaced the Africans in the slave population, traditional arrangements between slaves and free men, in the last quarter of the century, became dangerously outmoded. More slaves were able to resist in ways which challenged their masters' (and the society's) traditional sense of security. These developments, coupled with the changes in the economic and political realities of the revolutionary era, brought about Gabriel's Rebellion. Slavery in the nineteenth century would be based on a heritage more American than African. . . .

chapter 6

The Black Experience
Beyond Slavery

AMERICAN RACIAL SLAVERY held "black" and "slave" to be nearly synonymous terms and had no real social place for the half million blacks not in bondage. (The phrase "free Negro" will be used for convenience but with the realization that no black person actually lived in freedom.) The quarter million free Southern Negroes of 1860 ranging in numbers from 441 in Mississippi to 83,000 in Maryland aroused much hostility and fear among white Southerners and had gained their status through historical accidents and fortuitous circumstances rather than through the political consent of the ruling whites. With a few exceptions law and custom excluded all blacks from political and legal processes and kept them in a condition only somewhat less impoverished and repressed than the bondsmen. Political authorities treated the black man as a slave unless he could prove otherwise, enacted statutes for voluntary enslavement, frequently discussed the expulsion of all non-slave blacks, and passed many laws which either made manumission virtually impossible or forced the freed slave out of the state. Free Negroes, who lived constantly with the threat of violence and the possibility of kidnaping for sale into slavery, generally had to rely on the arbitrary "paternalism" of one or more white patrons in order to survive.

The other quarter million free Negroes lived in the North and the West under conditions less oppressive than in the South but still extremely harsh. Blacks frequently could not find access to education or to most jobs, serve on juries or in the militia, vote, give testimony against whites, use public accommodations freely, or marry white persons. Despite all of these restrictions, much white hostility and a substantial measure of racial violence, a small black intelligentsia emerged which created institutions such as the African Methodist Episcopal Church, Masonic and other fraternal organizations, moral reform societies, schools, national conventions, antislavery societies, a few newspapers and more pamphlets and books, and a large number of underground railroad stations to rescue slaves and prevent kidnaping. Naturally, many of these institutional arrangements had a precarious existence and a brief lifespan, but the surprising thing was that they existed at all. Just as slaves had forged the rudiments of an Afro-American culture from an oppressive bondage, so the nonslave blacks of the North articulated basic black experiences in institutional forms in the midst of poverty, small numbers, and a hostile white environment.

Among the most important efforts of the new black elite were the historical articles, pamphlets, books, and arguments which served as instruments of the black struggle for liberation. Because white America ignored contemporary black institutions and capabilities and used history as a racist weapon, blacks had to challenge a body of historical beliefs which denied the existence of a meaningful black history, insisted on the incapability of Africans for even the lowest ladder of civilization, and rejected the very humanity of black people. Although some writers stressed the lives of gifted black men such as Benjamin Banneker or discussed the contributions of blacks to the building of America, most time and energy went to attacking the general conception of whites as the exclusive carriers of history and civilization in critiques which demonstrated that ancient Egyptians had been dark skinned people or that Africans such as Hannibal loomed large on the world stage. A summary account of the findings of half a century of embattled black scholarship can be found in George Washington Williams' impressive two volume work of 1883.

After the post-Reconstruction triumph of Southern caste and at the nadir of black life during the early twentieth century, black historians such as Carter G. Woodson faced the same task as their intellectual ancestors of trying desperately to establish and defend a black past in the context of a hostile white culture and historical scholarship. Men of the next generation such as Charles H. Wesley continued the struggle. After World War II and the emergence of dozens of new Afro-Asian nations, the decline of ideological racism and the dramatic rise of the civil rights and black power movements in the United States, hundreds of black and white scholars turned their attention to recapturing the black past. By the mid 1960s it became clear that the contradictions of modern times between democratic theory and white racist practices, between racial repression and the capabilities and aspirations of black people, had existed throughout American history. Moreover, the two dominant political movements in the black community during the 60s, black demands for full human and constitutional rights and black nationalism, had their roots in the earliest years of the United States. In a very real sense Martin Luther King and the early leadership of the Student Nonviolent Coordinated Committee (SNCC) marched behind W. E. B. DuBois and the Niagara movement of the early twentieth century and the black abolitionists of the 1840s. Behind the Muslims and other contemporary black nationalist groups stood Marcus Garvey's United Negro Improvement Association of the 1920s, Bishop Henry M. Turner's African migration movement of the 1890s and Martin Delany's black separatism of the 1850s. In antebellum times as in other eras separatism and militant protest for human rights in America were not mutually exclusive ideologies but rather different human and intellectual strategies for survival with one being stressed over the other in accordance with the most pressing of immediate demands and pressures. Martin Delany, as one learns in Howard H. Bell's essay (Selection 2), served as a leader of black abolition in the 1840s; turned to Africa after the passage of the Fugitive Slave Act, the up-swing in Southern oppression and the increasing signs of national indifferences or hostility; and then returned to America to become the ranking black officer in the Union Army and one of the architects of black Reconstruction in South Carolina.

Beyond the question of historical heritage and cultural heroes, the 1960s gave birth to a passion to unearth every significant aspect of the black past. For a time most scholarly energy went into establishing the facts of black oppression and bad national faith, the part played in these matters by presidents, congressional leaders, state politicians and various white factions, and defensive responses by black groups and individuals. Recently, however, a number of scholars have become more concerned with the internal history of the black community, with the concrete details of the manner in which slaves painfully created a culture in the house of bondage and with the specific ways that free Negroes organized protest and established basic social institutions. The structure of general events had been presented by Woodson, Wesley, and more recently by John Hope Franklin; and a host of black and white scholars too numerous to list here built on that framework. Benjamin Quarles (Selection 1), one of the most prolific scholars in America, provided in his book on the black abolitionists a fascinating panoply of black radicals and reformers, of moral reform societies and determined vigilance committees, and perhaps most importantly, of black men and women attempting to create the social instruments for survival and ultimate liberation.

BIBLIOGRAPHY

Works Discussed in This Chapter

Bell, Howard H., "Introduction" to Martin R. Delany and Robert Campbell, *Search for a Place* (1860 [mod. ed., 1969]).

Franklin, John Hope, *From Slavery to Freedom: A History of Negro Americans* (3rd ed., 1967), and other works.

Quarles, Benjamin, *Black Abolitionists* (1969) and other works.

Wesley, Charles H., revision of Woodson, *The Negro in Our History* (10th ed., 1962) and other works.

Williams, George Washington, *History of the Negro Race in the United States from 1610 to 1880* (2 vols., 1883).

Woodson, Carter G., *The Negro in Our History* (1928) and other works.

Suggested Readings

Among *general works* for a useful antebellum anthology see John Bracey, Jr., August Meier, and Elliott Rudwick, eds., *Free Blacks in America, 1800–1869* (1971). The best general collection for black protest is still Herbert Aptheker, ed., *A Documentary History of the Negro People in the U.S.* (1951).

For an excellent collective biography see Edgar A. Toppin, *A Biographical History of Blacks in America Since 1528* (1969). See also Lerone Bennett, Jr., *Pioneers in Protest* (1968).

Among *general anthologies of scholarly essays* see Melvin Drimmer, ed., *Black History* (1968); Peter I. Rose, ed., *Americans From Africa* (2 vols., 1970); and Okon E. Uya, ed., *Black Brotherhood: Afro-Americans and Africa* (1971).

Among *general black histories* see Lerone Bennett, Jr., *Before the Mayflower* (4th rev. ed., 1969); other works by Bennett; C. Eric Lincoln, *The Negro Pilgrimage in America* (1967); J. Saunders Redding, *They Came in Chains* (1950); Earl E. Thorpe, *The Mind of the Negro* (1961); and three volumes by Charles H. Wesley, *In Freedom's Footsteps* (1968), *Negro Americans in the Civil War* (1967), and *The Quest for Equality* (1968).

Five useful *interpretative and bibliographical essays* are Ernest Kaiser, "The Negro Impact on Western Civilization," *Science and Society* (1972); George Ravick, "The Historical Roots of Black Liberation," *Radical America* (1968); Robert S. Starobin, "The Negro: A Central Theme in American History," *Journal of Contemporary History* (1969); Starobin and Dale Tonick, "Black Liberation Historiography," Ibid. (1968); and H. E. Morill and J. Donaldson, "Geographical Perspectives on the History of Black America," *Economic Geography* (1972).

On *blacks, Indians and whites* see the essays by Charles Crowe, William S. Willis and others in Charles Hudson, ed., *Red, White and Black* (1972) and *Three Centuries of Southern Indians* (1975). See also Gary B. Nash, *Red, White and Black* (1974).

For interesting materials in the realm of *comparative history* see the thought-provoking and very useful David W. Cohen and Jack P. Greene, eds. *Neither Slave Nor Free: The Freedman of African Descent in the Slave Societies of the New World* (1972). See also Herbert S. Klein, "The Colored Freedmen in Brazilian Slave Society," *Indiana Magazine of History* (1969).

Colonization was initially a hostile white idea, but P. J. Staudenraus in *The African Colonization Movement, 1816–1865* (1961), a very unsatisfactory book, argued for white benevolence. For some black responses see Tom L. McLaughlin, "Sectional Responses of Free Negroes to the Idea of Colonization," *Washington State U. Research Studies* (1966); William A. Poe, "A Look at Louisiana Colonization in Its African Setting," *Louisiana Studies* (1972); and Marilyn Baily, "From Cincinnati, Ohio to Wilberforce, Canada: A Note on Ante-Bellum Colonization," *Journal of Negro History* (1973).

For a brief and informative but unsatisfactory and not very sympathetic account of *black separatism* see Theodore Draper, *The Rediscovery of Black Nationalism* (1969). For more knowledgeable and sympathetic essays see Robert Weisbord, *Ebony Kinship: Africa, Africans and the Afro-American* (1973); Howard H. Bell, "Negro Nationalism in the 1850s," *Journal of Negro Education* (1966); Floyd J. Miller, "John B. Vashon, The Father of Black Nationalism," *Civil War History* (1971); Archie Epps, "A Negro Separatist Movement of the Nineteenth Century," *Harvard Review* (1966); Jane H. Pease and William H. Pease, "Black Power—The Debate in 1840," *Phylon* (1968); and Richard K. McMaster, "Henry Highland Garnett and the African Civilization Society," *Journal of Presbyterian History* (1970). Dated but still useful is Henry M. Sherwood, "Paul Cuffee," *Journal of Negro History* (1923). Sympathetic but completely undocumented and curiously dogmatic is Victor Ullman, *Martin R. Delany and the Beginning of Black Nationalism* (1971).

On *black communal enterprises* in Canada see William H. Pease and Jane H. Pease, *Black Utopias* (1963). On the Negro convention movement, see Howard H. Bell, *A Survey of the Negro Convention Movement, 1830–1861* (1969) and William H. Pease and Jane H. Pease, "Negro Conventions and the Problems of Black Leadership," *Journal of Black Studies* (1971).

On *black antislavery* see George A. Levesque, "Black Abolitionists in the Age of Jackson," *Journal of Black Studies* (1970); Charles H. Wesley, *Richard Allen, Apostle of Freedom* (1935); William Still, *The Underground Railroad* (1872, 1968); Robert B. Toplin, "Peter Still versus The Peculiar Institution," *Civil War History* (1967); William E. Farrison, *William Wells Brown; Author and Reformer* (1969); Lerone Bennett, Jr., *Before the Mayflower* (1966); Richard Grau, "The Christiana Riot," *Journal of the Lancaster County Historical Society* (1964); Allen Peskin, ed. *North Into Freedom: The Autobiography of John Malvin, Free Negro, 1795–1880* (1966); and J. Reuben Sheeler, "The Struggle of the Negro in Ohio for Freedom," *Journal of Negro History* (1946).

On *Jim Crow discrimination* see Leon F. Litwack, *North of Slavery* (1961); Louis Ruchames, "Jim Crow Railroads in Massachusetts," *American Quarterly* (1956); and Harold B. Hancock, "Not Quite Men: The Free Negroes in Delaware in the 1830s," *Civil War History* (1971).

On *social thought and self-improvement* one of the best essays is Frederick Cooper, "Elevating the Race: The Social Thought of Black Leaders, 1827–1850," *American Quarterly* (1972). See also Richard W. Pih, "Negro Self-Improvement Efforts in Ante-Bellum Cincinnati, 1836–1850," *Ohio History* (1966); Dorothy Provine, "The Economic Position of Free Blacks in the District of Columbia, 1800–1860," *Journal of Negro History* (1973); and Jacqueline Halstead, "The Delaware Association for the Moral Improvement and Education of the Colored People," *Delaware History* (1972).

On *black institutions* see Carol V. R. George, *Segregated Sabbaths: Richard Allen and the Emergence of Independent Black Churches, 1760–1840* (1973); Daniel Perlman, "Organization of the Free Negroes in New York City, 1800–1860," *Journal of Negro History* (1971); Martin E. Dean, ed., *The Black Press 1827–1890* (1971); Dorothy Porter, "The Organized Educational Activities of Negro Literary Societies, 1828–1846," *Journal of Negro Education* (1936); Carter G. Woodson, *The Education of the Negro Prior to 1861* (1915, 1969); and Emma Lou Thornbrough, *The Negro in Indiana* (1957). Dated and condescending are Charles T. Hickok, *The Negro in Ohio* (1896) and Edward R. Turner, *The Negro in Pennsylvania* (1911).

On *Southern nonslave blacks* much of the older white scholarship is badly marred by racism and some of the older black studies are dated. Still useful are John Hope Franklin, *The Free Negro in North Carolina, 1790–1860* (1943); Carter G. Woodson, *Free Negro Owners of Slaves in the U.S. in 1830* (1925); Woodson, *Free Negro Heads of Families in the U.S. in 1830* (1925); Alice Dunbar Nelson, "People of Color in Louisiana, *Journal of Negro History* (1916); Part II, Ibid. (1917); Luther P. Jackson, *Free Negro Labor and Property Holding in Virginia, 1830–1869* (1942); and James H. Johnston's Ph.D. dissertation recently published but done over 30 years earlier, *Race Relations in Virginia and Miscegenation in the South* (1969). Studies that must be used with considerable caution are Charles S. Sydnor, "Free Negroes in Mississippi," *American Historical Review* (1927); James M. Wright, *The Free Negro in Maryland, 1634–1860* (1921); and John H. Russell, *The Free Negro in Virginia, 1619–1865* (1913). See also W. Harrison Daniel, "Southern Presbyterianism and the Negro in the Early National Period," *Journal of Negro History* (1973).

The *best of modern studies on Southern blacks* are Richard C. Wade, *Slavery in the Cities* (1964); Constance M. Green's book on Washington, *The Secret City* (1967); Edwin A. Davis and William R. Hogan, *The Barber of Natchez*

(1954); John Hope Franklin, "James Boon, Free Negro Artisan," *Journal of Negro History* (1945); Letitia W. Brown, *Free Negroes in the District of Columbia, 1790–1846* (1972); Edmund Berkeley, Jr. "Prophet Without Honor: Christopher McPherson, Free Person of Color," *Virginia Magazine of History and Biography* (1969); Roland C. McConnell, *Negro Troops of Ante-Bellum Louisiana* (1968); Donald J. Senese, "The Free Negro and the South Carolina Courts, 1790–1860," *South Carolina Historical Magazine* (1967); James B. Sellers, "Free Negroes of Tuscaloosa County Before the Thirteenth Amendment," *Alabama Review* (1970); and Sing-nan Fen, "Notes on the Education of Negroes in N. C. During the Civil War," *Journal of Negro Education* (1967). Difficult to classify and curious for deleting evidence of black resistance is James H. Brewer, *The Confederate Negro* (1969). See also H. E. Ster, *The Free Negro in Ante-Bellum Louisiana* (1972) and Joseph E. Walker, "A Comparison of Negro and White Labor in a Charcoal Iron Community," *Labor History* (1969).

On *blacks in early America* see Lorenzo J. Greene, *The Negro in Colonial New England* (1942, 1968); Thad W. Tate, *The Negro in Eighteenth Century Williamsburg* (1965); Winthrop D. Jordan, *White Over Black* (1968); Robert C. Twombley and Richard H. Moore, "Black Puritan: The Negro in Seventeenth Century Massachusetts," *William and Mary Quarterly* (1967); Benjamin Quarles, *The Negro in the American Revolution* (1961); and Silvio Bedini, *The Life of Benjamin Banneker* (1972).

On *blacks in the West* see Kenneth W. Porter, *The Negro on the Frontier* (1971); the more popular Phillip Durham and Everett L. Jones, *The Negro Cowboys* (1965); and E. Daniel and Annette Potts, "The Negro and the Australian Gold Rush, 1852–1857," *Pacific Historical Review* (1968).

For a useful bibliographical essay see Clarence L. Mohr, "Southern Blacks in the Civil War: A Century of Historiography," *Journal of Negro History* (1974).

Black Abolitionists*

Benjamin Quarles

. . . The black abolitionist phalanx was not just another group of camp followers. The Negro was, in essence, abolition's "different drummer." To begin with, his was a special concern; he felt that the fight against slavery was the black man's fight. Not all Negroes were abolitionists; far from it. But their general attitude was not incorrectly sensed by the British re-

---

former, John Scoble, after a first-hand observation: "The free people of color, with few exceptions, are true to their brethren in bonds," he wrote in 1853, "and are determined to remain by them whatever the cost." Although, as Scoble pointed out, the free Negroes felt a special kinship to the slave, their sense of concern was often rooted in a broad humanity: "I am opposed to slavery, not because it enslaves the black man, but because it enslaves *man*," wrote Daniel A. Payne in 1839. And to John Mercer Langston the abolitionist movement was designed not only for the liberation of the slave but for "the preservation of the American Government, the preservation of American liberty itself."

Aside from his varied role as a participant, the black abolitionist constituted a symbol of the struggle. Many of the Negro leaders in the crusade were former slaves, men and women who brought to the platform an experience that in its way was as eloquent, however broken the English, as the oratory of Wendell Phillips. Moreover, it was the Negro membership in the newer abolitionist movement of the Garrison years that marked one of its greatest differences with earlier abolitionist effort, one in which the Negro was regarded as a recipient of good works rather than as an expounder of the faith. And finally an account of the rich role of the Negro participant in the abolitionist crusade would add an element that heretofore has been incomplete or absent in the telling.

The chief reason for the neglect of the Negro abolitionist was the contemporary white media, which took its cue from the Southern press. In Southern thinking the abolitionists loomed large, almost to the point of obsession. But the abolitionists whom the Southerners paraded in such constant if disorderly array were, like so much else in the land of cotton, overwhelmingly of white hue. The white Southerner had to ignore the Negro as abolitionist wherever possible, for to do otherwise would have been to unhinge a cardinal tenet of the Southern faith—the concept of the contented slave and the impassive black. To picture the Negro as civic-minded, as a reformer, might arouse interest in him as a human being and sympathy for him as a figure battling against the odds. Outside the South this neglect of the Negro reformer was less studied but scarcely less prevalent. Indeed, white abolitionists, even those who would never have consciously borrowed anything from the South, would have been more than human had they not inclined to take at face value the ego-soothing role of exclusivity thrust upon them by the supporters of slavery. . . .

[*Black Underground Railroad Operators.*] Any balanced analysis of underground railroad operations must include its Negro workers. In Ohio, for example, black people were particularly active. Abolitionist leader James G. Birney noted in February 1837 that slaves were escaping in great numbers to Canada by way of Ohio. And, he added, "such matters are almost uniformly managed by the colored people. I know nothing of them generally till they are past." The fugitive slaves who made their way through Sandusky were aided almost wholly by the town's one hundred Negroes, led by a barbershop owner, Grant Richie. The state numbered not fewer than one hundred Negro underground railroad workers. In

Missouri the loose network included a cluster of all-Negro associations in St. Louis which sped the fugitive to Chicago and points north.[1]. . .

Of the variety of ways to assist fugitives, one in particular was suited to the Negro operator—that which entailed going into the South and making contact with those who were escape-minded. The slave was more likely to place his trust initally in a black face. Moreover, some Negro conductors were former slaves who were familiar with the territory in which they operated. Some of these secret returnees were willing to run this special risk in order to rescue their wives and children.

The most renowned of these black conductors was Harriet Tubman who, like Nat Turner, was given to dreams and to prayers. Herself an escapee from Dorchester County, Maryland, in 1849, she made some fifteen excursions into slave territory and brought back more than two hundred fugitives. Short and spare, she hardly looked like a person with a price on her head. But she was skillful in avoiding detection, her coolness in a tight spot matching her courage. To her abolitionist associates she became something of a legend, Thomas Wentworth Higginson calling her the greatest heroine of the age.[2]

A less noted and less lucky conductor was Leonard A. Grimes, a free Negro. Grimes became a hackman in Washington, D. C., eventually owning a number of horses and carriages, all as available for rescuing slaves as for conveying paying passengers. In one of his ventures in Virginia, his native state, he was seized after spiriting a slave family away in a hack. Grimes spent two years in the state prison at Richmond. He then went to Boston and became the pastor of the Twelfth Baptist Church. But, as in Washington, he neglected no opportunity to assist a runaway.

Most of the conductors whose names are lodged in record were based in the free states and hence were engaged in speeding the slave on his way rather than leading him out of the South. These "middlemen" included George L. Burroughs of Cairo, Illinois, whose job as a sleeping-car porter between Cairo and Chicago gave him an unusual opportunity for smuggling slaves. The most enterprising conductor in Salem, Ohio, was George W. C. Lucas, whose false-bottomed wagon conveyed fugitives to Cleveland, Sandusky, and Toledo.[3] At Elmira, New York, former slave John W. Jones secreted slaves in baggage cars bound for Canada.

For some black conductors the water was the freedom route. Slaves were carried across the Ohio on skiffs from Kentucky to Indiana. Negro crewmen might bring slaves aboard as stowaways on vessels leaving Southern ports and bound for the North. Elizabeth Barnes, who worked

---

[1] Birney to Tappan, Feb. 27, 1837, Dwight L. Dumond, ed., *Letters of James Gillespie Birney* (2 vols., New York, 1938), 1, 376. Benjamin G. Merkel, "The Underground Railroad and the Missouri Borders, 1840–1860," *Missouri Historical Review*, April 1943 (37), 278. Rush R. Sloane, "The Underground Railroad of the Fireland," *Magazine of Western History*, May 1888 (8), 38. E. Delorus Preston, Jr., "The Underground Railroad in Northwest Ohio," *Journal of Negro History*, October 1932 (17), 411.

[2] Earl Conrad, *Harriet Tubman* (Washington, D.C. 1943), 232. Mary Thatcher Higginson, ed., *Letters and Journals of Thomas Wentworth Higginson, 1846–1906* (New York, 1921), 81.

[3] Siebert, *Underground Railroad*, 70. Ibid., 296.

for a ship captain at Portsmouth, Virginia, hid slaves on vessels sailing for Boston and New Bedford. New Yorkers Edward Smith and Isaac Gansey of the schooner *Robert Centre* were charged by the Virginia Governor Thomas W. Gilmer with having abducted slave Isaac, and $3,000 was offered for their delivery to the jailer at Norfolk.[4]

Shipping slaves from one Northern port to another was far more common than the intersectional traffic, not to say less hazardous. James Ditcher piloted slaves along the Ohio from Portsmouth to Proctorville. Fugitive slaves were a common sight on the canal boat running from Cleveland to Marietta and owned by Negro abolitionist John Malvin.

It is to be noted that many runaways never left the cotton kingdom, taking refuge either in the towns or the swamp lands. Other slaves preferred Mexico as their destination. A letter from a "free, colored Floridian," in an abolitionist journal in October 1831, urged slaves to turn toward Mexico because of its convenient location, its mild climate, its generous land policy, and its freedom from color prejudice. But to the great majority of footloose slaves, the region above the Ohio River had one irresistible attraction that Mexico lacked—a substantial black population like themselves in language and outlook and one whose feeling of "sympatico" needed no proving. . . .

[*Black Vigilance Committees.*] Individual assistance to runaway slaves was supplemented by the work of vigilance committees, and here too the black people in the North played a distinctive role.[5] A vigilance committee aided the fugitives in a variety of ways—boarding and lodging them for a few days, purchasing clothing and medicine for them, providing them with small sums of money, informing them as to their legal rights and giving them legal protection from kidnapers. A primary function of the vigilance committee was to help a slave establish himself in a new location, to furnish him with letters of introduction, to help him find a job, and to give him guidance and protection while he was thus engaged in getting started. Hence a vigilance committee was a combination underground and upperground railroad, the latter comprising its efforts to help the slave locate within the United States. "The time has come to stop running," announced Jermain W. Loguen, manager of the Fugitive Aid Society of Syracuse.[6]

Many of the vigilance committees had a totally or predominantly Negro membership. The greatest of these Negro-run organizations was the New York Committee of Vigilance, founded in November 1835, with David Ruggles as its secretary and general agent. At its monthly meetings the committee listened to speakers like James Emerson, a seaman who had almost been sold into slavery after accepting work on a ship running to Petersburg, Virginia. Appearing at committee meetings were speakers

---

4 Wilbur Siebert, "The Underground Railroad in Massachusetts," *Proceedings of the American Antiquarian Society,* new series, 1936 (45), 29. Luther R. Marsh, ed., *Writings and Speeches of Alvan Stewart on Slavery* (New York, 1860), 219–20.

5 These abolitionist outfits are not to be confused with the horse-thief societies so common to the rural America of that day.

6 *Douglass' Paper,* Apr. 6, 1855.

like the wife of kidnaped Peter John Lee, her fatherless sons at her side.[7]

The committee listened to stories of colored children who had been hired as domestics and then carried into the South and sold. The committee publicized descriptions of missing Negroes, and informed its members as to the arrival and departure dates of ships suspected of harboring slaves. At one of its meetings three destitute Africans were introduced, with a plea for funds to help them return to their native land. On one occasion Isaac Wright told his story of being rescued by an agent of the committee after having been sold into slavery at New Orleans by the captain of the *Newcastle,* J. D. Wilson. It was through the committee that Wilson was arrested and detained for the illegal sale of Wright and two other Negro seamen. To attend a meeting of the Vigilance Committee tended to tear at the heart strings. At the annual meeting in 1837 at the Zion Church, Alvan Steward, founder in 1835 of the New York Anti-Slavery Society, was deeply moved by the strong emotions of gratitude expressed by the fugitives whom the committee had assisted. "I could almost submit to become a slave for the privilege of making such a friendship," he said to the gathering.[8]

Much of the success of the New York Committee of Vigilance could be credited to David Ruggles. "He is a General Marion sort of man," wrote a contemporary editor, "for sleepless activity, sagacity and talent." Ruggles personally gave assistance to hundreds of runaways. The case of Frederick Douglass was a typical one. Ruggles sheltered the young Douglass for nearly two weeks, made his marriage arrangements, and sent the newlyweds to New Bedford, Massachusetts, with a five-dollar bill and a letter of introduction to a locally prominent Negro, Nathan Johnson....

[*Black and White Relations.*] Social intermingling between whites and blacks in the abolitionist movement had its special perils. A few white abolitionists, troubled because their colored fellow workers faced discrimination in public places, made it a point to appear with them, courting their lot. Still fewer, like Theodore D. Weld, ate at Negro homes and attended their parties, weddings, and funerals. At the marriage of Weld and Angelina Grimké on May 14, 1838, Grace Douglass and Sarah M. Douglass were among the nearly fifty guests and Theodore S. Wright was one of the two clergymen offering prayers. But such conduct was as unpopular as it was uncommon. When the just-completed Pennsylvania Hall in Philadelphia was sacked and burned two days after the Weld-Grimké wedding, the newspapers charged the abolitionists with bringing it about by having Negroes seated side by side with whites at meetings and by condoning if not fostering interracial arm-in-arm walking in the streets adjacent to the building.[9]

The charge of social intermingling was emotion-laden and hence likely to lead to trouble. In the early days of the movement, abolitionism was

---

7 *Emancipator,* January 26, 1837. Ibid.

8 Wilson's arrest in *Colored American,* July 21, 1838. *Emancipator,* June 1, 1837.

9 *Liberator,* June 28, 1834.

synonymous with amalgamationism in the popular mind. Indeed, a white who worked for the repeal of an intermarriage law had as his real object, a Negro wife, ran a familiar bit of popular lore. It was unfounded. . . .

Even when they worked side by side, white and Negro abolitionists scarcely sustained a peer relationship. Whites tended to be paternalistic, reflecting a "father knows best" attitude. They tended to praise an above-average Negro almost to the point of eulogy, as if in surprise that he revealed any ability at all. And like the earlier abolitionists they were fond of giving advice to Negroes, their remarks interlarded with beatitudes.[10] The advice might have been good—certainly it was much like that given by Negro leaders themselves. But if one Negro criticized another for patronizing a Dan Rice minstrel show while ignoring a magic lantern exhibition on slavery being held in the same block, the whole thing somehow seemed freer of racial connotations.

The chief criticism against the white abolitionists by their black counterparts was their halfheartedness in carrying out the second of their twin goals—the elevation of the free Negro. Equal rights for Negroes was an essential corollary of abolitionism—improving the lot of the Northerners of color was a clearly stated goal. The Maine Union in Behalf of the Colored Race, formed in Portland in 1835, was a reflection of this outlook.[11] Aware of this dual commitment, nearly every abolitionist society had a special committee on the welfare of the free Negro. But in most instances this is about as far as it went—such committees, as a rule, simply did not function.

Hence, in this quarter the abolitionists were vulnerable. In their strong campaign against slavery in the South, "they half overlooked slavery in the North," wrote a Negro editor in 1839. The Negro people needed jobs, as their spokesmen constantly stressed. In 1831 Maria W. Stewart asked "several women" to hire colored girls. Abolitionists were asked to give Negro apprentices and mechanics an equal chance at least, and a preference if possible—their "being a neglected people." In an editorial that brought a flood of approving letters, an Albany weekly informed the white abolitionists that Negroes did not expect to ride in their carriages or sup at their parties, but they did hope that avenues of employment would be opened up by their alleged friends.[12]

Such thrusts, sharp as they were, brought few changes. Most white abolitionists simply did not think in terms of the workingman, white or

---

[10] See, for example, *Address of the People of Color in the City of New York, By Members of The Executive Committee of the American Anti-Slavery Society* (New York, 1834), 5–6.

[11] *Proceedings of the Convention which Formed the Maine Union in Behalf of the Colored Race* (Portland, 1835). Apparently this was a short-lived organization. Dwight L. Dumond's comprehensive compilation of printed antislavery literature, *A Bibliography of Antislavery in America* (Ann Arbor, 1961), lists a single entry for it.

[12] *Herald of Freedom*, June 1, 1839. *Liberator*, November 17, 1832. *Colored American*, September 1, 1838. *Northern Star and Freeman's Advocate*, March 3, 1842, and March 31, 1842.

colored. Men of great understanding in some things, they never seemed to fully sense that economic freedom was coequal with, if not basic too, all other freedoms.

To be sure, there were a few gestures by individuals and organizations. In isolated instances an abolitionist might employ a skilled Negro. Lewis Tappan, for example, paid Patrick H. Reason $70 to do a steel engraving of his brother, Benjamin. The Tappans were pleased with the product, and Lewis thought that the antislavery cause would be advanced if it were known that a Negro was capable of such craftsmanship. But, he added in his letter to Reason, "perhaps it will be best to wait until you have engraved two or three more before the secret is let out."[13]

Abolitionist organizations made some token efforts to help the black workingman. Following an address by Charles Lenox Remond in November 1837, the Rhode Island Anti-Slavery Society voted to aid Negroes to get jobs as clerks. *The Philanthropist,* organ of the Ohio society, made its office into a referral agency at which employers willing to take colored apprentices might leave their names and colored parents with sons to be apprenticed might follow suit.[14] . . .

[*Summary Statement.*] "Our National Sin has found us out," ran an editorial in *Douglass' Monthly* for May 1861. In this Old Testament sense, war had indeed come as sort of an atonement for a fall from grace, an act of redemption, no matter how untoward its expression. But in a sense less retributive and more peculiarly American, the Civil War was a phase of the continual striving for the goals for which this country had been conceived. The downfall of slavery would thus bring additional strength for the tasks ahead. Viewed in this light, the abolitionist crusade itself was but a continuing phase of the revolution of 1776, an attempt to put into practice the doctrine of man's essential equality.

"We have good cause to be grateful to the slave for the benefit we have received to *ourselves,* in working for *him,*" wrote Abby Kelley. "In striving to strike *his* chains off, we found, most surely, that *we* were manacled ourselves."[15] Miss Kelley's sentiment bespoke a largeness of mind and of spirit. But, written in 1838, it did not fully encompass the role of the black American in the abolitionist crusade. More than an unhappy pawn, he had known that he must work to forge his own freedom. And to this task he had brought special skills. The struggle to make man free was a grim business, but he was accustomed to grim businesses. The struggle to make men free might entail armed resistance, but he was crisis-oriented from birth. To the extent that America had a revolutionary tradition, he was its protagonist no less than its symbol.

---

13 Tappan to Reason, July 11, 1840, Tappan Papers, Library of Congress.

14 *Colored American,* November 25, 1837. *Philanthropist,* May 26, 1841.

15 "Anti-Slavery Album of Contributions from Friends of Freedom, 1834–1858," Manuscripts Div., Library of Congress.

Martin Delany and
Black Nationalism*
Howard H. Bell

Often, present-day black separatists look for ways to restore the balance of justice for centuries of oppression by penalizing the white man. Their counterparts a century ago looked often for a place beyond the borders of the United States where they might develop a powerful black nation, the products of which would compete economically with those of the slave South, and where the Negro's genius for politics and government would be unhampered by meddling whites.

Mindful always of their responsibility to those still in slavery, the Negro separatists of that era reasoned that uplift of the black race, whether in Canada, the Caribbean, Central America, or Africa would have a "reflex influence" on the plight of those still held in bondage and on those only partly removed from its curse in America. A black nation would in time accomplish the goals which an oppressed people could not accomplish for themselves. To support this thesis they pointed to such examples as the Puritans who had been unable to throw off the yoke of oppression in England until some of their number had braved the dangers of a new land and had established a viable government of their own. Of such conviction were Martin R. Delany and Robert Campbell, two black Americans who penetrated into the Egba and Yoruba areas of what is now western Nigeria in the search for a place where, in the Biblical language so meaningful to Americans of the mid-nineteenth century, "Ethiopia might stretch forth her hand." . . .

No one year can be singled out as the beginning of a new era in Negro interest in areas beyond the borders of the United States, but the birth of the government of Liberia in 1847 was significant. No longer to be considered only as a white man's attempt to siphon off the free black, Liberia now emerged as a black nation and therefore a place to which the Negro American could look with hope—even with pride. Henry Highland Garnet launched one of the most spectacular challenges to the philosophy of staying at home while black governments were being born, and black men could be building for a brighter future. In articles in *The North Star* for January 26 and March 2, 1849, he made it clear that he still opposed the American Colonization Society in its philosophy that the Negro could never rise to equality in America, but he was now ready to accept the long-suspect society's ministrations "to the land of my

---

* Howard H. Bell, Introduction to Martin R. Delany and Robert Campbell, *Search for a Place: Black Separatism and Africa, 1860* (Ann Arbor: University of Michigan Press, 1968). By permission of the publisher.

fathers," and like "Augustine" a decade earlier he would rather be free in lands beyond the borders than a slave in the United States. He now looked to Liberia to become a great commercial and political benefit to Africa, and he expected the new government to check the slave trade "by the diffusion of light and knowledge, and by turning the attention of the black traders to some other and honorable business, and by sweeping off the white ones as with the hands of an avenging God."

Garnet's new stand on emigration was followed by a feverish decade of proposals and counterproposals relating to emigration, always with the view that emigration and Negro nationalism went hand in hand. Information on politics and on the agricultural or horticultural potential of Liberia and news of educational advances in the new nation, which hitherto had always been rebuffed by the abolitionist press, now received a respectful hearing by at least some Negro editors; other blacks, especially the younger generation, put their new interest to practical account by trying their luck on foreign soil.

Martin R. Delany with his great pride in the black race was not slow to accept the new interest, and once having done so he became the embodiment of Negro separatism to the great discomfiture of those dedicated to leading the Negro into full equality in the United States. In 1852 he published a booklet entitled *The Condition, Elevation, Emigration, and Destiny of the Colored People of the United States*. Here he claimed credit for having planned at an earlier date an East African commercial-colonization project based on a transcontinental railway reaching from the Red Sea to the west coast. Now willing to suspend the original venture, so long as the black man got credit for the plan, he turned his attention to the more urgent need for developing a powerful and respected Negro nation in the tropics of the Western Hemisphere. But whether his interests lay in the American tropics early in the decade or in Africa in the latter part, he saw the need to develop a strong support from black America. He must change the philosophy which had bound the black man to the area where he could be a symbol of hope to the enslaved and a threat to the enslaver. He must persuade blacks to change an attitude which made them reluctant to lead in any venture, but willing to follow if the white man led the way. He must persuade Negro Americans that once the colored people got together in the American tropics they would be beyond the grasp of the United States. And above all he must persuade them that it was the will of God. He warned against resisting lest "[God's] protecting arm and fostering care . . . be withdrawn from us."

As to those who remained in bondage in America, Delany recognized that blacks must ever be mindful of their condition, but the "reflex influence" would be at work to mitigate ther plight. In his words "the redemption of the bondmen depends entirely upon the elevation of the freeman; therefore, to elevate the free colored people of America, anywhere upon this continent, forbodes the speedy redemption of the slaves." . . .

Thus, Delany and Garnet became rivals in an effort to explore within the Niger area. Delany had the formidable task of selecting capable members for the expedition, with no organizational backing for either men or money. Garnet had the support of the African Civilization Society, with access to money from interested whites. But if the two men were rivals, they still had much in common. Both had had an honorable career in efforts to improve the position of the blacks in America. Both had opposed emigration. Both had come to believe in emigration as a legitimate way of progress and to believe in a Negro nation. Both now looked to Africa as the land of promise.

Neither man expected miracles in planning for a home in Africa. They did not expect to lead a mass emigration. Both expected to develop small settlements of American blacks in Africa—people carefully chosen who would demonstrate Christianity, morality, and good character. They should have skills in agriculture, the mechanical arts, and commerce; they should come well recommended. It was expected that these enclaves of Americans would influence the people of Africa to accept their way of life. Meantime, the new community would raise cotton or other crops to compete with the American South and thus hasten the day when slavery would be no more. And if there were still slaves being put on board ship from Africa, that curse could also be eliminated by the influence of the new settlers.

Delany's unwillingness to use money from whites quickly got him into financial difficulties which Garnet's easier acceptance of proffered aid allowed him to avoid. In fact, it was Garnet's organization, the African Civilization Society, which put up the money necessary to send one of Delany's chosen colleagues on his way to Africa via England. This was, of course, without Delany's consent. The man in question was Robert Campbell. . . .

In reporting on their sojourn in Africa, whether in Liberia or in Egba-Yoruba area from Lagos to Ilorin, Delany seldom forgets his mission. He must develop a Negro nation. He must read into the record the achievement of the black man and his plans for the future, for white historians had deprived the Negro of his rightful place in history by simply failing to record the accomplishments of other groups than their own. He suffered for the race when he recounts how his young colleague had taken things into his own hands and had, in his estimation, sullied the banner of Negro nationalism by accepting money from, and thereby an obligation to, the African Civilization Society.

Delany reports courteous treatment at the hands of the Liberians, even though his fame as an opponent of the American Colonization Society's child had preceded him. He found it possible to explain his position to their satisfaction and his role as an emissary from American blacks to inspect the land for future settlement. . . .

On the way home the two explorers stopped off in England in May 1860 and were assured of the interest of Englishmen in developing the cotton industry in Africa. They were told that the African Aid Society would be at their service in exploiting the resources of the continent. What neither report records is that within a few months the African kings reneged on their treaty, the British government began to pressure the African Aid Society into withholding further succor for the would-be immigrants, and Delany made a kind of peace with the African Civilization

Society after he had dictated some modification of the constitution requiring that blacks be in command. By that time the American Civil War had begun, and the interest in Africa had to take second place in the lives, though perhaps not in the hearts, of men like Martin Delany. When he died in 1885, somewhat past the Biblical three score years and ten, he was once again involved in an enterprise concerning blacks beyond the borders of the United States.

Delany's report preserves information on the history of the separatist movement, culminating in the effort to transfer Christian black communities from America to Africa. Delany remained defensively aware of his own place in history and defensively aware of the Negro's struggle for recognition and fulfillment. . . .

[*The Modern and the Antebellum.*] . . . Black nationalist movements, separated by the Civil War and more than a century of unkept promises, have more in common than at first meets the eye. Both have elements of pride in race, which has been too often lacking among the oppressed. Both look to the Negro as the means of salvation, not only for Africa but also for America. Both are aggressively aware of black unity which scoffs at claims of white superiority, but is ready to accept black superiority. Both demand the fulfillment of economic and social equality. Both are disdainful of white-led, or even white-participating efforts at betterment of conditions for the Negro. Both demand black leadership for black projects.

Black nationalism of the 1960s is, however, better educated, more aggressive, more sophisticated, more ruthless than the Negro nationalism of the 1850s. Whitfield and Holly and Delany looked for a place where the black man might prove his capacity for government; the black nationalist of today is more likely to suggest that a substantial portion of the United States be assigned to Negroes for past misdeeds of the nation.

Perhaps one of the greatest differences, and one of the happiest, between the nationalists of the 1850s and those of today is the greater confidence which the twentieth century has brought to the black man. One cannot read Delany without being painfully aware of his great sense of hurt and frustration, but there were relatively few who believed him when he spoke of the great soul and the potentially great accomplishments of the blacks. Today there are literally millions of people in the United States and Africa who do believe what only the few believed about the black man's greatness a century ago.

This new confidence is in part due to the development of Africa during the intervening years. The Negro nationalists of the 1850s had to persuade themselves, and seek to persuade others, that their confidence in the black man would be vindicated. It is somewhat ironic that the "reflex influence" which was cited so often by Negro nationalists of the past century came to fruition only in the 1960s after Africa had suddenly spawned its independent members of the family of nations. It is even more ironic that, except for Liberia, the reflex influence came not from the emigrant American black men, but from the native population which had emerged to independence under the aegis of European powers.

Even though Delany and Campbell failed to lead many emigrants to

Africa, the back-to-Africa movement of the period should not be written off as inconsequential. There were in Africa at that time thousands of blacks who made their way back from the Western Hemisphere and had settled in Liberia, or Sierra Leone, or the Niger River area. They had come not only from the United States but from Latin America and British American areas as well.

This return to Africa was nationalistic, as portrayed in the lives of men like Delany and Campbell. It had a strong economic bent as demonstrated by a Negro emigrationist's reference to the meeting between Diogenes and Alexander the Great, when Diogenes had asked the great one to get out of his light: "We, too, asked this [of the whites] a long time; finding, however, they wouldn't mind us, we came around to the east, so as to get between them and the sun, and get the early sun on our sugar, coffee, and cotton, that by and by we may somewhat obstruct their view" (*African Repository*, February 1860, p. 56). Finally, the return to Africa was never devoid of the religious element. The bondage and redemption of the children of Israel had too many similarities to the later bondage and hopeful redemption of the blacks to escape notice. . . .

chapter 7

The Abolitionists Reconsidered

EXCEPT FOR OUTCASTS such as the blacks no other group in American history has been presented so frequently in a hostile context than the abolitionists. Until a generation ago only black writers and Marxist scholars maintained traditions of sympathetic consideration, and during the 1940s and 1950s only Richard Hofstadter's pioneer essay on Wendell Phillips, Irving H. Bartlett's splendid biography of Phillips, Russell B. Nye's capable account of Garrison, and a few other studies escaped the general hostility against the antislavery leadership. Avery O. Craven in 1939 described the abolitionists as "violent demagogues" who saw that "false propaganda took the place of truth" and made Southern masters do "scapegoat service for all aristocrats and sinners." William B. Hesseltine in 1948 dismissed the whole complex web of commitment and action as "mere humanitarian gabble," Craven indicated that Garrison badly needed psychiatric help, and one Hesseltine student, Hazel Wolf, announced in 1952 that the abolitionists were essentially sick men with "a mania for uniqueness and attention" as well as a "martyr complex" which caused them to "glory in persecution" and to compete vigorously in "bidding for a martyr's crown."

The abolitionists have been described by various scholars as gullible, naive, mistaken, dangerous, ignorant, self-righteous, inflexible, fanatical, dogmatic, vituperative, humorless, aggressive, and violent men, who succeeded only in arousing Southerners to militant counter-attacks, in riveting the chains of slavery more firmly to black men, and in providing one cause, possibly the major cause, of the mass slaughter of a "needless" Civil War. In a 1963 biography of Garrison, John L. Thomas explained Garrison in terms of "the longings of an authoritarian mind concerned with getting and using power over others" and placed much of the blame on the abolitionists for a Civil War "without any clear sense or purpose." As recently as 1969 David B. Davis presented a subtle and sophisticated version of the old themes of antislavery "irrationality" in

The Slave Power Conspiracy and the Paranoid Style. More than a few scholars argued that the "worst" of the abolitionists, men such as John Brown, really belonged in the insane asylum. So notable a modern scholar as C. Vann Woodward in 1960 seriously considered the theory of Brown's insanity and seemed to give at least limited credence to the idea.

David Donald leaned heavily upon mental pathology in the prize-winning and much lauded first volume of his Charles Sumner biography (1960) which left strewn on the psychological battlefield damaging images of emotional impotence, latent homosexuality and the sick escapism of a man who fled from his own neuroses into reform politics. "This holy, blissful martyr," a "specimen of prolonged and morbid juvenility," went armed in the political world with "unvarnished egotism" and the weapons of "moral terrorism." A few years earlier Donald had undertaken to expose true motives from the vantage point of consensus notions about "status politics." The radicals as descendents of old and once dominant Federalist families turned out to be a "displaced elite" without power or satisfactory political functions, men for whom "agitation allowed the only chance for personal and social fulfillment." When Lincoln finally emancipated the bondsmen he served as "the killer of the abolitionist dream" whose policies robbed the agitators of "the great crusade that had brought purpose and joy." (In *Charles Sumner and the Rights of Man*, 1970, Donald was not quite so overtly hostile.)

A different "social science" approach, which avoided the old cant about "neurotic" reformers, was presented in a chapter of Stanley Elkins' influential book on slavery. Elkins admired the British abolitionists who presumably used institutions such as the Church of England in the sober and responsible march to gradual abolition through modest, step-by-step reforms. By contrast the ultra-individualistic, guilt-ridden, and hopelessly anti-institutional American radicals preferred to passionately pursue grand abstractions rather than be effectual in advocating limited but possible reforms. Elkins' book appeared on the eve of a radical change in the direction of antislavery scholarship. During the 60s a number of able scholars set out to clear the debris of generations of hostile presentations and to reconsider the abolitionists with new perceptions and a new sympathy. Martin Duberman (Selection 1) in 1960 published the first important interpretative essay, a cautious but clearly sympathetic effort to indicate that many leaders in history display at some time in their lives elements of "pathological" conduct and that "healthy" minded persons (including radicals) might reasonably aim at distant goals requiring the maintenance of inner tensions. Duberman, asserting that past psychological generalizations lacked credibility because so little was known about many abolitionists, discussed his own research into the life of the most unneurotic, warm, witty, confident, and happily married James Russell Lowell and suggested that studies of other abolitionists would make the inadequacies of the old stereotypes increasingly apparent.

Duberman's observations were borne out by significant new books and articles on Thomas Wentworth Higginson, the Grimké sisters, James

Russell Lowell, Franklin Giddings, Benjamin Lundy, William Lloyd Garrison, Wendell Phillips, Lewis Tappan, John Brown, Owen Lovejoy, John P. Hale, John G. Palfrey, and others. The new biographical data about abolitionists made it possible to refute David Donald's status politics thesis. As early as 1959 Robert A. Skotheim listed a number of Donald's methodological weaknesses including an arbitrary definition of "leader," failure to list the "106 hard core leaders" for other scholars to check, generalizations about the entire movement from a study of only the leadership, refusal to consider men converted to the cause after 1838, and the lack of a nonabolitionist control group. Gerald Sorin made an even stronger case against Donald's theory in 1970 with a book on 100 Liberty Party leaders who had at least as much status as their fathers and appeared to be motivated by ideological commitment rather than by status anxieties or the need of disturbed persons to release inner tensions.

Howard Zinn (Selection 2) in 1965 examined the whole range of anti-abolitionist charges from extremism and emotionalism to irrationality and the agitator's distortions of the facts, and found them in the main to be arbitrary. Emotionalism as a neutral instrument could be attached to the best and the worst of human acts and that which gained the label of extreme in one era became conservative in another. (Even Garrison regarded black suffrage as an excess of reform in 1830.) Extremely evil institutions such as slavery demanded an extreme response and surely men of conscience should respond to the destruction of millions of human lives in bondage with considerable emotion.

In 1967 and 1972 Aileen S. Kraditor (Selection 3) from a different vantage point than Zinn or Duberman stressed institutions and tactics in the most systematic and effective critique of Elkins. She noted that Elkins presented Transcendentalist ultra-individualism and then illogically projected this ideology into the antislavery camp where at best it fitted a few men such as Stephen S. Foster. Most antislavery leaders actually sought to reform and purify institutions, abandoned them only when they could not be pulled toward the abolitionist cause, and then returned to churches, political factions, and the Federal Union itself when these entities served the interests of human freedom. The Garrisonians, she insisted, could not follow the path of either English abolitionists or American humanitarian reformers who pursued gradualist, piecemeal reform through existing institutions. Because the American abolitionists faced a nation flawed at the center by slavery and racism and wished to thoroughly restructure the national society, the Garrisons had to treat slavery as a moral issue, assault existing institutions, deal heavily in abstractions and grope for revolutionary solutions. Moreover, guilt had an objective reference and "the anomaly of the most rigidly institutionalized form of slavery existing within the most fluid, least institutionalized social structure had to make slavery wrong to those who took their Declaration of Independence seriously." Just as in the case of the anti-Nazi Germans during the 1930s guilt was a realistic response and in both cases the dissenters rather than the phlegmatic majority merited the censure of scholars. Tilden G. Edelstein agreed that "in

times of social injustice it may be the inactive individual, not the reformer, who is mentally disturbed."

Many of the modern revisionists such as Zinn and Duberman had
clearly gone to school not only in the Nazi era but also in the struggles for
black freedom and for peace in their own times. Zinn called his book on
the civil rights struggle, *SNCC: The New Abolitionists;* Bertram Wyatt-
Brown traced the ideological foundations of nonviolent confrontation
from Garrison to Tolstoy to Ghandi to King; and Carlton Mabee drew similar parallels in his study of the nonviolent abolitionists. In the works of
many scholars the abolitionists emerged with a new importance and dignity and in 1972 William H. Pease and Jane H. Pease, once fairly skeptical about the abolitionists and still in doubt about the Garrisonians, portrayed both radicals and moderates of the 1850s as very essential and
effective disturbers of the political peace. The Peases noted that "when the
reality of events run counter to the moral imperative of an era, reasonable
men join fanatics in rejecting quiet argument for more vigorous action."
Many scholars insisted that the large accomplishments of the abolitionists
in antebellum times as well as during Civil War and Reconstruction be-
lied the charges of Elkins and his supporters. In 1968 Merton L. Dillon,
who had written a decade earlier about the "failure" of antislavery, asserted that historians now generally regard the abolitionists as "important
historical figures worthy of respect and admiration rather than as fanatics and irresponsible agitators."

The new wave of sympathy for the abolitionists touched even the old
revolutionary John Brown who became during the 1960s a frequent topic
of scholarly discussion as well as a political symbol to both white and
black radicals. In more than a century since Brown's death the numerous
biographies, except one by the black scholar DuBois and a second by an
aging abolitionist, had been hostile and during the last generation the
best known authority on Brown, James Malin of Kansas, devoted a large
part of his scholarly life to the denigration of the antislavery rebel. Stephen B. Oates in a carefully researched and brilliantly written biography
of 1970 carefully examined the old myths and rejected nearly all of them.
In the final analysis, however, the book was not a work in the tradition
of Zinn and Duberman, and Oates kept his distance from Brown. It was
in a brief essay by Louis Ruchames (Selection 4) that Brown received
fully sympathetic consideration as a revolutionary leader in a desperate
struggle and in a historical context which called for revolutionary tactics
and men.

At a moment when a positive historical judgment on the antislavery
cause seemed close to complete triumph, several scholars presented evidence on racism in the movement, on a common refusal to employ and
to associate closely with blacks, and on a tendency to treat the black man
as innately inferior and to meet him with regal paternalism, condescension, or scorn. James M. McPherson made an early attempt to defend the
abolitionists on the charge in an explanation limited in its persuasiveness
because of McPherson's narrow and naive working definition of racism.
To date no scholar has dealt satisfactorily with this interpretative prob-

lem. On the heels of the charges about racism, the climate of opinion which had given birth to a reconsideration of abolitionists during the 1960s changed again as liberal and left hopes collapsed and the age of Nixon arrived. In 1971 C. Vann Woodward described "the Northern crusade against slavery" as "corrupted and frustrated . . . by an old sickness endemic among the crusaders" and raised the spectre of the presumably long buried "needless war" doctrine of the 1930s by suggesting that "it also seems rather more difficult than it was before to be confident in justifying the sacrifice of those 600,000 lives." Even more useful as an intellectual barometer for the 70s were two essays in 1973 by Bertram Wyatt-Brown, one accepting several of the hostile charges made by Stanley Elkins in 1959 and the other expressing some distaste for the "strangely sterile . . . accepted canon" of modern antislavery scholarship which revealed "an unwillingness to accept the integrity of the past." (The last phrase often served as a key to much conservative writing of the 1960s.) In brief, it seems likely that the abolitionists will get more unsympathetic attention in the mid and late 70s unless dominant political opinion changes substantially.

A major work which did not spring from neoconservative sensibilities but which did suggest new directions for scholarship on the abolitionist movement was Leonard L. Richards' monograph of 1970 (Selection 5) about the mobs of the 1830s against antislavery people and blacks. Richards used and extended insights of the 1960s in carefully demonstrating the pervasiveness of violence during the Jacksonian era, in proving many of the mob leaders to be "gentlemen of property and standing," and in revealing the fact that these highly placed instigators of violence often attacked abolitionists as general threats to the standing social and political order, the family, and even male dominance. Richards departed from the main trends of the 1960s by using so many of the approaches and techniques of the new social history. He stressed sociological and psychological issues rather than political factions, abandoned narrative for analytical history, and relied heavily on quantitative methods to establish generalizations. *Gentlemen of Property and Standing* may well represent the wave of the future in antislavery studies.

BIBLIOGRAPHY

Works Discussed in This Chapter*

Bartlett, Irving H., *Wendell Phillips, Brahmin Radical* (1961).

Craven, Avery O., *The Repressible Conflict* (1939).

Davis, David B., *The Slave Power Conspiracy and the Paranoid Style* (1969).

Dillon, Merton L., "The Abolitionists: A Decade of Historiography, 1959–1969," *Journal of Southern History* (1969).

Donald, David, *Charles Sumner and the Coming of the Civil War* (1960), "Toward a Reconsideration of the Abolitionists," in *Lincoln Reconsidered* (1956), and *Charles Sumner and the Rights of Man* (1970).

---

* In this rather long list, Craven, Hesseltine, Wolf, and Malin represent the older hostility toward the abolitionists and Woodward, Donald, Elkins, Thomas and Davis, are the modern skeptics. The other writers are generally sympathetic.

Duberman, Martin, "The Abolitionist and Psychology," *Journal of Negro History* (1962).

DuBois, W. E. B., *John Brown* (1909).

Edelstein, Tilden G., *Strange Enthusiasm: A Life of Thomas Wentworth Higginson* (1968).

Elkins, Stanley, *Slavery* (1959).

Hesseltine, William B., *Lincoln and the War Governors* (1949).

Hofstadter, Richard, "Wendell Phillips," in *The American Political Tradition* (1948).

Kraditor, Aileen, *Means and Ends in American Abolitionism: Garrison and His Critics on Strategy and Tactics* (1969), and "A Note on Stanley Elkins and the Abolitionists," *Civil War History* (1967).

Mabee, Carlton, *Black Freedom: The Non-Violent Abolitionists From 1830 Through The Civil War* (1970).

McPherson, James M., *The Struggle for Equality: Abolitionists and the Negro in Civil War and Reconstruction* (1964).

Malin, James C., *John Brown and the Legend of the Fifty-six* (1942).

Nye, Russell B., *William Lloyd Garrison and the Humanitarian Reformers* (1955).

Oates, Stephen B., *To Purge This Land With Blood: A Biography of John Brown* (1970).

Pease, William H., and Pease, Jane H., "Confrontation and Abolition in the 1850s," *Journal of American History* (1972).

Richards, Leonard L., *Gentlemen of Property and Standing: Anti-Abolitionist Mobs in Jacksonian America* (1970).

Ruchames, Louis, *A John Brown Reader* (1959).

Skotheim, Robert A., "A Note on Historical Method," *Journal of Southern History* (1959).

Sorin, Gerald, *The New York Abolitionists* (1970), and *Abolitionism, A New Perspective* (1972).

Thomas, John L., *The Liberator: A Biography of William Lloyd Garrison* (1963).

Woodward, C. Vann, "John Brown's Private War," in *The Burden of Southern History* (1960, 1968), and *American Counterpoint* (1971).

Wyatt-Brown, Bertram, "Abolitionism: Its Meaning for Contemporary American Reform," *Midwest Quarterly* (1966), "Stanley Elkins' Anti-Slavery Interpretation Re-examined," *American Quarterly* (1973), a review-essay in *The American Historical Review* (April 1973), and "New Leftists and Abolitionists: A Comparison of American Radical Styles," *Wisconsin Magazine of History* (1970).

Zinn, Howard, "Abolitionists, Freedom-Riders and the Tactics of Agitation," in Martin Duberman, ed., *The Anti-Slavery Vanguard* (1965), and *SNCC: The New Abolitionists* (1964).

Suggested Readings

For three brief and useful *anthologies* see Richard O. Currey, ed., *The Abolitionists* (1973); Hugh Hawkins, ed., *The Abolitionists: Means, Ends, and Motivations* (2d ed., 1972); and Louis Ruchames, ed., *The Abolitionists* (1963). For an excellent collection of documents see William H. and Jane H. Pease, eds., *The Anti-Slavery Argument* (1965).

For materials on *comparative antislavery* see Christine Bolt, *The Anti-Slavery Movement: A Study in Anglo-American Cooperation, 1833–1877*

(1969); Betty Fladeland, *Men and Brothers: Anglo-American Anti-Slavery Co-operation* (1973); Robert B. Toplin, "The Specter of Crisis: Slaveholder Reaction to Abolitionism in the U.S. and Brazil," *Civil War History* (1972); and Claude Levy, "Slavery and the Emancipation Movement in Barbados, 1650–1833," *Journal of Negro History* (1970).

Several important works on the *Garrisonians* are Robert D. Marcus, "Wendell Phillips and American Institutions," *Journal of American History* (1969); James B. Stewart, "Peaceful Hopes and Violent Experiences: The Evolution of Reforming and Racial Abolitionism, 1830–1837," *Civil War History* (1971); Stewart, "The Aims and Impact of Garrisonian Abolitionism, 1849–1860," *Civil War History* (1969); Robert H. Abzug, "The Influence of Garrisonian Abolitionist Fear of Slave Violence on the Anti-Slavery Arguments, 1829–1840," *Journal of Negro History* (1970); and Lewis Perry, *Radical Abolitionism: Anarchy and the Government of God in Anti-Slavery Thought* (1973).

On the *origins of antislavery* see Bertram Wyatt-Brown, "Prelude to Abolitionism: Sabbatarian Politics and the Rise of the Second Party System," *Journal of American History* (1971); Walter M. Merrill, ed., *The Letters of William Lloyd Garrison, I Will Be Heard, 1822–1835*, Vol. I (1971); Louis Ruchames, ed., *The Letters of William Lloyd Garrison, A House Divided Against Itself, 1836–1840*, Vol. II (1971); Bernard Rosenthal, "The Puritan Conscience and New England Slavery," *New England Quarterly* (1973); Bruce Rosen, "Abolition and Colonization . . . 1829–1834," *Phylon* (1972); Ferenc M. Sasz, "Ante-Bellum Appeals to 'Higher Law'," *Essex Institute Historical Collections* (1974); Arthur Zilversmit, *The First Emancipation: The Abolition of Slavery in the North* (1968); David B. Davis, cited later; Winthrop D. Jordan, *White over Black* (1968); and Donald L. Robinson, *Slavery in the Structure of American Politics, 1676–1820* (1971).

On *religion and slavery* see Donald G. Mathews, *Slavery and Methodism* (1965).

For a pro-Elkins work on *ideology* see William H. Pease and Jane H. Pease, *The Anti-Slavery Argument* (1965).

On *Southern antislavery* see Gordon Finnie, "The Anti-Slavery Movement in the Upper South Before 1840," *Journal of Southern History* (1969).

On the *abolitionists in Civil War and reconstruction,* see McPherson above and Willie Lee Rose, *Rehearsal for Reconstruction; The Port Royal Experiment* (1964).

On *black and white* see Chap. 6 and William H. Pease and Jane H. Pease, "Ends, Means and Attitudes: Black and White Confrontation in the Anti-Slavery Movement," *Civil War History* (1972).

In no other field of American history have so many *biographies* of note been written in so short a time period. See Martin Duberman, *James Russell Lowell* (1966); Edelstein and Oates listed earlier; Gerda Lerner, *The Grimké Sisters From South Carolina: Rebels Against Slavery* (1969); James B. Stewart, *Joshua R. Giddings and the Tactics of Radical Politics* (1970); Bertram Wyatt-Brown, *Lewis Tappan and the Evangelical War Against Slavery* (1969); Jane H. Pease and William H. Pease, *Bound With Them in Chains: A Biographical History of the Anti-Slavery Movement* (1973); Merton L. Dillon, *Benjamin Lundy and the Struggle for Negro Freedom* (1966); Richard H. Sewall, *John P. Hale and the Politics of Abolition* (1965); Edward Magdol, *Owen Lovejoy, Abolitionist in Congress* (1967); Edmund Fuller, *Prudence Crandell* (1971); Betty Fladeland, *James Gillispie Birney: Slaveholder to Abolitionist* (1955); and Frank O. Gatell, *John Gorham Palfrey and the New England Conscience* (1963).

More works of note on *John Brown* are Richard O. Boyer, *The Legend of John Brown* (1973); Betty L. Mitchell, "Massachusetts Reacts to John Brown's Raid," *Civil War History* (1973); Benjamin Quarles, *Allies for Freedom: Blacks and John Brown* (1974); and Truman Nelson, *The Old Man: John Brown at Harper's Ferry* (1973).

For several interesting *Northern antislavery* works see Thomas D. Morris, *Free Men All, The Personal Liberty Laws of the North: 1780–1861* (1973); and Thomas Graham, "Harriet Beecher Stowe and the Question of Race," *New England Quarterly* (1973).

There are many *selected scholarly works* for the period 1949–1965. For a regional study see Lawrence Lader, *The Bold Brahmins: New England's War Against Slavery, 1831–1863* (1961). Larry Gara, *The Liberty Line: The Legend of the Underground Railroad* (1961) demonstrated that much of the rescue work was actually in the hands of blacks. The indispensable book for ideas, interpretations, and new insights, *The Antislavery Vanguard* (1965), edited by Martin B. Duberman, contains an important essay by Duberman on "The Northern Response to Slavery." A widely used narrative history of the movement is Louis Filler, *The Crusade Against Slavery* (1960). For a discussion of the great variety of persons involved in the antislavery movement see Betty Fladeland, "Who Were the Abolitionists" *Journal of Negro History* (1964).

The most useful bibliographies are in McPherson and Filler, both cited earlier. On the Negro in antislavery, see the essays by Leon F. Litwack and James M. McPherson in the Duberman anthology cited earlier; Litwack, *North of Slavery* (1961); Howard H. Bell, "National Negro Convention of the Middle 1840's: Moral Suasion vs. Political Action," *Journal of Negro History* (1957); and "Expressions of Negro Militancy in the North, 1840–1860," *Journal of Negro History* (1960). For several recent and important accounts of developments within the antislavery movement, see David B. Davis, "The Emergence of Immediatism in British and American Antislavery Thought," *Mississippi Valley Historical Review* (1962) and John Demos, "The Antislavery Movement and the Problem of Violent Means," *New England Quarterly* (1964). David A. Williams provided an interesting account of changing scholarly opinion on Garrison; see "William Lloyd Garrison, the Historians, and the Abolition Movement," *Essex Institute Historical Collections* (1962).

For information on the attempt of abolitionists to gain greater consistency by extending the freedom struggle to the North see Leonard W. Levy and Harlan B. Phillips, "The Roberts Case: Source of the 'Separate by Equal' doctrine," *American Historical Review* (1951) and Louis Ruchames, "Race and Education in Massachusetts," *Negro History Bulletin* (1949). On the last remnants of antislavery activity in the South, see Fletcher M. Green, "Northern Missionary Activities in the South, 1846–1861," *Journal of Southern History* (1955). Maryland was a microcosm of the divided and changing nation as Charles L. Wagandt indicated in *The Mighty Revolution: Negro Emancipation in Maryland* (1964). On abolition and civil rights in a Northern state, see Stanley I. Kutler, "Pennsylvania Courts, The Abolition Act, and Negro Rights," *Pennsylvania History* (1963). The decline of antislavery in the South was charted by Kenneth M. Stampp in "The Fate of the Southern Antislavery Movement," *Journal of Negro History* (1943). For a general discussion of the emancipation question in the North and the South, see Edgar A. Toppin, "Negro Emancipation in Historical Retrospective: Ohio," *Journal of Human Relations* (1963). Gilman M. Ostrander wrote a good summary of the dramatic response of New England intellectuals to John Brown, see "Emerson, Thoreau, and John Brown," *Mississippi Valley Historical Review* (1953). For a rare example of mass emancipation and resettlement see Ralph L. Ketcham, "The Dictates of Conscience: Edward Coles and Slavery," *Virginia Quarterly Review* (1960). See also David B. Davis, *The Problem of Slavery in Western Culture* (1966).

Abolitionist Motives and Personalities*

Martin B. Duberman

Out of their heightened concern with the pressing question of Negro rights, a number of historians, especially the younger ones, have begun to take a new look at the abolitionists, men who in their own day were involved in a similar movement of social change. About both them and ourselves we are asking anew such questions as the proper role of agitation, the underlying motives of both reformers and resistants, and the useful limits of outside interference. From this questioning a general tendency has developed to view the abolitionists in a more favorable light than previously. As yet, however, it is a tendency only, and hostility to the abolitionists continues to be strong among historians. . . .

With barely a redeeming hint of uncertainty, many historians list a group of "similar traits" which are said to characterize all abolitionists: "impractical," "self-righteous," "fanatical," "humorless," "vituperative," and,—if they are very modern in their terminology—"disturbed." The list varies, but usually only to include adjectives equally hostile and denunciatory. The stereotype of the "abolitionist personality," though fluid in details, is clear enough in its general outlines.

But did most abolitionists really share these personality traits? The fact is, we know much less about the individuals involved in the movement than has been implied. Some of the major figures, such as Joshua Leavitt, have never received biographical treatment; others—the Tappans, Edmund Quincy, and Benjamin Lundy, for example—badly need modern appraisal. And the careers and personalities of the vast majority of significant secondary figures—people like Lydia Maria Child, Sidney Gay, Maria Weston Chapman, Henry B. Stanton, and Abby Kelley Foster

---

* Martin Duberman, "The Abolitionists and Psychology," *Journal of Negro History* (1962). This is a slightly revised version of Duberman's "The Abolitionists and Psychology." Among the footnotes in the original article were references to Gordon W. Allport, *Becoming, Basic Considerations for a Psychology of Personality* (1960); Philip Rieff, *Freud: the Mind of the Moralist* (1959); O. Hobart Mowrer, "Psychiatry and Religion," *Atlantic Monthly* (1961); Erich Fromm, *Psychoanalysis and Religion* (1959).

—have been almost totally unexplored. Whence comes the confidence, then, that allows historians to talk of "the abolitionist personality," as if this had been microscopically examined and painstakingly reconstructed?

Certainly the evidence which we do have does not support such confident theorizing. In order to adhere to this conceptual straitjacket, it is necessary to ignore or discount much that conflicts with it—the modesty of Theodore Weld, the wit of James Russell Lowell, the tender humanity of Whittier, the worldly charm of Edmund Quincy. This does not mean that we need leap to the opposite extreme and claim all abolitionists were saints and seraphs. But if some of them were disagreeable or disturbed, we want, instead of a blanket indictment, to know which ones and in what ways; we want some recognition of the variety of human beings who entered the movement. . . .

. . . Let the evidence at least precede the judgment. And let us also show a decent timidity in applying the label "neurotic." Psychiatrists, dealing with a multitude of evidence and bringing to it professional insights, demonstrate more caution in this regard than do untrained historians working with mere traces of personality. If the disposition to be hostile exists, "neurosis" can almost always be established. Under the Freudian microscope, it would be a rare man indeed whose life showed no evidence of pathological behavior. (Think, for one, of the admirable William James, who, as his devoted biographer, Ralph Barton Perry, has shown, was subject to hypochondria, hallucinations, and intense oscillations of mood.) . . . I mean . . . to warn that, given the double jeopardy of a hostile commentator and the weight of a hostile historical tradition, we must take special precaution not to be too easily convinced by the "evidence" of neurosis in the abolitionists.

And even were we to establish the neurotic component of behavior, the story would certainly not be complete. To know the pathological elements in an individual's behavior is not to know everything about his behavior. To say that Garrison, in his fantasy world, longed to be punished and thus deliberately courted martyrdom, or that Wendell Phillips, alienated from the "new order," sought to work out his private grievances against the industrial system by indirectly attacking it through slavery is hardly to exhaust their range of possible motives. We know far too little about why men do anything—let alone why they do something as specific as joining a reform movement—to assert as confidently as historians have, the motives of whole groups of men. . . .

. . . Gordon Allport . . . summarizing current opinion, suggests that behavior does not result solely from the need to reduce tension, but may also aim (especially in a "healthy" person) at distant goals, the achievement of which can be gained only by maintaining tension. . . . His hypotheses are at least suggestive as regards the abolitionists, for their motives, rather than being solely the primitive ones of eliminating personal tension (under the guise of ethical commitment), may also have included a healthy willingness to bear tension (in the form of ostracism, personal danger and material sacrifice) in order to persevere in pursuit of long-range ideals.

Acceptance of these suggestions runs into the massive resistance of neo-Freudian cynicism. How old-fashioned, it will be said, to talk in terms of "ideals" or "conscience," since these are only unconscious rationalizations for "darker" drives which we are unable to face. How old-fashioned, too, to talk as if men could exercise choice in their conduct, since all our behavior is determined by our antecedents.

But the surprising fact is that such views are not old-fashioned. On the contrary, they have recently returned to favor in psychoanalytical circles. Increasing dissatisfaction with the ability of behaviorist theory fully to explain human action has led to a reconsideration of the role of reason and the possibilities of purposive, deliberate behavior. The result is the influential new school of "ego psychology," which views man as endowed with a considerable margin of freedom and responsibility, and which has restored to the vocabulary such "old fashioned" terminology as character, willpower, and conscience. Moral earnestness, moreover, is no longer equated with self-deception. As Allport has said, the very mark of maturity "seems to be the range and extent of one's feeling of self-involvement in abstract ideals." Some of these new emphases had been prefigured in the work of such philosophers as Sartre, who have long stressed social action as a sign of "authenticity" in man. . . .

. . . A connection between inner problems and outer convictions probably always exists to some degree. But an individual's public involvement is never completely explained by discussing his private pathology. Yet it is just this that historians have frequently done, and to that degree, they have distorted and devalued the abolitionist commitment. . . .

. . . [James Russell Lowell's] history seems to me convincing proof that at least some people became abolitionists not primarily out of an unconscious need but rather from deliberate, rational commitment to certain ethical values—recognizing, as I have said, that the two are never wholly unrelated. Lowell's active life as a reformer came during the period of his greatest contentment—secure in a supremely happy marriage, and confident of his talents and his future. His contemporaries agree in describing him as a gay, witty, warm man, without serious tensions or disabling anxieties. I have come across so little evidence of "pathology" in the Lowell of these years that when the standard picture of the abolitionist as a warped eccentric is applied to him, it becomes absurd.

And he *was* an abolitionist, though various arguments have been used to deny this. Lowell, it has been said, came to the movement late—and only at the instigation of his bride, Maria White, who was a confirmed reformer; he never fully committed himself to abolition, and finally left the ranks in the early 1850s. There may be some justice to these charges, but on the whole the argument is not persuasive. Given Lowell's youth (he was born in 1819) he could not have joined the movement much earlier than he did (which was around 1840), and there is evidence that he was involved in the cause before he met Maria White. The important point is that for roughly ten years he was unquestionably a serious abolitionist, both as an active member of the Massachusetts Anti-Slavery Society, and as a frequent contributor to abolitionist periodicals. The reasons for his drifting out of the movement are complex, but turn largely on the fact that his wife's death in 1853 destroyed the structure of his life and left him apathetic to public issues. (Might not this give added weight to the argument that it takes a reasonably contented man to interest himself in the problems of others?)

Even when it is admitted that Lowell was an abolitionist, he is dismissed as not having been a "typical" one. But who was the typical abolitionist? . . .

. . . We know so little about the individual personalities and careers of the majority of abolitionists that it seems like putting the cart before the horse to even talk about a composite portrait. Certainly the one which is now commonly accepted ("impractical"; "self-righteous," etc.) fails adequately to describe many of the abolitionists about whom we do have information. I mean here not only Lowell, but a number of others. What I have seen in my researches into papers of people like Edmund Quincy, Lydia Maria Child, or Maria Weston Chapman (to name only a few of the more prominent), has created the strong suspicion in my mind that if their personalities were to be investigated in depth, they too would be found to deviate from the accepted portrait in so many significant ways as further to undermine its reliability. . . .

Opinions will continue to differ as to the best way of achieving desired social change. Our own generation's confrontation with segregation has made this clear. Many of us feel as strongly about the evil of that practice as the abolitionists did about the institution of slavery. Like them, too, we have scant faith in Southern voluntarism or the benevolent workings of time; patience and inactivity have not done their work. Naturally we would like to believe that our sense of urgency comes from concern for the Negro rather than from a need to escape from some private torment of our own. Because of this we are admittedly prone to credit our historical counterparts with the kind of good motives we would like to impute to ourselves. Our wish to think well of them may account for our doing so. But as Erich Fromm has said, "the fact that an idea satisfies a wish does not mean necessarily that the idea is false." There is much in the new psychology to encourage the belief that the idea is not false. At any rate, if we are to find out, we need less dogma, more research, and a chastening sense of wonder at the complexities of human nature.

The Tactics of Agitation*

Howard Zinn

Few groups in American history have taken as much abuse from professional historians as that mixed crew of editors, orators, runaway slaves, free Negro militants, and gun-toting preachers known as the abolitionists. Many laymen sympathetic to the Negro have been inspired by Garrison, Phillips, Douglass, and the rest. Scholars, on the other hand (with a few exceptions), have scolded the abolitionists for their immoderation, berated them for their emotionalism, denounced them for bringing on the Civil War, or psychoanalyzed them as emotional deviates in need of recognition.

It is tempting to join the psychological game and try to understand what it is about the lives of academic scholars which keeps them at arm's length from the moral fervor of one of history's most magnificent crusades. Instead, I want to examine in fact the actions of the abolitionists, to connect them with later agitators against racial exclusiveness, and try to assess the value of "extremists," "radicals," and "agitators" in the bringing of desired social change.

At issue are a number of claims advanced by liberal-minded people who profess purposes similar to the radical reformers, but urge more moderate methods. To argue a case too heatedly, they point out, provokes the opponent to retaliation. To urge measures too extreme alienates possible allies. To ask for too much too soon results in getting nothing. To use vituperative language arouses emotions to a pitch which precludes rational consideration. To be dogmatic and inflexible prevents adjustment to rapidly changing situations. To set up a clash of extremes precipitates sharp conflict and violence.

All of these tactical sins, adding up to immoderation, extremism, impracticality, have been charged, at different times, by different people, to the American abolitionists. . . .

THE ABOLITIONISTS

There is no denying the anger, the bitterness, the irascibility of the abolitionists. William Lloyd Garrison, dean of them all, wrote in blood in the columns of the *Liberator* and breathed fire from speakers' platforms all over New England. He shocked people: "I am ashamed of my country." He spoke abroad in brutal criticism of America: "I accuse the

---

* Howard Zinn, "Abolitionists, Freedom-Riders and the Tactics of Agitation," in Martin Duberman, *The Anti-Slavery Vanguard* (1965). Reprinted by permission of the Princeton University Press. Copyright 1965 by the Princeton University Press.

land of my nativity of insulting the majesty of Heaven with the greatest mockery that was ever exhibited to man." He burned the Constitution before several thousand witnesses on the lawn at Framingham, calling it "source and parent of all other atrocities—a covenant with death and an agreement with hell" and spurred the crowd to echo "Amen!" . . .

Gradualism was not for [Wendell] Phillips. "No sir, we may not trifle or dally. . . . Revolution is the only thing, the only power, that ever worked out freedom for any people." The piety of New England did not intimidate him: "The American church—what is it? A synagogue of Satan." He scorned patriotic pride: "They sell a little image of us in the markets of Mexico, with a bowie knife in one side of the girdle, and a Colt's revolver in the other, a huge loaf of bread in the left hand, and a slave whip in the right. That is America!"

Phillips did not use the language of nonresistance as did Garrison. On that same green where Garrison burned the Constitution, Phillips said: "We are very small in numbers; we have got no wealth; we have got no public opinion behind us; the only thing that we can do is, like the eagle, simply to fly at our enemy, and pick out his eyes." . . .

But even Garrison and Phillips seem moderate against the figure of John Brown, lean and lusty, with two wives and 20 children, filled with enough anger for a regiment of agitators, declaring personal war on the institution of slavery. . . . On his way to the gallows, after the raid on the Harpers Ferry arsenal in Virginia in the fall of 1859, he wrote: "I John Brown am now quite certain that the crimes of this guilty land will never be purged away; but with Blood."

The Negro abolitionist Frederick Douglass, newly freed from slavery himself and long a believer in "moral suasion" to free others, talked with John Brown at his home in 1847 and came away impressed by his arguments. Two years later, Douglass told a Boston audience: "I should welcome the intelligence tomorrow, should it come, that the slaves had risen in the South, and that the sable arms which had been engaged in beautifying and adorning the South, were engaged in spreading death and devastation." . . .

These are the extremists. Did they hurt or help the cause of freedom? Or did they, if helping this cause, destroy some other value, like human life, lost in huge numbers in the Civil War? To put it another way, were they a hindrance rather than a help in abolishing slavery? Did their activities bring a solution at too great a cost? . . .

WHAT IS EXTREMISM?

The first four pages of a well-known book on Civil War politics (T. Harry Williams, *Lincoln and the Radicals*) refers to abolitionists, individually and collectively, in the following terms: "radical . . . zealous . . . fiery . . . scornful . . . revolutionary . . . spirit of fanaticism . . . hasty . . . Jacobins . . . aggressive . . . vindictive . . . narrowly sectional . . . bitter . . . sputtering . . . fanatical . . . impractical . . . extreme."[1] Such words,

---

[1] T. Harry Williams, *Lincoln and the Radicals* (Madison, Wis., 1941), pp. 3–6.

in different degrees of concentration, are used by many historians in describing the abolitionists. . . .

"Extremist" carries a psychological burden when attached to political movements, which it does not bear in other situations. A woman who is extremely beautiful, a man who is extremely kind, a mechanic who is extremely skillful, a child who is extremely healthy—these represent laudable ideals. In politics, however, the label "extremist" carries unfavorable implications. It may mean that the person desires a change in the *status quo* which is more sweeping than that requested by most people. For instance, in a period when most people are willing to free the slaves, but not to enfranchise them, one wanting to give them equal rights would be considered an extremist. Or it may mean someone who urges a more drastic action to attain a goal shared by most people; that is, someone who advocates slave revolts (like John Brown) rather than compensated emancipation followed by colonization abroad (like Lincoln).

Yet, in any given political situation, there is a very large number of possible alternatives, both in desired goals and in the means of achieving them. The actual alternatives put forward in any one situation are usually much fewer than the total range of possibilities. And the most extreme suggestion put forward at the time will be labeled "extremist" even though it may be far less sweeping than other possible courses of action.

For instance, William Lloyd Garrison, looked upon both by his antagonists and by modern historians as an "extremist," did not seek goals as far reaching as he might have. He explained, around 1830, his stand for "immediate abolition" as follows: "Immediate abolition does not mean that the slaves shall immediately exercise the right of suffrage, or be eligible to any office, or be emancipated from law, or be free from the benevolent restraints of guardianship." Yet the ideas of suffrage and officeholding were not too much for Thaddeus Stevens and Charles Sumner—nor for Garrison—in 1865, when actual freedom had come for the slaves. . . .

Consider how movements denounced as radical begin to look moderate as soon as still more radical movements appear. The NAACP, denounced all over the South as virtually Communist, began to look respectable and legalistic when the sit-inners and Freedom Riders moved into mass, extra-legal action in 1960 and 1961. And the White Citizens Councils of the South could lay claim to being "moderate" segregationists so long as the KKK was around. . . .

If the notion of "extremism" is too nebulous to sustain a firm judgment on a goal or a tactic, how do we judge? One point of reference might be the nature and severity of the problem. Even that moderate, Lao Tzu, said you use a boat for a stream and a litter for a mountain path; you adapt your means to your problem. While more modest evils might be dislodged by a few sharp words, the elimination of slavery clearly required more drastic action. The abolitionists did not deceive themselves that they were gentle and temperate; they quite consciously measured their words to the enormity of the evil.

Garrison said in 1833: "How, then, ought I to feel and speak and write, in view of a system which is red with innocent blood drawn from the bodies of millions of my countrymen by the scourge of brutal drivers. . . ."

How evil was slavery? It was a complex phenomenon, different in every individual instance, with the treatment of slaves varying widely. But the whole range of variation was in a general framework of unspeakable inhumanity. Even at its "best," slavery was a ferocious attack on man's dignity. . . .

And at its worst, slavery was, as Allan Nevins has said: ". . . the greatest misery, the greatest wrong, the greatest curse to white and black alike that America has ever known."[2] Ads for fugitive slaves in the Southern press (5,400 advertisements a year) contained descriptions like the following to aid apprehension: ". . . Stamped N. E. on the breast and having both small toes cut off. . . . Has some scars on his back that show above the skin, caused by the whip. . . . Has an iron band around his neck. . . . Has a ring of iron on his left foot. . . . Has on a large neck iron, with a huge pair of horns and a large bar or band of iron on his left leg. . . . Branded on the left cheek, thus 'R,' and a piece is taken off her left ear on the same side; the same letter is branded on the inside of both legs." One plantation diary read: ". . . whipped every field hand this evening."[3] A Natchez slave who attacked a white man was chained to a tree and burned alive.

Against this, how mild Garrison's words seem.

EMOTIONALISM AND IRRATIONALITY

. . . Fanaticism, irrationality, emotionalism—these are the qualities attributed again and again, in a mood of sharp criticism, to the abolitionists; and, indeed, to radical reformers in general. How valid is the criticism? . . .

. . . I would suggest . . . that emotion is a *morally neutral* instrument for a wide variety of ends; that it serves a positive purpose when linked to laudable goals; that it is not "irrational" but "nonrational" because, being merely an instrument, its rationality is derived only from the value with which it is linked.

. . . There is no necessary connection between emotionalism and irrationality. A lie may be calmly uttered, and a truth may be charged with emotion. Emotion can be used to make more rational decisions, if by that we mean decisions based on greater knowledge, for greater knowledge involves not only extension but intensity. Who "knows" more about slavery—the man who has in his head all the available information . . . and calmly goes about his business, or the man who has less data, but is moved by a book (Harriet Beecher Stowe's) or by an orator (Wendell Phillips) to *feel* the reality of slavery so intensely that he will set up a station on the underground railroad? Rationality is limited by time,

---

[2] Allan Nevins, *Ordeal of the Union* (New York, 1947), 1, 461.
[3] Ralph Korngold, *Two Friends of Man* (1950), p. 85.

space, and status, which intervene between the individual and the truth. Emotion can liberate it.

DOES THE AGITATOR DISTORT THE FACTS?

Abolitionist reformers, and those who supported them, historian Avery Craven wrote in *The Coming of the Civil War,* spread thousands of distortions about the South. . . . Craven's thesis is that the war was repressible, but abolitionist (and slaveholder) exaggerations brought it about.[4] . . .

Because the reformist agitator is so often charged with distortion and exaggeration, and because thinkers with an abiding concern for truth are often led by such charges to keep a safe distance from such agitators, it is essential to discuss this point.

Distinctions ought first to be made between outright misstatements of fact and personal slander on the one hand, and, on the other, exaggerations of the truth and the singling out of those aspects of a complex truth which support the viewpoint of the reformer. It needs to be acknowledged that false statements have at times been made by radical reformers, and this is unpardonable, for if the reformer speaks the truth, then material exists on all hands to support him, and he needs no falsification of the evidence to back his case. As for character denigration, it is not only repugnant to truth-seekers, but makes explanation embarrassing when the attacked person is revealed as something different. . . .

More serious, and more frequent, however, are charges of exaggeration and distortion leveled at the radicals. At the root of this problem is that once we get past simple factual statements ("On March 3, 1851, field hand . . . was whipped by his master") and begin to deal with general characterizations of social institutions (like Nevins' statement about slavery being "the greatest misery, the greatest curse. . . .") we are in a realm where words like "true" and "false" cannot be applied so simply. Slavery was a complex institution, and no one statement can describe it fully. . . .

There is an answer to the problem of how to state simply a complex truth—but this requires an activist outlook rare among scholars. It means deciding from a particular ethical base what is the action-need of the moment and concentrating on that aspect of the truth-complex which fulfills that need. If we start from the ethical assumption that it is fundamentally wrong to hold in bondage—whether kindly or cruelly—another human being, and that the freeing of such persons requires penetrating the moral sensibilities of a nation, then it is justifiable to focus on those aspects of the complexity which support this goal. When you teach a child to be careful crossing the street, and say, "You can be killed by an automobile," you are singling out of the totality of automobile behaviors that small percentage of incidents in which people are killed. You are not telling the whole truth about automobiles and traffic. But you are

---

4 Avery Craven, *The Coming of the Civil War* (N.Y., 1942), 2.

emphasizing that portion of the truth which supports a morally desirable action.

. . . The scholar who accepts no harsh judgment because it does not do justice to the entire complex truth, can really accept no judgments about society, because all are simplifications of the complex. The result is scholarly detachment from the profound ethical conflicts of society and from that human concern without which scholarship becomes a pretentious game.

HISTORICAL PERSPECTIVE AND THE RADICAL

It is paradoxical that the historian, who is presumably blessed with historical perspective, should judge the radical from within the narrow moral base of the radical's period of activity, while the radical assesses his immediate society from the vantage point of some future, better era. If progress is desirable, and if escape from the bonds of the immediate is healthy, whose perspective is more accurate—that of the agitator, or that of the scolding historian?

James Russell Lowell wrote in 1849: ". . . the simple fact undoubtedly is that were the Abolitionists to go back to the position from which they started, they would find themselves less fanatical than a very respectable minority of the people. . . ."[5]

Garrison himself took note of the profound change in the nation by 1860, . . . "Whereas, ten years since, there were thousands who could not endure my lightest rebuke of the South, they can now swallow John Brown whole, and his rifle into the bargain."

The historian too often moves back a hundred years into a moral framework barbarian by modern standards and thinks inside it, while the radical shakes the rafters of this framework at the risk of his life. Wendell Phillips, speaking affectionately of the abolitionist leader Angelina Grimké, said: "Were I to single out the moral and intellectual trait which won me, it was her serene indifference to the judgment of those about her." That kind of indifference (David Riesman calls it inner-directedness) is hard to find in contemporary scholarship.

COMPROMISE

The argument over the wisdom of radical agitation in the tactics of social reform was aptly expressed in Boston in pre-Civil War years by two leading figures. Samuel May, speaking of Garrison, said: ". . . he will shake our nation to its center, but he will shake slavery out of it." Reverend Lyman Beecher said: "True wisdom consists in advocating a cause only so far as the community will sustain the reformer."[6] . . .

The abolitionist took an advanced position so that even if pushed back by compromise, substantial progress would result. Garrison wrote: "Urge

---

[5] James Russell Lowell, *Anti-Slavery Papers* (1902), 2, 53.
[6] Ibid., p. 80.

immediate abolition as earnestly as we may, it will be gradual abolition in the end." And Phillips said: "If we would get half a loaf, we must demand the whole of it." The Emancipation Proclamation itself was a compromise . . . and only the compelling force of the abolitionist intransigents made it come as soon as it did.

. . . There is a huge difference between the passive wisher-for-change who quietly adds up the vectors and makes a decision as to which is the composite of all existing forces, and the active reformer who pushes so hard *in the course of adding-up* that the composite itself is changed. The latter—the radical—is viewing compromise as a dynamic process, in which his own actions are part of the total force being calculated. He bases his estimate of what is possible on a graph in which his own action and its consequences are calculated from the first.

MODERATION AS TACTIC

Does the agitator alienate potential allies by the extremism of his demands, or the harshness of his language? . . .

But who? The slaveholder? The slave? The moderate reformer? The open-minded conservative? It needs to be acknowledged that different sections of the population will respond differently to the same appeal, and in judging the effect of bold words upon the population, this population must be broken up into parts, based on the varying degrees of receptivity to the ideas of the reformer. Why should the radical soften his language or his program to please that element of the population which cannot possibly be pleased by anything short of total surrender of principle, whose self-interest in fact dictates rejection of any reform? . . .

. . . The slaveholders themselves pointed to the impossibility of their being won over by moderate overtures. In 1854, the editor of the Richmond *Enquirer* wrote: "That man must be a veritable verdigreen who dreams of pleasing slaveholders, either in church or state, by any method but that of letting slavery alone."[7] . . .

With a population of diversified interests, tactics must be adapted and focused specially for each group, and for the group most inimical to reform, it is doubtful that moderation is effective. With the intransigents, it may be only the most powerful action that impels change. It was Nat Turner's violent slave revolt in Virginia in 1831 that led the Virginia legislature into its famous series of discussions about the abolition of slavery. "For a while indeed," Ralph Korngold writes, "it seemed that what years of propaganda by the Quakers had failed to accomplish could come as a result of Turner's bloodletting."[8] . . .

. . . If neither extreme opposition nor hard-and-fast friends can be moved by tactics of moderation, this leaves, as a decisive group, that large part of the population which is at neither end of the ideological spectrum, which moves back and forth. . . .

Garrison was quite aware that most of the American population to

---

[7] Korngold, *Two Friends of Man*, p. 89.
[8] Ibid., p. 54.

which he was appealing was not sympathetic with his views, and he was completely conscious of how distant were his own fiery convictions from those of the average American. But he was persuaded, as were Phillips and other leading abolitionists (John Brown felt it, and acted it, if he did not express it intellectually) that only powerful surges of words and feelings could move white people from their complacency about the slave question. . . . To his friend Samuel May, who urged him to keep more cool, saying: "Why, you are all on fire," Garrison replied: "Brother May, I have need to be all on fire, for I have mountains of ice about me to melt."

We have the historical record as a check on whether the vituperative language of Garrison, the intemperate appeals of Wendell Phillips, hurt or advanced the popular sentiment against slavery. In the 1830s a handful of men cried out against slavery and were beaten, stoned, and shot to death by their Northern compatriots. By 1849, antislavery sentiment was clearly increasing, and some of the greatest minds and voices in America were speaking out for abolition. . . . And by 1860, with millions of Americans convinced that slavery was an evil, open insurrection by John Brown brought more public support than had the mere words of Garrison 30 years before. . . .

The politician is annoyed and angry at the pushing of the radical reformer, and the moderate observer thinks the radical unfair and injudicious in making extreme demands of the man in office, but both critics fail to distinguish between the social role of the politician and that of the agitator. . . .

Abolitionist Guilt Was Realistic*

Aileen S. Kraditor

. . . [Stanley] Elkins contrasts the structure of American society with the structure of British society in the middle of the nineteenth century, and he finds that by then the power of many American institutions had melted away. The church had broken into denominational fragments. The legal profession was not the strong institution it was in England. Political parties were dissolving and changing their forms. Old classes were declining and new ones rising. The result, according to Elkins, was that traditional institutions were so weak, fragmented, and shifting that Americans of that day easily imagined that institutions as such were not

---

* Aileen S. Kraditor, "A Note on Elkins and the Abolitionists," *Civil War History*, 13 (1967) 330–39. By permission of the Kent State University Press.

necessary to a society's stability. "In the America of the 1830s and 1840s there was no other symbol of vitality to be found than the individual, and it was to the individual, with all his promise, that the thinker, like everyone else, would inexorably orient himself." Individualism, self-reliance, abstractionism, disregard of the responsibilities and uses of power— "Such was the state of mind in which Americans faced the gravest social problem that had yet confronted them as an established nation," slavery.[1] . . .

The question is whether the abolitionists as a group did have an anti-institutional bias. Elkins prejudges the issue in his query: "Why should the American of, say, 1830 have been so insensitive to institutions and their function?"[2] "The American" turns out, according to the evidence Elkins provides, to be a tiny group of Concord Transcendentalists and a handful of abolitionists, whose ideas and attitudes were uncharacteristic not only of the overwhelming majority of Americans but even of the majority of abolitionists. He discusses such Transcendentalists as Emerson and Theodore Parker and their refusal to use institutional means to effect reforms and to think in institutional terms, and he admits that "their relationship with abolition societies was never anything but equivocal."[3] But if the Transcendentalists did not generally join abolition societies their intellectual affinities with the abolitionists, according to Elkins, were very significant. It would seem, then, that he discusses the Transcendentalists in order to provide a foundation for his contention that the abolitionists themselves were anti-institutionalists. This inference is strengthened by his reference to "Transcendentalism and other reform movements," despite the notorious fact that the Transcendentalists lacked the commitment to action that characterizes movements for change. Stating that any other movement concerned with social policy "would have" found no better source of wisdom than the Transcendentalists, that a formidable abolitionist movement "might thus have" gathered both strength and weakness from them, and that the abolitionists "could not have duplicated the intellectual pattern of the Transcendentalists more precisely if they tried," Elkins then transforms all those conditionals into declaratives.[4] Moreover, he believes it significant that "the very time at which they [the Transcendentalists] flourished coincides with the launching of the great reform impulses." We are half persuaded already; the Transcendentalists, it appears, were both logical models for and contemporaries of the abolitionists. Evidence from the abolitionists' own writings is almost superfluous.

But "evidence" is furnished, from the speeches and writings of William Lloyd Garrison, Wendell Phillips, and Stephen S. Foster, and from the doctrines of Nathaniel P. Rogers, the last two of whom were undoubtedly anti-institutionalists; and from the writings of Theodore D. Weld, William Jay, and James G. Birney, who were not. A thorough study of the

---

1 Elkins, *Slavery,* pp. 27–34.

2 Ibid.

3 Ibid., pp. 164–175. I might add that they refused to use *any* means to effect reforms; few of them were activists.

4 Ibid., pp. 164–165.

latter three and even a cursory glance at the scores of political abolitionists who worked through such institutions as the Democratic and Whig parties, or who formed new institutions such as the Liberty party and the Liberty League, would have destroyed Elkins' thesis.

. . . Elkins' application of this analysis to the Transcendentalists, and by later implication and logical leap to the abolitionists, is suggested in the title of the next section of the chapter in which that quotation appears: "Intellectuals with Responsibility." The picture is completed in "The Abolitionist as Transcendentalist," a section containing many highly anti-institutionalistic statements by some abolitionists, as well as quotations that could be interpreted otherwise.

All this might justify Elkins' generalization concerning abolitionist anti-institutionalism if the bulk of the movement shared Garrison's repudiation of human government (as construed by Elkins), withdrew from all organized churches as he and Foster did, and relied solely on moral suasion to induce slaveholders to repent their sin. Unfortunately for the theory, this was not the case. The Rogerses and Fosters were a tiny minority of the movement even in New England, their stronghold. The Garrisonian perfectionists (who, incidentally, insisted they were not anti-institutionalists) were but a small coterie even in Massachusetts. The overwhelming majority of members of antislavery societies evidently believed that slavery would not be abolished unless the political power of the slaveowners was destroyed by political means, for they continued to work within the major parties and later in the Free Soil and Republican parties. Most of them believed that the respectability and influence of the slaveowners could be destroyed not by withdrawing from the compromising churches but by working within them, to persuade them to exert pressure on their southern wings and refuse fellowship with slaveowning clergymen and members. In other words, the vast majority of abolitionists did not repudiate institutions or institutional means to effect the desired change; they valued institutions as potential weapons, and where existing institutions seemed too corrupted they tried to replace them with new institutions through which collective efforts could be exerted. Most of them harbored no illusions about the possibility of convincing the slaveowners, by mere exhortation, of the error of their ways. When they advocated moral pressure on the owners they usually explained that this meant worldwide ostracism, disruption of economic and social contacts, and an unremitting propaganda offensive—something quite different from the naive sermons on brotherhood that, according to some historians, abolitionists were content to rely on.[5] And most abolitionists who advocated

---

[5] See, for example, "To the Abolitionists of Massachusetts," an open letter from the Board of Managers of the Massachusetts Anti-Slavery Society, in *The Liberator*, Aug. 10, 1838: "We would make the public sentiment of the North a tonic, instead of an opiate to southern conscience, we would unite and concentrate it, until it shall tell, in a manner perfectly irresistible, upon the sense of right, the pride of social standing, and character, even upon the interest of the slaveholder, until it shall help to make real to his mind, and he shall feel, in the air around him, the guilt, the danger, the deep disgrace, the ruinous impolicy of the relation he sustains. . . ." Frederick Douglass' writings are full of such statements. Another theme frequently found in abolitionist writings is that abolitionists should endeavor to ostracize slaveholders at northern resorts like Newport.

this tactic urged that it be accompanied by efforts to win elections, pass laws, dominate political parties, reform the churches, and in other ways use institutions to destroy slavery. . . .

Far from repudiating institutions, most abolitionists wished to purify them. Consider, for example, a passage from William Goodell's *Slavery and Anti-Slavery* (1852), an extremely influential book by a prominent abolitionist:

> This great question is to be decided, mainly, by the concurrent action of the two great social institutions of the country, the Church, and the State, the ecclesiastical and the civil power.
>
> It is for THE PEOPLE of the non-slaveholding States to say whether those two social institutions shall be redeemed from the foul embraces of slavery, and wielded for their heaven-appointed ends, or whether they shall remain, as at present, in the hands of their enemies.[6]

Such statements abound in antislavery literature. Even the Garrisonian, James S. Gibbons, could write: "Organization, Concert, is at the base of the divine economy."[7]

Another sort of statement frequently encountered is the accusation by some abolitionists that others were anti-institutionalists. At the height of the controversy over the woman question and perfectionism, the Rev. James T. Woodbury, an abolitionist, asserted that in the opinion of Garrison and his friends: "Slavery is not merely to be abolished, but nearly everything else. . . . *We* are not willing, for the sake of killing the rats, to burn the house down with all it contains."[8] The "Appeal" of some abolitionists at Andover Theological Seminary, published in *The Liberator* of August 25, 1837, included the statement that the appellants had read, in antislavery publications, "speculations which lead inevitably to disorganization and anarchy, unsettling the domestic economy, removing the landmarks of society, and unhinging the machinery of government."[9] The targets of these accusations pleaded innocent[10] (sometimes, in my opinion, convincingly), but Elkins himself could not have penned a severer indictment of anti-institutionalism than this group of abolitionists directed against their fellows. While many non-Garrisonians thought the Andover Appeal in bad taste, they agreed with its substance. What inferences, then, can be drawn concerning the thinking of the movement as a whole?

Only a minority of abolitionists reacted to the hostility they encountered by rejecting not the *compromising* churches and the *proslavery* government but churches and governments—institutions per se. The vast majority never did so. And when the northern wings of some churches

---

[6] Goodell, p. 584. Emphasis in original.

[7] Gibbons to William Lloyd Garrison, March 30, 1841, in Anti-Slavery Letters to Garrison and Others, Boston Public Library.

[8] *The Liberator,* September 1, 1837. Emphasis added.

[9] See also letter from "Alethea," ibid., May 26, 1837; and Elizur Wright, Jr., "Judge Lawless and the Law," *Quarterly Anti-Slavery Magazine,* 1 (1836), 400–409, esp. pp. 400–402. Many other examples could be cited.

[10] See Garrison's reply to Dr. Osgood, *The Liberator*, August 2, 1839; and "To the Abolitionists of Massachusetts," cited in footnote 5.

and parties, and later the Federal government, moved closer to their position, that majority and even some of the minority ceased their attacks. When abolitionists supported the Union in the Civil War, it was usually because the institutions, not the abolitionists, had changed.

Radicals have always been accused of wanting to undermine institutions. What is true about most radicals, including most Garrisonians and many other abolitionists, is that they did not share the conservatives' reverence for institutions as such. Specific traditions, customs, and institutions they were willing to judge by transcendent ethical criteria and condemn if found wanting. Garrisonians, for example, repeatedly disclaimed hostility to the clergy and the church and reiterated that they deplored only the perversions of these institutions.[11] It may be argued that the Garrisonians were anti-institutionalists despite their disclaimers. In the case of Henry C. Wright, I think that is true. In other cases it is a matter of definition. This question is peripheral, because of the Garrisonians did not represent the entire movement, Elkins' discussion of their attitude toward institutions proves nothing about American abolitionism as a whole. The bulk of the movement, those who followed the more conservative leaders such as Birney and the Tappan brothers, found no need even to make public disclaimers. Unless a desire to abolish completely an inherently evil institution like slavery and an insistence that all other institutions be purged of its influence are defined as anti-institutionalism, the majority of abolitionists do not merit that label. If such desire and insistence do add up to anti-institutionalism, the label must be applied to every movement for change that does not visualize the proposed change as piecemeal, gradual, and reformist. But to do that is to contradict the word's denotation and to attach to it an invidious connotation in the guise of objective historiography.

Elkins regrets that slavery was not ended gradually, by piecemeal adjustments of the institutional arrangements that supported it. He offers "a catalogue of preliminaries—a series of separate short-term reforms rather than root-and-branch abolition" that might have solved the problem. For example, the churches could have insisted that slaves be instructed in Christian morality and given a dignified spiritual life. They could have required regular marriage and guaranteed the sanctity of the family. Laws could have been passed to mitigate cruelty and recognize the slaves' humanity. Slaves might have been given the right to earn enough money to buy their freedom.[12] He points out that such schemes were in fact proposed in the United States and were put into practice in other countries. As a result slavery died peacefully in the British West Indies and in Latin America. But, he adds, this process was not possible here. There was no national church, no national focus of social and financial power, no national bar—in short, no other national institutions such

---

[11] See, for example, Garrison's editorial, "Clerical Protest, No. 2," ibid., Sept. 8, 1837; and "To the Abolitionists of Massachusetts," cited in fn. 12: ". . . the abolitionists form the only great party, in our age, who, aiming at a wide social reform, and operating on and through social institutions, yet rest their efforts and their hopes professedly on religious grounds. . . ."

[12] Elkins, *Slavery*, pp. 194–96.

as existed in other slaveholding countries—that could have mediated the conflicting interests or wielded the necessary power. The absence of such institutions forced the opponents of slavery to see it in abstract terms, in terms of "sin" on the part of the slaveholder and of "guilt" on the part of northerners. Since this view of the abolitionists' conception of sin, guilt, and morality is a principal corollary of Elkins' anti-institutionalism thesis, it is appropriate at this point to consider its validity.

The contrast between the United States and other nations in which slavery existed is valid up to a point; certainly institutions here were much more fluid and in the period under discussion were changing drastically. But no society, no matter how structured, provides institutional means or moral justifications for its own subversion. The significant point is not that American society was relatively "devoid of structure," as Elkins correctly states, but that slavery in this country was part of what structure it had, such an integral part that a movement to destroy it was not a reform movement but a radical one. It judged the institution of slavery not by the moral criteria of the society within which slavery had a legitimate place, but by a higher law that rejected those very criteria. Slavery not only was involved inextricably in the economic and political structure of the entire nation, but was also the social and economic base of a class that wielded almost total power in its own section and tremendous influence in the North and the Federal government. The abolitionists' situation was, therefore, different from that of all the other movements for change in that day—women's rights, temperance, trade-unionism, prison reform, and so on. They were reform movements; abolitionism was radical (more radical than many abolitionists realized). The reformers' goals were attainable without touching the basic structure of American society; abolition could be attained only by overturning that structure in part of the country and shifting power drastically in the remainder.[13]

Elkins thus misconstrues what he regards as the abolitionists' penchant for moral abstractions, their moral absolutism, and their guilt feelings. . . . The guilt feelings of the abolitionists may be explained in terms other than psychological. If slavery was an integral part of the institutional structure of the nation as a whole, the average northerner had as realistic a basis for guilt feelings as the average German of the 1930s. By the same token, the minority of northerners who were aware of their section's complicity in the crime of slavery and who worked in a variety of ways to publicize that complicity and end it were no more pathological than German antifascists thirty years ago. The unrealism was not the abolitionists' for feeling guilty but their neighbors' for *not* feeling guilty.

. . . The anomaly of the most rigid, institutionalized form of slavery existing within the most fluid, least institutionalized social structure had

---

13 As to the reasons why slavery ended peacefully in the West Indies and Brazil, E. D. Genovese . . . in *Science & Society*, 25 (1961), 47, [explains that] "The peaceful solution in the British Caribbean . . . followed from the political weakness of the ruling planters. In Brazil, the slaveowners lacked a contiguous territory and were isolated and subjected to a crushing defeatism by the failure of the Confederate cause."

to make slavery seem morally wrong to those whites who took the Declaration of Independence seriously. This anomaly suggests that the abolitionists' reaction was realistic, not a pathological attitude forced on them by the absence of institutionalized ways to oppose a social anachronism, and that whatever one may say of the tactics they employed, they were correct in insisting that individuals who shut their eyes to the crime of slavery were to that extent guilty of its perpetuation. It may be argued further that slavery was objectively a moral problem precisely because it was anomalous and anachronistic and involved basic questions of men's relations to one another.[14] And if that is so, a movement to abolish it could not, without distorting the nature of the problem, have dealt with it other than as largely a moral problem. That is, the charge of "abstractionism" could be leveled at a movement that did *not* make the moral aspect central.

The moral aspect of slavery thus was not something the abolitionists superimposed on a problem that was difficult enough to solve without it; nor was it imposed by the lack of institutional structure in the abolitionists' society. It was inherent in the nature of slavery itself. And it appealed with irresistible force to those who accepted literally the teachings of their religion that God created all men in his own image and that Christ died for all. The central place that the abolitionists gave to the religious and moral aspect of their crusade also explains why they always accompanied their demand for abolition with the demand for equal rights for the Negro and the ending of racial prejudice. Chattel slavery was simply the worst form of the sin they wanted to eradicate, the sin of denying the humanity of the Negro and the equality of all men as children of God. But Elkins' advice was followed a century before it was offered. The nation failed to respond to the moral appeal and preferred to approach the problem of slavery "as a question of institutional arrangements." This meant separating what the abolitionists insisted on combining—the legal status of the Negro, and the moral condition of American society as reflected in its treatment of the Negro. When the nation altered the former and left the latter unchanged, it distorted the nature of the problem and insured fulfillment of an ominous prophecy (somewhat exaggerated) uttered by Lydia Maria Child twenty-three years before the Thirteenth Amendment was ratified.

> Great political changes may be forced by the pressure of external circumstances, without a corresponding change in the moral sentiment of a nation; but in all such cases, the change is worse than useless; the evil reappears, and usually in a more aggravated form.[15]

---

14 Acceptance of the objective reality of the moral aspect of slavery is gaining currency among historians. The most recent statements of it are in David Brion Davis, *The Problem of Slavery in Western Culture* (Ithaca, 1966). . . .

15 "Dissolution of the Union," reprinted from *The National Anti-Slavery Standard* in *The Liberator*, May 20, 1842.

John Brown and the American Tradition*

Louis Ruchames

. . . As a symbol, Brown's desperate attack upon Harpers Ferry on Sunday night, October 16, 1859, has had different and frequently contradictory meanings for different groups. To the slaveholder and his sympathizers, both North and South, it was a criminal and murderous attack upon an institution sanctioned by law and justified by an ideology which regarded slavery as part of the very nature of things, with the white man born to rule and the Negro to serve. Brown was therefore a murderer and criminal who sought "to incite slaves to murder helpless women and children." His courageous behavior at his trial and execution was no more worthy of veneration than the similar behavior of any criminal. . . .

On the other hand, in Northern antislavery circles, Brown represented the highest idealism: the willingness to sacrifice one's life and possessions for the freedom and welfare of one's fellow men. In a lecture on November 8, 1859, in Boston, Emerson referred to Brown as "The Saint, whose fate yet hangs in suspense, but whose martyrdom, if it shall be perfected, will make the gallows as glorious as the Cross." In an address delivered in Concord almost two weeks after Harpers Ferry, Thoreau remarked that "when I think of him, and his six sons, and his son-in-law, not to enumerate the others, enlisted for this fight, proceeding coolly, reverently, humanely to work, for months, if not years . . . without expecting any reward but a good conscience, while almost all America stood ranked on the other side,—I say again, that it affects me as a sublime spectacle." Thoreau indeed anticipated his friend Emerson in comparing Brown to Jesus. "Some eighteen hundred years ago Christ was crucified; this morning, perchance, Captain Brown was hung. These are the two ends of a chain which is not without its links. He is not Old Brown any longer; he is an angel of light." Wendell Phillips, who had devoted the previous 25 years to the antislavery movement, went so far as to regard Harpers Ferry as the beginning of emancipation. Invoking Brown as a "marvellous old man," he said: "History will date Virginia Emancipation from Harpers Ferry. True, the slave is still there. So, when the tempest uproots a pine on your hills, it looks green for months, a year or two. Still, it is timber, not a tree. John Brown has loosened the roots of the slave system; it only breathes—it does not live—hereafter."

Few events in American history provide so vivid an illustration of the thesis that the historian's evaluations of men and events are dependent not upon facts alone but upon the basic premises from which he views those facts. . . . To those who regarded slavery as "the sum of all villainies," as legalized kidnapping maintained by jails, the lash, and, ultimately, the death penalty for those who sought to secure their freedom or to help others do so, Brown's action was one of great idealism and placed him in the company of the great liberators of mankind. Theodore Parker . . . expressed this point of view as ably and frankly as anyone. . . . "A man held against his will as a slave," he wrote, "has a natural right to kill every one who seeks to prevent his employment of liberty. The freeman has a natural right to help the slaves recover their liberty, and in that enterprise to do for them all which they have a right to do for themselves." . . . In the light of these opinions one can well appreciate Parker's final judgment that "there have been few spirits more pure and devoted than John Brown's, and none that gave up their breath in a nobler cause. Let the American State hang his body, and the American Church damn his soul; still, the blessing of such as are ready to perish will fall on him, and the universal justice of the Infinitely Perfect God will take him welcome home. The road to heaven is as short from the gallows as from a throne; perhaps, also, as easy." Even men like Garrison, who were non-resistants, and did not themselves wish to use force to achieve freedom for the slave, cheered Brown's effort as a valid alternative to continued slavery. "Rather than see men wearing their chains in a cowardly and servile spirit," he said at a meeting memorializing Brown, "I would, as an advocate of peace, much rather see them breaking the head of the tyrant with their chains. Give me, as a non-resistant, Bunker Hill, and Lexington, and Concord, rather than the cowardice and servility of a Southern slave-plantation." . . .

The conflict of ideologies has continued to our own day. . . .

In opposition to . . . [those who cherish Brown] stands James Malin,[1] the foremost anti-Brown historian, who seems unable to forgive the North for having used force against Southern secession, or the abolitionists for having taught that the abolition of slavery would be a step forward for American society, or the Negro for having believed that his welfare would be furthered by the forceful elimination of slavery. To Malin, minor errors of date or place committed by writers who have a high regard for Brown are frequently labeled deliberate falsehoods, while the errors of Brown-haters are simply unintentional blunders. Very few antislavery leaders and writers emerge unscathed under Malin's furious onslaught. Typical of his method are his comments on Emerson, Thoreau, Parker and the other leaders of New England opinion, whom he contemptuously refers to as the "New England Transcendental Hierarchy, the self-appointed keepers not only of New England culture, but, according to their own estimates, of national civilization." Following in the footsteps of earlier anti-Brown biographers, such as Hill Peebles Wilson and Robert Penn Warren, Malin refers to the sympathetic evaluation of Brown as "the John

---

[1] James C. Malin, *John Brown and the Legend of Fifty-Six* (Philadelphia: American Philosophical Society, 1942).

Brown legend," a "hoax" created largely by the above-mentioned "hier-archy." To expose the "hoax," he concludes, would result in breaking "the spell of its authority" and deflating "other fakes and fakers" as well. . . .

[My position is] that the abolitionists and other antislavery leaders, who devoted their lives to the achievement of freedom for the slave and equality of opportunity for Negro and white alike, seeking through their writings and lectures to educate the American public to the evils of slavery, were not paranoiacs or narrow-minded fanatics, but men and women who were devoted to the highest ideals of equality and democracy, influenced by the best in the Judeo-Christian tradition and all that was good and noble in the thoughts and actions of the Founding Fathers. John Brown was one of this company of antislavery men. . . .

[John Brown] was found guilty . . . of three crimes: conspiring with slaves to rebel, murder, and treason. Though his lawyers sought to enter a plea of insanity on the basis of affidavits received from residents of Ohio, he rejected the attempts and refused to permit any such plea. Con-cerning the trial itself, Richard B. Morris, the well-known historian notes that it was "flagrantly unfair."

The right of the accused to a reasonable time to prepare for trial was shockingly violated. Brown was forced to stand trial the very same day he was indicted. Scrupulous though the court was to provide the accused with competent trial counsel, it erroneously denied him the right to en-gage lawyers of his own choice. When, finally, his own counsel took over, they were given no time to familiarize themselves with the case against their client.

To this catalogue of judicial errors must be added a last one: John Brown was tried and sentenced for a crime of which he could not con-ceivably have been guilty. How the accused could have committed treason against Virginia when he was neither a citizen nor a resident of that state and owed it no allegiance was never clarified by the law-enforcement authorities. Objectivity and reason gave way to hysteria and vigilantism. This was no time for technicalities. It was enough that John Brown be convicted of a crime carrying the capital penalty and that the sentence of the court be carried out with expedition.[2] . . .

As to whether Brown was or was not insane, the best answer lies in an examination of his behavior at the trial and afterward. Certainly, his remarks and actions at the trial show no indication of insanity, nor has it ever been alleged that they do. His speech to the court before sentence was pronounced is regarded by many as one of the finest utterances in American literature; Emerson, indeed, compared it in later years to Lin-coln's Gettysburg address. His letters from prison are models of lucidity and breathe a rare nobility of thought and character. "No lunatic," writes Villard, "ever penned such elevated and high-minded, and such consist-ent epistles." Brown's concentration upon slavery and its evils through-out the latter part of his life, which is the usual reason given for alleging his insanity, was indeed intense and unusual for his day. But it was not

---

2 Richard B. Morris, *Fair Trial* (New York: Alfred A. Knopf, 1953), pp. 259–60.

unusual when compared to that of such men and women as William Lloyd Garrison, Wendell Phillips, Lydia Maria Child, Theodore Parker, Charles Sumner, Maria Weston Chapman, and Parker Pillsbury, to name but a few, who devoted their lives to the antislavery cause, suffered hardships and privations for its sake, and on various occasions were also accused of being fanatics and insane on the subject of slavery. The lesson to be learned from their example is simply that to be deeply sensitive to injustice, to be willing to devote one's life to an unpopular cause, to give up the pursuit of one's own gain to alleviate the suffering of others involves running the risk of being called fanatic and even insane by the smug, the callous, and the well-placed members of society. "The prophet is a fool, the man of the spirit is mad!" has echoed through the ages, from the days of Hosea to our own.

Finally, perhaps the most important evidence as to the nature of John Brown's mind and character is to be found in the devotion to him of the 21 young men—intelligent, able, and high-minded—who lived with him and knew him as a leader and a friend, and who followed him even unto death.[3]

John Brown's end came on December 2, on a scaffold in Charlestown. His execution served as a visible demonstration by the state of Virginia of the condign punishment ultimately in store for those who sought to tamper with the institution of slavery; for the slave seeking to escape from bondage and for the free man, white or colored, who dared to aid him.

To the North, however, Brown's execution brought a far different lesson. For in John Brown, whose venture at Harpers Ferry it first saw as the desperate act of a demented old man oblivious to the realities of the world, the North came to see the embodiment of all that was noble, courageous, and self-sacrificing in man's love for his fellow man. It saw beyond the bloodshed and death into the heart of a man who had identified himself with the poorest, the lowliest, the most forsaken people of the land, had thrown in his lot with theirs, had given up his home, his possessions, his ambitions, his wife and children whom he loved, even life itself, to bring freedom and dignity to men, women, and children who

---

[3] Among recent historians, Professors C. Vann Woodward and Allan Nevins have emphasized the case for Brown's insanity. Professor Vann Woodward has made much of the 19 affidavits testifying to insanity in Brown's family, especially on his mother's side, and to Brown's own insanity or "monomania" on the question of slavery. Putting aside the basic question of whether one's insanity may be established by the presence or absence of insanity in one's family, it may be noted that the affidavits are highly suspect as valid evidence. Their primary purpose was to save Brown from execution by showing him to be insane. . . .

. . . Professor Nevins writes that Brown "was subject to extravagant religious fixations. In 1852, worried because his son John did not exhibit piety, he spent an entire month writing a letter of pamphlet length to him, composed largely of scriptural quotations. We might question the sanity of a nearly penniless man with a large family who devotes a month to such an exhortation—which proved futile." A close reading of the letter in question, which is printed in full in F. B. Sanborn's *John Brown*, pp. 45–51, reveals the very opposite of what Professor Nevins believes it to prove. . . . Prof. Vann Woodward's discussion of Brown is in "John Brown's Private War," *America in Crisis*, ed. by Daniel Aaron (New York: Alfred A. Knopf, 1952), 109–30. Professor [Allan] Nevins evaluates Brown in *The Emergence of Lincoln* (New Work and London: Charles Scribner's Sons, 1950), 2, 5 ff.

had known only the bitterness and hopelessness of slavery. As they saw the state of Virginia, in all of its majesty, proceed in indecent haste to exact the life of the man who had threatened its power, the people of the North learned, as little else could have taught them, that the structure of slavery remained intact primarily through the power of the whip, the gun, and the gallows and that when these were gone there was little else left. They learned, too, that wealth and happiness derived from the sweat of slaves was not less easily relinquished than that gotten through more honorable means, and that the slaveholder would fight desperately, with all the means at his disposal, to maintain the foundation of his wealth and power. It was then that many in the North realized that the issue of slavery and freedom would be decided by the weapons that the South had chosen. The battle at Harpers Ferry demonstrated what those weapons were.

When the war came, almost two years later, the man who had been hanged rose, as it were, from his grave to march again with those who had finally taken up the cause for which he had fought, and, by proffering the example of his life and work, helped to achieve the victory which he had lost in life but gained in death.

Anti-Abolitionist Mobs*

Leonard L. Richards

It is particularly noteworthy . . . that the peak of both anti-abolition and other mobs came in the summer of 1835, for after June of that year, organized antislavery was unquestionably the paramount issue of the day. Almost every major city and town in the nation held anti-abolitionist rallies. From Maine to Missouri, from the Atlantic to the Gulf, crowds gathered to hear mayors and aldermen, bankers and lawyers, ministers and priests denounce the abolitionists as amalgamationists,[1] dupes, fanatics, foreign agents, and incendiaries.[2]

---

* From "Gentlemen of Property and Standing": Anti-Abolition Mobs in Jacksonian America by Leonard L. Richards. Copyright © 1970 by Oxford University Press, Inc. Reprinted by permission.

[1] "Amalgamation" was the ante-bellum equivalent of "miscegenation," which did not come into use until the Civil War. See Sidney Kaplan, "The Miscegenation Issue in the Election of 1864," Journal of Negro History 34 (July 1949), 274–343.

[2] For further commentary, see Nye, Fettered Freedom, Chapter 5; Clement Eaton, "Censorship of the Southern Mails," American Historical Review, 48 (January 1943), 266–80; Bertram Wyatt-Brown, "The Abolitionists' Postal Campaign of 1835" Journal

By mid-August, emotions had reached high tide. Fiery speeches and torchlight parades became everyday news. Citizens formed vigilance committees to patrol Negro quarters, to question strangers, and to search post offices, ships, and stages for antislavery literature. Southern vigilance committees offered rewards for leading abolitionists. In East Feliciana, Louisiana, citizens posted $50,000 for the delivery of Arthur Tappan, the president of the American Anti-Slavery Society, dead or alive; in Mount Meigs, Alabama, $50,000 for Arthur Tappan or any other prominent abolitionist; in New Orleans, $100,000 for Tappan and LaRoy Sunderland, the editor of *Zion's Watchman*. The grand jury of Tuscaloosa, Alabama, demanded that R. G. Williams, the publishing agent of the American Anti-Slavery Society, be sent south for trial. Forty angry citizens of Hinds County, Mississippi, promised Williams a taste of Kentucky hemp if he ever ventured south. And a Virginia grand jury indicted and demanded the extradition of all the key personnel of the Anti-Slavery Society.[3]

In New York City, the home base of Arthur Tappan, R. G. Williams, and the American Anti-Slavery Society, excitement became so intense by mid-August that Elizur Wright, the society's corresponding secretary, barricaded his doors with "bars and planks an inch thick." From sundown to sunup the Mayor of Brooklyn patrolled the neighborhood where Tappan lived, and a relay of men stood ready to carry his messages to the Brooklyn Navy Yard. The "least spark," merchant Philip Hone confided to his diary, "would create a flame in which the lives and property of Arthur Tappan and his associates would be endangered." Under the present circumstances, William Leggett, editor of the *Evening Post*, cautioned his readers, "a few inflammatory phrases might easily set men's minds on fire." "I have not ventured into the city," wrote abolitionist Lydia Maria Child, ". . . so great is the excitement here. . . . 'Tis like the times of the French Revolution, when no man dared to trust his neighbors."[4] . . .

This fear of assimilation, of being "mulattoized," of losing one's sense of identity, existed long before . . . Northerners had ever heard of the

of Negro History, 50 (October 1965), 227–38; William Freehling, *Prelude to Civil War* (New York, 1966), Chapter 10; Charles M. Wiltse, *John C. Calhoun: Nullifier, 1829–1839* (Indianapolis, 1947), Chapter 20; Samuel Eliot Morison, *Life and Letters of Harrison Gray Otis* (2 vols.; Boston, 1913), Vol. 2, Chapter 32; W. Sherman Savage, *The Controversy over the Distribution of Abolition Literature, 1830–1860* (n.p., 1938), 15–26, and *passim;* Thomas M. Owen, "An Alabama Protest Against Abolitionism in 1835," *Gulf States Historical Magazine,* 2 (July 1903), 26–34; Edwin A. Miles, "The Mississippi Slave Insurrection Scare of 1835," *Journal of Negro History,* 42 (January 1957), 48–61; N. Dwight Harris, *The History of Negro Servitude in Illinois* (Chicago, 1904), 69–71.

3 Nye, *Fettered Freedom,* 180; *Alabama Senate Journal* (November 1835), 12; *New York Assembly Journal* (1836), 38–48; Charles Zebina Eastman, *Messages from the Governors* . . . (11 vols.; Albany, 1909), Vol. 3, pp. 594–604; Thomas Harney and others to R. G. Williams, Clinton, Mississippi, August 28, 1835, quoted in Washington *United States Telegraph,* September 24, 1835; New York *Evening Post,* August 26, October 12, 1835.

4 Lewis Tappan, *Arthur Tappan* (New York, 1870), 249–50; Allan Nevins, ed., *Diary of Philip Hone,* Vol. 1, p. 173 [entry for August 26, 1835]; *Evening Post,* August 26, 1835; Lydia Maria Child to Mrs. Ellis Gray Loring, August 15, 1835, *Letters of Lydia Maria Child* (Boston, 1883), 15.

Liberator. Everywhere in the North, as countless travelers noted, Negrophobia and racism flourished, and Northern whites—either legally or illegally—made the lot of the Negro miserable in "a thousand ways." Indeed, it was largely because Northern Negrophobia was so vicious and so pervasive that colonizationists insisted that their cause was holy. Anything as unyielding and malicious as Northern fear and hatred of the free Negro, they argued, was obviously "an ordination of Providence, and no more to be changed than the laws of nature." . . .

Northern Negrophobia was not manifested merely in social and legal prescription, in barring Negroes from jury boxes and election polls, in excluding Negroes from white men's schools and railroad cars, in limiting Negroes to "Nigger work" and "Nigger pews." It hounded Northern Negroes from cradle to grave. Indicative was a potter's field in Cincinnati, where whites were buried east to west and blacks north to south.[5] Among the dead, Northerners insisted that white supremacy must prevail.

This antipathy frequently expressed itself in violence. Often whites suffered from black felons, who apparently abounded under these circumstances. And in September, 1824, about 150 Philadelphia Negroes attacked white officials as they were taking a runaway to jail.[6] But in nine instances out of ten, whites were the aggressors, and blacks the victims. Northern law and custom left Negroes unprotected, and they suffered continually at the hands of frustrated whites, practical jokers, and village sadists.

Occasionally whites tried to expel free Negroes forcibly from their communities. In Providence, where anti-Negro feeling was "very bitter," several attempts were made in the 1820s.

The most serious incident of this kind occurred in Cincinnati in August, 1829. For two decades the city fathers had ignored the provision of Ohio's infamous Black Laws that compelled free Negroes entering the state to post a $500 bond as guarantee of their good behavior and providence. But between 1826 and 1829, which were the years of greatest Negro migration to the state, Cincinnati's Negro population suddenly jumped from about 4 to 10 percent of the total population. White citizens became alarmed. The Cincinnati Colonization Society, which had been formed in 1826 for the express purpose of "forwarding to Africa the free blacks of Cincinnati," received increasing support, and the number of local colonization societies in Ohio increased from one in late 1825 to forty-five by 1830. In 1828, the city council appointed a committee to consider a petition asking for measures to stop the inpouring of free blacks. In the spring of 1829, the Negrophobes scored heavily in a ward election that centered around the question of enforcing the Black Laws. And in July, the city fathers responded positively to this sentiment; in their role as Overseers of the Poor, the Trustees of Cincinnati announced that after thirty days they would enforce the $500 bond requirement.[7]

---

5 Abdy, *Journal*, Vol. 3, p. 7.

6 *Niles' Register* 27 (September 11, 1824), 32.

7 E. Drake and E. D. Mansfield, *Cincinnati in 1826* (Cincinnati, 1827), 57–58, 37; *The Cincinnati Directory for the Year 1829* (Cincinnati, 1829), n. p.; Alice D.

Almost immediately, white bands began raiding Negro quarters. These assaults reached a climax on the weekend of August 22, when several hundred whites invaded "Bucktown," spreading terror and destruction. By the end of 1829, about half of the Negro population had left the city. Unfortunately, wrote the editor of the Cincinnati *Gazette*, the "sober, honest, industrious, and useful portion of the colored population" left, and thus the enforcement of the Black Laws, which he had supported, only served "to lessen much of the moral restraint, which the presence of respectable persons of their own color, imposed on the idle and indolent, as well as the profligate." But never again in the ante-bellum period did Cincinnati's Negro population exceed 5 percent of the total, and for many whites this fact alone justified the excesses.[8]

. . . Antislavery men did not cause Northern Negrophobia, as some of their opponents later argued; they merely inherited it. And it was this legacy of fear and hate—rather than any concern about the practicality or the impracticality of immediate emancipation—that caused many Northerners to side with the colonizationists in their war with the abolitionists. It was not the doctrine of immediatism, as Gilbert Hobbes Barnes insists, but the heritage of racism that generated much of the controversy in the North.

. . . Anti-abolition journals invariably supported ill-conceived plans for transporting millions of unwilling American Negroes to Africa, Brazil, or Central America. And mobs constantly thundered their approval of the same schemes. For most anti-abolitionists, it seems that a plan's practicality depended on whether it promised an all-white America.

It is also clear that before the New York philanthropists assumed control of the antislavery movement, a community's initial response to immediatism hinged largely on the race question. That is, it depended primarily on whether the doctrine was identified with Negro uplift or racial assimilation. . . .

In Connecticut, the promotion of immediate abolition coincided with an attempt to establish a Negro college in New Haven. In June, 1831, Simeon S. Jocelyn, a white pastor of a New Haven Negro church, Arthur Tappan, and Garrison proposed such a college to a Negro national con-

---

Adams, *The Neglected Period of Antislavery in America, 1808–1831* (Boston, 1908), 106; Staudenraus, *African Colonization Movement,* 137; Henry N. Sherwood, "The Movement in Ohio to Deport the Negro," *The Quarterly Publication of the Historical and Philosophical Society of Ohio,* 7 (June 1912), 55ff.; *African Repository,* 5 (1829), 248; Richard C. Wade, "The Negro in Cincinnati, 1800–1830," *Journal of Negro History* 39 (January 1954), 48–57; Allan Peskin, ed., *North Into Freedom: The Autobiography of John Malvin, Free Negro, 1795–1880* (Cleveland, 1966), 38–40, 47–48; "Public Warning to Cincinnati Negroes and Commentary on Their Reaction," *Journal of Negro History* 8 (July 1923), 331–32.

[8] Cincinnati *Gazette,* September 17, 1829, quoted in Wade, "The Negro in Cincinnati," 56–57; Abdy, *Journal,* Vol. 2, pp. 381–83; Charles Cist, *Cincinnati in 1851* (Cincinnati, 1851), 46.

Invariably historians maintain that the extreme racism that prevailed in Cincinnati was due to a large number of settlers from Virginia and Kentucky. The argument is false. Less than 15 percent of the city's adult population was Southern-born. For every Southerner in Cincinnati, there were three or four settlers from the Northeast. See the tables of nativity for adult males in *The Cincinnati Directory for 1825,* 7, and *The Cincinnati Directory . . . for 1840,* 484.

vention. The enterprise would "produce a band of educated men to take up the pen" for Negro rights. New Haven, they agreed, was an ideal site because of its location, its intellectual fame, and the "friendly, pious, generous, and humane" character of its inhabitants.[9]

The friendly inhabitants disagreed. Almost immediately they became alarmed, and after the Nat Turner insurrection broke out in Virginia in August, their apprehension increased. In September, a month before Boston officials had heard of the *Liberator*, the mayor and alderman of New Haven called a town meeting. And by a vote of approximately 700 to 4, the citizens of New Haven denounced the proposal for a Negro college and denounced Garrison and the abolitionists for "unwarrantable and dangerous interference with the concerns of other states." Calling "the institution a *College*," Jocelyn reported to Garrison, "touched the very *quick* of oppression," for "it carries the assurance of equality with it."[10]

Although Jocelyn, Garrison, and the other abolitionists accepted defeat and abandoned the project, local newspapers continued to berate them for sponsoring amalgamation and causing New Haven Negroes to become "impudent and insolent." Several newspapers demanded the suppression of vice in "New Liberia," the Negro ghetto. Finally, in October, 1831, one mob stoned Arthur Tappan's house on Temple Street, another tore down a Negro shanty on "Sodom Hill," and still another invaded "New Liberia" and attacked amalgamation where it actually existed, capturing four white women and fourteen white men.[11]

A year and one-half later, but still six months before the New York City mob of October, 1833, an almost identical reaction occurred in nearby Canterbury, Connecticut. This was the famous Prudence Crandall incident. In the spring of 1833, Miss Crandall, a young Quaker schoolmistress, who had just been publicly rebuked for admitting a Negro day student, decided to challenge the community's prejudice in a radical way. Securing the support of antislavery leaders, she opened her boarding school exclusively to black girls.

Immediately the townfolk, led by Andrew T. Judson, town selectman and later United States district judge, Democratic politician, and an officer of the local colonization society, called a town meeting and denounced the scheme. Ignoring this condemnation and pleas from angry citizens, Miss Crandall received between ten and twenty girls. To offset this devilish plot to make "New England . . . the Liberia of America," the town fathers called a second meeting, which condemned the school as a "rendezvous . . . designed by its projectors . . . to promulgate their disgusting doctrines of amalgamation and their pernicious sentiments of subverting the Union." The angry citizens drew up a petition to the General Assembly

9 *Minutes and Proceedings of the First Annual Convention of the People of Colour* (Philadelphia, 1831), 5–7.

10 *Connecticut Journal,* July 20–September 13, 1831; Robert Austin Warner, *New Haven Negroes: A Social History* (New Haven, 1940), 53–56; *College for Colored Youth: An Account of the New Haven City Meeting and Resolutions* (New York, 1831); W. P. and F. J. Garrison, *Garrison*, Vol. 1, p. 260n.

11 *Connecticut Journal,* September 20–November 1, 1831; Tappan, *Tappan,* 258; Warner, *New Haven Negroes,* 57–59.

"deprecating the evil consequences of bringing from other states and towns, people of color for any purpose, and more especially for the purpose of disseminating the principles and doctrines opposed to the benevolent colonizing system." In May, the state legislature, responding to pressure, enacted a statute designed to outlaw Miss Crandall's boarding school.[12]

Miss Crandall defied the law, was twice tried, and finally was found guilty. . . . Eventually, in late 1834, an appellate court quashed the case on a technicality.[13]

Meanwhile, the exasperated citizens of Canterbury resorted to violence. Townfolk harassed Miss Crandall continuously. Vandals filled the school's well with manure, stoned the schoolhouse frequently, and even tried to burn it down. All these efforts, however, failed to stop Miss Crandall. Finally, in September, 1834, a band of men attacked her house at night and rendered it uninhabitable; Miss Crandall at last gave way and departed for Illinois.[14]

Connecticut remained the most inhospitable of the New England states. From 1833 through 1837, antislavery journals reported 16 antiabolition and anti-Negro mobs there.[15] . . .

Even in Cincinnati, which bordered a slave state and depended heavily on the Southern trade, there was little reaction to immediatism until it became associated with amalgamation and Negro uplift. . . .

It was not until the Lane students opened schools in "Little Africa" or "Bucktown" and associated publicly with Negroes, particularly "sable belles," that the editor of the *Journal* and other Cincinnatians expressed alarm. Weld often visited Negro homes, and Augustus Wattles, the most zealous supporter of Negro education and uplift, boarded with a Negro

---

[12] Prudence Crandall to Simeon S. Jocelyn, February 26, April 9, April 17, 1833, in "Abolition Letters Collected by Captain Arthur B. Spingarn," *Journal of Negro History* 17 (1933), 80–84; Prudence Crandall to Garrison, March 19, 1833, Garrison Papers; *Liberator*, April 6, 1833; *A Statement of Facts, Respecting the School for Colored Females, in Canterbury, Ct.* (Brooklyn, Connecticut, 1833), Ralph Foster Weld, *Slavery in Connecticut* (New Haven, 1935), 20–21. Of the many accounts of this whole affair, perhaps the most useful is May, *Reminiscences*, 40ff.

[13] May, *Reminiscences*, 54ff.; Helen T. Catterall, ed., *Judicial Cases Concerning American Slavery and the Negro* (5 vols.; Washington, D.C., 1926–1937), Vol. 4, pp. 415–16, 430–33.

[14] May, *Reminiscences*, 50–51, 70–71; W. P. and F. J. Garrison, *Garrison*, Vol. 1, pp. 317n., 321; Abdy, *Journal*, Vol. 1, pp. 199–203, Vol. 3, pp. 208–13, 303–7; George Benson to William Lloyd Garrison, March 5, 1833, Henry E. Benson to Samuel J. May, March 31, 1833, Almira Crandall to Henry E. Benson, April 30, 1833, Almira Crandall to George Benson, July 9, 1834—all Garrison Papers.

[15] Information on mobs computed from data, *Liberator*, 1833–1837, *Emancipator*, 1833–1837, and *Philanthropist*, 1836–1837. I arrived at the number of auxiliaries by taking the listing given in American Anti-Slavery Society, *Fifth Annual Report* (New York, 1838), 128–52, and subtracting the number formed before January 1833 as reported in the *First Annual Report . . . of the New England Anti-Slavery Society* 43.

Connecticut	(46 auxiliaries—16 mobs)
New Hampshire	(79—13)
Rhode Island	(26—4)
Maine	(48—4)
Massachusetts	(243—17)
Vermont	(104—7)

family. One student, who had been seen leaving town with a black girl and returning with her a few hours later, caused a stir; few believed his claim that he was only giving directions. On another occasion, a carriage of Negro students visited Lane Seminary, and it soon became common gossip that the Lane students paid "marked attention" to the girls. And thus rumor followed rumor, and gossip became nastier and nastier.[16] ...

... Cincinnati, which had anti-abolition and anti-Negro riots in 1836, 1841, and 1843, remained sensitive to questions of Negro uplift and racial assimilation. Repeatedly cries of "Amalgamationists! Amalgamationists! Amalgamationists!" rang through the Queen City. The "bugbear of 'amalgamation,'" reported one traveler, permeated southern Ohio. Even the notable Lyman Beecher was "so far jaundiced" that he supported African colonization, because "he considered it a salutary preventive of that amalgamation, which would confound the two races and obliterate the traces of their distinction."[17] And after the riot of September, 1841, which was the most violent and destructive of Cincinnati's outbursts, zealous Negrophobes organized themselves into the Anti-Abolition Society of Cincinnati. The society's primary goal was to secure the expulsion of the Negro from Ohio, either by the enactment of harsher anti-Negro legislation or by enforcement of the Black Laws of 1804 and 1807. Its only enemies, the society declared, were those "white traitors" who favored a "mixture of races." After the same riot, Dr. Gamaliel Bailey, the editor of the *Philanthropist,* issued a public declaimer. It began: "We are not *amalgamationists.*"[18]

Across the nation, abolitionists made the same disclaimer time and again, but to no avail. Throughout the ante-bellum period, anti-abolitionists repeated no charge with greater pertinacity than that of amalgamation, and none could more effectively stir up the rancor and the brutality of a mob. It was this charge—rather than any complaint about the technical difficulties of immediate emancipation or the future of the Southern trade—that generated the more savage anti-abolition mobs, such as those in New York City in July, 1834, and in Philadelphia in May, 1838.

For many Northerners, the probable alternative to slavery and African colonization was *either* race war *or* miscegenation. For Northern anti-

---

16 Theodore Dwight Weld to Lewis Tappan, March 18, 1834, March 9, 1836, in Barnes and Dumond, *Weld-Grimké Letters,* Vol. 1, 133–35, 273; *Proceedings of the Ohio Anti-Slavery Convention Held at Putnam* (Cincinnati, 1835), 34; *Fifth Annual Report of Lane Seminary, Nov. 1834* (Cincinnati, 1834), 38–41; *Cincinnati Journal,* October 17, 1834.

17 Abdy, *Journal,* Vol. 2, pp. 399–400. Amalgamation, Abdy added, was "neither to be dreaded nor deprecated, as it would destroy animosity by destroying its causes." Cincinnatians may have had reason to be extremely sensitive on questions of race, sex, and marriage. According to Abdy, one justice of the peace performed four interracial marriages in the course of one winter. See Vol. 3, pp. 17–18. And, judging from innuendoes in the press, illicit relationships between white men and Negro women apparently abounded. In the 1850 census, Cincinnati had fourteen mulattoes for every ten blacks; Connecticut, three for ten; New York City, three for ten.

18 *Daily Cincinnati Enquirer,* September 21, 25, 1841; *Cincinnati Post, and Anti-Abolitionist,* January 22, February 12, March 26, 1842; Bailey's disclaimer appeared in the *Cincinnati Daily Gazette,* September 17, 1841.

abolitionists, this alternative was as immutable as the law of gravity or the Ten Commandments: if slaves were freed, it followed that the two races must completely separate or wholly merge. To free millions of slaves and then leave them as a distinct race, to leave them in wretchedness and disgrace as the North had done with its few Negroes, was nothing less than to build a house with powder kegs. Destruction was certain.

The slave, as anti-abolitionists saw him, was contented and cowardly; he had been, as one ardent defender of the Lovejoy mob put it, "despoiled by Slavery."[19] But once the spirit of freedom and hope revived his dormant passions, he would be a new creature. He would never be satisfied with a few limited freedoms. He would want more and more. He would, in fact, never be content until he had access to women of both races, as white men had had for centuries, and particularly until he married the master's daughter. Onto the Negro the anti-abolitionists projected their own view of the American way. Marrying "well," they assumed, was the only real sign that an "inferior" had arrived. And since all "inferior" nationalities and classes measured their standing on the basis of their access to a "superior's" women, it followed that the most "inferior" of all would do likewise.

Once the slave became a new creature, he would also wield the sword with all the terror and the ferocity of deep revenge. The anti-abolitionist imagery of racial war, of slaughter, of carnage rested on the foreboding that the Negro had a score to settle with the white American. With dread anti-abolitionists looked forward to the day when the white man stood before the judgment seat of the black man. . . .

The only alternative to that day and the only penance for their sins, anti-abolitionists feared, was the horror of horrors—amalgamation. . . . For Americans who desperately dreaded being cut off from deep and permanent ties of family, clan, class, community, and position—amalgamation touched the heart of their passions: their dread of sinking below their forefathers' station and their nightmare of becoming cogs in a mass society.

For such men, African colonization offered the happy illusion of excluding the Negro not only from "society" but from the country as well. By attacking the American Colonization Society and by closely identifying themselves with the free Negro, the abolitionists made it clear that they entertained a far different vision. They proposed to lift the Negro not only out of bondage but out of the gutter as well. They proposed to give the free Negro citizenship—second-class citizenship to be sure, but citizenship nevertheless. Many anti-abolitionists were thus alarmed, and some resorted to violence. . . . We have seen in this chapter that the conventional picture of mobs painted by Le Bon and inherited by later social psychologists has little application to Northern anti-abolitionist mobs. Words such as "spontaneous," "unorganized," "fickle," "indiscriminate," and "purposeless" do not describe even the most impulsive anti-abolition mobs. "Murderous" has more meaning, but only when applied to mobs that encountered violent resistance. More useful are the terms

---

19 Austin, *Review of Channing's Letters to Phillips,* 67.

favored by George Rudé: nearly all anti-abolition mobs were "destructive," "discriminating," and "purposeful." In most respects, moreover, the lower-class anti-abolition mobs, such as the New York mob of 1834 and the Cincinnati mob of 1841, resembled the European mobs that Rudé describes.

Yet the conventional anti-abolition mobs, such as the Utica mob of 1835 and the Cincinnati mob of 1836, differed markedly from the mobs that interest Rudé. They were neither revolutionary nor lower-class. They involved a well-organized nucleus of respectable, middle-class citizens who wished to preserve the status quo rather than to change it. They met purposefully and often formally, and they coordinated their actions several days in advance. Frequently they had either the support or the acquiescence of the dominant forces in the community. Sometimes they represented the Establishment. More frequently they *were* the Establishment. . . . Anti-abolition mobs were often led by prominent citizens such as congressmen, attorneys general, judges, doctors, and mill owners. . . . Abolitionists thus erred in their appraisal of what epitomized the lower-class mob, but they were surprisingly accurate in their dissection of the more typical anti-abolitionist mob. We may regard the New York rioters as morally debauched, but they hardly represented "the sweepings of society," as antislavery men claimed. They were, on the average, very ordinary citizens who despised Negroes and dreaded the thought of miscegenation.

The more typical anti-abolition mob, whom the abolitionists seem to have known well, differed markedly from the lower-class mob. The rioters were rarely tradesmen or artisans; instead they were largely professional and commercial men. Many, as antislavery men insisted, were "gentlemen of property and standing" who regarded organized antislavery as a threat to their élite status. They were preservers of traditional forms, powers, and usages, and thus they deeply feared the invasion and development of mass media techniques, systematic agitation, and centralized organization and control. These forces, which organized antislavery so strongly personified, not only threatened their élite status and moral leadership but also undermined their values and traditions; these forces, said one anti-abolitionist spokesman after another, heralded the destruction of an older America.

chapter 8

Racism in America

FOUR HUNDRED YEARS OF WHITE VICTORIES against the colored peoples of the world in a framework of almost constantly expanding European capitalism and imperialism gave rise to a common scorn for nonwhites which became most virulent in South Africa and the United States. The sense of white supremacy which gained general sustenance throughout the Western World from European expansion at the expense of "the lesser breeds without" drew particular strength in America from the long and harsh tyranny of white masters over black slaves and from centuries of war, private violence and cultural aggression against the Indians. Yet the term "racism" scarcely existed before the 1930s, did not enter common usage until the 1960s, and still finds no favor among millions of Americans in the 1970s.

From the New Deal years onward a growing number of liberals displayed a willingness to discuss at least occasionally and superficially the status of blacks, but they generally used "soft" descriptive terms such as "prejudice" and "discrimination" in discussions which suggested the existence of minor flaws in American society. The intellectual foundation for the liberal position came from the struggle of pioneers such as Franz Boas and Melville Herskovits and the efforts of a small intellectual cadre of social scientists during the 1930s to pull social science from the bog of racism by disassociating culture and personality from biological "race." The mass murders of Hitler in the name of racism, the postwar emergence of colored nations, the Cold War diplomatic competition for "Third World" peoples, and modest economic and educational gains by segments of the black American populace, all provided the material conditions for the decline of ideological racism.

The fall from favor of formal racist thought actually helped to make possible until a few years ago the common American belief that unregenerate southern whites demonstrated the regional and transient nature of racial hostility. Scholarship between the two world wars tended to confirm this impression as did the two most notable books of the 1930s and early 40s relating to racism, William S. Jenkins' pedestrian but useful survey of proslavery arguments and W. J. Cash's provocative exploration of the Southern mind. Both writers were to a large extent immersed in racist opinions and presuppositions but their books still have some value today, particularly for insight into the opinions and sensibilities of the slaveowners. Among "mainstream" historians of the 40s and 50s only Richard Hofstadter came close to grasping the general facts about racism in several sections of his book on Social Darwinism (1944) and in the essay on Lincoln in *The American Political Tradition* (1948). Although a number of major scholars in the 50s such as Kenneth M. Stampp and Stanley M. Elkins broke free of old racist assumptions, they still tended to discuss racism in terms of slavery and Southern society.

The struggle for survival in America forced black writers to use their limited numbers and resources in the effort to present the past in a non-racist context. Sometimes tactical needs led black writers to stress the Southern citadel of racial aggression according to the example of Carl Rowan's *South of Freedom*. In the late 50s and in the 60s, however, an increasing number of black scholars placed racial thought in a national context as Rayford W. Logan did in his pioneer examination of white aggression in a great flood of books, magazines, pamphlets, newspapers, plays, songs, congressional speeches, Supreme Court opinions and presidential statements between Reconstruction and the First World War.

In 1960 William R. Stanton initiated modern scholarship on racism with a perceptive study of science and antebellum racial ideas. Although many of Stanton's scientists were Southerners, a considerable number worked in the North and Stanton's study reminded readers of the extent to which many of the social sciences entered the American intellectual scene as handmaidens of racism. Anthropologists, "craniologists," and miscellaneous students of society placed black men in the category of a separate species, classed blacks as enduringly inferior through thousands of years, and measured "internal skull capacity" with lead shot to place "Causasians" at the top and "Ethiopians" at the bottom of the human scale. Thomas F. Gossett in 1963 provided a general compendium of scholarship in a volume which indicated the prevalence in many generations of national life of WASP [White Anglo-Saxon Protestant] theories of superiority to Indians, Orientals, and the peoples of Eastern and Southern Europe, but the impact of Gossett's work was to some extent blunted because of a genial style and a tendency to assume that racist thought did not actually constitute a central theme in American history.

During the mid 60s current events once again informed the sensibilities of scholars when the black power movement turned from an emphasis on Southern white supremacy to stress racism as a central and pervasive force in all segments of American society. If racism afflicted California and New York in the 1960s, it seemed most probable that the same social ideas in more virulent forms, existed in the 1890s and the 1850s. As early as 1961 Leon Litwack (Selection 2) had pointed the way with his impressive study of extensive racial discrimination by the Northern states and the Federal government in the antebellum era. The perceptions of a number of scholars in the mid 60s bore fruit in a burst of important works which appeared in 1967 and 1968. In 1967 alone, V. Jacque Voegeli's volume demonstrated the existence of racist opinions, laws and customs in the midwest during the Civil War; Gilbert Osofski's volume of readings on *The Burden of Race* carefully documented the persistence of racist concepts and practices from early national history to the 1960s; Eugene H. Berwanger portrayed the West as so white supremacist that even the Oregon legislature felt compelled to express hostility toward the "menace" of the several dozen blacks in the territory during the 1850s; and Claude H. Nolen reminded Americans of the intensity of Southern racial hatreds after Civil War and Reconstruction as well as before and during that era.

Forrest G. Wood in 1968 extended Voegeli's study to the entire North and into the Reconstruction period and Winthrop D. Jordan's monumental work on racial attitudes from the beginning of the colonial period to the 1820s (Selection 1) proved how early and extensive the arrogance of white opinion and behavior had been. In 1971 John S. Haller took up the theme of science and racism where Stanton ended his study and discussed the very low regard of America's scientific elite at the end of the nineteenth century for blacks as "outcasts from evolution" locked into hopeless inferiority without any hope of evolutionary progress. Among the many books, articles, and anthologies of the era, H. Shelton Smith in 1972 displayed the intense racial hostilities among southern Protestant churches from the beginning of national history, William A. Osborne in 1967 presented the shabby record of American Catholic institutions, and Rubin Francis Weston traced the powerful influence of white supremacy concepts on U.S. foreign policy from the Hawaiian "revolution" of 1893 to the origins of the Cold War. In 1971 George M. Fredrickson (Selection 3) provided a useful compendium of scholarship from the previous decade on the century from Jefferson's era to the age of Wilson and added his own investigations and analysis of popular racism as "Herrenvolk democracy." As early as 1957 Robert F. Durden had suggested that all was not as scholars supposed on the question of the Republican Party and race and eight years later Hugh C. Bailey made the same point in his study of Hinton R. Helper as an "abolitionist racist." During the late 60s and early 70s some historians with vantage points ranging from C. Vann Woodward to Eugene Genovese began to postulate a racism even more intense in the North and the West than in the South, but Lawrence J. Friedman in 1971 placed a strong emphasis on "the white savage" of the postwar South. However unlikely Woodward's and Genovese's conclusion may seem to many scholars, it can nevertheless be taken as an index to the distance travelled from the easy assumption of many historians two decades ago that white racism was a minor affliction largely limited to the South.

BIBLIOGRAPHY

Works Discussed in This Chapter

Bailey, Hugh C., *Hinton Rowan Helper: Abolitionist Racist* (1965).
Berwanger, Eugene H., *The Frontier Against Slavery: Western Anti-Negro Prejudice and the Slavery Extension Controversy* (1967).

Boas, Franz, *The Mind of Primitive Man* (1911).

Cash, W. J., *The Mind of the South* (1941).

Durden, Robert F., *James Shepherd Pike, Republicanism and the Negro* (1957).

Elkins, Stanley M., *Slavery* (1959).

Fredrickson, George M., *The Black Image in the White Mind: The Debate on Afro-American Character and Destiny* (1971).

Friedman, Lawrence J., *The White Savage: Racial Fantasies in the Post-Bellum South* (1970).

Genovese, Eugene D., *The World the Slaveowners Made* (1969) and *In Red and Black* (1971).

Gossett, Thomas F., *Race: The History of an Idea in America* (1963).

Haller, John S., *Outcasts From Evolution: Scientific Attitudes of Racial Inferiority* (1971).

Herskovits, Melville, *The American Negro* (1928).

Hofstadter, Richard, *Social Darwinism in American Life* (1944) and *The American Political Tradition* (1948).

Jenkins, William S., *Pro-Slavery Thought in the Old South* (1935).

Jordan, Winthrop D., *White Over Black: American Attitudes Toward the Negro, 1550–1812* (1968) and *The White Man's Burden: Historical Origins of Racism in the U.S.* (1974).

Litwack, Leon, *North of Slavery: The Negro in the Free States, 1790–1860* (1961).

Logan, Rayford W., *The Negro in American Life and Thought: The Nadir, 1877–1901* (1954).

Newby, I. A., *Jim Crow's Defense: Anti-Negro Thought in America, 1900–1930* (1965), and *Challenge to the Court: The Social Sciences and the Defense of Segregation, 1954–1966* (1967).

Nolen, Claude H., *The Negro's Image in the South: The Anatomy of White Supremacy* (1967).

Osborne, William A., *The Segregated Covenant: Race Relations and American Catholics* (1967).

Osofsky, Gilbert, *The Burden of Race: A Documentary History of Negro-White Relations in America* (1964).

Rowan, Carl, *South of Freedom* (1952).

Smith, H. Shelton, *In His Steps, But . . . Racism in Southern Religion, 1790–1910* (1972).

Stanton, William R., *The Leopard's Spots: Scientific Attitudes Toward Race in America, 1815–1859* (1960).

Voegeli, V. Jacque, *Free But Not Equal: The Midwest and the Negro During the Civil War* (1967).

Weston, Rubin Francis, *Racism in U.S. Imperialism: The Influence of Racial Assumptions on American Foreign Policy, 1893–1946* (1972).

Wood, Forrest G., *Black Scare: The Racist Response to Emancipation and Reconstruction* (1968).

Woodward, C. Vann, *American Counterpoint* (1971).

Suggested Readings

Many titles listed in earlier and later chapters are germane, and in most sections of this chapter bibliography the editor lacks the space for complete listings.

Among the **general works** the most interesting collection of essays is Gary B. Nash and Richard Weiss, eds., *The Great Fear: Race in the Mind of America*

(1970). Three collections of documents are noteworthy: Louis Ruchames, ed., *Racial Thought in America From the Puritans to Abraham Lincoln* (1969); Otto H. Olsen, ed., *The Negro Question From Slavery to Caste, 1863–1910* (1971); and I. A. Newby, ed., *The Development of Segregationist Thought* (1968). The last volume extends from the 1890s to the 1950s. On racism in one state from the Civil War to the very recent past see Herman D. Bloch, *The Circle of Discrimination: An Economic and Social Study of the Black Man in New York* (1969). For a provocative work by a committed black scholar see Mary F. Berry, *Black Resistance/White Law: A History of Constitutional Racism in America* (1971). For the contribution of a psychiatrist see Joel Kovel, *White Racism: A Psycho-history* (1970). On white hostilities toward and exploitation of both blacks and Indians see essays by Charles Crowe and several others in Charles Hudson, ed., *Red, White and Black* (1972) and Hudson, ed. *Three Centuries of Southern Indians* (1974). See also Gary B. Nash, *Red, White and Black: The Peoples of Early America* (1974) and Wesley Frank Craven, *White, Red and Black: The Seventeenth Century Virginian* (1971). In a neglected volume Ruth Elson examined about every important 19th century textbook to study the ways in which images of race, religion etc. were communicated. See *Guardians of Tradition* (1964). Books which make few original contributions but are useful as summaries and popularizations are Sig Synnestvedt, *The White Response to Black Emancipation* (1972) and Dan Lacy, *The White Use of Blacks* (1972). A volume edited by Barry N. Schwartz and Robert Disch, *White Racism: Its History, Pathology and Practice* (1970) has only one historical section. A hastily contrived and inadequate anthology is Marvin Steinfield's *Our Racist Presidents From Washington to Nixon* (1972).

On *scientific racism* see Stanton, Haller and Newby, cited earlier; George W. Stocking, *Race, Culture and Evolution* (1968); and Mark Haller, *Eugenics: Hereditarian Attitudes in American Thought* (1963).

On *racism and religion* see David M. Reimers, *White Protestantism and the Negro* (1965); Andrew E. Murray, *Presbyterianism and the Negro* (1966); and Rufus Spain, *At Ease in Zion: Social History of the Southern Baptists, 1865–1900* (1967).

On *sex and racism* see Jordan's scholarly volume cited above. James Hugo Johnston's Ph.D. dissertation of the 1930s was published as *Race Relations in Virginia and Miscegenation in the South* (1970). For two popular books by journalists, see Calvin C. Hernton, *Sex and Racism in America* (1965) and Lawrence W. Baughman, *The Southern Rape Complex: A Hundred Year Psychosis* (1966).

For *colonial racism* see Jordan cited above and Thad W. Tate, *The Negro in Colonial Williamsburg* (1965).

For the *antebellum period* see Litwack, Stanton, Fredrickson as well as Eric L. McKitrick, ed., *Slavery Defended: The Views of the Old South* (1963); Frederick M. Binder's inadequate, *The Color Problem in Early National America As Viewed by Adams, Jefferson and Jackson* (1968); Harvey Wish, *George Fitzhugh, Propagandist of the Old South* (1943); Eric Foner, *Free Soil, Free Labor, Free Men: The Ideology of the Republican Party Before the Civil War* (1970); Joyce Adler, "Melville's Benito Cereno: Slavery and Violence in America," *Science and Society* (1974); and the less adequate Lorman Ratner, *Powder Keg: Northern Opposition to the Anti-Slavery Movement, 1830–1840* (1968).

For *Civil War and reconstruction* see Voegeli, Wood, Fredrickson, Haller, and Arthur Zilversmit, ed. *Lincoln on Black and White* (1972). For racism among the Radicals see William S. McFeeley, *Yankee Stepfather: General O. O. Howard and the Freedmen* (1968).

On *racism after reconstruction* see for the South Jack T. Kirby, *Darkness at the Dawning: Race and Reform in the Progressive South* (1972); Nolen and Friedman. For the North, see David W. Southern, *The Malignant Heritage: Yankee Progressives and the Negro Question, 1901–1914* (1968) and Herman D. Bloch, "Labor and the Negro, 1866–1910," *Journal of Negro History* (1965).

For *20th century racism* see both Newby monographs; Gilbert Osofsky, *Harlem The Making of a Ghetto* (1966); Allen H. Spear, *Black Chicago* (1967); Seth M. Scheiner, "President Theodore Roosevelt and the Negro," *Journal of Negro History* (1962); August Meier and Elliott Rudwick, "The Rise of Segregation in the Federal Bureaucracy, 1900–1930," *Phylon* (1967); Charles C. Alexander, *The Ku Klux Klan in the Southwest* (1965); David M. Chalmers, *Hooded Americanism: The History of the Ku Klux Klan* (1965); Leslie H. Fishel, Jr. "The Negro and the New Deal Era," *Wisconsin Magazine of History* (1964); Joseph Boskin, *The Life and Death of Sambo* (1971); and Charles Silberman, *Crisis in Black and White* (1964). The most recent period has been only very thinly researched.

Three useful anthologies on anti-black, anti-Indian, anti-Oriental racism, on *all major forms of racism*, are Bruce A. Glasrud and Alan M. Smith, eds., *Promises to Keep: A Portrayal of Nonwhites in the U.S.* 2 vols. (1972); Paul Jacobs, Saul Landau and Eve Pell, eds., *To Serve the Devil*, 2 vols. (1971); and Louis H. Carlsen and George H. Colburn, eds., *In Their Place: White America Defines Her Minorities, 1850–1950* (1972).

On *anti-Asian racism* see Gunther Barth, *Bitter Strength: A History of the Chinese in the U.S., 1850–1870* (1964); Stuart C. Miller, *The Unwelcome Immigrant: The American Image of the Chinese, 1785–1882* (1969); Alexander Saxton, *The Indispensable Enemy: Labor and the Anti-Chinese Movement in California* (1971); James W. Loewen, *The Mississippi Chinese: Between Black and White* (1971); Rogers Daniels, *The Politics of Prejudice: The Anti-Japanese Movement in California and the Struggle for Japanese Exclusion* (1969); and Daniels, *Concentration Camps, U.S.A.: Japanese-Americans and World War II* (1971).

On *anti-Indian racism* see Wilbur Jacobs, *Dispossessing the American Indian . . . On the Colonial Frontier* (1972); William T. Hagan, *Indian Police and Judges: Experiments in Acculturation and Control* (1966); Dee Brown, *Bury My Heart at Wounded Knee: An Indian History of the American West* (1970); Robert F. Berkhofer, *Salvation and the Savage: American Protestant Missions and Indian Assimilation, 1800–1890* (1963).

At times *nativist hostilities* approached the level of racial hatred. See John Higham, *Strangers in the Land: Patterns of American Nativism, 1869–1925* (1955) and Barbara Solomon, *Ancestors and Immigrants* (1956).

From the large literature on *race riots* (much of which is on recent black riots and hastily contrived) see for the antebellum period David Grimsted, "Rioting in Its Jacksonian Setting," *American Historical Review* (1972); and Leonard L. Richards, *Gentlemen of Property and Standing: Anti-Abolition Mobs in Jacksonian America* (1970); for the Civil War period, the popular account James McCague, *The Second Rebellion: The Story of the New York City Draft Riot of 1863* (1968); for Reconstruction riots see portions of Allen W. Trelease, *White Terror: The Ku Klux Klan Conspiracy and Southern Reconstruction* (1971); for the Progressive era two articles by Charles Crowe on the Atlanta Riot of 1906 in the *Journal of Negro History* (1968, 1969); for World War I, two excellent books, Elliott Rudwick, *Race Riot at East St. Louis—July 2, 1917* (1964) and William M. Tuttle, Jr. *Race Riot: Chicago in the Red Summer of 1919* (1970). Howard Sitkoff has written essays on World War II riots, and Pauline Meier, Joe M. Richardson, Herbert Shapiro, Jimmie

L. Franklin, Jack Holmes and others have written essays on riots in the various time periods.

On the *ghetto uprisings of the 60s,* perhaps the best single book is Robert M. Fogelson, *Violence as Protest* (1971), but see also Robert Conot on Watts, *Rivers of Blood, Years of Darkness* (1967) and John Hersey on Detroit in the *Algiers Motel Incident* (1968). Also very useful are the scholarly volumes edited by historians Hugh Davis Graham and Ted Robert Gurr for the National Commission on the Causes and Prevention of Violence. See especially *History of Racial Violence in America* (1968) which has many essays on general white violence. An excellent anthology of the same kind is Thomas Rose, ed. *Violence in America* (1969). Good but less comprehensive are Richard M. Brown, ed. *American Violence* (1970) and Richard Hofstadter and Michael Wallace, eds., *American Violence: A Documentary History* (1970). Ovid Demaris, *America the Violent* (1971) has faults but is worth looking at. No satisfactory account of lynching exists but see the startling news stories collected in Ralph Ginzburg, ed., *One Hundred Years of Lynching* (1962). On other Southern violence, see William F. Holmes, "Whitecapping: Agrarian Violence in Mississippi, 1902–1906," *Journal of Southern History* (1969) and Richard E. Rubenstein, *Rebels in Eden: Mass Political Violence* (1970).

On the *world context* see for comparative studies of racism in different countries, Michael Benton, *Race Relations* (1971) and Pierre L. van den Berghe, *Race and Racism: A Comparative Perspective* (1967). On the conflict between the nonwhite and poor and the rich, white peoples of the world, see Ronald Segal, *The Race War* (1967); Keith Irvine, *Rise of the Colored Races* (1970); and Frantz Fanon, *The Wretched of the Earth,* trans. by Constance Farrington (1961, Eng. ed. 1965).

The literature of *black responses* is vast, but some of the most important statements were made in major biographies, autobiographies and essays by Richard Wright, Ralph Ellison, James Baldwin, Malcolm X, Martin Luther King, and Eldridge Cleaver.

The Emergence of Racism*

Winthrop D. Jordan

The powerful impact which the Negro's color made upon Englishmen must have been partly owing to suddenness of contact. Though the Bible as well as the arts and literature of antiquity and the Middle Ages offered some slight introduction to the "Ethiope," England's immediate acquaintance with black-skinned peoples came with relative rapidity. While the

* Winthrop D. Jordan, *White Over Black: American Attitudes Toward the Negro, 1550–1812* (Chapel Hill: University of North Carolina Press, 1968). By permission of the publisher.

virtual monopoly held by Venetian ships in England's foreign trade prior to the sixteenth century meant that people much darker than Englishmen were not entirely unfamiliar, really black men were virtually unknown except as vaguely referred to in the hazy literature about the sub-Sahara which had filtered down from antiquity. Native West Africans probably first appeared in London in 1554; in that year five "Negroes," as the legitimate trader William Towrson reported, were taken to England, "kept till they could speake the language," and then brought back again "to be a helpe to Englishmen" who were engaged in trade with Negroes on the coast. Hakluyt's later discussion of these Negroes, who he said "could wel agree with our meates and drinkes" though "the colde and moyst aire doth somewhat offend them," suggests that these "blacke Moores" were a novelty to Englishmen.[1] In this respect the English experience was markedly different from that of the Spanish and Portuguese who for centuries had been in close contact with North Africa and had actually been invaded and subjected by people both darker and more highly civilized than themselves. The impact of the Negro's color was the more powerful upon Englishmen, moreover, because England's principal contact with Africans came in West Africa and the Congo where men were not merely dark but almost literally black: one of the fairest-skinned nations suddenly came face to face with one of the darkest peoples on earth.

Viewed from one standpoint, Englishmen were merely participating in Europe's discovery that the strange men who stood revealed by European expansion overseas came in an astounding variety of colors. A Spanish chronicle translated into English in 1555 was filled with wonder at this diversity: "One of the marveylous thynges that god useth in the composition of man, is coloure: whiche doubtlesse can not bee consydered withowte great admiration in beholding one to be white and an other blacke, beinge coloures utterlye contrary. Sum lykewyse to be yelowe whiche is betwene blacke and white: and other of other colours as it were of dyvers liveres."[2] As this passage suggests, the juxtaposition of black and white was the most striking marvel of all. And for Englishmen this juxtaposition was more than a curiosity.

In England perhaps more than in southern Europe, the concept of blackness was loaded with intense meaning. Long before they found that some men were black, Englishmen found in the idea of blackness a way of expressing some of their most ingrained values. No other color except white conveyed so much emotional impact. As described by the *Oxford English Dictionary*, the meaning of *black* before the sixteenth century included, "Deeply stained with dirt; soiled, dirty, foul. . . . Having dark or deadly purposes, malignant; pertaining to or involving death, deadly; baneful, disastrous, sinister. . . . Foul, iniquitous, atrocious, horrible,

---

[1] Hakluyt, *Principal Navigations*, 6, 176, 200, 217–18. Just how little Europeans knew about Africa prior to the Portuguese explorations is evident in T. Simar, "La géographie de l'Afrique central dans l'antiquité et au moyen âge," *La Revue Congolaise*, 3 (1912), 1–23, 81–102, 145–69, 225–52, 288–310, 440–41.

[2] Francisco López de Gómara, in Peter Martyr (D'Anghera), *The Decades of the Newe Worlde* . . . , trans. Richard Eden (London, 1555), in Edward Arber, ed., *The First Three English Books on America* . . . (Birmingham, Eng., 1885), 338.

wicked. . . . Indicating disgrace, censure, liability to punishment, etc."
Black was an emotionally partisan color, the handmaid and symbol of
baseness and evil, a sign of danger and repulsion.

Embedded in the concept of blackness was its direct opposite—whiteness. No other colors so clearly implied opposition, "beinge coloures utterlye contrary"; no others were so frequently used to denote polarization:

> Everye white will have its blacke,
> And everye sweete its sowre[3]

White and black connoted purity and filthiness, virginity and sin, virtue
and baseness, beauty and ugliness, beneficence and evil, God and the
devil.[4]

Whiteness, moreover, carried a special significance for Elizabethan
Englishmen: it was, particularly when complemented by red, the color
of perfect human beauty, especially *female* beauty. This ideal was already centuries old in Elizabeth's time,[5] and their fair Queen was its very
embodiment: her cheeks were "roses in a bed of lillies." (Elizabeth was
naturally pale but like many ladies then and since she freshened her
"lillies" at the cosmetic table.)[6] An adoring nation knew precisely what a
beautiful Queen looked like.

> Her cheeke, her chinne, her neck, her nose,
> This was a lillye, that was a rose;
> Her hande so white as whales bone,
> Her finger tipt with Cassidone;
> Her bosome, sleeke as Paris plaster,
> Held upp twoo bowles of Alabaster.[7]

Shakespeare himself found the lily and the rose a compelling natural
coalition.

> 'Tis beauty truly blent, whose red and white
> Nature's own sweet and cunning hand laid on.[8]

---

[3] Thomas Percy, *Reliques of Ancient English Poetry* . . . , ed. Robert A. Willmott
(London, 1857), 27 (Sir Cauline, pt. 2, stanza 1).

[4] Numerous examples in Middle English, Shakespeare, the Bible, and Milton are
given by P. J. Heather, "Colour Symbolism," *Folk Lore*, 59 (1948), 169–70, 175–78,
182–83; 60 (1949), 208–16, 266–76. See also Harold R. Isaacs, "Blackness and
Whiteness," *Encounter*, 21 (1963), 8–21; Caroline F. E. Spurgeon, *Shakespeare's
Imagery and What It Tells Us* (1968), 64, 66–69, 158. . . .

[5] Walter Clyde Curry, *The Middle English Ideal of Personal Beauty; As Found
in the Metrical Romances, Chronicles, and Legends of the XIII, XIV, and XV Centuries* (Baltimore, 1916), 3, 80–98.

[6] Elkin Calhoun Wilson, *England's Eliza* (Cambridge, Mass., 1939), 337; Charles
Carroll Camden, *The Elizabethan Woman* (Houston, N.Y., and London, 1952),
chap. 7; Cawley, *Voyagers and Elizabethan Drama*, 85; Elizabeth Jenkins, *Elizabeth
the Great* (London, 1958), 62, 100, 159, 296; Gamaliel Bradford, *Elizabethan
Women*, ed. Harold O. White (Boston, 1936), 82, 212; Violet A. Wilson, *Queen
Elizabeth's Maids of Honour and Ladies of the Privy Chamber* (N.Y., n.d.), 4–5.
Hugh Plat, *Delightes for Ladies, Written Originally by Sir Hugh Plat, First Printed
in 1602, London, England*, ed. Violet and Hal W. Trovillion (Herrin, Ill., 1939),
87–94, 99, 102–3, contains advice on cosmetics.

[7] [George Puttenham?], *Partheniades* (1579), quoted in Wilson, *England's Eliza*,
242.

[8] *Twelfth Night*, I, v, 259–60, W. J. Craig, ed., *The Complete Works of Shakespeare* [London, N.Y., Toronto, 1943]. For other expressions of this ideal, *A Mid-
summer-Night's Dream*, I, i, 128–29; III, i, 98–99; III, ii, 137–44.

By contrast, the Negro was ugly, by reason of his color and also his "horrid Curles" and "disfigured" lips and nose.[9] . . .

. . . Because Englishmen were Christians, heathenism in Negroes was a fundamental defect which set them distinctly apart. However much Englishmen disapproved of Popery and Mahometanism, they were accustomed to these perversions. Yet they were not accustomed to dealing face to face with people who appeared, so far as many travelers could tell, to have no religion at all.[10] Steeped in the legacy and trappings of their own religion, Englishmen were ill prepared to see any legitimacy in African religious practices. Judged by Christian cosmology, Negroes stood in a separate category of men.

The condition of savagery—the failure to be civilized—set Negroes apart from Englishmen in an ill-defined but crucial fashion. Africans were *different* from Englishmen in so many ways: in their clothing, huts, farming, warfare, language, government, morals, and (not least important) in their table manners. . . .

. . . The Negro's savagery . . . fascinated Englishmen from the very first. English observers in West Africa were sometimes so profoundly impressed by the Negro's deviant behavior that they resorted to a powerful metaphor with which to express their own sense of difference from him. They knew perfectly well that Negroes were men, yet they frequently described the Africans as "brutish" or "bestial" or "beastly." The hideous tortures, the cannibalism, the rapacious warfare, the revolting diet (and so forth page after page) seemed somehow to place the Negro among the beasts. The circumstances of the Englishman's confrontation with the Negro served to strengthen this feeling. Slave traders in Africa handled Negroes the same way men in England handled beasts, herding and examining and buying. The Guinea Company instructed Bartholomew Haward in 1651 "to buy and put aboard you so many negers as yo'r ship can cary, and for what shalbe wanting to supply with Cattel, as also to furnish you with victualls and provisions for the said negers and Cattel." Africa, moreover, teemed with strange and wonderful animals, and men that killed like tigers, ate like vultures, and grunted like hogs seemed indeed to merit comparison with beasts. In making this instinctive analogy, Englishmen unwittingly demonstrated how powerfully the African's different culture—for Englishmen, his "savagery"—operated to make Negroes seem to Englishmen a radically different kind of men. . . .[11]

If Negroes were likened to beasts, there was in Africa a beast which

---

9 *Love in Its Ecstacy,* quoted in Cawley, *Voyagers and Elizabethan Drama,* 86n; "A Letter written from Goa . . . by one Thomas Stevens . . . 1579," Hakluyt, *Principal Navigations,* 6, 384. . . .

10 For example, Hakluyt, *Principal Navigations,* 6, 144.

11 Ernest George Ravenstein, ed., *The Strange Adventures of Andrew Battell of Leigh, in Angola and the Adjoining Regions. Reprinted from "Purchas His Pilgrimes"* (ca. 1607) (*Works Issued by the Hakluyt Soc.,* 2d Ser., 6 [London, 1901]), 18. The term *bestiality* was first used to denote sexual relations with animals early in the 17th century; it was thus used frequently only for about 150 years! "A Description . . . of Guinea . . ." in Samuel Purchas, *Hakluytus Posthumus or Purchas His Pilgrimes, Contayning a History of the World in Sea Voyages and Lande Travells by Englishmen and Others,* 20 vols. (Glasgow, 1905–07), 6, 251.

was likened to men. It was a strange and eventually tragic happenstance of nature that the Negro's homeland was the habitat of the animal which in appearance most resembles man. . . . Englishmen were introduced to the anthropoid apes and to Negroes at the same time and in the same place. The startlingly human appearance and movements of the "ape"—a generic term though often used as a synonym for the "orang outang"—aroused some curious speculations. . . .

The sexual association of apes with Negroes had an inner logic which kept it alive without much or even any factual sustenance. Sexual union seemed to prove a certain affinity without going so far as to indicate actual identity—which was what Englishmen really thought was the case. By forging a sexual link between Negroes and apes, furthermore, Englishmen were able to give vent to their feeling that Negroes were a lewd, lascivious, and wanton people.

It was no accident that this affinity between Negroes and apes was so frequently regarded as sexual, for undertones of sexuality run throughout many English accounts of West Africa. To liken Africans—any human beings—to beasts was to stress the animal within the man. Indeed the sexual connotations embodied in the terms *bestial* and *beastly* were considerably stronger in Elizabethan English than they are today, and when the Elizabethan traveler pinned these epithets upon the behavior of Negroes he was frequently as much registering a sense of sexual shock as describing swinish manners. . . .

. . . Englishmen were unaccustomed to West African standards concerning suitable public attire. Many Negroes were (or perhaps merely appeared to trousered Englishmen) utterly "naked."[12] Fully as important were African matrimonial practices, which in fact frequently failed to match the accepted norm for Christian Englishmen. It may be that Englishmen found Negroes free in a primitive way and found this freedom somehow provocative; many chroniclers made a point of discussing the Negro women's long breasts and ease of child bearing. . . .

Male numerical predominance [in the New World] must surely have been conducive to development of a system of Negro concubinage and, concomitantly, to widespread acceptance of such a system—at least by its participants, which meant a major proportion of white men in the West Indies. As for white women there, a kind of psycho-sexual Gresham's law tended to drive them out of circulation. And while a high sex ratio must have contributed to the acceptability of miscegenation, it may by extension have enhanced the acceptability of mulatto offspring. . . .

Beginning in the 1730s the Jamaican legislature passed numerous private acts conferring upon the colored offspring and sometimes the colored mistress of such and such a planter the rights and privileges of white persons, especially the right to inherit the planter's estate.[13] . . .

---

12 "The First Voyage Made by Master William Towrson . . ." (1555), Hakluyt, *Principal Navigations*, 6, 184; "A voyage to Benin . . . Written by James Welsh . . ." (1589), ibid., 457.

13 *Acts of Assembly, Passed in the Island of Jamaica, from the Year 1681 to the Year 1769 Inclusive*, 2 vols. in 1, with an *Appendix: Containing Laws Respecting Slaves* (Kingston, 1787), 2, 36–39. For the private acts, the Table of Acts in ibid.;

The colonist on the American continent refused to make this extension of privilege. He remained firm in his rejection of the mulatto, in his categorization of mixed-bloods as belonging to the lower caste. It was an unconscious decision dictated perhaps in large part by the weight of Negroes on his community, heavy enough to be a burden, yet not so heavy as to make him abandon all hope of maintaining his own identity, physically and culturally. Interracial propagation was a constant reproach that he was failing to be true to himself. Sexual intimacy strikingly symbolized a union he wished to avoid. If he could not restrain his sexual nature, he could at least reject its fruits and thus solace himself that he had done no harm. Perhaps he sensed as well that continued racial intermixture would eventually undermine the logic of the racial slavery upon which his society was based. For the separation of slaves from free men depended on a clear demarcation of the races, and the presence of mulattoes blurred this essential distinction. Accordingly he made every effort to nullify the effects of racial intermixture. By classifying the mulatto as a Negro he was in effect denying that intermixture had occurred at all. . . .

By calling the Negro woman passionate . . . [white men] were offering the best possible justification for their own passions. Not only did the Negro woman's warmth constitute a logical explanation for the white man's infidelity, but, much more important, it helped shift responsibility from himself to her. If she was *that* lascivious—well, a man could scarcely be blamed for succumbing against overwhelming odds. Further reinforcement for this picture of the Negro woman came from the ancient association of hot climates with sexual activity,[14] a tradition which persists today despite the introduction of central heating. Operating less strongly in the same direction was the old equation of barbarism with sexual abandonment: Negro women seemed more natural and were sometimes described, for instance, as giving birth more easily than white women.[15]

Attitudes toward the Negro male were more complex and potentially far more explosive. The notion that Negro men were particularly virile, promiscuous, and lusty was of course not new in the eighteenth century, but the English colonists in America showed signs of adding a half-conscious and revealingly specific corollary: they sometimes suggested that Negro men lusted after white women. Again there was probably some ob-

---

in *Acts Jamaica* (1786); and in *Acts of Assembly, Passed in the Island of Jamaica, from the Year 1784 to the Year 1788 Inclusive* (Kingston, 1789). Also Edwards, *History of British West Indies,* 2, 22–23; [Long], *Jamaica,* 2, 320–23. [Long], *Jamaica,* 2, 332–35. This general picture is borne out by a work on a later period: Philip D. Curtin, *Two Jamaicas: The Role of Ideas in a Tropical Colony, 1830–1865* (Cambridge, Mass., 1955), chaps. 1–3.

14 J. W. Johnson, " 'Of Differing Ages and Climes,' " *Jour. Hist. Ideas,* 21 (1960), 474–75.

15 For example, [Long], *Jamaica,* 2, 380. Apparently this notion about parturition is incorrect: Julian H. Lewis, *The Biology of the Negro* (Chicago, 1942), chap. 6. Negro wet nurses for white babies, and objections to the practice, are noted in Luffman, *Brief Account of Antigua,* 36; Julia C. Spruill, *Women's Life and Work in the Southern Colonies* (Chapel Hill, 1938), 55–57; *Works of James Houstoun, M.D.* (London, 1753), 293–94; "Letters of Rev. Jonathan Boucher," *Maryland Historical Magazine,* 7 (1912), 6.

jective basis for the charge, since sexual intercourse with a white woman must in part have been for Negro men an act of retribution against the white man. For different reasons there was also good basis for the common feeling that only the most depraved white woman would consent to sleep with a Negro, since white women of the lowest class had the least to lose in flouting the maxims of society and the most reason to hate them. No matter how firmly based in fact, however, the image of the sexually aggressive Negro was rooted even more firmly in deep strata of irrationality. For it is apparent that white men projected their own desires onto Negroes: their own passion for Negro women was not fully acceptable to society or the self and hence not readily admissible. Sexual desires could be effectively denied and the accompanying anxiety and guilt in some measure assuaged, however, by imputing them to others. It is not we, but others, who are guilty. It is not we who lust, but they. Not only this, but white men anxious over their own sexual inadequacy were touched by a racking fear and jealousy. Perhaps the Negro better performed his nocturnal offices than the white man. Perhaps, indeed, the white man's woman really wanted the Negro more than she wanted him.

Significantly, these tensions tended to bubble to the surface especially at times of interracial crisis when the colonists' mundane control over their Negroes appeared in jeopardy. During many scares over slave conspiracies, for instance, reports circulated that the Negroes had plotted killing all white persons except the young women, whom they "intended to reserve for themselves."[16] In fact these charges were ill-founded at best, for there is no evidence that any Negroes in revolt ever seized any white women for their "own use," even though rebellious slaves certainly had opportunity to do so during the successful insurrections in the West Indies and also at Stono in South Carolina.

It is especially striking that in the eighteenth century, reports of sexual aims were confined to the continental colonies; in the seventeenth century, that is before the institutionalization of miscegenation in the West Indian islands, these reports circulated during two insurrections on Barbados, revealing a tension there which later remitted as Barbadians relaxed into an amiable attitude toward interracial sex and gradually accepted the fact that the island had been utterly given over to masses of slaves.[17] In the continental colonies there was a revealing overeagerness in the way the press in distant cities picked up the idea that Negro insurrectionaries in a certain locality had aimed at acquisition of white women. . . .

---

16 N.-Y. Gaz., March 25, 1734; Stephen Bordley to Matt Harris, Annapolis, January 30, 1739 [/40], Stephen Bordley's Letterbook, 1738–1740, Maryland Historical Society, Baltimore; [Horsmanden], Journal of the Proceedings, passim, especially p. 42 when the New York jury was told that "the White Men should be all killed, and the Women become a Prey to the rapacious Lust of these Villains!" N.-Y. Weekly Jour., June 15, 1741; Phila. American Weekly Mercury, June 18, 1741; Charleston S.-C. Gaz., July 30, 1741; Box 3, bundle: Minutes of Council in Assembly (1748–49), Including Papers on the Negro Conspiracy, [Pt. ii], 39, Parish Transcripts, N.-Y. Hist. Soc.

17 Great Newes from the Barbadoes . . . (London, 1676), 10; [John Oldmixon], The British Empire in America . . . (2 vols., London, 1708), 2, 47. . . .

. . . It seems more than likely that fears of Negro sexual aggression during periods of alarm over insurrection did not represent direct response to actual overt threat, but rather a complex of reactions in the white man. Any group faced with a real threat of serious proportions is inclined to sense, even on a conscious level, a sexual element in the opponents' aggressiveness—as many have identified Communism with free love. Any Negro insurrection, furthermore, threatened the white man's dominance, including his valuable sexual dominance, and hence the awful prospect of being overthrown was bound to assume a sexual cast. Although the white man's sexual anxiety focused on the Negro male, it could easily spill over into resentful suspicion of the supposed objects of the Negro's lust, as in a Maryland planter's sarcastic coda to his remarks on the folly of a white woman who had heard from her slave of a forthcoming revolt and who had done nothing to inquire into an affair which could have led to her death—"but perhaps She had a mind for a black husband."[18] And finally, white men anxious and guilty over their own sexual aggressiveness were quick to impute it to others especially at a time of interracial crisis. One has only to imagine the emotions flooding through some planter who had been more or less regularly sleeping with some of his slave wenches when he suddenly learned of a conspiracy among their male counterparts; it was virtually inevitable that his thoughts turn in a torrent of guilt to the "safety" of his wife.

The white man's fears of Negro sexual aggression were equally apparent in the use of castration as a punishment in the colonies. This weapon of desperation was not employed by angry mobs in the manner which became familiar after Emancipation. In a few instances, particularly in the West Indies, individual planters emasculated their slaves, sometimes in outbursts of sadism involving hideous tortures which planter society deplored but did not effectively control until the latter part of the eighteenth century. Far more significant, castration was dignified by specific legislative sanction as a lawful punishment in Antigua, the Carolinas, Bermuda, Virginia, Pennsylvania, and New Jersey.[19] . . .

It was the case with English confrontation with Negroes . . . that a society in a state of rapid flux, undergoing important changes in religious values, and comprised of men who were energetically on the make and acutely and often uncomfortably self-conscious of being so, came upon a people less technologically advanced, markedly different in appearance

---

18 Stephen Bordley to Matt Harris, Annapolis, January 30, 1739 [/40], Stephen Bordley's Letterbook, 1738–1740, Md. Hist. Soc.

19 Hans Sloane, *A Voyage to the Islands Madera, Barbados, Nieves, S. Christophers and Jamaica, with the Natural History* . . . , 2 vols. (London, 1707–25), I, lvii; Sainsbury, ed., *Cal. State Papers, 1708–09,* 470, 520, 1724–25, 56; James Ramsay, *An Essay on the Treatment and Conversion of African Slaves in the British Sugar Colonies* (London, 1784), 86, 282; Purdie and Dixon's Wmsbg. *Va. Gaz.,* December 23, 1773. *Acts Leeward Islands* (1734), 136 (1702—unspecific, allowing "any Member cut off" for injuring a white person); Cooper and McCord, eds., *Statutes S.C.,* 7, 360 (1696); Clark, ed., *State Recs. N.C.,* 23, 489 (1758); Sainsbury, ed., *Cal. State Papers, 1704–05,* 506–9 (1704, Bermuda); Hening, ed., *Statutes Va.,* 3, 461 (1705); Mitchell *et al.,* eds., *Statutes Pa.,* 2, 79 (1700); [*Acts of N.J. in 1704*], 18–20. The Virginia act provided for "dismembring," a term which seems usually to have been taken to mean castration but which may occasionally have encompassed punishments such as severing toes.

and culture. From the first, Englishmen tended to set Negroes over against themselves, to stress what they conceived to be radically contrasting qualities of color, religion, and style of life, as well as animality and a peculiarly potent sexuality. What Englishmen did not at first fully realize was that Negroes were potentially subjects for a special kind of obedience and subordination which was to arise as adventurous Englishmen sought to possess for themselves and their children one of the most bountiful dominions of the earth. When they came to plant themselves in the New World, they were to find that they had not entirely left behind the spirit of avarice and insubordination. Nor does it appear, in light of attitudes which developed during their first two centuries in America, that they left behind all the impressions initially gathered of the *Negro* before he became preeminently the *slave*. . . .

From the first, then, vis-à-vis the Negro the concept embedded in the term *Christian* seems to have conveyed much of the idea and feeling of *we* as against *they:* to be Christian was to be civilized rather than barbarous, English rather than African, white rather than black. The term *Christian* itself proved to have remarkable elasticity, for by the end of the seventeenth century it was being used to define a species of slavery which had altogether lost any connection with explicit religious difference. In the Virginia code of 1705, for example, the term sounded much more like a definition of race than of religion: "And for a further christian care and usage of all christian servants, *Be it also enacted, by the authority aforesaid, and it is hereby enacted,* That no negroes, mulattos, or Indians, although christians, or Jews, Moors, Mahometans, or other infidels, shall, at any time, purchase any christian servant, nor any other, except of their own complexion, or such as are declared slaves by this act." By this time "Christianity" had somehow become intimately and explicitly linked with "complexion."[20] The 1705 statute declared "That all servants imported and brought into this country, by sea or land, who were not christians in their native country, (except Turks and Moors in amity with her majesty, and others that can make due proof of their being free in England, or any other christian country, before they were shipped, in order to transportation hither) shall be accounted and be slaves, and as such be here bought and sold notwithstanding a conversion to christianity afterwards."[21] As late as 1753 the Virginia slave code anachronistically defined slavery in terms of religion when everyone knew that slavery had for generations been based on the racial and not the religious difference.[22]

It is worth making still closer scrutiny of the terminology which Englishmen employed when referring both to themselves and to the two peoples they enslaved, for this terminology affords the best single means of probing the content of their sense of difference. The terms *Indian* and

---

[20] Hening, ed., *Statutes Va.*, 2, 281 (1670), 155 (1662).

[21] Ibid., 3, 447–48 (1705), also 283, 5, 547–48, 6, 356–57. Lingering aftereffects of the old concept cropped up as late as 1791, when *Negro* was still contradistinguished by *Christian:* Certificate of character of Negro Phill, Feb. 20, 1791, Character Certificates of Negroes, Papers of the Pennsylvania Abolition Society, Historical Society of Pennsylvania, Philadelphia.

[22] Hening, ed., *Statutes Va.*, 6, 356–57.

Negro were both borrowed from the Hispanic languages, the one originally deriving from (mistaken) geographical locality and the other from
human complexion. When referring to the Indians the English colonists
either used that proper name or called them *savages*, a term which reflected primarily their view of Indians as uncivilized, or occasionally (in
Maryland especially) *pagans*, which gave more explicit expression to
the missionary urge. When they had reference to Indians the colonists
occasionally spoke of themselves as *Christians* but after the early years
almost always as *English*.

In significant contrast, the colonists referred to *Negroes* and by the
eighteenth century to *blacks* and to *Africans*, but almost never to Negro
heathens or *pagans* or *savages*. Most suggestive of all, there seems to
have been something of a shift during the seventeenth century in the
terminology which Englishmen in the colonies applied to themselves.
From the initially most common term *Christian*, at mid-century there
was a marked drift toward *English* and *free*. After about 1680, taking the
colonies as a whole, a new term appeared—*white*.

So far as the weight of analysis may be imposed upon such terms, diminishing reliance upon *Christian* suggests a gradual muting of the specifically religious element in the Christian-Negro disjunction in favor
of secular nationality: Negroes were, in 1667, "not in all respects to be
admitted to a full fruition of the exemptions and impunities of the English."[23] As time went on, as some Negroes became assimilated to the
English colonial culture, as more "raw Africans" arrived, and as increasing numbers of non-English Europeans were attracted to the colonies, the
colonists turned increasingly to the striking physiognomic difference. By
1676 it was possible in Virginia to assail a man for "eclipsing" himself in
the "darke imbraces of a Blackamoore" as if "Buty consisted all together
in the Antiphety of Complections." In Maryland a revised law prohibiting
miscegenation (1692) retained *white* and *English* but dropped the term
Christian—a symptomatic modification. As early as 1664 a Bermuda
statute (aimed, ironically, at protecting Negroes from brutal abandonment) required that the "last Master" of senile Negroes "provide for them
such accomodations as shall be convenient for Creatures of that hue and
colour untill their death." By the end of the seventeenth century dark
complexion had become an independent rationale for enslavement: in
1709 Samuel Sewall noted in his diary that a "Spaniard" had petitioned
the Massachusetts Council for freedom but that "Capt. Teat alleg'd that
all of that Color were Slaves."[24] Here was a barrier between "we" and

---

23 Ibid., 2, 267.

24 "History of Bacon's and Ingram's Rebellion," Andrews, ed., *Narratives of the
Insurrections*, 96; *Archives Md.*, 13, 546–49; Lefroy, comp., *Memorials Bermudas*,
2, 216; *Diary of Samuel Sewall, 1674–1729* (Mass. Hist. Soc., *Collections*, 5th Ser.
5–7 [1878–82]), 2, 248. In 1698 Gov. Francis Nicholson informed the Board of Trade
that the "major part" of Negroes in Maryland spoke English: *Archives Md.*, 23, 499.
For first use of "white" in statutes of various colonies, Bartlett, ed., *Recs. Col. R.I.*,
I, 243 (1652); *Archives Md.*, 7, 204–5 (1681); Aaron Leaming and Jacob Spicer,
eds., *The Grants, Concessions, and Original Constitutions of the Province of New
Jersey . . .* , 2d ed. (Somerville, N.J., 1881), 236 (1683); *Col. Laws N.Y.*, 1, 148
(1684); Cooper and McCord, eds., *Statutes S.C.*, 7, 343 (1691); Hening, ed., *Statutes
Va.*, 3, 86–87 (1691); *Acts of Assembly, Made and Enacted in the Bermuda or Sum-*

"they" which was visible and permanent: the Negro could not become a white man. Not, at least, as yet.

What had occurred was not a change in the justification of slavery from religion to race. No such justifications were made. There seems to have been, within the unarticulated concept of the Negro as a different sort of person, a subtle but highly significant shift in emphasis. Consciousness of the Negro's heathenism remained through the eighteenth and into the nineteenth and even the twentieth century, and an awareness, at very least, of his different appearance was present from the beginning. The shift was an alteration in emphasis within a single concept of difference rather than a development of a novel conceptualization. The amorphousness and subtlety of such a change is evident, for instance, in the famous tract, *The Negro's and Indians Advocate*, published in 1680 by the Reverend Morgan Godwyn. Baffled and frustrated by the disinterest of planters in converting their slaves, Godwyn declared at one point that "their *Complexion*, which being most obvious to the sight, by which the *Notion* of things doth seem to be most certainly conveyed to the Understanding, is apt to make no *slight* impressions upon rude Minds, already prepared to admit of any thing for *Truth* which shall make for Interest." Altering his emphasis a few pages later, Godwyn complained that "these two words, *Negro* and *Slave*" are "by custom grown Homogeneous and Convertible; even as *Negro* and *Christian*, *Englishman* and *Heathen* are by the like corrupt Custom and Partiality made Opposites."[25] Most arresting of all, throughout the colonies the terms *Christian*, *free*, *English*, and *white* were for many years employed indiscriminately as metonyms. A Maryland law of 1681 used all four terms in one short paragraph.[26]

Whatever the limitations of terminology as an index to thought and feeling, it seems likely that the colonists' initial sense of difference from the Negro was founded not on a single characteristic but on a congeries of qualities which, taken as a whole, seemed to set the Negro apart. Virtually every quality in the Negro invited pejorative feelings. What may have been his two most striking characteristics, his heathenism and his appearance, were probably prerequisite to his complete debasement. His heathenism alone could never have led to permanent enslavement since conversion easily wiped out that failing. If his appearance, his racial characteristics, meant nothing to the English settlers, it is difficult to see how slavery based on race ever emerged, how the concept of complexion as the mark of slavery ever entered the colonists' minds. Even if the colonists were most unfavorably struck by the Negro's color, though, blackness itself did not urge the complete debasement of slavery. Other qualities—the utter strangeness of his language, gestures, eating habits, and so on—certainly must have contributed to the colonists' sense that he

---

mer-Islands, from 1690, to 1713–14 (London, 1719), 12–13 (1690 or 1691). West Indian assemblies used the term in the 1680's and 1690's, possibly earlier. Officials in England were using "whites" and "blacks" as early as 1670 in questionnaires to colonial governors: Hening, ed., *Statutes Va.*, 2, 515; Trumbull and Hoadly, eds., *Recs. Col. Conn.*, 3, 293.

[25] Godwyn, *The Negro's and Indians Advocate*, 20, 36.
[26] *Archives, Md.*, 7, 204.

was very different, perhaps disturbingly so. In Africa these qualities had for Englishmen added up to *savagery;* they were major components in that sense of *difference* which provided the mental margin absolutely requisite for placing the European on the deck of the slave ship and the Negro in the hold.

The available evidence (what little there is) suggests that for Englishmen settling in America, the specific religious difference was initially of greater importance than color, certainly of much greater relative importance than for the Englishmen who confronted Negroes in their African homeland. Perhaps Englishmen in Virginia, living uncomfortably close to nature under a hot sun and in almost daily contact with tawny Indians, found the Negro's color less arresting than they might have in other circumstances. Perhaps, too, these first Virginians sensed how inadequately they had reconstructed the institutions and practices of Christian piety in the wilderness; they would perhaps appear less as failures to themselves in this respect if compared to persons who as Christians were *totally* defective. In this connection they may be compared to their brethren in New England, where godliness appeared (at first) triumphantly to hold full sway; in New England there was distinctly less contrasting of Negroes on the basis of the religious disjunction and much more militant discussion of just wars. Perhaps, though, the Jamestown settlers were told in 1619 by the Dutch shipmaster that these "negars" were heathens and could be treated as such. We do not know. The available data will not bear all the weight that the really crucial questions impose.

Of course once the cycle of degradation was fully under way, once slavery and racial discrimination were completely linked together, once the engine of oppression was in full operation, then there is no need to plead *ignoramus.* By the end of the seventeenth century in all the colonies of the English empire there was chattel racial slavery of a kind which would have seemed familiar to men living in the nineteenth century. No Elizabethan Englishman would have found it familiar, though certain strands of thought and feeling in Elizabethan England had intertwined with reports about the Spanish and Portuguese to engender a willingness on the part of English settlers in the New World to treat some men as suitable for private exploitation. During the seventeenth century New World conditions had exploited this predisposition and vastly enlarged it, so much so that English colonials of the eighteenth century were faced with full-blown slavery—something they thought of not as an institution but as a host of ever present problems, dangers, and opportunities. . . .

Racist Policies of the Federal Government*

Leon F. Litwack

In the absence of any clear constitutional or judicial directive, the federal government and the individual states separately defined the legal status of antebellum free Negroes. Prior to the Fourteenth and Fifteenth Amendments, each state determined their political and educational rights. In many cases, this resulted in disfranchisement, immigration restrictions, and public school segregation. Various branches of the federal government also confronted problems involving the constitutional rights of free Negroes, an aspect of federal policy that historians have generally neglected.

During the Missouri controversy of 1819–21, Congress exhaustively debated the Negro's legal status but failed to clarify it. Not until 1857, when the Supreme Court settled the Dred Scott case, did the federal government finally resolve the question. By then, Chief Justice Roger B. Taney could turn to federal legislation and "the conduct of the Executive Department" for precedents.

Reflecting the popular conception of the United States as a white man's country, early congressional legislation frequently excluded Negroes from federal rights and privileges. In 1790, Congress limited naturalization to "any alien, being a white person"; in 1792, it organized the militia and restricted enrollment to "each and every free, able-bodied white male citizen"; in 1810, it excluded Negroes from carrying the United States mails; in 1820, it authorized the citizens of Washington, D.C., to elect "white" city officials and to adopt a code governing free Negroes and slaves.[1] It repeatedly approved the admission of states whose constitutions severely limited the legal rights of Negroes.[2] On one occasion, however, the House of Representatives momentarily recognized Negro citizenship when it resolved in 1803 "to enquire into the expediency of

---

* Leon F. Litwack, "The Federal Government and the Free Negro, 1790–1860," *The Journal of Negro History* Vol. 43, No. 4 (October 1958), 261–78.

[1] *Appendix to the Annals of Congress*, 1 Cong., 2 Sess., 2 Cong., 1 Sess., 1392; 11 Cong., 1 and 2 Sess., 2569; 16 Cong., 1 Sess., 2600–10; 18 Cong., 2 Sess., 91.

[2] Charles H. Wesley, "Negro Suffrage in the Period of Constitution Making 1787–1865," *Journal of Negro History*, 32 (1947), 154. Vermont (1790), Kentucky (1792), and Tennessee (1796) made no provision in their constitutions excluding Negroes from the suffrage. With Maine (1819), they were the only states which entered the Union, prior to the admission of Nebraska in 1867, which did not restrict the suffrage to whites. Kentucky and Tennessee subsequently enacted such a restriction.

granting protection to such American seamen citizens of the United States, as are free persons of color."[3]

These measures elicited only minor discussion. But after 1821 legislation affecting the legal position of Negroes frequently involved Congress in lengthy and bitter debates. As abolition sentiment and agitation increased, southern and "Doughface" congressmen seized upon opportunities to show the inconsistency of pronouncements on equality and freedom with the treatment accorded free Negroes in the North. In the famous exchange between Daniel Webster and Robert Hayne, for example, the South Carolina senator defended Negro bondage and charged that slaves were induced to leave their masters and go North where they were treated as outcasts and assigned to "the dark and narrow lanes, and obscure recesses" of the cities. "Sir," he cried, "there does not exist on the face of the earth, a population so poor, so wretched, so vile, so loathsome, so utterly destitute of all the comforts, conveniences, and decencies of life, as the unfortunate blacks of Philadelphia and Boston."[4] Senator Felix Grundy of Tennessee observed in 1830 that the treatment of Negroes in the free western states proved that "general notions about the liberation of slaves are idle and visionary."[5] In denouncing northern interference with slavery, a Virginia Representative asked, "Do you permit the black man to sit on juries, to enter the learned professions, and to associate with you upon an equal footing, or, to worship by your side in the house of God? It is notorious you permit none of these things. . . . Go home, and emancipate your free negroes. When you do that, we will listen to you with more patience."[6]

After 1840, southern congressmen could assert that the federal government itself offered authoritative proof of the benign influence of slavery on Negroes. The Sixth Census of the United States, released in 1841, enumerated for the first time the mentally diseased and defective—or "insane and idiots" as they were then officially described—and contained the startling revelation that their prevalence among free Negroes was about 11 times higher than among slaves. In the southern states, the ratio of insane or idiotic among the Negro population stood at one to every 1,558; in the northern states, it was one to every 144.5.[7] In fact, the frequency of these afflictions among Negroes decreased from Maine to Louisiana with virtual mathematical precision. For example, it was found that in Maine every 14th Negro was either a lunatic or an idiot; in New

---

3 *Journal of the House of Representatives*, 8 Cong., 1 Sess., 224.

4 *Register of Debates*, 21 Cong., 1 Sess., 47.

5 Ibid., 215.

6 *Congressional Globe*, 30 Cong., 1 Sess., 602; 29 Cong., 2 Sess., 349.

7 Albert Deutsch, "The First U.S. Census of the Insane (1840) and Its Use as Pro-Slavery Propaganda," *Bulletin of the History of Medicine*, 15 (1944), 469–82. Aside from the Deutsch article, I am indebted for suggested references to William R. Stanton, *The Leopard's Spots: Science and the American Idea of Equality, 1815–1860* (Ph.D. dissertation, Brown University, 1955), 87–100. For the original returns, see *Compilation of the Enumeration of the Inhabitants and Statistics of the United States, as Obtained at the Department of State, from the Returns of the Sixth Census* (Washington, D.C., 1841), 4–104.

Hampshire every 28th; in Massachusetts every 43rd; in Connecticut every 184th; in New York every 257th; and in New Jersey every 297th. This was in sharp contrast with the South where the proportion ranged from one in 1,299 in Virginia and one in 2,477 in South Carolina to one in 4,310 in Louisiana.[8]

Such statistics not only offered obvious moral lessons but gave official credence to popular "scientific" ideas about the peculiar suitability of Negroes for slavery. One northern observer, in a letter to a New York business journal, explained that the prevalence of insanity among local Negroes resulted from "the rigors of a northern winter, which have no influence on the temperament of the whites," but "which affect the cerebral organs of the African race." He admitted, however, that slavery undoubtedly lessened such occurrences.[9] The *Southern Literary Messenger* printed the insanity returns, declared that the sectional disparity resulted from "moral causes, arising from their situation, and in no degree the effect of climate," and concluded "that where slavery has been longest extinguished, the condition of the colored race is worse." It painted a dark picture of what would happen in the event of emancipation. "Let us then suppose," it remarked, "a half of a million of free negroes suddenly turned loose in Virginia, whose propensity it is, constantly to grow more vicious in a state of freedom. . . . Where should we find Penitentiaries for the thousands of felons? Where, lunatic asylums for the tens of thousands of maniacs? Would it be possible to live in a country where maniacs and felons met the traveller at every cross road?"[10] In Congress, a Mississippian used the census tables to contrast "the happy, well-fed, healthy, and moral condition of the southern slaves, with the condition of the miserable victims and degraded free blacks of the North." Such must be the case, he declared, for "idiocy and lunacy . . . in the lower classes, had been shown by medical men to be invariably caused by vice and missery."[11]

. . . [John C.] Calhoun nevertheless lectured the English foreign secretary on the relative merits of slavery and freedom for the Negro population, and he used the latest statistics to support his argument. "The census and other authentic documents," he declared, "show that, in all instances in which the States have changed the former relation between the two races, the condition of the African, instead of being improved, has become worse. They have been invariably sunk into vice and pauperism, accompanied by the bodily and mental inflictions incident thereto—deafness, blindness, insanity and idiocy—to a degree without example."[12] . . .

---

8 "Reflections on the Census of 1840," *Southern Literary Messenger*, 9 (1843), 341; Edward Jarvis, "Insanity among the Coloured Population of the Free States," *American Journal of the Medical Sciences*, 7 (1844), 71–83.

9 "Table of Lunacy in the United States," *Hunt's Merchants' Magazine and Commercial Review*, 8 (1843), 460–61.

10 "Reflections on the Census of 1840," 342, 344, 346–47.

11 *Congressional Globe*, 28 Cong., 1 Sess., 239.

12 John C. Calhoun to Lord Richard Pakenham, April 18, 1844, "Proceedings of the Senate and Documents Relative to Texas," *Senate Document*, 28 Cong., 1 Sess.,

In the absence of any revision, the census of 1840 continued to serve
the purposes of anti-abolition orators and editors. In fact, a Georgia congressman reportedly admitted to Jarvis that the census contained numer-
our errors but he added, "It is too good a thing for our politicians to give
up. They had prepared speeches based on it, which they could not afford
to lose."[13]

The congressional debates on slavery expansion in the 1840s and
1850s had little significance for the political or economic progress of
northern Negroes. Most proponents of slavery restriction tried to make
it clear that their concern was not for the plight of the Negro but for the
welfare of the white race. When Representative David Wilmot of Pennsylvania introduced his proviso to exclude slavery from the territories
acquired from Mexico, he carefully explained that he did not propose
to interfere with southern institutions, and that he possessed "no squeamish sensitiveness upon the subject of slavery, no morbid sympathy for
the slave." What he wanted were free states for free white men. "I plead
the cause and the rights of white freemen," he declared in 1847. "I
would preserve to free white labor a fair country, a rich inheritance,
where the sons of toil, of my own race and own color, can live without
the disgrace which association with negro slavery brings upon free
labor."[14] The following year, a New York representative proposed that
Congress "inquire into the expediency of setting apart a portion of the
public lands for the exclusive use and possession of free black persons."[15]

In order to reserve the new territories for whites, Negroes would have
to be barred from the benefits of federal land policy. The Senate attempted this in 1841 when it voted to confine the privileges of the new
preemption law to whites. Augustus Porter of Michigan, the lone dis-
senter, observed that no previous act had embodied such a clause and
that it conflicted with the right to buy and dispose of property. While
Negroes enjoyed no political rights in his state, they were entitled, he
declared, to all the civil rights conferred by the Constitution, including
that of holding property. By "general consent," the Senate deleted the restriction from the bill before its final passage.[16] But it still required an
opinion from the Attorney General's office to qualify Negroes for the benefits of the act. In the 1850s Congress frequently tacked amendments onto
land and homestead bills excluding Negroes from their provisions, be-

---

no. 341 (1844), 50–53. . . . In Maine where every fourteenth Negro was supposedly
insane, the census listed six such Negroes in Scarsboro but no Negro population,
and credited Dresden with twice as many insane Negroes as Negro residents. In
Worcester, Massachusetts, the census found 133 insane out of a Negro population
of 161. Actually, this former number represented the white patients in the state hos-
pital for the insane at Worcester. *Compilation of the Enumeration of the Inhabitants
and Statistics of the United States,* 5, 7, 9, 11; Deutsch, "The First U.S. Census of
the Insane," 475–76.

[13] Wood, *Memorial of Edward Jarvis,* quoted in Deutsch, "The First U.S. Census
of the Insane," 478.

[14] *Appendix to the Congressional Globe,* 29 Cong., 2 Sess., 317.

[15] *Congressional Globe,* 30 Cong., 1 Sess., 778.

[16] Ibid., 26 Cong., 2 Sess., 77, 114; *Appendix,* 27.

cause granting them land would encourage and prolong "their common residence in this Confederacy" with white people.[17]

The Dred Scott decision dealt a severe blow to the Negro's preemption rights. The Secretary of the Interior had previously written a New York Negro that "there is nothing in the laws of the United States which would prevent you, as a Freeman of African descent, from settling upon land in the Territory of Minnesota, and acquiring a right of pre-emption." Soon after the Supreme Court ruling, however, the commissioner of the General Land Office announced that since Negroes were not citizens, they could not qualify for preemption benefits.[18]

As early as 1810 the federal government excluded Negroes from the postal service. Postmaster General Gideon Granger, in "a private representation" to Senator James Jackson of Georgia, declared in 1802 that objections existed to Negroes handling the mail, "of a nature too delicate to engraft into a report which may become public, yet too important to be omitted or passed over without full consideration." Granger feared that they would use the postal service to coordinate insurrectionary activities, particularly in the southern states. "Every thing which tends to increase their knowledge of natural rights," he warned, "of men and things, or that affords them an opportunity of associating, acquiring, and communicating sentiments, and of establishing a chain or line of intelligence" must excite alarm. As post riders, Negroes would mix with other people, acquire information, and "learn that a man's rights do not depend on his color."[19] Congress responded in 1810 by providing "that no other than a free white person shall be employed in conveying the mail."[20] Postmaster General John McLean instructed his deputies in 1828 to adhere strictly to this regulation. If Negro labor was required "to lift the mail from the stage into the postoffice," it must be "performed in the presence and under the immediate direction of the white person who has it in custody."[21]

Not until 1862 did Congress attempt [unsuccessfully] to abrogate the restriction. . . .

In citing "the conduct of the Executive Department" as a precedent for

---

[17] For examples, see *Congressional Globe*, 31 Cong., 1 Sess., 33 Cong., 1 Sess., 1057–58, 1071–73. Frederick Douglass and Rep. Gerrit Smith strongly condemned the "white" restriction in the Homestead Bill of 1854. *Frederick Douglass' Paper*, March 17, 1854.

[18] New York *Daily Times*, August 21, 1857; *Annual Reports of the American Anti-Slavery Society, . . . for the years ending May 1, 1857, and May 1, 1858* (New York, 1859), 130.

[19] *American State Papers, Documents, Legislative and Executive, of the Congresses of the United States . . .* (38 vols., Washington, D.C., 1832–61), Class 7: Post Office, 27.

[20] The restriction was reenacted without change in 1825. *Appendix to the Annals of Congress*, 11 Cong., 1 and 2 Sess., 2569; 18 Cong., 2 Sess., 91.

[21] William Jay, "A View of the Action of the Federal Government in Behalf of Slavery," in *Miscellaneous Writings on Slavery* (Boston, 1853), 233; William C. Nell, *The Colored Patriots of the American Revolution, with Sketches of Several Distinguished Colored Persons: To which is added a Brief Survey of the Condition and Prospects of Colored Americans* (Boston, 1855), 312.

his opinion, Chief Justice Taney referred specifically to the refusal of the State Department to grant passports to Negroes. Actually, Negroes secured passports in several cases as late as 1854.[22] However, the Secretary of State rejected the application of a Philadelphia Negro in 1839 on the grounds that the newly revised Pennsylvania Constitution did not recognize Negroes as citizens.[23] In 1847 Secretary of State James Buchanan clarified this policy when he declared that it was customary to grant free Negroes "not a passport, in the ordinary form, recognizing them as citizens, but a certificate suited to the nature of the case."[24] His successor, John M. Clayton, stated two years later that passports "are not granted by this department to persons of color, and that protections are only given to them when they are in the service of diplomatic agents, etc., of the United States going abroad."[25] This prompted one observer to write that "the colored man is not only insulted and wronged at home, and in half the Union is utterly defenceless, but if he would leave this cruel country he must go abroad as an outlaw."[26] Severely censured by several newspapers, Clayton justified his action with the assertion that this has been the "settled regulation of the Department."[27]

In the late 1840s and in the 1850s, numerous Negro leaders sought passports for England where they planned to lecture and raise money for the abolitionist cause, but in most cases their applications were rejected. . . . In 1861, the new secretary, William H. Seward, reversed State Department policy.

The opinions of the attorneys general demonstrated that differences did exist in the federal interpretation of Negro citizenship. In 1821, William Wirt ruled that free Negroes in Virginia were not citizens of the United States and, therefore, could not command vessels according to the acts regulating the foreign and coasting trade.[28] . . .

In 1822, the South Carolina legislature passed the first in a series of southern acts which provided for the imprisonment of free Negro seamen while their vessels remained in port. . . . Upon the receipt of another British protest in 1831, Secretary of State Edward Livingston asked the

---

[22] For example, the State Department issued passports to Robert Purvis in 1834; Peter Williams in 1836; William Wells Brown in 1849; and John Remond in 1854. Arnold Buffum to Roberts Vaux, May 16, 1834, Historical Society of Pennsylvania, Philadelphia; *The Liberator*, April 16, 1858.

[23] Sarah M. Grimké to Elizabeth Pease, August 25, 1839, in Gilbert H. Barnes and Dwight L. Dumond (eds.), *Letters of Theodore Dwight Weld, Angelina Grimké Weld and Sarah Grimké, 1822–1844* (2 vols.; New York, 1934), 2, 792–93. The Pennsylvania Constitutional Convention of 1837–38 restricted the suffrage to white males.

[24] James Buchanan to N. H. Davis, March 8, 1847, in John Bassett Moore (ed.), *The Works of James Buchanan* (12 vols.; Philadelphia, 1908–11), 7, 236.

[25] *The North Star*, July 20, August 24, 1849. See also *The Non-Slaveholder*, 4 (1849), 191, and *Eighteenth Annual Report, presented to the Massachusetts Anti-Slavery Society, . . . January 23, 1850* (Boston, 1850), 44–45.

[26] *The Non-Slaveholder*, 4 (1849), 191.

[27] John M. Clayton to the Editor of the Salem *Register*, in *The* [10th] *Annual Report of the American and Foreign Anti-Slavery Society, presented at New York May 7, 1850, . . .* (New York, 1850), 128–29.

[28] *Official Opinions*, 1, 506–9.

new attorney general, Roger Taney, for his opinion. . . . [He replied that] Negroes were "a separate and degraded people to whom the sovereignty of each state might accord or withhold such privileges as they deemed proper." Consequently, the framers of the Constitution had not regarded them as citizens and they "were evidently not supposed to be included by the term *citizens*."[29]

Attorney General Hugh Legare decided in 1843 that free Negroes were neither aliens nor citizens, but occupied an intermediate position.[30] . . .

The constitutional rights of free Negroes were finally recognized during the Civil War. Attorney General Edward Bates advised in 1862 that citizenship was "*not* dependent nor coexistent" with color, race, "the degradation of a people," or the legal right to vote and hold office. "Free men of color, if born in the United States, are citizens of the United States."[31] Six years later, the Fourteenth Amendment confirmed this opinion.

If any confusion existed in the federal government prior to 1857 on the constitutional rights of Negroes, it was finally dispelled by the decision of the Supreme Court in *Dred Scott* v. *Sanford*. The Missouri Compromise and Negro citizenship were both found to be unconstitutional.

Chief Justice Taney constructed his opinion on a review of the historical status of the Negro population, and he placed particular emphasis on their legal position at the time of the Constitutional Convention of 1787. For more than a century prior to that convention, Taney declared, Negroes had "been regarded as beings of an inferior order, and altogether unfit to associate with the white race, either in social or political relations; and so far inferior, that they had no rights which the white man was bound to respect." Colonial legislation demonstrated the extent of public apathy toward Negroes. Although the northern states abolished slavery, this resulted not from "any change of opinion in relation to this race" but from its unprofitability in the northern climate and economy. That no moral revolution had occurred, Taney continued, was nowhere more clearly demonstrated than in the laws passed by several states to control free Negroes.[32] "It cannot be supposed," he stated, that the framers of the Constitution intended to grant Negroes "rights, and privileges, and rank, in the new political body throughout the Union, which every one of them denied within the limits of its own dominion." Consequently, Negroes were "not intended to be included, and formed no part of the people who framed and adopted" the Declaration of Independence and the Constitution.[33]

---

[29] Carl Brent Swisher, *Roger B. Taney* (New York, 1935), 154.

[30] *Official Opinions*, 4, 147–48.

[31] Ibid., 10, 382–413.

[32] Taney cited as examples the Massachusetts and Rhode Island laws forbidding interracial marriages (1786 and 1822); the Connecticut law prohibiting the establishment of any school for the instruction of Negroes not inhabitants of the state (1833), and the decision of a Connecticut court upholding that law (1834); and the New Hampshire act barring Negroes from the militia (1815).

[33] *Dred Scott* v. *Sanford*, 19 Howard 407–10, 412–16.

. . . Had not Congress restricted naturalization to "free white persons"? Subsequent legislation and the practices of the Executive Department, Taney believed, confirmed his conclusion that Negroes "are not included, and were not intended to be included, under the word 'citizens' in the Constitution, and can therefore claim none of the rights and privileges which that instrument provides for and secures to citizens of the United States."[34] . . .

. . . Frederick Douglass declared that "the National Conscience" would not be silenced "by such an open, glaring, and scandalous tissue of lies as that decision is, and has been, over and over, shown to be."[35] But Robert Purvis, a colored abolitionist, warned his people not to comfort themselves with the thought that this decision was unconstitutional. It was, he declared, "in perfect keeping with the treatment of the colored people by the American Government from the beginning to this day."[36] This sentiment was shared by other Negro leaders who, while condemning the decision, expressed no great surprise. After all, one Negro protest declared, it was but "final confirmation of the already well known fact that under the Constitution and Government of the United States, the colored people are nothing, and can be nothing but an alien, disfranchised and degraded class."[37]

Herrenvolk Democracy and White Nationalism*

George M. Fredrickson

During the nineteenth century, race-thinking emerged for the first time as a central current in Western thought. Previously whites had encountered other races in the course of "the expansion of Europe" and had

34 Ibid., 404–6. Federal practices and legislation cited by Taney included the militia law of 1792; an act of 1813 prohibiting employment on vessels to "any person or persons except citizens of the United States, or persons of color, natives of the United States"; the Washington, D.C., administrative act of 1820; the opinions of Attorneys General Wirt and Cushing; and the passport policy of the State Department.

35 "The Dred Scott Decision, Speech delivered before the American Anti-Slavery Society, New York, May 11, 1857," reprinted in Philip S. Foner (ed.), The Life and Writings of Frederick Douglass (4 vols.; New York, 1950–55), 2, 411.

36 The Liberator, April 10, 1857.

37 Ibid.

* From pp. 1, 99–100, 132–34, 168–70, 185–89 in The Black Image In the White Mind by George M. Fredrickson. Copyright © 1971 by George M. Fredrickson.

characteristically subjugated, enslaved, or exterminated them. Out of these brutal and crassly exploitative contacts developed a set of attitudes about dark-skinned peoples which were "racist," if racism is regarded as synonymous with race prejudice and discrimination, but which might be considered preracist or protoracist, if one defines racism in a more restricted way—as a rationalized pseudoscientific theory positing the innate and permanent inferiority of nonwhites. Racism in this second sense had some roots in the biological thinking of the eighteenth century but did not come to fruition or exert great influence until well along in the nineteenth. In large part this book is a study of the development of intellectualized racist theory and ideology as it was applied directly and programmatically to the "problem" posed in the white mind by the presence of millions of blacks in the United States. . . .

To make certain that the debates and shifts of opinion are seen in proper perspective, we need only enumerate the basic white-supremacist propositions in a form likely to have been acceptable to almost all shades of white opinion—Northern and Southern, Negrophobe and "paternalist" —after the 1830s. Widespread, almost universal, agreement existed on the following points:

1. Blacks are physically, intellectually, and temperamentally *different* from whites.
2. Blacks are also *inferior* to whites in at least some of the fundamental qualities wherein the races differ, especially in intelligence and in the temperamental basis of enterprise or initiative.
3. Such differences and differentials are either permanent or subject to change only by a very slow process of development or evolution.
4. Because of these permanent or deep-seated differences, miscegenation, especially in the form of intermarriage, is to be discouraged (to put it as mildly as possible), because the crossing of such diverse types leads either to a short-lived and unprolific breed or to a type that even if permanent is inferior to the whites in those innate qualities giving Caucasian civilization its progressive and creative characteristics.
5. Racial prejudice or antipathy is a natural and inevitable white response to blacks when the latter are free from legalized subordination and aspiring to equal status. Its power is such that it will not in the foreseeable future permit blacks to attain full equality, unless one believes, like some abolitionists, in the impending triumph of a millenarian Christianity capable of obliterating all sense of divisive human differences.
6. It follows from the above propositions that a biracial equalitarian (or "integrated") society is either completely impossible, now and forever, or can be achieved only in some remote and almost inconceivable future. For all practical purposes the destiny of the blacks in America is either continued subordination—slavery or some form of caste discrimination—or their elimination as an element of the population. . . .

The doctrine of hierarchical biracialism, often expressing itself as the ideology of "*Herrenvolk* democracy," began as a defense of slavery widely accepted in the antebellum South. It was embraced by Northerners who valued an economic or political connection with the slave South or feared that emancipation would result in an inundation of the North by Southern blacks competing with white labor and threatening the status of lower-class whites. After the abolition of slavery, hierarchical biracialism was reaffirmed as "white supremacy" and the gospel of segregation. . . .

The ideal of homogeneity originated with men of a moderately reformist persuasion, for it derived initially from the conservative antislavery sentiment of the early Republic. Implicit in the initial colonizationist enterprise, it did not receive full articulation until it became an element in the nationalist thinking of many Republicans and free-soilers in the 1850s. The hope for an all-white America found a final outlet in the Darwinian speculation of the late nineteenth century about the disappearance of the American Negro in a "struggle for existence" with the superior whites. . . .

The attitudes toward blacks revealed by such conceptualizations had their origins in the institutionalization of slavery based on race during the seventeenth century. But racism did not come to full ideological consciousness until called forth by nineteenth-century developments and given shape and consistency by contemporary trends in scientific and social thought. Racialist thinking crystallized in nineteenth-century America mainly because the presence of blacks was a central fact in the great sectional conflict that almost destroyed the Union. . . .

In the pre-Civil War crisis, then, the South can be described as having manifested a desire for both slavery and Negroes, while a Northern majority provided indications that it wanted neither, at least not on a permanent basis. Abraham Lincoln, it should be recalled, affirmed in this period not only that slavery must be put on the path of "ultimate extinction" but also that blacks could never have equal rights as long as they remained in the United States and should therefore be colonized abroad. But contingencies arising from the war and the subsequent need to reconstruct the Union combined to give an influential segment of Northern opinion the idea that Southern blacks must be given equal rights, principally because their cooperation was essential to the establishment of Northern political, social, and ideological hegemony over the South. Accompanying this sense that blacks could be useful was the growth in popularity of the romantic stereotype of the blacks as a people whose peculiar virtues were submissive gratitude and undying loyalty to benefactors. Consequently, the Reconstruction era saw a temporary subordination of racial nationalism to the overriding political nationalism arising out of the Unionist fervor of the Civil War years. . . .

Notions of white or Anglo-Saxon superiority were common even among critics of the slave system.[1] Francis Lieber, a German-born political theorist who remained unsympathetic to slaveholding despite a long residence in the South, wrote in the 1850s of "Anglican liberty," that marvelous

---

[1] See Gossett, Race, p. 97; and Ray Allen Billington, The Protestant Crusade: 1800–1860 (New York, 1938). For a typical expression of antebellum Anglo-Saxonism, with its emphasis on the ability of Anglo-Saxons to assimilate other Caucasian groups without losing their innate characteristics, see "The Anglo-Saxon Race," North American Review, 72 (July 1851), 34–71.

combination of individual freedom with the capacity for national unity and cooperative action which was "common to the whole Anglican race" and which had been "evolved first and chiefly by this race." It was on this ethnic and historical basis that the United States, according to Lieber, had developed its Republican institutions.[2]

Theodore Parker, liberal Unitarian minister and militant abolitionist, went even further. The early settlers of Massachusetts Bay, he announced in 1854, "had in them the ethnologic idiosyncrasy of the Anglo-Saxon—his restless disposition to invade and conquer other lands; his haughty contempt of humbler tribes which leads him to subvert, enslave, kill, and exterminate; his fondness for material things, preferring these to beauty; his love of personal liberty, yet coupled with most profound respect for peaceful and established law; his inborn skill to organize things to a mill, men to a company, a community, tribes to a federated state; and his slow, solemn, inflexible, industrious, and unconquerable will." Only in America, he continued, did "the peculiar characteristics of the Anglo-Saxon" come to full development.[3] As a humanitarian and an antislavery radical, Parker was not entirely happy with the harshly exploitative and genocidal side of the Anglo-Saxon character, but he concluded in another address of the same year that "the Anglo-Saxon," as "the Caucasian's best," was "a good hardy stock for national welfare to grow on,"[4] and in a letter to an English friend in 1857 he wrote: "I look with great pride on this Anglo-Saxon people. It has many faults, but I think it is the best specimen of mankind which has ever attained great power in the world."[5]

The American "ethnologic" self-image, whether described as Anglican, Anglo-Saxon, Celtic-Anglo-Saxon, or simply Caucasian, was being formulated and popularized at the very time when the slavery controversy focused interest on the Negro character. No longer were Americans in general being characterized primarily by their adherence to a set of political and social ideals allegedly representing the universal aspirations of all humanity, but democracy itself was beginning to be defined as racial in origin and thus realizable perhaps only by people with certain hereditary traits. The heightened consciousness of what were supposed to be white racial characteristics undoubtedly helped make it easy for many, on both sides of the sectional debate over slavery, to accept a stereotype of the Negro which made him a kind of anti-Caucasian. . . .

. . . Americans who exploited the Negro economically or socially had no desire to get rid of the black population. Hoetink says that those whose economic or social position necessitates a subservient racial group, or groups, achieve a kind of "pseudo-homogeneity" by regarding "the other

2 Francis Lieber, *On Civil Liberty and Self-Government,* Enlarged Edition (Philadelphia, 1859), pp. 53–57.

3 Theodore Parker, "The Nebraska Question," sermon of February 12, 1854, *Collected Works,* ed. Francis P. Cobbe (London, 1863–1870), 5, 250.

4 Theodore Parker, "Dangers Which Threaten the Rights of Man in America," sermon of July 2, 1854, ibid., 6, 117.

5 Letter to Miss Cobbe, Dec. 4, 1857, in John Weiss, *Life and Correspondence of Theodore Parker* (New York, 1864), 1, 463.

segments" as "foreign bodies, outsiders, even aliens." In the nineteenth-century South, as we have seen, the presence of an egalitarian ethos seemed to require that the Negro be regarded, not merely as an alien, but as a creature not quite human.[6]

In nineteenth-century America, North and South, the equivalent of Hoetink's "pseudo-homogeneity" was often affirmed in the context of opposition to "amalgamation," or intermarriage. In the United States the racial ideal was of course lily-white, and legal barriers to intermarriage certified black exclusion from the "real" community, within which men and women were free to marry by choice. As James Kirke Paulding put it in 1836, amalgamation of the races would "destroy the homogeneous character of the people of the United States, on which is founded our union, and from which results nearly all those ties which constitute the cement of social life."[7] It never occurred to Paulding that the mere presence of the Negro as a slave in the South and a social pariah in the North in any way contradicted the notion that Americans were racially homogeneous. With the development in the 1840s and 1850s of scientific race theory and a new sense of Caucasian or Anglo-Saxon racial pride, it became possible to articulate such a concern for continued "homogeneity" with greater authority. In 1857 J. Aitken Meigs, . . . [cited Gobineau on] the national degeneracy that inevitably sets in when a people fails to preserve its "leading ethnical principle" and concluded that Americans needed to "provide intelligently for the amelioration of that disease whose seeds were planted when the Declaration of Independence was proclaimed and whose deadly influences threaten, sooner or later, like the Lianes of a tropical forest, to suffocate the national tree over which they are silently spreading."[8]

The "pseudo-homogeneity" that could be attained by the exclusion of the Negro from the community of citizens, through enslavement, patterns of discrimination, and ultimately through the absolute prohibition of intermarriage, did not satisfy all segments of anti-Negro opinion in the pre-Civil War period. Aberrant Southerners like J. J. Flournoy and Hinton Rowan Helper objected openly to the physical presence of blacks, however lowly and subordinate they might be, and advocated deportation of the entire race.[9] Such thinking was much more common in the North,

---

[6] Harmanaus Hoetink, The Two Variants in Carribean Race Relations (London, 1967), 106–10.

[7] James Kirke Paulding, Slavery in the United States (New York, 1836), p. 64.

[8] J. C. Nott and George R. Gliddon, eds., Indigenous Races of the Earth (Philadelphia, 1857), pp. 251–52. Meigs's reference to the Declaration of Independence is a little obscure, but presumably he was referring to its claim that "all men are created equal"—a doctrine which, if literally applied, might threaten what Meigs conceived of as the racial integrity of the nation.

[9] See E. Merton Coulter, John Jacobus Flournoy: Champion of the Common Man in the Antebellum South (Savannah, 1942); and Hinton Rowan Helper, The Impending Crisis of the South: How to Meet It, ed. George M. Fredrickson (Cambridge, Mass., 1968), pp. xxxi, 97, 182. Flournoy, a Georgian who published his views in pamphlet form in the 1830s, was a half-mad local eccentric whose theories were hardly noticed in the South. Helper's expulsionism is more significant because his doctrines attracted great attention and may have expressed the otherwise unarticulated desires of many nonslaveholding whites. But Helper's greatest visible impact was on Northern free-soil enthusiasts.

which lacked a direct dependence on Negro labor and consequently manifested a tendency to look on the free blacks as superfluous population. Negro exclusionist sentiments were particularly strong in the Midwest, where there were various efforts in the 1840s and 1850s to prevent Negro immigration and to remove the blacks who were already there. In 1851 Indiana prohibited all Negroes from entering the state, and Illinois followed suit in 1853. At about this same time, the Midwest saw an upsurge of the kind of colonizationist activity that was openly and explicitly concerned with simply getting rid of the local free Negroes by sending them anywhere outside the United States.[10] . . .

[Dr. Daniel] Drake spoke for many in his region in expressing the fear that, unless something were done, the Midwestern states might at some point be inundated by a flood of Negroes pouring across the Ohio River.[11] This sense of a black peril, building up in the South as slavery reached what were supposed to be its natural limits of expansion, haunted the popular imagination of the Midwest and reached panic proportions when the Civil War brought the prospect of emancipation.[12] . . .

. . . Colonizationists had always implied that a complete separation of the races was the only satisfactory answer, the only way to fulfill safely and adequately the popular desire for racial homogeneity that was assumed to exist. But something new was added in the 1840s and 1850s, giving greater impetus to the hope for homogenization through the removal or elimination of the Negro. Only in connection with larger historical developments can one understand why speculations which denied Negroes a continued existence in the United States were so frequently ventured and so widely accepted in the North during a period of sectional conflict climaxed by a somewhat reluctant acceptance of Negro emancipation.

One such development was the rise of a new sense of American nationalism that had clear racial overtones. . . .

. . . [The white nationalist] point of view was presented in classic form by John C. Calhoun in his Senate speech of January 4, 1848. Calhoun, like some other proslavery spokesmen, saw no future for the "peculiar institution" in such an arid country, and he opposed annexation because he regarded Mexicans as an inferior breed. The United States, he pointed out, had never "incorporated into the Union any but the Caucasian race. . . . Ours is a government of the white man. . . . in the whole history of man . . . there is no instance whatever of any civilized colored race, of any shade, being found equal to the establishment and maintenance of free government."[13] . . .

---

[10] See Eugene H. Berwanger, *The Frontier Against Slavery: Western Anti-Negro Prejudice and the Slavery Extension Controversy* (Urbana, Ill., 1967), pp. 44–59.

[11] Dr. Daniel Drake, "Letters on Slavery to John C. Warren of Boston," Reprinted from the *National Intelligencer,* April 3, 5, 7, 1851 (New York, 1940), pp. 29, 31, 32, 34, 37, 54–67.

[12] . . . V. Jacque Voegeli, *Free but Not Equal: The Midwest and the Negro during the Civil War* (Chicago, 1967), pp. 17–18.

[13] From John C. Calhoun's Senate speech against the annexation of Mexico, Jan. 4, 1848, in John C. Calhoun, *Works,* ed. Richard K. Crallé (New York, 1853–1857), 4, 410–411.

. . . It would be a mistake to assume that [during the Civil War] the old stereotype of the docile and inferior "Sambo" was now replaced by a radically new image of self-reliant and intelligent blacks in uniform. The Sambo image, rather than being abolished with slavery, was merely modified. The traditional view of innate Negro docility had actually been reinforced in the early stages of the war by the failure of the slaves to engage in massive rebellion once their masters had gone off to fight the Yankees. In 1862 the Reverend Joseph Henry Allen of Massachusetts had described the blacks as "a race that takes kindly to domestication, and receives its crumbs of a higher culture with grateful submissiveness." As evidence of such traits, he pointed to their passivity, docility, and "nonresistance" following the outbreak of the war. Submissiveness, he concluded, "was one of those characteristics of the race, on the right understanding of which our whole solution rests."[14] . . .

This image of innate black docility and inoffensiveness was, as it turned out, too deeply rooted to be demolished by the emergence of the Negro as a soldier. In fact, the potential or actual successes of black troops were often seen as the *result* of their submissiveness—which in a military context could mean the same thing as susceptibility to discipline. Since their units were officered by whites, the alleged willingness of blacks to submit to military rule could also be interpreted as an instinctive sense of racial subordination. In February, 1863, Jacob D. Cox, a Union general of antislavery background who later became Republican Governor of Ohio, endorsed the use of black troops by arguing "that blacks make excellent troops when well officered and disciplined, *that they are most easily ruled.*"[15] The Freedmen's Inquiry Commission came to a similar conclusion in its *Preliminary Report,* noting that the effectiveness of Negro troops depended to a large extent on the caliber of their white officers: ". . . colored regiments badly officered would be more liable to give way than badly officered regiments of the more self-reliant white race." To support this point of view, the commission quoted Colonel Thomas Wentworth Higginson, a fiery New England abolitionist and commander of the First South Carolina Volunteers, the earliest black regiment to be recruited in the South. In Higginson's view, Negro troops "will depend more upon their officers than white troops, and be more influenced by their conduct. If their officers are intimidated they will be; and if their officers stand their ground so will they. If they lose their officers the effect will be worse on them than upon white troops, not because they are timid, but because they are less accustomed to entire self-reliance."[16]

This paternalistic and condescending attitude toward blacks, who, it was claimed, knew how to follow orders but lacked Anglo-Saxon self-reliance, was reflected even more dramatically and with clearer racial

14 Joseph Henry Allen, "Africans in America and Their New Guardians," *Christian Examiner,* 232 (July 1862), 114–16.

15 Letter to Aaron F. Perry. February 9, 1863, Cox Papers, Oberlin College Library. (The italics are mine.)

16 *Preliminary Report . . . to the Secretary of War, by the Freedmen's Inquiry Commission, June 30, 1863* (New York, 1863), pp. 17–18.

overtones in Colonel Higginson's camp diary and journal of 1862 and 1863. Higginson, who described himself as having "a constitutional affinity for undeveloped races," professed to find the blacks attractive and was delighted to find no mulattoes among his recruits—"all looked as thoroughly black as the most faithful philanthropist could desire." He was also readily impressed with their aptitude for military drill: "To learn the drill, one does not want a set of college professors; one wants a set of eager, active, pliant schoolboys; and the more childlike these pupils are the better." He therefore predicted at the outset that blacks, whom he described as "simple, docile, and affectionate almost to the point of absurdity," would "surpass whites" in military drill. Further association did not change Higginson's opinion that his charges were "the world's perpetual children, docile, gay, and loveable," and he reveled in a sense of his absolute power over them. "They could be made fanatics if I chose," he noted; "but I do not choose. The whole mood is essentially Mohammedan, perhaps, in its strength and its weakness; and I feel the same degree of sympathy that I should if I had a Turkish command— that is, a sort of sympathetic admiration, not tending towards agreement, but towards co-operation."[17]

Higginson, it would appear, had a kind of sahib complex, suggestive of the pleasure derived during the same period by British officers in command of native troops in India and elsewhere. Indeed, an aura of pseudo-colonial paternalism surrounded the "Negro soldier cause" in New England, where the endeavor had its greatest popularity. *Noblesse oblige* was the characteristic note struck in New England's glorification of white "aristocrats" who officered black regiments—men like Higginson and the martyr Robert Gould Shaw, who led the ill-fated assault of black troops on Fort Wagner—and a prevalent attitude toward the loyal black followers was summed up by Charles Eliot Norton, man of letters and wartime propagandist, when he recommended Negro troops as "American Sepoys without any disposition to treachery."[18] Hence it was possible to advocate the use of Negro troops and glorify their achievements without giving up the cherished stereotype of black submissiveness and docility in the presence of "superior" whites.

. . . The operative Northern concept of equality was in fact doubly flawed in its application to the Negro: it gave prior sanction to social and economic inequalities which were likely to result from what was in fact —if not in theory—an unfair competition; and, in addition, it was compatible with a residual or hypothetical belief in racial inequality. The idea that equal rights led to equal opportunities was obviously not applicable to a people just released from slavery, but the prevailing belief in

---

[17] *Letters and Journals of Thomas Wentworth Higginson*, ed. Mary Thacher Higginson (Boston and New York, 1921), p. 213; Thomas Wentworth Higginson, *Army Life in a Black Regiment* (Boston, 1870), pp. 7, 10, 29, 54.

[18] See George M. Fredrickson, *The Inner Civil War: Northern Intellectuals and the Crisis of the Union* (New York, 1965), Chapter 10; Charles Eliot Norton is quoted in George Winston, "Broadsides for Freedom: Civil War Propaganda in New England," *New England Quarterly*, 21 (September 1948), 303.

the probability of racial inferiority provided an ideological escape valve, a ready explanation for future Negro failures which would not call the bourgeois ideology of "self-help" and "equal opportunity" into question.

Some of the callousness implicit in the notion that a race degraded by slavery and suspected to be biologically inferior should simply be given its formal rights and then forced to compete in a capitalistic free-labor society was manifested in the postwar comments of Horace Greeley, who became known as a principal advocate of "the root hog or die" approach to the Negro problem. "Freedom and opportunity—these are all that the best Government can secure to White or Black," Greeley wrote. "Give every one a chance, and let his behavior control his fate. If negroes will not work, they must starve or steal; and if they steal, they must be shut up like other thieves. If there be any among them who fancy that they, being free, can live in comfort without work, they have entered a school in which they will certainly and speedily be taught better." Greeley ended by indicating that all that needed to be done was to "clear away the wreck of slavery, dispel the lingering fear of a return to it, and we may soon break up our Freedmen's Bureaus and all manner of coddling devices and let negroes take care of themselves."[19]

Such an ideology helped shape Northern Reconstruction policy, as it developed in 1866 and 1867, by establishing limits beyond which the North was unwilling to go in its effort to aid and protect the Southern blacks. The Freedmen's Bureau was gradually weakened and phased out after 1866 and was replaced by "the safeguard of general laws," as provided by the Civil Rights Act of 1866 and the Fourteenth Amendment. But attempts to guarantee the Negro's equality before the law by Congressional action or amendments to the Constitution proved insufficient to protect him from the threat of oppression by Southern whites. . . .

. . . It seems likely . . . that the decisive factor which provided the necessary support for black enfranchisement was not a popular commitment to racial equality but a belief that Republican hegemony and the restoration of the Union on a safe and satisfactory basis could be accomplished only by subordinating racial prejudices to political necessities.

Whatever the motivation of Radical Reconstruction and however inadequate its programs, it was a serious effort, the first in American history, to incorporate Negroes into the body politic. As such, it inevitably called forth bitter opposition from hardcore racists, who attempted to discredit radical measures by using many of the same arguments developed as part of the proslavery argument in the prewar period.

The new cause was defined as "white supremacy"—which in practice allowed Southern whites to reduce the freedmen to an inferior caste, as they had attempted to do by enacting the "Black Codes" of 1865. To further this cause in 1868, Van Evrie simply reissued his book *Negroes and Negro "Slavery"* with a topical introduction and under the new title *White Supremacy and Negro Subordination*.[20] Nott also entered the Re-

---

[19] New York *Tribune,* May 25, 1865.

[20] John H. Van Evrie, *White Supremacy and Negro Subordination* (New York, 1868).

construction controversy. In an 1866 pamphlet he reasserted the "scientific" case for inherent black inferiority as part of an attack on the Freedmen's Bureau and other Northern efforts to deal with the Southern race question. "If the whites and blacks be left alone face to face," he wrote, "they will soon learn to understand each other, and come to proper terms under the law of necessity."[21]

Edward A. Pollard, a Richmond journalist and prewar fire-eater, also attacked Northern Reconstruction proposals on racial grounds. His book *The Lost Cause Regained*, published in 1868, contended that "the permanent, natural inferiority of the Negro was the true and *only* defense of slavery" and lamented the fact that the South had wasted its intellectual energy on other arguments. Before the war, Pollard had advocated a revival of the slave trade because it would deflate the pretensions of uppity house servants and town Negroes by submerging them in a flood of humble primitives; he now endorsed Van Evrie's thesis that white democracy depended on absolute black subordination, and concluded his discussion of Negro racial characteristics by asserting that the established "fact" of inferiority dictated "the true *status* of the Negro."[22] Other propagandists of white supremacy, North and South, joined the fray. A writer named Lindley Spring attacked Radical Reconstruction in 1868 with a lengthy discourse on the benighted and savage record of blacks in Africa; and a Dr. J. R. Hayes excoriated the proposed Fifteenth Amendment in 1869 with a rehash of all the biological "evidence" for Negro incapacity.[23]

Inevitably, the pre-Adamite theory of Dr. Samuel A. Cartwright and Jefferson Davis was trotted out. In 1866 Governor Benjamin F. Perry of South Carolina made it the basis of a defense of white supremacy; and in 1867 a Nashville publisher named Buckner Payne, writing under the pseudonym "Ariel," revived a controversy among racists by expounding the doctrine at some length in a pamphlet entitled *The Negro: What Is His Ethnological Status?*[24] Payne not only asserted that the Negro was "created before Adam and Eve" as "a *separate* and *distinct* species of *the genus homo*," but also argued that it was because some of the sons of Adam intermarried with this inferior species, related, as it was, to the "higher orders of the monkey," that God had sent the flood as a punishment for human wrongdoing. Like almost all the racist respondents to Reconstruction, he contended that Negro equality would lead inevitably to amalgamation, and that miscegenation, in addition to resulting in the debasement of the white race, would bring on catastrophic divine intervention: "The states and people that favor this equality and amalgamation of the white and black races, *God will exterminate*. . . . A man can

---

[21] Josiah C. Nott, *The Negro Race: Its Ethnology and History* (Mobile, 1866), p. 27.

[22] E. A. Pollard, *The Lost Cause Regained* (New York, 1868), pp. 114–15, 128; and *The Southern Spy, or Curiosities of Negro Slavery in the South* (Washington, 1859), pp. 37–40.

[23] Lindley Spring, *The Negro at Home* (New York, 1868); Dr. J. R. Hayes, *Negrophobia on the Brain, in White Men . . .* (Washington, D.C., 1869).

[24] John W. De Forest, *A Union Officer in the Reconstruction*, ed. James H. Croushore and David M. Potter (New Haven, 1948), p. 117; "Ariel" [Buckner H. Payne], *The Negro: What Is His Ethnological Status?* (Cincinnati, 1867); see also Wood, *Black Scare*, pp. 6–7.

not commit so great an offense against his race, against his country, against his God, . . . as to give his daughter in marriage to a negro—a beast. . . ."[25]

. . . To speed up the divinely ordained process of racial extermination, [Hinton] Helper proposed as immediate steps the denial of all rights to Negroes and their complete separation from the whites. All this of course went in the teeth of the emerging Reconstruction policies of what had been Helper's own party, and throughout the book he excoriated "the Black Republicans" for departing from the attitudes of the prewar period, a time when Republicans had billed themselves as "the white man's party." His heroes were "White Republicans" like Secretary of State Seward and those few Republicans in the House and Senate who had remained loyal to President Johnson. . . .

. . . When the Reconstruction governments foundered, many in the North were quick to say that the blacks had had their fair chance, had demonstrated their present incapacity for self-government, and could justifiably be relegated, for the time being at least, to an inferior status.[26]

[Albion W.] Tourgée probably understood better than anyone how tenuous and conditional the Northern commitment to Negro equality had been. His book *An Appeal to Caesar*, published in 1884, contended that the Northern people "have always reflected the Southern idea of the negro in everything except as to his natural right to be free and to exercise the rights of the freedman. From the first [the North] seems to have been animated by the sneaking notion that after having used the negro to fight its battles, freed him as the natural result of a rebellion based on slavery, and enfranchised him to constitute a political foil to the ambition and disloyalty of his former master, it could at any time unload him upon the states where he chanced to dwell, wash its hands of all further responsibility in the matter, and leave him to live or die as chance might determine."[27]

---

[25] "Ariel," *The Negro*, pp. 21–22, 23, 26–27, 47–48.

[26] The promulgation of such views in the North during the 1870s is described in Victor P. De Santis, *Republicans Face the Southern Question—The New Departure Years, 1877–1897* (Baltimore, 1959), pp. 44–45, 49–52.

[27] Albion W. Tourgée, *An Appeal to Caesar* (New York, 1884), p. 127.

chapter 9

Jefferson, Lincoln, and Equality

LONG ROWS OF LIBRARY SHELVES have been filled with books about Jefferson and Lincoln and nearly all of them are to some extent filiopietistic celebrations of these two symbols of the highest pretensions of the American republic. Jefferson scholars have commonly evaluated their "apostle of liberty and equality" in terms of his own words as a man who really did swear "eternal hostility to every form of tyranny over the mind of man." Tons of printers ink have been spilled in avoidance of the most elementary and indisputable facts about Jefferson as a believer in black inferiority, a national leader often involved in policies favorable to slavery interests, and a life-long slaveowner who exploited his bondsmen much as other masters did and left all but a few of them in servitude after his death. The dominant approach of historians has been to ignore or to evade the racial hostility and to rationalize the slaveowning. Charles M. Wiltse in 1935 could think of several reasons for Jefferson to keep his bondsmen, particularly the "fact" that "it seemed more humane to keep them than to let them go;" Adrienne Koch in 1950 invited her readers to speculate about the good fortune which might have overtaken the nation on slavery issues if "the enlightened legislation of the liberal Jefferson had been adopted;" and the renowned Jefferson biographer, Dumas Malone, suggested in 1962 that if Jefferson could be criticized as a slaveowner it might be because he "erred" on "the side of leniency."

Although the most recent major biography (1970) met high standards of scholarship and contained substantial criticisms of some Jeffersonian racial opinions, author Merrill D. Peterson continued the traditional tactic of rationalizing Jefferson's slavemaster role by portraying him as the puppet of history and circumstances unable to act effectively toward the extrication of the nation, Virginia, or even himself from the institution of human bondage but determined to live as a "lenient . . . kind and generous master" genuinely concerned for the health and welfare of the slaves, tolerant of the whipping post only "at the last resort," and filled

243

with plans to place the slaves (in Jefferson's own words) "on the comfortable footing of the laborers of other countries." If Peterson's book tended to ignore the critical scholarship of the 1960s on Jefferson, race and slavery, William W. Freehling in an essay of 1972 took a different tack by facing the critics and trying to refute some of their criticisms. In an article replete with dubious phrases such as "the Founding Fathers' antislavery dreams" and "their antislavery instincts," Freehling complained that the revisionists of the 1960s abandoned the proper historical task of "explaining" for the illegitimate activity of "judging." He insisted on the merits of "Jefferson and his contemporaries" for progressing from the slave republic of 1775 to a point where they could leave to posterity "a crippled, restricted, peculiar institution" with the African slave trade gone, slavery abolished in the Northeast and kept from the Northwest, and the uncompromising defense of slavery largely limited to the lower South. Jefferson's generation deserved the credit for initiating "the creeping antislavery process."

That the Jefferson myth had weaknesses in areas other than slavery and race Leonard W. Levy demonstrated in a monograph of 1963 which presented the alleged patron saint of civil liberties using institutional power to violate constitutional rights of individuals, to urge the repression of opposition newspapers, and to abridge intellectual and academic freedom. Levy himself, however, blunted the major point with the subtitle "The Darker Side" and with the suggestion that he had presented only "one side of the story." If Levy irritated the major guardians of Jeffersonian piety, Robert McColley disturbed them more with a volume in 1964 which demonstrated that the years of Republican ascendancy had been a time of maximum expansion of human bondage under the leadership of a racist and proslavery Virginia elite rather than an era in which Jeffersonians with antislavery sympathies presided over the decline of slavery. The liberal rhetoric espoused from time to time by a small minority had been in the main part for outside consumption and did not affect the fortunes of the peculiar institution. Jefferson aided slavery expansion as President, made only a few private criticisms of black bondage during the national period, and expressed doubt on slavery primarily because the institution corrupted the masters and posed the bloody threat of a servile rebellion. Moreover, he espoused a variety of racist and proslavery rationalization which fell substantially below the most thoughtful and humane opinion of both America and Virginia.

If Winthrop D. Jordan in his brilliant monograph of 1968, *White Over Black*, sometimes veered toward the old apologetics for Jefferson as a victim of circumstances he also provided a critique with devastating criticism on some important points. The central dilemma, according to Jordan, was that Jefferson "hated slavery but thought Negroes inferior to white men." Although many scholars today might question the depth, the intensity and even the existence of this alleged Jeffersonian hatred of black bondage, most of them would concede that Jordan provided a convincing analysis of "the most intense, extensive and extreme formulation of anti-Negro 'thought' in the thirty years after the Revolution." Jordan proved himself particularly skillful in placing fears for white identity and horror of miscegenation in the complex web of white power, aggression, fantasy, guilt and fear in the Jeffersonian mind. After so careful an examination of ideology and opinion, it seemed logical enough for William Cohen in his essay of 1969 (Selection 1) to observe Jefferson's role as a master on his own plantations. Cohen could find little if any difference between the actions of a planter such as Jefferson with alleged antislavery sentiments and those of "proslavery" planters. Slavemaster Jefferson bought and sold human beings, had his frequent runaways and other nonservile blacks flogged, hired slave catchers, functioned as a slave breeder, and refused to take any significant financial loss to keep slave families together. Finally, the master who freed only one slave in his lifetime and allowed only one person to purchase his liberty, left more than 260 people enslaved in a will which emancipated only 5 bondsmen who were probable relatives of the family. (Several may have been his own children.) As Jefferson's own words (Selection 2) indicate, he accepted many of the racist cliches common to each generation from the colonial era to the mid-twentieth century.

The child of another century, Abraham Lincoln, has been even more deeply enshrouded in myth as the very symbol of emancipation and human freedom, the saintly and suffering liberator of the great masses of black people from the house of bondage. School children still read about the horrified young Lincoln in New Orleans before the auction block swearing "to hit this thing hard" if ever he got the chance. Scholarly biographers have told about the Illinois legislator taking a stand for freedom in a resolution against the murder of abolitionist Elijah Lovejoy, the statesman who suffered "continual torment" from the memory of shackled slaves on an Ohio riverboat in 1841, the brave young Whig Congressman with his bill for the abolition of slavery in the District of Columbia, and the President of 1862 with his fervent wish that "all men everywhere should be free." From this background, according to conventional accounts, came the great emancipator with his splendid proclamation of 1862.

Yet, critical history tells quite another story. The New Orleans story seems to be a fable and the Illinois legislator on the occasion of Lovejoy's death objected as much to abolitionists as to slavery. The complaint of the Ohio riverboat slaves as "a continual torment" appeared in a context of special pleading 13 years after the event and the only letter Lincoln wrote soon after the journey described a group of "happy" slaves who proved that fate can make tolerable even the worst of human conditions. Moreover, the District of Columbia bill for compensated and very gradual emancipation rested on the impossible condition that the proslavery population of the District embrace the proposal at the polls. As late as the Matson case in 1847 Lincoln aided a slave owner in legal problems which sprang from the forcible return of a slave to Kentucky. Lincoln's cautious criticism of the peculiar institution in 1858 came wrapped in sympathetic words for the South and the emphatic rejection of "the social and political equality of the white and black races" along with the right of blacks to hold office, vote, serve on juries, or marry a white person. "Physical difference," he argued "forever forbid the races living together upon terms of social and political equality," and if the races *must* coexist, "I, as much as any man, am in favor of the superior [status] being assigned to the white man." In a White House interview of 1862 which blamed the war on the slaves Lincoln endorsed racial segregation to a black delegation and urged mass emigration from the country as his solution to "the race problem." One need not wonder, then, that Richard Hofstadter in 1948 had correctly noted Lincoln's prejudice toward blacks and asserted that the Emancipation Proclamation which freed no one immediately had "all the moral grandeur of a bill of lading." Historians generally ignored Hofstadter's remarks and paid only a little more attention to the conclusion of Ralph Korngold (Selection 3) in 1955 that Lincoln was a very reluctant emancipator taking a token step possibly to stave off more radical action from Congress.

As modern scholarship increased the awareness of Lincoln's flaws, the problem of bridging the chasm between the man and the myth became more difficult. Some scholars seemed to assume that the praise of even one black person such as Frederick Douglass would somehow erase all the racist remarks, the antiblack policies and the "darky" dialect stories Lincoln loved to tell, but the publication of Douglass' works in 1955 made clear to the careful reader that the great abolitionist had no lasting illusions about Lincoln. James G. Randall in his massive four volume study (1945–1955) of the Lincoln presidency granted the "prejudice" of the early years, quoted Douglass on the war period and concluded that Lincoln had "grown in office." Yet his own version of the emancipation issue in 1862 did not sustain the theory and Lincoln toyed with colonization of blacks at least as late as 1864. Moreover, Randall's last volume spoke of Lincoln's "fairness to the South," "conservatism," and "lack of vindictiveness" without explaining how such a man could fashion a revolutionary racial policy or how a person so concerned with the sensibilities of Southern masters could be "tormented" by the plight of their slave victims. A more plausible version of the "growth in office" theory was offered in 1958 by Richard N. Current (Selection 4), but the point is still in doubt. According to Ben Butler, Lincoln advocated colonization as late as February, 1865.

Norman Graebner, who joined Randall in 1959 in citing constitutional scruples as the reason for Lincoln's tardiness on the emancipation issue, argued for the wisdom and morality of an essentially conservative approach by Lincoln in opposing "all disrespect for property" and warning the Radicals that their emancipation policy constituted an intolerable "destruction of property." If this reasoning implicitly surrendered the conception of the Great Emancipator, David Donald in 1956 explicitly set aside the notion to praise Lincoln as a great man without firm principles, "an astute and dexterous operator of the political machine," a "pragmatist" whose avoidance of the pitfalls of "dogma" could be seen in the remark that "my policy is to have no policy." Donald also followed a curious version of the golden mean first developed in a 1952 biography by Benjamin Thomas which praised Lincoln for following a correct middle course between pro- and antislavery "extremists." In Donald's version Lincoln's policies on race and slavery took an admirable midposition between the ideology of proslavery apologetics and "the antislavery man's idealization of the Negro as God's image in ebony." One might respond to Donald with the suggestion that blacks as well as whites could be cast in God's image and to both Donald and Thomas that in a nation with democratic pretensions middle positions between the freedom or the bondage of millions of human beings are not acceptable compromises but betrayals of the most basic democratic values.

In the most recent, widely praised scholarly biography, an account of Lincoln in the 1850s, Don E. Fehrenbacher simply ignored most of the critical scholarship. Inexplicably he made the false assertion that the Illinois politician had "always opposed the institution of slavery" and on the debates of 1858 devised a curious explanatory framework which exonerated Lincoln from the "moral obtuseness" he attributed to Stephen A. Douglas. Fehrenbacher even seemed to regard as unobjectionable Lincoln's position that "the progressive degradation of all white men who earned their living by toil" was "more monstrous" than "the mere expansion of Negro servitude." As recently as 1971 C. Vann Woodward, who correctly described the pervasiveness of racism in antebellum America, implied that Lincoln both escaped and manipulated American racism for great ends. Lincoln, it seemed, was "the greatest artist of the possible" who "knew in his bones that unless he fought that war with the support of racists and in the name of white supremacy it would be his lost cause and not Jefferson Davis'." Unfortunately Woodward offered no definition of Lincoln's "cause" and no convincing evidence for his assertion.

Nevertheless, the late 60s displayed signs of the gradual expansion of a critical spirit. It became clear that if anything at all could be said for the argument that presidential growth in office brought Lincoln to an equalitarian position, the explanation would have to be limited to the President's last year and use as evidence his efforts for the 13th Amendment and his Second Inaugural Address which echoed abolitionist explanations of the war. Most of the evidence seems to indicate that Lincoln changed but not radically and that at the time of his death he leaned toward a very limited Southern black suffrage coupled with the same kind of conservative and half-hearted Reconstruction efforts advanced by Andrew Johnson shortly after Lincoln's death. Certainly this explanation is compatible with the realistic and critical estimates of Lincoln's racial views made in 1967 by V. Jacque Voegeli in his study of Midwestern racism and by black author Lerone Bennett, Jr. who maintained in 1968 that Lincoln had been consistently "a firm believer in white supremacy." Arthur Zilversmit's (1971) collection of all Lincoln's comments on race and slavery thoroughly confirms the recent findings of critical scholarship. Lincoln's own words (Selection 5), continue to provide the best introduction to his opinions on race and slavery.

BIBLIOGRAPHY

Works Discussed in This Chapter

On Jefferson

Cohen, William, "Thomas Jefferson and the Problem of Slavery," *Journal of American History* (1969).

Freehling, William W., "The Founding Fathers and Slavery," *American Historical Review* (1972).

Jefferson, Thomas, is best read in the modern edition of *Notes on the State of Virginia* ed. William Peden (1955).

Jordan, Winthrop D., *White Over Black: American Attitudes Toward the Negro: 1550–1812* (1968).

Koch, Adrienne, *Jefferson and Madison: The Great Collaboration* (1950).

Levy, Leonard W., *Jefferson and Civil Liberties: The Darker Side* (1963).

McColley, Robert, *Slavery and Jeffersonian Virginia* (1964).

Malone, Dumas, *Jefferson and His Times* (3 vols., 1948–62).

Peterson, Merrill D., *Thomas Jefferson and the New Nation: A Biography* (1970).

Wiltse, Charles M., *The Jeffersonian Tradition in American Democracy* (1935).

On Lincoln

Bennett, Lerone Jr., "Was Abe Lincoln a White Supremacist?" *Ebony* (February 1968).

Current, Richard N., *The Lincoln Nobody Knows* (1958).

Donald, David, *Lincoln Reconsidered* (1956).

Fehrenbacher, Don E., *Prelude to Greatness: Lincoln in the 1850s* (1962).

Foner, Phillip S., ed., *The Life and Writings of Frederick Douglass* (4 vols., 1950–55).

Graebner, Norman A., ed. *The Enduring Lincoln* (1959).

Hofstadter, Richard, "Lincoln" in *The American Political Tradition* (1948).

Lincoln, can best be studied in Roy P. Basler, ed., *The Collected Works of Abraham Lincoln* (9 vols., 1953–55).

Randall, James, *Lincoln the President* (4 vols., 1945–55).

Thomas, Benjamin P., *Abraham Lincoln* (1952).

Voegeli, V. Jacque, *Free But Not Equal: The Midwest and the Negro During the Civil War* (1967).

Woodward, C. Vann, *American Counterpoint* (1971).

Zilversmit, Arthur, ed., *Lincoln on Black and White: A Documentary History* (1971).

Suggested Readings

Works on Jefferson

Among the books which *portray Jefferson glowingly as antislavery* are Marie Kimball, *Jefferson and the Road to Glory, 1773–1776* (1943) and Gilbert Chinard, *Thomas Jefferson, The Apostle of Americanism* (rev. ed., 1939). Albert Jay Nock in *Jefferson* (1926) seems to share Jefferson's opinions in the few remarks on slavery and race in his book. Nathan Schachner in *Thomas Jefferson: A Biography* (1951) makes a few mildly critical remarks. Karl Lehmann in *Thomas Jefferson, American Humanist* (1947) does not seem to regard racial equalitarianism and antislavery as any essential parts of "humanism." Merrill D. Peterson in *The Jeffersonian Image in the American Mind* (1960) has a long and interesting account of Jefferson's reputation as foe or friend of slavery, but one may disagree with some of his conclusions. On Jefferson's slave mistress and children, see Pearl M. Graham "Jefferson and Sally Hemmings," *Journal of Negro History* (1961) and [Isaac Jefferson] *Memoirs of a Monticello Slave*, Rayford W. Logan, ed. (1951). Peterson and Winthrop D. Jordan seem too eager to dismiss the idea and require proof of paternity which is hardly available for any of us. Several noteworthy references to Jefferson are in David B. Davis, *The Problem of Slavery in Western Culture* (1966) and several interesting essays are in Merrill D. Peterson, ed. *Thomas Jefferson, A Profile* (1962). Some light on Jefferson and slavery is shed in John Fisher, "Slavery and the Slave Trade in the Louisiana Purchase, 1803–1812," *Essays in History* (1964). Other relevant works are Daniel J. Boorstin, *The Lost World of Thomas Jefferson* (1948); Richard B. Davis, *Intellectual Life in Jefferson's Virginia* (1964); and the indexed items on Jefferson in Irving Brant, *James Madison* (5 vols. 1941–61). Jefferson's most extensive remarks on race can be found in his *Notes on the State of Virginia*, William Peden ed. (1955). For the time period to the early 1790s, the definitive edition of Jefferson's papers is Julian Boyd et al. eds., *The Papers of Thomas Jefferson* (17 vols. to date, 1950–65). For most of Jefferson's life, scholars must still consult Paul L. Ford, ed., *The Writings of Thomas Jefferson* (10 vols., 1892–99) and A. A. Lipscomb and A. E. Bergh, eds., *The Writings of Thomas Jefferson* (20 vols., 1903). Information on Jefferson as a slaveowner can be found in Edwin M. Betts, ed., *Thomas Jefferson's Garden Book, 1776–1824* (1944) and Betts, ed., *Thomas Jefferson's Farm Book* (1953).

Works on Lincoln

The *basic work* is Roy P. Basler, ed. *The Collected Works of Abraham Lincoln* (9 vols.; 1953–55). Richard N. Current has a one volume condensation of Randall's four volumes under the title *Mr. Lincoln* (1957). See also Current, ed., *The Political Thought of Abraham Lincoln* (1967). The most persuasive evidence on Lincoln as a late-blooming equalitarian is the Wadsworth letter, but Ludwell H. Johnson denies its authenticity. In the Johnson exchange with Harold M. Hyman sympathies go easily to Hyman, but Johnson seems to have made the stronger case. See Johnson, "Lincoln and Equal Rights: The Authenticity of the Wadsworth Letter," *Journal of Southern History* (1966); Hyman, "Lincoln and Equal Rights . . . The Irrelevancy of the Wadsworth Letter," *Civil War History* (1966); Johnson, "Lincoln and Equal Rights: A Reply," *Civil War History* (1967). Another essay on Lincoln's racial opinions is Robert F. Durden, "A. Lincoln: Honkie or Equalitarian?" *South Atlantic Quarterly* (1972). Lincoln scholarship has been understandably thin in recent years. Lincoln is less troublesome as a nationalist. See Edmund Wilson's interesting and provocative essay, "Lincoln and the Union as Religious Mysticism," *Eight Essays* (1954). Reinhard Luthin was critical enough but faulty in scholarship and not much interested in the issues of this chapter. See Luthin, *The Real Abraham Lincoln* (1960). Carl Sandburg's romantic and enormously misleading work can be sampled in the one volume condensation of the earlier six volumes. See Sandburg, *Abraham Lincoln: The Prairie Years and the War Years* (1954). John Hope Franklin, *The Emancipation Proclamation* (1963) is particularly good for the world context.

Some recent books in the *tradition of piety toward Lincoln* are Paul Simon, *Lincoln's Preparation for Greatness: The Illinois Legislative Years* (1965); Don E. Fehrenbacher, ed. *The Leadership of Abraham Lincoln* (1970); Roy P. Basler, *A Touchstone for Greatness: Essays, Addresses and Occasional Pieces About Abraham Lincoln* (1973).

On *Lincoln and blacks,* see Gary R. Planck, "Abraham Lincoln and Black Colonization: Theory and Practice," *Lincoln Herald* (1970) and Ronald L. Satz, "The African Slave Trade and Lincoln's Company of 1858," *Journal of the Illinois State Historical Society* (1972).

For *mildly critical analyses*, see Donald W. Riddle, *Congressman Abraham Lincoln* (1957) and John S. Wright, *Lincoln and the Politics of Slavery* (1970). Two recent books of interest are Michael Davis, *The Image of Lincoln in the South* (1971) and David Elton Trueblood, *Abraham Lincoln: Theologian of American Anguish* (1973). The ultimate book for praising the "moderate" is T. Harry Williams, *Lincoln and the Radicals* (1941).

A great deal of information *on Lincoln and emancipation* can be found in Benjamin Quarles, *The Negro in the Civil War* (1953), and *Lincoln and the Negro* (1962). The best book on the subject as seen through the eyes of a Lincoln subordinate was written by Benjamin P. Thomas and Harold M. Hyman. See *Stanton: The Life and Times of Lincoln's Secretary of War* (1962). Harry V. Jaffa in *Crisis of the House Divided* (1959) attempted without much success to refute Hofstadter's comments on Lincoln's anti-equalitarianism. On the emancipation question in the 1864 election see William F. Zornow, *Lincoln and the Party Divided* (1954). On the Kentucky question, see Gary L. Williams, "Lincoln's Neutral Allies: The Case of the Kentucky Unionists," *South Atlantic Quarterly* (1974). In Grady McWhiney (ed.), *Grant, Lee, Lincoln and the Radicals* (1965), David Donald defended his thesis on the Radicals and T. Harry Williams defended a moderate version of his old assault on the Radicals, with Donald presenting the more plausible case. Dudley T. Cornish, *The Sable Arm; Negro Troops in the Union Army, 1861–1865* (1956), and James M. McPherson, (ed.), *The Negro's Civil War* (1965), suggested the very large part that Negroes played in their own emancipation.

Thomas Jefferson, Slaveowner*

William Cohen

It seems paradoxical that Thomas Jefferson, one of the enduring heroes of American democracy, should have been the owner of more than 180 slaves at the very time when he was proclaiming that all men were created equal and that they were "endowed by their Creator" with the "unalienable Rights" of "Life, Liberty and the pursuit of Happiness." Moreover, throughout his life he continued to hold that slavery was unjust and immoral. In 1785 he had used the phrase "avarice and oppression" to characterize the slaveholding interest, and he contrasted this with the "sacred side" of emancipation. A year later, he marveled at the fact that American patriots who had endured beatings, starvation, and imprisonment at the hands of their British oppressors could inflict "on their fel-

* William Cohen, "Thomas Jefferson and the Problem of Slavery," *Journal of American History*, 56 (1971), pp. 502–26. By permission of the publisher and the author.

low men a bondage one hour of which is fraught with more misery than ages of that which he rose in rebellion to oppose." In the final year of his life, he reiterated his belief that it was unlawful for "one man to appropriate to himself the faculties of another without his consent."[1]

Most Jefferson scholars have dealt with this contradiction by ignoring it, or by citing his views on abolition and holding that his role as an owner of men was entailed upon him. Born into a slave system, they argue, he could not in good conscience abandon his black charges; he made the best of a bad situation by behaving as a benevolent and indulgent master. Indeed, the most competent and scholarly biographer of Jefferson contends that "if the master himself erred [in handling his slaves] he did so on the side of leniency."[2] . . . *Malone*

This view of Jefferson as a proto-abolitionist master came under attack in 1961. Robert McColley's *Slavery and Jeffersonian Virginia* depicted the author of the Declaration of Independence as a man who believed in Negro inferiority and whose public actions frequently favored the slave system. Devoted to showing that the institution of slavery actually gained strength during the post-Revolutionary era, this work often used Jefferson as an example of the planter class and argued that political expediency and racist ideology prevented him from working effectively against the system.

More recently [1968], Winthrop Jordan devoted a chapter of his study [*White Over Black*] to an analysis of the contradiction within Jefferson's thought on the subject of black servitude. Accepting the traditional formulation that the Virginian was trapped by a system he abhorred, Jordan defined Jefferson's central dilemma as being that he "hated slavery but thought Negroes inferior to white men." . . .

Jordan's work is valuable for its analysis of Jefferson's intellectual entanglement with slavery, but it does not delve into Jefferson's day to day relationship with slavery. This is important because Jefferson's practical involvement with the system of black bondage indicates that, while his racist beliefs were generally congruent with his actions, his libertarian views about slavery tended to be more intellectual abstractions. This is particularly true for the years after 1785; and to a somewhat lesser degree, it holds true for the earlier period as well. . . .

On the whole . . . there was a significant gap between his thought and action with regard to the abolition question. He fully believed that it was morally and politically evil to hold another man in slavery, but he continued to do so. Believing that bondage should be abolished, he wrote an amendment which would have accomplished this gradually. But he kept it

---

[1] Thomas Jefferson to Edward Everett, April 8, 1826, Paul Leicester Ford, ed., *The Works of Thomas Jefferson* (12 vols., New York, 1904–1905), 12, 469. T. Jefferson to Richard Price, Aug. 7, 1785; T. Jefferson to Jean Nicolas Demeunier [June 26, 1786], Julian P. Boyd, ed., and Lyman H. Butterfield and Mina R. Bryan, associate eds., *The Papers of Thomas Jefferson* (17 vols., Princeton, 1950–1965), 8, 357, 10, 63.

[2] Dumas Malone, *Jefferson and His Time* (3 vols., Boston, 1948–1962), 3, 212. Dumas Malone is the most prominent advocate of the view which holds that, although T. Jefferson disliked his role as an owner of men, it was entailed upon him. . . . [See also biographies and studies by Henry S. Randall, Marie Kimball, Gilbert Chinard, Nathan Schachner, Adrienne Koch, and Albert Jay Nock.]

a secret for fear the public was not ready. Meanwhile, he codified Virginia's slave law and added to it harsh provisions aimed against free Negroes. He agreed to the desirability of keeping slavery out of the western territory, but his proposal would have allowed the disease a sixteen-year incubation period. . . .

Jefferson's views on slavery and race suggest that his libertarian sentiments were more than counterbalanced by his conviction that Negroes were members of a race so alien and inferior that there was no hope that whites and blacks could coexist side by side on terms of equality. Jefferson's libertarian views, however, had virtually no impact upon his actions after 1784, and his belief in the inferiority of the slaves was completely congruent with his behavior as both a planter and a politician.

In his daily life there were few differences between Jefferson's behavior as an owner of men and that of Virginia plantation masters who opposed his antislavery speculations. His bondsmen were well fed and clothed, and their work load was comparable to that of white freemen. In this regard their lot may have been easier than that of many other slaves in the state. Nevertheless, when he dealt with runaways, sales of slaves, breeding, flogging, and manumissions, his behavior did not differ appreciably from that of other enlightened slaveholders who deplored needless cruelty, but would use whatever means they felt necessary to protect their peculiar form of property.

During Jefferson's adult lifetime, more than forty of his Negroes attempted to escape. . . . [Jefferson] glosses over the fact that more than one-seventh of his blacks chose to follow the British army in 1781.[3] . . .

. . . Throughout his life Jefferson hired slave catchers and asked his friends to keep an eye peeled for his thralls when they struck out for freedom. In early September 1805, Jame Hubbard, a stout Negro who worked in the plantation nail factory, ran away, but was soon apprehended and returned. About five years later, he escaped again. A year passed before Jefferson learned that Hubbard was living in the area of Lexington and dispatched Isham Chisolm to retrieve the bondsman. It was too late, however; Hubbard had departed only a few days earlier for parts unknown. When Chisolm returned empty-handed, Jefferson offered him a bonus of twenty-five dollars to go after the man a second time. This time Hubbard was caught and brought back in irons, and Jefferson reported: "I had him severely flogged in the presence of his old companions. . . ." He then added that he was convinced that Hubbard "will never again serve any man as a slave. the [sic] moment he is out of jail and his irons off he will

---

3 This includes thirty slaves who went over to the British in 1781 and cases involving one or more runaways mentioned in the following sources: advertisement for a runaway named Sandy in the *Virginia Gazette*, Sept. 7, 14, 1769, George Wythe to T. Jefferson, Dec. 31, 1781, Boyd, ed., *Papers of Thomas Jefferson*, 6, 144; Daniel Bradley to T. Jefferson, Oct. 6, 1805, T. Jefferson to Joseph Daugherty, July 31, 1806, T. Jefferson to Mary Dangerfield, July 31, 1808, T. Jefferson to Jeremiah Goodman, July 26, 1813, Joel Yancey to T. Jefferson, May 22, 1821, Betts, ed., *Thomas Jefferson's . . . Writings*, 21, 22, 27, 36, 46. Two other runaways, Beverly and Harriet [Hemings] are listed in Jefferson, "Farm Book," 29, 130. See Thomas Jefferson to William Gordon, July 16, 1788, Boyd, ed., *Papers of Thomas Jefferson*, 13, 363–64. The figure of forty is probably conservative as it is based solely on a study of readily available sources.

be off himself." Before Jefferson could implement plans to have him sold out of the state, Hubbard disappeared again.[4]

In the abstract Jefferson did not believe one man had a right to own another, and, hence, no man had a right to sell another. He repeatedly expressed his dislike for this commerce, and he tried to avoid selling his human property except for misbehavior or at their own request.[5] Nevertheless, slaves were sold when he was pressed for cash, regardless of their wishes in the matter. . . . The underlying assumption . . . [in his letters] is that the slaves owe him a living and that, if they do not provide it, they will be the ones to suffer. A second implication is that he has the right to dispose of them as he thinks best. Acting upon this view in the years 1783–1794, he reluctantly sold about fifty slaves.[6]

When selling slaves, Jefferson did his best to keep families together if it did not entail a financial hardship for him. In 1792, he sold two males named York and Jame and offered to throw their superannuated parents, Judy and Will, into the bargain if they wished to go along with their sons. His gesture might have saved him money by taking from his shoulders the burden of caring for the old couple who were no longer good for much work. That Jefferson did not let scruples about breaking up families interfere with his business is shown by the fact that in the same lot of slaves with Jame and York was Dilcey, a twenty-three-year-old woman, whose valuable parents remained his property.[7] . . .

It may be argued that, although Jefferson deplored the institution of slavery and particularly the buying and selling of men, the purchases and sales he made were impossible to avoid, since they were for the purpose of paying off debts or uniting families. But in 1805, he said that he was "endeavoring to purchase young and able negro men" for his plantation.[8] Clearly then, he was not merely engaged in a holding operation designed to protect his slaves from a cruel and inhospitable world.

Like any other entrepreneur, Jefferson was concerned with the problem of increasing his capital assets—land and Negroes. Because he was always short of cash, it was difficult for him to increase his land holdings; and he never did. Slaves, however, increased of their own accord, and Jefferson took pains to make sure that this source of profit was not lost through shortsightedness.[9] . . .

---

[4] T. Jefferson to Bradley, Oct. 6, 1805, T. Jefferson to Reuben Perry, April 16, 1812, Sept. 3, 1812, Betts, ed., *Thomas Jefferson's . . . Writings*, 21, 34–36.

[5] T. Jefferson to John W. Eppes, June 30, 1820, T. Jefferson to Craven Peyton, Nov. 27, 1815, T. Jefferson to Thomas Mann Randolph, June 8, 1803, ibid., 45, 40, 19.

[6] Malone, *Jefferson and His Time*, 3, 207, 1, 443–44. References to sales of slaves appear in T. Jefferson to Alexander McCaul, Jan. 4, 1787, Boyd, ed., *Papers of Thomas Jefferson*, 11, 10; and T. Jefferson to James Lyle, April 25, 1793, Ford, ed., *Works of Thomas Jefferson*, 7, 278.

[7] T. Jefferson to Bowling Clarke, Sept. 21, 1792; Betts, ed., *Thomas Jefferson's . . . Writings*, 13; T. Jefferson, "Farm Book," 9, 24, 30. Bess was known as Betty in 1774. In 1795 T. Jefferson wrote the word "old" beside the names of Judy and Will indicating that they were not useful for labor anymore.

[8] Jefferson to Jordan, Dec. 21, 1805, Betts, ibid., 21.

[9] Jefferson to Yancey, Jan. 17, 1819, ibid., 43. Writing to Eppes on June 30, 1820, T. Jefferson said: "I know no error more consuming to an estate than that of stocking farms with men almost exclusively. I consider a woman who brings a child

. . . Between 1810 and 1822, about 100 slaves were born to Jefferson's "breeding women"; while only a total of thirty Negroes died, were sold, or ran away.[10]

Throughout his life, Jefferson appears to have emancipated only two slaves; and one of them bought his freedom in 1792 at the price of £60. Upon his death in 1826, Jefferson manumitted five more Negroes and willed over 260 bondsmen to his heirs. Of the total of seven slaves that he freed, at least five were members of a mulatto family named Hemings; and it seems well established that these favored individuals were directly descended from Jefferson's father-in-law. Nevertheless, several of them remained in servitude after Jefferson died. In 1822, two Hemings girls, tired of waiting for their freedom, ran away to Washington.[11]

Apparently, Jefferson's unwillingness to manumit his bondsmen arose, at least in part, from his reluctance to alter his standard of living and to bring his practices into line with his principles. He took much pride in the fine wines, good books, and generous hospitality to be found at Monticello; and he went to great lengths to preserve intact this inheritance for his posterity.[12] . . .

If self-interest played a major role in determining Jefferson's behavior as a plantation owner, it was equally important in shaping his stance as a national leader on questions involving slavery. After 1784, he refrained from discussing the issue publicly for political reasons, but the matter came up occasionally in the course of his official duties. As ambassador to France, he zealously sought to justify the American claim to compensation for slaves taken by the British in 1783; and he continued to press for satisfaction on this issue when he served as secretary of state. He then pressured the Spanish government into denying sanctuary in Florida to fugitive slaves from Georgia.[13]

Although Jefferson embraced the French Revolution, he shuddered with fear in August 1791 when slaves on the island of Santo Domingo

---

every two years as more profitable than the best man of the farm. What she produces is an addition to capital, while his labors disappear in mere consumption." Ibid., 45–46. T. Jefferson's keen awareness of the profit to be derived from the natural increase of his slaves is also shown in his observation that "our families of negroes double in 25 years which is an increase of the capital invested in them, 4 percent over and above keeping up the original number." See Jordan, *White Over Black,* 430.

[10] These figures are based on T. Jefferson, "Farm Book," 130–31.

[11] Ibid., 130. For the freedom papers of Robert and James Hemings (dated Dec. 12, 1794 and Feb. 5, 1796 respectively), see Betts, ed., *Thomas Jefferson's . . . Writings,* 15. For T. Jefferson's will, dated March 1826, see Ford, ed., *Works of Thomas Jefferson,* 12, 482. The relationship of the Hemings family to Jefferson and his relatives is discussed in Merrill D. Peterson, *The Jefferson Image in the American Mind* (New York, 1960), 185–86. See also Jordan, *White Over Black,* 464–68.

[12] In his will the Virginian went to elaborate lengths to see that his estate went to his daughter Martha and not to the creditors of her husband. Ford, ed., *Works of Thomas Jefferson,* 12, 479; McColley, *Slavery and Jeffersonian Virginia,* 23; Randall, *Thomas Jefferson,* 3, 332–33; Nock, *Jefferson,* 59.

[13] Amplification of Subjects Discussed with Vergennes [ca. Dec. 20, 1785], Jefferson to John Jay, April 23, 1786, Boyd, ed., *Papers of Thomas Jefferson,* 9, 111, 403–04; T. Jefferson to British Minister, May 29, 1792, Dec. 15, 1793, T. Jefferson to Governor of Florida, March 10, 1791, T. Jefferson to Governor of Georgia, March 26, 1791, Ford, ed., *Works of Thomas Jefferson,* 7, 41–46, 8, 95–97, 6, 212, 226–27.

revolted for their liberty, and he approved a grant of arms and ammunition to their embattled Gallic masters. . . .

. . . [A decade later] Jefferson became President, and he failed to use his office to avert the bloody scenes he had predicted. Deeply worried by the slave revolt of 1800, the Virginia legislature requested Governor Monroe to consult with the President about means of deporting Negroes involved in future outbreaks. Jefferson, a longtime colonizationist, then asked the American minister to England to negotiate with the Sierra Leone Company for the "reception of such of these people as might be colonized thither." After learning that the Company was unwilling to consider the proposal, the President abandoned his colonization efforts for the duration of his term.[14]

Jefferson's proslavery actions were particularly evident in the area of foreign policy, and the treaty which granted the Louisiana Territory to the United States contained a provision protecting the right of the Spanish and French inhabitants in the area to keep their slaves. The French insistence upon such a condition was understandable, and so was its acceptance by the United States, but the author of the Ordinance of 1784 made no move to limit the further introduction of bondage into the area.[15]

Napoleon had given up Louisiana largely because of his inability to crush the rebel forces on Santo Domingo. By 1806, he again entertained the hope of reconquering the island, and he asked the American government to cooperate by cutting off all trade with the black nation. Jefferson complied with this request and commended the measure to Congress, where it passed in the House by a vote of 93–26. The President supported France in this venture because he hoped that Napoleon would reciprocate by aiding the United States to acquire Florida, but Jefferson was surely aware of the fact that if the plan succeeded it would destroy the island's Negro regime, which stood as a beacon of hope to American slaves.[16]

Despite these actions, the dominant theme of Jefferson's administration on the subject of slavery was discreet silence. When citizens in the Indiana Territory were demanding that slavery be permitted throughout the Northwest Territory, the President made no comment. Although Jefferson privately continued to represent himself as a foe of human bondage and on rare occasions during his presidency voiced such sentiments in letters to men who shared his views, he was exceedingly careful to keep these thoughts from reaching the public. . . . In fact . . . Jefferson had already given up "the expectation of any early provision for the extinguishment of slavery among us," and his actions appear to have been designed more to mute the issue than to resolve it.[17]

Ten years after he left office, as the Missouri issue was dividing the nation, Jefferson again demonstrated his ability to mix vague abolition

---

[14] Ford, ed., *Works of Thomas Jefferson,* 9, 383–86. The quotation is to be found in T. Jefferson to John Lynch, January 21, 1811, ibid., 11, 179. The request of the Virginia legislature also asked that the matter of finding a place to which free Negroes could be sent should also be investigated.

[15] McColley, *Slavery and Jeffersonian Virginia,* 125.

[16] Ibid., 112.

[17] T. Jefferson to William A. Burwell, January 28, 1805, ibid., 10, 126.

sentiments with a position that worked to the advantage of the slave states. Recognizing that the dispute over the admission of Missouri heralded an era of increasing national division over the slavery issue, he likened the controversy to a "fire bell in the night" and warned of impending disaster for the Union. Speaking of slavery, he implicitly endorsed the moral position of the North when he described the dilemma of the South: "We have the wolf by the ears and can neither hold him, nor safely let him go. Justice is in the one scale, and self-preservation in the other." He indicated his willingness to give up his bondsmen if any *"practicable"* way of achieving their "emancipation and *expatriation*" could be found.[18]

Nevertheless, he endorsed the southern position and charged the Federalists with creating a geographical division based on an ostensibly moral question as a means of regaining their influence. He then denied that morality was involved because the limitation of the area of bondage would free no one. He also denied that the federal government could regulate the "condition of different descriptions of men composing a State," and he ruled out the only practical means by which emancipation might eventually have been brought about.[19]

It may be argued that Jefferson's position on the Missouri issue and also his inactivity as President may have been dictated by his strict construction of the Constitution. When the object was large enough, however, Jefferson could be quite flexible; and he did not allow such scruples to prevent the acquisition of the Louisiana Territory. Moreover, he believed that the expatriation of America's blacks was a subject which merited a similar elasticity.

Despite his support for the southern position on the issue of Missouri, in 1821 Jefferson could still write: "Nothing is more certainly written in the book of fate than that these people are to be free, Nor is it less certain that the two races, equally free, cannot live in the same government."[20] Thus, in the last years of his life he continued to insist that emancipation must be accompanied by expatriation. Nevertheless, he lacked enthusiasm for the plan to resettle the Negroes in Africa and believed that the distance of that continent would make it impossible for such an operation to succeed.[21]

Since African colonization seemed an impossibility, Jefferson suggested a plan which entailed "emancipating the afterborn, leaving them, on due compensation, with their mothers, until their services are worth their maintenance, and putting them to industrious occupations until a proper age for deportation." The individuals who would be "freed" immediately after their birth would eventually be sent to Santo Domingo which, according to the newspapers, had recently offered to open its doors to such persons. In effect, Jefferson was proposing that the federal gov-

---

18 T. Jefferson to John Holmes, April 22, 1820, ibid., 12, 159.
19 Ibid.; T. Jefferson to Albert Gallatin, December 26, 1820, ibid., 12, 187–89.
20 Ibid., 1, 77.
21 T. Jefferson to Jared Sparks, February 4, 1824, ibid., 12, 334–35.

ernment buy all newborn slaves from their owners (at twelve dollars and fifty cents each) and that it pay for their "nurture with the mother [for] a few years." Beyond this, the plan would not cost the government anything, for the young blacks would then work for their maintenance until deported. Santo Domingo had offered to bear the cost of passage.

Jefferson noted that a majority of Americans then living would live to see the black population reach six million and warned that "a million and a half are within their control; but six millions, . . . and one million of these fighting men, will say, 'we will not go.' " The Virginia statesman concluded his proposal by urging that neither constitutional problems nor human sentiment ought to be allowed to stand in its way. . . .

. . . Thus, only two and a half years before his death, Jefferson reiterated his long held belief that emancipation was imperative for the sake of the nation, but that it must be accompanied by colonization. Even here, however, his theory differed from his practice; and in this case his inconsistency would follow him beyond the grave for he did not offer to free his slaves on the condition that they leave the country. On the contrary, in his will he requested the Virginia legislature to grant special permission to the five slaves he manumitted to continue to live in the state.[22]

Jefferson was a man of many dimensions, and any explanation of his behavior must contain a myriad of seeming contradictions. He was a sincere and dedicated foe of the slave trade who bought and sold men whenever he found it personally necessary. He believed that all men were entitled to life and liberty regardless of their abilities, yet he tracked down those slaves who had the courage to take their rights by running away. He believed that slavery was morally and politically wrong, but still he wrote a slave code for his state and opposed a national attempt in 1819 to limit the further expansion of the institution. He believed that one hour of slavery was worse than ages of British oppression, yet he was able to discuss the matter of slave breeding in much the same terms that one would use when speaking of the propagation of dogs and horses.

From an intellectual point of view, his strong "suspicion" that the Negroes were innately inferior is probably of great significance in explaining his ability to ignore his own strictures about their rights. Thinking of them as lesser men, he was able to convince himself that his behavior toward them was benevolent and humane; and indeed it was, when judged by the traditional assumptions of the slaveholders. It is a mistake, however, to treat Jefferson's relationship to slavery in intellectual or psychological terms alone, for the institution shaped the warp and woof of life at Monticello and his abstract speculations about human freedom carried little weight when balanced against the whole pattern of his existence there.

Interacting with one another as both cause and effect to produce Jefferson's proslavery behavior was a complex set of factors which included his belief in Negro inferiority, a social environment which took for granted the enslavement of one race by another, and the fact that he owned

---

[22] T. Jefferson's will, March 1826, ibid., 12, 483.

10,000 acres of land and over 200 slaves.[23] His wealth, his status, and his political position were tied to the system of slavery, and never once did he *actively* propose a plan that would have jeopardized all this. More often than not, the actions he took with regard to slavery actually strengthened the institution. This can be seen in his authorship in 1778 of Virginia's slave code, in his support of the plantation owners of Santo Domingo, and in his position on the Missouri question.

Monticello was the workshop of the maker of the "agrarian dream." It was here that Jefferson conducted his agricultural and scientific experiments and offered a generous hospitality to visitors. It was here that he lived a bustling, but gracious life far from the money changers in the cities of the North. This was the life that he sought to preserve against the incursions of the forces of commerce and industry. But it should not be forgotten that Jefferson's world depended upon forced labor for its very existence.

Jefferson on Blacks: Notes on the State of Virginia (1785)

. . . It will probably be asked, Why not retain and incorporate the blacks into the state, and thus save the expense of supplying by importation of white settlers, the vacancies they will leave? Deep rooted prejudices entertained by the whites; ten thousand recollections, by the blacks, of the injuries they have sustained; new provocations; the real distinctions which nature has made; and many other circumstances, will divide us into parties, and produce convulsions, which will probably never end but in the extermination of the one or the other race. To these objections, which are political, may be added others, which are physical and moral. The first difference which strikes us is that of colour. Whether the black of the negro resides in the reticular membrane between the skin and the scarf-skin, or in the scarf-skin itself; whether it proceeds from the colour of the blood, the colour of the bile, or from that of some other secretion, the difference is fixed in nature, and is as real as if its seat and cause were better known to us. And is this difference of no importance? Is it not the foundation of a greater or less share of beauty in the two races? Are not the fine mixtures of red and white, the expressions of every passion by

---

23 This listing is not meant to exclude the effect of T. Jefferson's psychological make-up as a factor which influenced his behavior with regard to slavery. Jordan convincingly suggests that the Virginian's belief in Negro inferiority was partially rooted in his inner mind. See Jordan, *White Over Black*, 457–81.

greater or less suffusions of colour in the one preferable to that eternal monotony, which reigns in the countenances, that immoveable veil of black which covers all the emotions of the other race? Add to these, flowing hair, a more elegant symmetry of form, their own judgment in favour of the whites, declared by their preference of them, as uniformly as is the preference of the Oranootan [orangutan] for the black women over those of his own species. The circumstance of superior beauty, is thought worthy attention in the propagation of our horses, dogs, and other domestic animals; why not in that of man? Besides those of colour, figure, and hair, there are other physical distinctions proving a difference of race. They have less hair on the face and body. They secrete less by the kidneys, and more by the glands of the skin, which gives them a very strong and disagreeable odour. This greater degree of transpiration renders them more tolerant of heat, and less so of cold than the whites. Perhaps too a difference of structure in the pulmonary apparatus . . . may have disabled them from extricating, in the act of inspiration, so much of that fluid from the outer air, or obliged them in expiration, to part with more of it. They seem to require less sleep. A black after hard labour through the day, will be induced by the slightest amusements to sit up till midnight, or later though knowing he must be out with the first dawn of the morning. They are at least as brave, and more adventuresome. But this may perhaps proceed from a want of forethought, which prevents their seeing a danger till it be present. When present, they do not go through it with more coolness or steadiness than the whites. They are more ardent after their female: but love seems with them to be more an eager desire, than a tender delicate mixture of sentiment and sensation. Their griefs are transient. Those numberless afflictions, which render it doubtful whether heaven has given life to us in mercy or in wrath, are less felt, and sooner forgotten with them. In general, their existence appears to participate more of sensation than reflection. To this must be ascribed their disposition to sleep when abstracted from their diversions, and unemployed in labour. An animal whose body is at rest, and who does not reflect, must be disposed to sleep of course. Comparing them by their faculties of memory, reason, and imagination, it appears to me that in memory they are equal to the whites; in reason much inferior, as I think one could scarcely be found capable of tracing and comprehending the investigations of Euclid; and that in imagination they are dull, tasteless, and anomalous. . . .

. . . This unfortunate difference of colour, and perhaps of faculty, is a powerful obstacle to the emancipation of these people. Many of their advocates while they wish to vindicate the liberty of human nature are anxious also to preserve its dignity and beauty. Some of these, embarrassed by the question "What further is to be done with them?" join themselves in opposition with those who are actuated by sordid avarice only. Among the Romans emancipation required but one effort. The slave when made free, might mix with, without staining the blood of his master. But with us a second is necessary unknown to history. When freed, he is to be removed beyond the reach of mixture.

Lincoln: A Very Reluctant Emancipator*

Ralph Korngold

On September 17, 1862, the battle took place at Antietam. Lee's march through Maryland was halted, but McClellan's victory was inconclusive. The Confederate commander retreated in good order. His army remained intact and was destined to win important victories. Five days later, on September 22, 1862, Lincoln issued the famous preliminary Emancipation Proclamation. Secretary Chase tells us about it in his *Diary*. He quotes Lincoln as saying:

> The action of the army against the rebels has not been quite what I should have best liked. But they have been driven out of Maryland, and Pennsylvania is no longer in danger of invasion. When the rebel army was at Frederick, I determined, as soon as it should be driven out of Maryland, to issue a Proclamation of Emancipation such as I thought most likely to be useful. I said nothing to any one; but I made the promise to myself, and [hesitating a little]—to my Maker. The rebel army is now driven out, and I am going to fulfill that promise. I have got you together to hear what I have written down. I do not wish your advice about the main matter for that I have determined myself.[1]

There exists, however, a diary entry made by James C. Welling, editor of the *National Intelligencer*, concerning a statement made to him by Edward Stanly, military governor of North Carolina, to whom Lincoln gave an entirely different version about what prompted him to issue the proclamation. Since Welling and Stanly are reliable witnesses and since, as we have seen, Lincoln was in the habit of contradicting himself, it is the historian's duty to give both versions and to try to ascertain the truth in the matter.

Stanly had been a congressman from North Carolina. He was an avowed Unionist but was opposed to any interference with slavery. He had accepted the military governorship of his state at great personal sacrifice and only after Lincoln had given him the assurance that he had no intention of interfering with slavery. When the preliminary Emancipation Proclamation appeared he thought Lincoln had played him false. So he hastened to Washington with the intention of handing in his resignation. He had several interviews with Lincoln and decided to remain at his post. Having made that decision he went to the office of the *National In-*

* Ralph Korngold, *Thaddeus Stevens, A Being Darkly Wise and Rudely Great* (1955). Reprinted by permission of Virginia Rice. Copyright 1955 by Ralph Korngold.

[1] *Diary*, vol. 2, pp. 87–88.

telligencer and talked to Welling, who made the following entry in his diary:

> September 27th.—Had a call at the *Intelligencer* office from the Honorable Edward Stanly, Military Governor of North Carolina. In a long and interesting conversation Mr. Stanly related to me the substance of several interviews which he had had with the President respecting the Proclamation of Freedom. Stanly said that the President had stated to him that the proclamation had become a civil necessity to prevent the Radicals from openly embarrassing the government in the conduct of the war. The President expressed the belief that, without the proclamation for which they had been clamoring, the Radicals would take the extreme step in Congress of withholding supplies for carrying on the war—leaving the whole land in anarchy. Mr. Lincoln said that he had prayed to the Almighty to save him from this necessity, adopting the very language of our Saviour, "If it be possible, let this cup pass frome me," but the prayer had not been answered.[2]

The extreme reticence of Lincoln's biographers and Civil War historians in general concerning this and other contradictory statements made by Lincoln during this trying period makes it evident that they have found them embarrassing. They ill accord with the image of Lincoln they appear to have been determined to present to the public. To the author of this volume they make Lincoln more, not less, sympathetic, since they make him appear more human. He was not all-wise, he made mistakes, he often contradicted himself. Notwithstanding all this he went steadfastly toward his goal—the preservation of the Union. Emancipation and all else— even truth sometimes—were subordinated to this. He wished to preserve the Union without having to resort to general emancipation if at all possible because he feared the postwar consequences of that form of emancipation to the country and to the Negro. It does not appear unlikely that his persistence in this prolonged the war. Stevens and many others thought so, and they may have been right. Lincoln finally was to acknowledge that far from having the serious consequences he had so often predicted, the Emancipation Proclamation had the opposite effect.[3] Yet we shall see that after he issued the final document he continued trying to get the border states to adopt gradual emancipation. Had he succeeded it would have made the ratification of the Thirteenth Amendment abolishing slavery impossible and have led to serious complications.

Lincoln's statement to Stanly harmonizes with what we know concerning his dislike of general emancipation. It likewise harmonizes with his words and actions both before and after he issued the proclamation. The statement he made at the cabinet meeting does not. In corroboration of the version he gave to Stanly there can be cited his statement in his letter to Cuthbert Bullitt, July 28, 1862, in which he also expressed fear of congressional displeasure unless a change of policy is adopted by the administration. He wrote:

---

[2] Allen T. Rice, *Reminiscences of Abraham Lincoln*, pp. 532–33.
[3] See Lincoln's letter to James C. Conkling, Aug. 26, 1863.

> It is a military necessity to have men and money; and we cannot get either in sufficient numbers or amounts if we keep from or drive from our lines slaves coming to them.

Welling, who as editor of the *National Intelligencer,* an old and influential publication, had considerable inside information, and whose relations with members of Lincoln's cabinet were, as Allen Thorndike Rice assures us, "intimate and often confidential," was of the opinion that what Lincoln told Stanly accurately reflected his state of mind. He has written:

> The proximate and procuring cause of the proclamation, as I conceive, is not far to seek. It was issued primarily and chiefly as a political necessity, and took on the character of a military necessity only because the President had been brought to believe that if he did not keep the Radical portion of his party at his back he could not long be sure of keeping an army at the front.[4]

Congressman George W. Julian, who, although one of those whom Lincoln's young secretary Hay called "Jacobins," was on the best of terms with the President, was of the same opinion. He wrote:

> Mr. Lincoln feared that enlistments would cease, and that Congress would even refuse the necessary supplies to carry on the war, if he declined any longer to place it on a clearly defined antislavery basis.[5]

Lincoln's friend and partner William H. Herndon must have received information of a similar nature, for he wrote: "When he freed the slaves there was not heart in it."[6]

That unless McClellan won a decisive victory he would have to do something to placate the Radicals or there would be the devil to pay as soon as Congress met must have become obvious to Lincoln on September 17, 1862, the day the battle took place. While the guns were booming at Antietam, Stevens was speaking at Lancaster and what he said must have sounded ominous to the President. The Commoner made it plain that as soon as Congress reassembled he meant to strike where Lincoln was most anxious for Congress not to interfere—at slavery in the border states. Here is what he said:

> I have protested against the present policy, not only to the people, but to the face of the President and his Cabinet, and on the floor of Congress; . . . told them that they were exercising too much lenity at the request of border statesmen—not one of whom, in my judgment, has loyalty in his heart. I have accused the prime minister [Seward] to his face of having gone back from the faith he taught us, and instead of arming every man, black or white, who could fight for the Union, withholding a well-meaning President from doing so. . . . I have told these things to the President and Cabinet, and they replied—It may come to this. *"Come to this!"* when 200,000 men have melted away, and $2,000,000,000 spent! *"Come to this!"* when another half million lives have been lost, and a bil-

---

4 Rice, *Reminiscences of Abraham Lincoln,* pp. 530–34.
5 Ibid., p. 62.
6 *Life of Lincoln* (edition annotated by Paul Angle), p. 483.

lion dollars more laid upon you in taxation. *I cannot and will not stand this.*

He then told his constituents that if they returned him to Congress he would introduce a bill providing *"that every man be armed, black and white, who can aid in crushing the rebellion; that every inch of rebel soil be taken and sold to pay the debt of this war."*[7]

What did this mean?

It meant that Stevens intended to introduce a bill requiring the administration to draft into the armed forces not only white men but black men, *including all able-bodied slaves in the border states.* On June 16 of that year he had managed to have a bill adopted authorizing the President to employ persons of African descent in the armed forces and providing that

> when any man or boy of African descent shall render any such service . . . he, his mother, and his wife and children, shall for ever thereafter be free, any law, usage, or custom whatsoever to the contrary notwithstanding.

The bill had excluded slaves belonging to border state slaveholders, now the exclusion was to end. To draft able-bodied slaves in the border states, or even to permit them to enlist, meant the end of slavery in those states. Now Lincoln had pinned his hopes on the border states helping him to solve the slavery problem in the only way he considered practical—by the adoption of compensated gradual emancipation with federal aid. More than that! He believed that if they did so the war would be practically ended. If Stevens succeeded in getting his bill adopted all hope of reaching that solution would have disappeared. For if the President threatened to veto the bill, the powerful chairman of the Ways and Means Committee might answer with the threat of holding up appropriations for the Army. Now that McClellan's victory had proved indecisive there appeared to be only one way to head off Stevens—to issue a preliminary Emancipation Proclamation.

None of the calamities the President had predicted might happen if he issued an Emancipation Proclamation put in an appearance. Kentucky did *not* "go out to the South." Twenty thousand soldiers from that state did *not* "throw down their muskets." Half the officers did *not* "fling down their arms." Fifty thousand soldiers from the border states did *not* "go over to the rebels." The President's predictions—some of which were sufficiently publicized—added to assurances given by border state slaveholders led the Confederates to believe, however, that if they took advantage of the opportunity some of these things might come to pass. They promptly invaded Kentucky. But on October 12, 1862, the Confederate commander Braxton Bragg ruefully reported to Richmond:

> The campaign here was predicated on the belief and the most positive assurances that the people of Kentucky would rise in mass and assert their independence. No people ever had so favorable an opportunity, but I am distressed to add there was little or no disposition to avail of it.[8]

---

[7] *Liberator*, September 19, 1862. Italics in original.

[8] *Off.c. Rec.*, 1 ser., vol. 16, pt. 1, p. 1088.

In the fall elections, when Lincoln's own state went over to the opposition, Kentucky and other loyal border states sent an almost solid delegation of Unionists to Congress.

Stevens had always claimed that the President's anxiety concerning Kentucky and other loyal border states was exaggerated. As early as December 16, 1861, he said on the floor of Congress:

> I do not understand where the President gets the facts in this respect. I believe he has been misled. I believe he is laboring under a hallucination of mind upon the subject as fatal as that of Samson under the manipulation of Delilah.

The fact that in the Kentucky state elections of August, 1861, three-fourths of those elected to the legislature were Unionists makes his skepticism understandable. Lincoln appears to have used the border state argument to delay issuing the proclamation in the hope that the slaveholders of those states would have the wisdom and the patriotism to adopt the solution he so greatly favored.

On December 1, 1862, he again presented to Congress—and in doing so to the slave states, rebel as well as loyal—his compensated gradual emancipation plan. It evoked no response from the slave states and was coldly received by Congress. On January 1 of the new year, he issued the final proclamation. After the document had made its appearance, Adam Gurowski wrote in his *Diary:*

> The patriots of both Houses, as the exponents of the noble and loftiest aspirations of the American people, whipped in—and this literally, not figuratively—whipped Mr. Lincoln into the glory of having issued the Emancipation Proclamation. The laws promulgated by this dying Congress initiated the Emancipation—generated the Proclamation of the 22d of September, and of January 1st. History will not allow one to wear borrowed plumage.[9]

Robert Mallory of Kentucky, in a speech in the House on February 24, 1863, charged that the President had yielded to pressure from Stevens. The Commoner did not reply, and no supporter of the President ventured to contradict the charge. Mallory said in part:

> Soon after the War broke out, the gentleman from Pennsylvania and his great allies Horace Greeley and Wendell Phillips, and all his little allies in the House, began their pressure on the President and the Republican Party. In vain the President from time to time besought his friends, and those who had not been his friends, to relieve him from this pressure.
>
> The gentleman from Pennsylvania and his allies persevered. They demanded of the President his proclamation of emancipation. He refused. Again they demanded it; he refused again, but more faintly and exhibited himself in his letter to his "dear friend Greeley" in the most pitiable and humiliating attitude in which an American President was ever exhibited to the American people—But the gentleman from Pennsylvania still pressed him and educated him and the Republicans.
>
> The Committee of Divines from Chicago, armed with authority from

---

9 *Diary*, vol. 2, pp. 99–100.

the other but not the better world, was brought to aid in the pressure; but apparently in vain. Sir, do you remember the reply of the President to that committee? It was conclusive, unanswerable. The reasons given for refusing to proclaim the freedom of slaves in the rebel states are perfectly irrefutable. "I have not the power to do it," said the President, "and if I had, the proclamation would be impotent; it would be like the Pope uttering his Bull against the comet."

We then supposed the matter had been settled. But scarcely had this confidence entered the great conservative heart of the nation, when feeble or false, or both, or yielding to the teachings of the gentleman from Pennsylvania, he suddenly without notice, issued his celebrated Emancipation Proclamation.

The Kentucky representative was seriously mistaken in believing that in issuing the final proclamation Lincoln had given up the struggle and had adopted Stevens's program. As has already been remarked the President had a way of yielding so the advantage remained with him.

A Great Capacity for Moral Growth?*

Richard N. Current

Lincoln is a paradoxical hero. His name has been lighted down from generation to generation as a synonym for liberty and equality. His name also has been made to symbolize the opposite doctrine of white supremacy and black oppression.

Lincoln the friend of freedom is well and widely known. For most liberals, he occupies a place beside that of Thomas Jefferson. For many Negroes, he long has held a lone position as a kind of folk god. . . .

Less well known than Lincoln the slaves' chainbreaker is Lincoln the hero of Negro-baiters and white supremacists. Yet he has been that kind of image also. Few Negroes or friends of the Negro ever admired him more or praised him oftener than did a certain Mississippi advocate of white supremacy, James K. Vardaman.

In the early 1900s this long-haired, dramatic Great White Chief of Mississippi stood out as the most rabid racialist in the most racist-dominated Southern state. When Theodore Roosevelt dined with the Negro educator Booker T. Washington in the White House, Vardaman sneered

* From *The Lincoln Nobody Knows* by Richard Current. Copyright 1958 McGraw-Hill Book Company. Used by permission.

at the President as a "wild broncho buster and coon-flavored miscegenationist." . . . During World War I, he took every opportunity to expound his belief in a white man's country. Do not draft Negroes into the Army, he advised his fellow senators, for it is dangerous to give them a sense of citizenship and a training in the use of guns. Repeal the Fifteenth Amendment so that Negroes cannot even pretend to have the right to vote. Enforce segregation and do not let the races mix, for the Negro is by nature morally inferior and must never be allowed to corrupt the pure blood of the heaven-favored white. . . .

This Mississippian once made a pilgrimage to his hero's home town, to Springfield, Illinois. The year was 1909, the centennial of Lincoln's birth. The previous year had been a disgraceful one for Springfield. Municipal leaders were looking ahead to anniversary celebrations when, on a summer night, thousands of the townspeople suddenly went wild with hate. . . . It took 4,000 state troopers all of a week to quiet the city and end the so-called race riot. . . . When Vardaman visited Springfield the feeling among local Negrophobes still ran high, and a huge crowd came out to applaud his lecture on the inherent virtue of the white race.

Vardaman never tired of praising "the immortal Lincoln," never tired of quoting "the wise words of this wondrous man." He insisted that he and Lincoln saw eye to eye. "I have made a very careful study of Mr. Lincoln's ideas on this question," he declared in a Senate speech, "and I have said often, and I repeat here, that my views and his on the race question are substantially identical." Next to Thomas Jefferson, he thought, Lincoln understood the Negro problem better than anyone else of former days. To prove his point, Vardaman cited Lincoln's advocacy of Negro colonization. He explained the Lincoln policy thus:

> Up to the very time of Mr. Lincoln's death he told the Negroes who came to see him here in Washington, "You will not be permitted to share in the government of this country, and I am not prepared to say that you ought to be, if I had the power to give you that right."
> "The shackles of slavery will be stricken from your arms. You, the educated and more fortunate members of your race, take the others and go to some country"—his idea was the same that Jefferson's was—"and there work out your own salvation." I do not pretend to quote Mr. Lincoln literally. The great desire of his patriotic heart was that the friction might be avoided by deportation.

The words of Lincoln that Vardaman repeated oftenest, the words he knew almost by heart, came from the debate with Douglas at Charleston, Illinois, on September 18, 1858. These words formed for Vardaman a sort of golden text. Here they are, exactly as Lincoln uttered them:

> I will say then that I am not, nor ever have been in favor of bringing about in any way the social and political equality of the white and black races, [applause]—that I am not nor ever have been in favor of making voters or jurors of Negroes, nor of qualifying them to hold office, nor to intermarry with white people; and I will say in addition to this that there is a physical difference between the white and black races which I believe will forever forbid the two races living together on terms of social and political equality. And inasmuch as they cannot so live, while they

do remain together there must be the position of superior and inferior, and I as much as any other man am in favor of having the superior position assigned to the white race.

Yet, despite these contradictions, Lincoln does deserve his reputation as emancipator. True, his claim to the honor is supported very uncertainly, if at all, by the proclamation itself. The honor has a better basis in the support he gave to the Thirteenth Amendment. It is well founded also in his greatness as the war leader, who carried the nation safely through the four-year struggle that brought freedom in its train. But the best reason for his reputation is, perhaps, to be discovered in something else. Consider the example he set his fellow Americans by treating all men as human beings, regardless of the pigment of their skin.

The real and final emancipation of the Negro may depend more upon attitudes than upon laws. The laws, the constitutional amendments, are important, even indispensable. But, as the abolitionist Henry Wilson observed, many of those who voted for the Thirteenth Amendment and other antislavery measures did so without conversion or conviction. Many acted from a desire to hurt the slaveholder rather than to help the slave. Within their hearts still lurked the "foul spirit of caste," the spirit of race prejudice. Until this prejudice was overcome, the Negroes, though no longer the slaves of individual masters, would continue to be in a sense the slaves of the community as a whole.

Now, Lincoln himself was one of those who veered to an actively antislavery line for reasons of wartime expediency. He did not pretend to do otherwise. And he was well aware of race prejudices as an existing fact in the United States. Hence his pathetic eagerness to find new homes for freedmen in foreign lands. Yet he had the capacity to rise above prejudice, and he grandly rose above it. Again and again, during the last two years of his life, he made the White House a scene of practical demonstrations of respect for human worth and dignity. He proved that whites and Negroes, without the master-servant tie, could get along together happily in his own official home, no matter what the antagonisms that might trouble the nation at large. A kindly, unself-conscious host, he greeted Negro visitors as no President had done before.

The distinguished former slave Frederick Douglass called upon Lincoln several times at his summer cottage at the Soldiers' Home. Douglass made at least three visits to the White House. On the final occasion, when he tried to enter as an invited guest at the inaugural reception in 1865, policemen manhandled him and forced him out. Making his way in again, he managed to catch Lincoln's eye. "Here comes my friend Douglass," the President exclaimed, and, leaving the circle of guests he had been conversing with, he took Douglass by the hand and began to chat with him. Years later Douglass wrote:

> In all my interviews with Mr. Lincoln I was impressed with his entire freedom from popular prejudice against the colored race. He was the first great man that I talked with in the United States freely, who in no single instance reminded me of the difference between himself and myself, of the difference of color, and I thought that all the more remarkable because he came from a state where there were black laws.

There were black laws in Illinois indeed—laws that denied the Negro the vote and deprived him of other rights. Illinois in those days was a Jim Crow state. That was where Lincoln had spent most of the years of his manhood, among people who had migrated from slave country farther south, as he himself had done. Naturally he had shared some of the Negrophobic feeling of his neighbors in Kentucky, in southern Indiana, in central Illinois. That was where, in geography and in sentiment, he came from.

But he did not stay there. The most remarkable thing about him was his tremendous power of growth. He grew in sympathy, in the breadth of his humaneness, as he grew in other aspects of the mind and spirit. In more ways than one he succeeded in breaking through the narrow bounds of his early environment.

This helps to explain and to reconcile those conflicting images of Lincoln—on the one hand, the racist; on the other, the champion of the common man, black as well as white. The one view reflects the position he started from, the other the position he was moving toward. There is confusion regarding particular phases of his presidential career because nobody knows for sure just what point he had reached at any given moment. But there should be little question as to which way he was going.

To see Lincoln in this light is to make him more than ever relevant, more than ever inspiring, for us in the stormy present, in the fiery trial through which we too must pass. Lincoln, as a symbol of man's ability to outgrow his prejudices, still serves the cause of human freedom. He will go on serving so long as boundaries of color hem in and hinder any man, any woman, any child.

BIBLIOGRAPHICAL NOTE

All the biographers, of course, treat with comparative fullness the subject of Lincoln and slavery. A basic work, by a wartime Illinois congressman who knew the President, and who stressed the antislavery theme in his career, is Isaac N. Arnold's *The History of Abraham Lincoln and the Overthrow of American Slavery* (1866). A later work by Arnold, again emphasizing this theme, is *The Life of Abraham Lincoln* (1885). Another useful work by a contemporary antislavery politician is Henry Wilson's *History of the Rise and Fall of the Slave Power in America* (3 vols., 1872–77). Probably the best exposition of Lincoln's own, preferred emancipation plan is to be found in the second volume of Randall's *Lincoln the President.*

A recent and forthright statement of the view that Lincoln used his famous proclamation as a dodge to delay actual freedom is presented by Ralph Korngold in *Thaddeus Stevens* (1955). See especially Chapter VII, "The Truth about the Emancipation Proclamation." Some contemporary impressions of Lincoln's slow and incomplete conversion to the antislavery cause are recorded in *Reminiscences of Abraham Lincoln,* edited by Allen T. Rice (1885). On Lincoln's relationships with Negroes, see Frederick Douglass's recollections in the Rice volume; Benjamin Quarles's *The Negro in the Civil War* (1953); and Warren A. Beck's "Lincoln and Negro Colonization in Central America," in the *Abraham Lincoln Quarterly* (1950).

James K. Vardaman's views on Lincoln and the Negro are repeated and elaborated in a number of his Senate speeches, two of which have been noted in particular, those of February 6, 1914, and August 16, 1917, in the *Con-*

gressional Record. There is a sketch of Vardaman in the *Dictionary of American Biography,* and there are several contemporary magazine articles concerning him, but no full-length study of the man has yet been published.

Lincoln on Slavery, Race, and Emancipation

FOR WHITE SUPREMACY*

He [Lincoln] said the question is often asked, why this fuss about niggers? It is dictated that their position is a small matter, but let us inquire whether it is or not. . . . [After this reporter's notes given in the third person, Lincoln is directly quoted for the main part of the speech.]

. . . I will say then that I am not, nor ever have been in favor of bringing about in any way the social and political equality of the white and black races, [applause]—that I am not nor ever have been in favor of making voters or jurors of negroes, nor of qualifying them to hold office, nor to intermarry with white people; and I will say in addition to this that there is a physical difference between the white and black races which I believe will for ever forbid the two races living together on terms of social and political equality. And inasmuch as they cannot so live, while they do remain together there must be the position of superior and inferior, and I as much as any other man am in favor of having the superior position assigned to the white race. . . .

REJECTS ANTISLAVERY AND RACIAL EQUALITY†

. . . What a very mad-man your correspondent, Smedes is. Mr. Lincoln is not pledged to the ultimate extinctinction [*sic*] of slavery; does not hold the black man to be the equal of the white, unqualifiedly as Mr. S. states it; and never did stigmatize their white people as immoral & unchristian; and Mr. S. can not prove one of his assertions true. . . .

PROMISES PROTECTION OF SLAVERY‡

. . . Apprehension seems to exist among the people of the Southern States, that by the accession of a Republican Administration, their prop-

---

* *Carlinville Democrat,* September 2, 1858 (Speech, August 31, 1858: Carlinville, Illinois).

† Letter to Henry J. Raymond, December 18, 1860. Manuscript of the Abraham Lincoln Association.

‡ First Inaugural Address, March 4, 1861. James D. Richardson, ed., *Messages and Papers of the Presidents* (10 vols., 1909), 7, 3206–13.

erty, and their peace, and personal security, are to be endangered. There has never been any reasonable cause for such apprehension. Indeed, the most ample evidence to the contrary has all the while existed, and been open to their inspection. It is found in nearly all the published speeches of him who now addresses you. I do but quote from one of those speeches when I declare that "I have no purpose, directly or indirectly, to interfere with the institution of slavery in the States where it exists. I believe I have no lawful right to do so, and I have no inclination to do so." Those who nominated and elected me did so with full knowledge that I had made this, and many similar declarations, and had never recanted them. And more than this, they placed in the platform, for my acceptance, and as a law to themselves, and to me, the clear and emphatic resolution which I now read:

> Resolved, That the maintenance inviolate of the rights of the States, and especially the right of each State to order and control its own domestic institutions according to its own judgment exclusively, is essential to that balance of power on which the perfection and endurance of our political fabric depend; and we denounce the lawless invasion by armed force of the soil of any State or Territory, no matter under what pretext, as among the gravest of crimes.

I now reiterate these sentiments: and in doing so, I only press upon the public attention the most conclusive evidence of which the case is susceptible, that the property, peace and security of no section are to be in anywise endangered by the now incoming Administration. I add too, that all the protection which, consistently with the Constitution and the laws, can be given, will be cheerfully given to all the States when lawfully demanded, for whatever cause—as cheerfully to one section as to another. . . .

FOR COLONIZATION*

. . . Why should they [Negroes] leave this country? This is, perhaps, the first question for proper consideration. You and we are different races. We have between us a broader difference than exists between almost any other two races. Whether it is right or wrong I need not discuss, but this physical difference is a great disadvantage to us both, as I think your race suffer very greatly, many of them by living among us, while ours suffer from your presence. In a word we suffer on each side. If this is admitted, it affords a reason at least why we should be separated. You here are freemen I suppose.

A VOICE: Yes, sir.

The President—Perhaps you have long been free, or all your lives. Your race are suffering, in my judgment, the greatest wrong inflicted on any people. But even when you cease to be slaves, you are yet far removed from being placed on an equality with the white race. You are

---

* Advice to a black delegation to return to Africa, *New York Tribune*, August 15, 1862.

cut off from many of the advantages which the other race enjoy. The aspiration of men is to enjoy the equality with the best when free, but on this broad continent, not a single man of your race is made the equal of a single man of ours. Go where you are treated the best, and the ban is still upon you.

I do not propose to discuss this, but to present it as a fact with which we have to deal. I cannot alter it if I would. It is a fact, about which we all think and feel alike, I and you. We look to our condition, owing to the existence of the two races on this continent. I need not recount to you the effects upon white men, growing out of the institution of Slavery. I believe in its general evil effects on the white race. See our present condition —the country engaged in war—our white men cutting one another's throats, none knowing how far it will extend; and then consider what we know to be the truth. But for your race among us there could not be war, although many men engaged on either side do not care for you one way or the other. Nevertheless, I repeat, without the institution of Slavery and the colored race as a basis, the war could not have an existence.

It is better for us both, therefore, to be separated. . . .

REJECTS ABOLITION AS THE PRIMARY WAR AIM*

. . . I would save the Union. I would save it the shortest way under the Constitution. The sooner the national authority can be restored; the nearer the Union will be "the Union as it was." If there be those who would not save the Union, unless they could at the same time *save* slavery, I do not agree with them. If there be those who would not save the Union unless they could at the same time *destroy* slavery, I do not agree with them. My paramount object in this struggle *is* to save the Union, and is *not* either to save or destroy slavery. If I could save the Union without freeing any slave I would do it, and if I could save it by freeing *all* the slaves I would do it; and if I could save it by freeing some and leaving others alone I would also do that. What I do about slavery, and the colored race, I do because I believe it helps save the Union; and what I forbear, I forbear because I do *not* believe it would help to save the Union. I shall do *less* whenever I shall believe what I am doing hurts the cause, and I shall do *more* whenever I shall believe doing more will help the cause. I shall try to correct errors when shown to be errors; and I shall adopt new views so fast as they shall appear to be true views.

I have here stated my purpose according to my view of *official* duty; and I intend no modification of my oft-expressed *personal* wish that all men every where could be free. . . .

LINCOLN'S CONSERVATIVE RECONSTRUCTION PLANS†

I congratulate you on having fixed your name in history as the first-free-state Governor of Louisiana. Now you are about to have a Conven-

---

* Public letter to Horace Greeley, *New York Tribune*, August 22, 1862.

† Letter to Michael Hahn, March 13, 1864. Manuscript of Roger Barrett, Chicago, Ill.

tion which, among other things, will probably define the elective franchise. I barely suggest for your private consideration, whether some of the colored people may not be let in—as, for instance, the very intelligent, and especially those who have fought gallantly in our ranks. They would probably help, in some trying time to come, to keep the jewel of liberty within the family of freedom. But this is only a suggestion, not to the public, but to you alone.

AN ABOLITIONIST IN THE END[*]

. . . One eighth of the whole population were colored slaves, not distributed generally over the Union, but localized in the Southern part of it. These slaves constituted a peculiar and powerful interest. All knew that this interest was, somehow, the cause of the war. To strengthen, perpetuate, and extend this interest was the object for which the insurgents would rend the Union, even by war; while the government claimed no right to do more than to restrict the territorial enlargement of it. Neither party expected for the war, the magnitude, or the duration, which it has already attained. Neither anticipated that the *cause* of the conflict might cease with, or even before, the conflict itself should cease. Each looked for an easier triumph, and a result less fundamental and astounding. Both read the same Bible, and pray to the same God; and each invokes His aid against the other. It may seem strange that any men should dare to ask a just God's assistance in wringing their bread from the sweat of other men's faces; but let us judge not that we be not judged. The prayers of both could not be answered; that of neither has been answered fully. The Almighty has His own purposes. "Woe unto the world because of offences! for it must needs be that offences come; but woe to that man by whom the offence cometh!" If we shall suppose that American Slavery is one of those offences which, in the providence of God, must needs come, but which, having continued through His appointed time, He now wills to remove, and that He gives to both North and South, this terrible war, as the woe due to those by whom the offence came, shall we discern therein any departure from those divine attributes which the believers in a Living God always ascribe to Him? Fondly do we hope—fervently do we pray—that this mighty scourge of war may speedily pass away. Yet, if God wills that it continue, until all the wealth piled by the bond-man's two hundred and fifty years of unrequited toil shall be sunk, and until every drop of blood drawn with the lash, shall be paid by another drawn with the sword, as was said three thousand years ago, so still it must be said "the judgments of the Lord are true and righteous altogether." . . .

---

[*] Second Inaugural Address, March 5, 1865. Richardson, *Messages and Papers*, 7, 3477–78.

chapter 10

Feminism in the Age of Civil War and Reconstruction

DURING THE CENTURY AND A HALF OF FEMINIST STRUGGLE for sexual equality and full citizenship women have received little recognition from scholars. The historical neglect of nearly all aspects of women's history constituted a major aspect of feminine subordination which sprang largely from the fact that an overwhelmingly male profession reflected dominant social attitudes in supposing that women had no meaningful past. The notion of women as history-lacking creatures formed an important part of the identity cage in which women had to live and the general body of scholarly writing assisted society in keeping women "in their place." Even in some of the more thoughtful monographs and textbooks women entered the scene largely as wives of famous men, the dominant point of view served masculine interests, and chapter after chapter neglected or completely ignored topics and trends of particular importance to women. The intellectual problem extends beyond the human need of women to have historical identity because a truly adequate history of Civil War and Reconstruction cannot be written with token attention to half the nation. To delete the lives and activities of the Lucretia Motts and the Harriet Tubmans is to fail to understand abolition, to ignore antebellum feminism is to give a false portrait of the era, and to grant consideration to rather obscure male reformers while neglecting the Grimké sisters is to distort reality itself.

In recent years the attitudes of historians have begun to change, partly because of the efforts of scholars of the feminine past such as Gerda Lerner, Aileen Kraditor, William L. O'Neill, Anne F. Scott and others. Gerda Lerner's remarkable documentary history of black women disclosed the lives of slave women as double victims of a harshly exploitative social system. Major aspects of this oppression had been discussed in Frances Kemble's journal of a Georgia plantation, in sociologist E. Franklin Frazier's pioneer study of the black family, and in John W. Blassingame's recent book on the slave family. (Blassingame also stressed the strengths and accomplishments of black women in bond-age.) If the women of the slaveowning class were in several respects highly privileged, their position lost some of its substance in a system which dictated male dominance and tended to reduce wealthy wives to the condition of pampered pets rather than truly free persons. Moreover, as Anne F. Scott's book on the Southern lady and William R. Taylor's chapter on the same theme indicate, women displayed signs of dissatis-faction in a contradiction-ridden sexual and social order. The masses of "poor white" women with some caste gains and great class losses, strangely in the middle between the extremes of the crude exploitation of slaves and the manipulated pampering of ladies, have gotten almost no attention from historians.

In the new wave of interest in women's history Southern women have attracted the efforts of fewer scholars than the Northeastern women of the antislavery movement who gave birth to American feminism and seem so akin to the political activists of modern times. Once again a po-litical movement motivated and provided insights for scholarship. Just as the struggles of industrial workers in the 1930s forcefully reminded some scholars that labor had a history and just as the black movement of the 1960s forced the acknowledgment of the black past, so the wom-an's liberation movement demanded with some success the consideration of women in history. The fact that many leaders of the modern move-ment had come to political commitment through the black struggle of the early and mid 60s had a striking parallel in the emergence from the abolition struggle of antebellum feminism.

Gerda Lerner's biography of the Grimké sisters, her popular history of American women (Selection 2), and Alma Lutz's study of antislav-ery women provide interesting chronicles of women in these early strug-gles for black and feminine causes. William L. O'Neill (Selection 1) in his general history of American feminism also gave a brief ac-count of the abolitionist background to the emergence of feminism but he was more concerned with providing a complete explanation of all fac-tors. Although O'Neill gave due credit to antislavery, to the ideology of the American and French revolutions and to the industrial revolution which moved home handicraft production to the factories, he also in-sisted on the importance of "the transformation of the family from a loosely organized . . . adjunct of Western society into a strictly defined nuclear unit at the very center of social life . . . the conjugal family with its great demands of women."

All students of feminism agreed on the importance of specific histori-cal events which created the felt need to speak, petition, and agitate against slavery and thus led both to a new consciousness of feminine repression and to the desire of some to work for the rights of women as well as of blacks. As Mary Elizabeth Massey's study on women in the Civil War indicates, Southern women to some degree and Northern women to a much greater extent moved in substantial numbers away from several aspects of the old repression and seclusion from public af-fairs through involvement with organizations such as the U.S. Sanitary Commission and the Loyalty Leagues. Willie Lee Rose's study of Union forces in the Sea Islands provided only one instance in which large numbers of women assisted former slaves as teachers, missionaries, and welfare administrators. All of these activities in Civil War and Reconstruction both helped to make possible the rise of women's organizations and to create the great dilemma of postwar feminism.

Dominant leaders faced the dilemma of whether to insist on coupling demands for women's suffrage with the cause of the black vote or to acknowledge that "this is the Negro's hour" by refusing to burden a possible cause with an impossible one. Elizabeth Cady Stanton, Susan B. Anthony, and others whose commitment to antislavery had for many years been distinctly secondary to their feminism refused to subordinate women's rights and ended in the leadership of the new National Woman Suffrage Association (N.W.S.A.). Women with a more powerful abolitionist-Radical commitment joined by their sisters with a more conservative approach to women's rights than that of Stanton and Anthony formed a rival American W.S.A. and the breach was not healed until nearly the end of the century. A general narrative account of the suffrage movement as well as the earlier abolition struggles can be found in *A Century of Struggle* by Eleanor Flexner who tended to minimize the divisive power of race, class, ethnic origins, and nationality which make radical feminist movements so difficult. In Aileen Kraditor's more candid and analytical study of the ideas of the woman's suffrage movement at the turn of the century it is only too clear that middle and upperclass women reformers generally clung to class privilege, that Southern women nearly always made white supremacy issues paramount over feminist goals and that Northern women deferred to racism and frequently allowed nativism to destroy possibilities for recruiting immigrant women. However, if the movement at the turn of the century seemed unsuccessful, burdened with faulty leadership and enmeshed with conservative causes, brighter times were yet to come in the great mass movement of the Wilson years and the women's liberation movement of the 1960s.

BIBLIOGRAPHY

Works Discussed in This Chapter

Blassingame, John W., *The Slave Community* (1972).
Flexner, Eleanor, *A Century of Struggle* (1959).
Frazier, E. Franklin, *The Negro Family in the U. S.* (1939, 1966).
Kemble, Frances, *Journal of a Georgia Plantation* (1863, 1965).
Kraditor, Aileen S., *Ideas of the Woman's Suffrage Movement, 1890–1920* (1965).
Lerner, Gerda, *Black Women in White America: A Documentary History* (1972), *The Grimké Sisters of South Carolina: Rebels Against Slavery* (1967), and *The Woman in American History* (1971).
Lutz, Alma, *Crusade For Freedom: Women in the Anti-Slavery Movement* (1963).
Massey, Mary Elizabeth, *Bonnet Brigades* (1964).
O'Neill, William L., *Everyone Was Brave: A History of American Feminism* (1969).

Rose, Willie Lee, *Rehearsal for Reconstruction: The Port Royal Experiment* (1964).
Scott, Anne F., *The Southern Lady* (1972).
Taylor, William R. (section on Southern women), *Cavaliers and Yankees* (1961).

Suggested Reading

For the intellectual and historical *European background* to American feminism see Simone DeBeauvoir's imposing classic, *The Second Sex* (1949) and Susan G. Bell, ed. *Women from the Greeks to the French Revolution* (1973). The historical chapters in Kate Millet's *Sexual Politics* (1969) are most helpful and interesting. The selections are well chosen in Miriam Schneir, ed., *Feminism: The Essential Historical Writings* (1972). Mary R. Beard's *Women as a Force in History* (1946) was an important pioneer work. Among the important nineteenth century classics now in inexpensive paperback editions is John Stuart Mill and Harriet Taylor Mill, *Essays on Sex Equality* (1832, 1851, 1869. Mod. col., 1970).

Among *histories of American women* see William L. O'Neill's comparative study, *The Woman Movement: Feminism in the U.S. and England* (1969). Without some of the insights of recent years are Robert E. Riegel, *American Feminists* (1962); Page Smith, *Daughters of the Promised Land* (1966); and Andrew G. Sinclair, *The Emancipation of the American Woman* (1965); A gold mine of historical sources can be found in Susan B. Anthony, et al., *A History of Women's Suffrage* (6 vols. 1881-1922). Valuable information can be found in Robert Smuts, *Women and Work in America* (1959); Thomas Woody, *History of Women's Education in America* (2 vols., 1929); and Barbara Cross, *The Educated Woman in America* (1965).

Among the best of the recent *documentary histories* are Aileen S. Kraditor, ed., *Up From the Pedestal: Selected Writings in the History of American Feminism* (1968); Anne F. Scott, ed., *The American Woman: Who Was She?* (1971); and Wendy Martin, ed., *The American Sisterhood* (1972).

Among the more interesting *collections of historical essays* are Barbara Welter, ed., *The Woman Question in American History* (1973); Ronald W. Hogeland, ed., *Woman and Womanhood in American Life and Thought* (1973); and Jean E. Friedman and William G. Shade, eds., *Our American Sisters: Women in American Life and Thought* (1973).

For two important primary sources on *black women* see the William and Ellen Craft slave autobiography in Arna Bontemps, *Great Slave Narratives* (1969) and Ray L. Billington, ed., *A Free Negro in the Slave Era: The Journal of Charlotte Forten, 1854-1864* (1961). See also Earl Conrad, *Harriet Tubman* (1935) and Arthur H. Fauset, *Sojourner Truth* (1938).

On *Southern white women* see the modern publication of the antebellum journal, Mary B. Chesnut, *A Diary from Dixie* (1949). Much can be gleaned from W. J. Cash, *The Mind of the South* (1941) and Rollin G. Osterweis, *Romanticism and Nationalism in the Old South* (1949).

On *Western women* see Walter O'Meara, *Daughters of the County: The Women of the Fur Traders* (1968); William Sprague, *Women and the West* (1940) and Page Smith, cited above.

On *nineteenth century feminism*, see the most essential primary work Dwight L. Dumond, ed., *The Letters of Theodore Dwight Weld, Angelina Grimké and Sarah Grimké* (2 vols. 1966); the modern reprint of Margaret Fuller's *Women in the Nineteenth Century* (1971); Ross Evans Paulson, *Woman's Suffrage and Prohibition: A Comparative Study of Equality and Social Control* (1973); James P. Lewis, "The Roots of Feminism," *Civil War History* (1971); James M. McPherson, "Abolitionists, Women's Suffrage and the Negro, 1865–1869," *Mid-America* (1965). Older but informative works are Ida H. Harper, *The Life and Work of Susan B. Anthony* (3 vols. 1898–1908) and Harriet S. Blatch and Theodore Stanton, eds. *Writings of Elizabeth Cady Stanton* (1927). See also Elizabeth A. Dexter, *Career Women of America, 1776–1840* (1950).

A few *twentieth century works* worth mentioning are Christopher Lasch, *The New Radicalism in America, 1889–1963: The Intellectual as a Social Type* (1965); William H. Chaffee, *The American Woman: Her Changing Social, Economic and Political Roles, 1920–1970* (1972); June Sochen, ed., *The New Feminism in Twentieth Century America* (1971); David Morgan, *Suffragists and Democrats: The Politics of Woman Suffrage in America* (1972); and June Sochen, *The New Woman: Feminism in Greenwich Village, 1910–1920* (1972).

The Birth of American Feminism*
William L. O'Neill

. . . If we assume . . . that the conjugal family system with its great demands upon women was a fairly recent development and became general only in the nineteenth century, then the feminist response becomes explicable. In completing the transformation of the family from a loosely organized, if indispensable, adjunct of Western society into a strictly defined nuclear unit at the very center of social life, the Victorians laid a burden on women which many of them could or would not bear. The Victorians had attempted, moreover, to compensate women for their increased domestic and pedagogic responsibilities by enveloping them in a mystique which asserted their higher status while at the same time guaranteeing their actual inferiority. Hence the endless polemics on the moral purity and spiritual genius of woman which found their highest expression in the home, but which had to be safeguarded at all costs from the corrupting effects of the man-made world beyond the domestic circle. Unfortunately for the Victorians, this rationale was ultimately self-defeating, as William R. Taylor and Christopher Lasch have suggested.

> The cult of women and the Home contained contradictions that tended to undermine the very things they were supposed to safeguard. Implicit

---

* Reprinted by permission of Quadrangle/The New York Times Book Co. from *Everyone Was Brave* by William L. O'Neill. Copyright © 1969, 1971 by William L. O'Neill.

in the myth was a repudiation not only of heterosexuality but of domesticity itself. It was her purity, contrasted with the coarseness of men, that made woman the head of the Home (though not of the family) and the guardian of public morality. But the same purity made intercourse between men and women at last almost literally impossible and drove women to retreat almost exclusively into the society of their own sex, to abandon the very Home which it was their appointed mission to preserve.[1]

The libertarian rhetoric of the early feminists masked, therefore, separatist and sororital impulses which affected vast numbers. Discontented women first expressed themselves, as Taylor and Lasch point out, in literary pursuits and church work. By the end of the nineteenth century these small shoots had flowered into great national organizations like the National American Woman Suffrage Association (NAWSA), the Woman's Christian Temperance Union (WCTU), and the General Federation of Women's Clubs (GFWC), which took millions of women outside the home.

Feminism is, then, perhaps best understood as one reaction to the great pressures that accompanied the emergence of the nuclear family. It was not a rebellion born of ancient slavery but part of a collective response to the sexual awareness deliberately inspired by Victorian society in an attempt to foster what the twentieth century would consider an oppressive domesticity. The Victorians taught women to think of themselves as a special class. Having become conscious of their unique sexual identity, however—a consciousness heightened by the common experiences forced upon them by the cult of purity—they could no longer accept uncritically those role definitions drawn up for them by the alien male. Victorian society created The Woman, where before there had been only women. Yet the alternatives were even less agreeable. The worst thing about the situation of women in the nineteenth century was, as Ronald V. Sampson has pointed out, that because they were denied liberty they sought power, and, especially, power over their children.

> The Victorian family as depicted by [Samuel] Butler is essentially an unholy alliance between an overbearing but petty patriarch and a vain adulatory consort for the purpose of deceiving their offspring as to the real nature of their parents and of a society composed of them and their like.[2] . . .

. . . In [a] . . . very special sense . . . feminism was a radical movement. On the face of it, equal rights for women was not a demand likely to compromise the essential Victorian institutions. In fact, it threatened to do so because the Victorians had given the nuclear family a transcendent significance all out of proportion to its functional value. . . .

It is hard for us now to appreciate the strength and courage of the early feminists who set themselves against the network of ideas, prejudices, and almost religious emotionalism that simultaneously degraded

---

[1] William R. Taylor and Christopher Lasch, "Two 'Kindred Spirits': Sorority and Family in New England, 1839–1846," *New England Quarterly*, 36 (March 1963), 35.

[2] Ronald V. Sampson, *The Psychology of Power* (New York, 1966), p. 104.

and elevated women—"the cult of true womanhood," as one historian calls it, which made central virtues of piety, purity, submissiveness, and domesticity. Almost the only form of activity permitted women was religious work, because it did not take them away from their true "sphere." "From her home woman performed her great task of bringing men back to God."[3] Woman, it was believed, was morally and spiritually superior to man because of her highly developed intuition, refined sensibilities, and especially because of her life-giving maternal powers which defied man's comprehension. But woman was also physically weaker than man, inferior to him in cognitive ability, and wholly unsuited to the rough world outside the home. This was just as well, because women were largely responsible for The Family—the principal adornment of Christian civilization and the bedrock upon which society rested.[4]

While the Victorian conception of women as wan, ethereal, spiritualized creatures bore little relation to the real world where women operated machines, worked the fields, hand-washed clothing, and toiled over great kitchen stoves, it was endorsed by both science and religion. Physicians, clergymen, and journalists churned out a stream of polemical literature in support of this thesis. Even fashion conspired to the same end, for the bustles and hoops, the corsets and trailing skirts in which women were encased throughout much of the nineteenth century seemed designed to prevent all but the desperate from entering the vigorous world of men. . . . In the end, the fashion was self-defeating, for it aroused fears that women would become incapable of discharging their essential functions. The Civil War helped wake middle-class women from "their dream of a lady-like uselessness." . . .

The cult of delicacy was an extreme and transient expression of an enduring conviction that feminists had to deal with if they were to win equality. They could not admit that the differences between the sexes were so marked as to make women inherently and eternally inferior; neither could they escape the fact that women everywhere were subordinate to men. Moreover, the weight of opinion against them was so great that it was hard for even the most talented women to free themselves of the invidious assumptions that kept them in their place. . . .

Underneath the cheerful cant (which was to grow rather than diminish with time) about women's superior morality and intuitive genius, we can sense the first uncertain efforts of intelligent American women to find their true selves. The most alert feminists did not accept the prevailing sentiments as final, or worry about their inherent nature. They took the inferiority of women as an existential reality and concerned themselves with bringing women to an awareness of it. . . . In 1878 Joslyn Gage, corresponding secretary of the National Woman's Suffrage Association, told a committee of the New York Senate that the argument that women should not be given their freedom until they had become fit for

---

[3] Barbara Welter, "The Cult of True Womanhood: 1820–1860," *American Quarterly,* 18 (Summer 1966), 162.

[4] For a more elaborate survey of these ideas, see William L. O'Neill, *Divorce in the Progressive Era* (New Haven, 1967), Ch. 3.

it reminded her of Macauley's statement that "if men [or women] are to wait for liberty till they have become good and wise in slavery, they may indeed wait forever."[5]

The parallel with slavery which the early feminists drew again and again was, on the face of it, strained and unreal. Yet, even though *feeling* enslaved is clearly not the same as *being* enslaved, there were real similarities between the women's rights and anti-slavery movements. Not only were women, and usually the same women, active in both causes, but the causes themselves were in many respects alike. Both aimed at removing unconscionable handicaps imposed by law and custom on specific groups in American society. . . . While efforts to extend the rights and opportunities already enjoyed by white males to the rest of society were consistent with the essential premises of the American system, and therefore conservative, such attempts violated conventions and beliefs which, however much they compromised the spirit of the Constitution, were venerated equally with it. Thus, both abolitionists and feminists found themselves in the ironic but characteristically American position of those who put themselves outside the national consensus by a too literal rendering of its sacred texts.

If women were not slaves, to be at once patronized and discriminated against was bad enough. "While woman's intellect is confined, her morals crushed, her health ruined, her weaknesses encouraged, and her strength punished, she is told that her lot is cast in the paradise of women: and there is no country in the world where there is so much boasting of the 'chivalrous' treatment she enjoys." In brief, "indulgence is given her as a substitute for justice."[6] Since most Americans seemed ignorant of womankind's degraded state, the first tasks confronting feminists were relatively uncomplicated. They had, on the one hand, to agitate and propagandize against the prevailing system of ideas, and on the other to seize whatever private advantages they could for themselves. Religion formed the cornerstone of the case against feminine equality, and consequently the first major work by an American feminist, Sarah Grimké's *Letters on the Equality of the Sexes and the Condition of Women* (1838), was directed against those clergymen who believed God had ordained women's inferior state. . . .

Miss Grimké made no concessions whatever to masculine complacency. Man "has done all he could to debase and enslave her mind; and now he looks triumphantly on the ruin he has wrought and says, the being he has thus deeply injured is his inferior."[7] The burden of Miss Grimké's arguments was, however, scriptural. She insisted that false translations and perverse interpretations of the sacred writings had obscured God's true intent. It was perfectly clear to her that "whatsoever it is morally right for a man to do, it is morally right for a woman to do." . . .

---

5 Elizabeth Cady Stanton, Susan B. Anthony, and Matilda Joslyn Gage, eds., *History of Woman Suffrage, 1848–61* (New York, 1881), 3, 94, 860. . . .

6 Harriet Martineau, *Society in America* (1837) 1, 199.

7 Sarah M. Grimké, *Letters on the Equality of the Sexes and the Condition of Women* (Boston, 1838), p. 17.

While bold women were calling attention to the human record as a "history of repeated injuries and usurpations on the part of man toward woman, having in direct object the establishment of an absolute tyranny over her," and demanding for women "immediate admission to all the rights and privileges which belong to them as citizens of the United States," more were finding self-help and self-culture useful to their private emancipation.[8] Gradually their thirst for knowledge found expression in female seminaries and colleges (beginning with Emma Willard's Troy Female Seminary in 1821), in the admission of women to regular colleges and universities, and in the opening of professional training on a limited scale. Few women secured a good education before the Civil War, but by 1870 eleven thousand women were enrolled in some 582 institutions of higher learning, while many more had obtained enough formal schooling to become teachers themselves. Equally if not more important was the growth of women's clubs and societies which gave married women in particular outlets for their frustrated energies and sororital aspirations.[9]

By 1860 the emancipation of women was proceeding apace on two distinct levels. Privately, as students, teachers, and in a few cases professionals, and as members of small, often informal societies, middle-class women were enlarging their "sphere" and reaching out for wider opportunities beyond the domestic circle. Publicly, in their still-limited women's rights movement, in temperance work, and most strikingly of all as abolitionists, they were challenging Victorian stereotypes and laying the groundwork for that empire of women's organizations soon to be born. . . .

The case for women's rights, although far more offensive to Victorian sensibilities, was equally simple. It was based largely on the Declaration of Independence and the republican and egalitarian principles advanced since 1776. The force of an argument so framed could hardly be denied in America, and Victorians were forced to combat its lucid precepts with biblical citations of decreasing weight, and confused references to psychological, physiological, and anthropological principles of uncertain value. Democratic Americans did concede much of the feminist case in fact, however much they resisted it in principle, as the substantial number of legal reforms enacted from the 1830s on showed. The country held firm on woman suffrage, but otherwise reformers found it possible to improve property and marriage laws in state after state. The early feminists were thus encouraged to believe that equality could be won in their lifetimes.

The Civil War had a powerful effect on the fortunes of women. Having acquired some practical experience and some education outside the home, they were able for the first time to participate actively in a national enterprise. The Union's Sanitary Commission and other relief agencies,

---

[8] From the "Declaration of Sentiments" adopted by the first Woman's Rights Convention at Seneca Falls, New York, in 1848. *History of Woman Suffrage,* 1, 70–71.

[9] Mildred White Wells, *Unity in Diversity* (Washington, D.C., 1953), pp. 9–17. Some of these still exist, e.g., the Ladies Association for Educating Females of Jacksonville, Illinois, founded in 1833.

although controlled largely by men, gave vast numbers of women public work to do. Thousands served as nurses, and daring individuals such as Clara Barton, Mary Livermore, and Louisa May Alcott, not to mention the eccentric few who became spies, soldiers, and the like, distinguished themselves.[10] On the ideological front, Elizabeth Cady Stanton and Susan B. Anthony formed the National Woman's Loyal League to inspire patriotism, support the Thirteenth Amendment, and secure for women an honorable role in the war effort. Most importantly, perhaps, the war gave Union women a heroic myth which echoed down the generations. . . .

Portraits of Women as Abolitionists and Feminists*

Gerda Lerner

RESISTANCE TO OPPRESSION

Under slavery, few historical records were kept of individual slaves. Once in a while a spectacularly dramatic story would find its way into the columns of newspapers. One such story was that of Margaret Garner, a slave who had escaped to Cincinnati with her husband and four children, only to be recaptured. While her husband was led away, she killed her three-year-old girl, and was only prevented from killing the other children by being overpowered. When her captors transported her down the Ohio River back to slavery, she allowed her baby to fall overboard "by accident." The boat was later shipwrecked and Margaret Garner, eluding her captors and would-be rescuers, was finally able to find freedom in death.

Apart from individual desperate instances such as this of resistance to slavery, there were a few black women whose unbreakable spirit and lifelong dedication to the fight against oppression brought them enduring fame.

Harriet Tubman (c. 1820–1913). Born a slave in Maryland, Harriet Tubman is famous for being the most daring "conductor" on the Underground Railroad. After her master's death, she feared that she would be sold and decided to escape. Her husband, a freedman, refused to join

---

[10] The range of feminine activities is described in Mary Elizabeth Massey, *Bonnet Brigades: American Women and the Civil War* (New York, 1966).

* Gerda Lerner, *The Woman in American History* (Menlo Park, Calif.: Addison-Wesley Publishing Company, 1971). By permission of the publisher.

her, so she made her way to freedom without him. She returned repeatedly to her old plantation until she had rescued her entire family.

Due to an old head injury, incurred while aiding the escape of a slave, she was seriously handicapped by fainting spells that came upon her without warning. But with tremendous courage, tenacity, and practical wisdom she managed to overcome all obstacles in her effort to bring slaves north to freedom. She always carried a pistol with her. When a slave faltered under the hardships of the trip and proposed to return to slavery or begged to be left behind, she would draw her pistol on him and declare, "You go on or die." Nobody ever doubted that she would make good her threat. When carrying infants she would drug them into deep sleep and conceal them in a sack. The slaves called her "Moses" and credited her with supernatural powers. Over the years, the slaveholders offered a total of $40,000 in rewards for her capture. During a ten-year period Harriet Tubman made nineteen trips into slave territory and rescued over three hundred slaves. It was her pride that she never lost a single "passenger."

Harriet Tubman performed invaluable services as a scout and nurse during the Civil War and in old age organized and supported a home for aged freedmen.

Sojourner Truth (c. 1797–1893).   Another remarkable slave woman was Isabella Baumfree, known by her chosen name, "Sojourner Truth." Born a slave in the last years of the eighteenth century in Ulster County, New York, she saw all her twelve brothers and sisters sold off by her Dutch master. After his death, Belle was sold together with a herd of sheep to John Neely, who beat her for not understanding his English commands. Sold twice before the age of fourteen and raped by her master, Belle was then forcibly married to an older slave.

By 1817, when New York abolished slavery for adults, she had borne five children, of whom four were alive. She was freed with her youngest child, but learned that her boy, Peter, was still enslaved, although his owner had promised him his freedom. Determined to save him, Belle took the daring step of suing for his freedom in the state court, and won the case. She supported herself and her children as a domestic worker in New York City, joined a utopian religious colony and engaged in another spectacular law suit during which she sued a white man for slander and won complete vindication.

Her increasingly powerful, mystical visions convinced her that she must become an itinerant preacher. She adopted the name "Sojourner Truth" and began preaching for freedom all over the North. In 1851 the tall, thin woman appeared at a Woman's Rights Convention in Akron, Ohio, and asked to address the audience. The previous speaker, a clergyman, had ridiculed the weakness of women and argued that they could not be entrusted with equal rights. She answered him in these words:

> The man over there says women need to be helped in carriages and lifted over ditches, and to have the best place everywhere. Nobody ever helps me into carriages or over puddles, or gives me the best place—and ain't I a woman? Look at my arm! I have ploughed and planted and gathered into barns, and no man could head me—and ain't I a woman?

I could work as much and eat as much as a man—when I could get it —and bear the lash as well! And ain't I a woman? I have borne thirteen children, and seen most of 'em sold into slavery, and when I cried out with my mother's grief, none but Jesus heard me—and ain't I a woman?

Sojourner Truth's pithy arguments and dignified personality had tremendous impact on her audiences. She was fearless and had an overpowering self-confidence, which was based on her belief that God talked to her. This faith made her impervious to insults and attack. Once, after she had debated a bigoted lawyer, the man sneered contemptuously, "You think your talk does any good, old woman? Why, I don't care any more for it than for a fleabite." "Maybe not," Sojourner replied calmly. "But the Lord willing, I'll keep you scratching."

After the Civil War she was appointed by the Freedmen's Bureau to train black women for employment. Well over eighty, she made it her business to board the Jim Crow Washington streetcars, seat herself in the white compartment, and force the conductors to throw her off, protesting. Even though she could not single-handedly break this discriminatory law, she saw to it that every such incident became a lesson in cruelty and inhumanity which the white onlookers would not soon forget.

Sojourner Truth, whose life was an unceasing struggle against race prejudice, proved that extraordinary strength could overcome brutality, illiteracy, bitter poverty, and constant discrimination. The wizened old woman with her symbolic name and her shrewd folk wit was the voice of tens of thousands of anonymous suffering black women. . . .

ANTISLAVERY WOMEN

In 1833, when delegates met in Philadelphia to form the American Anti-Slavery Society, three women attended the convention as observers. A few days later twenty women met to form the Philadelphia Female Anti-Slavery Society. From that time on, northern women played an important part in the movement for the abolition of slavery and for the integration of the Negro into American society. In the next decade they set up a great number of female antislavery societies. By the 1840s there were roughly as many men as women organized into these groups.

The women very early began to use petitions as a means of influencing public opinion and gaining adherents. "The right of petition is the only political right that women have," Angelina Grimké pointed out. Many others agreed; tens of thousands of petitions against slavery flooded Congress and the state legislatures, serving to arouse public opinion and stir up debate on this highly controversial subject. Antislavery women also organized fairs and bazaars to raise funds and pioneered in setting up youth groups to educate a new generation of antislavery workers.

Lucretia Mott (1793–1880). The best in antislavery leadership was epitomized by Lucretia Mott. The mother of six children, she had the standing of a Quaker minister in her Philadelphia society and was experienced in public speaking. Her gentle, lady-like appearance concealed a razor-sharp mind and a stubborn determination. Mrs. Mott was known to stop mobs with the same firmness that she would use on an unruly child. She founded the Philadelphia Female Anti-Slavery Society and remained for over forty years its president and leading member. She was also instrumental in organizing the early Woman's Rights movement.

Lucretia Mott was a convincing speaker and frequently lectured to large audiences outside her Quaker circle, but her main impact was that of an organizer and pace-setter. One had only to look at the motherly, genteel Lucretia Mott and listen to her opinions and speeches to become convinced that it was possible for women to combine femininity with active participation in the political and social life of their time.

The antislavery women were as intrepid as their brothers and husbands when it came to meeting mobs or threats of violence. In fact, they developed what we know as nonviolent resistance to a fine art. A memorable occasion on which the technique was used was in Boston in 1835, when a furious mob of citizens surrounded a meeting of the Boston Female Anti-Slavery Society at which William Lloyd Garrison was featured as the speaker. Appeals to the mayor for protection proved fruitless. Instead, he informed the women that the presence of black women in their midst justifiably enraged the citizens and asked them to send their Negro members home. This the women refused to do and the chairman, Mrs. Chapman, replied, "If this is the last bulwark of freedom, we may as well die here as anywhere." The ladies continued their meeting for a time, but spirited Garrison away to another room. Then each white woman took a black sister by the hand, and they walked out through the mob in orderly procession, staring down their attackers with quiet dignity. Meanwhile, Garrison was dragged through the streets at the end of a rope and finally had to be lodged in the town jail for safekeeping. This Boston mob had the effect of winning important new adherents to the antislavery movement and made the courage of abolitionist women a legend.

The Grimké Sisters—Sarah M. Grimké (1792–1873) and Angelina E. Grimké Weld (1805–1879). The participation of women in political life was lifted to a new level during the winter and spring of 1837–1838, when the "woman question" was first raised as an issue confronting reformers. The crisis was precipitated by two most unlikely agents of social revolution, Sarah and Angelina Grimké, natives of South Carolina. The Grimké sisters were that greatest of rarities, southern abolitionists.

Daughters of the assistant chief justice of South Carolina, the Grimké sisters were raised in a typical plantation household. What they saw of slavery shocked them, and they attempted to convince others of the sinfulness of the system. Finally, realizing that they could not help to effect any changes while remaining in the South, the sisters chose exile in the North. They became Quakers and, much later, abolitionists. Angelina Grimké wrote a stirring antislavery appeal to southern women, which was publicly burned in Charleston. She was threatened with immediate imprisonment should she ever return. Before long both sisters had taken the decisive step of becoming "agents" and traveling lecturers of the American Anti-Slavery Society.

The sisters' spectacular lecture tour in New England attracted large audiences who came not only to hear what they had to say but to enjoy the unprecedented spectacle of women speaking in public. It was impossible to dismiss the pious, utterly respectable, and impeccably lady-like Grimké sisters as freaks and lunatics. In an effort to weaken their audience appeal, the Council of Congregationalist Churches issued a pastoral letter warning "against the dangers which at the present seem to threaten the female character with widespread and permanent injury." If a woman "assumed the place and tone of man as a public reformer," she would "fall in shame and dishonor into the dust."

While this blast did not have the desired effect on New England audiences, it did provoke a vigorous debate on the woman question in abolitionist circles. In this debate the Grimké sisters performed one of their most notable services by refusing in any way to disassociate their abolitionism from their insistence that as women they had a perfect right to speak in public. "Woman must feel that she is the equal and is designed to be the fellow laborer of her brother," Sarah Grimké declared. "I ask no favors for my sex. . . . All I ask our brethren is, that they will take their feet from off our necks, and permit us to stand upright on that ground which God designed us to occupy."

The sisters ended their speaking tour with Angelina Grimké presenting an antislavery petition, signed by twenty thousand women, to the Massachusetts legislature. It was the first time any woman had ever testified before a legislative committee.

It took two more years before the full impact of these pioneering events was felt in reform circles. By then, the Grimké sisters' example had influenced a number of women who would later lead the movement for woman's rights.

When the woman question exploded in reform circles, it raised an issue American society had complacently ignored for five decades. If all men were created equal, why not woman? If woman was equal, why should she not do anything men might do—speak in public, vote, hold office, even lead organizations? Once these questions had been raised, it was only a very short step to the next one: Why should not women organize to help themselves and gain the rights denied them? . . .

THE STRUGGLE FOR EQUALITY

In the Jacksonian era the United States was alive with a ferment of ideas. Demands were heard for all kinds of reforms, from free public schooling for every child to schemes for reforming the drunkard, freeing the slaves and abolishing war forever. Small wonder that women, too, began to question the position to which they had been relegated by tradition and habit.

In 1836, the first petition for a law granting married women the right to own property reached the New York state legislature. It carried the signatures of six women and had been written and circulated by Ernestine Rose, a recent immigrant. Ernestine Rose, a Rabbi's daughter from Poland, later became one of the most dynamic platform speakers of her day on behalf of woman's rights. She continued circulating petitions until the New York legislature finally, in 1849, enacted a law safeguarding married women's property. Soon Mississippi, Pennsylvania, California, and Wisconsin enacted similar measures. This was a small, but important step forward in giving women legal equality.

During the same period the right of divorce was first openly advocated. The passage of laws restricting child labor and making education compulsory in several states during the 1840s tended to weaken the absolute authority of the father over his children. From there it was an easy step to questioning the absolute authority of a man over his wife.

This questioning was evident even in areas of minor importance. When Angelina Grimké married abolitionist leader Theodore Weld, they devised a marriage ceremony that avoided the customary pledge of obedience by the wife to the husband. Instead, the couple pledged to love and cherish one another, and before their wedding signed an agreement whereby Weld renounced all claims to his wife's property. When Robert Dale Owen married Jane Robinson in 1832, he declared that he wished to be "utterly divested, now and during the rest of my life, of any such rights, the barbarous relics of a feudal, despotic system." When Lucy Stone and Henry Blackwell were married in 1855, they drew up a printed "protest" containing similar ideas. But Lucy Stone went further and, as a token of her independence, retained her maiden name after marriage.

The Right to Representation. To the thousands of educated volunteer workers in various reform organizations, the constant discrimination they suffered as women had become increasingly obnoxious. In 1840 the abolitionist movement split over the "woman question" when a woman was elected to the National Committee of the American Anti-Slavery Society. The actual causes of the division were much more profound than the question of a woman holding office, but the issue provided a handy excuse for precipitating a split. Henceforth there were two branches of the organized abolitionist movement, one permitting women to vote and hold office, the other exclusively male.

The woman's rights issue became international somewhat later that year when the Garrisonian abolitionists sent a number of women to the World Anti-Slavery Convention in London. After heated discussion, the credentials of the female delegates were refused and they were seated behind a curtain in the gallery. In protest, William Lloyd Garrison and several of his followers walked out and joined the ladies. Among those seated in the gallery were Lucretia Mott and the young wife of the abolitionist Henry Stanton, Elizabeth. The two women soon became friends and spent long hours discussing what might be done to break down the prejudice against women. The personality and intellect of the older woman left a profound impression on Elizabeth Cady Stanton. "When I first heard from the lips of Lucretia Mott that I had the same right to think for myself that Luther, Calvin, and John Knox had, and the same right to be guided by my own convictions . . . I felt at once a new-born sense of dignity and freedom." The two women decided that upon their return to the United States they would call together a convention of women to discuss their condition. But eight years passed before they could carry out their resolution.

Elizabeth Cady Stanton (1815–1902). A pretty, fun-loving girl, Eliza-

beth Cady grew up with four sisters in the well-to-do household of conservative Judge Cady, in upstate New York. The only boy in the family
had died as a youth, and nothing any of the girls did could ever make
up to Judge Cady for the fact that he had no son. Elizabeth grew up
keenly resentful of the inferiority attached to being a girl. As a child she
sat in her father's office and heard many female clients tell their sad
stories, asking for redress against abusive husbands. In each case Judge
Cady told them there were no laws which could give them aid. Young
Elizabeth was so incensed by this that she once seriously proposed cutting out all the "bad laws" from the books. Her father patiently explained
that this was not the way to change laws, and lectured her on the process
by which laws are made and amended. It was a lesson she never forgot.

She married Henry Stanton over the strong objections of her father,
who resented the young man's radical, abolitionist views. After their return from the London convention, the young couple set up housekeeping
in upstate New York. Henry Stanton became a lawyer, businessman, and
politician, while his wife was fully occupied with running the household
and taking care of her growing family of seven children. But she did not
forget her idea of bringing women together to discuss their problems.

A "public meeting for protest and discussion" was finally decided upon
by Mrs. Stanton and Lucretia Mott during a social visit. They and three
other women drafted a call for such a meeting, but in their inexperience
they did not trust themselves to find the proper words for defining their
purpose. After some thought they hit upon the idea of using the Declaration of Independence as a model. They paraphrased the original, sentence by sentence:

> We hold these truths to be self-evident: that all men and women are
> created equal: that they are endowed by their Creator with certain in-
> alienable rights: that among these are life, liberty and the pursuit of
> happiness. . . .
> The history of mankind is a history of repeated injuries and usurpa-
> tions on the part of man toward woman, having in direct object the es-
> tablishment of an absolute tyranny over her. To prove this, let facts be
> submitted to a candid world.

The Seneca Falls Convention. On July 19, 1848, almost three hundred persons, including forty men, gathered in a small chapel at Seneca
Falls, New York. Since none of the women felt equal to the task, the convention was presided over by James Mott. The speeches and resolutions
stated a bold doctrine: woman was the equal of man and had the right
and duty to participate "in all righteous causes," to speak in public, to
teach, and to write. Women also demanded "equal participation with
men in the various trades, professions and commerce."

The women who met at Seneca Falls were neither the most downtrodden nor the most abused of women. Yet each in her own way had
experienced discrimination, a sense of frustration and a feeling of being relegated to second-class citizenship. One of them, nineteen-year-old
Charlotte Woodward, the only one of those present who lived long enough
to see women get the vote in the United States, has left a moving account

of her reactions to the Seneca Falls convention. She, like so many others in the villages around Seneca Falls, had been employed as a homeworker, doing piecework for the glove factories. She recorded her feelings about her work:

> We women work secretly in the seclusion of our bed chambers be- cause all society was built on the theory that men, not women, earned money and that men alone supported the family. . . . But I do not be- lieve that there was any community in which the souls of some women were not beating their wings in rebellion. For my own obscure self I can say that every fibre of my being rebelled, although silently, all the hours that I sat and sewed gloves for a miserable pittance which, as it was earned, could never be mine. I wanted to work, but I wanted to choose my task and I wanted to collect my wages. That was my form of rebellion against the life into which I was born.

The most controversial of all the resolutions was offered by Elizabeth Cady Stanton: "It is the sacred duty of the women of this country to se- cure to themselves their sacred right to the elective franchise." It almost failed to be adopted; only the vigorous supporting speech of the ex-slave and great black leader, Frederick Douglass, helped to secure enough votes to pass it by a small majority. For most women, suffrage was a remote concept, not nearly as pressing as most of their demands. But Judge Cady's daughter had not forgotten what it takes to change the na- tion's laws. She could not foresee that it would take seventy-two years of struggle to have her resolution translated into actuality. But, as she had expected, that meeting in the little upstate village set forces into motion which became, in time, a tremendous mass movement on behalf of woman's rights, not only in the United States but across the world.

The movement started modestly enough with annual state and na- tional woman's rights conventions. While at the beginning these were nothing more than small local affairs subjected to bitter ridicule by the press and, at times, mob violence by an uncomprehending citizenry, they served an important function. As yet, only a very small minority of women were actively involved, and comparatively few were convinced of the justice of the demands being raised by the feminists. But the wom- an's rights conventions taught women to speak for themselves, to initiate broad mass campaigns, to engender public discussion and win male sup- porters, to make their voices heard in the legislative halls, and to stand up to the abuse of press and public.

After the Seneca Falls convention, talented individuals who wanted a chance for education and a wider sphere of activity than was offered by the home were no longer subject to the terrible loneliness and isolation that an earlier generation of women had experienced. They knew that there were others with similar strivings in small communities and in large cities, who gathered at least annually in woman's rights conven- tions. This knowledge was of tremendous importance in producing the generation of female leaders who initiated the campaign for woman's rights and after decades of hard and bitter struggle carried it to fulfill- ment.

THE IDEAS BEHIND THE MOVEMENT

A movement, in order to succeed, must have ideas which appeal to broad masses of people. The concepts of human equality and perfectability and of the right of the citizen to participate in government—ideas which powered the American and French Revolutions—inevitably influenced society's thinking in regard to women. The earliest and most comprehensive statement of feminism appeared in England in 1790 and reached America in 1792. Mary Wollstonecraft's *Vindication of the Rights of Women* had a decided influence on the popular American novelist Charles Brockden Brown, who felt inspired by it to write *Alcuin,* a tract setting forth ideas of female equality.

A generation of eighteenth-century revolutionaries from Voltaire to Thomas Paine, Benjamin Franklin, and Dr. Benjamin Rush, believing in the decisive influence of environment on the shaping of human destiny, had an equal faith in the potential intellectual equality of women, and spoke with conviction on their behalf. The contribution of Judith Sargent Murray, Mercy Warren, and Abigail Adams to this discussion have already been mentioned. Rationalist and egalitarian ideas were also brought to America by a number of visiting foreigners—Frances Wright, Harriet Martineau, and Frances Kemble.

Frances Wright's was the most important contribution. In her speeches, lectures, and articles, she developed between 1828 and 1834 a strong, logical, and coherent argument for woman's rights. As a rationalist, free-thinker, and confirmed revolutionary, she did not hesitate to develop her arguments to their ultimate extension: she advocated not only full equality for women, but also free love, birth control, and the right to divorce. She herself experienced a bitter divorce settlement: her husband, whom she had supported financially for over fifteen years, obtained every penny of her property and the custody of their child.

A similarly tragic divorce and public scandal involved Frances Kemble, a celebrated British actress who married Pierce Butler without realizing that he was a wealthy Georgian slave-holder. A brief stay on his plantation convinced her of the incompatibility of their views, and she asked for a divorce. Pierce Butler refused, and after a bitter and extended period of litigation Frances Kemble was deprived of her children and left without property, a living example of the humiliation the law could inflict on even the most educated and privileged woman.

Neither Frances Wright's nor Frances Kemble's advanced views drew much support from American women. On the contrary, Frances Wright's "bad reputation" and tragic personal fate were cited as a horrible example of feminine "notoriety" by a whole generation of American preachers and editorial writers.

While the influence of established religion generally tended to reinforce the ideas of woman's inferiority, contradictory trends appeared in the early nineteenth century. Revivalist ministers, preaching the need to translate religious conviction into practical reform activity, recommended the equal participation of women in revivalism and unleashed a tremendous source of female energy. The ideas that women were potentially the equal of men, and that they were morally obligated to strive for such equality, came out of this period of religious thought.

These ideas were most forcefully stated in what was the first fully developed feminist argument written by an American, Sarah Grimké's *Letters on the Equality of the Sexes,* which appeared in 1838. Sarah Grimké met the biblical arguments for the subordination of women head-on. She denied the Scriptures were divine in origin and pointed out that they were interpretations made by men of the word of God. She raised the moral argument for the equality of women and claimed: "God has made no distinction between men and women as moral beings. . . . To me it is perfectly clear that *whatsoever it is morally right for a man to do, it is morally right for a woman to do.*" Sarah Grimké's largely theological discussion was followed in short order by a different type of argument from the pen of Margaret Fuller.

Margaret Fuller's *Woman in the Nineteenth Century* appeared in print in 1844. Her book was a much greater popular success than Sarah Grimké's, although its argument is less lucid. Margaret Fuller's claim for the equality of women was based on their intellect. Every woman had "the same divine energy as man" and must be free to develop as fully as man. "What Woman needs is . . . as a nature to grow, as an intellect to discern, as a soul to live freely, and unimpeded to unfold such powers as were given her. . . ." But Margaret Fuller agreed with Sarah Grimké and other feminist spokesmen that women were entitled to equal opportunities with men: "If you ask me what offices they may fill, I reply—any. I do not care what case you put; let them be sea captains if you will."

After Seneca Falls, the lone voices of individual rebels had become an organized chorus. Admittedly, the lofty Declaration of Principles drawn up at Seneca Falls had overstated the subjection of women considerably in order to arouse sympathy for the new cause. Perhaps not all of history was simply a history of "the subjection of woman by man," but to a growing number of women the issue presented itself rather simply. When Susan B. Anthony was a self-supporting schoolteacher, her brother-in-law, in a typical expression of male prejudice, declared that he admired her for baking biscuits "rather than for solving Algebra problems." "There is no reason," Susan B. Anthony replied tartly, "why woman should not be able to do both." Many women saw the issue in these simple terms. . . .

chapter 11

Indians and White America

ALTHOUGH THE PROPAGANDA OF EUROPEAN IMPERIALISM contains an almost endless list of "savage" vices attributed to the native peoples of North America, some English colonial writers also acknowledged the existence of important Indian virtues such as courage, hospitality, generosity, and an admirable sense of communal sharing and caring. Settlers saw the red man primarily as a dangerous barbarian standing in the way of their righteous conquest, but men who attempted to infuse the white presence in the New World with conscience sometimes granted that Indians lived by moral values which Europeans merely professed. The seventeenth century poet Thomas Traherne compared Indian civility with the aggressive greed of the invaders and observed that "there is no Savage Nation under the Cope of Heaven that is more absurdly Barbarous than the Christian World." Gary B. Nash in his intellectually provocative study of 1974 on "red, white and black" in colonial America noted that Indians embodied many of the highest qualities which some Europeans had hoped to use as a foundation for their colonial culture before vaulting ambition and New World abundance pulled them in the direction of "individualism, disputatiousness, aggrandizement of wealth, and the exploitation of other humans." Nash concluded that the white settlers "had chosen productivity and acquisitiveness, both of which proceeded far. But it was obvious from looking in any direction that this had been accomplished at a terrible price in exploitation and human suffering, enslavement and alienation."

Major events and leaders during the first century of United States history had entirely different meanings for native peoples than for white Americans. Because the new nation in 1776 promised for Indians not "Life, Liberty and the pursuit of Happiness" but rather a more destructive threat than the old empire, many native peoples of the East with good reason supported the British. (After the war the U.S. dispossessed "loyal" Indians as readily as the "disloyal" ones.) The acquisition of Louisiana from France, the seizure of California and the U.S. Southwest from Mexico, the Oregon settlement with England, and the purchase of Alaska from Russia in 1867, all of which stimulated an exuberant optimism among white Americans merely provided for Indians the basic conditions for many decades of military defeat, violence, and cultural aggression. Cheyenne survivors of the Sand Creek massacre of 1864 could hardly have regarded Gettysburg as the major conflict of the 1860s and the Sioux people saw in George Custer an arrogant and implacable enemy rather than an idealistic young Civil War general thrust into fame by a combination of personal dash and antislavery sympathies.

An especially indefensible example of white arrogance and aggression can be found in the seizure of the Southeastern Indian homelands, an historical event which may have met the canons of honor among most white citizens but which seemed to the victims to be the ultimate betrayal of all good faith. These Indians, as R. S. Cotterill persuasively indicated in a monograph of 1954 on the Southern aborigines before removal, eliminated or altered many customs which the whites had condemned most harshly. However, the acquisition by the Cherokees with particular vigor of many aspects of "civilization" (including, in a peripheral way, slavery) did not prevent systematic treaty breaking, frequent violence from white Georgians, and the ultimate U.S. military deportation to the West on the "Trail of Tears" so well described in 1953 by Grant Foreman. The Choctaws, Creeks, and Chickasaws, according to Mary Elizabeth Young's impressive account in 1961 of the ill-fated Indian allotment system, fared little better in the greedy scramble for the lands of the native peoples in Alabama and Mississippi.

The most dramatic aspect of white expansion from the colonial era to the Civil War was war and violence but increasingly historians in recent years have turned to the study of white attitudes and cultural conflict. Roy Harvey Pearce in a seminal study of 1953 found a general and unquestioning faith in "the natural and divine superiority of a farming to a hunting culture" and in "the great and eternal frontier truth" of "civilization or death to all American savages." On the Indian question white Americans concluded that "they were destined to try to civilize him and, in trying, to destroy him, because he could not and would not be civilized." Robert F. Berkhofer, Jr., in a 1965 monograph on antebellum missionaries to the Indians, revealed the total nature of a conflict in which the whites demanded nothing less than cultural surrender. ("To become truly Christian was to become anti-Indian.") Some of the roots of this white hubris Wilcomb Washburn in an essay of 1959 and a book of 1971 traced to "a muscular, aggressive and didactic Christianity," cultural scorn for "savages" devoted to hunting and without settled habitations (a false idea of many native peoples), and the tendency to regard the Indians as "part of the landscape" to be "discovered," conquered, and manipulated at will.

Although Bernard Sheehan's monograph of 1973 on Indian-white relations in the early national period dubiously accepted "Jeffersonian philanthropy" as an important and pervasive reality and seemed to assume that this philanthropic bent rather than physical aggression constituted the most important relation between white and red, he made an interesting point in trying to demonstrate that "the white man's sympathy was more deadly than his animosity." Sheehan concluded his volume by quoting de Tocqueville's ironic observation on America's humanitarian pretensions about the Indians, that "it is impossible to destroy men with more respect to the laws of humanity." In 1968 Reginald Horsman had also noted in his study of U.S.–Indian relations to 1812 a rationale for dispossession in the idea of "expanding American freedom and civilization to new areas." Horsman, placing expansion in a larger context, noted that rationalizations invented to justify the conquest of the Indians were later extended to other despised, alien people such as the Mexicans and insisted that students of U.S. history see American aggression "as part of the expansion of Western Europe, particularly the so-called Anglo-Saxons, over peoples throughout the world." While Horsman did not develop the insight, he did accomplish that which every Indian scholar should have done but nearly all failed to do in linking the American conquest of the Indians directly to the general history of Western imperialism. Charles Crowe (Selection 1) and several other historians elaborated on the same point. In 1972 Wilbur R. Jacobs discussed the glorification of aggression in Indian dispossession and made a comparative analysis of destructive white excursions against the native cultures of North America, Australia, and New Guinea.

Themes explored by Horsman, Pearce, and their colleagues in the study of the 1776–1860 period were taken up by other scholars for the antebellum and postbellum eras. Between 1915 and 1925 Annie H. Abel wrote three volumes on the slaveholding Indians which displayed some errors and considerable prejudice but which contained much valuable information for readers willing to use the work with proper caution. When the Civil War came the five major tribes of the Indian territory consulted the record of Federal betrayal and the bright promises of Confederate Officials before the majority sided with the Confederacy. Moreover, the five tribes were largely ignored by the remote administration in Washington, misinformed by pro-Confederate U.S. agents and physically surrounded by Confederate political and military forces. (War decisions hardly seemed to matter in the long run since the Federal government punished many "loyal" Indians the most severely.) In Reconstruction, as M. Thomas Bailey indicated in a monograph of 1972, Washington demanded that the Indians give to blacks in their midst the land and full citizenship which they did not require from either the North or the South. Moreover political leaders followed time-worn traditions by using the occasion to make another massive grab of Indian lands.

For a brief time after the Civil War the attention of policy makers and the American public focused on the Indian territory but as time passed both groups turned increasingly to the final defeat and disposition of the Plains Indians and the major tribes of the far Southwest. During the last stage of military operations Sioux, Navajo, Arapaho, Cheyenne, Apache, Comanche, and other peoples fought the white invaders with great ingenuity and persistence under the able leadership of men such as

Sitting Bull, Crazy Horse, and Chief Joseph. Some of the major leaders gained an appropriately sympathetic chronicle in Alvin M. Josephy's volume of 1958 on *The Patriot Chiefs*. Dee Brown in 1971 provided a long and dramatic narrative of white aggression and Indian resistance from the Navajo conflict of 1860 to the last major white massacre at Wounded Knee in 1890.

During the 1880s open warfare became secondary to the expropriation of the more choice Indian lands and to U.S. campaigns against tribal cultures. The story of U.S. policy in the cultural struggle from the Civil War to the Dawes Severalty Act of 1887 for the division of tribal lands into individual plots has been told (though with some condescension and a dash of apologetics) by Loring Benson Priest and an account of all major aspects of the drive for "assimilation" from 1865 to 1890 has been presented by Henry E. Fritz. With a veneer of "philanthropy" Indians were penned more firmly into reservations and the cultural struggle began in earnest to transform tribal relatedness, communal ownership and Indian sense of community into the isolated individualism, the passion for private gain, and the love of private property which had always characterized the white man. In that struggle Indian agents, reservation schools, ministers, and priests and the persistent pressures of the private instrumentalities of white culture all played a part. By the beginning of the twentieth century many white Americans thought that the total defeat and the impending extinction of native cultures constituted the final solution to "the Indian problem."

In the nearly nine decades since the Dawes Act and the last major military actions American scholarship has generally favored imperialist values, but Helen Hunt Jackson initiated a significant minority tradition with an anti-imperialist orientation in *A Century of Dishonor* (1881), a chronicle of white greed, injustice, broken treaties, and massacres from the first colonial attacks on unoffending Indians to hostile Federal acts against the starving Utes in the winter of 1879. Jackson's contemporary Theodore Roosevelt, more in the mainstream with his multi-volume study of the West, denounced the "maudlin fanatics" and "foolish sentimentalists" who ignored Indian racial inferiority, "slandered their own countrymen" and gave currency to the absurd idea that "a few squalid savages" hunting aimlessly and sporadically over millions of acres had held title to the vast reaches of America. As late as 1947 the renowned Southern historian E. Merton Coulter expressed Rooseveltian values without apologies in a scathing attack on the "alien" and "semi-barbarous" Cherokees for the inexcusable crime of "getting in the way of Georgia" until the white people drove the tribe from the state and thus finally "won their freedom from Indians."

Although Coulter's open contempt and Helen Hunt Jackson's appeals to "the slumbering conscience of the nation" went out of fashion many years ago, both traditions in modified forms continue in our own times. While no reasonable person would confuse the excesses of Coulter with the thoughtful, and sophisticated work of a modern school of historians who insist on new approaches and wish in the words of Robert Berkhofer "to avoid the usual moral fable that masquerades as Indian history," the end result nevertheless was an explicit or implicit advocacy of pro-white and anti-Indian values which merits the label of "neo-imperialist." One of the more extreme productions of the new school was an essay of 1969 by Francis Paul Prucha which portrayed the dispossession and military deportation of the Cherokees as "a reasonable and necessary answer to the Indian problem" and attributed to the old Indian hater Andrew Jackson "the kindest feelings" of a statesman "genuinely concerned for the well-being of the Indians and their civilization." Four years earlier Alden T. Vaughn had attempted more plausibly in a thoroughly researched and skillfully reasoned monograph to provide a fresh interpretation of Puritan-Indian relations, but he rested much of his case on an arbitrary and pro-imperialist preference for the "unified, visionary, disciplined and dynamic" culture of the invaders over the "self-satisfied, undisciplined and static" native peoples.

A more calculated effort to dispose of the school of Helen Hunt Jackson appeared in an essay of 1969 by Bernard W. Sheehan who attempted to move the war-torn and bloody record of white-Indian relations from the realm of fact to the status of very dubious theory with rhetorical exorcism by speaking frequently of "the oppressor-victim interpretation," asserting that Alden Vaughn had "disposed of the guilty white man scheme," and so on. When reality comes garbed in rhetoric about "the suffering-Indian, wicked-white-man interpretation," the "moralistic dichotomy" of white aggressor and betrayed Indian, and "the alleged guilt of the frontiersman," then one is surely asked to believe that no one suffers and no one is evil or guilty. Moreover, according to Sheehan, the white man did not destroy his adversary for the simple reason that "the Indian disintegrated." How could the historian distribute blame when he truly understood that the red man had been "the victim of a process" and that "when the conflict is submerged in the process of cultural intermingling the moralistic dichotomy dissolves?" (This kind of reasoning needs to be tried with Nazis and Jews or with masters and victims in the African slave trade.) The dispossessed could easily insist that no amount of knowledge about cultural "contact" and "intermingling" altered the historical record or absolved the white man from responsibility.

Even as the neo-imperial school emerged a new Indian protest movement burst into the public arena with political action which ranged from symbolic demonstrations against the "discovery" arrogance of Columbus Day celebrations and Thanksgiving Day ceremonies at Plymouth ("We didn't land on Plymouth Rock, it landed on us.") to the physical "reoccupation" of Alcatraz and the violent confrontation at Wounded Knee. White writers on the left such as Paul Jacobs attempted to present truthful perspectives on "natives and slaves" and popular historians such as Dee Brown (Bury My Heart at Wounded Knee, 1971) wrote best selling chronicles of the history of crimes against native peoples. Most importantly, perhaps, a critical examination of history encouraged many Indians to create new organs of expression such as The Indian Historian and to heed a new generation of intellectual and political leaders such as Vine Deloria and Russell Means.

BIBLIOGRAPHY

Works Discussed in This Chapter

Abel, Annie H., *The Slaveholding Indians* (3 vols., 1915–25).

Bailey, M. Thomas, *Reconstruction in Indian Territory: A Story of Avarice, Discrimination and Opportunism* (1972).

Berkhofer, Robert F., Jr., *Salvation and the Savage: An Analysis of Protestant Missions and American Indian Response* (1965).

Cotterill, R. S., *The Southern Indians: The Story of the Civilized Tribes Before Removal* (1954).

Coulter, E. Merton, *Georgia, A Short History* (1947).

Crowe, Charles, "Indians and Blacks in White America," in Charles Hudson, ed., *Three Centuries of Southern Indians* (1975), and the Commentary in Hudson, ed., *Red, White and Black: Symposium on Indians of the Old South* (1971).

Deloria, Vine, *Custer Died For Your Sins: An Indian Manifesto* (1969).

Foreman, Grant, *Indian Removal: The Emigration of the Five Civilized Tribes of Indians* (1932, rev. ed., 1953).

Fritz, Henry E., *The Movement for Indian Assimilation, 1860–1890* (1963).

Horsman, Reginald, "American Indian Policy and the Origins of Manifest Destiny," *Birmingham Historical Journal* (1968) and *Expansion and American Indian Policy, 1783–1812* (1967).

Jackson, Helen Hunt, *A Century of Dishonor: A Sketch of the United States Government's Dealings with Some of the Indian Tribes* (1891).

Jacobs, Paul, et al., *To Serve the Devil: Natives and Slaves, A Documentary History of America's Racial History. . . .* (1972).

Jacobs, Wilbur, *Dispossessing the American Indian: Indians and Whites on the Colonial Frontier* (1972).

Josephy, Alvin M., Jr., *The Patriot Chiefs: A Chronicle of American Indian Resistance* (1958).

Nash, Gary B., *Red, White and Black: The Peoples of Early America* (1974).

Pearce, Roy Harvey, *Savagism and Civilization: A Study of the Indian and the American Mind* (1967), rev. ed. of *The Savages of America* (1953, 1965).

Priest, Loring Benson, *Uncle Sam's Stepchildren: The Reformation of U.S. Indian Policy, 1865–1887* (1942).

Prucha, Francis Paul, "Andrew Jackson's Indian Policy: A Reassessment," *Journal of American History* (1969).

Roosevelt, Theodore, *The Winning of the West* (Vol. I, 1889).

Sheehan, Bernard W., "Indian-White Relations in Early America: A Review Essay," *William and Mary Quarterly* (1969) and *Seeds of Extinction: Jeffersonian Philanthropy and the American Indian* (1973).

Vaughn, Alden T., *New England Frontier: Puritans and Indians, 1620–1675* (1965).

Washburn, Wilcomb E., "The Moral and Legal Justifications for Dispossessing the Indians," in James M. Smith, ed., *Seventeenth Century America* (1959) and Washburn, *Red Man's Land White Man's Law: A Study of the Past and Present Status of the American Indian* (1971).

Young, Mary Elizabeth, *Redskins, Ruffleshirts and Rednecks: Indian Land Allotments in Alabama and Mississippi, 1830–1860* (1961).

Suggested Readings

Among *general narrative histories* the most standard, brief work is William T. Hagan, *American Indians* (1961). An excellent work with a stress on Oklahoma Indians is Angie Debo, *A History of the Indians of the U.S.* (1970). An account by an Indian scholar worth consulting is D'Arcy McNickle *They Came Here First: The Epic of the American Indian* (1949).

Collections of historical essays worth noting are Francis Paul Prucha, ed., *The Indian in American History* (1971) and Louis Filler and Allen Guttmann, eds., *The Removal of The Cherokee Nation: Manifest Destiny or National Dishonor?* (1962). The Prucha book has a good bibliography and is useful despite the fact that the volume gives disproportionate space to the neo-imperialists. The Filler and Guttmann anthology has several useful essays and tells us something about the shortcomings of liberal scholarship in the early 1960s.

Several *documentary histories* are in print. Particularly good for white-Indian relations is Wilcomb E. Washburn, ed. *The Indian and the White Man* (1964) and Washburn, ed., *The American Indian and the U.S.: A Documentary History* (1973). Many selections in Jack D. Forbes, ed., *The Indian in America's Past* (1964) are damning evidence of pervasive white hostility. Perhaps the most eloquent volume is Shirley H. Witt and Stan Steiner, eds., *The Way: An Anthology of American Indian Literature* (1972). Also useful is Virgil J. Vogel, ed., *This Country Was Ours: A Documentary History of the American Indian* (1972). Books which stress contemporary conditions are Edgar S. Cahn and David W. Hearne, eds., *Our Brothers Keeper: The Indian in White America* (1969) and Hazel W. Hertzberg, *The Search for Indian Identity: Modern Pan-Indian Movements* (1971).

On *noble savage literature* Roy Harvey Pearce can be supplemented by Henri Baudet, *Paradise on Earth: Some Thoughts on European Images of Non-European Men* (1965) and David Bidney, "The Idea of the Savage in North American Ethnohistory," *Journal of the History of Ideas* (1954).

On *Indians in the colonial era,* see Hudson and Nash, cited earlier, and Wesley Frank Craven, *White, Red and Black: The Seventeenth Century Virginian* (1971).

For a useful essay on *Indian-white relations and ethical judgments,* see Wilcomb E. Washburn, "A Moral History of Indian-White Relations," *Ethnohistory* (1957). See also Robert W. Mardock's *The Reformers and the American Indians* (1971); Gary B. Nash, "Images of the Indian in the Colonial Mind," *William and Mary Quarterly* (1972); and Francis Paul Prucha, ed., *Americanizing the American Indians: Writings by the "Friends of the Indians,"* 1880–1890 (1973).

Works of interest on *Federal policy* and the dispossession of *Eastern Indians* are Grant Foreman, *The Last Trek of the Indians* (1946); Dale Van Every, *Disinherited: The Lost Birthright of the American Indian* (1966); and Francis Paul Prucha, *American Indian Policy in the Formative Years: The Indian Trade and Intercourse Acts, 1790–1834* (1962).

On *Western Indians* see Ralph K. Andrist's dramatic study of the Plains Indians, *The Long Death* (1964), Paul J. Wellman, *The Indian Wars of the West* (1954) and Louis O. Saum's sometimes anti-Indian, *The Fur Trader and the Indian* (1965).

In the late 1960s and early 1970s the *Chronicles of Oklahoma* published a number of articles on *reconstruction in Indian territory.* See for example Walt Willson, "Freedmen in Indian Territory During Reconstruction," *Chronicles of Oklahoma* (1971–72). See also Paul F. Lambert, "The Cherokee Reconstruction Treaty of 1866," and five other articles on the five tribes during Civil War and Reconstruction in the July, 1973 issue of *Journal of the West*.

The University of Oklahoma Press has published a number of volumes on the *history of Indian tribes* such as J. J. Mathews, *The Osages: Children of the*

Middle Waters (1961); Donald J. Berthong, *The Southern Cheyennes* (1963); and Angie Debo, *The Rise and the Fall of the Choctaw Republic* (1934).

The general modern literature on *European imperialism* is relevant. See in particular Albert Memmi, *The Colonizer and the Colonized*, trans. by Howard Greenfeld (1957, Eng. ed., 1967) and Frantz Fanon, *The Wretched of the Earth*, trans. by Constance Farrington (1961, Eng. ed., 1965).

American Imperialism and the Indian*

Charles Crowe

During the colonial period of American history the aggressive confrontation of English imperialists with red and black men not only shaped American nationalism but also created the "white" man, the "Indian" and the "Negro." Although racial prejudices certainly existed in the Tudor era, the Englishman regarded other factors as more fundamental than skin color. The imperial experience made "whiteness" the primary category of self-perception for Europeans and compelled the victims to consider their "blackness" and "redness." Before the catastrophe contacts with Europeans the native peoples of North America lacked a sense of common interest as well as collective names for themselves. Cherokees and Narragansetts did not and could not call themselves "Indians," and similarly Ashantis and Ibos lacked any knowledge of either Africa or Negritude. "Discovery," defeat, and ultimate condemnation to plantations and reservations by Europeans gave to vastly different peoples the enduring names of Indian and Negro. Jean-Paul Sartre had something like this process in mind when he observed in a discussion of the Nazi era that "the anti-Semite creates the Jew" and in a prefatory analysis of imperialism for Frantz Fanon's most celebrated book extended the same observation to settlers and "natives."[1]

Sartre's idea does not reveal the whole truth. History cannot be en-

---

* By permission of the author. A longer version of the essay included blacks and appeared in Charles Hudson, ed., *Three Centuries of Southern Indians* (Athens: University of Georgia Press, 1974).

[1] Jean-Paul Sartre, "Portrait of the Anti-Semite," *Partisan Review* (1946); and Sartre's preface to Frantz Fanon, *The Wretched of the Earth*, trans. Constance Farrington (1965), 26–84. On American Indians and Blacks see William S. Willis "Divide and Rule: Red, White, and Black in the Southeast," *Journal of Negro History* (1963), 157–76; and Charles M. Hudson, ed., *Red, White and Black: Symposium on Indians in the Old South* (1971).

compassed in a simple chronicle of oppressors and their victims, and human creativity often transcends the most tyrannical circumstances. Black people, acting from desperately felt needs, combined what they could use from the house of bondage with African remnants to establish a new Afro-American culture. Among the many creative responses of native Americans was the case of the Plains Indians who made the white man's horse the central feature in dynamic new life patterns. Although Europeans created the Negroes and Indians they knew, conventional white chronicles failed to consider the most important facts about these peoples. The victims have a separate history which is an essential part of the contemporary struggle to define the future. In certain respects the red man's internal history even predated the arrival of the Europeans, found expression during the 17th and 18th centuries in the Iroquois, Creek, and Cherokee confederacies, and continues in the present with native American movements. Still, these developments happened contrary to or apart from the will of the conquerors.[2]

When the Revolution established American nationality during the 1770s, the new citizen recognized himself first as a white man. Long before independence had become an American dream, color was the dominant badge of status in a society strongly oriented toward white supremacy. (This powerful sense of whiteness even made the status of some Europeans suspect. Benjamin Franklin described Germans as "swarthy," fretted over the "very small" number of whites in the world, and admitted only Englishmen and "Saxons" to the racial elite.) The "whiteness" which emerged from the conquest and exploitation of red and black man, symbolized a conviction of superiority over "lesser breeds" around the world as well as dominion over the North American continent and its "inferior" peoples.[3]

Indians had no reason whatsoever to rejoice over the birth of a new nation destined to advance destructively from the Appalachian mountains to the Pacific Ocean, killing and dispossessing the red man as an obstacle to "the course of civilization" and America's "manifest destiny." The Declaration of Independence made it clear that "the merciless Indian savage" who conspired with George III in "domestic insurrections" was no part of the new republic. The U.S. Constitution in the enumeration of Congressional powers left the status of Indians extremely ambiguous by speaking of commerce "with foreign nations, and among the several states and with the Indian tribes." The treaty making process dealt with Indians as foreign nations and the very first Congress, President, and Commissioner of Indian Affairs (Secretary of War Henry

---

[2] On black nationalism see Edwin S. Redkey, *Black Exodus, 1890–1910* (1969); and John Bracey, Jr., et al., *Black Nationalism in America* (1970). On Indians during early American history, see Gary B. Nash, *Red, White and Black: The Peoples of Early America* (1974).

[3] Franklin in Leonard Labaree, et al., *The Papers of Benjamin Franklin*, 4 (1963), 225–34. On color symbolism, see Arrah B. Evarts, "Color Symbolism," *The Psychoanalytic Review*, 6 (1919), 129–34, and the extensive notes and bibliography in Harold B. Isaacs, *The New World of Negro Americans* (1963).

Knox) all began with the announcement of their intention to grant Indians the conventional rights of foreign peoples. Secretary Knox's assertions that Indian lands "cannot be taken from them unless by their free consent or by right of conquest in case of a just war," and that Indians *"ought to be* [note the choice of words] considered as foreign nations, not as subjects of any particular state," did not in fact guide Knox or any other major official in Indian policy. The Act of Congress (one of the first passed) to which Knox was responding is worth quoting: "The utmost good faith shall always be observed toward the Indians; their land and property shall never be taken from them without their consent; and in their property, rights, and liberty, they shall never be invaded or disturbed, unless in just and lawful wars. . . ." As Congress and Secretary Knox may have foreseen, "ought" is not a very binding word, "consent" might be gained by fraud, intimidation, or force, and all wars undertaken by whites turned out to be "just and lawful."[4]

In commenting upon the native peoples already extinct Knox expressed his "regret" over the fact that "if the same causes continue the same effects will happen" to other Indian cultures. More candid and explicit was the toast in the officers' mess of the 1779 force sent to burn Iroquois villages in upstate New York, "Civilization or death to all American savages." (For "civilization" one may substitute "subordination to the master race.") Even in times of peace the frontiersman and his sympathizers agreed with the officers of 1779. Hugh Henry Brackenridge referred to the red men as "the animals vulgarly called Indians" and described their most useful function as providing fertilizer: "The Indians' bones must enrich the soil before the plough of civilized man can open it." The Jacksonians resorted to this kind of violent rhetoric even more frequently. President Jackson himself privately abused the red man and in public messages phrased the fundamental question of white-red relations in this way: "What *good* man would prefer a country covered with forests and ranged by a few thousand savages to our extensive Republic, studded with cities, towns, and prosperous farms . . . occupied by more than 12,000,000 people and filled with all the blessings of liberty, civilization, and religion." Seemingly, all righteous forces would laud the white man who dispatched the "squalid savages" as quickly as possible.

Thomas Hart Benton, like many of his contemporaries, drew a moral for the world from white-Indian relations in America: "the white race alone received the divine command to subdue and replenish the earth . . . civilization or extinction has been the fate of all people who have found themselves to be in the path of advancing whites." Red and black men, presumably, should have been grateful for the option of mass destruction or total subordination to white "civilization." An ordinary Ohio farmer, when asked if a wretched handful of surviving Miamis ever caused any trouble, replied, "No . . . if any . . . displease us, we take them

---

[4] For the Knox quotations see *American State Papers, Indian Affairs*, 1, No. 4, 53. See also Roy H. Pearce, *The Savages of America* (1953). For Congress, see *A Sketch of the Development of the Bureau of Indians Affairs* . . . (Bureau of Indian Affairs, Dec. 1956), 1–3.

out of doors and kick them a little, for they are like dogs, and will love you better for it."[5]

In books and articles remote from public policy, the frontier and the battlefield, quite a different Indian, the noble and virtuous savage, served as a foil to the decadent "civilized" men in the many thousands of pages devoted to the theme. The Kansas senator who measured sympathy for the Indian by the amount of distance between the white sympathizer and the "noble redskin" had a point. The defender of the Indian seldom got near the object of his concern, and the actual history of the red man centered around the violence and aggression inflicted on him by the constantly encroaching whites. Writers, artists, and publicists often seemed merely to be specializing in a different kind of exploitation—one which was intellectual rather than economic or political.

Even in politics the self-appointed friend of the Indian generally turned out to be destructive, and the depredations of white power can be seen more effectively in the allegedly sympathetic Franklins and Jeffersons than in the overtly hostile Brackenridges and Jacksons. Franklin certainly expressed sympathy toward the native American on many occasions, and wrote the oft-quoted indictment of the Paxton boys who massacred men, women, and children from the small remnants of a defeated and peaceful Indian tribe. In several essays and letters, Franklin even made an effort to imagine himself as an Indian, but he also discussed in a matter-of-fact manner the doom which he anticipated for the native American. With a humor which might escape the victim he described rum as "the appointed means" of fulfilling "the design of Providence to extirpate these savages in order to make room for the cultivators of the earth." As one might expect, he assumed that the continent belonged to the white man and advanced this goal more than once.[6]

If the Indian had a "best friend" among the whites it was Thomas Jefferson, who repeatedly exempted the native American from the gross inferiority which he attributed to the black man. Jefferson returned again and again throughout his long life to the theme of Indian virtues—intellect, imagination, fortitude, courage, great capacity for human growth, and a "sublime oratory" comparable to the best of Demosthenes and Cicero. Yet, quite another Jeffersonian point of view lurks in the vast corpus of his letters and papers. The accusation in the Declaration of Independence has already been noted, and later in the same year when Indian warfare threatened his home country, he insisted that "nothing will reduce those wretches so soon as pushing the war into the heart of their country. But I would not stop there. I would never cease pursuing them while one of them remained on this side of the Mississippi. . . . [They] are a useless, expensive, and ungovernable ally."

A few years later in a sharp reversal of opinion Jefferson proved him-

5 For Knox, *American State Papers, Indian Affairs,* 1, No. 2, 13. For the officers' toast, Frederick Cook, ed., *Journals of the Military Expedition of Major General John Sullivan* (1897), pp. 225–26. For Brackenridge, *Indian Atrocities* (1782) (1867), 62. For the Ohio farmer, see R. G. Thwaites, ed., *Early Western Travels* (1904), 4, 263.

6 *The Autobiography of Benjamin Franklin,* Max Farrand, ed. (1949), 149.

self the poorest of prophets: "It may be regarded as certain that not a foot of land will ever be taken from the Indians, without their own consent. The sacredness of their rights is felt by all thinking persons in America. . . ."

Yet Jefferson himself did more than most chief executives to plunder the Indian by aiding or allowing the seizure of 100 million acres of land through "persuasion," intimidation, bribery, and hastily devised "treaties" often forced upon "chiefs" who failed to understand the white man's concept of property and lacked the authority to surrender the tribal heritage. Jefferson repeatedly expressed the belief that the Indians would continue to be crushed as long as they caused trouble for the inevitably dominant whites. The major hope for the red man, it seemed, lay in retreating to lands west of the Mississippi which the whites did not want. All of this was said and done by a President who lived in a kind of cloud cuckoo land inhabited by highly favorable reports about the growing friendship of whites and Indians. In 1803 he promised "to live in perpetual peace with the Indians, to cultivate an affectionate attachment . . . by everything just and liberal." The gap between rhetoric and action is astonishing, but not even the rhetoric always held up. In 1812 he noted that the "backward" Indian would be thrust into new retreats by the whites: "They will relapse into barbarism and misery . . . and we shall be obliged to drive them with the beasts of the forest into the stony mountains." Jefferson's relative lack of bigotry did not mean much to the Indians who suffered the disastrous results of his policies. Moreover, Jefferson thought that the highest praise to be bestowed on those magnificent, courageous, and eloquent people was that with enough high-minded striving and effort they might ultimately hope to cease being Indians and become instead fully assimilated "sodbusters."[7]

The five "civilized" tribes in the South made an impressive attempt to follow Jefferson's advice. The Cherokees, by conventional American standards, acquired at least as high a level of "civilization" as their white Georgia adversaries, even to the point of acquiring a substantial number of black slaves and a few cotton plantations. Unfortunately, Cherokee newspapers, schools, farms, and skilled trades did not stop the insatiable land-grabbers, President Jackson and, ultimately, Federal troops. John Marshall accepted the Cherokees as a "domestic dependent nation" (a phrase that almost defies rational analysis) with a treaty binding on the United States, but his decision had no force and after the Civil War Congress passed a law asserting the power to unilaterally "abrogate" Indian treaties. (So much for "dependent domestic nations.") Although the 14th Amendment accepted the citizenship of "all persons born in the United States," that status was not even abstractly extended to native Americans until the 1920s.[8]

[7] All the Jefferson quotations are from Foley, *The Jefferson Cyclopedia*, pp. 420–23. On Jefferson and race, see Winthrop D. Jordan, *White Over Black* (1968) and Bernard Sheehan, *Seeds of Extinction* (1973).

[8] See Mary Elizabeth Young, *Redskins, Ruffleshirts, and Rednecks; Indian Allotments in Alabama and Mississippi* (1961); Albert K. Weinberg, *Manifest Destiny* (1935); and the excellent short history, William T. Hagan, *American Indians* (1961).

Jefferson might praise the noble red man, Jackson might denounce the devious savage, and Lincoln might promise new policies but warfare and aggression devastated the Indians under all three administrations. Ironically, the Radical Republican era marked the beginning of a new cycle of repression. Still to come were the last battles, scattered lynchings, unprovoked massacres of men, women, and children at Sand Creek, Wounded Knee, and elsewhere, as well as an incredible amount of private aggression and random violence, but 300 years of military struggle had nearly come to an end. The old land frauds would continue (by 1934, 86 million acres were gone, the best of 138 million left after the Dawes Act) as wretched and starving bands huddled together in reservations increasingly too small to sustain the old ways. "Honest" officials of the Office of Indian Affairs often aided the despoilation of tribes, while corrupt agents diverted rations, appropriated cattle, and plundered natural resources. The post-Reconstruction era gave birth to a cultural war against the Indians in which the U.S. government launched systematic assaults on Indian religions, languages, and customs. Boarding schools were established which taught English and as well as cultural shame to the possessors of "the barbarous dialects." Agents and teachers ridiculed the ancient ways, forbade children to practice the old rituals, and cut their students' hair—sometimes at gunpoint. Usually Federal employees were assisted by hordes of aggressively competitive Baptist, Methodist, Mormon, and Catholic missionaries.

The Dawes Act, aimed at forcing Indians to divide communal lands into individual plots, was to be the final solution to the Indian problem. By division and purchase the Federal government "recovered" 17 million acres in one year (1890), but the private land-grabbers got a larger quantity from the five civilized tribes alone. Physical force, squatting, corrupt contracts, and myriad forms of deception all brought millions of acres into white hands, and when new legislation made outright "purchase" difficult, leasing became the new vehicle of fraud. Among the weapons for squeezing profits from leasing were excessive fees, illegal mortgages and liens, forged wills, and the "guardianship of minors and incompetent Indians."

Despite all that the white man did, the often demoralized and half-starved red men continued to share food with his hungry ones, support the old people, and cling to other members of his tribe. In brief he cherished his ancient original sin of preferring communal life to private property, possessive individualism, and competitive lifestyles.[9]

---

[9] See Hagan, Ibid., and Edward H. Spicer, *A Short History of the Indians of the U.S.* (1969). Two excellent anthologies are Wilcomb E. Washburn, ed., *The Indian and the White Man* (1964) and Jack D. Forbes, ed., *The Indian in America's Past.*

chapter 12

Sectional Strife and the Nature of the Civil War

DURING THE 1930s AND 1940s James G. Randall, Avery O. Craven, Allan Nevins, and other leading historians rejected the old idea of the Civil War as an "irrepressible conflict" between free labor and slavery. Determined to dismiss slavery as the major cause of the conflagration, they sometimes went so far as to echo proslavery apologetics in explaining the "needless war," the "repressible conflict," which lacked "real issues" and could be traced to the "emotionalism," the "irrationality," and the "uncontrolled fanaticism" of abolitionists and Southern "fire-eaters" as well as to the "irresponsible" political leaders of "a blundering generation." Randall, influenced by revisionist diplomatic historians intent on exploding the myth of German war guilt and on assigning responsibility for the catastrophe of 1914 to all the great powers, placed the Civil War in the same category with World War I as a senseless blood bath. The American conflict developed from "crisis psychosis," the "despairing plunge," the "unmotivated drift," the "highly artificial, almost fabricated issue of slavery," the "advocate of rule or ruin," and the "reform-your-neighbor prophet." The needless war school evoked in 1949 a telling critique by Arthur Schlesinger, Jr. (Selection 1) which persuasively portrayed Randall and Craven as too callously indifferent to the oppressiveness of human bondage to perceive slavery as a social evil and a moral dilemma. Unfortunately Schlesinger, then in the process of becoming a leading cold war intellectual, placed antebellum abolitionists and modern anticommunists in the same general category with the implication that American cold warriors stood single-mindedly for freedom while Communists continued the old slavocracy's war on human values.

Obstacles to more adequate explanations of the Civil War had been erected before Randall and Craven by the giants of early historical writing, Frederick Jackson Turner and Charles and Mary Beard. Turner's romantic celebration of the frontier as the crucible which created American democracy from European raw materials, neglected capitalism, urbanism, immigration, and the harsh realities of class, ethnic, and racial conflict. Contrary to Turner's reports, the frontier experience everywhere contained much private violence as well as nearly incessant warfare against the Indian and in the South the oppressive institution of slavery with masters and slaves rather than subsistence farmers doing much of the pioneering. (As Staughton Lynd phrased the point, "Simon Legree was a frontier farmer.")

Both Turner and the Beards saw America at the beginning of national history as an "agrarian" democracy of small self-sufficient farmers and both scholars regarded slavery and abolition as relatively minor matters in comparison to the grand issues. The Beards found the central theme of American history from the Revolution to the Populist revolt of the 1890s in the conflict between the elitist commercial-capitalist interests and the majority variously described as "agrarians," "agricultural interests," or "farmers and mechanics." The fact that "agrarian leadership" from the 1770s to the 1850s generally fell to masters of slaves and great plantations created much confusion, sometimes made the Beards allies of John C. Calhoun and the proslavery argument, and led them to conclude that the entire process of Civil War and Reconstruction had been a "Second American Revolution" which ended with the complete triumph of capitalist plutocracy over the South as the last stronghold of "agrarianism." For the Beards, Republican and Radical pretensions had been shields for an economic conspiracy which enabled business men to defeat and plunder the South and to enact a battery of national procapitalist laws under the cover of the bogus cause of black freedom.

In the late 1950s and in the early 1960s a group of economic historians, partly in reaction to the scorn for Reconstruction stimulated by the Dunning School (see chapter 13) and partly from the pull of consensus history which tended to homogenize the past, attacked the very idea of a monolithic set of capitalist interests. Thomas C. Cochran suggested that the Civil War had actually *retarded* economic growth. Bray Hammond described Greenback currency as an emergency measure often denounced as "immoral" rather than a business conspiracy; Robert P. Sharkey disclosed the extent to which currency and tariff issues divided businessmen and Republican leaders; Irwin Unger discovered not an economic revolution between 1860 and 1880 but rather an impressive continuity of economic ideas and events; and Stanley Coben found in the era of Radical Reconstruction a business community far too fragmented for monolithic machinations. Still, these scholars appear to have been too influenced by the pull toward consensus and they may have proven less than they thought. Certainly they indicated some of the pitfalls of naive Marxist approaches and the many difficulties in the Beards' simplistic analysis of "agrarianism" and "capitalism," but they did not preclude more sophisticated and precise economic explanations. A more damaging critique of the Beards was provided by Staughton Lynd (Selection 2) who persuasively criticized the Beards and Turner for neglecting slavery and abolition and Beard for lumping into a single mass the very distinct rural groups of Southern planters, Northern commercial farmers, and frontier subsistence farmers.

In recent analyses of the Civil War and its origins scholars have tended to accept Lynd's emphasis on the slavery issue and to add their own stress on Southern white supremacy. As William W. Freehling demonstrated in 1966 even the South Carolina nullification controversy of the 1830s traditionally traced to inexplicably powerful emotions about tariffs actually developed from that emotional thicket of anxiety, guilt, and aggression centering around slavery and white dominion. Deeply disturbed by Denmark Vesey and Nat Turner and irrationally alarmed by a small, marginal Northern abolitionist movement as an "immediate" threat, South Carolinians risked civil war because they saw the tariff as an expression of a Northern hostility which might well lead to slave revolts, colonization schemes, and ultimately a national emancipation policy generative of "race war" and the destruction of "white civilization."

South Carolina secession in 1860, according to Steven A. Channing's study of 1970, was "the product of logical reasoning within the framework of irrational perception" which could hardly distinguish between Abraham Lincoln and John Brown and firmly predicted that the reign of "Black Republicanism" would soon lead to servile uprisings. Although the reader is struck by the contrast between hysterical Southern rhetoric and Lincoln's calm willingness to promise constitutional guarantees for slavery and vigorous enforcement of the fugitive slave act, to compromise almost everything except the goal of keeping slavery out of the territories, it is still possible to agree with several reviewers of Channing's book that Southern perceptions may not have been quite so irrational. Much of the dominant Southern leadership despised compromise, bristled with aggressiveness, and called for nothing less than a government which would give sustenance to slavery in the territories, in the North or wherever slaveowners chose to take their chattels. No major politician, not even the conservative and racist Democrat Stephen A. Douglas, could have granted Southern demands. Moreover, the loss of the Presidency, in Southern or doughface hands most of the time since 1789, might signal the impending loss of Congress and the Supreme Court and the beginning of an intolerable drift toward a national policy of gradual and compensated emancipation.

For an account of the nation as a whole we must add to Channing's study of a "blundering generation" of Southern planters and politicians fanatically rushing toward civil conflagration, Eric Foner's sympathetic monograph of 1970 (Selection 3) on Northern ideas and motives. Charles Beard had seen in Republicanism sordid motives and the first act of an unhappy drama which would bring the industrial plutocracy to power, but Foner presented a Republican affirmation of success, opportunity and the self-made man sanctified not by the imperial goals of big business but by a middle class ideology which promised social mobility to the worker and the primacy of the small entrepreneur over the man of great wealth. Convinced of their inherent progressiveness, Northerners placed the American combination of dynamic, expanding capitalism with democratic institutions in the forefront of a world-wide movement from absolutism to democracy, aristocracy to equality and backwardness to modernity. (Some like William H. Seward saw the success of American capitalism and democracy as the foundation of a great and allegedly benevolent overseas empire.) In the Republican mind "free labor civilization" needed to fear only a decadent and stagnant South with its hordes of ignorant and degraded slaves and vast numbers of impoverished whites cheated of social mobility. Foner found it perfectly natural that the slavocracy should rebel and that the North should resist.

Foner forcefully characterized the opinions of many Northerners in a generally persuasive book but his interpretation had distortions and oversights. Some readers will reject Foner's sympathy toward a Republican version of manifest destiny which glorified so completely the rapacious thrusts against Indians, Mexicans, and anyone else who got in the way. It is also possible to doubt, as several reviewers did, that any very large number of Northerners were so concerned about the triumph of free labor in the South. Finally, Foner did not deal satisfactorily with racism. While other scholars such as Eugene Genovese and C. Vann Woodward recently argued that the North displayed the most intense racism, Foner goes to the opposite and equally improbable extreme of setting aside a score of scholars to insist that racism did not play a large part in Republican thought.

A more general set of explanations about Civil War and Reconstruction than Channing's or Foner's can be found in political scientist Barrington Moore's comparative study of *The Social Origins of Dictatorship and Democracy*, a world survey of the major revolutionary upheavals of modern times. Moore drew upon both Marxist and Beardian traditions but followed Marx rather than Beard in seeing slavery as the central issue and in accepting Northern victory as the triumph of progressive forces over the reactionary South. For Moore the Civil War was "the last capitalist revolution. . . . the last revolutionary offensive of bourgeois democracy" in the tradition of the English Puritan struggle in the seventeenth century and the French Revolution of 1789. The central question in America did not involve a capitalist North versus a feudal South but rather three often harmonious "forms of capitalist growth," the plantation South, the farming Midwest and the rapidly industrializing Northeast with the slave South for many decades sustaining American industrial growth and supporting the settlement of the Midwest. Indeed, the United States was long open to an enduring and ultraconservative alliance between rising industrialists and the Southern rulers of unfree labor of the kind formed in Germany by emerging capitalists and the Junker masters of the peasantry. However, economic and political changes in sectional alliances and deepening contradictions between the slave South and the more equalitarian North made a slaveowner-Northern capitalist settlement virtually impossible. The South became increasingly unsympathetic toward Western growth not directly beneficial to slavery as the Northeast and the Midwest pushed for expansion and moved toward a mutually profitable exchange of manufactured goods and farm products. Both sections felt the impact of the burgeoning antislavery movement which aroused so much hatred in the South. If the Civil War was not a struggle of capitalists against anticapitalists, it did represent "a sharp break between the two major segments of the ruling classes" which both made war and emancipation possible and a radical alternation of the class structure among whites unlikely. Moore assumed that the economic and social differences among classes provided the basic material of human struggle and left for other scholars the question of whether or not racist ideology and institutions provided independent causal forces in history. After perusing Moore the reader was left with the impression that both sections and general economic explanations could be studied with profit. If Turner's account of the frontier seems largely misleading he still left valid a heritage of concern with sectionalism and if large parts of the Beards' theories must be abandoned they left a challenge for those who would give proper stress to slavery and provide a more complex and sophisticated set of economic interpretations.

BIBLIOGRAPHY

Works Discussed in This Chapter

Beard, Charles A., and Beard, Mary, *The Rise of American Civilization* (2 vols., 1940).

Channing, Steven A., *Crisis of Fear: Secession in South Carolina* (1970).

Coben, Stanley, "Northeastern Businessmen and Radical Reconstruction," *Mississippi Valley Historical Review* (1959).

Cochran, Thomas C., "Did the Civil War Retard Industrialism?" *Mississippi Valley Historical Review* (1961).

Craven, Avery O., *The Coming of the Civil War* (1942).

Foner, Eric, *Free Soil, Free Labor, Free Men: The Ideology of the Republican Party Before the Civil War* (1970).

Freehling, William W., *Prelude to Civil War: The Nullification Controversy in South Carolina, 1816–1836* (1966).

Genovese, Eugene, *In Red and Black: Marxian Explorations in Southern and Afro-American History* (1971).

Hammond, Bray, "The North's Empty Purse, 1861–62," *American Historical Review* (1961), and *Banks and Politics in America from the Revolution to the Civil War* (1957).

Lynd, Staughton, "On Beard, Turner and Slavery," *Journal of Negro History* (1963).

Moore, Barrington, *The Social Origins of Dictatorship and Democracy* (1967).

Nevins, Allan, *Ordeal of the Union* (1947).

Randall, James G., "The Blundering Generation," *Mississippi Valley Historical Review* (1940).

Schlesinger, Arthur, Jr., "The Causes of the Civil War," *Partisan Review* (1949).

Sharkey, Robert P., *Money, Class and Party* (1959).

Turner, Frederick Jackson, *The Frontier in American History* (1920).

Unger, Irwin, "Businessmen and Specie Resumption," *Political Science Quarterly* (1959) and *The Greenback Era* (1964).

Woodward, C. Vann, *American Counterpoint: Slavery and Racism in the North-South Dialogue* (1971).

Suggested Readings

For early works on *Civil War causation* the chief work is Thomas J. Pressly's *Americans Interpret Their Civil War* (1954). A symposium of 1960 found great difficulties in any causal theory. See Cushing Strout's and Lee Benson's fine essays on "Causation and the American Civil War," *History and Theory* (1961). Peter Geyl was critical of Randall and Craven in "The American Civil War and the Problem of Inevitability," *New England Quarterly* (1951) and Geyl, "Synopsis: The American Civil War Viewed from the Netherlands," *Proceedings of the American Philosophical Society* (1962). See also Thomas N. Bonner, "Civil War Historians and the Needless War," *Journal of the History of Ideas* (1956). In 1960 David Donald in "American Historians and the Civil War," *South Atlantic Quarterly*, wondered why historians wrote less and less about the theme. See also Howard K. Beale, "What Historians Have Said About the Causes of the Civil War," *Theory and Practice in Historical Study, Social Science Council Publication* (1946) and David M. Potter, "The Background of the Civil War," *Yearbook of the National Council for the Social Studies* (1961). For a recent antiradical and antiabolitionist essay see John S. Rosenberg, "Toward a New Civil War Revisionism," *The American Scholar* (1969). See the summary article by Joel H. Silbey, "The Civil War Synthesis in American Political History," *Civil War History* (1964).

For *anthologies on the causes of the Civil War* see Kenneth M. Stampp, ed., *Causes of the Civil War* (1959); Edwin C. Rozwenc, ed., *Causes of the American Civil War* (1961); William R. Brock, ed., *The Civil War* (1969); and Hans L. Trefousse, *Causes of the Civil War: Institutional Failure or Human Blunder?* (1971). For a good general bibliography see David Donald, *The Nation in Crisis, 1861–1877* (1969).

For *other causal ideas* see Arthur Bestor, "The American Civil War as a Constitutional Crisis," *American Historical Review* (1964); Paul W. Gates "The Struggle for Land and the Irrepressible Conflict," *Political Science Quarterly* (1957); Wallace D. Farnam's stress on the weakness of American Institutions in "The Weakened Spring of Government: A Study in Nineteenth Century American History," *American Historical Review* (1963); and A. E. Campbell's stress on "isolation" in "An Excess of Isolation: Isolation and the American Civil War," *Journal of Southern History* (1965). See also C. Vann Woodward "Reflections on Two Centennials: The American Civil War," *Yale Review* (1961). For Allan Nevins' changing opinions see his many volumes in the 20 year period from 1947.

Among *recent "needless war" works* see Elbert B. Smith, *The Death of Slavery in the U.S.* (1967); Norman A. Graebner, *Politics and the Crisis of 1860* (1961); David B. Davis, *The Slave Power Conspiracy and the Paranoid Style* (1969); and Roy F. Nichols, *The Disruption of American Democracy* (1948). For a healthy antidote to Davis, etc., see Lara Gara, "Slavery and the Slave Power: A Crucial Distinction," *Civil War History* (1969). See also George Woolfolk, *The Cotton Regency* (1958).

On *Turner and the Beards* see Charles Crowe, "The Emergence of Progressive History," *Journal of the History of Ideas* (1966); Richard Hofstadter, *The Progressive Historians: Turner, Beard, Parrington* (1968); and Bernard C. Borning, *The Political and Social Thought of Charles A. Beard* (1962). For background to Turner and Beard, see Richard Slotkin, *Regeneration Through Violence: The Mythology of the American Frontier, 1600–1860* (1973).

For *Marx's comment on Civil War issues* see the several anthologies of his writings and Gerald Runkle, "Karl Marx and the American Civil War," *Comparative Studies in Society and History* (1964).

For *criticism of the modern economic revisionists* see the attack on Cochran's thesis in Pershing Vartanian, "The Cochran Thesis: A Critique in Statistical Analysis," *Journal of American History* (1964); Allan Solganick, "The Robber Baron Concept and the Revisionists," *Science and Society* (1965); and

Hal Bridges, "The Robber Baron Concept in American History," *Business History Review* (1958).

Two *recent books on the Union war effort* are Eugene Murdock, *Patriotism Limited, 1862–65* (1968) and Murdock, *One Million Men: The Civil War Draft in the North* (1971).

Several *Civil War social and intellectual* titles worth mentioning are George M. Frederickson, *The Inner Civil War, Northern Intellectuals and the War* (1965); Lorman Ratner, *Pre–Civil War Reform, The Variety of Principles and Programs* (1967); and Frank Freidel, ed., *Union Pamphlets of the Civil War, 1861–65* (2 vols., 1967).

Two interesting essays on the *Copperheads* are Robert N. Abzug, "The Copperheads: Historical Approaches to Civil War Dissent in the Midwest," *Indiana Magazine of History* (1970) and Richard O. Curry, "The Union as It Was: A Critique of Recent Interpretations of the Copperheads," *Civil War History* (1967).

On the *international context* see Harold M. Hyman, ed., *Heard Round the World: The Impact Abroad of the American Civil War* (1969) and Joseph M. Hernon, Jr., *Celts, Catholics and Copperheads: Ireland Views the American Civil War* (1969).

On the *Confederacy* see James H. Brewer, *The Confederate Negro: Virginia's Craftsmen and Military Laborers, 1861–1865* (1969) which is painstakingly researched but curiously silent on black resistance. Emory H. Thomas in his thought provoking and imaginatively reasoned but not entirely persuasive *The Confederacy as a Revolutionary Experience* (1971) argues for "an unintended revolution" in which states rights, agrarianism, patriarchy, and an aristocratic and stable society based on slavery, were substantially altered toward centralized nationalism, industrialism, "an incipient proletariat," and a changed status for women. The Confederacy even stood on the verge of abandoning racial slavery. The last point is persuasively disputed by Robert F. Durden in *The Gray and the Black, The Confederate Debate on Emancipation* (1972).

In the current trend toward *political quantification* several works are worthy of attention. Joel Silbey in *The Shrine of Party: Congressional Voting Behavior, 1841–1852* (1967) granted more to party loyalty than to sectionalism. On Northern elites Edward Pessen in *Riches, Class and Power Before the Civil War* (1973) showed that in an alleged age of social mobility men of wealth in an overwhelming majority of cases came from families of affluence and high social status. Thomas B. Alexander in *Sectional Stress and Party Strength: A Computer Analysis of Roll Call Voting Patterns in the U.S. House of Representatives, 1836–1860* (1967) argues for stronger sectional influences in the 1840s and a triumph of sectionalism from 1850 on. See also Allen G. Bogue, "Bloc and Party in the U.S. Senate, 1861–1863," *Civil War History* (1967); Glenn M. Linden, "Radicals and Economic Policies: The House of Representatives, 1861–1873," *Civil War History* (1967); Leonard P. Curry, "Congressional Democrats, 1861–1863, *Civil War History* (1966); and Dean Yarwood, "Legislative Persistence: A Comparison of the U.S. Senate in 1850 and 1860," *Midwest Journal of Political Science* (1968).

On *Northern Doughface* support of the South by businessmen see Thomas O'Connor, *Lords of the Loom: The Cotton Whigs and the Coming of the Civil War* (1968) and Kinley J. Brauer, *Cotton versus Conscience: Massachusetts Whig Politics and Southwestern Expansion, 1843–1848* (1967).

Among the works on *expansion and sectionalism* are Robert W. Johannsen, *Stephen A. Douglas* (1973); Gerald W. Wolff's critiques of the slave power, "Party and Section; The Senate and the Kansas-Nebraska Bill," *Civil War His-*

tory (1972); and "The Slavocracy and the Homestead Problem of 1859," *Agricultural History* (1966). For a critical essay and a sympathetic book on Manifest Destiny, see M. L. Wilson, "Ideological Fruits of Manifest Destiny," *Journal of the Illinois State Historical Society* (1970) and Frederick Merk, *Slavery and the Annexation of Texas* (1972). James A. Rawley thought that emotional hysteria, political irrationality, etc. sprang from a universal American racism. See *Race and Politics, Bleeding Kansas and the Coming of the Civil War* (1969). According to Joseph G. Rayback, responses to the Wilmot Proviso shaped the campaign of 1848. Chaplain W. Morrison makes the Proviso even more central. See Rayback, *Free Soil: The Election of 1848* (1970) and Morrison, *Democratic Politics and Sectionalism: The Wilmot Proviso Controversy* (1967). See also Eric Foner, "The Wilmot Proviso Revisited," *Journal of American History* (1969). On the Fugitive Slave Act and sectionalism see Stanley W. Campbell, *The Slave Catchers: The Enforcement of the Fugitive Slave Law, 1850–1860* (1970).

Several works of the 1960s on the *sectional struggle and secession* are worth examining. George Dangerfield, in *The Awakening of American Nationalism, 1815–1828* (1965), argued that the Compromise of 1820 was probably a mistake which made the Civil War inevitable, and that slavery expansion could have been checked if the North had held firm. Ralph A. Wooster attempted to demonstrate that secession was the will of the Southern white majority. See *The Secession Conventions of the South* (1962). Hamilton Holman, probing the crisis of 1850 in *Prologue to Conflict: The Crisis and the Compromise of 1850* (1964), left the impression that the compromise was unwise, unstable, and possible only through the bribery of certain key Southern congressmen. The "abstract" defenders of slavery were presented as dangerously aggressive in Robert R. Russell, "The Issues in the Congressional Struggle over the Kansas-Nebraska Bill of 1854," *Journal of Southern History* (1963). Robert W. Johannsen was kinder with the "Douglas Democracy" but found flaws there as well as still larger faults among the aggressive defenders of slavery, in "The Douglas Democracy and the Crisis of Disunion," *Civil War History* (1963). Warren J. Donnelly summarized the long debate over "Conspiracy or Popular Support: The Historiography of Southern Support for Secession," *North Carolina Historical Review* (1965). Richard N. Current, in an attempt to pin down Lincoln's role in the coming of the war, followed the President's day-by-day activities during the few weeks before Sumter in *Lincoln and the First Shot* (1963). See also Robert Cruden, *The War That Never Ended: The American Civil War* (1973).

Slavery a Most Pressing Moral Issue*

Arthur M. Schlesinger, Jr.

The Civil War was our great national trauma. A savage fraternal conflict, it released deep sentiments of guilt and remorse—sentiments which
have reverberated through our history and our literature ever since. Literature in the end came to terms with these sentiments by yielding to the
South in fantasy the victory it had been denied in fact; this tendency culminated on the popular level in *Gone with the Wind* and on the highbrow
level in the Nashville cult of agrarianism. But history, a less malleable
medium, was constricted by the intractable fact that the war had taken
place, and by the related assumption that it was, in William H. Seward's
phrase, an "irrepressible conflict," and hence a justified one.

. . . [In the 1930s and 1940s] the writing of history would succumb
to the psychological imperatives which had produced *I'll Take my Stand*
and *Gone with the Wind;* and Professor [James G.] Randall would emerge
as the leader of a triumphant new school of self-styled "revisionists." . . .
[Randall's and Avery Craven's books] brought about a profound reversal
of the professional historian's attitude toward the Civil War. Scholars now
denied the traditional assumption of the inevitability of the war and
boldly advanced the thesis that a "blundering generation" had transformed a "repressible conflict" into a "needless war."

The swift triumph of revisionism came about with very little resistance
or even expressed reservations on the part of the profession. . . . By 1947
Professor Allan Nevins . . . could define the basic problem of the period in
terms which indicated a measured but entire acceptance of revisionism. . . .

The revisionist case, as expounded by Professors Randall and Craven,
has three main premises. First:

(1) that the Civil War was caused by the irresponsible emotionalization
of politics far out of proportion to the real problems involved. The war, as
Randall put it, was certainly not caused by cultural variations nor by
economic rivalries nor by sectional differences; these all existed, but it
was "stupid," as he declared, to think that they required war as a solution. . . .

Nor was the slavery the cause. The issues arising over slavery were in
Randall's judgment "highly artificial, almost fabricated. . . . They produced quarrels out of things that would have settled themselves were it
not for political agitation." Slavery, Craven observed, was in any case a
much overrated problem. It is "perfectly clear," he wrote, "that slavery

* Arthur M. Schlesinger, Jr., "The Causes of the Civil War," *Partisan Review,* 16,
10 (October 1949), 969–81. By permission of the author.

played a rather minor part in the life of the South and of the Negro."

What then was the cause of war? "If one word or phrase were selected to account for the war," wrote Randall, ". . . it would have to be such a word as fanaticism (on both sides), misunderstanding, misrepresentation, or perhaps politics." . . . The "molders of public opinion steadily created the fiction of two distinct peoples." As a result, "distortion led a people into bloody war."

If uncontrolled emotionalism and fanaticism caused the war, how did they get out of hand? Who whipped up the "whipped-up crisis"? Thus the second revisionist thesis:

(2) that sectional friction was permitted to develop into needless war by the inexcusable failure of political leadership in the fifties. "It is difficult to achieve a full realization of how Lincoln's generation stumbled into a ghastly war," wrote Randall. . . .

It was the politicians, charged Craven, who systematically sacrificed peace to their pursuit of power. . . . "These uncalled-for moves and this irresponsible leadership," concluded Craven, blew up a "crack-pot" crusade into a national conflict.

It is hard to tell which was under attack here—the performance of a particular generation or democratic politics in general. But, if the indictment "blundering generation" meant no more than a general complaint that democratic politics placed a premium on emotionalism, then the Civil War would have been no more nor less "needless" than any event in our blundering history. The phrase "blundering generation" must consequently imply that the generation in power in the fifties was *below* the human or historical or democratic average in its blundering. Hence the third revisionist thesis:

(3) that the slavery problem could have been solved without war. For, even if slavery were as unimportant as the revisionists have insisted, they would presumably admit that it constituted the real sticking point in the relations between the sections. They must show therefore that there were policies with which a non-blundering generation could have resolved the slavery crisis and averted war; and that these policies were so obvious that the failure to adopt them indicated blundering and stupidity of a peculiarly irresponsible nature. . . .

The revisionists have shown only a most vague and sporadic awareness of this problem. "Any kind of sane policy in Washington in 1860 might have saved the day for nationalism," remarked Craven; but he did not vouchsafe the details of these sane policies; we would be satisfied to know about one.[1] Similarly Randall declared that there were few policies of the fifties he would wish repeated if the period were to be lived over again; but he was not communicative about the policies he would wish pursued. . . .

In view of this reticence on a point so crucial to the revisionist argument, it is necessary to reconstruct the possibilities that might lie in the

---

[1] It is fair to say that Professor Craven seems in recent years to have modified his earlier extreme position; see his article "The Civil War and the Democratic Process," *Abraham Lincoln Quarterly* (June 1947).

back of revisionism. Clearly there could be only two "solutions" to the slavery problem: the preservation of slavery, or its abolition.

Presumably the revisionists would not regard the preservation of slavery as a possible solution. Craven, it is true, has argued that "most of the incentives to honest and sustained effort, to a contented, well-rounded life, might be found under slavery. . . ." . . . But Craven would doubtless admit that, however jolly this system might have been, its perpetuation would have been, to say the least, impracticable.

If, then, revisionism has rested on the assumption that the nonviolent abolition of slavery was possible, such abolition could conceivably have come about through internal reform in the South; through economic exhaustion of the slavery system in the South; or through some government project for gradual and compensated emancipation. Let us examine these possibilities.

(1) *The internal reform argument.* The South, the revisionists have suggested, might have ended the slavery system if left to its own devices; only the abolitionists spoiled everything by letting loose a hysteria which caused the southern ranks to close in self-defense.

This revisionist argument would have been more convincing if the decades of alleged antislavery feeling in the South had produced any concrete results. . . .

In any case, it is difficult for historians seriously to suppose that northerners could have denied themselves feelings of disapproval over slavery. To say that there "should" have been no abolitionists in America before the Civil War is about as sensible as to say that there "should" have been no anti-Nazis in the 1930s. . . .

. . . And, just as abolitionism was inevitable, so too was the southern reaction against it—a reaction which, as Professor Clement Eaton has ably shown, steadily drove the free discussion of slavery out of the South. The extinction of free discussion meant, of course, the absolute extinction of any hope of abolition through internal reform.

(2) *The economic exhaustion argument.* Slavery, it has been pointed out, was on the skids economically. It was overcapitalized and inefficient; it immobilized both capital and labor; its one-crop system was draining the soil of fertility; it stood in the way of industrialization. As the South came to realize these facts, a revisionist might argue, it would have moved to abolish slavery for its own economic good. As Craven put it, slavery "may have been almost ready to break down of its own weight."

This argument assumed, of course, that southerners would have recognized the causes of their economic predicament and taken the appropriate measures. Yet such an assumption would be plainly contrary to history and to experience. . . . Nothing in the historical record suggests that the southern ruling class was preparing to deviate from its traditional pattern of self-exculpation long enough to take such a drastic step as the abolition of slavery.

(3) *Compensated emancipation.* Abraham Lincoln made repeated proposals of compensated emancipation. In his annual message to Congress of December 1, 1862, he set forth a detailed plan by which states, on an agreement to abolish slavery by 1900, would receive government bonds

in proportion to the number of slaves emancipated. Yet, even though Lincoln's proposals represented a solution of the problem conceivably gratifying to the slaveholder's purse as well as to his pride, they got nowhere. Two-thirds of the border representatives rejected the scheme, even when personally presented to them by Lincoln himself. And, of course, only the pressure of war brought compensated emancipation its limited hearing of 1862.

Still, granted these difficulties, does it not remain true that other countries abolished slavery without internal convulsions? . . . . Brazil and Russia were able to face servitude "as a national question" because it was, in fact, a national question. Neither country had the American problem of the identification of compact sectional interests with the survival of the slavery system. In the second place, there was no race problem at all in Russia; and, though there was a race problem in Brazil, the more civilized folkways of that country relieved racial differences. . . .

. . . The hard fact, indeed, is that the revisionists have not tried seriously to describe the policies by which the slavery problem could have been peacefully resolved. They have resorted instead to broad affirmations of faith: if only the conflict could have been staved off long enough, then somehow, we could have worked something out. It is legitimate, I think, to ask how? where? what?—at least, if these affirmations of faith are to be used as the premise for castigating the unhappy men who had the practical responsibility for finding solutions and failed. . . .

The revisionists first glided over the implications of the fact that the slavery system was producing a closed society in the South. . . . Professor Frank L. Owsley, the southern agrarian, has described inadvertently but accurately the direction in which the slave South was moving. "The abolitionists and their political allies were threatening the existence of the South as seriously as the Nazis threaten the existence of England," wrote Owsley in 1940. . . . With the book burning, the censorship of the mails, the gradual illegalization of dissent, the South was in process of creating a real machinery of repression in order more effectively "to defend its existence." No society, I suppose, encourages criticism of its basic institutions. Yet, when a democratic society acts in self-defense, it does so at least in the name of human dignity and freedom. When a society based on bond slavery acts to eliminate criticism of its peculiar institution, it outlaws what a believer in democracy can only regard as the abiding values of man. When the basic institutions are evil, in other words, the effect of attempts to defend their existence can only be the moral and intellectual stultification of the society.

A society closed in the defense of evil institutions thus creates moral differences far too profound to be solved by compromise. Such a society forces upon every one, both those living at the time and those writing about it later, the necessity for a moral judgment; and the moral judgment in such cases becomes an indispensable factor in the historical understanding.

The revisionists . . . tried hard to pronounce no moral judgments at all. . . . Slavery became important, in Craven's phrase, "only as a very ancient labor system, probably at this time rather near the end of its existence"; the attempt to charge this labor system with moral meanings was "a creation of inflamed imaginations." Randall, talking of the Kansas-Nebraska Act, could describe it as "a law intended to subordinate the slavery question and hold it in *proper* proportion" (my italics). I have quoted Randall's even more astonishing argument that, because major controversies between downstate and metropolis in Illinois stopped short of war, there was reason to believe that the Civil War could have been avoided....

Because the revisionists felt no moral urgency themselves, they deplored as fanatics those who did feel it, or brushed aside their feelings as the artificial product of emotion and propaganda....

By denying themselves insight into the moral dimension of the slavery crisis . . . the revisionists denied themselves a historical understanding of the intensities that caused the crisis. . . . To say that the Civil War was fought over the "unreal" issue of slavery in the territories is like saying that World War II was fought over the "unreal" issue of the invasion of Poland. The democracies could not challenge fascism inside Germany any more than opponents of slavery could challenge slavery inside the south; but the extension of slavery, like the extension of fascism, was an act of aggression which made a moral choice inescapable. . . . Every historian . . . imports his own set of moral judgments into the writing of history by the very process of interpretation; and the phrase "every historian" includes the category "revisionist." . . . The whole revisionist attitude toward abolitionists and radicals, repeatedly characterized by Randall as "unctuous" and "intolerant," overflows with the moral feeling which is so virtuously excluded from discussions of slavery.

An acceptance of the fact of moral responsibility does not license the historian to roam through the past ladling out individual praise and blame. . . . But it does mean that there are certain essential issues on which it is necessary for the historian to have a position if he is to understand the great conflicts of history....

. . . And human slavery is certainly one of the few issues of whose evil we can be sure. It is not just "a very ancient labor system"; it is also a betrayal of the basic values of our Christian and democratic tradition. No historian can understand the circumstances which led to its abolition until he writes about it in its fundamental moral context....

. . . The unhappy fact is that man occasionally works himself into a logjam; and that the logjam must be burst by violence. We know that well enough from the experience of the last decade. Are we to suppose that some future historian will echo Professor Nevins' version of the "failure" of the 1850s and write: "The primary task of statesmanship in the 1930s was to furnish a workable adjustment between the United States and Germany, while offering strong inducements to the German people to abandon the police state and equal persuasions to the Americans to help the Nazis rather than scold them?" . . .

The problem of the inevitability of the Civil War, of course, is in its essence a problem devoid of meaning. The revisionist attempt to argue that the war could have been avoided by "any kind of sane policy" is of interest less in its own right than as an expression of a characteristically sentimental conception of man and of history....

We delude ourselves when we think that history teaches us that evil will be "outmoded" by progress and that politics consequently does not impose on us the necessity for decision and for struggle. If historians are to understand the fullness of the social dilemma they seek to reconstruct, they must understand that sometimes there is no escape from the implacabilities of moral decision. When social conflicts embody great moral issues, these conflicts cannot be assigned for solution to the invincible march of progress; nor can they be bypassed with "objective" neutrality. . . .

To reject the moral actuality of the Civil War is to foreclose the possibility of an adequate account of its causes. More than that, it is to misconceive and grotesquely to sentimentalize the nature of history. . . . Man generally is entangled in insoluble problems; history is consequently a tragedy in which we are all involved, whose keynote is anxiety and frustration, not progress and fulfillment. Nothing exists in history to assure us that the great moral dilemmas can be resolved without pain; we cannot therefore be relieved from the duty of moral judgment on issues so appalling and inescapable as those involved in human slavery; nor can we be consoled by sentimental theories about the needlessness of the Civil War into regarding our own struggles against evil as equally needless. . . .

Turner and Beard
Neglected Slavery*

Staughton Lynd

The significance of slavery in American history is a largely unexplored theme. Despite the recent increase of interest in such topics as abolitionism, prejudice, and the plantation as a social system, these subjects tend to be kept separated (one might almost say, segregated) from the rest of American history. We have not yet begun to view slavery as a key to the meaning of our national experience.

The thesis of this essay is that the significance of slavery in American history has been obscured partly because the twin giants of modern American historiography, Frederick Jackson Turner and Charles Beard, systematically minimized its importance. Believing that a sentimental memory of the Civil War was being used to veil an emerging conflict between the capitalist and the common man, these two great historians

---

* Staughton Lynd, "On Turner, Beard, and Slavery," *Journal of Negro History* (1963).

went to an opposite extreme. Turner, I shall argue, attempted to shift attention from slavery to the frontier, and in so doing tended to forget that there was a Southwestern as well as a Northwestern frontier[1] and that Simon Legree was a frontier farmer. Beard, similarly, portrayed slavery both in the era of the Revolution and at the time of the Civil War as merely a form of "agrarianism." Thereby Beard blurred the fact that the Constitution was not a victory of capitalism over slavery, but a compromise between capitalism and slavery, and accomplished the difficult feat of presenting the Civil War as a revolution, while deftly moving offstage the abolitionist revolutionaries who made it. By minimizing the significance of slavery, Turner and Beard inevitably also minimized the significance of abolitionism, and paved the way for the revisionist view of the abolitionist as an impractical fanatic.

For both Turner and Beard, the characteristic social struggle in American history was that between the Eastern financier and the Western farmer. "We may trace the contest between the capitalist and the democratic pioneer from the earliest colonial days," Turner wrote; and Beard set this quotation at the beginning of his *Economic Origins of Jeffersonian Democracy*.[2] Both were heavily influenced by the Populist Revolt of the 1890s, and tended to use the Populist analogy in interpreting earlier American history. Thus Beard entitled the chapter of his *Rise of American Civilization* which dealt with the 1780s, "Populism and Reaction." Turner, likewise, said in an introduction to Orin Libby's pathbreaking study of the vote on the United States Constitution:[3]

> the present Populistic agitation finds its stronghold in those western and southern regions whose social and economic conditions are in many respects strikingly like those existing in 1787 in the areas that opposed the ratification of the Constitution.

The Populist analogy led both historians to believe that throughout American history "the democratic party was the agrarian element."[4] And in their histories those aristocratic agrarians, the slaveholders of the South, quietly drop out of sight.

The ironic result was that although Turner and Beard called for a new history written from the standpoint of "the fourth estate, the great mass of people,"[5] they ended in directing attention away from the most exploited group in our history: the Negroes. In their indifference to the Negro, Turner and Beard were typical of Northern liberals at the turn of the century. This attitude was also common among historians. Turner, as

---

[1] Avery Craven has commented on Turner's tendency to assume that his native Middle West was typical. . . . (Introduction to Frederick Jackson Turner, *The United States, 1830–1850: The Nation and its Sections* [New York, 1935], vii.)

[2] Turner used this phrase in his "Social Forces in American History" (1911), *The Frontier in American History* (New York, 1920), 325.

[3] Orin G. Libby, *The Geographical Distribution of the Vote of the Thirteen States on the Federal Constitution, 1787–8* (Madison, 1894), vi–vii.

[4] Charles A. Beard, *An Economic Interpretation of the Constitution of the United States* (New York, 1913), 258.

[5] Turner, "The Significance of History" (1891), *The Early Writings of Frederick Jackson Turner,* ed. Everett E. Edwards and Fulmer Mood (Madison, 1938), 47. . . .

will appear, followed his University of Wisconsin colleague Ulrich Phillips' appraisal of slavery, and Beard's views on Reconstruction were akin to those of his fellow Columbians, Burgess and Dunning. Yet there was special irony in the fact that as Turner and Beard were neglecting the Negro and exalting the frontier Populist, many real Populists in the South were building a new, if fleeting, unity between white and Negro tenants. Equally paradoxical was the fact that the Negro's betrayal by the Republican Party had been engineered by the same force which Turner and Beard denounced: capitalist finance.[6] In their neglect of the Negro, therefore, Turner and Beard reflected the viewpoint of a social group which they opposed and ignored the efforts of a group which they championed; in this aspect of their writings, they stood not with the farmer but with the financier.

In "The Significance of the Frontier in American History," Turner made it quite clear that he sought to displace a view of American history which stressed the struggle over slavery, a view symbolized at that time by the writing of Edward Von Holst. "When American history comes to be rightly viewed," Turner said, "it will be seen that the slavery question is an incident."[7] . . . For a generation since 1861, slavery has been cast as the central character of the historical drama. Now, in the belief that he expressed the new needs of a new day, Turner brought the frontier forward in its stead.

The most troublesome obstacle to Turner's frontier thesis was the Southwestern frontier with its plantation pioneers. Here the covered wagons had been followed by long lines of slaves; here, as Jefferson Davis observed in 1861, it was slaves not freemen who had made farms out of the wilderness; here the structure of power was aristocratic not egalitarian,[8] here the effect of frontier life was to coarsen and brutalize the peculiar institution, not to humanize it. Great historian that he was, Turner sensed this contradiction in his argument. His answer was that there had originally existed in the Southern uplands a democratic frontier society similar to that in the Northwest, but that the advance of slavery had overlaid and destroyed it. . . . Again and again in later writings Turner repeated the thought that originally, before "the fall" as it were, the Southern frontier like the Northern frontier had been a place of democracy and freedom.[9]

---

6 The most recent study concludes: "Far from being the exclusive work of social and intellectual forces, the sectional realignment of the last quarter of the nineteenth century was largely the product of powerful economic forces. More than any other Northern groups, merchants engaged in Southern trade and Eastern industrialists frustrated Republican attempts to stress the war issues." (Stanley P. Hirshson, *Farewell to the Bloody Shirt: Northern Republicans and the Southern Negro, 1877–1893* [Bloomington, 1962], 252).

7 "The Significance of the Frontier in American History" (1893), *Early Writings*, 213.

8 For a recent, well-documented exposition of this point, see Stanley Elkins and Eric McKitrick, "A Meaning for Turner's Frontier. Part II: The Southwest Frontier and New England," *Political Science Quarterly*, 69 (1954), 565–83.

9 See "Problems in American History" (1904), *The Significance of Sections in American History* (New York, 1932), 12–13; "Is Sectionalism Dying Away?" (1908),

The belief that slavery was a late-coming and transitional force in the Southern interior underlay Turner's conception of Andrew Jackson, a key to the whole of Turner's thought. For Turner, Jackson was a personification of frontier ideals of "human rights" and "democracy." . . . . Throughout his life Turner vigorously defended the proposition that as late as 1830 the small farmer was the dominant social type of the Southwest, his "persistent content against slavery" still in doubt.[10]

Turner's picture of the Southwest in Jackson's day is not convincing. Professor Abernethy has recently summed up a lifetime of research on the problem with the statement that by 1820 "the slave-owning planter was now the pioneer."[11] During Turner's lifetime, Edward Channing suggested that Jackson was a slaveholder who represented not frontier farmers but a solid slave South. . . . [Turner, however, insisted that] Andrew Jackson "was not so much a cotton planter and slaveholder as a personification of Western wishes and Western will."[12]

. . . The old division of the South into democratic upland and aristocratic Black Belt still revealed itself, said Turner, in primary elections "in which the negro issue is eliminated," although that division had been "obliterated in large measure in the era of civil war and reconstruction and in the later Solid South under the influence of the negro problem."[13] Is it merely hypersensitiveness that makes the reader today perceive in these words a wish that not only "the Negro problem" but the Negro himself could, somehow, be "eliminated" from the American scene? Perhaps not; for coincidentally with the founding of the National Association for the Advancement of Colored People, Turner was writing:[14]

> the negro is still the problem of the South and while he remains there will be a Southern sectionalism. If the negro were removed, it seems not unlikely that the unity of the Mississippi Valley would once more have free play.

Turner went so far as to perceive in the triumph of the red-neck and Jim Crow a victory for frontier egalitarianism. . . . Only a man profoundly

---

ibid., 293–95; "The Problem of the West" (1896), *The Frontier in American History*, 216–17; "The Old West" (1908), ibid., 91 ff., 114 ff.; "Dominant Forces in Western Life" (1897), ibid., 241; *The Rise of the New West, 1819–1829* (New York, 1906), 52–53, 183; *The United States, 1830–1850*, 18, 30–31.

10 *The United States, 1830–1850*, 18; "The Old West" (1908), *The Frontier*, 122.

11 Thomas Perkins Abernethy, *The South in the New Nation, 1789–1819* (Baton Rouge, 1961), 475. See also Abernethy, *From Frontier to Plantation in Tennessee* (Chapel Hill, 1932), 208: "Slaves had been brought out by Robertson and the earliest settlers and figured in the life of the frontier stations. . . . In 1795 the slave population of Middle Tennessee was more than 20 percent of the whole. . . .

In 1820, there were more than 350,000 slaves in the states and territories of the frontier South (Kentucky, Tennessee, Alabama, Mississippi, Louisiana, Arkansas, Missouri, and western Georgia). In none were slaves less than 10 percent of the total population; in Mississippi and Louisiana they were more than 40 percent. (For these statistics, see Bureau of the Census, *A Century of Population Growth* . . . [Washington, 1909], 82, 133, 222). . . .

12 *The United States, 1830–1850*, 31–32.

13 "Geographical Influences in American Political History" (1914), *Sections*, 190.

14 "Is Sectionalism in America Dying Away?" (1908), ibid., 307.

insensitive to the experience of one-fifth of his fellow citizens could have spoken, in 1904, of "the wonderful development of the nation since the Reconstruction period," or could have called the generation 1889–1924 "these marvelous years."[15]

Tolerance toward the institution of slavery and intolerance toward the abolitionist movement are attitudes usually found together, for they support and supplement each other. So it was with Turner. . . . Most explicitly, Turner wrote:

> It would seem that Northern men, in their conclusion that the slave was unhappy, tended to attribute to him their own feelings and reactions to the conditions under which he lived. In general, he was sufficiently fed, with a coarse diet, adequately clothed, but poorly housed (though not to such a degree as to produce discontent in the slave's mind), and allowed opportunity for expressing the natural joyousness of the African temperament; and hardship was felt rather by individuals than by the mass of slaves.[16]

Abolitionism, accordingly, was mentioned by Turner (on the rare occasions when he mentioned it at all) as a diversion of the energies of American reform from its proper ends. . . .

It would have been difficult for any historian who identified himself so completely with the advance of the white settler across the continent to avoid insensitivity toward the victims of this process. Though he departed from the emphasis on Teutonic institutions prominent in the late nineteenth century, Turner did not altogether escape the biological presuppositions of the "germ" theory. "American colonization," he wrote in the early 1890s, "is part of a great historic movement—the Aryan migrations."[17] The American Indian was for Turner an obstacle in the path: Red Cloud of the Sioux, for example, was described by Turner as one who resisted "the march of civilization."[18] Most flagrant, perhaps because Turner's hero Jackson was involved, was Turner's attitude toward the removal of the Cherokees from Georgia. His account of the expulsion of this civilized nation, possessed of an alphabet, a newspaper, and a written constitution, began as follows: "From the beginning of the nation, the Indians on the borders of the settled area of Georgia were a menace and an obstacle to her development."[19] Turner was, in fact, very much a believer in Manifest Destiny. . . .

. . . [Turner] confined his sympathies to those of his countrymen who were also white, and cut him off from the new viewpoints toward American history suggested by the experience of "the fugitive slave, and the

---

15 "Problems in American History" (1904), *Sections*, 19; "Since the Foundations" (1924), ibid., 215.

16 *The United States, 1830–1850*, 16.

17 Introduction to extension lectures (1891), quoted in *Early Writings*, 33 n.

18 "The Middle West," *The Frontier*, 144.

19 See the combined excerpts from Turner's writings on the Cherokee removal in *The Removal of the Cherokee Nation*, ed. Louis Filler and Allen Guttmann (Boston, 1962), 102–5.

Mexican prisoner on parole, and the Indian come to plead the wrongs of his race."[20]

Charles Beard . . . characterized the attitude of slaves during the Civil War as a blend of contentment, affection for their owners, inertia, and helplessness.[21] Beard's approach to slavery, whether in the era of the American Revolution or in the period of the Civil War, was characterized above all by a tendency to regard slavery as merely a form of "agrarianism" [and] . . . to lump together three very different groups: frontier subsistence farmers, Northern commercial farmers, and Southern plantation owners. . . .

. . . Describing the irrepressible conflict as one between Northern capitalism and Southern agrarianism, Beard argued that "the institution of slavery was not the fundamental issue" on the ground that no major political party, including the Republican Party of 1860, put the abolition of slavery in its platform.[22] This was strange reasoning for a historian whose stock-in-trade was to discern the economic motives which underlay men's declared intentions. And why did Beard take at face value the planks on tariffs, railroads, and homesteads in the platform of the Republican Party, but disregard the equally explicit statements of Alexander Stephens and Jefferson Davis that slavery was the cornerstone of the Confederacy? . . .

If for Beard the Civil War was a bloodbath inspired by sordid motives, Reconstruction was an equally self-interested attempt by Northern capitalists to ensure the fruits of victory. Don Fehrenbacher comments that "by disparaging the outcome of the war and the motives of Radical Republicanism, the Beard thesis tended to merge with the Dunning interpretation of Reconstruction."[23] Particularly noteworthy is Beard's remark about Negro suffrage in the Reconstruction period, that it "was tried with results which, to a large degree, would have been ludicrous if they had not been pitiable."[24] Beard's shallow and essentially uninterested attitude toward the adventure of Black Reconstruction is another illustration of the point made earlier, that to minimize the significance of slavery is to miss the meaning of the struggle against slavery, too.

Less obvious is the fact that Beard also neglected the impact of slavery in his most famous historical analysis, *An Economic Interpretation of the Constitution of the United States.* Here Beard's self-alienation from the abolitionist tradition cost him dearly, for he neglected entirely the abolitionist critique of the Constitution as a covenant with death and an agree-

---

[20] The quoted phrase is, of course, from Henry David Thoreau's *Essay on Civil Disobedience.*

[21] Charles and Mary Beard, *The Rise of American Civilization* (New York, 1940), 2, 116. At the same point Beard says of the slaves before the Civil War: "At any rate they had made no striking development in intelligence."

[22] Beard, *Rise of American Civilization,* 2, 40.

[23] Don E. Fehrenbacher, "Disunion and Reunion," *The Reconstruction of American History,* ed. John Higham (New York, 1962), 110.

[24] *American Government and Politics* (New York, 1910), 86.

ment with hell because of its compromise with slavery. Beard noted the
clauses of the Constitution protecting slavery; but slavery as an independent force in the shaping and ratification of the document escaped
him, because it could not be fitted into the conflict of capitalism and
agrarianism which, in this connection as in others, he considered quintessential.

Precise in so much else, Beard's famous book is strangely vague and
confused in its handling of slavery. Was property in slaves "personalty"
or "realty"? Beard wavered. . . .

This ambiguity in the economic analysis of slavery led to confusion in
Beard's treatment of the politics of the slaveholders in the ratification
struggle. Indeed, it would be more accurate to say that Beard nowhere
squarely confronted the question of whether the Southern slaveholders
were Federalists or Anti-Federalists. In surveying the ratification process
in the several states, Beard built on Libby's conclusion that voters favoring the Constitution were concentrated near the coast; but, following
Libby, he chose to consider Tidewater-Virginia as "the region of the large
towns, and where commercial interests were predominant" rather than
as the region of densest slaveholding, and to characterize coastal South
Carolina by saying, "its mercantile and commercial interests were important."[25] Libby's map should have made clear to Beard what has since
been demonstrated in detail, that the great slaveholders were for the most
part Federalist,[26] but . . . in *The Economic Origins of Jeffersonian Democracy* Beard came down on the wrong side. . . . [of] the familiar capitalist-
agrarian dualism.[27] . . . Beard went on . . . to reiterate his view that the
core of both the Anti-Federalists of 1788 and the Jeffersonian Republicans of 1800 was made up of "backwoods agrarians" and "farmers." . . .
[Then he introduced] the idea of "the agrarian masses led by an aristocracy of slave-owning planters." . . .

. . . Turner . . . had set these two groups in fiercest opposition, and
Beard himself conceded that antagonism between them was "natural."
But, Beard went on, "in a conflict with capitalism, the agrarians rallied
around that agrarian class which had the cultural equipment for dominant direction," and so, by "a curious freak of fortune," the most aristocratic group in the nation became the spokesman for frontier democracy.[28] This was a suggestive formulation. It helped to explain how slaveowning Andrew Jackson had become a spokesman for the hill farmers
of Tennessee. But it did *not* explain why the Southern slaveholders, enemies of Hamiltonian Federalism in 1800, had worked with the Federalists

---

[25] These phrases are Libby's, quoted by Beard, *Economic Interpretation*, 285, 288.

[26] See Main, *Antifederalists*, 219 n., 232, 245. It is possible that Beard picked up
the idea that Southern slaveholders largely opposed the Constitution from Federalist
polemics of the 1790s. . . .

[27] *The Economic Origins of Jeffersonian Democracy* (New York 1915), 464–65.

[28] Ibid., 398–99. Schlesinger repeats this formulation in his *Age of Jackson*, 20:
"Only in the planting South did agriculture possess concentrated holdings, alert
leadership and a compulsion to run the state. To the Southern planters thus fell the
main responsibility of opposing the Hamiltonian tendencies in the government."
Beard himself quotes Richard Hildreth, *History of the United States* (1856 ed.), 4,
348–50.

to make the Constitution in 1788. Beard wrongly supposed that the clash of 1800 was a continuation of the alignment of 1788, whereas in fact the party battles of the 1790s represented a breaking-up of the coalition which drafted and promoted the Constitution.

Adequately to explain the forces behind the Constitution, Beard would have had to jettison his fundamental dichotomy of "personalty" and "realty," and to recognize that men of wealth, rural as well as urban, had joined to make a stronger national government. This would have been just as "economic" an interpretation as the interpretation Beard proposed.[29] But Beard like Turner was wedded to a particular economic interpretation which aligned all agrarians, rich or poor, freehold-farming or plantation-owning, against capitalism. And so, Beard failed to see that the Constituton was a compromise between capitalists and slaveholders, the product as much of James Madison and the South Carolina Pinckneys as of Hamilton, Gouverneur Morris, and James Wilson. . . .

In summary, it is clear that Turner and Beard sought to turn the attention of historians away from slavery toward the struggle of "capitalism" with "agrarianism." Much was gained thereby; but any sharply defined insight must throw some things into shadow as it illuminates others, and the effect of the neglect of slavery by Turner and Beard has been to postpone the day when slavery will be recognized as one of the two or three distinctive themes of the American experience. When that day comes, it will seem grotesque that historians of the 1950s proposed "equality" as the concept which best enclosed the meaning of American history, or found the uniqueness of the American story in the absence of feudalism, while forgetting the presence of slavery.

It is past time for American historians to expose themselves to the presence of slavery, to the full force and the pain of it. Only then can they begin to understand the meaning for all American history of the great and terrible reality which the Founding Fathers of this country did not hesitate to call its original sin.

---

[29] E. James Ferguson, for example, interprets the Constitution from an economic standpoint but sharply disavows Beard's dichotomy of "personalty" and "realty" ("The Forces Behind the Constitution," *William and Mary Quarterly,* 3rd Series, 19 [1962], 436).

The Free Labor North Versus the Slave South*

Eric Foner

. . . The concept of "free labor" lay at the heart of the Republican ideology, and expressed a coherent social outlook, a model of the good society. Political anti-slavery was not merely a negative doctrine, an attack on southern slavery and the society built upon it; it was an affirmation of the superiority of the social system of the North—a dynamic, expanding capitalist society, whose achievements and destiny were almost wholly the result of the dignity and opportunities which it offered the average laboring man.

The dignity of labor was a constant theme of ante-bellum northern culture and politics. . . .

Belief in the dignity of labor was not, of course, confined to the Republican party or to the ante-bellum years; it has been part of American culture from the very beginning. In large part, it can be traced to the fact that most Americans came from a Protestant background, in which the nobility of labor was an article of faith. One does not need to accept in its entirety Max Weber's association of the "Protestant ethic" with the rise of capitalism in Europe to believe that there is much validity in Weber's insight that the concept of "calling" provided the psychological underpinning for capitalist values. Weber pointed out that in Calvinist theology each man had an occupation or calling to which he was divinely appointed. To achieve success in this calling would serve the glory of God, and also provide visible evidence that an individual was among the few predestined to enter heaven. The pursuit of wealth thus became a way of serving God on earth, and labor, which had been imposed on fallen man as a curse, was transmuted into a religious value, a Christian duty. And the moral qualities which would ensure success in one's calling— honesty, frugality, diligence, punctuality, and sobriety—became religious obligations. Weber described the Protestant outlook on life as "worldly asceticism," since idleness, waste of time, and conspicuous display or expenditure for personal enjoyment were incompatible with its basic values.[1] . . .

* By permission of the publisher from *Free Soil, Free Labor, Free Men: The Ideology of the Republican Party Before the Civil War* (New York: Oxford University Press, 1970). Copyright by Eric Foner.

[1] Max Weber, *The Protestant Ethic and the Spirit of Capitalism* (New York, 1958 ed.), passim. Cf. Christopher Hill, "Protestantism and the Rise of Capitalism," in Frederick J. Fisher, ed., *Essays in the Economic and Social History of Tudor and Stuart England* (Cambridge, 1961), 15–39; Stuart Bruchey, *The Roots of American Economic Growth 1607–1861* (New York, 1965), 42–43, 197.

Contemporaries and historians agree that the average American of the ante-bellum years was driven by an inordinate desire to improve his condition in life, and by boundless confidence that he could do so. Economic success was the standard by which men judged their social importance, and many observers were struck by the concentration on work, with the aim of material advancement, which characterized Americans. . . .

The Republican idea of free labor was a product of this expanding, enterprising, competitive society. It is important to recognize that in ante-bellum America, the word "labor" had a meaning far broader than its modern one. Andrew Jackson, for example, defined as "the producing classes" all those whose work was directly involved in the production of goods—farmers, planters, laborers, mechanics, and small businessmen. Only those who profited from the work of others, or whose occupations were largely financial, or promotional, such as speculators, bankers, and lawyers, were excluded from this definition. . . . In general . . . Republicans would agree with Horace Greeley that labor included "useful doing in any capacity or vocation." They thus drew no distinction between a "laboring class" and what we could call the middle class. With Webster, they considered the farmer, the small businessman, and the independent craftsman, all as "laborers."[2]

If the Republicans saw "labor" as substantially different from the modern-day notion of the "working class," it was partly because the line between capitalist and worker was to a large extent blurred in the ante-bellum northern economy, which centered on the independent farm and small shop. Moreover, for the Republicans, social mobility was an essential part of northern society. The ante-bellum Republicans praised the virtues of the enterprising life, and viewed social mobility as the glory of northern society. . . .

In the free labor outlook, the objective of social mobility was not great wealth, but the middle-class goal of economic independence. For Republicans, "free labor" meant labor with economic choices, with the opportunity to quit the wage-earning class. A man who remained all his life dependent on wages for his livelihood appeared almost as unfree as the southern slave.[3] There was nothing wrong, of course, with working for wages for a time, if the aim were to acquire enough money to start one's own farm or business. . . .

The contradictions and ambiguities of the free labor ideology, the tension between its conservative aspects and its stress on equality of opportunity and an open society, reflected the world view of the northern middle class. If the social outlook of the Republican party was in many ways conservative, it was not because it defended privilege but because Republicans were satisfied with the economic and social order they per-

---

[2] Springfield *Republican*, January 16, 1858; Horace Greeley, *Hints Towards Reforms* (New York, 1850), 9. Cf. Bernard Mandel, *Labor: Free and Slave* (New York, 1955), 13.

[3] Arnold W. Green, *Henry Charles Carey, Nineteenth Century Sociologist* (Philadelphia, 1951), 118–19; Greeley, *Hints*, 354; *The Address of the Southern and Western Liberty Convention to the People of the United States; the Proceedings and Resolutions of the Convention* . . . (Cincinnati, 1845), 21.

ceived in the North. In post-war years, the same cult of the self-made man and of economic success would come to be a justification of every action and privilege of the business class, but in the ante-bellum world of the Republicans, the promise of economic advancement implied not the rise of big business but the guarantee of mobility to the laborer. . . .

To the self-confident society of the North, economic development increasing social mobility, and the spread of democratic institutions were all interrelated parts of nineteenth century "progress." . . . The important point was that material and moral developments were but two sides of the same coin. "Good roads and bridges," wrote the New York *Tribune*, "are as necessary an ingredient to the spread of intelligence, social intercourse, and improvement in population, as schools and churches." An Indiana Republican Congressman declared on the eve of the Civil War that throughout the world, manufactures and commerce were "the missionaries of freedom," and William Henry Seward agreed that "popular government follows in the track of the steam-engine and the telegraph."[4] It was but a short step, and one which Republicans took almost unanimously, to the view that for a society as for individuals, economic progress was a measure of moral worth. As Henry Adams later recalled, he was taught in his youth that "bad roads meant bad morals." On this basis, northern society was eminently successful. But when Republicans turned their gaze southward, they encountered a society that seemed to violate all the cherished values of the free labor ideology, and seemed to pose a threat to the very survival of what Republicans called their "free-labor civilization."[5] . . .

The whole mentality and flavor of southern life thus seemed antithetical to that of the North. Instead of progress, the South represented decadence, instead of enterprise, laziness. "Thus it appears," wrote the anti-slavery writer and historian Richard Hildreth, "that one plain and obvious effect of the slaveholding system is to deaden in every class of society that *spirit of industry* essential to the increase of public wealth."[6] To those with visions of a steadily growing nation, slavery was an intolerable hindrance to national achievement. Seward, who believed that a stable and prosperous American nation could serve as the base for an overseas empire which would spread American influence and power throughout the world, saw most clearly the way in which slavery stood in the way of national greatness.[7] Slavery, he declared, was "incompatible with all . . . the elements of the security, welfare, and greatness of nations." It im-

---

4 Carey, *Past, Present, Future*, 415; Greeley, *Hints*, 49; New York *Tribune*, August 22, 1856; *Congressional Globe*, 36 Congress, 2 Session, 1042; Seward, *Seward*, 2, 359.

5 [Henry Adams], *The Education of Henry Adams* (Boston, 1918), 47; *Congressional Globe*, 36 Congress, 1 Session, 1914.

6 Hildreth, *Despotism*, 115–16. Cf. William Stocking, ed., *Under the Oaks* (Detroit, 1904), 46; Cleveland *Leader*, January 29, 1856; George N. Fuller, ed., *Messages of the Governors of Michigan* (4 vols.: Lansing, 1925–27), 2, 293.

7 On Seward's view of empire, see Glyndon G. Van Deusen, *William Henry Seward* (New York, 1967), 206–11; Baker, ed., *Seward Works*, 1, 57, 250; 3, 12–13, 188; 4, 166–70, 333; Walter La Feber, *The New Empire* (Washington, 1963), 24–32.

paired the strength of the entire country and subverted the "intelligence, vigor, and energy" which national growth required. This was why, as early as 1845, Seward declared that abolition was the most important object which could occupy the attention of American statesmen. The question of restricting and ultimately abolishing slavery, he declared, was the question of "whether impartial public councils shall leave the free and vigorous North and West to work out the welfare of the country, and drag the reluctant South up to participate in the same glorious destinies."[8] . . .

The Republican critique of southern society thus focused upon the degradation of labor—the slave's ignorance and lack of incentive, and the laboring white's poverty, degradation, and lack of social mobility. The result was not only regional economic stagnation, but a system of social ethics entirely different from that of the North. The moral qualities of free labor, hard work, frugality, and interest in economic advancement seemed absent in the South. When Republicans visited the slave states they were struck by the character of the people even more than the poverty of the region. The Cincinnati *Gazette's* traveling correspondent reported in 1858 that he was astonished by the "lack of invention and resource, the clinging to old and now unprofitable ways" among southern laborers, and he added that there seemed to be "a sort of sluggish inactivity" throughout slave society.[9] . . .

If Republicans were anxious to reshape southern society in the image of the North, they were doubly determined that the slave system should not expand beyond its existing borders. It is impossible to understand the intensity of Republican opposition to the expansion of slavery into the West without bearing in mind their image of southern society, as well as their conviction that free land in the West provided an insurance of continuing social mobility in the North. . . .

In the eyes of many Republicans, the development of the West held the key to America's future. "The wealth and political power of the country," wrote Frank Blair in 1854, "will in a little time reside at its Geographical centre . . ." and most Republicans agreed that the sectional contest would be decided by the new states of the West. William Seward, for example, said he looked to the new states "to finally decide whether this is to be a land of slavery or of freedom. The people of the northwest are to be the arbiters of its destiny. . . ."[10] . . .

The question of slavery in the territories was thus one of potentialities. Whatever the actual number of slaves involved, the character of institutions which would affect the lives of millions of Americans was being

---

8 Baker, ed., *Seward Works*, 1, 76, 4, 395; *The Address of the Southern and Western Liberty Convention to the People of the United States; the Proceedings and Resolutions of the Convention* . . . (Cincinnati, 1845), 18; Seward, ed., *Seward Autobiography*, 717. . . .

9 Cincinnati *Gazette*, August 25, 31, September 3, 1858.

10 Francis P. Blair, Jr., to Edward L. Pierce, April 28, 1854, E. L. Pierce Papers, Houghton Library, Harvard University; Baker, ed., *Seward Works*, 4, 346–47. Cf. Henry Nash Smith, *Virgin Land* (Cambridge, 1950) 191–92.

determined. In taking this position, Republicans often compared the territories to children, whose upbringing would determine their future development. . . .

The Republicans saw their anti-slavery program as one part of a worldwide movement from absolutism to democracy, aristocracy to equality, backwardness to modernity, and their conviction that the struggle in the United States had international implications did much to strengthen their resolve. They accepted the characteristic American vision of the United States as an example to the world of the social and political benefits of democracy, yet believed that so long as slavery existed, the national purpose of promoting liberty in other lands could not be fulfilled. Lincoln declared in 1854 that slavery "deprives our republican example of its just influence in the world—enables the enemies of free institutions to taunt us as hypocrites," and Charles Sumner agreed that the institution "degrades our country, and prevents its example from being all-conquering."[11] William Seward believed that the spread of American economic influence would be accompanied by the export of America's egalitarian political institutions. The nation, he wrote, had a mission and responsibility "to renovate the condition of mankind" by proving at home that the "experiment in self-government" could succeed, and by aiding abroad "the universal restoration of power to the governed." Just as slavery stood in the way of achieving the nation's imperial destiny, so it interfered with the nation's mission of spreading democracy.[12] Yet as they looked at the world around them, Republicans could not but be confident that they were on the side of history. . . . The Republicans were confident that in the sectional struggle, which one newspaper summarized as a contest between "Northern Progress and Southern Decadence," southern civilization must give way before the onslaught of the modern world.[13] . . .

The decision for civil war in 1860–61 can be resolved into two questions—why did the South secede, and why did the North refuse to let the South secede? As I have indicated, I believe secession should be viewed as a total and logical response by the South to the situation which confronted it in the election of Lincoln—logical in the sense that it was the only action consistent with its ideology. In the same way, the Republicans' decision to maintain the Union was inherent in their ideology. For the integrity of the Union, important as an end in itself, was also a prerequisite to the national greatness Republicans felt the United States was destined to achieve. With his faith in progress, material growth, and the spread of both democratic institutions and American influence throughout the world, William Seward brought the Republican ideology to a kind of culmination. Although few Republicans held as coherent and far-reaching a world view as he, most accepted Lincoln's more modest view

---

[11] Basler, ed., *Lincoln Works*, 2, 255; Sumner to Francis Bird, September 11, 1857, Francis Bird Papers, Houghton Library, Harvard University.

[12] Baker, ed., *Seward Works*, 3, 292–93; 5, 221, 228. Cf. 3, 23, 132, 504.

[13] Frederic Bancroft, ed., *Speeches, Correspondence, and Political Papers of Carl Schurz* (6 vols.: New York, 1913), 1, 156–58; Chicago *Democratic Press*, May 2, 1857.

that the American nation had a special place in the world, and a responsibility to prove that democratic institutions were self-sustaining. Much of the messianic zeal which characterized political anti-slavery derived from this faith in the superiority of the political, social, and economic institutions of the North, and a desire to spread these to their ultimate limits.

When a leading historian says, therefore, that the Republican party in 1860 was bound together "by a common enmity rather than a common loyalty," he is, I believe, only half right.[14] For the Republicans' enmity toward the South was intimately bound up with their loyalty to the society of small-scale capitalism which they perceived in the North. It was its identification with the aspirations of the farmers, small entrepreneurs, and craftsmen of northern society which gave the Republican ideology much of its dynamic, progressive, and optimistic quality. Yet paradoxically, at the time of its greatest success, the seeds of the later failure of that ideology were already present. Fundamental changes were at work in the social and economic structure of the North, transforming and undermining many of its free-labor assumptions. And the flawed attitude of the Republicans toward race, and the limitations of the free labor outlook in regard to the Negro, foreshadowed the mistakes and failures of the post-emancipation years.

---

[14] William B. Hesseltine, *Lincoln and the War Governors* (New York, 1948), 4.

chapter 13

The Meaning of Reconstruction

THE STRUGGLE FOR EQUALITY which inspired first the antislavery movement and then the Radical wing of the Republican party reached a climax in Reconstruction. In 1865 nearly all white Southerners and most citizens of the North rejected the concept of "racial equality," but with slavery a casualty of the war the nation had no other choice than to allow a new status for the former slave. Millions of Americans, whatever their opinions on race and equality, had come to accept the Civil War as an abolitionist crusade, and the equalitarians now faced the difficult task of harnessing this sentiment to the cause of equal citizenship. The United States had been a slave republic in 1776 and when the "peculiar institution" was finally banished from the last states in 1865, it left behind deep wells of racial hostility. Two centuries of slavery and four centuries of European conquests over "the lesser breeds without" left a powerful heritage of white supremacist attitudes.

Thus the equalitarians had to contend with racism and caste as well as with the legal remnants of slavery. Some of the abolitionists were themselves tainted with a sense of racial superiority, but few revolutionists are able to move into a new era free from all opinions and attitudes shaped in the old social order. When all was said and done, the abolitionists and the Radical Republicans were still the bearers of a revolution which promised to bring freedom and equality to the most oppressed group in the Western world. The obstacles to revolution were truly formidable. Dominant conceptions of property and the state thwarted the movement at every turn; millions of freedmen had been degraded by slavery and all Negroes had been compelled to cope with a society ruled by an imperious racism in most areas from popular speech and songs to the highest expressions of culture. Although war and emancipation did affect the attitudes of vast numbers in the North, these events altered few Southern opinions about the all important superiority of the white man and the barbarous inferiority of the black man. The situation became graver still when the drive for equality encountered increasing Southern hostility interacting with the policies of an unexpectedly antipathetic President. The task was also complicated by laissez-faire conceptions of politics which denied the power of the federal government to take sweeping and effective action and by conventional and conservative notions of property rights at war with the desperate need of freedmen for justice and land. Often the revolution hinged precariously on political development such as a new wave of Southern violence, a lessening of Negrophobia in Ohio, another sign of presidential intransigence from Andrew Johnson, or a change of opinion among political or business leaders in New York.

Yet the American Negro had already traveled far from the violence of capture and sale in Africa, the bloody squalor of "the middle passage," and the misery of bondage in the New World. Now he spoke as much of the new tongue as many of his white countrymen, and was perhaps even more attached to American soil. With a basic knowledge of farming and with a thirst for land and education, he looked away from the harshness of slavery toward a new era of freedom. While grievances against former masters may have lingered, they were more than balanced by the common desire for a free and peaceful life on terms of mutual goodwill with the white man. Against the epic background from which the American Negro people emerged the problems of 1865 did not appear to be insurmountable. Many Negroes as well as the most committed Radicals across the country, in the Union army, and in the Congress, looked to the future with great expectations.

The dream failed so completely that Americans nearly forgot that it had ever existed, and by the end of the nineteenth century Southerners had developed new forms of social subordination for the Negro. Northern and Southern white men who purchased unity at the expense of Negro freedom certainly did not propose to return to slavery days, but on many issues they attempted to turn the clock back to 1865. As the abolitionists and the most idealistic Radicals died or lapsed into silence, the new vogue of Social Darwinism, crystallizing and intensifying the old racism, predicated a racial struggle which made the subordination of the black man seem a natural phenomenon. The United States, having completed the last battles against the Indians, joined the major imperial powers in 1898 at a time when Europe was consolidating and extending imperial rule in Africa and Asia. Under the circumstances the American Negro's power was too insubstantial and his voice too frail to turn the tide of hostile acts and images which began to enshroud the freedom struggle. The historian played his part in rationalizing the new bondage, and from the 1890s until recent years the overwhelming majority of scholars explained Reconstruction in hostile terms.

Presumably, the "ignoble" experiment included bad civil government and massive corruption as well as military misrule and offensive "Negro domination." In this historical portrait a great many Northerners from veteran abolitionists to young opportunists were portrayed as vicious Yankee "carpetbaggers" feeding with abandon on the prostrate South, and an equally varied group of Southern white men who cooperated in small or large ways with Reconstruction were depicted as unscrupulous "scalawags." In the most hostile accounts, the scalawags were invariably portrayed as lower class traitors to the South, the memory of the Confederacy, and the future of "the Caucasian race." In league with the carpetbagger and scalawag was the grossly "inferior" Negro, sometimes seen as a betrayed dupe and sometimes as a sinister and swaggering sharer in the spoils. All three groups lorded it over the disfranchised Confederate who longed only for the restoration of the old Union and for honest local government in his own capable and loyal hands. When all the "Force Acts" proved to be failures and federal troops were withdrawn, the white Southerner rose up in righteous wrath to claim his government from corruption and misrule.

For nearly a half century versions of Reconstruction similar to this characterization dominated American historical thought, and traces of the old conceptions still mark many textbooks. In 1906 James Ford Rhodes, who has often been credited with "abolitionist" sympathies and did indeed claim the Union cause as his own, rejected the Reconstruction experiment with evident distaste. He doubted the Negro's "capacity" and "nature," insisted that universal Negro suffrage had been an obvious "failure," and argued that in the final analysis Radical policies did "no real good to the Negro." John W. Burgess, a Southerner with somewhat weaker Union sympathies, expressed in 1902 even more aversion to "Black Republicanism" and described the Radical program as an effort "to establish barbarism in power over civilization." For Burgess the enslavement of an "inferior race" such as the Negroes was no great matter but the attempt to place the superior white race under the rule of their black inferiors was unnatural and repugnant. For several decades William A. Dunning continued the pattern of negative stereotypes and trained many of the most active Reconstruction scholars. The ideas of "the Dunning School" which shaped the dominant tradition, reached a lurid climax in 1929 with the work of Claude G. Bowers. "The tragic era" was a time of almost unrelieved shabbiness and sordidness in public and private life when "brutal, hypocritical, and corrupt" Republicans ruled and "the Southern people literally were put to the torture." Bowers' book constantly expressed hostility toward Negroes and Republicans, described Andrew Johnson as a man moved only by high constitutional scruples, and accepted as true nearly every malicious rumor about Radical leaders. Men such as Thaddeus Stevens, corrupted by an "obsession on Negro rights to absolute equality," were thoroughly ignorant of Southern conditions in contrast to the native white men who "understood the Negro best." Republican politicians who urged Negroes to use streetcars or theater facilities were described as "teachers of hate" making "incendiary speeches."

Scholarly books of the 1930s and 1940s were not ridden to the same extent with blatant and sharply etched prejudices but leading scholars such as James G. Randall carried on the hostile traditions in a quieter way. Now and then a historian who perpetuated most of the preconceptions in his own work would call for the revision of one or several stereotypes. A few scholars wrote monographs which suggested new modes of

understanding and pointed to inadequacies in the conventional interpretations. Still the old traditions reigned and the only two general works on
Reconstruction published between 1945 and 1950 were similar to past
productions of the Dunning School. As recently as 1959 Bernard A. Weisberger in an interpretive analysis complained that most textbooks did
not display the monographic discoveries of the 1950s which cried out for
major changes in general patterns of explanation. Several challenges of
1939 and 1940 which called upon scholars to escape timeworn habits of
thought had still not been met in 1959. Yet even while Weisberger wrote
the revisionist stream threatened to become a flood, as virtually every
group and major issue of the postwar era came under new critical scrutiny—Johnson and his supporters, carpetbaggers, scalawags, redeemers,
readjustors, Southern blacks, home rule, the 14th and 15th Amendments,
federal legislation, and most major political events of the era. In 1959
Carl N. Degler skillfully used and advanced the new scholarship with
an essay which described Reconstruction as "a political Cold War" between Radicals and Southern white supremacy forces, demolished the
myth of "Negro domination" in showing that Black Reconstruction had
not been very black, insisted that black enfranchisement could no longer
be regarded as very radical, and concluded that "the tragedy of Reconstruction was that it failed."

Six years later with the tide of revisionist scholarship running even
stronger Kenneth M. Stampp (Selection 1) published an up-to-date scholarly summary along with his own analysis of "the tragic legend of Reconstruction" which qualified as tragic because it had been used for several generations to justify the surrender of the black man to Southern
caste and to rationalize his continuing subordination. Stampp dismissed
ultra-romantic images of the war as "harmless" and addressed himself
only to Reconstruction, but Staughton Lynd in 1965 insisted on the existence of many legends about the age of Civil War and Reconstruction.
The revisionist interpretive essays of Stampp, Lynd, and Degler gained
widespread acceptance during a time when the old stereotypes of Reconstruction as a sordid piece of national shame were rapidly expiring and
a growing number of scholars had begun to describe the Radical venture
as one of the most momentous struggles of modern times against oppression.

The soaring political hopes for blacks at mid-decade in the 1960s undoubtedly influenced the tone and the quantity of the sympathetic monographs and readers on Radicals, abolitionists and the cause of black freedom. Before the decade ended, however, new doubts, indifference, and
pessimism inaugurated the era in which we now live, an age which may
reflect the attrition of the spirit from the long years of waging war on
Vietnamese peasants and mark the distance traveled between the almost
messianic optimism of the march on Washington in the summer of 1963
and the unhappy reflections on the blazing anger of burning ghettoes in
Newark and Detroit during a very different summer in 1967. No better
illustration for the history of sensibilities and responses relating to Reconstruction during the last 70 or 80 years can be found than in a chronicle of writings on the Freedman's Bureau. In 1903 the black intellectual

W. E. B. DuBois made virtually the last sympathetic remarks of that agency for half a century and his words sank beneath the sea of general hostility. DuBois' white contemporary John W. Burgess took a relatively moderate stance in describing the Bureau as the product of good intentions which did a brief season of useful disaster relief work before turning destructive. In Burgess' narrative the freedmen with guarantees of free food and shelter, "like the children they were . . . thought that the New Jerusalem would last forever," refused to work and became "a privileged class" on Federal bounty until the South was "driven to some legislation to prevent the whole Negro race from becoming paupers and criminals." (Thus we are introduced to the counter-revolution of Southern white supremacy.)

A generation later, according to Claude G. Bowers' popular and representative account of 1929, Bureau agents disrupted the labor supply intolerably and served as "teachers of hate" for whom "the simple-minded freedmen were easy victims of guile. . . ." and often "coercion." Radical politicians, it seemed, took the blacks from both honest labor and the wise counsel of "native whites who understood them best." As recently as 1955 George W. Bentley in the first monograph on the Freedman's Bureau concluded that the agency "sought too much for the Negro too soon" and exploited the black man to benefit the Radical Republican "bent on the political and economic exploitation" of the South where blacks of necessity had to live. By pushing the black man into politics and by refusing to allow him "to be influenced by the . . . politicians representing the people of his homeland. . . . the Freedman's Bureau had fed the flame of race hostility and had cancelled out much of the good it had otherwise accomplished."

Even before Bentley's book appeared in print, John and LaWanda Cox published an essay in 1953 entitled "The Misrepresented Bureau" and five years later LaWanda Cox extended the analysis in an article, "The Promise of Land for the Freedman," which suggested that if the Bureau had carried out the Congressional intent of the "Forty-Acre Program" America in the twentieth century might not have so monumental a race problem. Not until the mid 60s, however, did the Coxes' pioneer perceptions become the dominant thrust of Reconstruction historiography (just as the black Southern Civil Rights movement reached an apex). In 1964 John A. Carpenter, writing on O. O. Howard and the Freedman's Bureau, declared the courageous Howard to have been an authentic hero and the badly harassed Bureau to have "performed near miracles" in "trying to check atrocities against the freedman," in "insisting on equality before the law," and in helping former masters and exslaves "to adjust to a free labor system."

A few years later in a time of greater doubt and pessimism William S. McFeely (Selection 2), equally in sympathy with the freedmen and in retreat from the racism of earlier scholarship, came to very different conclusions about General Howard and the Bureau. McFeely, noting that the work of the agency often "served to preclude rather than to promote Negro freedom," concluded that agency leaders failed their moral and legal obligation to guide the former slaves to land and liberty. In the final analysis McFeely could not find heroes, miracles, or even "adjust-ment" to "a free labor system," but rather a betrayal in which the Radi-cals turned the helpless freedmen over to the Southern states and Howard and his associates cooperated closely with the planters in the mixture of pressure and duress, wage labor, and sharecropping which became the new system of black bondage.

The vast intellectual distances from Bowers to Stampp to McFeely suggested the most sweeping changes in American sensibilities as well as in historiography. Stampp's essay which seemed to promise the ban-ishment of racist perceptions from historical writings sprang naturally from a time in which many men thought that contemporary racism could easily be defeated and expelled from American society, and McFeely's book represented the sceptical detachment born of a climate of opinion in which white racism and black problems seemed far more intractable. For a moment in the mid 60s civil rights victories and a new sense of black past enabled black writers such as Lerone Bennett, Jr., to celebrate Reconstruction as a joyful epoch of Black Power, a golden age in which former slaves seized the reins of power and began to move rapidly toward the construction of a truly humane social order. (Ernest Kaiser in 1972 applied the insight to the stage of world history.) Yet when the revision-ist smoke and dust cleared one could see that, while much radical change had been hoped for and may have been possible, Reconstruction only established for a brief time the rudiments of Black Power in some parts of the South. The radicals brought not a revolution but only the modest beginnings of a just social order. Indeed there had been no "negro domi-nation,"—only one full U.S. Senate term here, a lieutenant governorship there, a few Congressmen during a 30-year-period, the substance of Black Power in scattered communities, a precarious suffrage and a small mi-nority of local and Federal offices nearly all lost by the end of the cen-tury, minor modifications in required caste behavior, and the small be-ginnings of land ownership and a rudimentary educational system. If the gains were often exaggerated, they still existed. The successes of "the Second Reconstruction" (to use a term popularized by Woodward) dur-ing the 1960s now also seem to have been limited ones, but hope remains and reasons for pride in the precedents and accomplishments of both Reconstructions. A Third Reconstruction seems inevitable and when it arrives the luster of that first and aborted Revolution may be rediscovered.

BIBLIOGRAPHY

Works Discussed in This Chapter

Bennett, Lerone, Jr., *Black Power U.S.A.: The Human Side of Reconstruction, 1867–1877* (1967).
Bentley, George R., *A History of the Freedman's Bureau* (1955).
Bowers, Claude G., *The Tragic Era* (1929).
Burgess, John W., *Reconstruction and the Constitution, 1866–1876* (1902).
Carpenter, John A., *Sword and Olive Branch: Oliver Otis Howard* (1964).
Cox, John, and Cox, LaWanda, "General O. O. Howard and the Misrepresented Bureau," *Journal of Southern History* (1953).

Cox, LaWanda, "The Promise of Land for the Freedman," *Mississippi Valley Historical Review* (1958).

Degler, Carl N., *Out of Our Past* (1959).

DuBois, W. E. B., *The Souls of Black Folk* (1903).

Dunning, William A., *Reconstruction, Political and Economic, 1865–1877* (1907).

Kaiser, Ernest, "The Negro Impact on Western Civilization: A Review Essay," *Science and Society* (1972).

Lynd, Staughton, "Rethinking Slavery and Reconstruction," *Journal of Negro History* (1965).

McFeely, William S., *Yankee Stepfather: General O. O. Howard and the Freedman* (1968).

Randall, James G., *Civil War and Reconstruction* (1937).

Rhodes, James Ford, *History of the United States from the Compromise of 1850 to the McKinley-Bryan Campaign of 1896*, Vol. 7 (1906).

Stampp, Kenneth M., *The Era of Reconstruction* (1965).

Weisberger, Bernard A., "The Dark and Bloody Ground of Reconstruction Historiography," *Journal of Southern History* (1959).

Woodward, C. Vann, "From the First Reconstruction to the Second," *Harper's Magazine* (1965).

Suggested Readings

Among the many works of *traditional racist explanation* a few examples will suffice. Many Johnson biographers enhanced the President's reputation at the expense of Negroes and radicals. See Robert W. Winston, *Andrew Johnson, Plebeian and Patriot* (1928); Lloyd P. Stryker, *Andrew Johnson: A Study in Courage* (1929); and George F. Milton, *The Age of Hate* (1930). The generally hostile attitudes of the Dunning School toward Reconstruction were continued by E. Merton Coulter in *The South During Reconstruction* (1947) and Hodding Carter, *The Angry Scar: The Story of Reconstruction, 1865–1890* (1958). The work and attitudes of this school can be found in a concise summary by A. B. More, "One Hundred Years of Reconstruction in the South," *Journal of Southern History* (1943). Nearly every book in the Dunning tradition contained examples from James S. Pike, *The Prostrate State: South Carolina under Negro Government* (1874) to show that even a Republican could see the sordid mess of Reconstruction. (In 1957 Robert F. Durden's *James Shepherd Pike* revealed that Pike's book was hastily assembled to embarrass the Grant administration.)

Among *pioneer revisionist works* the Marxists had a tradition of dissent and at least one of the works from this school is still well worth reading: see James S. Allen, *Reconstruction: The Battle for Democracy 1865–1876* (1937). Although Paul Lewinson's *Race, Class, and Party* (1932) fell into no neat category, the book made a serious attempt to rise above the standard stereotypes, and it is still useful as an account of Negro disfranchisement. Other monographs which broke some new ground in the 1930s were Francis B. Simkins and Robert H. Woody, *South Carolina During Reconstruction* (1932); Roger W. Shugg, *Origins of Class Struggle in Louisiana* (1939); and C. Vann Woodward, *Tom Watson, Agrarian Rebel* (1938). The two most widely noted calls for general revisions in thinking about Reconstruction were Francis B. Simkins, "New Viewpoints of Southern Reconstruction," *Journal of Southern History* (1939) and Howard K. Beale, "On Rewriting Reconstruction Historiography," *American Historical Review* (1940). A decade earlier Beale himself had included nearly all the hostile notions in *The Critical Year: A Study of Andrew*

Johnson and Reconstruction (1930). For some of the monographs and articles which led to the revisions of Weisberger, Stampp, Lynd, and others, see the bibliography to the next chapter.

The most important pioneer revisionist *works by black scholars* extended from 1910 to 1948. See W. E. B. DuBois, "Reconstruction and its Benefits," *American Historical Review*, (1910); John Lynch, *The Facts of Reconstruction* (1913); A. A. Taylor, *The Negro in South Carolina During the Reconstruction* (1924); and Taylor, *The Negro in the Reconstruction of Virginia* (1926). The monograph *Black Reconstruction in America* (1935) by W. E. B. DuBois, then a Marxist, has an implausible theory of the Southern proletariat, but the book is valuable and one chapter, "The Propaganda of History," is a telling indictment which should be read today by students of the period. From the 1930s on, the most blatant cliches were occasionally challenged: See Horace Mann Bond, "Social and Economic Forces in Alabama Reconstruction," *Journal of Negro History* (1938) and John Hope Franklin, "Whither Reconstruction Historiography?" *Journal of Negro Education* (1948).

The two best early accounts of Negro *disfranchisement* and the violent methods used to achieve it were written by William A. Russ, Jr. See "The Negro and White Disfranchisement During Radical Reconstruction," *Journal of Negro History* (1934) and "Registration and Disfranchisement under Radical Reconstruction," *Mississippi Valley Historical Review* (1934).

The number of *interpretive essays* since 1966 has diminished but is still substantial. A general article of note is Thomas J. Pressly, "Radical Attitudes, Scholarship, and Reconstruction: A Review Essay," *Journal of Southern History* (1967). In an essay which has little to say about race and racism, Larry Kincaid, "Victims of Circumstances: An Interpretation of Changing Attitudes Toward Republican Policy Makers and Reconstruction," *Journal of American History* (1970) attributes much of the hostility toward Radicals and Reconstruction to nationalist historians such as Rhodes seeking sectional reconciliation and to Dunning's Southern students espousing sectional apologetics. An interesting summary of Soviet views can be found in John V. Bratcher, ed. & trans., "A Soviet Historian Looks at Reconstruction," *Civil War History*, (1969). Other significant essays are John G. Clark, "Historians and the Joint Committee on Reconstruction," *The Historian* (1961); August Meier, "Negroes in the First and Second Reconstruction of the South," *Civil War History* (1967); C. Vann Woodward, "Seeds of Failure in Radical Race Policy," *American Philosophical Society Proceedings* (1967); and Woodward, *American Counterpoint* (1971).

More general essays on *racism, historians, and American history* which bear on Reconstruction are I. A. Newby, "Historians and Negroes," *Journal of Negro History* (1969); Robert S. Starobin, "The Negro: A Central Theme in American History," *Journal of Contemporary History* (1969); and C. Vann Woodward, "Clio With Soul," *Journal of American History* (1969). The English scholar W. R. Brock has a brief and lucid summary in "Race and the American Past: A Revolution in Historiography," *History* (1967). See also Richard O. Curry, "The Abolitionists and Reconstruction: A Critical Appraisal," *Journal of Southern History* (1969) and Stuart M. Jones, "The Schlesingers on Black History," *Phylon* (1972).

On *racism and the black suffrage* see Forrest G. Wood, "On Revising Reconstruction History: Negro Suffrage, White Disfranchisement and Common Sense," *Journal of Negro History* (1967) and John and LaWanda Cox, "Negro Suffrage and Republican Politics: The Problems of Motivation in Reconstruction Historiography," *Journal of Southern History* (1968).

The Tragic Legend of
Reconstruction*

Kenneth M. Stampp

. . . How, until recently, reconstruction was portrayed in both history and legend, how sharply it was believed to contrast with the years of the Civil War, is evident in the terms that were used to identify it. Various historians have called this phase of American history "The Tragic Era," "The Dreadful Decade," "The Age of Hate," and "The Blackout of Honest Government." Reconstruction represented the ultimate shame of the American people—as one historian phrased it, "the nadir of national disgrace." It was the epoch that most Americans wanted to forget.

Claude Bowers, who divided his time between politics and history, has been the chief disseminator of the traditional picture of reconstruction, for his book, *The Tragic Era,* published in 1929, has attracted more readers than any other dealing with this period. For Bowers, reconstruction was a time of almost unrelieved sordidness in public and private life; whole regiments of villains march through his pages: the corrupt politicians who dominated the administration of Ulysses S. Grant; the crafty, scheming northern carpetbaggers who invaded the South after the war for political and economic plunder; the degraded and depraved southern scalawags who betrayed their own people and collaborated with the enemy; and the ignorant, barbarous, sensual Negroes who threatened to Africanize the South and destroy its Caucasian civilization.

Most of Bowers' key generalizations can be found in his preface. The years of reconstruction, he wrote, "were years of revolutionary turmoil, with the elemental passions predominant. . . . The prevailing note was one of tragedy. . . . Never have American public men in responsible positions, directing the destiny of the nation, been so brutal, hypocritical, and corrupt. The constitution was treated as a doormat on which politicians and army officers wiped their feet after wading in the muck. . . . The southern people literally were put to the torture . . . [by] rugged conspirators . . . [who] assumed the pose of philanthropists and patriots." The popularity of Bowers' book stems in part from the simplicity of his characters. None are etched in shades of gray; none are confronted with complex moral decisions. Like characters in a Victorian romance, the Republican leaders of the reconstruction era were evil through and through, and the helpless, innocent white men of the South were totally noble and pure.

If Bowers' prose is more vivid and his anger more intense, his general

* Kenneth M. Stampp, *The Era of Reconstruction* (New York: Alfred A. Knopf, 1965). By permission of the publisher.

interpretation of reconstruction is only a slight exaggeration of a point of view shared by most American historians from the late nineteenth century until very recently. Writing in the 1890s, James Ford Rhodes, author of a multi-volumed history of the United States since the Compromise of 1850, branded the Republican scheme of reconstruction as "repressive" and "uncivilized," one that "pandered to the ignorant negroes, the knavish white natives and the vulturous adventurers who flocked from the North." About the same time Professor John W. Burgess, of Columbia University, called reconstruction the "most soul-sickening spectacle that Americans had ever been called upon to behold."[1] Early in the twentieth century Professor William A. Dunning, also of Columbia University, and a group of talented graduate students wrote a series of monographs that presented a crushing indictment of the Republican reconstruction program in the South—a series that made a deep and lasting impression on American historians. In the 1930s, Professor James G. Randall, of the University of Illinois, still writing in the spirit of the Dunningites, described the reconstruction era "as a time of party abuse, of corruption, of vindictive bigotry." "To use a modern phrase," wrote Randall, "government under Radical Republican rule in the South had become a kind of 'racket.' " As late as 1947, Professor E. Merton Coulter, of the University of Georgia, reminded critics of the traditional interpretation that no "amount of revision can write away the grievous mistakes made in this abnormal period of American history."[2] Thus, from Rhodes and Burgess and Dunning to Randall and Coulter the central emphasis of most historical writing about reconstruction has been upon sordid motives and human depravity. Somehow, during the summer of 1865, the nobility and idealism of the war years had died.

A synopsis of the Dunning School's version of reconstruction would run something like this: Abraham Lincoln, while the Civil War was still in progress, turned his thought to the great problem of reconciliation; and, "with malice toward none and charity for all," this gentle and compassionate man devised a plan that would restore the South to the Union with minimum humiliation and maximum speed. But there had already emerged in Congress a faction of radical Republicans, sometimes called Jacobins or Vindictives, who sought to defeat Lincoln's generous program. Motivated by hatred of the South, by selfish political ambitions, and by crass economic interests, the radicals tried to make the process of reconstruction as humiliating, as difficult, and as prolonged as they possibly could. Until Lincoln's tragic death, they poured their scorn upon him—and then used his coffin as a political stump to arouse the passions of the northern electorate.

The second chapter of the Dunning version begins with Andrew Johnson's succession to the presidency. Johnson, the old Jacksonian Unionist

---

[1] James Ford Rhodes: *History of the United States from the Compromise of 1850* . . . (7 vols.; New York, 1893–1906), Vol. 7, p. 168; John W. Burgess: *Reconstruction and the Constitution* (New York, 1902), p. 263.

[2] James G. Randall: *Civil War and Reconstruction* (Boston, 1937), pp. 689, 852; E. Merton Coulter: *The South during Reconstruction, 1865–1877* (Baton Rouge, 1947), p. xi.

from Tennessee, took advantage of the adjournment of Congress to put Lincoln's mild plan of reconstruction into operation, and it was a striking success. In the summer and fall of 1865, Southerners organized loyal state governments, showed a willingness to deal fairly with their former slaves, and in general accepted the outcome of the Civil War in good faith. In December, when Congress assembled, President Johnson reported that the process of reconstruction was nearly completed and that the old Union had been restored. But the radicals unfortunately had their own sinister purposes: they repudiated the governments Johnson had established in the South, refused to seat southern Senators and Representatives, and then directed their fury against the new President. After a year of bitter controversy and political stalemate, the radicals, resorting to shamefully demagogic tactics, won an overwhelming victory in the congressional elections of 1866.

Now, the third chapter and the final tragedy. Riding roughshod over presidential vetoes and federal courts, the radicals put the South under military occupation, gave the ballot to Negroes, and formed new southern state governments dominated by base and corrupt men, black and white. Not satisfied with reducing the South to political slavery and financial bankruptcy, the radicals even laid their obscene hands on the pure fabric of the federal Constitution. They impeached President Johnson and came within one vote of removing him from office, though they had no legal grounds for such action. Next, they elected Ulysses S. Grant President, and during his two administrations they indulged in such an orgy of corruption and so prostituted the civil service as to make Grantism an enduring symbol of political immorality.

The last chapter is the story of ultimate redemption. Decent southern white Democrats, their patience exhausted, organized to drive the Negroes, carpetbaggers, and scalawags from power, peacefully if possible, forcefully if necessary. One by one the southern states were redeemed, honesty and virtue triumphed, and the South's natural leaders returned to power. In the spring of 1877, the Tragic Era finally came to an end when President Hayes withdrew the federal troops from the South and restored home rule. But the legacy of radical reconstruction remained in the form of a solidly Democratic South and embittered relations between the races.

This point of view was rarely challenged until the 1930s, when a small group of revisionist historians began to give new life and a new direction to the study of reconstruction. The revisionists are a curious lot who sometimes quarrel with each other as much as they quarrel with the disciples of Dunning. At various times they have counted in their ranks Marxists of various degrees of orthodoxy, Negroes seeking historical vindication, skeptical white Southerners, and latter-day northern abolitionists. But among them are numerous scholars who have the wisdom to know that the history of an age is seldom simple and clear-cut, seldom without its tragic aspects, seldom without its redeeming virtues. . . .

What is perhaps more puzzling in the legend of reconstruction is the notion that the white people of the South were treated with unprecedented brutality, and that their conquerors, in Bowers' colorful phrase, literally put them to the torture. . . . [In fact] the great mass of ordinary Southern-ers who voluntarily took up arms, or in other ways supported the Confed-eracy, were required simply to take an oath of allegiance to obtain pardon and to regain their right to vote and hold public office. . . .

What then, constituted the alleged brutality that white Southerners endured? First, the freeing of their slaves; second, the brief incarceration of a few Confederate leaders; third, a political disability imposed for a few years on most Confederate leaders; fourth, a relatively weak military occupation terminated in 1877; and, last, an attempt to extend the rights and privileges of citizenship to southern Negroes. Mistakes there were in the implementation of these measures—some of them serious—but bru-tality almost none. In fact, it can be said that rarely in history have the participants in an unsuccessful rebellion endured penalties as mild as those Congress imposed upon the people of the South, and particularly upon their leaders. After four years of bitter struggle costing hundreds of thousands of lives, the generosity of the federal government's terms was quite remarkable.

If northern brutality is a myth, the scandals of the Grant administra-tion and the peculations of some of the southern reconstruction govern-ments are sordid facts. Yet even here the Dunningites are guilty of distor-tion by exaggeration, by superficial analysis, and by overemphasis. They make corruption a central theme of their narratives, but they overlook constructive accomplishments. They give insufficient attention to the men who transcended the greed of an age when, to be sure, self-serving politicians and irresponsible entrepreneurs were all too plentiful. Among these men were the humanitarians who organized Freedmen's Aid Soci-eties to help 4 million southern Negroes make the difficult transition from slavery to freedom, and the missionaries and teachers who went into the South on slender budgets to build churches and schools for the freedmen. Under their auspices the Negroes first began to learn the responsibilities and obligations of freedom. Thus the training of Negroes for citizenship had its successful beginnings in the years of reconstruction.

In the nineteenth century most white Americans, North and South, had reservations about the Negro's potentialities . . . and assumed that after emancipation he would be relegated to an inferior caste. But some of the radical Republicans refused to believe that the Negroes were innately in-ferior and hoped passionately that they would confound their critics. . . . Here, surely, was a projection into the reconstruction era of the idealism of the abolitionist crusade and of the Civil War.

Radical idealism was in part responsible for two of the most momen-tous enactments of the reconstruction years: the Fourteenth Amendment to the federal Constitution which gave Negroes citizenship and promised them equal protection of the laws, and the Fifteenth Amendment which gave them the right to vote. The fact that these amendments could not have been adopted under any other circumstances, or at any other time, before or since, may suggest the crucial importance of the reconstruction era in American history. Indeed, without radical reconstruction, it would be impossible to this day for the federal government to protect Negroes from legal and political discrimination.

If all of this is true, or even part of it, why was the Dunning legend born, and why has it been so durable? Southerners, of course, have contributed much to the legend of reconstruction, but most Northerners have found the legend quite acceptable. Many of the historians who helped to create it were Northerners, among them James Ford Rhodes, William A. Dunning, Claude Bowers, and James G. Randall. Thus the legend cannot be explained simply in terms of a southern literary or historiographical conspiracy, satisfying as the legend has been to most white Southerners. What we need to know is why it also satisfies Northerners. . . .

That the reconstruction era elicits neither pride nor sentimentality is due only in part to its moral delinquencies—remember, those of the Civil War years can be overlooked. It is also due to the white American's ambivalent attitude toward race and toward the steps that radical Republicans took to protect the Negroes. Southern white men accepted the Thirteenth Amendment to the Constitution, which abolished slavery, with a minimum of complaint, but they expected federal intervention to proceed no further than that. They assumed that the regulation of the freedmen would be left to the individual states; and clearly most of them intended to replace slavery with a caste system that would keep the Negroes perpetually subordinate to the whites. Negroes were to remain a dependent laboring class; they were to be governed by a separate code of laws; they were to play no active part in the South's political life; and they were to be segregated socially. When radical Republicans used federal power to interfere in these matters, the majority of southern white men formed a resistance movement to fight the radical-dominated state governments until they were overthrown, after which southern whites established a caste system in defiance of federal statutes and constitutional amendments. For many decades thereafter the federal government simply admitted defeat and acquiesced; but the South refused to forget or forgive those years of humiliation when Negroes came close to winning equality. In southern mythology, then, reconstruction was a horrid nightmare.

. . . A considerable number of [Northern whites] . . . shared the racial attitudes of the South and preferred to keep Negroes in a subordinate caste. For a time after the Civil War the radical Republicans, who were always a minority group, persuaded the northern electorate that the ultimate purpose of southern white men was to rob the North of the fruits of victory and to re-establish slavery and that federal intervention was therefore essential. In this manner radicals won approval of, or acquiescence in, their program to give civil rights and the ballot to southern Negroes. Popular support for the radical program waned rapidly, however, and by the middle of the 1870s it had all but vanished. In 1875 a Republican politician confessed that northern voters were tired of the "worn-out cry of 'southern outrages,'" and they wished that "the 'nigger' the 'everlasting nigger' were in—Africa." As Northerners ceased to worry about the possibility of another southern rebellion, they became increasingly receptive to criticism of radical reconstruction.

The eventual disintegration of the radical phalanx, those root-and-branch men who, for a time, seemed bent on engineering a sweeping reformation of southern society, was another important reason for the denigration of reconstruction in American historiography. To be sure, some of the radicals, especially those who had been abolitionists before the war, never lost faith in the Negro, and in the years after reconstruction they stood by him as he struggled to break the intellectual and psychological fetters he had brought with him out of slavery. Other radicals, however, lost interest in the cause—tired of reform and spent their declining years writing their memoirs. Still others retained their crusading zeal but became disenchanted with radical reconstruction and found other crusades more attractive: civil service reform, or tariff reform, or defense of the gold standard. In 1872 they repudiated Grant and joined the Liberal Republicans; in subsequent years they considered themselves to be political independents.

This latter group had been an important element in the original racial coalition. Most of them were respectable, middleclass people in comfortable economic circumstances, well educated and highly articulate, and acutely conscious of their obligation to perform disinterested public service. They had looked upon Senator Charles Sumner of Massachusetts as their political spokesman, and upon Edwin L. Godkin of the New York *Nation* as their editorial spokesman. Like most radicals they had believed that the Negro was what slavery had made him; give the Negro equal rights and he would be quickly transformed into an industrious and responsible citizen. With the radical reconstruction program fairly launched, they had looked forward to swift and dramatic results.

But reconstruction was not orderly and the Negro's progress was not nearly as swift and dramatic as these reformers had seemed to expect. The first signs of doubt came soon after the radicals won control of reconstruction policy, when the *Nation* warned the Negroes that the government had already done all it could for them. They were now, said the *Nation*, "on the dusty and rugged highway of competition"; henceforth "the removal of white prejudice against the Negro depends almost entirely on the Negro himself." By 1870 this bellwether of the reformers viewed with alarm the disorders and irregularities in the states governed by Negroes and carpetbaggers; by 1871 it proclaimed: "The experiment has totally failed. . . . We owe it to human nature to say that worse governments have seldom been seen in a civilized country." . . .

Actually, neither the obvious shortcomings of reconstruction nor an objective view of the Negro's progress in the years after emancipation can wholly explain the disillusionment of so many former radicals. Rather, their changed attitude toward the Negro and the hostile historical interpretation of reconstruction that won their favor were in part the product of social trends that severely affected the old American middle classes with whom most of them were identified. These trends had their origin in the industrial revolution; they were evident in the early nineteenth century but were enormously accelerated after the Civil War. Their institutional symbols were the giant manufacturing and railroad corporations.

In the new age of industrial enterprise there seemed to be no place for the old families with their genteel culture and strong traditions of disinterested public service. On the one hand, they were overshadowed by new and powerful industrial capitalists whose economic strength brought with it vast political influence. Legislative bodies became arenas in which the political vassals of oil, steel, and railroad barons struggled for special favors, while the interests of the public—and the old middle classes liked to think of themselves as *the public*—counted for nothing. On the other hand, they were threatened by the immigrants who came to America to work in the mines and mills and on the railroads—Italians, Slavs, and Jews from Poland and Russia. The immigrants crowded into the tenements of eastern cities, responded to the friendly overtures of urban political bosses, and used their ballots to evict the old middle-class families from power. Here was a threat to the traditional America that these families had loved—and dominated—to that once vigorous American nationality that was Protestant, Anglo-Saxon, and pure. . . .

Soon the new immigrant groups had become the victims of cruel racial stereotypes. Taken collectively, it would appear that they were, among other things, innately inferior to the Anglo-Saxons in their intellectual and physical traits, dirty and immoral in their habits, inclined toward criminality, receptive to dangerous political beliefs, and shiftless and irresponsible.

In due time, those who repeated these stereotypes awoke to the realization that what they were saying was not really very original—that, as a matter of fact, these generalizations were *precisely* the ones that southern white men had been making about Negroes for years. And, in their extremity, the old middle classes of the North looked with new understanding upon the problems of the beleaguered white men of the South. Perhaps all along Southerners had understood the problem better than they. Here, then, was a crucial part of the intellectual climate in which the Dunning interpretation of reconstruction was written. It was written at a time when xenophobia had become almost a national disease, when the immigration restriction movement was getting into high gear, when numerous northern cities (among them Philadelphia and Chicago) were seriously considering the establishment of racially segregated schools, and when Negroes and immigrants were being lumped together in the category of unassimilable aliens.

Several other attitudes, prevalent in the late nineteenth century, encouraged an interpretation of reconstruction that condemned radical Republicans for meddling in southern race relations. The vogue of social Darwinism discouraged governmental intervention in behalf of Negroes as well as other underprivileged groups; it encouraged the belief that a solution to the race problem could only evolve slowly as the Negroes gradually improved themselves. A rising spirit of nationalism stimulated a desire for sectional reconciliation, and part of the price was a virtual abdication of federal responsibility for the protection of the Negro's civil and political rights. An outburst of imperialism manifested in the Spanish-American War and the annexation of the Hawaiian Islands, found one of its principal justifications in the notion that Anglo-Saxons were superior to other peoples, especially when it came to politics. In the words of Senator Albert J. Beveridge of Indiana:

God has not been preparing the English-speaking and Teutonic people for a thousand years for nothing but vain and idle self-admiration. No! He has made us the master organizers of the world to establish system where chaos reigns. . . . He has made us adepts in government that we may administer government among savages and senile peoples.

What folly, then, to expect Italians and Slavs to behave like Anglo-Saxons—or to accept the sentimental doctrine that Negroes deserve to be given the same political rights as white men!

Finally, at this critical juncture, sociologists, anthropologists, and psychologists presented what they regarded as convincing evidence of innate racial traits—evidence indicating that Negroes were intellectually inferior to whites and had distinctive emotional characteristics. The social scientists thus supplied the racists of the late nineteenth and early twentieth centuries with something that antebellum pro-slavery writers had always lacked: a respectable scientific argument.

In this social atmosphere, armed with the knowledge of race that the social scientists had given them, historians exposed the folly of radical reconstruction. At the turn of the century, James Ford Rhodes, that intimate friend of New England Brahmims, gave his verdict on Negro suffrage—on that the Dunningites would soon develop into the central assumption, the controlling generalization, of the reconstruction legend.

> No large policy in our country [concluded Rhodes] has ever been so conspicuous a failure as that of forcing universal negro suffrage upon the South. . . . From the Republican policy came no real good to the negroes. Most of them developed no political capacity, and the few who raised themselves above the mass did not reach a high order of intelligence. . . . The negro's political activity is rarely of a nature to identify him with any movement on a high plane. . . . [He] has been politically a failure and he could not have been otherwise.[3] . . .

---

[3] Rhodes: *History of the United States*, vol. 7, pp. 168–70.

The Nation Failed the Black Man:
O. O. Howard and the
Freedman's Bureau*

William S. McFeely

Black Americans did not have much of a chance on their drive to achieve equality in the First Reconstruction. At the close of the Civil War, many white Americans were happy to help them celebrate their emancipation, but the freedmen were neither invited to share a reconstructed land nor given the opportunity to build their own new Canaans on empty lands, as Englishmen had been able to do two centuries before. The experience of slavery had given the Negroes little to equip them to assert their demands on the nation, and neither they nor their white friends could make such an assertion without other white men feeling that their interests were being threatened.

As the war ended, the nation did make one attempt to build an institution that would enable Negro Americans to struggle, with some hope of success, for the social, economic, and political rewards in a community offering equal opportunities to its citizens. In May 1865 Congress created the Bureau of Refugees, Freedmen and Abandoned Lands, which everyone called the Freedmen's Bureau. This national effort preceded the experiments of Radical Reconstruction which, if nothing else, gave the American Negroes of the Second Reconstruction, a century later, a political past to reactivate. Despite the great worth of such innovations as the grant of the franchise to the freedmen, the radical program for the rebuilding of the South did represent a national responsibility shrugged off on the states. Congress was the architect of the effort but it did not hold the nation to the task of sustaining the egalitarian programs it called on the southern states to undertake. The Freedmen's Bureau, the national institution designed to bring the new black citizens into the nation, came earlier.

In 1903, in W. E. B. DuBois' *The Souls of Black Folk* was an elegant essay, "Of the Dawn of Freedom." As he described his "tale," it was "an account of that government of men called the Freedmen's Bureau—one of the most singular and interesting attempts made by a great nation to grapple with vast problems of race and social condition."[1] To DuBois the

---

* William S. McFeely, *Yankee Stepfather: General O. O. Howard and the Freedman's Bureau* (New Haven: Yale University Press, 1968). By permission of the publisher.

[1] W. E. B. DuBois, "Of the Dawn of Freedom," *The Souls of Black Folk* (Chicago, 1903), pp. 13–40. Originally entitled "The Freedmen's Bureau," the essay first appeared in 1901, *Atlantic Monthly*, 87 (March 1901), 354–65.

Bureau had been the freedmen's, and its purpose had been to make them truly free. It had failed. "For this much all men know: despite compromise, war and struggle, the Negro is not free."

By "black farmers are peons" and Negroes "are a segregated, servile caste" DuBois meant that the Freedmen's Bureau had not done what it should have. Its legacies were two: the still unsolved problems of the American Negroes and the striving necessary to solve them. DuBois considered that the Bureau had sought to do its task, but forces outside the agency had prevented it from succeeding. He called on his own long generation to do the work the Bureau "did not do because it could not."[2]

To DuBois, the Bureau had failed because it did too little. Making prophecy of history, he wanted the beginnings he thought had been made by the Bureau to predict the great changes necessary if the Negroes were to gain their freedom. He saw that the Bureau should have been a medium of social change and not just the agent of reconciliation between ex-slaves and their former masters. Fifty years later, when a full study of the Freedmen's Bureau was written, this view of the agency was still rejected. George R. Bentley had a different use in mind in *A History of the Freedmen's Bureau*. Judging the agency by its effect on white Southerners and their mores, as he understood them, Bentley concluded that the agency "sought too much for the Negro too soon."[3] Claiming that Negro aspirations were exploited by radical Republican outside agitators, he did not appreciate, as did DuBois, that those aspirations were no less real because they were exploitable. . . .

. . . Bentley retained his commitment to the old claim that the white South knew best about its Negroes. The nation, he concluded, would have been better advised to leave the freedmen "free to be influenced by the normal wiles of politicians representing the people of his home land."[4]

One of the theses of this study is that the Freedmen's Bureau did acquiesce to exactly what Bentley prescribed. Before 1865 was over, Andrew Johnson, with great skill and understanding of southern politics, put the freedmen under the discipline of southern politicians whom he had restored to power. The Freedmen's Bureau had not stopped the delivery of the Negro labor force into the hands of Johnson's planter and businessman allies. On the contrary, it was used by the President to accomplish this purpose.

The Freedmen's Bureau . . . banked the fires of the freedmen's aspirations. Only the freedmen prevented the fire from going out. By insisting that the Freedmen's Bureau was theirs, even in the face of evidence that it was not, the Negroes forced the men of the Bureau to reckon with them and attempt to reverse the national government's course. But this attempted reversal came only after enormous damage had been done. The white men of the Freedmen's Bureau had let great opportunities go by.

---

2 DuBois, p. 40.

3 George R. Bentley, *A History of the Freedmen's Bureau* (Philadelphia, 1955), p. 214.

4 Bentley, p. 214.

By staying doggedly loyal to the Freedmen's Bureau and its Commissioner, the Negroes forced the nation to recognize that they had economic, political, legal, and educational needs and that there was a national obligation to meet them. As long as the agency existed, that obligation, however dishonored, was still on the books. To remove it, the Freedmen's Bureau was destroyed.

This is a study of those years in the Freedmen's Bureau in which [O. O.] Howard had the power to change the freedmen's position in the nation. It is not an exposé of a knave, but rather a record of naïveté and misunderstanding, timidity, misplaced faith, disloyalty to subordinates who were loyal to the freedmen, and an attempt to diminish the Negroes' aspirations. The sobering fact is that it is the record of the man regarded with remarkable unanimity by Americans as the best man for the job.

The services of Oliver Otis Howard were what the nation was prepared to give its freedmen. By taking measure of Howard and his work in the Bureau, we make a troubling assessment of America during Reconstruction. . . .

. . . By 1867, when Howard called himself a radical, he had long allowed his agency to be used to prevent the Negroes from becoming landowners and to keep them in their places as subservient agricultural laborers. Indeed, the whole contract system was a denial of the principal of individual farm ownership.

The bureau agents negotiated and enforced the contracts under which the freedmen worked. There can be no doubt that the contract system prevented many freedmen from having to work under more repressive conditions, but this does not alter the fact that the Freedmen's Bureau was engaged in the pacification of the freedmen. Much of the energy of Howard's Bureau was directed toward making the freedmen agree to work for their former masters. A student of the agency's work in Florida concluded that "the Bureau literally forced the Negroes to work for the planters."[5] Freedmen who experienced better conditions were discontented with the Freedmen's Bureau labor system. The Wadmalaw, Ossabow, and St. Catherines farmers demonstrated this when they departed for Savannah. They preferred to leave their houses, their furniture, and their crops, standing in the fields, rather than to sign contracts with their old masters as the Bureau urged them to do.[6] The Bureau hoped for good wages and compliance with the terms of the contracts, but this would not have permitted the freedmen to use pressure for bettering their position. Although many bureau agents individually rendered valuable service to the freedmen, it was far from the goal of advancement that Howard proclaimed when he became Commissioner.

Howard deplored keeping the Negroes at the "bare subsistence" level. Yet when freedmen struck to force a rise in their standard of living—and did so at the point in the crop year when their work stoppage most affected the planters and might have brought concessions—the Bureau

    5 Joe M. Richardson, "The Freedmen's Bureau and Negro Labor in Florida," *Florida Historical Quarterly*, 39 (October 1960), 170.

    6 *New Orleans Times*, 20 November 1865.

sent in troops as strikebreakers.[7] Even though Howard was unhappy about the planters' organization that enforced maximum wages, he swiftly removed bureau agents who encouraged the freedmen to meet in bureau offices and resist the planters.[8]

The freedmen were deprived even when the Freedmen's Bureau, as their protector in their relations with the planter, protected them effectively. The Negroes did not learn how to protect themselves. When the bureau personnel in South Carolina during Saxton's regime assumed logically that a black man should the the third member of the boards to supervise contracts along with a planter and a bureau agent, they were soon overruled. Removing the Negro member from an already unbalanced board left the freedmen unrepresented in their own affairs. The white planters seem to have feared most giving a voice to the Negroes in labor matters. Their dislike of the Bureau was largely based on the belief that it would teach the freedmen to organize in their own behalf.[9] Those bureau agents who sought to teach the Negroes independence were quickly weeded out of the agency. When the Bureau, which they had come to depend upon, was gone, the freedmen, uninstructed, were on their own.

Another service that Howard might have rendered the freedmen called for a tactical change in lobbying for them. Instead of constantly playing down their demands to convince white audiences that there was nothing intrusive inherent in their quest for a new place in the society, he could have faced up to the fact that there was and called on white America to help make the change required. General Howard, a popular figure at the end of the war, could command audiences wherever he spoke in the North. Instead of repeatedly lecturing to raise money for the symbolic victory of building, against the opposition of his Abolitionist minister and much of his denomination, an integrated First Congregational Church of Washington, he could have used his influence in the North to make the nation face the realities in the South.[10] By citing the Negro farmers on the Sea Islands as evidence of success, he could have publicly stressed the wisdom of the congressional mandate to divide the abandoned lands on which some Negroes could start their own farms. Instead of endlessly praising the Emancipation Proclamation, he could also have borrowed from his friend Lyman Trumbull's fear that slaverey was not yet a dead issue and admitted that some planters were distorting his contract system to continue the restraints of slavery in all but name. And, speaking as a major general, he might have used the courage of which he was capable and told the people of the North about the widespread antiNegro incidents

---

[7] O. O. Howard to W. H. Trescot, 14 January 1866, BRFAL; J. E. Cornelius to H. W. Smith, 1 July 1866, BRFAL; O. O. Howard to Davis Tillson, 8 December 1865, AJ Papers.

[8] O. O. Howard circular letter to assistant commissioner, 16 January 1868, BRFAL; Williamson, *After Slavery*, p. 87.

[9] Wharton, *The Negro in Mississippi*, p. 79.

[10] The time and effort spent by Howard on this project was immense and the correspondence involved equally enormous. Three full volumes of "Letters Received, 1866–68," devoted exclusively to the church building drive and integration controversy, stand in the OOH Papers as interesting response to Howard's vigorous letter-writing campaign, which is documented throughout his letter books.

committed by the army men stationed in the South. Further, Howard might have revealed the President's subversion of the agency. That this would have caused Johnson to try to remove Howard is of course almost certain, but it is possible that Howard might have proved a difficult man to fire in 1865 or 1866. . . .

Had he spoken out, Howard would have been removed by the President, but not before the Commissioner had made it clear that the freedmen needed the help of a federal agency and that Johnson was the chief obstacle to their getting it. If the issue causing Howard's removal had been the treatment of the freedmen, emphasis would have been clearly focused on the Negro as the man crucial to all Reconstruction issues. Rather than being blurred in a morass of tenure of office and impeachment matters, the lines of Reconstruction dispute might have been clearly drawn and the deterioration of the freedmen's condition made brightly visible.

By not speaking up, Howard contributed immensely at a critical moment to the process—in the end it defeated Reconstruction—by which the nation pulled the wool over its eyes with respect to the freedmen. As long as the good General commanded the Freedmen's Bureau, many Americans felt free of the obligation to meet the plight of the ex-slaves. Perhaps the nation would not have met the obligation even if Howard defined it. Perhaps, but the test was never made. Because of his eternal hopefulness and his faith in the efficacy of his kind paternalism, Howard spared the nation the full force of the moral test that he had originally posed for it. . . .

. . . The Freedmen's Bureau could have been the builder but it was not, and a radical Congress gave that job to southern legislatures. Radical Reconstruction, with its achievements and failures in the states of the South, took the place of national responsibility. It introduced the freedmen to American politics; but as the nation's Negroes were given the chance to fend for themselves as southern voters, they lost an institution that might have made permanent their claim to be represented in the nation as a whole.

When that claim was entered again, it was made by the Negroes themselves. The Freedmen's Bureau had been theirs, but it failed them by substituting paternal supervision for man to man respect. As one of the Negroes, who most importantly entered the claim in behalf of his people, said of the Freedmen's Bureau: "The passing of a great human institution before its work is done, like the untimely passing of a single soul, but leaves a legacy of striving for other men. The legacy of the Freedmen's Bureau," wrote W. E. B. DuBois, "is the heavy heritage of this generation."[11]

---

11 DuBois, *Souls of Black Folk*, p. 39.

chapter 14

The Issues of Reconstruction

ANY CONTEMPORARY ACCOUNT OF RECONSTRUCTION must begin by noting that most of the traditional interpretations have been abandoned. As early as 1944 David Donald published an essay on Mississippi "scalawags" which traced much of the white Republican leadership to very respectable Whig political and social origins. Donald's thesis has been criticized and it obviously cannot be extended to other areas without substantial amendment, but it is no longer possible to think of the scalawags after the old conception of unsavory poor whites. In 1947 Vernon L. Wharton published an account of the Negro in postwar Mississippi which challenged the cliches about "Negro domination," massive corruption, shocking misrule, and the nature and extent of violence by white Southerners. These two studies have been multiplied many times and today we have fresh ideas and new research on nearly all the protagonists of the era. Thaddeus Stevens, Benjamin Wade, and other radicals are no longer commonly associated with sinister fanaticism or buffoonery. If no historian has given us a fully satisfactory study of black Reconstruction, much useful research has been done, and the old tone of general hostility has been replaced by more judicious perspectives. Recent studies of abolitionists, missionaries, teachers, young businessmen, and adventurers who went South because of ideology, opportunity, adventure, or exploitation demonstrate how misleading it was to place so many types of men under the single label of "carpetbagger" and to describe the entire lot as a predatory and malicious band. In 1961 John Hope Franklin summarized the work of many colleagues in a book which stressed the substantial accomplishments of Reconstruction constitutional conventions and legislatures, and helped lay to rest the ancient ghost of pervasive and extraordinary corruption.

During the 1960s a larger number of scholars made headway against the once dominant interpretations. In 1968 Stanley A. Kutler's monograph demonstrated the large inadequacies of conventional images of a

U.S. Supreme Court resentful of Radical excesses but deprived of power and largely cowed into inaction by Congress. Kutler's basic conclusions were strengthened and extended in a section of Harold M. Hyman's 1973 survey of the grand constitutional issues of Civil War and Reconstruction. Allen H. Trelease and Otto H. Olsen in essays of 1963 and 1966 suggested that David Donald had exaggerated the numbers and influence of affluent "old-line Whigs" among the "scalawags" but they joined Donald in the complete rejection of stereotypes on Southern Republicans as merely unprincipled, malodorous, and disloyal lower class whites. Otto H. Olsen's 1965 biography of the young Ohio lawyer, Union officer, and North Carolina Republican leader, Albion W. Tourgee, provided an account of an attractive person who combined idealism and a search for good health with the quest for opportunity generally urged upon Americans in the nineteenth century. Richard N. Current in a major monograph of 1967 on three Northern born governors of Southern states virtually laid to rest the carpetbag stereotype with convincing portraits of political figures who were almost too diverse to classify but reasonable men, conscious of principle, and neither cynical demagogues nor corrupt would-be dictators.

It would be erroneous to assume that the new conceptions emerged quickly and conquered all opposition at once. Political transformations may take place overnight but change comes to the general structure of American historical interpretation only by degrees and over a period of time. The point can be illustrated by examining three major works of scholarship printed between 1960 and 1963 on Andrew Johnson and the first year of his presidency. Although the authors all rejected the cliches describing Johnson as a courageous constitutionalist cast in the role of both hero and victim, each approached the topic from a somewhat different point of view. The first of the three books, written by Eric L. McKitrick and published in 1960, bore no traces of racial stereotypes or the cant which placed so heavy a burden of social evil on the Radicals. The book contained some sharp criticism of the President and presented new ideas, insights, and approaches, but the author perpetuated several traditional judgments and sympathies which many contemporary scholars reject. The central tragedy, according to McKitrick, sprang from the fact that the reunification of the North and the South came not in 1865 but slowly and painfully a generation later. Yet the chief movers of the times, the equalitarian Radicals, regarded citizenship for the Negro as a more important goal than the immediate reunification of Northerners and Southern white men. More recently, scholars have sympathized with radicals and traced the major tragedy of Reconstruction to the ultimate surrender of the freedman into new forms of bondage.

In a perceptive account of different Northern and Southern psychological interpretations of victory and defeat, McKitrick argued convincingly that Northerners expected a recognition of error, or at least a symbolic expression of defeat and repentance. Southerners, who had no consciousness of wrongdoing, disappointed Northern expectations by acting as if defeat meant no more than the grudging surrender of secession and the right of individuals to hold slaves. A "total" surrender of the type Germany made in 1945, McKitrick asserted, would have been "grotesque" and a tragic barrier to sectional reunification. Skeptics may wish to question this conclusion after considering that a sense of wrongdoing could have been manipulated to create a more substantial local foundation for black citizenship. Southern "innocence" coupled with an intense devotion to white supremacy contributed much to the ultimate defeat of Reconstruction.

Despite a barrage of criticism directed against Johnson, McKitrick clearly preferred the President's initial impulse toward "moderation" over the "harsh" plans of the Radicals. This is a preference which many scholars do not share. Certainly one may ask if the evidence sustains the notion that the best hope for the Republic lay in the crystallization of common action between Northern "moderates" and Southern counterparts such as Wade Hampton of South Carolina. McKitrick regretted "the ruthless quality" of Reconstruction and confessed that "the North for three generations has had something on its conscience which will probably never be exorcised." Curiously enough, the notion of guilt seems to refer not to the abandonment of black people but to Reconstruction itself. The most militant of the Radicals proposed the revolutionary change of bringing Negroes to the freedom and equality of full citizenship in the face of bitter and determined opposition, and it is difficult to imagine how this could have been accomplished except by "harsh" methods.

A significant number of white Southerners cooperated with Reconstruction from a great variety of motives ranging from sheer opportunism and "the acceptance of the inevitable" to the wish for national unity and an authentic desire to help the freedman establish himself in a new life. In New Orleans even famous Confederate generals such as Longstreet and Beauregard supported integrated schools and black participation in politics. Much of the willingness to cooperate, however, sprang from the belief that the federal government meant to *insist* on making the former slave a citizen. When the federal presence was removed or when Republican leaders wavered, white Southern cooperation tended to melt away. In the long run blacks stood to gain very little from Southern "moderates," and turned naturally enough to the more determined Radicals.

If McKitrick gave due consideration to Northern Negrophobia and the mixture of motives in the minds of many Radicals, he failed to take into account the intensity of Southern race consciousness or the fierce desire to keep Negroes in firm subordination. One may well ask if plans "milder" than the Radical program could have worked any major social changes at all. The "moderate" Wade Hampton came to power in South Carolina with a number of promises to Negroes, some of which he kept, but far more important to his political victory in 1876 was the prophetic wave of terror and coercion sponsored by his military bands of "Red Shirts." In brief, while McKitrick's theory of moderation seems dubious, his book opened new areas of debate and destroyed the myth of Andrew Johnson as the injured leader of high states' rights principles undone by the unscrupulous Radicals.

In 1963 an English scholar, William R. Brock, provided a more stringent analysis of Johnson and his policies. It seemed unlikely to Brock that any "centrist" or "moderate" policy led by Johnson and based on "moderate" Republicans and Democrats would have been feasible or desirable. Indeed, such a political coalition would have sounded the death knell of Reconstruction. Brock, even more critical than McKitrick of Johnson, described him as ignorant of Southern conditions and incapable of foreseeing or understanding Northern responses. Like McKitrick, Brock began with Northern and Southern psychological expectations at the end of the war, but he argued that without Northern demands for repentance and the substitution of national sentiment for provincial loyalty, Reconstruction would have been impossible. He also insisted that the Northern commitment to a higher status for the Negro, however vaguely defined or grudgingly granted, was a powerful force in the postwar era. Unlike nearly all the scholars before him, Brock understood the unity in the minds of many Republicans between their "materialistic" and their "idealistic" interests. The Radicals, who saw no conflict between assisting business prosperity and defending the cause of freedom, thought that moral progress joined to material advances would bring the Republic to a new pinnacle of human civilization. In the final analysis the Republican belief in the sanctity of property hindered considerably the effort to give black freedom an effective economic base, but the Radicals were still the best hope the freedman had. Brock answered an old complaint that the Radicals were a conspiratorial minority who came to power through devious means by explaining that the Radicals not only had the advantages of a dynamic ideology and Johnsonian blunders but that they also gained much from simply knowing the congressional ropes and the best uses of legislative rules and procedures.

LaWanda and John Cox joined the growing circle of Johnson critics in 1963 (Selection 1). They too saw Johnson as an inept politician whose blunders hurt the nation grievously, and they outlined several of his faults with a new clarity. Johnson, it seemed, was motivated by suspicion and hostility toward Negroes, by the insecurities and the vanity of a man who had risen from the grinding poverty of Southern "poor white" origins to hold in his hands the fate of all Southern "aristocrats." The President, consumed by political ambition, worked incessantly to preserve his power and to gain renomination in 1868 by means of a new coalition of Democrats and conservative Republicans. Fortunately for the country Johnson lacked the ability to execute his own ill-conceived and dangerous plans.

The Coxes proved that the basic split between Congress and Johnson came over the issue of civil rights, and James M. McPherson in 1964 demonstrated the reality of equalitarian ideology as a fundamental cause of Reconstruction. Johnson, who opened hostilities with the initially well-disposed radicals, staked his grand political design on the immediate "restoration" of the old Confederate states to the Union. Consequently Southerners had free rein to work out a system for replacing individual slave ownership with collective subordination. When Johnson vetoed the Civil Rights Act, he declared himself against "the Africanization of half the United States" and took a position fraught with racist concepts. Black prospects for a higher status in the South were dim without federal help, and the passage of legislation over the executive veto owed much to equalitarian thought. If the conflict of the President and Congress involved several major issues, the chief one was the struggle of racist and equalitarian ideologies. The veto and the repassage of the Civil Rights Bill marked the real beginning of Reconstruction, and made the struggle for freedom and equality the central issue of the times.

After the scholarship of the past two decades, the timeworn notions about Johnson's role as the heir to Lincolnian "moderation" seem extremely unlikely. On the face of the matter, one can see that "moderation" to most white Southerners meant harshness to the freedmen, and that sympathetic help to freedmen meant "harshness" to the great majority of Southern whites. The theory of Johnsonian and Lincolnian "moderation" was often spun around Lincoln's remark in the Second Inaugural Address which called for a peace with malice toward none and charity for all. In the sentence immediately prior to this much quoted remark, Lincoln suggested that the war might well be a terrible punishment sent to both North and South for the monstrous sin of slavery. He concluded the thought with the observation that if the conflict cost all of the wealth piled up by two-and-one-half centuries of bondage and if all the blood shed in slavery had to be repaid on the field of battle, then Americans could only say that God was just. After this thought the "charity" remark certainly seems poor evidence for a hypothetical postwar toleration of Southern intransigence by Lincoln. Much evidence points to the possibility that Lincoln considered a "sterner" policy for the South just before his death, but the nature of his "Pragmatic" bent, the ability to act with the Radicals today and the "moderates" tomorrow while keeping on good terms with all factions, makes any speculation about Lincoln's postwar conduct hazardous. Still it is difficult to imagine that Lincoln would have been as dogmatic, inflexible, and politically unwise as Johnson.

Although both Lincoln and Johnson were tossed on the tide of turbulent times which carried them beyond their expectations, Lincoln could ride with the tide while Johnson fell prey to the illusion that he could stem the surge of events. After Johnson tried to oppose the Freedmen's Bureau and the implementation of the Civil Rights Act by inattention, obstruction, and the appointment of hostile officials, both he and Congress carried their respective cases to the country and in the fall of 1866 the Radicals won a smashing victory at the polls. Obviously not all the Republican voters were equalitarians—far from it—but Johnson and the Southerners appeared to many Northerners as men who would undo the results of victory and challenge the peace. When the South resisted the Civil Rights Act, Radical leaders decided to commit its substance to the Constitution in the form of the 14th Amendment. After the Southern states rejected the amendment and met the drive for Negro citizenship with the kind of violence described in a 1962 article by John A. Carpenter, it became clear that only military reconstruction would be effective.

Harold M. Hyman in an essay of 1960 demonstrated that Southern violence and harassment seriously affected the Union army, and actually helped to bring about a powerful alliance between the Radicals and the military. It was Johnson's determination to remove from the South the military commanders sympathetic to Reconstruction and to replace Secretary Stanton in the War Department with a man hostile to the Radicals which persuaded Congressional leaders to attempt the impeachment of the President. If Johnson prevailed, the Republican program was undone. In retrospect it seems probable that the impeachment trial represented the high-water mark of Reconstruction, and that both the Radicals and the struggle for Negro citizenship suffered a major defeat in Johnson's acquittal. In 1958 a Jack B. Scroggs essay (Selection 2) made very clear the desperate need of Southern radicals for the federal presence and a sympathetic president. Thirteen years later in 1971 an impressive and painstakingly researched 553-page monograph by Allen W. Trelease on Klan violence (Selection 3) explored the dimensions of the terror first unleashed against blacks and their white allies in the Johnson administration.

The belief that Johnson's impeachment would have been tragic for the country, a traditional interpretation much weakened by the scholarship of the 1960s, seemed completely implausible after Michael Les Benedict's book of 1973 on the President's trial. Older historical works held that irresponsible Radicals with hastily contrived and ill founded charges were prevented from doing the most deplorable damage to the American form of government only by one or several heroic Senators. Benedict, who demonstrated that Congress repeatedly indulged Johnson with proposals for an easy way out, made a persuasive case for radical impeachment on the legal ground that Johnson clearly violated a statute in removing Secretary of War Stanton from office and on the more important political ground that the President persisted in an intolerable war against the Reconstruction so desperately needed by the nation. (Demands for the impeachment of Richard M. Nixon in 1973 and 1974 stimulated extra interest in Benedict's book.) Grant's more-active-than-supposed role during the impeachment crisis and the remainder of the Johnson presidency provided a major theme for Martin E. Mantell's 1973 study of Johnson, Grant, and Reconstruction politics.

Continuing Southern intransigence and violence, some Republican Congressional losses in 1867 and 1868, and the narrowness of Grant's victory in 1868, kept alive fears about the preservation of the fruits of Union victory and about future material and moral progress in general. A Democratic resurgence would, of course, destroy the Republican majority which provided the foundation for all policies and hopes. Consequently Congress to protect that majority as well as to advance black rights in both the South and the North passed the 15th Amendment and a series of Enforcement Acts between 1870 and 1873. As Everette Swinney's 1962 essay (Selection 4) indicated, the enforcement of the amendment and the laws depended largely upon the quantity of persistent energy and sustained local action allocated to the task by the Federal government. Although the Republicans did not enact the last major Civil Rights Act until 1875, the crucial year turned out to be 1873. Grant, alternately slack and vigorous in enforcement during the past, now allowed the panic of 1873, political scandals, and a growing Northern impatience with Southern issues, to distract his administration from Reconstruction. (The Democratic capture of the House of Representatives in 1874 did not help matters.) Some of the causes and conditions of the drift can be seen in Martin E. Mantell's book and in Keith Ian Polakoff's monograph of 1973 on the 1876 election and the end of national Reconstruction, but much work remains to be done on the Grant years. Revisionist scholarship which cast so much light on the first phases of Reconstruction during the 1950s and 1960s seemed in the mid 1970s to be turning to a close scrutiny of the middle and later phases.

In the late 1960s and the early 1970s monographs on American racism such as Forrest G. Wood's 1968 study of racist responses to emancipation and Reconstruction altered the attitudes of many scholars toward the post-Civil War era. During two brief decades, a number of historians began with hostile attitudes, moved toward at least a tentative recognition of black and white radical efforts as a struggle for human freedom, and ended by doubting Reconstruction as a tainted crusade irretrievably flawed by the racism of the crusaders. That racism existed among Senators and Representatives cannot be doubted, but some scholars lacked a proper perspective for this fact because they failed to perceive racism as a dominant ideology and a force which permeated American society. Still, the Reconstruction generation paid less homage to master race ideology than the generations before and after, Republicans invoked white supremacy ideas less frequently than Democrats, and the Radicals were the least racist group of leaders in national history. If some Radicals displayed racial condescension and even hostility, a significant number of men in the same faction struggled valiantly and with substantial success to achieve a genuinely equalitarian position.

On a second major point the attempt to escape old mistakes led to several new errors. The effort to dispose of the ancient canard of "Negro domination" led to a correct realization of the impressive achievements of Reconstruction governments, of the tendency of white radicals to occupy most important offices, and of the fact that blacks dominated no states and only a modest number of local governments. Some revisionists, however, used these facts incorrectly to understate the role of blacks and to characterize them as largely passive before events. Corrective ideas and information can be found in the recent internal histories of black groups which focus on the responses and actions of blacks rather than whites. The new trend was one of emphasis rather than of difference in kind and scholars could begin with useful general compilations of existing knowledge about black Reconstruction such as the black journalist Lerone Bennett's dramatic account of 1967 and white historian Robert Cruden's capable summary of 1969 (Selection 5). Moreover, any scholar could profit from the modern foundation stones of black history in Reconstruction, Joel Williamson's brilliant study of South Carolina blacks and Joe M. Richardson's useful and informative monograph on Florida blacks (both published in 1965). The most important recent monographic contribution was John Blassingame's excellent 1973 study on the almost uniquely rich institutional life of black New Orleans between 1860 and 1880. In Peter Colchin's monograph of 1972 on black responses in Alabama to emancipation and Reconstruction we encounter not a largely passive populace overly deferential to white leadership but rather people capable of vigorous independence and a vital role in shaping Reconstruction. In recent biographies such as Okon Edet Uya's 1971 study of Robert Smalls we find political leaders of large ability and in essays such as Marjorie Morris' article of 1967 on the Louisville demonstrations of 1870 and 1871 we see blacks acting energetically against white caste claims.

BIBLIOGRAPHY

Works Discussed in This Chapter

Benedict, Michael Les, *The Impeachment and Trial of Andrew Johnson* (1973).

Bennett, Lerone, Jr., *Black Power: The Human Side of Reconstruction* (1967).

Blassingame, John, *Black New Orleans, 1860–1880* (1973).

Brock, William R., *An American Crisis: Congress and Reconstruction, 1865–1867* (1963).

Carpenter, John A. "Atrocities in the Reconstruction Period," *Journal of Negro History* (1962).

Colchin, Peter, *First Freedom: The Response of Alabama's Blacks to Emancipation and Reconstruction* (1972).

Cox, John, and Cox, LaWanda, *Politics, Principles and Prejudices, 1865–1866* (1963).

Cruden, Robert, *The Negro in Reconstruction* (1969).

Current, Richard N., *Three Carpetbag Governors* (1967).

Donald, David, "The Scalawags in Mississippi Reconstruction," *Journal of Southern History* (1944), and the Donald-Trelease items, *JSH* (1964).

Franklin, John Hope, *Reconstruction After the Civil War* (1961).

Hyman, Harold M., *A More Perfect Union: The Impact of Civil War and Reconstruction on the Constitution* (1973), and "Johnson, Stanton and Grant: A Reconsideration of the Army's Role in Events Leading to Impeachment," *American Historical Review* (1960).

Kutler, Stanley A., *Judicial Power and Reconstruction Politics* (1968).

McKitrick, Eric L., *Andrew Johnson and Reconstruction* (1960).

McPherson, James M., *The Struggle for Equality: The Abolitionists in Civil War and Reconstruction* (1964).

Mantell, Martin E., *Johnson, Grant and the Politics of Reconstruction* (1973).

Morris, Marjorie M., "An Early Instance of Non-Violence: The Louisville Demonstrations," *Journal of Southern History* (1967).

Olsen, Otto H., "Reconsidering the Scalawags," *Civil War History* (1966), and *Carpetbagger's Crusade: The Life of Albion W. Tourgeé* (1965).

Polakoff, Keith Ian, *The Politics of Inertia: The Election of 1876 and the End of Reconstruction* (1973).

Richardson, Joe M., *The Negro in the Reconstruction of Florida, 1865–1877* (1965).

Scroggs, Jack B., "Southern Reconstruction: A Radical View," *Journal of Southern History* (1958).

Swinney, Everette, "Enforcing the Fifteenth Amendment, 1870–1877," *Journal of Southern History* (1962).

Trelease, Allen W., "Who Were the Scalawags?" *Journal of Southern History* (1965), and *White Terror: The Ku Klux Klan Conspiracy and Southern Reconstruction* (1971).

Uya, Okon Edet, *From Slavery to Public Service: Robert Smalls, 1839–1915* (1971).
Wharton, Vernon L., *The Negro in Mississippi, 1865–1890* (1947).
Williamson, Joel, *After Slavery: The Negro in South Carolina During Reconstruction, 1861–1877* (1965).
Wood, Forrest G., *Black Scare: The Racist Response to Emancipation and Reconstruction* (1968).

Suggested Readings

The most useful *general accounts of Reconstruction* are still John Hope Franklin, *Reconstruction After the Civil War* (1961) and Kenneth M. Stampp, *The Era of Reconstruction* (1965). Franklin tends to stress narrative and Stampp analysis. Both books could profit from revision. Two more recent surveys are Rembert W. Patrick, *The Reconstruction of the Nation* (1967) and Michael Perman's *Reunion Without Compromise: The South and Reconstruction* (1973). Robert Cruden's *The Negro in Reconstruction* (1968) provides a survey of black history.

Among *general works on Civil War and Reconstruction* the most extensive and detailed, James G. Randall and David Donald *The Civil War and Reconstruction* (2nd ed., 1961) is dated in many respects but useful on some points and has a bibliography comprehensive up to the late 1950s. A concise and very useful survey of the war and postwar era is Emory M. Thomas' well written *The American War and Peace, 1860–1877* (1973). Also brief but with more antebellum material is David Lindsey, *American Conflict: The Civil War and Reconstruction* (1974). Three books which like other recent surveys have merit but fail to assimilate much important revisionist scholarship are Thomas H. O'Conner, *The Disunited States: The Era of Civil War and Reconstruction* (1972); Robert H. Jones, *Disrupted Decades: The Civil War and Reconstruction Era* (1973); and David M. Potter, *Division and the Stresses of Reunion, 1845–1876* (1973).

Among brief *collections of documents* the best volumes are Richard N. Current, ed., *Reconstruction, 1865–1877* (1965) and James P. Shenton, ed., *Reconstruction: A Documentary History of the South After the Civil War* (1963). See also Robert W. Johannsen, ed., *Democracy on Trial, 1845–1877* (1966). Heavily slanted toward white supremacy is Walter L. Fleming, ed. *A Documentary History of Reconstruction* (2 vols., 1966). The defense of Fleming in David Donald's preface is not convincing.

Among *collections of essays* the most useful brief volumes are Staughton Lynd, ed., *Reconstruction* (1967) and Seth M. Scheiner, ed., *Reconstruction: A Tragic Era?* (1968). Irwin Unger's *Essays on the Civil War and Reconstruction* (1969) is also worth noting and several essays in Harold Hyman, ed., *New Frontiers of Reconstruction Historiography* (1966) strike out in new directions. The most extensive and best chosen anthology of modern writings is Kenneth M. Stampp and Leon Litwack, eds., *Reconstruction: An Anthology of Revisionist Writings* (1969) but the utility of the book is restricted by the absence of introductory and bibliographical material.

On *Southern violence and repression* the best book is Allen W. Trelease's volume on the Klan. See also Herbert Shapiro, "The K.K.K. During Reconstruction—the S. C. Episode," *Journal of Negro History* (1964); Shapiro, "Afro-American Responses to Race Violence During Reconstruction," *Science and Society* (1972); Jack D. L. Holmes, "The Effects of the Memphis Race Riots of 1866," *West Texas Historical Society Papers* (1958); and Jerrell H. Shofner,

"Fraud and Intimidation in the Florida Election of 1876," *Florida Historical Quarterly* (1964). For a curious and thoroughly unpersuasive effort to vindicate the infamous Black Codes, see Theodore Wilson, *The Black Codes of the South* (1965). For a more reasonable approach, see Joe M. Richardson, "The Florida Black Codes," *Florida Historical Quarterly* (1969).

Among works on *early Reconstruction policy and experiments* the best book is Willie Lee Rose's important and beautifully written *Rehearsal for Reconstruction: The Port Royal Experiment* (1964). For a fine, ground-breaking essay on Sumner's brainchild, the Freedman's Inquiry Commission, see John G. Sproat, "Blueprint for Radical Reconstruction," *Journal of Southern History* (1957). Also worthy of note is Louis S. Gerteis, *From Contraband to Freedman: Federal Policy Toward Southern Blacks, 1861–1865* (1973). On quasi-communal experiments, see Martha M. Bigelow, "Freedmen of the Mississippi Valley, 1862–1865," *Civil War History* (1962) and "Plantation Lessee Problems in 1864," *Journal of Southern History* (1961). See also Richard B. Drake, "Freedman's Aid Societies and Sectional Compromise," Ibid. (1963); Hans L. Trefousse, "The Joint Committee on the Conduct of the War, A Reassessment," *Civil War History* (1964); John G. Clark, "Radicals and Moderates on the Joint Committee on Reconstruction," *Mid-America* (1963); and J. Thomas May, "Continuity and Change in the Labor Program of the Union Army and the Freedman's Bureau," *Civil War History* (1971).

Among the works on *freedom amendments and laws* the best account of the three Reconstruction amendments are as follows: John and LaWanda Cox *Politics, Principles and Prejudices, 1865–1866* (1963); Jacobus tenBroek, *The Antislavery Origins of the Fourteenth Amendment* (1951); Joseph B. James, *The Framing of the Fourteenth Amendment* (1965); and William Gillette, *The Right to Vote: Politics and Passage of the Fifteenth Amendment* (1965). See also Alfred H. Kelly, "The Fourteenth Amendment Reconsidered: The Segregation Question," *Michigan Law Review* (1956) and Robert Harris, *The Quest for Equality* (1960). On the Civil Rights Act of 1866 see LaWanda and John Cox; for the Civil Rights Act of 1875, see James M. McPherson, "The Abolitionists and the Civil Rights Act of 1875," *Journal of American History* (1965); Bertram Wyatt-Brown, "The Civil Rights Act of 1875," *Western Political Quarterly* (1965); and Ronald B. Jager, "Charles Sumner, the Constitution, and the Civil Rights Act of 1875," *New England Quarterly* (1969).

The best *state and local studies on Reconstruction* are by Vernon L. Wharton, Joel Williamson, and Joe M. Richardson, listed earlier. See also Richard L. Hume, "The Arkansas Constitutional Convention of 1868: A Case Study in the Politics of Reconstruction," *Journal of Southern History* (1973). W. McKee Evans' *Ballots and Fence Rails: Reconstruction on the Lower Cape Fear* (1967) is an interesting and useful study. Carol K. R. Bleser does a competent job in *The Promised Land: The History of the South Carolina Land Commission, 1860–1890* (1969). The English scholar Alan Conway, *Reconstruction in Georgia* (1967) used little revisionist scholarship and produced a dated study. Also based on "moderate" scholarship and perceptions are Jack P. Maddex, Jr., *The Virginia Conservatives, 1867–1879* (1970); Elizabeth Nathans, *Losing the Peace: Georgia Republican and Reconstruction* (1968); and William C. Harris, *Presidential Reconstruction in Mississippi* (1967).

Among the best studies on "*carpetbaggers*" *and* "*scalawags*" are the works by David Donald, Allan W. Trelease, Richard N. Current, and Otto H. Olsen discussed in the chapter introduction. See also Sarah Van Woolfolk, "Five Men Called Scalawags," *Journal of Negro History* (1964); Thomas B. Alexander, "Persistent Whiggery in the Confederate South, 1860–1877," *Journal of Southern History* (1961); other works by Alexander; John Hope Franklin's introduction to a new ed. of Tourgee's *A Fool's Errand* (1961); and Lillian A. Pereyra, *James Lusk Alcorn: Persistent Whig* (1966).

For surveys of *black Reconstruction* see Robert Cruden and the collection edited by Emma Lou Thornbrough, *Black Reconstructionists* (1972). The best state study is Joel Williamson's volume on South Carolina. Also very good is Joe M. Richardson's book on Florida blacks, and the somewhat dated but still useful volume of 1947 on Mississippi by Vernon L. Wharton. Lerone Bennett Jr.'s book of 1967 on black Reconstruction is a dramatic and useful survey. For a fine article on a key topic, see Louis R. Harlan, "Desegregation in the New Orleans Public Schools During Reconstruction," *American Historical Review* (1962). The best biography of a black leader is Okon Edet Uya's study of Robert Smalls. Two significant recent studies are Peggy Lansome, *The Glorious Failure: Black Congressman Robert Brown Elliot and the Reconstruction in South Carolina* (1973) and William Warren Rogers and Robert David Ward, *August Reckoning: Jack Turner and Racism in Post-Civil War Alabama* (1973).

For *black war and postwar activities* which contributed to Reconstruction see Dudley T. Cornish, *The Sable Arm: Negro Troops in the Union Army, 1861–1865* (1956); James M. McPherson, ed., *The Negro's Civil War* (1965); Martin Abbott, "Freedom's Cry: Negroes and their Meetings in South Carolina, 1865–1869," *Phylon* (1959); Benjamin Quarles, "The Abduction of the Planter," *Civil War History* (1958); Alan F. Westin, "Ride-In!" *American Heritage* (1962); and Elsie M. Lewis, "The Political Mind of the Negro, 1865–1900," *Journal of Southern History* (1955). Two recent items of interest on black politics are Elizabeth Balanoff, "Negro Legislators in the N. C. General Assembly, 1868–1872," *North Carolina Historical Review* (1972) and Melvin Urofsky, "Blanche K. Bruce: U.S. Senator, 1875–1881," *Journal of Mississippi History* (1967). On black education see James M. McPherson, "White Liberals and Black Power in Negro Education, 1865–1915," *American Historical Review* (1970). Against the idea of great numbers of roving blacks see Richard J. Hopkins, "Occupational and Geographic Mobility in Atlanta, 1870–1896," *Journal of Southern History* (1968). On economic conditions see Christie Farnum Pope, "Southern Homesteads for Negroes," *Agricultural History* (1970); Roger L. Ransom and Richard Sutch, "Debt Peonage in the Cotton South After the Civil War," *Journal of Economic History* (1972); and Thomas Wagstaff, "Call Your Master—'Master'—Southern Political Leaders and Negro Laborers During Presidential Reconstruction," *Labor History* (1969); and Edward F. Sweat, "Francis L. Cardoza—Profile of Integrity in Reconstruction Politics," *Journal of Negro History* (1961). For a worthwhile monograph on a neglected topic see Otis A. Singletary, *The Negro Militia in Reconstruction* (1957). For ultra-racist history and a few useful footnotes see E. Merton Coulter, *Negro Legislators in Georgia During the Reconstruction Period* (1968).

On *Northern blacks* see Leslie H. Fishel, Jr., "Repercussions of Reconstruction, The Northern Negro, 1870–1883," *Civil War History* (1968), and Howard H. Bell, *A Survey of the Negro Convention Movement* (1969).

The key work on *border state Reconstruction* is Richard O. Curry, ed., *Radicalism, Racism and Realignment: The Border States During Reconstruction* (1969). See also the useful works by Rosa A. Webb, *Benjamin Helm Bristow: Border State Politician* (1969); William E. Parrish, *Missouri Under Radical Rule, 1865–1870* (1965); Norma L. Peterson, *The Political Career of B. Grantz Brown* (1965); and Victor B. Howard, "The Black Testimony Controversy in Kentucky, 1866–1872," *Journal of Negro History* (1973).

On *radical Republicans* the key works are Hans L. Trefousse, *The Radical Republicans: Lincoln's Vanguard for Racial Justice* (1969); James C. Mohr, *The Radical Republicans and Reform in New York During Reconstruction*

(1973); Harold M. Hyman, ed., *The Radical Republicans and Reconstruction, 1861–1870* (1967); Trefousse, ed., *Background for Radical Reconstruction* (1970); Michael Les Benedict, "The Rout of Radicalism: Republicans and the Elections of 1867," *Civil War History* (1972); Edward L. Gambill, "Who Were the Senate Radicals?" Ibid. (1966); Lee A. Dew, "The Reluctant Radicals of 1866," *Midwest Quarterly* (1968); Glenn M. Linden, " 'Radicals' and Economic Policies: The House of Representatives, 1861–1873," *Civil War History* (1967); Linden, " 'Radicals' and Economic Policies: The Senate," *Journal of Southern History* (1967); Linden, "Radical, Political and Economic Policies: The Senate, 1873–1877," *Civil War History* (1967). Equally important are three fine biographies, Ralph Korngold, *Thaddeus Stevens: A Being Darkly Wise and Rudely Great* (1955); Fawn M. Brodie, *Thaddeus Stevens: Scourge of the South* (1959); and Benjamin P. Thomas and Harold M. Hyman, *Stanton: The Life and Times of Lincoln's Secretary of War* (1962). Also useful despite David Donald's hostility is Donald's *Charles Sumner and the Rights of Man* (1970); Hans L. Trefousse, *Benjamin F. Wade: Radical Republican from Ohio* (1963); John A. Carpenter, *Ulysses S. Grant* (1970); Patrick W. Riddleberger, *George Washington Julian, Radical Republican* (1966); Richard H. Abbott, *The Life of Henry Wilson* (1972); and Mark M. Krug, *Lyman Trumbull, Conservative Radical* (1965). Some of the more important articles are David Montgomery, "Radical Republicanism in Pennsylvania, 1866–1883," *Pennsylvania Magazine of History and Biography* (1961); Ira V. Brown, "William D. Kelley and Radical Reconstruction," Ibid. (1961); and Robert Kirkwood, "Horace Greeley and Reconstruction in 1865," *New York History* (1959). See also Ernest McKay, *Henry Wilson, Practical Radical: A Portrait of a Politician* (1971); and Sister Mary Karl George, *Zachariah Chandler* (1969).

On the *Freedman's Bureau* see the titles in the last chapter; Martin Abbott, *The Freedman's Bureau in South Carolina, 1865–1872* (1967); Howard Rice, *The Freedman's Bureau in Louisiana* (1970); and Alton Hornsby, Jr., "The Freedmen's Bureau Schools in Texas, 1864–1870," *Southwestern Historical Quarterly* (1973).

The most important recent works on *national Reconstruction politics* are John and LaWanda Cox, Stampp, Franklin, McKitrick, Stanley I. Kutler, W. R. Brock, cited elsewhere. See also William H. Ahern, "The Cox Plan of Reconstruction: A Case Study of Ideology and Race Relations," *Civil War History* (1970) and Kenneth B. Shover, "Maverick at Bay: Ben Wade's Senate Re-election Campaign, 1862–63," Ibid. (1966). Avery O. Craven makes a persistent but not very successful effort to cope with revisionist scholarship in *Reconstruction: The Ending of the Civil War* (1969). David Donald, *The Politics of Reconstruction, 1863–1867* (1965) attempts to quantify Congressional voting patterns but does not come up with many conclusions. Herman Belz tries to demonstrate a closeness of thought of Lincoln and the radicals in *Reconstructing the Union: Theory and Policy During the Civil War* (1969). Charles Fairman, *History of the Supreme Court of the U.S., Reconstruction and Reunion, 1864–1888*, Vol. 6, Part 1, (1971), a vast storeroom of hastily presented information, contains a number of racist observations. Other recent studies are James E. Sefton, *The U.S. Army and Reconstruction, 1865–1867* (1967); Kenneth E. Davison, *The Presidency of Rutherford B. Hayes* (1972); and Felice A. Bonard, *North of Reconstruction: Ohio Politics, 1865–1870* (1970).

The major work on *Johnson's impeachment* is Michael Les Benedict, *The Impeachment and Trial of Andrew Johnson* (1973). See also Ralph J. Roske, "The Seven Martyrs?" *American Historical Review* (1959); Harold M. Hyman, "Johnson, Stanton and Grant: A Reconsideration of the Army's Role in the

Events Leading to Impeachment," Ibid. (1960); Hans L. Trefousse, "The Acquittal of Andrew Johnson and the Decline of the Radicals," *Civil War History* (1968); and Eric L. McKitrick, *Andrew Johnson and Reconstruction* (1961). The Coxes and Brock cited earlier are also useful.

Among general studies of the *Reconstruction era* see the fine studies by Ralph E. Morrow, *Northern Methodism and Reconstruction* (1956); Winthrop S. Hudson, "Reconstituting the Nation: Religion and Reconstructon," *Foundations* (1966); Walter T. K. Nugent, *The Money Question During Reconstruction* (1967); Nugent, *Money and American Society, 1865–1880* (1968); and David Montgomery, *Beyond Equality: Labor and the Radical Republicans, 1862–1872* (1968).

On the *liberal Republicans and the stalwarts* see Richard A. Gerber, "Liberal Republicanism, Reconstruction and Social Order: Samuel Bowles as a Test Case," *New England Quarterly* (1972); William G. Eidson, "Who Were the Stalwarts?" *Mid-America* (1970); Matthew T. Downey, "Horace Greeley and the Politicians: The Liberal Republican Convention in 1872," *Journal of American History* (1967). James M. McPherson's "Grant or Greeley, The Abolitionist Dilemma in the Election of 1872," *American Historical Review* (1965) is less useful.

On *Indians and Reconstruction* see W. McKee Evans, *To Die Game: The Story of the Lowry Band, Indian Guerrillas of Reconstruction* (1971) and M. Thomas Bailey, *Reconstruction in Indian Territory: A Story of Avarice, Discrimination and Opportunism* (1972).

Civil Rights Was the Issue*
LaWanda and John H. Cox

Even the Republican papers that remained friendly in their attitude toward the President made clear their own support for some form of national guarantee of the freedmen's rights. A few reconciled their own attitude with that of the President by pointing to his concluding promise, the one Johnson had incorporated from Seward's draft, and insisting that the President was not opposed to federal protection. Most of the Republican press, however, saw the veto as drawing a sharp line between the position of the President and that of their party.[1]

What had been taking place in the Republican party since the close of

---

* Reprinted with permission from *Politics, Principles and Prejudices, 1865–1866* by John and LaWanda Cox. Copyright 1963 by The Free Press of Glencoe, a division of The Macmillan Company.

[1] These generalizations are based primarily upon the extensive press clippings on the Civil Rights veto.

the civil conflict was a gradual metamorphosis, similar to the one that had taken place during the war. The war years transformed the Republicans, a political amalgam originally united on the principle of opposition to the extension of slavery, into a party committed to the destruction of slavery. This objective had been formally embodied in the party platform of 1864. The platform, however, had not included a plank supporting equal legal status for the freed slaves, despite the fact that such a plank was offered and considered. By the winter of 1865, Republicans generally had expanded their repudiation of slavery into a condemnation of legal discriminations which by then seemed to them the last vestiges of slavery. Important elements within the party held that the freedmen's rights must include an equality of suffrage, but on this more advanced position, Republicans were not yet agreed. They had, however, come to identify Republicanism with a defense of basic civil rights for the freed slave.[2] Sometimes this identification of Republicanism with the principle of equal status before the law was stated explicitly; sometimes it was expressed through generalizations that invoked liberty, freedom, or humanity. A characteristic argument, advanced by one Republican paper, was that if the position on equal civil rights embodied in Johnson's veto message were correct, then "all the principles of democracy and freedom upon which our creed of Republicanism rests are false and we must recant them."[3] When Republicans accused Johnson of treachery to the Republican party and Republican principles, or with greater forbearance simply asked that he give them some unmistakable evidence so that they might "continue to confide in him as a *Republican*,"[4] they were identifying their party with the principle of equality in legal status for all freedmen.

Thus what had once been an advanced, or "Radical," position within Republican ranks, by 1866 had become accepted and moderate. To most opponents of equal civil status, however, the principle still appeared "Radical." Herein lies one clue to the confusion in the use of the term "Radical" which plagues any serious student of the period. The term is inescapable; yet a man labeled a "Radical" by one set of contemporaries or historians is often found designated a "moderate" by another group of contemporaries or historians. All would agree that Charles Sumner, Thaddeus Stevens, and Wendell Phillips, extreme men though not of one mind, were the prototypes of Radicalism. The term *Radical*, however, has often been used to identify, and castigate, all Republican opponents of

2 Before the opening of Congress in December 1865, Schuyler Colfax, Speaker of the House, made a speech which was widely regarded as a statement of majority Republican opinion. He abjured any inflexibility of policy, spoke warmly of what the President had already accomplished in securing commitments from the Southern states, but made clear that some additional assurances were considered necessary. The first of these, and indeed the only one that was substantive, was that "the Declaration of Independence be recognized as the law of the land" by the protection of the freedmen in their rights of person and property including the right to testify. He made no mention of suffrage for the Negro nor of any punitive action against the South. For text of speech, see *New York Times*, November 19, 1865.

3 Clipping from a Buffalo paper, March 29, 1866, Scrapbook, Johnson MSS.

4 Chicago *Evening Journal*, March 28, 1866, ibid.

Andrew Johnson. Many of these men were almost as critical of Sumner, Stevens, and Phillips as were their Conservative adversaries. Few followed Stevens in his demand for confiscation; most were ready to abandon or drastically compromise Sumner's aim of Negro suffrage. Though they wished to proceed with caution, there was no strong desire among them for an indefinite postponement of restoration by reducing the South to the status of "territories" or "conquered provinces." In other words, many Radicals were moderate men. The Radical opponents of President Johnson were united in one demand—that of national protection for the freedmen. On other issues of Reconstruction they held widely divergent views.

It has sometimes been assumed that a common economic attitude united Radicals and marked them off from pro-Johnson men. This assumption is demonstrably false. Some were protariff men, some antitariff men; some advocated cheap money, some upheld a sound gold standard; some were spoilsmen, others were among the spoilsmen's bitterest critics. . . .

Although [Henry J.] Raymond's break with Johnson did not come over the civil rights issue, his defection to the opposition was consonant with his basic convictions in respect to equality of citizenship for the Negro. Most other key Republican moderates who took their stand against Johnson shared those convictions. Senator John Sherman had long been troubled by the probability that freedmen would be oppressed if they had no share of political power. As for the Civil Rights Bill, he wrote, "I felt it so clearly right that I was prepared for the very general acquiescence in its provisions both North and South. To have refused the Negroes the simplest rights granted to every other inhabitant, native or foreigner, would be outrageous."[5] The veto was a major factor in Sherman's repudiation of Johnson, whom he had hitherto defended. "The President's course on the Civil Rights Bill and constitutional amendment was so unwise that I could not for a moment allow anyone to suppose that I meant with him to join a coalition with the rebels and Copperheads."[6] Senators Lyman Trumbull of Illinois, James Grimes of Iowa, and William Fessenden of Maine were all men of moderation and principle, able to withstand terrific pressures, as their votes against Johnson's conviction on impeachment charges later made amply clear; their principles included a commitment to basic civil rights for the freedmen. . . .

Behind conciliatory Republican leaders whose personal attitudes might in other circumstances have enabled them to accept a solution which would leave the future status of the freedmen in the hands of Southern whites, there was the pressure of mass Republican opinion. The overwhelming preponderance of Republican sentiment was behind a national guarantee for basic civil equality, short of suffrage, for the freedmen. This sentiment is unmistakable in newspaper editorials and private cor-

---

[5] J. Sherman to W. T. Sherman, May 16, 1865, April 23, 1866, *The Sherman Letters*, pp. 251, 270; see also John Sherman, *Recollections of Forty Years in the House, Senate and Cabinet: an Autobiography* (2 vols.; Chicago, 1895), 1, pp. 364, 366–67, 369.

[6] J. Sherman to W. T. Sherman, October 26, 1866, *The Sherman Letters*, p. 278.

respondence;[7] it was also reflected in the congressional vote on what was to become the Fourteenth Amendment. In the Senate, Republicans divided thirty-three to four in its favor. The "nays" were those of Senators Cowan, Doolittle, Norton of Minnesota and Van Winkle of West Virginia. Senator Dixon was absent and not voting. In the House, 138 Republican votes were cast for the Amendment; not a single Republican voted against it.[8] This vote was taken *before* Johnson made clear his political intentions by issuance of the call for the Philadelphia Convention.

After the Civil Rights veto, Republican opinion had crystallized in a determination to set further conditions before accepting Southern representatives back into the counsels of the nation, but not just any conditions.[9] The matters dealt with in sections two and three of the Fourteenth Amendment, namely the basis of future Southern representation, the granting of suffrage to the Negro, and the degree of proscription of Confederate leaders were negotiable; the question of equality before the law, federally enforceable, was no longer open to compromise. The issue of civil rights and national protection for the freedmen was not, as has sometimes been implied, the product of campaign propaganda and exaggeration, nor even of the shocking impact of the Memphis and New Orleans riots. The civil rights issue predated those developments.

Although in deference to Seward and Raymond the pro-Johnson leaders had attempted to evade discussion of the Fourteenth Amendment, it was generally recognized as being at stake in the ensuing campaign. After Radical victories in the states that voted in September and early October, pressure was put upon the President to accept the Amendment. As early as September 19, Bennett in the *Herald* foresaw defeat unless the President would "take up" the proposed Fourteenth Amendment and "push it through all the still excluded Southern States as rapidly as possible" with the kind of pressure he had used in behalf of the Thirteenth Amendment. Bennett at last deplored the condition he had done so much to provoke, "the widening of his [Johnson's] conflict with the radicals to a conflict with Congress." He now viewed the Amendment as "not a radical measure, but a measure of the Republican conservatives of Congress."[10] When Samuel S. Cox asked the President about the rumors that he would modify his opposition to the amendment in keeping with "the poplar [sic] current," Johnson "got as ugly as the Devil. He was regularly mad. . . . There's no budge in him. Browning's letter is his view."[11]

S. L. M. Barlow's attitude toward the Amendment's role in campaign strategy is pertinent. He was much opposed to the President's yielding unless the Johnson forces should suffer defeat in New York. In that event, he thought the President might be "compelled to yield on the Constitutional amendment, but to yield to the pressure now, before our election, would destroy him & be in gross bad faith . . . as we are making a good

---

[7] See footnotes 4–9, 20–23, 27, 31–49 in the Coxes' book.

[8] McPherson, *Handbook of Politics for 1868*, p. 102.

[9] Compare McKitrick, *Andrew Johnson and Reconstruction*, p. 443.

[10] New York *Herald*, September 19, 1866.

[11] Cox to Marble, October 9, 1866, Marble MSS. See also Barlow to R. Taylor, October 26, 1866, Barlow MSS.

fight & cannot now change our course."[12] If faced with defeat in November, however, Barlow thought Johnson could say to the South, "While I have not thought the ratification of the amendment necessary . . . the Northern people have decided otherwise—You must be represented. . . . Ratify the amendment therefore." Barlow explained that Johnson could "be supported in this, if necessary, *after* November, not only here but by the ablest presses of the South in New Orleans, Mobile, Charleston & Richmond—To change *now* would deprive him, practically of every paper and every voter—The Radicals would not be won back to him and he would lose the whole power of the Democratic party."[13]

Browning's letter, to which Representative Cox referred, is additional proof of the importance of the Amendment as a campaign issue. It is also, and more importantly, added evidence that the opposition of the pro-Johnson forces to the Amendment was not merely limited to a distaste for section three, which denied Southern leaders state and national office. The heart of Browning's argument, approved by the President, was that section one, the civil rights guarantee, would restrict the states in functions properly their own. It would subject the "authority and control of the States over matters of purely domestic and local concern . . . to criticism, interpretation and adjudication by the Federal tribunals, whose judgments and decrees will be supreme."[14]

Johnson's refusal, despite great pressure and much advice, to capitulate on the Fourteenth Amendment after his election defeat cannot be attributed alone to his stubborn nature. The explanation that he decided for reconciliation, then reversed course on the basis of the Radicals' behavior, is exploded by the identification of the early conciliatory draft message as the work of Seward.[15] Another factor entered into policy considerations, the hope of ultimate victory and the tactical advantage to be gained by encouraging extreme action on the part of the opposition with a view to ultimate popular reaction against it. Doolittle wrote Browning on November 8:

> The elections are over and we are beaten for the present. But our cause will live. If all the states not represented refuse to ratify the amendment . . . the extreme Rads will go . . . for reorganizing the southern states on negro suffrage. . . . That will present the issue squarely of forcing negro suffrage upon the South and upon that we can beat them at the next Presidential election.[16]

---

12 Barlow to R. Johnson, October 24, 1866, Barlow MSS.

13 Barlow to T. J. Barnett, September 27, 1866, ibid.

14 Browning to W. H. Benneson and H. V. Sullivan, October 13, 1866, printed in *New York Times*, October 24, 1866. See also the earlier public statement of Democratic and Conservative members of Congress to the effect that the "dignity and equality of the States" must be preserved, including "the exclusive right of each State to control its own domestic concerns"; published in the New York *Herald*, July 4, 1866.

15 Professor Beale erroneously assumed that Seward's unidentified draft message had been prepared by Johnson and had reflected his views. *The Critical Year*, pp. 400–403.

16 Doolittle to Browning, November 8, 1866, Doolittle MSS; see also James, *Framing of the Fourteenth Amendment*, p. 178, and McKitrick, *Andrew Johnson and Reconstruction*, pp. 464–65, especially footnote 38.

A short time later, Weed was writing Seward that he had rebuffed Senator Morgan's suggestion of an organization in Congress against "extreme men." Weed explained, "I think that if the pressure should be withdrawn the Radicals would hang *themselves*."[17] From Ohio the prediction reached the President that "If Congress resorts to rash and violent means to carry out the destructive purposes of the radicals, their own party will break to pieces."[18] From New York came more positive advice:

> Are those proposed amendments to be adopted, changing the whole nature of our government? I trust not. I think a year or two of Radicalism more, will satisfy the country that the principles contained in that old instrument are too dear to us to be frittered away. . . . I believe that with you standing firmly on the ground you have assumed and each state organizing her conservative men on the Philadelphia platform, two years more will have seen the end of the Radical race.[19]

Analysts of the 1866 election returns pointed out to the President that if the potential vote of the unrepresented South were added to the Conservative vote in the North, a large majority of the nation supported the President and opposed the amendment, and that ultimately the President must triumph.[20]

Raymond's editorials in the *Times* had urged the President to accept the decision of the people in favor of the Amendment, and either to recommend its ratification by the Southern states or to stand aside while they made a settlement with Congress upon the basis of its principles. By the end of December, however, Raymond had come to the conclusion that Johnson's opposition to the Amendment was unyielding. The President, he explained, intended to hold to his earlier position in the conviction that his policy would ultimately prevail. Johnson believed that the Supreme Court would set aside any conditions Congress might impose upon the South or, failing such a resolution of the conflict, that the use of military power to enforce congressional policy would become so "expensive, odious and intolerable" that the voters would expel from power the party responsible for such a policy.[21]

The losses which the Radicals sustained in the state elections of 1867 seemed to justify the President's hope of victory and the strategy of no compromise. News of the defeat of the Radicals in Connecticut's April election of that year was received by Johnson as "the turn of the current" and by Welles as "the first loud knock, which admonishes the Radicals of their inevitable doom."[22] Welles believed that the returns from Pennsylvania and Ohio in October "indicate the total overthrow of the Radicals

---

17 Weed to Seward, November 24, 1866, Seward MSS. By the end of February, Weed was apprehensive of congressional reconstruction proposals and uncertain of the best presidential tactics; Weed to Seward, February 21, 1867, ibid.

18 P. W. Bartley to Johnson, November 9, 1866, Johnson MSS.

19 S. Smith to Johnson, November 10, 1866, ibid.

20 T. S. Seybolt to Johnson, November 8, 1866, F. A. Aiken to Johnson, November 26, 1866, ibid.

21 *New York Times*, October 31, 1866, November 3, 9, 12, 17, 19, 1866, December 4, 27, 31, 1866.

22 *Diary of Gideon Welles*, 3, p. 78.

and the downfall of that party."[23] In November, 1867, Johnson celebrated the election results by a victory speech before a group of serenaders in which he held that "the people have spoken in a manner not to be misunderstood."[24] The President's "stubbornness" of the previous November seemed to have prepared the way for success in the presidential election of 1868. The hope proved an illusion; but the hope was present, and died hard.[25]

In refusing to accept the equal rights provisions of the Civil Rights Act or of the Fourteenth Amendment, Johnson won lasting gratitude from white Southerners to whom the concept of equality between the races was anathema,[26] and this despite the ordeal of military government and immediate universal Negro suffrage which they in all likelihood would have been spared had Johnson's course been different. But with this decision, the President lost the confidence and respect of moderate Republicans. Lyman Trumbull and John Sherman both felt a sense of betrayal in Johnson's veto of the Civil Rights Bill. "Besides," confided Sherman to his brother, "he [Johnson] is insincere; he has deceived and misled his best friends."[27] The confidence in Johnson's assurances of justice for the freed people, which characterized Republican opinion, except that of extreme Radicals, in December, 1865, turned to mistrust. No longer were misgivings directed toward Presidential policy alone; they came to embrace the President's intention and integrity, and corroded his public influence. "The truth is," Senator Fessenden wrote to Senator Morgan in mid-1867, "Mr. Johnson has continued to excite so much distrust that the public mind is easily played upon by those who are seeking only the accomplishment of their own purposes."[28] By standing adamant against a federally enforceable pledge of minimum civil equality for the Negro as a prerequisite to restoration of the secession states, Johnson precipitated a great issue of moral principle central to the battle over Reconstruction; and he brought upon himself an unparalleled humiliation.

---

[23] Ibid., p. 232.

[24] *New York Times*, November 14, 1867; McKitrick, *Andrew Johnson and Reconstruction*, p. 498.

[25] See pp. 95–106 in the Coxes' book.

[26] Of the 65 votes which Johnson obtained on the first ballot for the presidential nomination of the Democratic party in 1868, all but four were from Southern delegates. Charles H. Coleman, *The Election of 1868: The Democratic Effort to Regain Control* (New York, 1933), pp. 164, 208.

[27] J. Sherman to W. T. Sherman, July 8, 1866, *The Sherman Letters*, p. 276. For Trumbull's reaction see *Congressional Globe*, 39th Cong., 1st sess., p. 1761 (April 4, 1866); and C. H. Ray to M. Blair, April 10, 1866, enclosure in Blair to Johnson, April 15, 1866, Johnson MSS. A digest and explanation of the bill, unsigned, but in Trumbull's handwriting, is in the Johnson MSS; see Cox, "Andrew Johnson and His Ghost Writers," p. 473.

[28] Fessenden to Morgan, June 26, 1867, Morgan MSS. The distrust, of course, involved party as well as principle. By mid-1866, it was widely believed that Johnson intended to bring the Democracy back into national power and ascendancy, and that he had deliberately sought to wreck the party that had elected him.

Southern Radicals Fight for Reconstruction*

Jack B. Scroggs

The advent of Radical Republican leadership in the reconstruction of the recently rebellious states of the South in early 1867 resulted in sweeping changes in both the form and substance of government in this conquered area. Of revolutionary political significance, this shift brought to the fore a new group of leaders gathered from Negroes, the heretofore politically submerged class of native whites, and recently arrived Northerners. The fortunes of this unusual alliance, especially during the early phase of Reconstruction, depended largely upon the success of the Radical party in Congress, a circumstance which led to widespread efforts by state leaders to establish a close liaison with the national party. Correspondence from the Southern Republicans to congressional Radicals discloses many of the problems which they encountered and presents Reconstruction from a point of view frequently ignored by many historians. Here is found an intimate record of local political leaders striving to revamp Southern political institutions despite the determined opposition of Southern spokesmen trained in the school of conservatism. This task, ambitious at best, was made increasingly difficult by intraparty factionalism on the state and local level and by the failure to maintain close cooperation between the national Republican leadership and the Radical party in the South. A cross section of regional Radicalism, based on the voluminous correspondence from the South Atlantic states—Virginia, North and South Carolina, Georgia, and Florida—clearly reveals these difficulties inherent in the organization of state parties dedicated to radical reform within the framework of a national party rapidly evolving as the agent of conservative interests.

The return to power of traditional political leaders in 1865 and 1866 touched off an initial storm of protest from Southern Radicals. Union men vigorously charged that these former rebels continued to be hostile toward the government and could not be trusted with the job of reconstructing the economy, politics, and society of the South. From North Carolina and Virginia came complaints that rebels held the offices of "trust, honor, or emolument" to the exclusion and proscription of men loyal to the Union.[1] An observer in North Carolina asserted that "the feel-

* Jack B. Scroggs, "Southern Reconstruction: A Radical View," *Journal of Southern History,* 24 (November 1958), 407–29. Copyright 1958 by the Southern Historical Association. Reprinted by permission of the Managing Editor.

[1] John Robinson to Thaddeus Stevens, February 22, 1866; Augustus Watson to Stevens, May 3, 1866, in Thaddeus Stevens Papers (Manuscripts Division, Library of Congress).

ings of by far the larger proportion of the people of this State are disloyal to the Govt—and enamored by the bitterest hatred towards the North." He expressed the view that the duplicity of Southern leaders led observers like General Grant to form hasty and erroneous opinions of their loyalty.[2] Thaddeus Stevens, Radical leader in the House, received a report from Georgia that the rebellious spirit in that state was greater than when the states seceded from the Union.[3] Former rebels were accused of tampering with the mails and practicing discrimination in the courts; one North Carolinian expressed fear of mob violence should the rebels discover that he had written to Charles Sumner.[4]

Initially this proscriptive attitude was displayed most prominently toward Southerners who had resisted the Confederacy,[5] but Northerners and freedmen complained of similar treatment. The assistant superintendent of the Freedmen's Bureau at Harpers Ferry declared that "to be an Officer of the U S [sic] is to subject one to continual insult, without the power of redress."[6] Protesting against the action of the Georgia convention of 1865 in requiring two years prior residence for voting, a recent immigrant to that state wrote to Thaddeus Stevens: "The loyal men thousands in number now residing in Georgia appeal to you to save them from this rebel act which has been passed to disfranchise them because they are loyal."[7] The former rebels were accused not only of being unwilling to extend any considerable rights and privileges to the Negroes but also of subjecting them to abuse and refusing to encourage them to labor for themselves.[8] A Georgia correspondent, refuting the claim that the Negro was indolent, maintained that "the Southern people as a whole, are not faithful or true exponents of the negroe's [sic] character or his ability."[9] Negro testimony in a similar vein came from freedmen at Halifax, North Carolina, who requested aid from Elihu B. Washburne in collecting a fund to allow them to emigrate to Liberia. They complained that landowners would not let land to black men and they were unable to collect their wages, in arrears for two years. Seeing no hope for freedom in the South, they lamented: "There is nothing in this country for a black-

---

[2] G. F. Granger to Stevens, January 11, 1866, ibid. In November, 1865, General Grant had made a hurried trip through some of the Southern states and had made a report highly favorable to the former rebellious citizens.

[3] L. Black to Stevens, December 18, 1865, ibid.

[4] Marion Roberts to Stevens, May 15, 1866, ibid.; W. T. Laflin to Charles Sumner, February 25, 1867, in Charles Sumner Papers (Houghton Library, Harvard University). From a lower stratum of society came a more fervent plea: "I ask is thar no protection to union men my god how long shall I be prosacuted by Secessions." J. W. Ragland to Stevens, February 8, 1866, in Stevens Papers.

[5] See Roberts to Stevens, May 15, 1866, in Stevens Papers, for an account of Southern reaction to returning western North Carolina veterans of the Union army.

[6] A. [F.] Higgs to Elihu B. Washburne, December 27, 1866, in Elihu B. Washburne Papers (Manuscripts Division, Library of Congress).

[7] Frank S. Hesseltine to Stevens, April 26, 1866, in Stevens Papers.

[8] Granger to Stevens, January 11, 1866, ibid. See also Dexter E. Clapp to Benjamin F. Butler, November 9, 1865, in James A. Padgett (ed.), "Reconstruction Letters from North Carolina," in North Carolina Historical Review, 19 (October, 1942), 398–99.

[9] William Strother to Stevens, April 28, 1866, in Stevens Papers.

man that has comon sence [sic] but cruelty starvation & bloodshed."[10] Also from North Carolina came the warning that the "protection afforded on account of property interest, and the social attachments of Master & Slave are destroyed, and now God have mercy on the blacks, if they are turned over to the government of their old masters, who seem determined to prove emancipation a curse."[11] Southern Radicals argued that Congress should remove the ex-Confederates from office and place Reconstruction in the hands of loyal Union men.[12] Although not wholly responsible for the changing attitude of Congress, these pleas undoubtedly exerted considerable influence in crystallizing congressional action against the relatively lenient policies of President Johnson.

With the overthrow of the Johnson-supported state governments by the Reconstruction Acts of 1867, the three factions of Southern Republicans saw no further impediment in the path toward reform and personal aggrandizement.[13] The exuberant Radicals suggested that the incumbent state officers be immediately dismissed and replaced by loyal Republicans.[14] Although congressional Radicals refused to aid Southern Republicans to this extent, the influence of Radicals in the South began to show a remarkable growth. Negro meetings called by Southern Conservatives tended to evolve into Radical rallies. The freedmen, safely under the control of carpetbag leadership, refused to respond to Conservative overtures, preferring to remain with the party which promised to preserve their political and civil rights.[15] . . .

True to pre-election predictions, the people of the South voted [in 1868] for conventions and returned large Republican majorities in each of the South Atlantic states, but exultant reports of victory from Southern Radicals were intermingled with their charges of fraud by the Conservative opposition. . . . John C. Underwood, carpetbag leader in Virginia, complained that the state judiciary was "most unrelenting in the persecution of every white or colored voter who is favorable to the Republican party." He further alleged that "thousands have been discharged for the avowed reason that they voted the Republican ticket in October."[16]

---

10 Charles Snyder et al. to Washburne, February 1, 1868, in Washburne Papers.

11 Clapp to Butler, November 9, 1865, in Padgett, "Reconstruction Letters from North Carolina" in *North Carolina Historical Review*, 19 (October, 1942), 398–99.

12 Watson to Stevens, May 3, 1866, in Stevens Papers. Watson wrote: "The true and simple *policy* is to declare every citizen (irrespective of color) a *voter*, and disfranchise every rebel both in the state and National Governments."

13 Joseph H. Williams to Sumner, March 15, 1867; J. B. Hall to Sumner, March 17, 1867, in Sumner Papers; S. A. Daniel, Jr., to John Sherman, March 13, 1867, in John Sherman Papers (Manuscripts Division, Library of Congress); W. F. Henderson et al. to Stevens, March 4, 1867, in Stevens Papers.

14 Henderson et al. to Stevens, March 4, 1867, in Stevens Papers; J. Bowles to Saul Shellabarger, October 11, 1867, in Washburne Papers.

15 Thomas W. Conway to Salmon P. Chase, April 23, 1867, in Padgett (ed.), "Reconstruction Letters from North Carolina," in *North Carolina Historical Review*, 21 (July, 1944), 233–35; Daniel Richards to Washburne, November 13, 1867, in Washburne Papers.

16 John C. Underwood to Washburne, December 16, 1867, in Washburne Papers. This charge was bolstered by similar complaints against officials of the Petersburg area. James H. Platt, Jr., to George F. Edmunds, December 28, 1867, in Sherman Papers.

Faced with heightening Conservative opposition, Southern Radicals became more insistent upon assurances from Congress of continued support during this inchoate period of their new governments. In Virginia, Underwood wrote of threats "that if the colored and poor laboring people continued to vote against the land holders . . . they would find themselves between the upper & nether mill stones & would be ground to powder." A Conservative member of the Virginia constitutional convention was charged with declaring that no such voter could live upon his land and that he "would sooner see it all grow up in broom sedge & scrub pine." Underwood declared: "These threats are made boldly & defiantly by those who hold all the offices with very rare exceptions & who are at heart just as rebellious as when they were in arms against us." Faced with these threats to the rising power of the Radicals, Underwood asked, "Can Congress save us from annihilation?"[17] . . .

Despite such warnings of tightening opposition, the constitutional conventions which met to reform the state governments were safely in the control of the Radicals, and reports received by congressional leaders were optimistic of the ultimate success of the Republican party in the South. Although the South Carolina group contained a Negro majority, congressional Radicals were assured by a leading white member that "we have now a convention composed of better material than any other Southern state."[18] Urged by Elihu B. Washburne to finish the Florida constitution in time to get it ratified before the Chicago Republican convention, a Radical leader from that state predicted early agreement on the new frame of government.[19] Virginia Radicals wrote for advice on the further disfranchisement of rebels; many Virginia Republicans favored disfranchisement but hoped to avoid anything that would injure the Republican party or "impede its glorious march toward human freedom."[20] North Carolina leaders were optimistic, but Albion W. Tourgée, outstanding carpetbag leader in that state, advised congressional Radicals to defer action on Sherman's Alabama Bill until after all the state elections in order to lull the Conservatives into a continuation of their policy of inaction. . . .

The campaign for ratification of the new state constitutions revealed a growing Conservative opposition which gave rise to another flurry of protests from Southern Republicans. A Savannah resident wrote that organized clubs of Conservatives were using all sorts of spurious promises to win Negro support and by the use of threats were making freedom of speech impossible. Merchants in Savannah were reportedly advertising that they did not want any further trade from Radicals.[21] Another Georgia observer declared: "These are parties of rebels now going about through the state murdering loyal citizens in their houses at night and shooting

---

17 Underwood to Washburne, December 9, 16, 1867, in Washburne Papers.

18 J. P. M. Epping to Washburne, February 22, 1868, in Washburne Papers.

19 Richards to Washburne, January 27, 1868, ibid.

20 J. W. D. Bland to Washburne, March 15, 1868, ibid.

21 J. S. Powell to "The Reconstruction Committee," February 18, 1868, in Stevens Papers.

them from bushes during the day. . . . These murdering parties are said to be chiefly composed of slave holders sons."[22] . . . Thaddeus Stevens was urgently requested to curb further the power of President Johnson as a requisite to victory in South Carolina.[23]

The ratification contest also brought a renewal of party strife in Florida. . . . Washburne's faithful reporter, the carpetbagger Richards, warned that "a perfect reign of terror is most imminent." He pointed out that Klan outrages were applauded in Florida and that "threats of violence against all those who dare oppose the adoption of the Rebel Constitution come from high quarters so that we are not permitted to question their purposes."[24] Richards later reported that "the rebels are organizing rapidly and will all support the Constitution," and that their leaders were sponsoring Reed meetings. The Conservatives not only used threats and intimidation, but the Reed Republican faction boasted of their employment of force and their own control of the election boards. And yet, even though the Negro leader Saunders deserted them, the Radicals remained optimistic of a shift in the tide.[25]

Despite internal party divisions and growing Conservative opposition, the ratification elections resulted in Republican victories in each of the states except Virginia, where the election was postponed. A combination of factors contributed to this victory, but Republican reports particularly stressed the value of the Union League organizations in achieving ultimate victory.[26] . . .

With an apparent victory won in the battle for state reorganization, congressional and local Radicals began to show increasing concern over the approaching presidential election. For a time there was some doubt among Southern Radicals as to whether they should support Grant or Chase for the nomination.[27] Grant's nomination by the Chicago Republican convention resolved this doubt, but left the Radicals to face the twin difficulties of Conservative opposition in the South and dissension within their own state organizations. . . .

Political conditions in South Carolina during the presidential campaign became so chaotic as to justify the dispatch of a special Radical agent and observer to that state. This observer, John M. Morris, reported that the Democrats were very active and well supplied with money—the "rich rebels coax with one breath and threaten with the next." As to in-

---

22 Joseph McKee to Stevenson [Stevens], April 16, 1868, ibid.

23 Samuel Linsley to Stevens, March 15, 1868, in Stevens Papers.

24 Richards to Washburne, April 14, 1868, in Washburne Papers.

25 Richards to Washburne, April 14, 20, 21, 1868, ibid.

26 H. P. Farrow of Georgia proclaimed that the "Union League has again saved us." J. M. Edmunds, head of the National Union League, announced in a report to Chandler that testimony from every Southern state witnessed the fact that the Union League was responsible for the Republican sweep in the delegate and constitutional elections. In contrast to most estimates, Farrow announced that the Conservatives of Georgia had secured the support of about 20,000 Negroes. Farrow to Chandler, April 28, 1868; Edmunds to Chandler, June 13, 1868, in Chandler Papers.

27 Washburne, the central power behind the early Grant boom, was informed of the Chase campaign in the South. . . . Deweese to Washburne, October 30, 1867.

timidation by the Democrats, Morris declared: "All that is said in the North is true. It is not safe for me to go alone unarmed into the up country here. Negroes are daily shot dead or wounded. Nobody is convicted because no adequate testimony is found or the magistrates don't prosecute. . . . I fear that thousands of voters will be kept away or driven away from the polls."[28] The carpetbag leadership in the state reported that the malignancy of the Democrats was growing and that they were openly proclaiming that no Negro would be allowed to approach the polls.[29] Governor Robert K. Scott warned: "The rebels did not misrepresent the fact when they said they were not whipped but only overpowered."[30] Nor was evidence lacking to corroborate these charges. In Abbeville County, B. F. Randolph, colored state senator and chairman of the Republican state central committee, while on a speaking tour was murdered by a group of undisguised whites.[31] A congressional representative from the state reported: "Three members of the General Assembly and one member of the late Constitutional Convention have been murdered secretly." He added that the "whole upper portion of the State is said to be in such a condition that it is regarded as unsafe for Republicans to go there to speak." It was impossible, he said, to punish the murderers because of the sympathy of their white neighbors.[32] . . .

The position of the party in Georgia caused further anxiety to the national Radicals. The Negroes of that state were of doubtful value to the Republicans, and the white members of the party were hopelessly at odds. The Democrats, on the other hand, were well organized. Ex-governor Joseph E. Brown predicted a difficult campaign to swing the state to Grant, and, in a plea for funds, declared that all the money in Georgia was concentrated in the hands of the Democrats.[33] . . .

The success of the Democrats in the newly elected Georgia legislature served to heighten the anxiety of the Radicals. Close division not only made it impossible for the Republican administration to carry out an effective program, but ultimately led to the expulsion of the Negro members of both houses by the Democrats, and thus to an absolute Democratic majority.[34] The Radicals hoped that this move would "arouse the colored race to sense of their danger, and . . . stimulate them in the cause of their own defense, and that of the Republican party."[35] Actually, Democratic assumption of control in the legislature caused talk of calling a "white

---

[28] John M. Morris to William Claflin, September 14, 1868, in Chandler Papers.

[29] B. F. Wittemore to Chandler, September 16, 1868; N. G. Parker, D. H. Chamberlain, C. C. Bowen to Chandler, September 12, 1868, ibid.

[30] R. K. Scott to T. L. Tullock, October 20, 1868, ibid.

[31] A. J. Ransier to Tullock, October 19, 1868; Scott to Tullock, October 20, 1868, ibid.; Francis B. Simkins and Robert H. Woody, South Carolina During Reconstruction (Chapel Hill, 1932), 446.

[32] F. A. Sawyer to Chandler, October 22, 1868, in Chandler Papers.

[33] Joseph E. Brown to Tullock, June 29, 1868, ibid.

[34] Caldwell to Claflin, September 1, 3, 1868; J. E. Bryant to [Chandler], October 5, 1868; Spalding to Chandler, September 5, 1868, ibid.

[35] Spalding to Chandler, September 1, 1868, ibid.

man's" constitutional convention. A Republican observer declared: "It is manifestly the intention of the Rebel leaders, to defy the power of the U.S. Govt. and to set at naught the laws of Congress."[36]

Democratic success in Georgia brought an increased volume of Republican protests against frauds, violence, and intimidation. . . . Joseph E. Brown feared that the Negroes would be driven from the polls either by intimidation or by force. In the event of a free election the state would go Republican by a 10,000 majority, but, Brown declared: "There is . . . a reign of terror and violence in some parts of the state, and Republicans cannot hold meetings and discuss the questions involved in the canvass without actual violence or such threats of it as drive off the timid from the meetings.[37] Foster Blodgett, notorious Georgia scalawag, echoed the former governor's observations. "The rebellious spirit is more intense and bitter now than in 1860 and 1861," he said. "Negroes are killed almost every day while white Republicans are threatened [with] abuse and maltreated to an extent that is alarming.[38] John H. Caldwell, Republican candidate for Congress, reported that Democratic methods in Georgia included "bribery, threats, and when they can do so unmolested, actual violence, as well as fraud in the election."[39] . . .

The election resulted in a Grant victory in three of the five states. Through intimidation of the Negroes and a tightly knit white organization the Democrats secured the ascendancy in Georgia; Virginia, not yet readmitted to the Union, was not entitled to a vote.

With the Republicans in control in North Carolina, South Carolina, and Florida, and the status of Virginia and Georgia not fully decided, correspondence between the Radicals of the South and congressional Republicans began to dwindle. No longer were Southern Republicans entirely dependent upon Northern arms for their support. And, with Grant safely elected, congressional Radicals were largely content to allow their Southern colleagues free sway in the former rebellious states—their electoral votes would not be required again until 1872.

Only in Virginia and Georgia did Southern Radicals still urgently petition congressional aid. In a bid for further help, a prominent Georgia Republican, early in 1869, reported that "There is no split in the Republican Party of Georgia. . . . There has never been a question as to whether Georgia is reconstructed." His solution of the problem called for the convening of the old constitutional convention to complete the work of reconstruction.[40] The strife in Georgia led Congress, after a year of vacillation, again to impose military rule in that state. Even so, the state Radicals were still unable to cooperate, and a combination of anti-Bullock Republicans and Democrats brought about the overthrow of the Radical

---

36 Spalding to Chandler, September 5, 1868, ibid.

37 Brown to Chandler, October 8, 1868, ibid.

38 Blodgett to Chandler, September 13, 1868, ibid.

39 Caldwell to Claflin, July 4, 1868, ibid. Caldwell reported that there was a Democratic plot to murder him which failed when rains delayed his campaign trip. Caldwell to Chandler, October 10, 1868, ibid.

40 Farrow to Washburne, February 26, 1869, in Washburne Papers.

administration in the state election of December, 1870.[41] In Virginia, the disputed sections on disfranchisement in the 1868 constitution de-layed the ratification vote until 1869, when a combination of conservative Republicans and Democrats secured the defeat of these provisions and elected a compromise governor and a Democratic legislature.[42]

The presidential election of 1872 brought another attempt to affect a liaison between national Radical leaders and Southern Republicans to assure the reelection of Grant. Southern Republicans again poured forth tales of Democratic violence and intimidation and bemoaned the dissen-sion within the Radical group of the South. From North Carolina came an early request for protection from the outrages of the Ku Klux Klan. . . . The Radicals of South Carolina bitterly complained of their lot. A promi-nent Republican editor of Columbia, protesting continued Klan activity, declared:

> There has never, during my four years residence here, been a more in-tolerant and vindictive spirit manifest than is exhibited now. The threat is openly made, that if Mr. Greeley is elected President the northern men will all be driven out of the state, the negroes degraded from office, and all the old Southern rebel element put into power again.[43]

Despite the seriousness of a growing party schism in South Carolina, however, national Radicals refused to intercede in aid of either group. William E. Chandler informed Franklin J. Moses that local politics were of no concern to the party leadership so long as the state was won for Grant. . . .

Republican hopes for the capture of Georgia were dissipated by the results of the state election in August. Democrats again asserted their power. One Radical, reporting to Chandler, declared: "To say that the election was a farce, fails to express the truth, it was a mob, controlled by the Democratic bullies, and ended in *crime*." The "straights," he com-plained, either stayed at home or were bullied into the Democratic ranks.[44] A South Carolinian observing the Georgia election reported:

> Never since the formation of this government was there a more shame-ful outrage upon free suffrage than the one just perpetrated in Georgia in the name of democracy. The colored men were intimidated and driven away from the polls by the hundred and one devices of the democrats, and where words would not do, bloody deeds soon taught the negroes that to vote against the wishes of their white employers and neighbors was to risk death.[45]

---

[41] C. Mildred Thompson, *Reconstruction in Georgia* (New York, 1915), 255–75; M. M. Hale to Chandler, March 25, 1872, in Chandler Papers.

[42] L. E. Dudley to Chandler, August 1, 1868, in Chandler Papers; James B. Hope to Washburne, December 21, 1868; J. K. Gilmer to Washburne, January 16, 1869, in Washburne Papers; Eckenrode, *The Political History of Virginia During the Recon-struction* (Baltimore, 1904), 87–128.

[43] L. Cass Carpenter to Chandler, August 6, September 21, 1872, in Chandler Papers.

[44] Scruggs to Chandler, October 5, 1872, in Chandler Papers.

[45] Carpenter to Chairman, National Executive Committee, October 6, 1872, ibid.

Despite internal Republican dissension, the political picture in Florida was cause for Radical optimism. A Tallahassee carpetbagger wrote of the improving political sagacity of the Negro: "The opposition may talk of the everlasting 'nigger' but it is beginning to learn that it has in the black man a foe whose opinions are born of honesty and whose native instincts assisted by six years' education in the exercise of the suffrage, and his naturally Christian heart, make him at this time their most formidable enemy, and the finest and most progressive friend of the Republican party."[46] . . .

Notwithstanding the favorable turn of events in Florida, and continued strong Radical influence in North and South Carolina, Republican prospects generally were not thought to be as bright as in 1868. . . .

Doubtless these local Radical apprehensions had a salutary effect upon the activities and contributions of national Republicans, for the efforts of the Democrats and "straight-outs" to recapture these Southern states were in vain except in Georgia. In that state, although it was a center of insurgent Democratic activity, the regular Democrats produced a sizable majority for Greeley.

After the reelection of Grant in 1872, the tie between the congressional Radicals and Southern Republicans rapidly deteriorated. Southern Radicals, gradually losing power through the South Atlantic states, discovered that Congress was reluctant to act except during periods of national party crisis, and their complaints and pleas gradually lessened. Indeed, when in 1874 the Democrats captured the lower house of Congress, Radical congressional action was no longer possible.

As the election of 1876 approached, Democratic leaders displayed a determination to oust the Republicans regardless of methods. A Florida Radical, despairing of victory with two Republican electoral tickets in the field, informed Chandler that the strong opposition was composed of young men who had grown up in postwar conditions and who blamed all the ills of the South on Yankees and Negroes, and a Virginia observer told John Sherman that there was great danger of open revolt in the South if the Democrats failed to win the election.[47] In South Carolina, Governor Daniel H. Chamberlain, candidate for reelection, faced Wade Hampton's formidable "red-shirts," undergoing personal abuse and even threats on his life. Chandler received a report that at one Republican rally in Barnwell County 600 mounted Democrats had taken over the meeting and heaped abuse upon the carpetbaggers and scalawags. The governor was denounced as "a Carrion Crow, a Buzzard who has come down here to prey upon our people and steal from them their substance," and amidst frequent rebel yells it was suggested that the crowd hang him and his entourage on the spot. An observer of the affray declared that the Republicans of the state were no longer willing to undergo such punishment unless the North came to their aid.[48] An Atlanta Republican sug-

---

[46] Sid L. Bates to Chandler, April 15, 1872, ibid.

[47] Alex River to Sherman, July 25, 1875, in Sherman Papers; Rollins to Chandler, August 9, 1876, in Chandler Papers.

[48] Carpenter to Chandler, August 26, 1876, in Chandler Papers.

gested that Northern speakers be sent South: "The ignorant masses here (mostly Republicans) require instruction in their political rights and duties as free citizens, and encouragement to stand up like men for their rights."[49]

The determination of Southern Democrats plus the dissension within the Southern Republican party ultimately led to the defeat of the Radicals in each of the South Atlantic states by 1876. Contested election returns from both South Carolina and Florida for a time beclouded the political scene, but the repudiation of the Radical state leaders by the Hayes administration brought a quick collapse of the remaining Radical organizations.

Although Southern Radical Republican correspondence necessarily presents a distorted picture of the full process of Southern Reconstruction, it is nevertheless an invaluable source for a study of that much-disputed period of American history. From no other source is the historian able to secure so complete a picture of the motives, emotions, and reactions of the members of the three factions who composed the Southern wing of the postwar Republican party. This correspondence, along with other contemporary sources, reveals a much more complex social, economic, and political evolution than is found in partisan accounts by historians who neglect material prejudicial to their sectional sympathies.

Several factors of primary importance are disclosed by these Radical letters from the South. In the first place they reveal a problem of adjustment of interests which plagued the party until its overthrow in 1876—a problem which undoubtedly contributed much to that downfall. A contemporary North Carolinian phrased the difficulty thus: "The problem of adjusting the balance between the three constituent elements of the Republican party South is certainly one pregnant with danger, therefore claiming imminent solution from the hands of the national leaders of our party."[50] That the national leaders were either unable or unwilling to undertake this task is evidenced by the inability of the state organizations to follow consistently a policy of cooperation.

These communications further reveal a lack of close cooperation between the leading Radicals of the South and the congressional Radicals. Most frequently the correspondence was from less influential Republicans often in opposition to dominant groups. The urgency of pleas and complaints from these Southern Radicals obviously was important in helping to shape the opinions of congressional leaders, but, after 1868, the pleas received a favorable response only when the strength of the national party was threatened. Intrastate party difficulties were, in the main, left to the solution of local leaders; national leaders refused to become involved in party splits such as occurred in Florida and South Carolina. Central direction was difficult to achieve, particularly as the Southern Radicals became increasingly a burden and an embarrassment to the

---

[49] Spalding to Chandler, June 26, 1876, ibid.

[50] E. M. Rosafy to Butler, March 28, 1874, in Padgett (ed.), "Reconstruction Letters from North Carolina," in *North Carolina Historical Review*, 20 (October 1943), 365–70.

national party.[51] Personal ambition and differences in ideology worked to produce antagonistic groups within the party in each of the Southern states, and astute Conservative politicians proved to be adept at widening the gaps. This intraparty division ultimately proved disastrous to the Republicans in all of the South Atlantic states, especially in South Carolina, Georgia, and Florida, where conflicting groups struggled for power throughout the Reconstruction years.

Southern Radical correspondence further reveals the effectiveness of the campaign developed by the Redeemers in their struggle to capture control of the state governments. Radical accounts of intimidation, fraud, and violence, while undoubtedly exaggerated, demonstrate an early reinvigoration of local political leadership. The evidence indicates that state Radicals, especially the carpetbag leaders, grossly underestimated the abilities and strength of this Conservative leadership in all of the South Atlantic states. The immigrants from the North seized upon the Reconstruction Acts as an opportunity to revamp Southern political and social standards, but their methods were revolutionary in character and took little account of past development and of national trends in political economy. Ultimately cultural forces of the past, and long-standing mores, in league with newly evolving economic combinations, led to repudiation of Southern Radicalism by the national party leaders and the emergence of conservative whites of the South as the stronger force.

Reconstruction and the White Terror*

Allen W. Trelease

. . . The Ku Klux Klan was . . . a terrorist organization aiming at the preservation of white supremacy and . . . a counter-revolutionary device to combat the Republican party and Congressional Reconstruction policy in the South. For more than four years it whipped, shot, hanged, robbed, raped, and otherwise outraged Negroes and Republicans across the South in the name of preserving white civilization.

The Klan could not have launched this career, much less persisted in it

---

51 C. Vann Woodward, *Reunion and Reaction: The Compromise of 1877 and the End of Reconstruction* (Boston, 1951), deals extensively with this party problem.

* From pp. xi–xii "Preface" and pp. xv–xvii, xx–xxiii, xliii–xlviii "Introduction" in *White Terror: The Ku Klux Klan Conspiracy and Southern Reconstruction* by Allen W. Trelease. By permission of Harper & Row, Publishers, Inc.

for so long, without widespread public support in the areas where it flourished. . . . In effect the Klan wrapped itself in the Stars and Bars, recited the racist litanies which had been devised to justify Negro slavery, threatened death to unbelievers, and thereby rendered itself unassailable by orthodox Southerners. Willingly or unwillingly, they entered into a conspiracy to protect the Klan and advance its works.

The roots of this conspiracy ran so deep that, wherever it extended, the traditional system of local justice was undermined and subverted. In most places the reign of terror exceeded the power even of state governments to control, and federal intervention was required to bring it to a close. Even then the spirit which had animated it carried on and soon triumphed by other means. . . .

. . . This story is central to the history of Reconstruction after the Civil War. The Ku Klux Klan terror colored nearly every aspect of Southern life and politics, often far beyond the immediate range of terrorist activity. It was therefore central to the formulation and implementation of Reconstruction policy in Washington.

My attitude toward the Ku Klux Klan terror is in keeping with that of most recent historians of the Reconstruction period; it is impossible any longer to embrace the opposite view which for so long celebrated the Ku Klux Klan and its civilizing mission in the South. If I differ with my contemporaries at all in this respect, I suspect that the distinction arises from the heightened awareness of the magnitude and power of the Ku Klux conspiracy which this study has engendered. It has put the plight of Southern Republicans in clearer perspective and brought Republican men and measures into a still more favorable light than is customary. By the same token it has revealed still further the degrading effects of racism in societies which fall prey to that virus. . . .

Compared with Reconstruction, no period better exemplifies historian Ulrich B. Phillips' dictum of forty years ago that the "central theme of Southern history" was a determination always to keep the section "a white man's country."[1] Hardly an issue arose that did not involve the race question directly or indirectly and that was not fought out largely on that ground. The Louisiana Democratic party platform of 1865 proclaimed: "That we hold this to be a Government of white people, made and to be perpetuated for the exclusive benefit of the white race. . . ." The same view was expressed by Alexander H. Stephens of Georgia, recent vice-president of the Confederacy: "Equality does not exist between blacks and whites. The one race is by nature inferior. . . . [and] It is useless to war against the decrees of nature in attempting to make things equal which the Creator has made unequal. . . ."[2] . . .

Few persons were as perceptive or candid as George Washington Cable, the New Orleans writer, who pointed out in the 1880s that Negroes had never advocated black supremacy during Reconstruction; their goal was

---

[1] "The Central Theme in Southern History," *American Historical Review* 34 (1928), pp. 30–43.

[2] Myrta L. Avary, *Recollections of Alexander H. Stephens* (New York, 1910), p. 207.

equality.[3] Most Southern whites were unwilling to concede—even unable to comprehend—that freedom for the Negro could mean the same thing as freedom for them. Slaveholders could part with slavery as an economic institution—even welcome its passing in many cases—but to see the ex-slave compete for lands, jobs, and profits, to see him enter the professions and hold political power—that was quite another matter. . . .

After promoting for a generation and more the idea of innate Negro inferiority in order to justify slavery, Southerners could hardly be expected suddenly to abandon it with the coming of emancipation, especially in the wake of military defeat.[4] The newly freed slave, regarded as occupying an intermediate stage between humanity and the lower orders of animal life, fell into a niche already prepared for him—that of the antebellum free Negro. . . . In effect Negroes were now the slaves of every white man. As subordination and discipline had been enforced by the lash before, it continued to be so now, but without the restraining influence of the slaveholder's self-interest. . . . Certainly whipping and corporal punishment were regarded as the white man's right and duty, emancipation or no emancipation; organized regulators or vigilantes took up this task with the advent of emancipation, and the Klan further institutionalized the practice.[5]

. . . For all the talk of white suffering during the Reconstruction era, it was the black man who experienced the greatest deprivation and mistreatment, first and last. But it was a rare freedman who regretted emancipation; stories to the contrary could almost invariably be traced to white men's rationalizations of slavery.

Negroes wanted the same freedom that white men enjoyed, with equal prerogatives and opportunities. The educated black minority emphasized civil and political rights more than the masses, who called most of all for land and schools. In an agrarian society, the only kind most of them knew, landownership was associated with freedom, respectability, and the good life. It was almost universally desired by Southern blacks, as it was by landless peasants the world over.[6] Give us our land and we can take care of ourselves, said a group of South Carolina Negroes to a Northern journalist in 1865; without land the old masters can hire us or starve us as they please.[7] A major failure of Reconstruction was that, except for a favored few, they never got it. Not only did they lack money or credit, but the government made no substantial effort to help them obtain it. Whites in many areas refused to sell, lease, or even rent land to Negroes when they did not have the means to buy, and often actively conspired to keep them from acquiring it. Negro landownership would have enhanced the economic and social well-being of the entire section, but it smacked too

---

3 George Washington Cable, *The Negro Question* (mod. ed., New York, 1958), pp. 140, 170–73.

4 See Joel Williamson, *After Slavery* (Chapel Hill, N.C., 1965), pp. 241–46.

5 *KKK Report,* Alabama, pp. 93, 456; Georgia, p. 32.

6 See August Meier and Elliott M. Rudwick, *From Plantation to Ghetto* (New York, 1968), p. 134.

7 Whitelaw Reid, *After the War* (mod. ed., New York, 1965), p. 59.

much of equality and independence. Some Negroes who did acquire farms of their own were driven off by mobs or the Ku Klux Klan. . . .

Whites of every class united in opposition to what they called social equality—a completely integrated society—as leading inevitably to inter-marriage and degeneration of the white race. In that event, a South Caro-linian declared, "we shall become a race of mulattoes . . . another Mexico; we shall be ruled out from the family of white nations. . . . It is a matter of life and death with the Southern people to keep their blood pure."[8] . . .

Emancipation increased the Southern white rape complex because free-dom presumably stimulated the Negro's innate passion for white women and removed external restraints. This was the supreme taboo, which evoked white supremacy in its most virulent form. Whether or not Negro rape of white women actually increased during Reconstruction, it cer-tainly was not widespread; more important was the fact that whites *thought* it was on the increase.[9] The only penalty sufficient to deter the tendency was violent and speedy death—lynching without the delay and dignity of formal trial. The Fayetteville (Tennessee) *Observer* echoed widespread opinion when it condoned the lynching of an alleged Negro rapist in 1868: "The community said amen to the act—it was just and right. We know not who did it, whether Ku Klux or the immediate neigh-bors, but we feel that they were only the instruments of Divine vengeance in carrying out His holy and immutable decrees."[10] Here too the Ku Klux Klan helped to institutionalize a practice which preceded and long out-lived it.

The physical and psychological necessities of keeping Negroes in sub-ordination led to the wildest inconsistencies of attitude and expression. On the one hand the black man was best fitted by nature and tempera-ment for a life of servility and happiest in his carefree dependence on white protectors. On the other hand he was only a degree removed from the wild beasts of the jungle, and the most constant surveillance was needed to keep him from bursting the bonds of discipline and turning upon his friends and protectors in a bloody insurrection. The first theory was necessary to rationalize slavery and the ensuing peonage, but as it never fully squared with the facts, the second argument served to justify necessary repressive measures. Both reinforced Negro subordinance.

Eternal vigilance is the price of despotism or white supremacy as well as of liberty. White men were never fully convinced by their own claims of affection for those they held in subjection, or by the accompanying be-lief that they were the Negroes' best friends, and they expected, at least subconsciously, that the blacks would react to slavery or white supremacy just as they liked to think *they* would if the shoe were on the other foot. This fear thus led to further aggression against the blacks in order to fore-stall any rebelliousness. Whenever Negroes did show evidence of discon-tent, whites were apt to react with disproportionate severity, regarding it as a symptom of greater discontent than the facts warranted. "I have

---

[8] David Macrae, *The Americans at Home* (New York, 1952), pp. 296–97.

[9] *KKK Report,* Georgia, p. 124.

[10] June 25, 1868.

heard planters complain very earnestly of the insubordinate spirit of their colored laborers," Carl Schurz reported in 1865, "because they remonstrated against the practice of corporal punishment. This was looked upon as a symptom of an impending insurrection.[11] . . .

. . . In these periods of imagined crisis the courts were often ignored and mobs of vigilantes reigned supreme. Both Negroes and whites were terrorized and even lynched on the slightest suspicion of knowledge of or complicity in some rumored plot. . . .

Such fears continued during the war and redoubled in the wake of Emancipation. In 1865 a general rising was again anticipated at Christmastime. Governor Humphreys of Mississippi called out the state militia and ordered it to patrol the roads and search Negro cabins for arms. This it did, in some cases with great brutality. Much the same thing happened in South Carolina and other states. Investigation revealed no evidence whatsoever to justify the panic, but fear recurred in 1866 and again in 1867. The advent of Radical Reconstruction in 1868 led to enhanced anxiety, which continued sporadically for years. Almost invariably the newspapers played a major role in spreading the terror. Over the years thousands of innocent Negroes were harassed, tortured, or dealt the extreme penalty. In this respect too the Ku Klux Klan for a time institutionalized a white vigilantism which long preceded and followed it. There was often no basis whatever for the fear; even the most peaceable Negro gatherings for political and other legal purposes were assumed to be incendiary conspiracies. On occasion, however, white terrorism itself drove desperate freedmen to organize militarily for their own protection. . . .

. . . Although the Southerner may have known the Negro as a slave, he did not know him as a man. The misconception, which endured for generations, probably arose from a need to rationalize white supremacy. It led to constant surprise and disillusionment over Negro behavior, which then had to be explained in terms of Negro ignorance and ingratitude as well as the machinations of outside agitators.

Northern Reconstruction policy evolved against this background of myths and realities. Again, the race question was crucial. The North began fighting the Civil War to defeat secession and ended by abolishing slavery as well. Emancipation brought the unavoidable problem of defining the freedmen's status. Northern Democrats generally shared the racial views of the white South and sanctioned the most minimal adjustments required by the ending of legal servitude. This was also the tendency of Abraham Lincoln and of Andrew Johnson afterward. Most Republicans fell between this conservatism and the Radicals' advocacy of full legal and political equality at war's end, but they were gradually driven toward egalitarianism by the course of events between 1865 and 1867. And as theirs was the majority party in the North, that drift determined federal government policy. . . .

Negroes were elected to office in every state, leading Conservatives in moments of bitter abandon to characterize the whole policy as one of

---

[11] *Senate Executive Documents*, 39th Congress, list sess., no. 2, pp. 31–32. See also Dollard, *Caste and Class in a Southern Town*, pp. 287, 319–20.

"Negro rule," an accusation made partly for political effect but also arising from the common conviction that racial sovereignty was indivisible. If
whites did not rule blacks, it must therefore be the other way around. The
charge of Negro rule was absurd, for blacks never held office in proportion
to their total number and they rarely held the most prominent posts. . . .
The quality of these Negro officeholders high and low who did pass the
barrier was not notably better or worse than that of white men who held
comparable posts at that time, before, or later. Some, especially in the
lower levels, were illiterate, but so were some of their white counterparts
of both parties. Incompetent and illiterate officials did not begin or end
with Reconstruction, nor were they typical of that period.[12]

The so-called carpetbagger—Northerners who settled in the South
during and after the war and affiliated with the Republican party—were
only a tiny minority numerically. They had great influence, however, particularly in the deep South where the Negro population was heavy and
there was no significant native white Republican element to provide leadership. The term "carpetbagger" was another canard. These men supposedly descended on the South like a swarm of locusts, bringing no more
than they could carry in a carpetbag; their purpose was to prey on the
defenseless region through political manipulation of the gullible freedmen. Actually most of these persons moved South by 1866, well before
Radical Reconstruction was conceived or the Republican party was even
organized in most of the South. Some were stationed there by the Army or
Freedmen's Bureau, but most moved South for the same reasons of economic betterment that led greater numbers to go West. When the Republican party was organized and new governments were in process of
formation these men filled a need for educated and occasionally experienced leadership. In fact, they usually raised the caliber of Radical government rather than lowering it. Of course their motives, abilities, and
accomplishments ran the usual human scale; along with the incompetent
or corrupt there were honest and highly able men whom posterity would
have celebrated under other circumstances. Active Republicans required
a tough skin and often great physical courage to withstand the social
ostracism, economic boycott, verbal abuse, character assassination, and
physical violence to which they were commonly subjected by Southern
whites. In a few cases at least, this courage was inspired by a high degree
of dedication. . . .

The native white Republicans—scalawags to their enemies—were
drawn from every walk of Southern life. Some had been Democrats and
others were Whigs before the war. A few had served the Confederacy in
conspicuous fashion, but most were wartime Unionists; the more uncompromising their Unionism had been the more apt they were to embrace
the Republican party afterward. . . . The Appalachian highlands from
western Virginia to northern Alabama and the Ozark Mountains of Arkansas were the major strongholds of white Republicanism. . . . The term

---

12 See Wharton, *The Negro in Mississippi*, pp. 167–72, 179; Williamson, *After
Slavery*, pp. 376–81; Samuel D. Smith, *The Negro in Congress, 1870–1901* (Chapel
Hill, N.C., 1940).

"scalawag" was of course another form of political abuse; the personal character of Southern Republicans did not suffer by comparison with their accusers. Many joined the Republican party because it was the Unionist party and it opposed the planter interest as they themselves had done for years. . . . A few members of the ante-bellum ruling class, usually ex-Whigs who had not been enthusiastic secessionists, also joined the Republican party, hoping to hold it to a moderate course and exercise a paternalistic rein on the Negroes while profiting by their strength at the polls. Such men carried great prestige and were given some of the highest offices in an effort to make the party more appealing to the white population generally, but the number of these converts was small. Governor James L. Alcorn of Mississippi belonged to this class, as did former Governor Lewis E. Parsons of Alabama and James L. Orr of South Carolina.[13]

In terms of ideology, Republicans were clearly the democratic party of the Reconstruction South. . . .

Radicalism was also aimed less spectacularly at raising the status of poorer whites. Within limits the Republican party was a poor man's party which sought to obliterate racial lines as much as popular prejudice made it politically safe to do. Democrats defeated the effort, as they later did when the Populists tried it, by crying "nigger"; most Southern whites placed white supremacy above all other issues.

Many public offices which had been appointive were now made elective, sometimes at the cost of efficiency. In some states, but not all, more home rule was extended, making local government more responsive to local wishes and less subject to central control. Property qualifications for office-holding, where they still existed in 1867, were removed. Legislatures were reapportioned to provide more equal representation, although Negro counties in some states were slighted. By far the most important democratic extension was the granting of Negro suffrage. This had been required by the Reconstruction Acts, and it was incorporated in all the new constitutions.

. . . The Radical governments made no effort to outlaw the Conservative opposition or create a dictatorship. On the contrary, they were too lenient in enforcing law and order against those who used force to overthrow them.

There was corruption, electoral as well as financial, in nearly every state during the period of Republican control. Conservatives at the time succeeded in pinning on the Radical regimes a blanket charge of dishonesty which has never worn off, but the actual picture was not so simple. Corruption was rampant throughout the country after the war, and Democrats North and South were about as guilty as Republicans. The Tweed Ring in New York City supposedly stole more than all Southern politicians combined, if only because New York had more to steal. Within the South corruption varied widely from state to state. It flourished most in South Carolina, where it had been comparatively unknown, and in Louisiana, where it was endemic. In South Carolina the Republicans at least

---

[13] See Lillian A. Pereya, *James Lusk Alcorn* (Baton Rouge, 1966); Williamson, *After Slavery*, pp. 374–75.

partially cleaned their own house under Governor Chamberlain after 1874. In Louisiana both parties were corrupt and remained so for generations. In Mississippi an honest Republican administration gave way to less honest Democratic regimes after 1875. During the period of Republican control, moreover, minority Democratic officials were sometimes as venal as their Republican counterparts, and Democratic businessmen sometimes offered the bribes that Republicans accepted. In the matter of electoral, as opposed to fiscal, corruption generalization is easier. Republicans were occasionally guilty of manipulating election returns, but these practices paled in comparison with the massive campaigns of fraud and intimidation, symbolized by the Ku Klux Klan, with which Democrats sought to return to power in nearly every state. It was largely owing to these methods that they did assume power in one state after another during the 1870s.[14] . . .

Actually it was white men who committed most of the violence, and much of it was racially and politically inspired. When these overtones were not present, it was punished about as effectively, or ineffectively, in areas of Republican control as Democratic, and as was true in earlier and later periods of Southern history.[15] A great deal of violence was deliberate and organized, however, committed by mobs and by armed bands in and out of disguise. A disproportionate share was directed at Negroes and white Unionists, partly to avenge real or imaginary injuries arising from the war, partly to keep the Negro "in his place" economically and socially, and partly to overthrow the Republican party by intimidating, exiling, or assassinating its members. The Ku Klux Klan exemplified this kind of violence in the most spectacular way, but it extended far beyond the Klan. The greatest short-run deficiency of the Republican regimes— it would soon prove fatal—was their physical weakness. In the face of implacable white resistance they proved unable to preserve law and order, or their own existence, against attempts at violent overthrow. In certain parts of the South the authorities were almost paralyzed by organized lawlessness.

When conspiracies to obstruct justice assumed this dimension the only solution was armed force. Republican officials repeatedly called on the Army for help in suppressing combinations which they could not handle by the usual means, but the results were usually discouraging. In the first place, too many troops were mustered out of service too quickly amid the euphoric celebration of victory in 1865. Only 20,000 troops remained on duty in the South by the fall of 1867, and this number gradually fell to 6,000 by the fall of 1876; moreover, one-quarter to half of these were stationed in Texas, chiefly on frontier duty.[16] A much larger

---

[14] On corruption, see Wharton, *The Negro in Mississippi*, p. 179; Roger W. Shugg, *Origins of Class Struggle in Louisiana* (Baton Rouge, 1939), pp. 226–27; Current, *Three Carpetbag Governors*; Williamson, *After Slavery*, pp. 382–405.

[15] *KKK Report*, Committee Report, pp. 2, 92; *Congressional Globe*, 42nd Congress, 1st sess., Appendix, p. 28.

[16] James E. Sefton, *The U.S. Army and Reconstruction, 1865–1877* (Baton Rouge, 1967), pp. 261–62.

occupation force would have had trouble in maintaining order throughout the South. . . .

In the last analysis, Radical Reconstruction failed because the seed of
biracial democracy which it planted fell on barren ground in the South,
and the artificial nurture it received from the federal government was
soon discontinued. . . .

Conservatives mercilessly pilloried the Negroes, carpetbaggers, and
scalawags who staffed and supported the Republican regimes. The Democratic newspaper press—which far outstripped the Southern Republican
press in numbers and circulation—played a vital role in stimulating and
disseminating hatred of all things Radical. The wildest allegations and
ad hominem arguments were at least half believed and unblushingly
broadcast because they fit preconceived notions. . . . Radical regard for
the civil liberties of ex-Confederates enabled the latter to sabotage the
Reconstruction program almost from the start. Democrats had full access to the polls almost everywhere after 1868 and controlled hundreds
of county and local governments throughout the period; they exercised
the right to express themselves freely on every occasion, and they controlled the great majority of the section's newspapers. When they were
charged with illegal activity and violence they had full access to the
courts—in fact often dominated them. In such cases it was often impossible to get grand juries to indict, prosecutors to prosecute, or petit
juries to convict, even if sheriffs were willing to arrest or judges to try
them. This was even true in Republican-controlled localities. All of the
safeguards for the accused in the Anglo-Saxon system of justice were
mobilized to enforce the higher law of white supremacy. The Republicans themselves insisted upon certain limits to federal authority, and
this was another source of weakness. Conservative violence against Negroes and Radicals involved crimes which had always fallen within state
rather than federal jurisdiction, and as a result the federal government
refused to intervene soon enough or strongly enough to check the terror
effectively. Thus the Radicals were defeated within a few years by their
very conservatism and unwillingness to employ more than halfway measures.[17] . . .

The most common type of coercion at first, which did not always wait
for peaceful persuasion to have its day, was economic pressure. From
one end of the South to the other white landlords threatened their Negro
laborers with discharge if they cast Republican ballots. This movement
was often well organized by state and local party agencies, and sometimes employers were themselves coerced into joining by threats of ostracism and boycott. . . .

The last resort was physical intimidation and violence. These were not
new to the South during Reconstruction. The Old South had emphasized
individualism and self-reliance in personal relationships, but it also had
demanded conformity of ideas. Nowhere in America was there a greater
manifestation of that tyranny of the majority which de Tocqueville set

---

[17] See the Alfred H. Kelley essay in Harold M. Hyman, ed., *New Frontiers of the
American Reconstruction* (Urbana, Ill., 1966), pp. 41–57.

forth as a national characteristic in the 1830s. Intolerance was always greatest in the area of race relations. Slavery by 1860 had become a sacred institution, the rock upon which Southern civilization rested. Those who questioned or attacked it did so in the face of emphatic public displeasure and at great personal risk. There was no free speech on this or any other topic which threatened to subvert established ways. Men of every station sanctioned lynch law when it suited their purpose. Jefferson Davis once told a New York audience that Northern politicians who proclaimed a higher law than the Constitution, condemning slavery on moral grounds, *"should be tarred and feathered, and whipped. . . . The man who . . . preaches treason to the Constitution and the dictates of all human society, is a fit object for a Lynch law that would be higher than any he could urge."*[18] Newspapers condoned and even encouraged mob violence against the few hardy souls who spoke out against slavery. In following this course they reflected general community sentiment. Such persons were public enemies who could not safely be trusted to the delays and uncertainties of legal due process. . . .

. . . [In Reconstruction] white men could and did commit the most brutal forms of aggression, convinced all the while that they were acting defensively.[19]

This aggression took every conceivable form, from individual assaults and minor street encounters through mob lynchings to pitched battles involving hundreds on either side. These attacks were seldom punished; it simply was not a punishable offense in the eyes of many whites to attack or even kill a Negro. Late in 1866 Freedmen's Bureau officials reported in detail the murders of 33 freedmen by whites since the war in Tennessee, 29 in Arkansas, 24 in South Carolina, 19 in Kentucky. In February 1867 General Joseph A. Mower reported 70 such murders in Louisiana, giving specific information; the actual total, he said, might have been twice that number. In addition he told of 210 cases of whipping, beating, and stabbing, almost all of them unpunished.[20] In the guise of preserving the peace, legally constituted militia of the Johnson governments commonly went about disarming Negroes and frequently committing violence in the process. . . .

The larger interracial collisions or riots increasingly showed signs of white organization and advance planning. The Negroes almost invariably suffered most of the casualties, but they were less responsible for initiating violence. Whites commonly believed otherwise, even when they consciously hurled the first stone or fired the first shot; for them the very fact of a League parade or a militia muster was an act of aggression that justified violence in self-defense. In many cases, however, whites deliberately covered their trail and sought to blame their antagonists for in-

---

[18] Quoted in Avery Craven, *The Growth of Southern Nationalism, 1848–1861* (Baton Rouge, La., 1953), pp. 394–95.

[19] See Dollard, *Caste and Class in a Southern Town*, pp. 319–20; and Myrdal, *An American Dilemma*, 1, xcviii–xcix.

[20] John A. Carpenter, "Atrocities in the Reconstruction Period," *Journal of Negro History*, 47 (1962), pp. 236–44. See also Joe M. Richardson, *The Negro in the Reconstruction of Florida, 1856–1877* (Tallahassee, 1965), pp. 161–64.

stigating hostilities. If this required the distortion of facts or outright lying, it was but another regrettable outgrowth of Negro emancipation. Sometimes one must level a few buildings to save the town from fire.

Many of the so-called riots came close to being massacres. Such was the case in Memphis between April 30 and May 2, 1866, when 46 Negroes were killed and more than 80 wounded as against one white man injured. So also in New Orleans the following July 30, when the toll was about 34 Negroes killed and more than 200 injured as against 4 white dead and 10 injured. Other riots which gained nationwide attention took place in Camilla, Georgia, in September 1868; Laurens, South Carolina, and Eutaw, Alabama, in October 1870; Meridian, Mississippi, in March 1871; Colfax, Louisiana, in April 1873; Vicksburg, Mississippi, in December 1874; Clinton, Mississippi, in September 1875; and Hamburg, South Carolina, in July 1876. . . . The purpose, and to a great degree the result, of these battles was to demoralize and intimidate the freedmen. Some, like Clinton and Vicksburg, were part of a larger campaign to carry elections by storm and thus return the Democratic party to power in the face of Negro Republican majorities which other methods had failed to sway. . . . White Republicans, who took the place of both abolitionists and Unionists, were subjected to ostracism, boycott, threats, and physical attack. It was dangerous for them to campaign in many regions, or even to express their opinions openly. . . . Newspapers and public opinion often condoned even the bloodiest outrages if they did not positively encourage them. . . . As Floridians were quoted more succinctly as saying, "The damned Republican party has put niggers to rule us and we will not suffer it."[21]

The violence became more organized. In South Carolina white rifle clubs were organized, replacing the dissolved state militia. Eventually similar organizations would spring up in other states of the deep South, and they contributed importantly to the final overthrow of Reconstruction. But the more immediate source of harassment for Negroes and white Republicans throughout the South was the secret societies epitomized by the Ku Klux Klan. . . .

A Freedmen's Bureau official reported in March 1866 that in some counties of Kentucky "there are organized bands of men called 'rangers,' 'moderators,' 'nigger killers,' who have driven the freedmen entirely out of certain sections, and begin at last to threaten and intimidate Union white men."[22] . . .

Some of these groups were sufficiently organized to adopt a certain ceremony and ritual in their proceedings, and to bear such names as (in Alabama) the Black Cavalry and the Men of Justice. Most of them lost their separate identity (at least to outsiders) in 1868 when the Ku Klux Klan became famous. But they generally carried on as before, and one, the Knights of the White Camellia in Louisiana and elsewhere, was large enough to be famous in its own name. Still other societies continued to

---

21 *KKK Report,* Florida, p. 94.

22 *House Executive Documents,* 29th Congress, 1st sess., No. 70, pp. 202–8 (quotation from p. 202).

form in 1868 and afterward, all more or less local in character. Even the Ku Klux Klan was so decentralized that it is hardly proper to refer to it in the singular number. But its name attracted so much attention that common usage after 1868 made it synonymous with all nocturnal regulators, regardless of what they called themselves.

The overriding purpose of the Ku Klux movement, no matter how decentralized, was the maintenance or restoration of white supremacy in every walk of life. . . .

Economic and social objectives too preceded Radical Reconstruction. Klansmen sometimes disciplined recalcitrant Negro laborers whose employers could not or would not do so themselves. (Some slaveholders had been helped in the same way.) This activity was commonly defended as a means of keeping Negro labor docile and on the job. . . . The Klan in some places inherited the function of driving off Negro laborers in favor of poor whites. It prevented Negroes from owning or even renting land of their own in some areas. As a device for keeping blacks within their proper social bounds, the Klan lynched Negro men who cohabited with white women and frequently punished these women too, as well as white prostitutes who took Negro customers. It punished Negro assertions of social equality and real or imaginary insolence. It conducted a vendetta against the teachers of Negro schools.

The one really new ingredient of regulator activity after 1867 was political opposition to the Radicals. . . . The Klan became in effect a terrorist arm of the Democratic party, whether the party leaders as a whole liked it or not.

. . . Klansmen repeatedly attacked Negroes for no other stated offense than voting, or intending to vote, the Republican ticket. . . . In some states and many localities, after Democratic persuasion and economic pressure had failed to sway Negro voters, terrorism represented the only remaining way of seizing political control. . . .

The Ku Klux Klan was a mass movement of many sides, but nearly all of them slanted toward white supremacy. . . . It grew naturally out of the folk beliefs and practices of the old South, compounded by the topsy-turvy conditions of Reconstruction. It provided a collective means to do a job that many Conservatives felt needed to be done. As an organization, it freed its members to commit atrocities which many of them would have shrunk from as individuals:

> There is no telling to what extremes of cruelty and ruthlessness a man will go when he is freed from the fears, hesitations, doubts and the vague stirrings of decency that go with individual judgment. When we lose our individual independence in the corporateness of a mass movement, we find a new freedom—freedom to hate, bully, lie, torture, murder and betray without shame and remorse.[23]

This is a fitting characterization of the Klan in action, stripped of the heroic imagery with which apologists then and later obscured it.

---

[23] Eric Hoffer, *The True Believer*, 93.

Enforcing the Fifteenth Amendment*

Everette Swinney

. . . Begun in March, 1867, and completed by the summer of 1870, the Reconstruction settlement showed signs of crumbling at its foundation even before the edifice was completed. The election of 1868 amply demonstrated the tenuous nature of Republican supremacy upon which the success of the radical program rested. President Andrew Johnson's amnesty proclamations of September 7 and December 25, 1868, restoring the suffrage to most former Confederates did not help matters, and the victory of the Democratic party in 1869 and 1870 at the polls in Virginia, North Carolina, and Georgia was discouraging. But most alarming of all was the way in which the Ku Klux Klan and other similar extralegal bodies were, by violence and intimidation, preventing Negroes from voting.[1]

In the face of these cumulative threats to Republican ascendancy, Congress moved expeditiously, passing within a 12-month period in 1870–71 three laws designed to protect the Negro in the enjoyment of his newly won political and civil rights. The First Enforcement Act, which became law on May 30, 1870, was long and complex. It forbade state officials to discriminate among voters on the basis of race or color in the application of local election laws, outlawed "force, bribery, threats, and intimidation" of voters, and made it a misdemeanor to deprive a citizen of "employment or occupation" in order to control his vote. Most important, the law prohibited disguised groups from going "upon the public highways, or upon the premises of another" with intent to interfere with constitutional liberties.[2] The Second Enforcement Act, passed following the disheartening midterm elections of 1870, extended further the federal control of the voting process. Supervisors of election, to be stationed in cities where election irregularities were considered likely, were to stand guard over and scrutinize registration and voting procedures and to certify returns.[3] The third law, popularly known as the Ku

---

* Everette Swinney, "Enforcing the Fifteenth Amendment, 1870–1877," *Journal of Southern History,* 27 (May 1962), 202–18. Copyright 1962 by the Southern Historical Association. Reprinted by permission of the Managing Editor.

[1] See Charles H. Coleman, *The Election of 1868; the Democratic Effort to Regain Control* (New York, 1933); Jonathan Truman Dorris, *Pardon and Amnesty Under Lincoln and Johnson: The Restoration of the Confederates in Their Rights and Privileges, 1861–1898* (Chapel Hill, 1953), 339–61; and James A. Rawley, "The General Amnesty Act of 1872: A Note," *Mississippi Valley Historical Review,* 47 (December 1960), 480–84.

[2] *Statutes at Large of the United States,* 16 (1871), 140–46.

[3] Ibid., 433–40.

Klux Act, made it a federal offense to conspire to "overthrow . . . or destroy by force the government of the United States" or to conspire to prevent persons from holding offices, serving on juries, enjoying equal protection of the laws, or voting.[4] The three laws provided for extensive enforcement machinery. The President was given authority to call out the Army and Navy and to suspend the writ of habeas corpus; United States marshals were authorized to use the *posse comitatus;* and federal troops were empowered to implement court orders. In the hope of reducing the effect of local pressures against enforcement, exclusive original jurisdiction in all suffrage cases was reserved to the federal courts.

Historians have been far from favorable in their evaluation of this legislation. William W. Davis, whose study published in 1914 has been somewhat of a standard account of the enforcement program, wrote, "The enactment of the law and its enforcement meant the desertion, for the time being, by the national government of certain principles in political procedure which make working democracy in America a practical possibility." He found "considerable similarity between the arbitrary order and mailed fist in the South during the seventies and the past oppression of Ireland by England, of Bohemia and Italy by Austria, of Finland and Poland by Russia, of Alsace and Lorraine by Germany.[5] His interpretation has been perpetuated in textbooks where the terms "harsh," "drastic," or "iniquitous" are commonly used to describe the laws.

The Acts were comprehensive it is true; but the fact is that they did not go beyond the intent of the Fifteenth Amendment, which took a moderate and statesmanlike position on voting. The Fifteenth Amendment, unlike the Reconstruction Act of 1867, did not grant the Negro the right to vote; it merely outlawed the use of race as a test for voting. The Enforcement Acts of 1870–71 accorded with the Fifteenth Amendment in leaving to the state full freedom to restrict suffrage on any basis except race or color. . . .

. . . Finally, the provisions for enforcement of the acts of 1870–71— with the exception of the authorization to suspend the writ of habeas corpus, which was done only once—were not innovations but were consistent with traditional usage. Whatever the motives of those who promoted the legislation, the laws as enacted were essentially in accord with the democratic credo.

Under these laws the Department of Justice made a determined effort to enforce the Fifteenth Amendment. Between 1870 and 1896, when the bulk of the legislation was repealed, 7,372 cases were tried, and hundreds of offenders who were never brought to trial were arrested.[6] Despite this widespread activity, the disfranchisement of the Negro proceeded apace. By 1877 the Negro vote had been largely neutralized and a solid Democratic South assured. Complete disfranchisement of the Negro was to follow. The few historians who have attempted to evaluate the operation

---

[4] Ibid., 17 (1873), 13–15.

[5] William W. Davis, "The Federal Enforcement Acts," *Studies in Southern History and Politics; Inscribed to William A. Dunning* (New York, 1914), 205.

[6] Davis, "Federal Enforcement Acts," 224.

of the Enforcement Acts have emphasized the fact that there were relatively few convictions. . . . E. Merton Coulter, generalizing upon [William H.] Dunning's calculations, observed that "in all the trials throughout the South for the next few years, only about 10 percent of the defendants were convicted." He concluded that "arrests were made more to terrorize the people and to promote the Radical party than to secure actual justice."[7]

These assertions give a distorted picture. The percentages hold true only for the years after 1874. In 1870 the government won 74 percent of its enforcement cases; in 1871, 41 percent; in 1872, 49 percent; and in 1873, 36 percent. After 1874, it is true, convictions seldom passed the 10 percent mark and were often considerably below it.[8] If, as Dunning and Coulter aver, the low percentage of convictions proved the iniquity of the laws, one would have to conclude that the laws became iniquitous only after 1874.

The proper explanation is somewhat less absurd and more complex. In the first place, by 1874 the government was ready to pursue a more moderate policy. Attorney General George Williams justified this change in strategy by two arguments, both of which were probably fallacious. He took the position that the worst of the Ku Klux activity had been brought under control and that it was safe for the government to relax its vigilance. . . . Most scholars have accepted the view that the backbone of the Klan proper was broken by the initial impact of the prosecutions; it is certain, however, that violence continued and that the Negro's position in Southern society was anything but secure. Williams also sought to justify the change in policy on the grounds that the government's enforcement program had proved to be an irritant which provoked disrespect for authority and incited lawlessness. . . . [But] the South was determined to have a free hand in settling the Negro question, and nothing approaching real peace would come to that section until this was realized.

The Attorney General's arguments disguised rather than revealed the government's real motivation. . . . Expediency was the primary consideration. The South had remained obdurate in its opposition to enforcement; and the North, preoccupied with the depression, was beginning to lose interest. Erstwhile friends of coercion like Carl Schurz and E. L. Godkin had become critical before the time of the Liberal Republican revolt. Williams himself, a fairly influential Radical at the time of his appointment, was now in 1874 one of the most unpopular men in the country. A congressional committee questioned him about alleged excesses in the use of troops, and . . . the year before, in 1873, the Senate

---

7 E. Merton Coulter, *The South During Reconstruction, 1865–1877* (Baton Rouge, 1947), 171.

8 *Annual Report of the Attorney General, 1870, House Exec. Docs.,* 41st Cong., 3rd sess., No. 90 (Serial 1454); 1871, ibid., 42d Cong., 2d sess., No. 55 (Serial 1510); 1872, *Senate Exec. Docs.,* 42d Cong., 3rd sess., No. 32 (Serial 1545); 1873, *House Exec. Docs.,* 43rd Cong., 1st sess., No. 6 (Serial 1606); 1874, ibid., 43rd Cong., 2d sess., No. 7 (Serial 1638); 1875, ibid., 44th Cong., 1st sess., No. 14 (Serial 1686); 1876, ibid., 44th Cong., 2d sess., No. 20 (Serial 1751); 1877, ibid., 45th Cong., 2d sess., No. 7 (Serial 1802); 1878, ibid., 45th Cong., 3rd sess., No. 7 (Serial 1852), passim.

had rejected his appointment to the Supreme Court. The point is that the Republicans controlled Congress by a scant 35 votes with the midterm elections approaching. Under the circumstances, it is not surprising that in the spring and summer of 1874 Williams instructed district attorneys to dismiss all indictments "excepting such as involve charges of high crime committed in furtherance of the object of the conspiracy." They were told to "enter a *nolle prosequi*" in all cases in which the charge was "merely that of belonging to the Ku Klux Klan . . . of cooperating in its general purposes, or of committing some minor misdemeanor."[9] Many of the indictments which never came to trial were dismissed as a direct result of changing policy.

A second and perhaps more important reason for the abrupt decline in the number of convictions was that adverse court rulings made successful prosecutions after 1874 almost impossible. . . . [In 1873 the government lost the Reese case and] *United States* v. *Cruikshank et al.* was taking shape in Louisiana. The bloody Colfax massacre of April, 1873 . . . had resulted in the slaughter of about 60 Negroes. At the April, 1874, term of the circuit court for the district of Louisiana more than 100 persons were indicted under sections five and six of the First Enforcement Act.[10] Supreme Court Justice Joseph P. Bradley, who was reputed to believe the law unconstitutional, sat in on the trial. . . . In a closely reasoned opinion Bradley questioned the scope of the Fifteenth Amendment.[11] . . .

While the Reese and Cruikshank cases were pending before the Supreme Court (1874–76), the enforcement program was arrested. "As I do not believe any convictions can be obtained under existing circumstances," Williams informed district attorneys, ". . . I am of the opinion that criminal prosecution under these acts ought to be suspended until it is known whether the Supreme Court will hold them constitutional or otherwise."[12] The Supreme Court decisions, rendered in the spring of 1876, constituted a major reversal for the radicals. Chief Justice Morrison R. Waite, speaking for the court in both cases, adopted the narrow interpretation of the Fifteenth Amendment adumbrated in Bradley's opinion in the Louisiana case two years before. "The Fifteenth Amendment," he argued, "does not confer the right of suffrage upon any one." The right to vote comes from the states; only "the right of exemption from the prohibited discrimination comes from the United States." Congress can legislate only to prevent official discrimination by the states or the United States but not to prevent obstructions and discriminations generally, as it had done in the First Enforcement Act.[13] Technically, just two sections of the act were declared unconstitutional, but the whole law had been brought under a shadow. The effect of the decisions was

---

9 Williams to Lusk, April 25, 1874, in Instructions, D, 511.

10 Robert Selph Henry, *The Story of Reconstruction* (Indianapolis, 1938), 484–92.

11 *United States* v. *Cruikshank et al.*, 25 Fed. Cas. 707 (1874), quotation on p. 710.

12 Williams to W. W. Murray, May 5, 1875, in Instructions, E, 443–44.

13 *United States* v. *Reese et al.*, 92 U.S. 214 (1875), and *United States* v. *Cruikshank et al.*, 92 U.S. 542 (1875).

to bring to a close the active policy of the government to enforce the Fifteenth Amendment.

By going behind the statistics one discovers that there were other factors which made successful prosecutions difficult. White Southern Democrats insisted from the outset that the enforcement laws were unconstitutional, oppressive, and not worthy of respect. . . .

With such a view widely held it was extremely difficult to gather evidence. Native whites were usually uncooperative, and Negroes were often reluctant to testify in the face of white hostility. Those witnesses who were persuaded to testify might find their property and lives in danger. In 1872 G. Wiley Wells, district attorney of the northern district of Mississippi saw his case fall apart when five key witnesses were murdered. "I cannot get witnesses," he reported to Washington, "as all feel it is sure death to testify before the Grand Jury."[14] Frightened witnesses appealed to the President and Department of Justice for protection, but they received little comfort. The best the Attorney General could do was to exhort Negro witnesses to have courage, to "take the position that the country is as much yours as it is theirs—that you have as good a right to live in it as they—and that you are determined to live in it, and enjoy all your rights; or to die in it, bravely asserting your rights."[15]

State and local authorities often failed to cooperate with federal officials; indeed, on numerous occasions they impeded the operation of the federal program. In virtually every Southern state, at one time or another during the decade of the 1870s, federal deputy marshals, supervisors of election, or soldiers were arrested by local law enforcement officers on charges ranging from false arrest or assault and battery to murder. In South Carolina no less a figure than Major Lewis Merrill, commander of the troops stationed in York County during the period of martial law, was taken into custody for false arrest. A favorite stratagem was to prosecute for perjury Negroes who had testified against Klan members before United States commissioners.[16] The government never worked out a reliable device for combating these practices. . . .

Securing juries that would convict was a perennial problem. In the words of Judge Amos Morrill of Texas, "Jurors drawn at random from the list of voters . . . would not be convinced that any man had violated the revenue acts or the enforcement acts by any testimony.[17] . . . Even ostensibly friendly juries were anything but reliable. In 1876 a grand jury in Mississippi refused to indict several persons for violations of the Enforcement Acts even though, as the foreman admitted, the evidence was overwhelming. The reason given was that key witnesses, fearful of reprisals, would not agree to testify in open court, and the jury saw little use in involving the government in the expense of an abortive trial.[18] . . .

---

14 G. Wiley Wells to Williams, January 17, 1872, in Source-Chronological for Mississippi.

15 Cummings and McFarland, *Federal Justice*, 238.

16 Bristow to Wells, September 19, 1871, in Instructions, C, 370.

17 Amos Morrill to Williams, April 3, 1873, in Source-Chronological for Texas.

18 James R. Cavett to Alphonso Taft, August 28, 1876, in Source-Chronological for Mississippi.

Only in those districts where officials were willing to impanel all-Negro juries, fully protected by federal troops in the courthouses, could convictions be relied upon. . . .

Intimidation of witnesses and juries might have been prevented had marshals enjoyed sufficient power to guarantee protection. Indeed, in theory the marshal had ample resources, but in practice he was often impotent. He could call upon the *posse comitatus,* but social pressure made the bystanders reluctant and undependable. Federal troops were stationed throughout the South, but they were seldom available for routine police duty. Securing troops involved much red tape, and requests for them were turned down as often as they were granted. . . .

Perhaps more basic in the failure of enforcement than the unavailability of troops to protect witnesses and juries was the lack of money. The enforcement program was expensive, as a sampling of court costs in the South reveals. . . . Congress, harried by demands for lower taxes, was reluctant to provide adequate funds. . . . Consequently, the Attorney General was forced to urge economy from the beginning, and starting in 1873 marshals were required to make financial reports weekly. Soon the necessity for economy affected the program. Because of high costs Attorney General Williams in 1873 instructed district attorneys that "no case be prosecuted under the Enforcement Acts . . . unless the public interest imperatively requires it."[19] Emergency requests for money made by marshals and attorneys were halved and sometimes quartered before being approved. After the Democrats gained control of the House in the elections of 1874, a congressional committee was set up to investigate the expense of the Department of Justice, and the judicial appropriation for 1876–1877 was cut by a half million dollars. . . .

The enforcement program was further handicapped by the inadequacies of the federal court system. The Enforcement Acts imposed an unmanageable extra burden on an antiquated judicial structure. The attorneys general frequently complained of the inability of courts to clear their dockets. By October, 1870, some 472 persons had been arrested in South Carolina for alleged violation of the Enforcement Act. At the November term of the circuit court, 420 were indicted, but at the end of the one month session only five had been brought to trial.

> With the caution and deliberation which the law wisely observes in criminal proceedings [Attorney General Akerman wrote], it is obvious that the attempt to bring to justice . . . even a small portion of the guilty in that state must fail. . . . If it takes a court over one month to try five offenders, how long will it take to try four hundred, already indicted, and many hundreds more who deserve to be indicted?[20]

Similar problems arose in North Carolina and Mississippi. Faced by this dilemma, the Attorney General had little choice but to compromise. District attorneys were instructed in 1871 to prosecute vigorously only such

---

[19] Williams to All Marshals, March 8, 1873, and Williams to William H. Smyth, February 5, 1873, in Instructions, C, 645, 608.

[20] *Annual Report of the Attorney General,* 1871, 4–5.

persons "as appear to have been leaders in the conspiracies." Others were ordered to be "released on light bail" and their cases pushed to trial only if time allowed. "Those whose connection with the conspiracies was compulsory and reluctant" were not even to be indicted.[21] . . .

The administration was sensitive to charges of partisanship and consistently sought to control overzealous authorities. . . . As the election of 1874 approached, Attorney General Williams urged district attorneys and marshals in Alabama, South Carolina, Louisiana, Kentucky, and Tennessee "to proceed with all possible energy and dispatch to detect, expose, arrest, and punish" Ku Klux marauders, but he added, "You understand, of course, that no interference whatever with any political or party action not in violation of the law" should be undertaken.[22]

Moderates, conservatives, and even a few Democrats were to be found among the federal authorities in the South. The judiciary in particular was dominated by conservative ideas, and several judges endeared themselves to the Southern population by their refusal to embrace doctrines of social equality and constitutional change. . . . George W. Brooks, judge of the district of North Carolina, was a Johnson appointee with a reputation for industry and sound judgment. In 1870 Governor W. W. Holden declared two counties under martial law and sent in troops; Brooks released the prisoners under writ of habeas corpus basing his action on the Fourteenth Amendment to protect the personal liberties of white men.[23] . . . Other judges like John Erskine of Georgia, who never took an enforcement case when he could avoid it, and Robert A. Hill of Mississippi, who enforced United States laws with as much leniency as possible, won the confidence, respect, and gratitude of the Southern people.

Some marshals and district attorneys were either sensitive to Southern public opinion or in substantial agreement with it. . . . [One] Mississippi marshal supported the Democratic ticket in the election of 1872, and the marshal and district attorney of the eastern district of Texas packed juries with Democrats in order to prevent convictions.[24] . . .

Although the Department of Justice was involved in none of the great scandals of the Grant administration, there was to be found among department personnel some of the low morality characteristic of the age. . . .

In attempting to reach a fairer evaluation of the enforcement program, one additional factor must be considered. As in other phases of Southern history it is dangerous to overwork the concept of the "Solid South." Although the South ultimately presented a united front on the race question, there was initially considerable difference of opinion on this matter between the Black Belt planter and the upcountry farmer. . . . Since the Enforcement Acts were essentially, although not exclu-

---

[21] Akerman to D. T. Corbin, November 10, 1871, in Instructions, C, 33–34.

[22] Williams to District Attorneys and Marshals, September 3, 1874, in Instructions, E, 13–14.

[23] J. G. de Roulhac Hamilton, *Reconstruction in North Carolina* (New York, 1914), 525–30.

[24] Williams to Marshal Robert J. Alcorn, July 8, 1873, in Instructions, D, 115, and Governor E. J. Davis to Williams, February 2, 1872, in Source-Chronological for Texas.

sively, designed to combat the Klan, it is not surprising to find that outside of the former nonslaveholding areas there was relatively little activity under the legislation. The following table shows the number of cases instituted in each of the Southern states during 1870–77.[25]

South Carolina	1,387	Florida	41
Mississippi	1,175	Texas	29
North Carolina	559	West Virginia	27
Tennessee	214	Virginia	16
Alabama	134	Louisiana	4
Kentucky	116	Arkansas	3
Georgia	73	Missouri	3
Maryland	56		

These statistics reveal a correlation between Klan concentration and enforcement activity and suggest that prosecutions were more justified than Coulter, Dunning, and others have admitted.

In conclusion, it may be pointed out that most exciting studies of the federal enforcement policy in the 1870s were written at a time when disfranchisement and Jim Crowism were accepted as the normal state of affairs in both North and South; political and social inequality, it was assumed, was the logical result of racial inferiority. Such attitudes affected the validity of scholarly findings. . . .

In 1870, measures to preserve the Negro's constitutional rights were desperately needed, and Congress responded with the passage of the Enforcement Acts of 1870 and 1871. These laws, essentially sound, worked fairly well for three or four years. Implementation, however, was difficult. The Grant administration, whose radicalism has perhaps been overemphasized, used federal power conspicuously on a few well-known occasions, but shortages of troops, money, and courts plagued law enforcement officers from the beginning. After 1874, the Acts were virtually dead letter. In the final analysis, Southern intransigence and Northern apathy together brought about the collapse of the enforcement program; white supremacy proved to be a more vital principle than Republican supremacy. The South, in its determination to win home rule, was willing to face the prospect of race war; the North was not. In the end, the policy of enforcement failed; but this does not mean that the policy was iniquitous nor that its failure was a blessing. A complete re-examination of the subject should tell us much about the later Reconstruction period and might well provide useful object lessons for the present.

---

[25] *Annual Report of the Attorney General,* 1870–1877, passim.

Black Reconstruction
and Its Results*

Robert Cruden

How is Reconstruction to be appraised in terms of its significance to American black men?

Fundamentally, it represented the first major test of black belief that white Americans would honor the national commitment to equality set forth in the Declaration of Independence and applied specifically to black men in the Reconstruction amendments. Black men, for the most part, believed they could successfully integrate themselves into American life as equals. In so doing they would also solve the problem of identity by demonstrating that above all they were Americans. . . .

. . . Thanks in large part to their efforts Southern political life was democratized and infused with a social content to an extent hitherto unknown in Southern experience. Black children—and adults—swarmed into the schools, and many went on to the normal schools, colleges, and universities opened to them by Reconstruction governments. This, in turn, helped to swell the ranks of the miniscule black middle class of doctors, lawyers, merchants, and teachers. Black craftsmen and professional men sought, unsuccessfully, to identify themselves with their white counterparts.

The mass of blacks labored on construction gangs, in workshops, on fields and plantations, hoping to ameliorate their lot through economic and political action. A small number of them were able to acquire their own land; a very few, exemplified by Senator Bruce of Mississippi, became wealthy.

This was an impressive record for a people only a few years away from slavery. The fact that it had been made in the face of white hostility gave black men confidence in their abilities and helped nourish a sense of black worth and dignity. Indeed, they could hope that they were in process of overcoming white prejudice. . . .

Dominant though the sentiment for integration may have been, there were also within the black community strong currents of separatism, deriving from various sources. One source was the deep psychological need of black people to nurture their own institutions and direct their own affairs, to have some place of their own where they could be their own selves. Thus, the rapid development of the Negro church. Another source was the rejection of blacks by white society. The color line was

---

* Robert Cruden, *The Negro in Reconstruction* (Englewood Cliffs, N.J.: Prentice-Hall, Inc., 1969). By permission of the publisher.

drawn in social life, in the workshops and professions, and eventually in politics. Black men, perforce, were compelled to organize their own unions and professional associations and to develop a social life of their own. . . .

Some, like Henry M. Turner, were separatists on principle. Disillusioned with white men and white policies, they held America had little to offer black men save subordination. To them, there was only one way out, the ultimate in separatism—return to Africa, the black homeland. Black identity was not with America, but with Africa.

Such a view was unacceptable to the mass of blacks, who, making progress, slow though it may have been, believed the goal of integration to be realistic. As it turned out, their faith proved to be unrealistic. Why?

It must be recalled that the basic problem confronting the nation after the war was the place of the black man in American society. The Thirteenth Amendment made him free. Was he also a citizen? The Fourteenth Amendment declared that he was. Was he a full citizen, with rights and responsibilities equal to those of white men? The Fifteenth Amendment and the supporting body of Reconstruction legislation answered in the affirmative.

Yet Reconstruction was fundamentally a white man's policy. To be sure, state and national conventions of black men had repeatedly demanded citizenship and the ballot, but no black men sat in the Congress which shaped the basic laws. Black men, in later Congresses, backed legislation promoting black rights, but passage of such laws was conditioned upon white interests, and their enforcement and interpretation were entirely in white hands.

. . . Some, like Stevens and Sumner, had a genuine interest in black welfare as such. Most white politicians were concerned rather with how black political power could be used to subdue still rebellious Southern whites and to serve the mundane interests embraced within the Republican party. . . .

On such pragmatic basis America met the issue of the place of the black man in its society: expediency forced assertion of principle—but we must not lose sight of the fact that the principle enunciated was equality.

White opinion, however, while willing to tolerate the formal principle, was not prepared to accept it in practice. Expediency thus dictated masking the principle, even to the point of its tacit disavowal, as when Republicans sold the Reconstruction policy to Northern voters by appealing to racist fears. In the South, where such an approach was impractical, application of the principle was vitiated from the beginning by failure to give land to the freedmen. In neither section was much effort made, except by individual teachers and preachers, such as Wendell Phillips and Gilbert Haven, to persuade whites that Reconstruction presented opportunity for a great experiment in shaping a bi-racial society of free and equal Americans. This in turn derived from the failure of white leadership to envision Reconstruction in such terms.

It followed, then, that whites assumed that while black men were free and were citizens they were also "naturally" inferior and thus would accept subordinate status. When it became clear that black men not only sought equality, but were attaining it in such visible areas as public office, white fears of black men revived. Northerners, disabused of their fears of black hordes pouring across the Ohio river, were the more ready to believe Southern Conservatives that equality meant black oppression of whites. Whites in all sections were convinced that behind the demand for equality lurked a desire for racial amalgamation—and their ears were walls to all black arguments to the contrary. Thus, support for Reconstruction waned, and after the collapse of 1873 Northerners, preoccupied with their own problems, were content to let white men run the South in their own way. . . .

Another factor in the frustration of black hope for integration was that its attainment involved basic changes in American society which Americans were not prepared to make. Those abolitionists who entertained notions of equality after emancipation thought of it, for the most part, in terms of legal equality and equality of opportunity. They sought to help the black make the most of it by providing the rudiments of education and inculcating the puritan virtues of industry, thrift, frugality, sobriety, and self-discipline. Men so trained and so self-disciplined, it was believed, would in time acquire property and become respected members of their communities. Full equality would follow as a matter of course.

Some few, Thaddeus Stevens and Thomas Wentworth Higginson among them, thought this inadequate and unrealistic. It assumed that, given emancipation, Southern society would be an open society, when in fact it was a closed society, so far as the black man was concerned. It ignored the reality that no matter how good a man's character might be, if he lacked land, capital, and the knowledge of how to use them, he was at the mercy of those who did have them. And there was no denying that the mass of black men lacked all three.

If freedom were to be meaningful and equality assured, then the federal government must assume physical protection of the black man, promote his welfare, and underwrite his independence by land distribution. . . .

When these were raised as practical political issues it became clear that forces other than race feeling stood in the way of such a program for racial equality. Men on both sides of the issues perceived, however dimly, that their adoption entailed the remaking of American society.

The proposal for land confiscation touched an extremely sensitive point—the sanctity of private property. Northern leaders, having already "confiscated" more than a billion dollars of private property through emancipation, were little inclined to provide still another example for agrarian reformers and socialist spokesmen in the cities.

It was clear also that land distribution could be only a first step. Since black men lacked capital to work the land, it would have to be furnished. Two sources were open: private and public. If private, then the Federal Government, to protect the black man from usury, must oversee the transactions, just as it supervised labor contracts under the Freedmen's Bureau. If public, then government, federal or state, must regulate its use. . . . All of these possibilities represented, as did the Freedmen's Bureau, a turning away from free enterprise in the direction of social control.

White America was no more ready for such a step than any Western European nation. It was not simply a matter of race. It was also a matter of ideology and principle. This was the heyday of almost religious belief in the efficacy of the "hidden hand" of self-interest in bringing about social well-being, intensified by faith in the survival of the fittest as the test of social evolution. Both reinforced the inherited Puritan teachings of the individual's responsibility for his well-being, spiritual and material. If an individual fell by the wayside, it was basically due to his own weaknesses, not to social ills. Thus was ruled out governmental intervention on behalf of the poor, white or black. It helps explain why Reconstruction lacked social content.

General acceptance of the social philosophy of *laissez-faire* meant distress for poor people generally. For propertyless blacks, subject to racial animosity, it was well-nigh disastrous. When the hope of land distribution proved illusory, they were at the mercy of a "free" labor market dominated by planters and employers. In that market there was little hope for progress, for equality.

The tragedy of black leadership was that it failed to perceive this. It, too, believed in *laissez-faire*. The educated elite, who set the tone for other black leaders, were products of colleges and universities, either in the North or abroad, which produced white elites. Like the whites, blacks accepted the teachings of Adam Smith as social and economic law. They, too, shared in the Puritan ethic of work as the way to moral and material well-being—and the individual's responsibility for both. . . .

Among those who had been slaves, there were a few, such as Senator Bruce of Mississippi, who had gone on to become wealthy. It was easy for such self-made men to assume that because they had succeeded, others could also, providing they possessed the necessary character, shrewdness, and fortitude. . . .

. . . While the elite emphasized civil and political rights, the masses interpreted it in economic terms. They wanted land of their own—and they looked to government to provide it. Given their poverty and the conditions of Southern society they knew they had small chance of acquiring it on their own. In this context, *laissez-faire* was an impediment to realization of black hope. . . .

. . . Victims of a *laissez-faire* system in which their leaders believed, blacks were fragmented, and thus unable to confront successfully the Conservative-Republican coalition which effectively destroyed black political power and frustrated the black hope for integration into American society on the basis of equality.

The impact on black attitudes of what T. Thomas Fortune, the noted black editor, called the "betrayal" of 1876, cannot be overestimated. If it signalled the end of the hope for integration, it likewise marked the latest in what blacks considered to be a series of broken white pledges, beginning with the failure to grant land. . . .

True, for a generation after 1876 black men voted, held public office, and sat in Congress—but in ever diminishing numbers and on terms reflecting an understanding between such blacks and Southern Conservatives. For a time there was some respect for black civil rights. What remained of those, as well as of black political rights, were consumed in the flames of the political warfare of the 90s, when white Bourbons and white Populists fought for control of the South. No matter which side won, the black man lost. In state after state his degradation was written into law—and approved by the United States Supreme Court.

Nor was there much room for black men in the protest movements of the day. Populism attracted large numbers of black farmers until the white Populists turned on them. A few Negroes turned socialist, but the party was little interested in blacks as such. Many of the leaders were openly racist, and even Eugene V. Debs, who sympathized deeply with black men, thought they had no problems substantially different from those of white workers. The American Federation of Labor practiced segregation and its leaders were increasingly racist in public utterances.

Black hope for integration had proved unrealistic. Reality was the emergence of a color-caste system imbedded in the laws, behavior and attitudes of white America.

How did black men respond to this thwarting of their hope?

To some, the answer was separatism. Turner's project for a return to Africa took on a new lease of life; in 1886 an association formed for that purpose appealed to Congress for funds to help blacks emigrate. Others sought escape within the United States. In 1879, under conditions of incredible hardship, thousands fled the South for the prairies of Kansas in the first mass migration organized and directed by black men. There they hoped, vainly, to find the security and opportunity denied them in the South. Later, some blacks advocated migration to the Oklahoma territory, where they proposed to establish a separate Negro state. . . .

Other blacks [such as Frederick Douglass] equally sensitive to the decline in black fortunes, warned that giving way to counsels of despair was fatal. The proper answer, they said, was not withdrawal, but militancy. . . .

Even more militant was T. Thomas Fortune, who, in 1884, advocated the unity of black and white poor to end the economic system which impoverished them. . . .

There were still other leaders who felt that political activity was futile and that emphasis should be placed on self-help: the development of character, morality, and race pride through black economic activity. One such approach was that of Alexander Crummell, a famous Episcopalian priest who formulated an early version of black nationalism; another was that of Booker T. Washington.

Crummell exhorted his fellows to cease depending on white men and to develop their own business enterprises, employing black capital and black labor, in both industry and agriculture. Such cooperation, he thought, would forge racial solidarity, stimulate a sense of black pride, develop black character, and eventually win recognition of black equality from whites. Washington denied that blacks could attain their goals without "a certain extent" of white cooperation. But he, too, laid emphasis on the need for blacks to develop their own resources, material, moral, and intellectual. . . .

The last type of self-help appealed strongly to the emerging black bourgeoisie. . . . But always there was the color line. The response of many such blacks was particularly destructive to black psychological wholeness: they blamed the color line not on whites, but on the mass of blacks, who by their presumed vulgarity, laziness, thriftlessness, and immorality held back decent and industrious blacks from achieving their due. . . .

As for the masses, their reaction to the collapse of black hope was withdrawal: they were in American society, but not of it. They adjusted themselves to the ways of white supremacy through a subtle and complex code of behavior toward whites which satisfied white men while it enabled black men to keep a measure of self-respect. The tensions inherent in such a delicate situation were eased in the outlets of revivalistic religion and in development of black standards of behavior within the black community—the standards which so offended middle class blacks. . . .

Reconstruction, then, to the black man was only a beginning. It was a faltering, but decisive, step from formal freedom to meaningful freedom, based on the civil and political equality of black men. The means necessary to provide a firm economic foundation for such equality—land for the farmer and workshops open to the craftsman—were denied, and thus helped frustrate the hope of black men for integration as equals into American society. But even this, and the later reaction against black rights, could not erase the commitment made by the nation to the principle of equality. . . .

chapter 15

The Retreat from Reconstruction

IN THE CASE OF RECONSTRUCTION the roots of failure go deeply into American culture. From the earliest days of the Republic most Southerners *and* Northerners subscribed to racial opinions which denied the democratic creed to Negroes, and only the upheaval of Civil War made the revolutionary dream of emancipation a living possibility. The flight of slaves to Union lines forced federal commanders to ask whether or not they wished to aid the enemy by returning valuable slave property. The desperate need for manpower, the early and successful experiments in the use of black troops, and the clamorous antislavery agitation—all helped to bring a skeptical administration gradually to the policy of emancipation. It soon became clear, however, that the Proclamation and the 13th Amendment alone would not make citizenship a reality for the former slaves, and Southern violence followed by presidential blunders stimulated Northern fears that the results of the war would be reversed or damaged without a Reconstruction program.

Unfortunately Reconstruction never progressed far enough to secure land for the freedman. Charles Sumner and a few others saw the importance of providing an economic foundation for freedom but most Radicals, like the overwhelming majority of Americans, regarded conventional property rights as nearly sacred and would not sanction the proposal to turn confiscated plantation lands over to the freedman. In the final analysis the leaders of the Republic proved to be less perceptive than the czar of Russia, who at that very time had begun to allow newly emancipated serfs to purchase land and become landowners. There were several notable exceptions to the general rule, and Willie Lee Rose in 1964 (Selection 1) examined the most favorable of the land distribution experiments in a study of the South Carolina Sea Islands. Here at least some of the freedmen gained land which gave them a more hopeful future than most American Negroes were to know in the decades to come. Still, the experiment enjoyed only a limited success. The plots were small and often threatened by further subdivision and legal disputes, and the Sea Islands had to compete with new cotton areas of the world for a declining market. Most importantly, these small enclaves of black ownership and independence found survival difficult in the shadow of the larger and unsympathetic communities of South Carolina, the South, and the United States at large.

As a Patrick M. Riddleberger essay indicated in 1960, the abandonment of Reconstruction began as early as the Liberal Republican party secession of 1872. The Liberal Republican mind, so astutely explored in John G. Sproat's monograph of 1968, expressed high-minded elitist devotion to self-help, "decent" acquisitiveness, and "clean" and efficient government. With a completely inadequate understanding of the human devastation of slavery or the consuming Southern passion for racial mastery, the Liberals fully expected blacks to lift themselves by their own bootstraps into full citizenship and prosperity. Consequently they called for an end to military Reconstruction on the grounds that the three amendments and the various pieces of federal legislation had brought freedom to the Negro, and there was no longer any need for "special assistance." The North grew weary of violence, social conflict, and Southern issues in general, and a spokesman for President Grant indicated that "we are tired of these annual outbursts" of Democratic violence against Negro Republican voters. The spokesman did not mean that the country had become so weary of violence by white men as to act more effectively to stop it, but that the government was tired of having to act and think about the fate of the freedman. Then too, the Republicans had some white Southern voters and politicians were constantly tempted by the possibility of expanding this segment of support. The Radicals had gone to so much trouble to secure the franchise partly because they needed black assistance to stay in power, and free elections continued to be an issue until 1896 when the Republicans secured a solid national majority without black support. Subsequently Republican leaders ceased to be seriously concerned about Southern support of any kind.

While the withdrawal of federal troops in 1877 struck a damaging blow to the Radical cause, Reconstruction had not yet run its course. As books by Vincent P. De Santis in 1959 and Stanley P. Hirshson in 1962 demonstrated, every president from Hayes to Harrison gave some attention to "the Negro problem," and white Southerners could not be reasonably sure until the 1890s that the nation would not attempt to interfere with Southern racial domination. In 1877 a part of "the bargain" which brought Hayes to the White House was the promise of Southerners to respect the rights of the Negro. Despite all evidence to the contrary, Hayes seems to have seriously believed that the "redeemers," "conservatives," and Democrats who made this pledge would abide by it, and the President urged Congress several times to use federal support of education as a supplementary means of improving the status of the freedman. No doubt some Southern leaders meant to keep the pledges made in 1876, but as the North grew increasingly disinterested and as the concrete pressures lessened, the politicians tended to follow the desire of the white majority for more and more subordination of Negroes. The Republican political creed advocated both moral and material progress, and this belief did not die on Inauguration Day, 1877. As time passed moral idealism did diminish, the desire to have "business as usual" increased, and the amount of real concern for the Negro declined, but Rutherford B. Hayes, Chester A. Arthur, James G. Blaine, and even Benjamin Harrison made proposals relating either to voting rights or to educational opportunities. Hopes for a federal education bill died a lingering death in the 1880s, and Senator Henry Cabot Lodge introduced the last serious "force" bill to protect black voting rights in 1890.

For nearly 20 years after 1877 at least a few Republican politicians tried to keep alive the grand issues of Civil War and Reconstruction, an effort which led to the creation of another term of political abuse to use along with "carpetbagger" and "scalawag." The phrase "waving the bloody shirt" was applied to Northern politicians who raised the ghost of presumably dead "war" issues (such as Negro voting rights) for purely demagogic purposes. By implication, the new term denied the existence of any real issues, suggested that news of violence and caste subjugation from the South was somehow misleading or false, and impugned the motives of Republicans who made speeches on "war issues." Here is another instance of a rationalization which served to conceal the fact that a single society harbored both democratic values and social oppression. Men such as John Sherman, James G. Blaine, and George F. Hoar fell below the high moral standards of Garrison, Douglass, and Phillips and failed to operate on the same plane of momentous political leadership as Sumner and Stevens, but one should not assume that these men were totally devoid of principle and completely hypocritical in their speeches on Southern violence and the status of the Negro. If moral idealism was waning in the North between 1875 and 1895, the fact remained that the Negro had no one else to turn to other than the "wavers of the bloody shirt." Moreover, even if all the motives of the dwindling Republican minority who kept "war issues" alive were bad, did not their speeches refer to the real issue of Negro freedom? Were not the lynchings and acts of terror reported by the "bloody shirt" politicians events which actually took place?

The Supreme Court, which preceded the Republican Party in the abandonment of the Negro, initiated an anti-equalitarian trend of thought as early as 1873. The Court in the Civil Rights cases of 1883 virtually destroyed the Civil Rights Act of 1875, and rendered many parts of the 14th Amendment inoperative. Hostile legal reasoning reached a climax in the Plessy case of 1896 after a fashion which Barton J. Bernstein discussed in 1963 (Selection 3) and Otto H. Olsen analyzed and documented in 1968. The "separate but equal" formula was accepted despite the sharp protest of Justice John Marshall Harlan who identified segregation laws as oppressive measures contrary to the 14th Amendment. Did the Court or any other group of informed Northerners or Southerners really imagine that the facilities in any area of Southern life were in fact equal or likely to become so? It seems most improbable, and certainly "the separation of the races" makes sense only in the context of belief in racial superiority and inferiority. The Supreme Court's rationalization that "social equality" between "the races" could not be legislated represented surrender by the national government to regional forces intent on an increasingly firm subordination of Negroes.

The fate to which nation and Congress, Republican Party, and Supreme Court, abandoned Southern blacks has been defined commonly in terms of "Jim Crow" and "segregation." In 1954 soon after the Supreme Court seemingly issued a sweeping challenge to Southern white supremacy by ruling against school segregation, C. Vann Woodward gave a series of lectures at the University of Virginia which appeared in print the following year as *The Strange Career of Jim Crow*. During the troubled 1950s Northern liberals and the small minority of Southern "moderates" willing to sanction some change found reasons for hope in Woodward's discussion of a Dixie racial system based, not rigidly on slavery and the time-worn customs of many generations, but more flexibly on laws and social practices which made men of middle years and older "contemporaries of Jim Crow" who "grew up along with the system." Several monographs supported Woodward and much of the evidence seemed to bear out his thesis. Many segregation laws got on the books in relatively recent years such as 1890, 1915, or 1935; many blacks voted and used public facilities as late as the 1890s; the last black Congressman served until 1901; the state disfranchisement process did not take place until the 1890–1910 period; and Dixie politicians were still building the segregation edifice during the 1950s.

Yet Joel Williamson in his 1965 study of South Carolina blacks in Reconstruction demonstrated the existence of very extensive segregation in 1865 and concluded that turn-of-the-century laws merely codified old customs. Richard Wade in a monograph of 1964 on slavery in the cities and Roger A. Fischer in a 1969 essay on antebellum New Orleans proved the prevalence of urban Jim Crow laws and customs before the Civil War. Woodward in 1971 and 1974 modifications of his position clung to the essence of his thesis in an essay centered around "paternalistic" and "competitive" models of race relations which made the nineteenth century North more hostile to blacks than the allegedly paternalistic South. Moreover, according to the Woodwardian line of reasoning, Southern Populism created a humane biracial coalition which promised to provide a bridge to a more reasonable modern society until the collapse of both Populism and paternalism reversed the situation and gave the South competitive racial patterns harsher than those which prevailed elsewhere in America.

Woodward provided provocative discussions of Populism and paternalism, but he failed to persuade many scholars. A Charles Crowe essay in 1970 (Selection 2) insisted that Populists were as wedded to white supremacy as conservatives; Claude H. Nolen's 1967 volume on Southern images of blacks indicated the existence of venomous racial attitudes among all classes and types; a Lawrence J. Friedman study of 1970 on "racial fantasies" described even "paternalists" and "moderates" of the George W. Cable school as "white savages" with their own formulas for racial exploitation; and William Ivy Hair's monograph of 1969 on Louisiana Bourbonism and agrarian protest revealed a ruling elite devoted to rabid racism and the interests of the rich without any real pretenses toward noblesse oblige or racial paternalism. In a 1970 study of New South ideology, Paul M. Gaston analyzed the ways in which optimistic programs and proposals for economic progress and better race relations became "myths" and "ritualistic incantations" worlds apart from the realities of racism, stifling conformity, and economic stagnation. Pathetically marginal reform elements hardly helped the situation more than conservatives did. Jack T. Kirby's monograph of 1972 on race and reform in the Progressive South explained how the first elements of a regional dawning in reform encountered disastrously "the dark whirlwind of racism," and Bruce Clayton's study of the same year on intellectual leaders of the Populist-Progressive eras such as Woodrow Wilson, President Edwin A. Alderman of the University of Virginia, and the Rev. Edgar Gardner Murphy of Alabama, demonstrated that these men with their vague aspirations for an improved Southern society failed to challenge seriously the sterile and oppressive orthodoxies and actually helped to secure more rigidly the chains of color caste. Even Carl N. Degler's sympathetic account of 1974 on Southern dissent traced the limits of Reconstruction Republicans and of Populists and could find little to commemorate beyond these two marginal groups.

Some parts of Woodward's explanation of Jim Crow as a relatively recent "system" survived the scholarship of the 1960s and the early 1970s. Many segregation statutes and rituals clearly did have recent origins and the South did experience some kind of turn-of-the-century repression, but far more important than the shifting means of racial control from slave codes to new-style segregation laws was the fanatical Southern determination in all historical eras to rule blacks. A rural and seemingly stable antebellum South with its patterns of local mastery, slave patrols, and state slave codes had little need of elaborate Jim Crow laws and highly formalized customs but a New South looking toward industry, urban growth and more efficient government needed the more recent laws and mores to preserve and promote white supremacy. The key to the situation cannot be found in radical changes in Southern white opinion. To understand the Populist-Progressive South we must see that when it became reasonably clear that no significant national institution would intervene, Southern Democrats proceeded to do what they had wanted to do since 1865 and improved a set of social controls by law and private action which made the South a fortress of white supremacy ruled by formal expressions of caste which the nation would not have tolerated during Reconstruction and would have found highly dubious in the Post-Reconstruction era.

The closure of many choice occupations coupled with the establishment of invariably inferior educational systems sharply curtailed the Negro's hopes for a better life. Joblessness, low wages, and frequent threats to male independence sustained patterns of family instability inherited from slavery, and the assault on black dignity in the condescending ridicule or the harsh aggression of stories, songs, and maxims demoralized the lives of both men and women. To prevent or to destroy any form of group unity inimical to the interests of the dominant caste, local authorities generally kept Negro communities under surveillance.

The occasional practice of holding any Negro or even an entire community responsible for the actions of one person and the general failure to police Negro neighborhoods encouraged "displaced aggression" by men who lacked the power to direct hostile emotions toward their oppressors and consequently turned against each other.

"Segregation" seems an inadequate word to describe this new system of bondage which developed so many harsh and cruel institutions. The hated practice of using chain gangs for public works and leased convict labor for private wealth were not examples of isolated abuse but part of a complex pattern of social domination. In the midst of general poverty and at a time when wealth was rare, few could resist the temptation to exploit—and often to cheat—the illiterate and helpless sharecroppers and laborers. The debt peonage system, analyzed in 1972 and 1973 by Pete Daniel and by the economists Roger L. Ransom and Richard Sutch, harshly ruled the lives of millions of blacks. Economic and political systems simply did not compel white men to observe agreements faithfully, and the Negro had few means of redress after he had been excluded from the polls, the jury box, and the right to a trial before unbiased judges and juries. Invariably white men transformed Negro losses into personal advantage. The economic benefits to the dominant caste were dramatically evident, and they increased with the passing of every decade. The task of measuring white status gains achieved at the expense of Negro dignity and security is more difficult, but John Dollard in 1937 made an excellent analysis of the whole pattern of caste gain.

The pervasiveness and the frequency of violence provided the most demoralizing aspects of the system, and often lynchings became virtually public ceremonies led by local officials and attended by thousands of men, women, and children. To read the history of Southern racial violence is to read a catalog of the excessive acts of savagery of which humanity is capable—men emasculated, burnt alive, toes and fingers chopped from living persons and corpses to be used as souvenirs, the sustained torture of persons until death came from shock, and the occasional lynching of women and children as well as men. Frequently the killings went beyond the conceivable needs of a system of caste control and served either as a barbarous outlet for the most sadistic segment of the community or as a kind of ritual murder in the religion of white supremacy. Information on some forms of violence can be found in Allen W. Trelease's 1971 monograph on the Klan and in 1968 and 1969 essays on race riots by Charles Crowe.

It is quite true that many white citizens regretted these "acts of excess" but few made serious efforts to stop the violence, and juries almost always freed both leaders and members of the mobs. Rayford W. Logan in 1954 (Selection 4) traced the web of responsibility far beyond the Mason-Dixon line to a Supreme Court which did not protect constitutional rights, to a Congress which failed to pass anti-lynching laws, and to the general majority of Americans who belonged to the high age of imperialism when white men from America to Germany enjoyed a new peak of power and self-esteem. Most Northerners were perfectly willing to grant that the Southerner, as the man who "knew" the Negro best, should handle "race relations." Americans often acknowledged the inferiority of the Negro and just as frequently conceded that Reconstruction had been a mistake.

The South was the home of most Negroes and the storm center of violence, but men were lynched elsewhere. The years from 1880 to 1910 saw a general retrogression in the status of Northern Negroes, as state civil rights bills became hollow pretenses and universities closed doors which had once been open. According to David W. Southern's 1968 report on the Yankee Progressives, even reformers expressed the gospel of racism to a receptive white populace. The oppressed black urban ghettoes destined to expand so dramatically in the twentieth century had roots in the previous century as Gilbert Osofsky's book of 1966 on Harlem and Allen Spear's monograph of 1967 on black Chicago demonstrates. Northern abolitionist sympathizers had always been a minority, death and old age removed many from the political scene and a consequential number of the survivors were gradually persuaded by the new wave of racist opinion which marked the 1880s and 90s. Some, without conscious hypocrisy, began to grant the need for more segregation and to recommend "self-help" coupled with "better morale" as the only solution. A history of Negro labor in the North is in large part a history of violent displacement by the most recent and poverty-stricken immigrant group. On the New York docks, for example, Negroes could work as longshoremen until they were driven from their jobs by Irishmen; later they were able to reclaim some of the jobs only to be thrust out again by later waves of immigration. In general the racial concepts which dominated the South ruled the minds of most Americans. Between 1895 and 1919 nearly every major Northern and Middle Western city which contained Negroes experienced the kind of racial violence usually described as a "race riot" but which often represented the effort of a mob of white men to injure or kill Negroes and to destroy their possessions.

Some black leaders, as Emma Lou Thornbrough's 1972 biography of T. Thomas Fortune indicated, responded by continuing to demand militantly all the political and human rights promised in Reconstruction. The black nationalist, Bishop Henry M. Turner of Georgia, followed the way analyzed in Edwin M. Redkey's monograph on back-to-Africa movements and angrily turned away from an oppressive white America to follow the dream of establishing a black homeland across the Atlantic. Most Southern black men of education and standing probably took the path explored in Louis Harlan's 1972 study on Booker T. Washington of accommodation to Southern whites, stress on building black institutions and sporadic objection to some of the harsher applications of color caste.

American blacks moved into the twentieth century as an oppressed minority, deprived in almost every area—education, income, economic opportunity, and individual human dignity. Nevertheless, the Civil War and Reconstruction had created some permanent gains. The old system of slavery had been destroyed; and the freedman had gained a precarious economic independence and mobility of person, the rudiments of an educational system, and the hope for a better future. A small black middle class existed even in antebellum days, and it grew steadily through the postwar decades. The literacy rate increased with each decade, and modern measures such as social security and general community welfare which were certainly not created with the black in mind nonetheless often helped him. The New Deal and the post World War II eras brought a less hostile political climate, a Supreme Court willing to reverse its predecessors, an international situation favorable to the black cause, and above all the political movement which broke out among American blacks in the late 50s and the early 60s under the leadership of Martin Luther King, Jr. and the young men of the Student Non-Violent Coordinating Committee (SNCC) and the Congress of Racial Equality (CORE).

BIBLIOGRAPHY

Works Discussed in This Chapter

Bernstein, Barton J., "Plessy v. Ferguson: Conservative Sociological Jurisprudence," *Journal of Negro History* (1963) and "Case Law in Plessy v. Ferguson," ibid. (1962).

Clayton, Bruce, *The Savage Ideal: Intolerance and Intellectual Leadership in the South, 1890–1914* (1972).

Crowe, Charles, "Tom Watson, Populists and Blacks Reconsidered," *Journal of Negro History* (1970), "Racial Violence and Social Reform—Origins of the Atlanta Race Riot of 1906," ibid. (1968), and "Racial Massacre in Atlanta: September 22, 1906," ibid. (1969).

Daniel, Pete, *The Shadow of Slavery: Peonage in the South, 1901–1969* (1972).

Degler, Carl N., *The Other South: Southern Dissenters in the Nineteenth Century* (1974).

DeSantis, Vincent P., *The Republicans Face the Southern Question: The New Departure Years, 1877–1897* (1959).

Dollard, John, *Caste and Class in a Southern Town* (1937).

Fischer, Roger A., "Racial Segregation in Ante-Bellum New Orleans," *American Historical Review* (1969).

Friedman, Lawrence J., *The White Savage: Racial Fantasies in the Post-Bellum South* (1970).

Gaston, Paul M., *The New South Creed: A Study in Southern Myth-Making* (1970).

Hair, William Ivy, *Bourbonism and Agrarian Protest: Louisiana Politics, 1877–1900* (1969).

Harlan, Louis, *Booker T. Washington: The Making of a Black Leader, 1856–1901* (1972).

Hirshson, Stanley P., *Farewell to the Bloody Shirt: Northern Republicans and the Southern Negro, 1877–1893* (1962).

Kirby, Jack T., *Darkness at the Dawning: Race and Reform in the Progressive South* (1972).

Logan, Rayford W., *The Negro in American Life: The Nadir, 1877–1901* (1954), revised and expanded as *The Betrayal of the Negro* (1965).

Nolen, Claude F., *The Negro's Image in the South: The Anatomy of White Supremacy* (1967).

Olsen, Otto H., ed., *The Thin Disguise: Turning Point in Negro History. Plessy v. Ferguson: A Documentary Presentation, 1864–1896* (1967).

Osofsky, Gilbert, *Harlem: The Making of a Ghetto, Negro New York, 1890–1930* (1966).

Ransom, Roger L., and Sutch, Richard, "Debt Peonage in the Cotton South After the Civil War," *Journal of Economic History* (1972).

Redkey, Edwin S., *Black Exodus: Black Nationalism and Back-to-Africa Movements, 1890–1910* (1969).

Riddleberger, Patrick W., "The Radicals' Abandonment of the Negro During Reconstruction," *Journal of Negro History* (1960).

Rose, Willie Lee, *Rehearsal for Reconstruction: The Port Royal Experiment* (1964).

Southern, David W., *The Malignant Heritage: Yankee Progressivism and the Negro Question, 1901–1914* (1968).

Spear, Allan H., *Black Chicago: The Making of a Negro Ghetto, 1890–1920* (1967).

Sproat, John G., *'The Best Men': Liberal Reformers in the Gilded Age* (1968).

Thornbrough, Emma Lou, *T. Thomas Fortune: Militant Journalist* (1972).

Trelease, Allen W., *White Terror: The Ku Klux Klan Conspiracy and Southern Reconstruction* (1971).

Wade, Richard, *Slavery in the Cities, 1820–1860* (1964).

Williamson, Joel, *After Slavery, The Negro in South Carolina During Reconstruction, 1861–1877* (1965).

Woodward, C. Vann, *The Strange Career of Jim Crow* (1955; 2nd rev. ed., 1966; 3rd rev. ed., 1974), *American Counterpoint: Slavery and Racism in the North-South Dialogue* (1971), and *Tom Watson, Agrarian Rebel* (1938).

Suggested Readings

On *national politics* see Robert H. Wiebe, *The Search for Order, 1877–1920* (1967), and H. Wayne Morgan, *From Hayes to McKinley: National Party Politics, 1877–1896* (1969) for an able but implausibly optimistic survey. For the compromise of 1876–1877 see C. Vann Woodward, *Reunion and Reaction: The Compromise of 1877 and the End of Reconstruction* (1951). On Liberal Republicanism see Sproat, cited earlier, Patrick Riddleberger, "The Break in the Radical Ranks: Liberals vs. Stalwarts in the Election of 1872," *Journal of Negro History* (1959). For a moderate revision of the old stereotype on "waving the bloody shirt" see Sam Ross, *The Empty Sleeve: A Biography of Lucius Fairchild* (1964). See also Herbert J. Clancy, *The Presidential Election of 1880* (1958).

On the *Supreme Court, race and inequality* the most important book is Loren Miller, *The Petitioners: The Story of the Supreme Court of the United States and the Negro* (1966). See also Robert Harris, *The Quest For Equality* (1960).

On the *Blair education and Lodge Federal election bills* see Allen J. Going, "The South and the Blair Bill," *Mississippi Valley Historical Review* (1957); Daniel Crofts, "The Black Response to the Blair Education Bill," *Journal of Southern History* (1971); and Richard E. Welch, Jr., "The Federal Elections Bill of 1890: Poscripts and Prelude," *Journal of American History* (1965).

Among *Southern state and local studies* see Joy J. Jackson, *New Orleans in the Gilded Age: Politics and Urban Progress, 1880–1896* (1969) for a jungle of unsolved urban problems and an irresponsible New South ruling elite. For the idea that Southern Protestants were mostly "national," see W. Harrison Daniel, "Virginia Baptists and the Myth of the Southern Mind, 1865–1900," *South Atlantic Quarterly* (1974). C. Vann Woodward's *Origins of the New South, 1877–1913* (1951) continues to be a useful book for Southern state politics. See also Melton Alonzo McLaurin, *Paternalism and Protest: Southern Cotton Mill Workers and Organized Labor, 1875–1905* (1971).

On *sharecropping and peonage* see the Daniel book cited earlier; the Ransom and Sutch article cited earlier; Richard Sutch and Roger L. Ransom, "The Ex-Slave in the Post-Bellum South: A Study of the Economic Impact of Racism in a Market Environment," *Journal of Economic History* (1973); Joseph D. Reid, "Sharecropping as an Understandable Market Relation—The Post-Bellum South," *Journal of Economic History* (1973); William W. Brown and Morgan O. Reynolds, "Debt Peonage Reexamined," *Journal of Economic History* (1973).

On *segregation, caste and violence* see Trelease and Crowe, cited earlier; the chapter on racism; the modern edition of late nineteenth century pamphlets edited by Alfreda M. Duster, *Crusade for Justice: The Autobiography of Ida B. Wells* (1970); William F. Holmes, "Whitecapping in Mississippi: Agrarian Violence in the Populist Era," *Mid-America* (1973); Arthur F. Raper, *The Tragedy of Lynching* (1933); Ralph Ginzburg, ed., *One Hundred Years of Lynching* (1962); Glenn S. Sisk, "Crime and Justice in the Alabama Black Belt, 1875–1917," *Mid-America* (1958); F. Gavin Davenport, "Thomas Dixon's Mythology of Southern History," *Journal of Southern History* (1970); Linda M. Matthews, "Keeping Down Jim Crow: The Railroad and the Separate Coach Rule in South Carolina," *South Atlantic Quarterly* (1974); Roger L. Rice, "Residential Segregation by Law, 1910–1917," *Journal of Southern History* (1968); the works of C. Vann Woodward cited earlier; John Hope Franklin, "Jim Crow Goes to School," *South Atlantic Quarterly* (1959); Herbert Aptheker, ed., *A Documentary History of the Negro People in the U.S.* (1951); Louis R. Harlan, *Separate and Unequal: Public School Campaigns and Racism in the Southern Seaboard States, 1901–1915* (1958); William F. Holmes, *The White Chief: James Kimble Vardaman* (1969); Albert Kirwan, *Revolt of the Rednecks, Mississippi Politics, 1876–1925* (1951); and Francis B. Simkins, *Pitchfork Ben Tillman: South Carolinian* (1944).

On *Southern "moderates" and "paternalists"* see William J. Cooper, Jr., in *The Conservative Regime in South Carolina, 1877–1890* (1968). Cooper correctly sees no radical conflict of commercial and "agrarian interests" but argues for a measure of conservative "paternalism" on race. Hugh C. Bailey looks for the silver lining on race during the Bourbon era in *Edgar Gardner Murphy, Gentle Progressive* (1968) and *Liberalism in the New South* (1970) as does C. Vann Woodward in his 1964 edition of Lewis Henry Blair, *A Southern Prophecy* (1899) and other works. See also Charles E. Wynes, *Race Relations in Virginia, 1870–1902* (1961), and Wynes, ed., *Forgotten Voices: Dissenting Southerners in the Age of Conformity* (1967).

On *Southern Populists and Progressives* see the Crowe essay cited earlier; Herbert Shapiro, "The Populists and the Negro: A Reconstruction" in August Meier and Elliott Rudwick, eds., *The Making of Black America* (2 vols., 1969); William Warren Rogers, *The One-Gallused Rebellion: Agrarianism in Alabama, 1865–1900* (1970); Robert Sanders, "Southern Populists and the Negro, 1893–1905," *Journal of Negro History* (1969); and William H. Chaffee, "The Negro and Populism: A Kansas Case Study," *Journal of Southern History* (1968). C. Vann Woodward's *Tom Watson: Agrarian Rebel* (1938) is very dated and Sheldon Hackney's rather pedestrian volume, *From Populism to Progressivism in Alabama* (1969), is particularly weak on racism for a modern study.

On the *black urban South* see John W. Blassingame, "Before the Ghetto: The Making of the Black Community in Savannah, Georgia, 1865–1900," *Journal of Social History* (1973); Richard J. Hopkins, "Occupational and Geographical Mobility in Atlanta, 1870–1896," *Journal of Southern History* (1968); and Robert E. Perdue, *The Negro in Savannah, 1865–1900* (1973).

On *Southern black protest* see Clarence A. Bacote, "Negro Proscriptions, Protests and Proposed Solutions in Georgia, 1880–1908," *Journal of Southern History* (1950); and August Meier and Elliott Rudwick, "The Boycott Movement Against Jim Crow Street Cars in the South, 1900–1906," *Journal of American History* (1969).

On *black economic and social history* see Bettye C. Thomas, "A Nineteenth Century Black Operated Shipyard, 1866–1884," *Journal of Negro History*, (1974); Walter B. Weare, *Black Businessmen in the New South: A Social History of the N. C. Mutual Life Insurance Company* (1973); Roger L Williams, *The Bonds, An American Family* (1971); John Hope Franklin, ed., *Reminiscences of An Active Life: The Autobiography of John Roy Lynch* (1970); and Paul David Nelson, "Experiment in Inter-racial Education at Berea College, 1858–1908," *Journal of Negro History* (1974).

Among *state and local studies of Southern blacks* see I. A. Newby, *Black Carolinians: A History of Blacks in South Carolina from 1898 to 1968* (1973); Margaret Law Callcott, *The Negro in Maryland Politics, 1880–1912* (1969); Helen C. Edmonds, *The Negro and Fusion Politics in North Carolina, 1895–1901* (1951); Frenise A. Logan, *The Negro in North Carolina, 1876–1894* (1964); George B. Tindall, *South Carolina Negroes, 1877–1900* (1952); and Lawrence D. Rice's rather hastily put together volume, *The Negro in Texas, 1874–1900* (1971).

On *black soldiers* see Willard B. Gatewood, ed., *'Smoked Yankees' and the Struggle for Empire: Letters from Negro Soldiers, 1898–1902* (1971); Arlen L. Fowler, *The Black Infantry in the West, 1869–1891* (1971); William H. Leckie, *The Buffalo Soldiers: A Narrative of the Negro Cavalry in the West* (1967); and Lewis N. Wynne, "Brownsville: The Reaction of the Negro Press," *Phylon* (1972).

Among other *studies on Southern blacks* see Eugene D. Genovese, Herbert Aptheker, C. Vann Woodward, and Frank Kofsky, "The Legacy of Slavery . . ." *Studies on the Left* (1966); William F. Cheek, "A Negro Runs for Congress: John Mercer Langston and the Virginia Campaign of 1888," *Journal of Negro History* (1967); and Louis R. Harlan, "Booker T. Washington and the White Man's Burden," *American Historical Review* (1966).

On the *Northern black ghettoes* see Osofsky and Spear cited earlier. Gilbert Osofsky in "The Enduring Ghetto," *Journal of American History* (1968) finds the basic structure of the ghetto to have existed throughout American history. Two other significant studies are Seth M. Scheiner, *Negro Mecca: A History of the Negro in New York City, 1865–1920* (1965) and Constance M. Green, *The Secret City: A History of Race Relations in the Nation's Captol* (1967).

On *black life and thought* see Elinor M. Gersman. "The Development of Public Education for Blacks in Nineteenth Century St. Louis," *Journal of Negro Education* (1972); June Sochen, *The Unbridgeable Gap: Blacks and Their Quest for the American Dream, 1900–1936* (1972); Kenneth W. Porter, "Negro Leaders in the Western Cattle Industry, 1866–1900," *Labor History* (1969); Leslie H. Fishel, Jr. "The Negro in Northern Politics, 1870–1900," *Mississippi Valley Historical Review* (1955); E. Franklin Frazier, *The Negro Church in America* (1964); Robert L. Factor, *The Black Response to America: Men, Ideals and Organizations from Frederick Douglass to the NAACP* (1970); Phillip S. Foner, ed., *W. E. B. DuBois Speaks* (2 vols., 1970); and August Meier, *Negro Thought in America, 1885–1915* (1963).

On *Northern racism* see the earlier chapter on racism; Irving Dillard, "Civil Liberties of Negroes in Illinois Since 1865," *Journal of the Illinois State Historical Society* (1963); James L. Crouthamel, "The Springfield Race Riot of 1908," *Journal of Negro History* (1960); Elliott M. Rudwick, *Race Riot at East St. Louis, July 2, 1917* (1964); Herman D. Bloch, "The New York City Negro and Occupational Eviction 1860–1910," *International Review of Social History* (1960); William P. Vaughn, "Partners in Segregation: Barnabas Sears and the Peabody Fund," *Civil War History* (1964); Louis D. Rubin, *Teach the Freedman: The Correspondence of Rutherford B. Hayes and the Slater Fund for Negro Education, 1881–1887* (2 vols., 1959); and Valeria W. Weaver, "The Failure of Civil Rights, 1875–1883 and Its Repercussions," *Journal of Negro History* (1969). On the persecution and court martial of a pioneer West Point black cadet in the 1870s, see John F. Marszlek, Jr., *Court-Martial: A Black Man in America* (1972).

The Aftermath of Reconstruction at Port Royal*

Willie Lee Rose

. . . What had gone wrong? The future had seemed so promising back in 1868 when the radical Republican government had begun its course. Part of the initial exhilation had been sheer relief. All the fears for the freedmen associated with Saxton's last months in office, when he had tried manfully to block President Johnson's land restoration policy, were banished. The colored people had not been relegated to the tyranny of their late owners, and in the islands near Beaufort the freedmen had retained their land. President Johnson had been a poor politician and had understood little of the national sentiment in the year following the war; he had prescribed too mildly for the returning South. In the pivotal election of 1866, the radical reconstructionists had been returned to Congress in such strength that the meager alterations Johnson had conceived were swept from the board, and stern measures were promptly enforced. The radicals had, by a series of acts of 1867 and the enforcement of the Fourteenth Amendment, banished the old leading class from political power and "reconstructed" the South on the basis of an electorate composed, to all practical purposes, of enfranchised Negroes and Northerners in residence.

Back in 1864 James Thompson had written in passionate conviction of the great future in store for South Carolina with the overthrow of slavery. "To make another Massachusetts of South Carolina it is only necessary to give her freedom and education. To these ends we devote our best efforts."[1] For many idealists who converged on Columbia in 1868 to write

---

* Willie Lee Rose, *Rehearsal for Reconstruction: The Port Royal Experiment*, (Indianapolis, Ind.: The Bobbs-Merrill Co., 1964). By permission of the publisher.

[1] Beaufort *Free South*, January 2, 1864.

a new constitution for the state, these words were as meaningful as they had been for young Thompson, a Gideonite. The radicals, who included among their number many of the missionaries sent South by the freedmen's aid societies, wrote an excellent constitution, based upon the most modern concepts of popular government. No good Gideonite could have asked for more. Every disability of race was demolished, and the legal foundation for a universal free system of public education was laid.[2] The evangels had approached their part in the Reconstruction with confidence.

Laura Towne wrote Edward Pierce of her feelings. She congratulated her old friend on a radical speech he had made in the fall elections and said she was sorry to be so far from the great events in the North, where men like Pierce were "moulding the destinies" of America. But she added, "We are doing a little moulding in a small way ourselves. Isn't South Carolina loyal, and are not the states where there are no 'Yankee schoolmarms' disloyal? Won't we grow in loyalty as the rising generations come up?" The satisfaction of most evangels regarding universal suffrage was strongly predicated upon the assumption that they would remain the controlling influence among the freedmen. For as Reuben Tomlinson wrote, although he was "a universal suffrage man," he didn't "care a cent for it unless we can keep Northern influence here along with it." The Northern influence would remain, and the radicals would have their chance. E. L. Pierce was exultant. "How great [are] these days!" He thought he could see the end of the contest "concerning the African race in this country" and was confident that there had never been since Christian martyrdom or the Reformation the "opportunity for equal devotion —or like exhilaration of the moral sentiments." The Negroes of the South were "at last upon their feet provided with all the weapons of defense which any class or race can have."[3]

Pierce did not see the danger. The whole North seemingly joined him in thinking that, with the granting of suffrage, the slaves of a few years before were well "on their feet." By 1868, when the radical government of South Carolina went into effect, the Freedmen's Bureau, except for two more years of assistance to education, had already finished its work.[4] The charitable organizations were left alone in the field, and their days were numbered. In fact, the great American Freedmen's Union Commission was hardly organized before it began to disintegrate. In early 1867 the Western branches at Chicago and Cincinnati forsook the nonsectarian commission and joined forces with the American Missionary Association. By fall of that year the American Freedmen's Union Commission was restating its goals in such modest terms that it was possible to claim that the commission had actually done what it had set out to do. It was a bad thing, thought the officers, to continue to press the cause of the

---

2 Simkins and Woody, *South Carolina During Reconstruction*, pp. 93–100.

3 Laura Towne to E. L. Pierce, December 6, 1867, Pierce MSS; Reuben Tomlinson to J. M. McKim, December 4, 1866, and E. L. Pierce to McKim, April 20, 1867, McKim MSS.

4 John Cox and LaWanda Cox, "General O. O. Howard and the 'Misrepresented Bureau,'" *Journal of Southern History*, 19 (November 1953), 442.

black man before the public, because pressure might hasten a reaction against him. The triumph of the Republican party on President-elect Grant's "Let us have peace" slogan in the fall elections and the formation of reconstructed governments in the South were thought to have removed the necessity of Northern efforts for freedmen's schools. The organization had provided a model for the new state governments. "The skeleton of an educational system will be already there, waiting only to be filled up." At the close of its work the officers congratulated the organization mildly, and deceptively, on having "checked, if it has not altogether overcome, that spirit of denominationalism which endangered the whole movement."[5] Honesty should have compelled the officers to admit that the organized churches had triumphed and that nearly all that would be done in the future by the North for Negro education would come through the American Missionary Association and other denominational groups.[6]

Gone were the grand claims of making a new New England of the South. What had happened in the North is much more clearly seen in the statements of the officers of the New England branch of the Commission, a branch that struggled on alone until 1874. As early as the fall of 1866 the editors of its journal, the *Freedmen's Record*, were complaining of public indifference to the cause: "were the tidings to come, as they did last year, that thousands were suffering from hunger, cold, and nakedness, the appeal would probably be responded to as generously as it was then. The great mass of people do not, as yet see that in the education of . . . freedmen is to be found the solution of some of the weightiest public questions of the day." If the freedmen could not even read a newspaper, would they not become political pawns, perhaps in the hands of their late masters?[7] The society rallied, however, and spent an all-time high budget of nearly $76,000 for Southern education in the year 1866–67. The contributions tumbled sharply in the succeeding winter, dwindling to approximately $29,000. The society again recovered some lost ground, but not for long. Edward Hooper, the treasurer, was writing a supporter in early 1873, in great complacency: "The New England Freedmen's Aid Society has had so much money from the good people of Boston during the past ten years that it no longer thinks it fair to urge its friends to continue their gifts. The Society has reduced its work very much, having turned over to the local authorities in the South as many of its schools as they would take." A year later, at the annual meeting, a letter was read concerning the transfer of the society's "Robert Gould Shaw Memorial School" to the city of Charleston. Then the question was put whether the society should disband. The first vote was to continue. The secretary then recorded, "These votes not seeming on the whole to

[5] See the *American Freedman*, 2 (November 1868), *passim*, and quotations from this issue of the *American Freedman* in the *Freedmen's Record*, 4 (November 1868), 169–170; Synopses of School Reports, 1, 158, entry 158, Education Division, BRFAL MSS.

[6] Richard Bryant Drake, "The American Missionary Association and the Southern Negro, 1861–1888" (Ph.D. dissertation, Emory University, 1959), pp. 20–24; *A History of the American Missionary Association: Its Churches and Educational Institutions among the Freedmen, Indians and Chinese* (New York, 1874), pp. 13–14.

[7] *Freedmen's Record*, 2 (November 1866), 198.

reflect the exact feelings of the meeting[,] they were subsequently reconsidered, and instead it was voted, to discontinue the Society in its present form." Adjournment followed, "*sine die*."[8]

The North had plainly concluded that in granting the franchise the national obligation to the freedmen had been fulfilled. Edward King pointed out the folly of the federal government's granting voting rights without providing the means for national assistance to education, thrusting upon the impoverished South the responsibility for a public school system that it had not possessed in its flourishing days. By the time King came to South Carolina, the state had been on its own for five years, the state school system was simply one more tool in the hands of the corrupt, and Laura Towne was writing, "The need of education here seems to be greater than ever—the means less, friends fewer. . . ." Editor Thompson posited that "the fault of the North in its treatment of the South seems to us to be an indifference to it. This is a result of a reaction." The North was not completely oblivious of the South and its problems in the early 1870s, but there was an inclination to blame the sad state of affairs in the late slave states on the ignorance of the electorate and on renegade Northerners who used them as tools. The North was not so much indifferent as tired, and the nation seized simple excuses that left the Northern conscience easier. Thompson, however, brought up the point of Northern indifference in order to scold Southern conservative white people who persisted in making no difference between Northerners of honesty and good will and those who were no credit to any section. The editor of the *Republican* was angry because the conservatives had failed to come to the polls to help put in a reform Republican government in South Carolina in 1872. Thompson advised them "to give up looking for extraneous aid. . . . Quit sitting at home, thanking God that you were born between the Pedee and the Savannah, grumbling over the present and sighing for the past. No one cares for a self-made martyr."[9]

What had happened to bring James Thompson to such a pass that he cried out to the old planter class to aid Gideon's Band? He was smarting from the results of the failure in 1872 to elect his old friend Reuben Tomlinson to the governorship on a reform ticket. The results of the election, at least in Beaufort County, had made a certain matter completely clear, one that should have been foreseen by the Gideonites long ago. Northern "evangels," however high-minded, could not control the Negro vote. Robert Smalls had become the greatest political force in the region; and he had swung the colored vote for the "regular" Republicans, galvanizing the opposition to Tomlinson and his own opponent for the state senatorship, a Northern Negro lawyer named W. J. Whipper, with cries that the freedmen could not trust outsiders, that they should vote

8 Financial statement in Synopses of School Reports, 1, 341, Educational Division, BRFAL MSS; Edward Hooper to Miss M. G. Chapman, March 10, 1873, Weston MSS; Minutes of the New England Freedmen's Aid Society, March 20, 1874, NEFAS MSS, Sturgis-Hooper Papers.

9 Towne to F. R. Cope, April 9, 1873, Towne MSS; Beaufort *Republican*, November 21, 1872; King, *Southern States*, p. 602.

for none but Southern men.[10] It had worked. If Tomlinson had been known anywhere in South Carolina as a just and honorable man it would have been at Port Royal, where he had worked with the freedmen since 1862 with much credit and universal acclaim among his fellow evangels. He had received in Beaufort County a meager vote of 1,445 to 4,995 for Franklin J. Moses, as blatant a swindler as ever sat in any gubernatorial chair, and a native white Southerner. In the "Brick Church" precinct, near his old headquarters as General Superintendent under Saxton, Tomlinson received only 62 votes, to 631 for Moses. Editor Thompson saw that the votes had been divided between the two men largely on the basis of color, with the white people voting for Tomlinson and the colored voters, following Smalls, voting for Moses.[11] Smalls had called for reform too, and in the murky waters of Reconstruction it was impossible sometimes for even well-educated men to differentiate between the degrees of corrupt associations that clouded the reputations of nearly all politicians. To the Negro electorate Smalls was a hero, the brave skipper of the *Planter* and "the smartest *cullud* man in Souf Car-lina."[12] If a Yankee missionary named Reuben Tomlinson, Gideonite, was remembered at all, it was not very distinctly.

It is also impossible to say that the instincts of the Republican majorities were completely wrong. Still being for the most part illiterate, they probably never read the aspersions of Editor Thompson against Smalls in the *Republican*. In truth, although Smalls was identified with the regular Republicans rather than with the reformers, he emerged from the Reconstruction era convicted of only one serious charge, that he had bribed the clerks of the House and Senate to state that a claim of his for $2,250 had been passed and approved. Smalls, self-educated, had become a self-possessed speaker; he was a man of undoubted intelligence and ready wit. The radical politician may well have been as deeply involved as most of his fellows in the depressing round of graft that characterized the government at Columbia; his conduct of the printing committee was at once politically successful and morally blameworthy. To the Sea Islanders, however, it was thrilling to have a leader who spoke to them in their own Gullah dialect, a powerful man who was known to the conservative editor of the Charleston *News* as the "King" of Beaufort County.[13]

---

[10] Beaufort *Republican*, July 11, August 1, 1872; Simkins and Woody, *South Carolina During Reconstruction*, pp. 466–67. The authors list Smalls as among the bolters from the party, but on the local level he worked to defeat the movement, perhaps because his own opponent, Whipper, associated himself more closely with the reformers, and the carpetbag element was, as Thompson put it, "the heart of the reform movement. . . ." Beaufort *Republican*, August 22, 1872, and September 26, 1872.

[11] Ibid., October 24, 1872.

[12] [Justus Clement French], *Steamer Oceanus*, p. 86.

[13] Simkins and Woody, *South Carolina During Reconstruction*, pp. 133, 476, 543; [French], *Steamer Oceanus*, p. 86; George B. Tindall, *South Carolina Negroes 1877–1900* (Columbia, South Carolina, 1952), pp. 54–55; Beaufort *Tribune*, May 12, 1875, quoting the *News*. The printing swindles were not exposed until after the election of 1872. Smalls was chairman of the printing committee. See Beaufort *Republican*, December 5, 1872, and Port Royal *Commercial*, April 9, 1874.

On the other hand, the so-called reform wing of the party included in its ranks numerous unsavory characters. In actuality, Tomlinson himself was connected strategically with an extremely lucrative swindle. . . .

The truth was simple: The voters of Beaufort had less confidence in the white people than in Negroes. Ten years of exposure to the social and political ideas of Northern radicals had not made them more confident of the ultimate intentions of their teachers. Just as the immigrant population of New England in a later day would follow on faith the city "boss" who understood them, so Port Royalists accepted the leadership of their own people who won power. Perhaps nothing illustrates better the naïveté of certain evangels than their failure to foresee this eventuality.

When the Republican party organized on St. Helena Island in 1867, Laura Towne reported that at a meeting of Negroes, with only a handful of whites present, one man rose to say "he wanted no white man on their platform." He was talked down by his more generous fellows, who said, according to Miss Towne, "What difference does skin make, my bredren. I would stand side by side with a *white* man if he acted right," and pleaded that the Negroes not be prejudiced "against their color." Another said, "If dere skins *is* white, dey may have principle."[14]

Laura Towne found it amusing. It was more significant than she imagined. The colored people were speaking the language of New England liberals, but the resentment of the member who "wanted no white man" was more widespread than the generous Miss Towne had reason to know. She had simply assumed that the whites would lead.[15] . . .

When even Gideonites could not with certainty identify virtue among candidates and good policy among the parties and factions, it is not astonishing that the largely uninformed Negro electorate was at a loss. In an age when corruption was rampant in nearly every state legislature and when "Grantism" came to signify demoralization in the national administration, the Southern states under Reconstruction drew a disproportionate degree of criticism. The opportunities for plunder afforded by the new and rapid growth of capitalism left the reputations of few public figures a decent covering. The voters of South Carolina were hardly more responsible for the chicanery of the Greenville and Columbia Railroad ring than were the voters of New York State at a time when Jim Fiske and Jay Gould could arrive at Albany and buy the legislature to do the will of the Erie Railroad ring.

The colored voters of Beaufort County did have the real issues placed before them in the spirited contests between 1868 and 1877, and if they could not determine precisely what occurred at Columbia after the successful candidates took office, they were little more confused than the mass of voters over the nation. The three most persistent local issues on the Sea Islands were discussed at nearly every meeting. They were corruption on state and local levels, exorbitant taxes, and the still unresolved controversy over the lands seized and sold under the Direct Tax Laws.

---

14 Holland (ed.), *Towne*, p. 182.
15 Letter of Laura Towne of June 7, 1867, in *Pennsylvania Freedmen's Bulletin,* 3 (October 1867), 8.

On the head of corruption, the voters frequently heard charges flung directly at opposing candidates at political rallies, and staunch "regulars" warned the electorate just as freely as did the "reformers" not to send bad men to the legislature, on the ground that they "might steal." Of such a meeting Editor Thompson fulminated, "No allusion was made to the present splendid financial condition of the State, and no doubt many a hearer went away from the meeting with the impression that everything was going on as smoothly as possible in our State. . . ."[16] The voters of Beaufort County threaded their way through the confusion by trusting the skipper of the *Planter* to recognize the scoundrels, and they regularly returned the men he backed to the state offices. On the local level, the town and county offices usually went to carpetbaggers who managed with indifferent success. John Hunn and H. G. Judd, both of Gideon's Band, were local officers who managed badly but were apparently honest. The town went in and out of bankruptcy, and George Holmes, not of Gideon's Band, was certainly guilty of withholding teachers' salaries under the pretext of low funds and profiting from buying up teachers' pay certificates at a discount.[17] . . .

The incessant litigation over the status of the Direct Tax lands troubled Negroes and whites alike. Throughout the Reconstruction period the dispossessed whites worked under the leadership of Richard DeTreville to break the tax laws under which the confiscation of their estates had been effected. Using the house in Beaufort in which Robert Smalls had been reared as a slave and which the Negro leader had bought at the government tax sales, DeTreville fought the case through the state courts and lost. When the claim on the Prince Street house came into the possession of William DeTreville upon the death of Richard DeTreville, the case at last, in 1878, reached the Supreme Court, where it was defeated. The freedmen and Northerners who had benefited from the tax sales retained their land, and Port Royal became, in respect of landownership, very much what the Gideonites had hoped it would become. By 1890 Elizabeth Botume reported that three-fourths of the land in Beaufort County was owned by Negroes.[18]

As years passed, the animosities of war cooled, at least as far as the victors were concerned. In Beaufort County nothing demonstrated the mellowing attitude better than the growing sense among many resident Northerners that the local Southern white people had in the loss of their property, suffered an unfair amount of punishment. In January of 1872 Editor James Thompson was still reminding them that there had been a certain "poetic justice" in the fact that "the hot-bed of rebellion" had "received the worst punishment" and that the former owners had no claim

---

16 Beaufort *Republican,* July 11, 1872.

17 Beaufort *Tribune,* June 14, 1876, and February 3, 1875; Sworn affidavit of D. H. Hyatt, March 20, 1875, Education Petitions, State Archives, Columbia; Beaufort *Republican,* November 14, 1872.

18 *DeTreville* v. *Smalls,* 98 U.S.; *First Mohonk Conference on the Negro Question, June 4, 5, 6* (Boston, 1890), p. 24. The records of the Direct Tax Commission include a notebook that outlines the tangled legal history of the Direct Tax lands. Records of the Fifth Special Agency, United States Archives.

to the restoration of their lands. But he was already speaking of a possible money compensation.[19]

. . . Thompson was glad when a plan was effected whereby the old owners were allowed to redeem by paying the tax on those parts of their property that had not been sold, and he explained just how they ought to go about making their claims. Afterward, the government would be free to sell what remained of the property, and Thompson joined the clamor for a financial settlement for those whose property had been sold outright before the end of hostilities.[20]

There were other signs of peaceful coexistence. Indigent Southern whites accepted positions teaching in the Negro schools. Within the county, of the nineteen teachers reporting in 1870 all but five Negro teachers and two Northern whites were Southern whites. Thomas Chaplin came back to St. Helena; living in an overseers' house on a plantation neighboring his own old home, he taught "a large school for Negro children."[21] The signs of peace were even more pronounced in the religious life of the community. . . .

Not every white resident shared the amicable spirit; a young Southern white woman wrote in 1876 that spring had come to Beaufort—"Drumfish is scarce, but Yankees abundant. . . ." She had "not the *horror* of being acquainted with one of them." Neither was Laura Towne prepared to conciliate. When an affable young scion of the Rhett family made overtures to Miss Towne and said he was sorry to have been unable to call upon her, she said that that was just as well, for "our ways are not their ways, and it is troublesome to know them."[22] Most Northerners were not responding in like manner. The death of S. C. Millett, a young carpetbagger who had steered clear of politics and advanced the commercial interests of the region by his able management of the new Port Royal railroad, was regretted by all. His eulogy in the *Port Royal Commercial* stated that under Millett's management "all" employees on the road had been "Southern boys of integrity, sobriety, honesty, and position." Millett had "spurned and despised the oppression of our poor South, as much as do the dearest of our own."[23] . . .

. . . [Republicans seemed to know little] of the impending counter-revolution, [but] the Democratic clubs were arming themselves, they were wearing red shirts, and they intended to banish the Republican party from South Carolina.

After a fall campaign notorious for the fraudulent practices and violence of both parties, the Democrats, with the cooperation of the federal government, accomplished their purpose. The attempt to remodel South

---

19 Beaufort *Republican*, January 11, 1872.

20 Ibid., July 24, 1873, and June 6, 1872; Jan. 25, 1872. W. M. French, editor of the Beaufort *Tribune*, took the same view. See the *Tribune*, May 19, 1875.

21 Teachers' Monthly School Reports, State Archives, Columbia. Chaplin MS diary, final entry, January 1, 1886, relating the salient events of Chaplin's life during the Reconstruction.

22 [?] to Emily Elliott, April 12, 1876, Elliott–Gonzales MSS; Laura Towne to "L," October 29, 1876, Towne MSS.

23 *Port Royal Commercial*, March 19, 1874.

Carolina along the lines of Massachusetts was officially interred. The North would not protest when their "kindred people" snatched the reins of political power from Northerners and Negroes, nor lift a hand to prevent the "redemption" of the state where Reconstruction began first and lasted longest. By 1876 even a few Negroes and carpetbaggers who had been associated with the Port Royal movement seemed ready to acquiesce to the counterrevolution. . . .

But not all evangels were "redeemed," or "reconciled" to the overthrow of their hopes. Reuben Tomlinson went North and attempted to rouse popular indignation against President Rutherford Hayes, the Republican whose elevation to office had been part and parcel of the compromise that returned South Carolina to the rule of the white native population of the state. In vain did Tomlinson suggest that under the administration of Republican Governor Daniel Chamberlain the state had already been well on the way to good government and honest reform; in vain did he point to the violence that had marked the overthrow of the Republican party. He was astonished that the North should have acquiesced to a policy "which nullified some of the most important results of the war." For Tomlinson the Southern Question was not settled. Was the federal government not failing in its "promises to protect the millions of colored people at the South in their civil and political rights?" He pointed out that "States rights and home rule in the South mean the right of the rich and intelligent and powerful to trample under foot the poor and ignorant and weak."[24]

Protests availed little, for the nation was almost as weary of Reconstruction as were South Carolina Bourbon Redeemers. . . .

Reconstruction had begun first on the Sea Islands, and it did not end there, suddenly, with the victory of Wade Hampton for the governorship in 1876. Well into the evening of the century Negroes in Beaufort County were a political force, and the two old rivals, W. J. Whipper, carpetbag Negro, and Robert Smalls, ex-slave, were regularly returned to the state legislature. Smalls was United States Congressman from 1875 to 1879 and served again to complete a vacated term in 1884. He was reelected for his last full term in 1884.[25] Near the end of the century, however, the story of Negro participation in South Carolina political life came to an end. In 1895, under the leadership of Governor Ben Tillman, a constitutional convention was held, and South Carolina effectually nullified the Fifteenth Amendment by erecting such requirements for voting that Negroes saw the futility of even trying. True to its reputation as the strongest black district, Beaufort had sent five of the six Negro representatives present at this convention, Whipper and Smalls among them. With wit and skill the two men eventually obliged the delegates to drop the

---

[24] Tomlinson was active in the North for several years following the campaign of 1876, attempting to draw public attention to the dangers inherent in the triumph of the Democrats in South Carolina for the Negroes. See the Boston *Advertiser*, January 28, 1878, for the speech from which the quotations are taken.

[25] George Brown Tindall, *South Carolina Negroes, 1877–1900* (Columbia, South Carolina, 1952), p. 55, and Appendix, "Negro Members of the South Carolina General Assembly after Reconstruction," pp. 309–10.

cant about establishing fair practices of universal application with regard
to suffrage; they pressed the issue forward until one white delegate said,
in exasperation, "We don't propose to have any fair elections. We will get
left every time." Robert Smalls had his chance to say the many good things
that could be said for the radical constitution of 1868, which had, after
all, served nearly 20 years after the resumption of white control. He
pleaded no special defense for his race, but asked only "an equal chance
in the battle of life." He was proud to be a Negro. "I stand here the equal
of any man." It was brave whistling in the wind. The new constitution
was adopted, and by 1903 a citizen of Beaufort reported that even though
literate male Negroes in the county numbered 3,434 to 927 white voters,
the "registration officials do not allow registered Negro voters to outnum-
ber the whites."[26] . . .

The islanders could no longer vote, but in a signal respect they were
more fortunate than other Negroes of the South. They owned their own
land, and upon it they could support themselves. They came in time to
constitute a "black yeomanry," although they did not prosper as their best
Northern and Southern white friends had hoped they might. They had
been granted a chance to become free and independent in a span of years
when even the most able and experienced white Sea Island planters were
at a loss to meet the terrible readjustments required of them. They had
had to help restore prosperity to a region that had been in an unfavorable competitive position even before the war, and to achieve this in spite
of a national depression, the loss of the fine seed that had been the main
element in successful long-staple cotton farming, and the capture of the
long-staple cotton market by the producers in other parts of the world.
Unfortunately for the freedman, these events had coincided with his entry
into the political picture, and most observers, North and South, in explaining the problem, had seized the simple but inadequate excuse that the
freedmen were not working. . . .

The Sea Islanders had learned the lessons of freedom, and they became, in their own way, as self-governing as many a small New England
town. The church remained for them a greater force in the conduct of
men than man-made law, a law with which they would have less and
less to do. Scholars who studied the islands closely in the 1920s found that
nearly all disputes were settled by committees within the churches and
that among "members" the collective wisdom of the elders constituted the
recognized law and reduced crime to a minimum. The Baptist church was
essentially democratic; its elders were the choice of the local members,
and it was the only denomination that had a considerable following on the
islands. To the islanders, the secular law was the "unjust" law; the church
law was the "just" law.[27]

The efforts of Gideon's Band had not gone for nothing, although
Pierce's evangels might not have understood the fruit of their labor. The
freedmen had become self-supporting if not wealthy. They paid their

---

[26] Ibid., pp. 81–89, quotations, in order, from pp. 87, 86, 88.

[27] Johnson, *Social History*, pp. 209–10; T. J. Woofter, *Black Yeomanry* (New
York, 1930), pp. 239–40.

taxes, and they took care of their local troubles with aplomb. In addition to owning their land, they enjoyed yet another advantage over many American Negroes, North or South, at the end of the century. Living almost isolated from their white neighbors on the mainland, they were spared contacts at a time when race relations in America reached their most disgraceful depths. Perhaps Suzie King Taylor, far away in Boston, experienced more painful knowledge of the frightful abuse of her people than her old neighbors on the islands ever endured. In 1902 she wrote her reminiscences of the life she had led as a little slave girl on St. Simon's Island, how she had come to Beaufort, "liberated," and had worked as a laundress and unofficial schoolteacher for the first Negro troops. She remembered that "glorious day" on the Smith plantation when the Sea Islanders had first heard the Emancipation Proclamation. At the time of writing she knew that Negroes traveling in the South always rode second-class, and that small excuse was required to set off a lynching bee. She knew that in the South the time had come again when there were few liberties of Negroes that white people were bound to respect. She could not understand. "There is no redress for us from a government which promised to respect all under its flag. It is a mystery to me."[28]

There was really no mystery. The nation had forgotten. Thomas Wentworth Higginson, who wrote the introduction to Mrs. Taylor's little book, had even in 1863 feared for the "ultimate fate" of the liberated Negroes, remembering that "revolutions may go backward."[29] The regression had simply taken longer than Higginson had imagined it might.

The Failure of Southern Reform: Tom Watson, Populists, and Blacks[*]

Charles Crowe

At the time of his death in 1922, Tom Watson of Georgia symbolized the most implacable group hatreds in America. During the Progressive Era he raged because the White House had become "little more than an annex of the Vatican," denounced the Pope as "the fat old Dago" who

---

[28] Suzie King Taylor, *Reminiscences of My Life in Camp* (Boston, 1902), p. 61.

[29] Thomas W. Higginson, *Army Life in a Black Regiment* (Cambridge, 1900), pp. 63–64.

[*] By permission of the author. An earlier and longer version of the essay was published under the title, "Tom Watson, Populists, and Blacks Reconsidered," *Journal of Negro History*, 55 (1970) 99–116.

lived with "voluptuous women," informed Cardinal Gibbon of "my loathing for that stupid, degrading faith of yours," and tried to awaken his
countrymen to the menace of "foot kissers" and "bull-necked convent
keepers" determined to force women "behind the bars of convent dun-
geons . . . at the mercy of priests."[1] In 1914 and 1915 after the conviction
by a mob-dominated court of the Atlanta Jewish pencil manufacturer Leo
Frank for the murder of a 16 year old Protestant employee named Mary
Phagan, Watson wrote hundreds of pages on "the animal sexuality" and
"unspeakable lusts" of "the lascivious pervert Frank" and on "the crum-
pled frail white form," the "ravaged innocence," and "the torn garment
spotted with the virginal blood" of Mary Phagan. When a mob which he
helped to arouse lynched and mutilated Frank, Watson composed an
eight page apologia under the caption, "The Voice of the People Is the
Voice of God."[2] (Watson's hate campaign aided the rebirth of the Ku Klux
Klan in Atlanta during 1915.) Less frequently but with nearly as much
venom Watson tried to warn his followers that socialists and immigrants
as well as Catholics and Jews threatened the Republic. He "exposed" socialists as "Goths, Huns and Vandals" moved by "the lust for loot" and
the desire to make war on "Caucasion civilization," the "Christian home,"
and the "racial purity of white women." The "mongrel hordes" of Southern and Eastern Europe, he insisted, provided "a huge mass of living
dynamite" which threatened to destroy the nation.[3]

In the Watsonian canon the ultimate threat came from the "animal-
istic blacks" with their "innate stupidity," "inhuman ugliness," "lascivious
sexual habits," "inability to understand religion," and so on. Watson's
favorite theme on black women involved attacks on the institutions of
the black "mammy" as a cruel surrender of helpless white children to the
torments of these "lustful, brutal and besotted" women with their "root
and branch" hatred of the white family. The black male fared even worse
at the hands of Watson who insisted on the frequent use of brute force
to "control" blacks and on flogging, when other reasons did not exist,
simply for "their color and their smell." During the Georgia gubernatorial
campaign of 1906 which led to the disfranchisement of the small number
of Georgia blacks still voting in the unimportant general elections, he
called on white Georgians (in his own headline style) to "FIGHT THE

---

[1] For anti-Catholic remarks and similar ones by Watson, see *Watson's Jeffersonian Weekly*, December 16, 1909, June 22, 1911, January 25, 1912, April 16, 1914,
October 21, 1915, December 23, 1915; and *Watson's Jeffersonian Magazine*, 14
(1912), 996, 1000 and 18 (1914), 225.

[2] On the Frank case and Watson's anti-Semitism, see *Watson's Jeffersonian
Weekly*, March 19, June 11, November 19, 1914; March 25, June 3, June 24, August
19, August 26, September 2, September 9, October 7, 1915; August 3, August 17,
August 24, October 29, 916; January 11, 1917. See also *Watson's Magazine*, 21
(1915), 156, 22; *Atlanta Constitution*, September 17–20, 1915; and *New York Times*,
August 20–24, 1915. See also Leonard Dinerstein, *The Leo Frank Case* (1968).

[3] For Watson's comments on socialism, see Watson to John N. Taylor, April 23,
1910, Watson Papers, University of North Carolina at Chapel Hill; *Watson's Jeffersonian Magazine*, 3 (1909), 914, and 4 (1910), 4, 93, 267–77, 360, 451–52, 537–40,
and De Leon *Watson on the Gridiron* (1926), 20–43. For a few choice Watsonian
remarks on European "mongrels" and the immigrant "menace" see *Watson's Jeffersonian Magazine*, 3 (1906), 821–39.

HIDEOUS, OMINOUS MENACE OF NEGRO DOMINATION." When the campaign combined with other forces to trigger the Atlanta race riot of 1906 with its 25 black persons dead and hundreds more wounded, the "sage of Hickory Hill" had no apologies to make.[4] Moreover Watson with all of his violent hatreds stood before his times not as an isolated crank but rather as an important Progressive political leader of public opinion with a mass following, and in the Populist era of the 1890s he had been the movement's major Southern leader as well as one of the most important national figures.

Although the closing chapters of C. Vann Woodward's 1938 biography provided unsettling glimpses of Watsonian hatreds, Woodward generally placed the venomous bigot of the Progressive period in the shadows and left the center of the political stage to the Populist leader allegedly motivated by democratic impulses and broad human sympathies, "perhaps the first native white Southern leader to treat Negro aspirations with the seriousness that human strivings deserve."[5] Thus Woodward in effect conjured up from the same man an admirable Populist Dr. Jekyll and a demonic Progressive Mr. Hyde.[6]

The problem of interpreting Watson according to Woodward's conceptions is made vexing by the fact that the man's political career prior to 1892 adds more to the image of Hyde than to the portrait of Jekyll. During the 1880s Watson spent much of his public energy in developing the conservative themes of the "professional Southerner" rather than in fighting for reform politics. In this role he celebrated the nostalgic dream of Eden in "the old time" slave South and denounced New South publicists as "unpaternal" and "patricidal" traitors who offered "abject submission" and "sycophancy" to the North. Any "patriot" would feel shame for "Southern men who go to Northern Banquets and glory in our defeat."[7] As a member of the planter class by birth and one of the largest exploiters of oppressed labor in the state, Watson shared the obsessions of his peers in a hatred of Reconstruction and black aspirations and in a consistent devotion to white supremacy. Nothing in his career prior to 1890 would lead one to suspect him of racial heresy or a radical future.[8]

In Woodward's curious attempt to find the roots of Watson's alleged radicalism, he traced Populist "rebellion" to two primal antecedents: the

---

[4] On Watson and the origins of the Atlanta riot, see the *Atlanta Journal* July 13, 1906 and August 1, 1906; and Charles Crowe "Racial Violence and Social Reform—Origin of the Atlanta Riot of 1906," *Journal of Negro History*, 53 (1968), 234–56. For examples of Watson's comments on Negroes, see *Watson's Jeffersonian Magazine*, 1 (1907), 847, 3 (1909), 97, 5 (1910), 629–32; *Watson's Jeffersonian Weekly*, June 17, 1909, May 25, 1911, January 11, 1912, May 15, 1913, January 4, 1917.

[5] Woodward relies a good bit on the one article which Watson wrote for a national periodical during the nineties. (See Watson's "The Negro Question in the South," *Arena*, 6 [1892], 540–55.) For coverage of similar local speeches, see the *People's Party Paper*, November 3, 1893, and May 24, 1894.

[6] See Woodward's three page preface to *Tom Watson, Agrarian Rebel*.

[7] Tom Watson, Ms. Journal, 2 (1883), 296, 317–31, 407, 409. Watson Papers, University of North Carolina at Chapel Hill.

[8] Woodward, *Watson*, 417–20. See also Watson to John N. Taylor, July 15, 1909, October 5, 1910, and January 7, 1915, Watson Papers, University of North Carolina at Chapel Hill.

history of "the game Independent" and "the tradition of the Lost Cause." He also gave a sympathetic presentation to Watson's racist glorification of plantation life and slavery, and even went so far as to describe this "vision of agrarian bliss" as a major cause of Watson's individual "rebellion." We are assured that in the 1880s "the first expression of his agrarianism . . . found utterance in the Confederate creed, and was indistinguishable from the doctrine of Robert Toombs and C. C. Jones," and that after the election of 1896 "the next step was the rehabilitation of the Lost Cause."[9]

The Watson-Woodward account of the origins of Watson's Negrophobia merely provided another stereotype which served the same function as "Negro domination" or "carpetbagger" in guiding men away from genuine explanation and toward racist rhetoric. In truth, Populists as well as Democrats violated state election laws, stuffed ballot boxes and bribed and intimidated black voters. Seldom, if ever, did fully honest elections take place in the South during this era. (The old post-Reconstruction tale which contrasted the inherently and inevitably "corrupt and purchasable black vote" with the "honest," "responsible," and "civilized" white electorate was another white supremacy myth.) Civic corruption has been commonplace in American politics, but it is doubtful that many political factions exceeded the corruption of Southern white supremacy regimes of the 80s and 90s. Ironically enough, black voters during this period when given even the rudiments of political choice often voted their own interests with surprising rationality despite the violence, fraud, and intimidation.

In all fairness to Woodward, the racist assumptions inherent in his explanation of Watson's "disillusionment" with black political participation must be examined in the milieu of the 1930s. At a time when historical scholarship was heavily burdened with racist assumptions, Woodward expressed sympathy for black aspirations in a volume which turned out to be one of the most perceptive studies of the decade. The pervasiveness of white supremacy opinions during the 30s is to be measured less by the tendency of Americans to "demonstrate" the wickedness of Reconstruction with citations from obvious works of excess such as Claude G. Bowers' *The Tragic Era* (1929) than by the willingness of Samuel Eliot Morison and other sophisticated and urbane scholars to assure a generation of students that "Sambo" suffered less from "the peculiar institution" than his master did.[10] An even better barometer for the prevailing climate of opinion was Paul Buck's Pulitzer prize-winning book, *The Road to Reunion* (1937), which deplored the "failure" of North and South to reunite after the Civil War and rejoiced over a reconciliation of Northern and Southern whites in the 1890s which was won at the expense of black freedom.

When the illusion of uniqueness has been stripped from Watson and the Populists, key portions of Woodward's interpretation quickly collapse. The Populists represented, to be sure, a kind of culmination to inde-

---

9 Woodward,*Watson*, 371, 433.

10 See any one of the first four editions, S. E. Morison and H. S. Commager, *The Growth of the American Republic*, Vol. 1.

pendent politics in the post-Reconstruction era, but the movement grew upon traditions which had existed among Republicans and independents for nearly two decades before the birth of Southern Populism. In Georgia, where William H. Felton served as an independent Congressman from 1875 to 1881 and Emory Speer nearly as long, rebellious independency came close to dominating state politics. Among other Congressmen, Greenbackers W. M. Lowe of Alabama and Washington Jones of Texas played prominent parts in their state delegations during the late 1870s. At the Virginia polls in 1879 William Mahone and his Re-adjustors actually captured control of the state. Greenback and Greenback-Labor tickets polled significant numbers of votes across the South in the elections of 1880 and 1884; the Republican Party made consequential gains during 1888 in several Southern states, the Alliance movement became a major political force between 1888 and 1891; and the Populists emerged in the early nineties as the most dynamic of all the challengers of the Democrats.[11]

Moreover, conservative Democrats continued to compete for black votes in the 80s and 90s. The Mississippi entente created by Lucius Q. C. Lamar and Blanche K. Bruce in the 70s and sustained by others for more than a decade served to preserve some black political gains as well as to keep a modest number of state and local offices in black hands. This alliance of blacks and white planters with its center of strength in the Delta country sent six blacks to the state legislature as late as 1890. Similar political alliances elected black candidates to legislative office in nearly every Southern state during the 80s and 90s and in McIntosh County, Georgia, as late as 1906. Although conservative whites resorted to violence and fraud, they nevertheless accepted black suffrage as an established reality and often tried to win black votes by promises and pledges as well as by force. Thus Watson and the Populists did nothing startlingly novel in making appeals and offering concessions to the black electorate; they merely entered the competitive lists as the most recent contender in the old struggle by conservatives and independents for black votes.

Woodward fostered illusions about Watson and the Populists in other ways by stressing the "singular" use of violence in the elections of 1892 and 1894, by insisting on the great risks Watson took in inviting black cooperation, and by emphasizing Watson's courage in sheltering on his own farm a black supporter, H. S. Doyle. The political violence cited by Woodward was commonplace in Southern politics rather than extraordinary. Illustrations could be cited almost endlessly but a few randomly selected cases will make the point: the Louisiana election of 1878 took a toll of 30 to 40 lives; Bayou Teche, Louisiana alone six years later yielded the bodies of 16 political victims; Wilmington, North Carolina whites in

---

11 C. Vann Woodward, *Origins of the New South* (1951) and Vincent P. DeSantis, *The Republicans Face the Southern Question; The New Departure Years, 1877–1897* (1959). Most of the state studies which involve discussions of independent movements are not really helpful. (See for example A. M. Arnett, *The Populist Movement in Georgia* (1922). On the response of Negroes to Georgia Independency, see C. A. Bacote, "The Negro in Georgia Politics, 1880–1908," Ph.D. Thesis, Univ. of Chicago, 1955.

1898 killed 20 blacks and mobbed or drove from the cities thousands of persons; white Democrats in Phoenix, South Carolina, during the same year killed more than two dozen men; and as late as 1921 an Ocoee, Florida, mob murdered 12 persons because blacks attempted to vote.[12]

A careful examination of the Doyle incident casts much light on Watson and the allegedly extraordinary dangers of black and white cooperation. Much of the information we have on this episode is available because Watson's enemies publicized it in 1906 as proof of his allegedly inadequate devotion to white supremacy. In response to headline charges that he entertained Doyle as a "HOUSE GUEST" and "HAD DINNER WITH BLACK PREACHER," Watson "corrected" the record with a statement which freely granted the need and propriety for the Southern white man to protect "his darky." However, he went on to insist that he had greeted Doyle with the curt command to "go back in that nigger house" behind his plantation home. When the black preacher protested, "Mr. Watson, I am an educated man, I went to college," Watson supposedly replied in a stern manner, "I can't help that, Doyle—I'll protect you but get in that nigger house." All the details of this account cannot be confirmed but the truth of its essence can be checked in Watson's brief report of October 28, 1892, in the *People's Party Paper* which indicated that Doyle had been taken under Watson's protection and was told to "take up quarters in a negro house on the lot." State and local newspapers confirm this account and also make it clear that Watson did not defy the authorities of his community or run any really serious risk of violence in sheltering Doyle. Before befriending the black preacher he sought and secured the full cooperation of the Democratic mayor, the Populist county sheriff and other local officials who reprimanded the more violent Democrats. Several almost unprecedented arrests of these would-be "lynchers" indicate the extent of community support for Watson's actions.[13]

A careful scrutiny of Doyle and Anthony Wilson, his black colleague on the Populist platform, reveals a new set of ambiguities in Watson's "alliance" of black and white. First of all, it seems strange that these two men should constitute the sum total of Watson's campaign staff for an appeal to black voters in a district with a large black majority. Doyle and Wilson, who were compensated for their efforts, functioned more as employees than as allies and were accused by black politicians of being bribed into Watson's service. When Watson and his two assistants spoke to black audiences they sometimes had to face difficult questions: Didn't Watson have an anti-Negro record as a state legislator? Why

----

12 On the violence in Louisiana, see *Senate Reports*, 45th Cong., 3 Sess., IV, 28–37; and the Louisville *Courier-Journal*, November 3, 1884. For a long account of the Wilmington riot, see Helen G. Edmonds, *The Negro and Fusion Politics in North Carolina* (1951) 158–78. On the Phoenix riot, see the *New York Times*, November 9–10, 1898; and on the Ocoee violence see *The Ku Klux Klan*, Hearings Before the Committee on Rules, House of Representatives, 67th Cong., 1st Sess., 63, 66.

13 On Watson's 1906 version of the incident, see the *Atlanta Journal*, August 4, 1906. Several references by Watson to "the boy" (Doyle) are worth noting in the *Macon Telegraph*, October 26, 1892. The mayor of Thomson actually offered police protection to Watson and Doyle, but Watson refused the offer. It is possible that the incident was contrived by Watson as the *Augusta Chronicle* insisted on October 24, 1892 and the *Macon Telegraph* on October 26, 1892. See also *The Contested Election of Thomas E. Watson* v. J. C. Black (1896), 669–796.

had he ignored an unquestioned popular mandate in refusing to grant a legislative seat to the very same Anthony Wilson who now campaigned for him? Why had Watson voted against a bill for Negro branch colleges and against appropriation bills for black schools?

Watson's efforts to explain his record were almost pathetically inadequate. It seemed that Georgia could not afford black branch colleges because the state was "already committed" to an expensive state house and appropriations for black schools had to be kept to a minimum. Also taxes could not be raised above a level already intolerably burdensome to the exploited taxpayer. As a private person Watson knew that Anthony Wilson won his legislative seat with a large majority but as a lawyer he felt compelled to vote against seating Wilson because he had failed to prove his case by "strictly legal testimony." Although Watson did call for lower taxes and higher prices for farm products "to help both races," few blacks and less than a majority of whites had crops to sell or owned land to pay taxes on. Watson was also extremely vague about how he would advance these goals as a Congressman in Washington. When black questioners asked what he had done for Georgia blacks, he answered with rather feeble retorts such as the oft-used claim to have been the first Georgia Congressman to send free seeds to black constituents. Under fire, Doyle and Wilson were reduced to even feebler arguments and could only reply that Watson "was not the same man" but rather a person transformed by a great political regeneration.[14]

The difficulties which Woodward and those who followed his lead experienced in interpreting Watson also extended to Southern Populism in general. Indeed, Woodward himself briefly acknowledged as much in *Origins of the New South* by noting that "the barriers of racial discrimination mounted in direct ratio with the tide of political democracy" and by granting that this popular white hostility provided "one of the reasons" for the tendency of blacks to ally themselves with "reactionary" whites rather than with Populists. Woodward also admitted that at least a few Populists despised blacks and that some Populists imitated Democratic force and fraud but he did not reconcile these newly created contradictions. Consequently, the reader was left with warring impressions of popular white supremacy and of Populists somehow exempt from the new political conditions. Woodward, unable to surrender the old image of the Populists, asserted without adequate explanation that the political future after 1896 belonged to white supremacists such as "the Heflins" rather than to "fallen Populists" or to "patricians." Little was said about the political composition of this new group, "the Heflins," and no serious attempt was made to explain how the upsurge of democracy created both racist extremes and the tolerant Populists.[15]

When the difficult questions are brought to the Alliance movement

[14] For two accounts of a Doyle speech in Thomson, see the *Augusta Chronicle,* October 26, 1892 and the *Atlanta Constitution,* October 26, 1892. On the hostile charges against Watson and his black aides, see the *Atlanta Constitution,* August 24, August 26, 1892, and the *Atlanta Journal,* September 2, September 24, 1892.

[15] See Ch. XII, "The Mississippi Plan as the American Way of Life" in Woodward, *Origins of the New South* (1951), 321–49. For a characteristic Watsonian appeal for black votes, see the *Atlanta Journal,* August 10, 1892.

from which Populism emerged, the old interpretive approach encounters even larger obstacles. The Alliance in Georgia as in other Southern states consistently and openly expressed hostility toward the idea of black participation, and Negroes had no choice other than to join a separate Colored Alliance movement organized by white men and vastly unequal in wealth, influence, and prospects for political power. White Alliances felt free to ask the support of the Negro groups for their policies and candidates but seldom if ever asked the advice or offered to aid the goals of the black groups. Often the two organizations found themselves in complete opposition to each other, and particularly on the last two grand proposals of the nineteenth century to aid the black masses, the Blair Education Bill and the Lodge Federal Election Bill. Alliance men who sat in the Georgia legislature voted overwhelmingly in 1891 for the largest number of antiblack bills ever passed during a single year in the history of the state. The most important single piece of legislation was an act on state primaries which left all the basic rules to the discretion of the po- litical party and thus opened the way for the Democratic white primary. (Atlanta and several other cities took advantage of the new statute almost immediately.) Other laws established the first state-wide Jim Crow re- quirements for trains, reinstituted the dreaded practice of working con- victs under whipping bosses, and spitefully created a black normal school in Athens simply to receive Federal funds taken away from Atlanta Negro colleges because their white professors sent sons and daughters to the black schools. Among the unsuccessful bills were many proposals to carve out new areas of compulsory segregation and a dangerous plan to virtually destroy black schools by limiting their budgets to the small sums collected in taxes from black property holders.

The Alliance origins of most Populist leaders gave black voters ample reason to distrust Populist overtures. Moreover, some Populist candidates with notorious anti-Negro records gave black leaders such as W. H. Styles, a Republican candidate for the state senate, cause to complain that it would be absurd for black voters to support men who "were in the front rank when that army of oppression came against the Negro." Neither the presence of two lonely and isolated blacks in the state con- vention of 1892 nor the total absence of blacks from the list of Populist candidates did much to alleviate Negro suspicions. Populist insistence on segregation at political meetings also seemed to show a lack of good faith. Finally, the Populists rejected the idea of a state Fusion ticket with the Republicans despite the persistent requests of black leaders and a widespread feeling that only Fusion and a biracial ticket offered any prospects for victory at the polls. Even President Harrison overcame his loathing for the Populists sufficiently to sanction a Fusion ticket in Geor- gia, an action he lived to regret bitterly because of Populist and Demo- cratic fraud and force. The President reportedly asserted that "I have washed my hands of the south. It is a land of rebels and traitors who care nothing for the sanctity of the ballot, and I will never be in favor of making an active campaign down there until we can place bayonets at the polls." Certainly, it had been a larger gamble for the ultra conservative chief executive to risk the danger of "obnoxious" reforms in Georgia to strengthen Presidential Republicanism than for the allegedly radical Populists to risk the unpleasantness of a few black officeholders to increase enormously their prospects for establishing a state reform regime. The fact that most Georgia leaders refused even to discuss Fusion seriously both confirmed their devotion to white supremacy and called into question their radicalism.[16]

Only in North Carolina through Fusion politics and biracial tickets, (demanded by Republicans rather than Populists) did the People's Party actually succeed in making social changes. From this coalition, whites regained the local government which had been taken from them by conservatives and the blacks made more gains than in any Southern state since Reconstruction. Blacks gained a significant number of state and local offices, and they and low income whites also won in communities such as Wilmington an almost unprecedented measure of police protection, public safety and justice from biracial police and courts. That North Carolina's success was Georgia's failure Woodward and other scholars failed to see. In *Origins of the New South* Woodward spoke of the "temptation" to make corrupt "deals" with Republican "bosses" and of the ways in which Populists were sometimes driven to "surrender principle" to Fusion forces from "despair of coping with the Democratic use of the Negro." Quite the reverse was actually the case, for only through Fusion could leaders of the People's Party hope for the success that would make any kind of reform possible. Most of the Populists were simply more committed to white supremacy than to reform and many black voters seemed well aware of this fact. Because the Populists in no Southern state offered black voters enough to tempt the majority, blacks generally continued to try and secure modest gains through the Democratic and Republican parties.

When the Georgia Populist leadership in 1892 continued to insist on black endorsement without Fusion or black candidates, most of the black Republicans on the state executive committee joined W. A. Pledger in rejecting the Populist appeals. Populist delegates who went to President E. S. Richardson and other officers of the Colored Alliance for official endorsement gained their unenthusiastic consent. A few black leaders on their own initiative also quietly sought out W. L. Peek, the Populist gubernatorial candidate, but he offered a very cool reception and would promise little more than a reformation of the convict lease system. By contrast the Democratic incumbent William J. Northen, who had increased black school appropriations and denounced lynching, promised an anti-lynching bill and more school money for black children. In the election that followed black voters consulted their own self-interest, chose the lesser of the two evils, and cast most of their votes for Northen and other Democratic candidates.

---

16 On Jim Crow legislation, see the *Atlanta Constitution*, July 21–24, 1891; *Savannah Tribune*, November 28, 1891; *Georgia Laws* 1890–91, 1, 211–13; *Acts of the Georgia General Assembly*, 1890–91, 1, 114–15. On W. H. Styles, see the *Atlanta Journal*, December 7–8, 1893. J. L. Reddick, "The Negro and the Populist Movement," M.A. thesis, Atlanta University, 1937, has several references to Harrison and Fusion.

Nevertheless, Populist candidates won enough black votes to encourage them in more strenuous efforts to gain voters in 1894 by admitting 24 black delegates to the state convention and one of that number to the party executive committee. Unfortunately for the cause of Populism, the black delegation still represented token seating for a small and isolated minority whose requests for black candidates and issues were largely ignored by the convention. The new Populist candidate for governor did not treat black leaders quite so cooly, but he and many other office seekers continued to compete with the Democrats in attacking blacks before white audiences. The token efforts of the Populists in 1894 and the promises of a few of their prominent leaders to come out for Fusion and black representation on the ticket in 1896 did succeed in bringing a larger number of Georgia blacks to the People's Party in 1894 than in any other election.[17]

Populist tactics were inadequate to the task of drawing mass black support for several reasons, beginning with the fact that black leaders frequently doubted the sincerity of white Populists. In 1894 while accusing the Democrats of racial duplicity and fraudulent appeals to blacks, the Populists called on black voters to oppose the Democrats because the governor had pardoned a white man sentenced for killing a black person and appealed to whites to reject the Democrats because the same governor had freed a black man convicted of murdering a white person. While the Populists imitated the Democrats in opening rallies and barbecues to blacks and in using black speakers, they failed to convert large numbers of blacks through these tactics. A few white leaders made honest attempts to divide Populist Party offices on the county level, but these efforts generally failed. When Populist officers in predominantly black Greene County agreed to divide equally the places on the county committee, the enraged white rank and file walked out of the mass meeting called to ratify the agreement. Many Populist speakers attacked blacks before white audiences with all the venom of militant white supremacy Demo-

---

[17] For some interesting comments on black support of Northen and the Democrats, see the *Bulletin of Atlanta University*, November 1892, p. 4. For Bishop Turner's opposition to the Populists, see the *Atlanta Journal*, September 30, 1892, and for Pledger's position, see the *Atlanta Journal*, September 19, 1892. For comments on the support given to Northen by the Georgia Negro Press Association, see the *Savannah Tribune*, July 1, 1893. On the Colored Alliance and the Populists, see the *Atlanta Journal*, September 27, 1892. On Democratic attempts to woo black voters, see the *Atlanta Constitution*, July 1, 1892; the *Atlanta Journal*, August 15, 18, 25, September 2, 1892; and Georgia Writer's Program, *The Story of Washington-Wilkes County* (1943), 60–72. Richardson seems to have led the state Alliance better than many other Colored Alliance leaders. The organization had been formed by a white Baptist missionary, R. M. Humphrey, who at times seemed willing to serve his constituents and other times willing to betray them at the drop of a hat. (See the *National Economist*, 1 (1889) 6–7 and the *Richmond Dispatch*, August 19, 1891.) At most national Alliance and Populist meetings Southern white hostility was all too evident. At the crucial Populist convention at St. Louis in February, 1892, Humphrey corruptly sold all the Colored Alliance credentials to a white Georgian named J. L. Gilmore. Richardson led his Georgia delegation in their protest refusal to participate in the convention. When Gilmore cast all 97 votes allocated to the Colored Alliance for the third party against the will of nearly all the black delegates and the third party caucus then expelled the blacks, virtually the whole black delegation walked out. (See the *Atlanta Constitution*, May 2, May 21, 1891; February 23, 26, 1892.)

crats and in Washington and other communities whites left Populist rallies to attack blacks for attending Democratic meetings. In 1896 one large Populist delegation from all over the northern and central portions of the state asked William H. Felton, a former Independent congressman, to run for congress as a Populist and to join them in a crusade against Cleveland because the "nigger-lovers" had taken over the national party. As evidence for their contention, the delegation pointed to the stories about Cleveland's appointment of blacks to office and entertainment of Frederick Douglass and his white wife at the White House. Less hostile Populists might have offset some of the angry speech and action with symbolic gestures such as attending Negro conventions and meetings, but the only instance of this kind was provided by the attendance of maverick Joseph C. Manning of Alabama at several sessions of the National Afro-American Council.[18]

When Georgia Populist leaders in 1896 betrayed the promises made two years earlier by arrogantly rejecting all Fusion schemes and by reducing the small number of blacks in Populist councils, black support for the party fell off sharply. By 1898 the Populist black minority had become completely disillusioned with Fusion as well as with Populism and the radically decimated People's Party substituted for the old appeals to black voters bitter denunciations of the whole idea of Negro suffrage.

It is clear that Populist leaders wished to harvest black votes without compromising any major doctrines or practices of white supremacy. But what of Tom Watson? Was he a unique exception to the general rule or a confirmation of it? Although Woodward did quote Watson accurately and Watson did make conciliatory remarks in 1892 and 1894, the collation of all the surviving speeches and newspaper accounts of public meetings suggests a pattern of duplicity in which Watson made three kinds of speeches, one for whites, one for blacks, and one which featured the perilous attempt to accommodate simultaneously both white supremacy and black aspirations. It is instructive to examine a speech of 1892 to a largely black audience of Sparta in which he assured the audience of his sympathy for black aspirations toward "political equality" and of his acceptance of the fact that "the color line has been broken." In the next few days, Watson was to be denounced all over the state so vehemently that he felt compelled to issue an apologetic statement, but the first strong response to his suggestions came from the black audience who lingered behind after his departure to debate the meaning of the two sensational phrases. Several dozen black men and women, hardly knowing whether to believe the evidence of their senses, decided to resolve their doubts by seeking out the candidate at The Drummer's House where

---

[18] It is interesting to note the bitter denunciations by white Populists of a Colored Alliance proposal to call a strike of black cotton pickers. (See the *Atlanta Constitution*, September 15, 1891; and the *National Economist*, September 26, October 10, 1891.) On white Populist violence against blacks at Washington, Georgia, see the *Atlanta Constitution*, August 25, 1892, and for other similar incidents, see the *Augusta Chronicle*, October 6, 1892; and the *Farmer's Light*, October 20, 1892. On Felton and the Populist delegation, see Rebecca Felton, *Memoirs of Georgia Politics* (1911), 659.

he had a room. When Watson's hostess came to the *front* door and found a black crowd expecting to be invited into the hotel lounge to discuss with the candidate the precise meaning of his speech, she flew into a rage over so gross a violation of caste etiquette and ordered the blacks away in very insulting terms. The delegation, bewildered by the contrast between Watson's warm appeal and his hostess's angry conduct, began to remonstrate with her and called for Watson to come out. The candidate did not leave the hotel until the local sheriff arrived on the scene to disperse the "mob" and arrest its leaders, and then he appeared only to apologize to whites in the community who might have misunderstood his speech as an invitation to loathsome "social equality" rather than as a purely political invitation for the blacks to support the Populist ticket.[19]

Watson's campaign contained many appeals for black votes and many assurances of his basic commitment to white supremacy. Frequently he had to answer from the stump white complaints that the People's Party was in the throes of becoming a "nigger party" and that biracial political cooperation would lead to "negro supremacy, mongrelism and the destruction of Anglo-Saxon wives, daughters, and womanhood." Whenever Watson heard these complaints from predominantly white audiences, he assured them that Populism opposed "social equality and miscegenation," that the blacks themselves rejected social equality, and that in any event blacks could not gain this equality without the white consent which would never be given. Not content to rest here, Watson went on to tell his listeners that whites and blacks had the same community of interests as during the Civil War when white men fought to save Southern society and black people ignored opportunities for vengeance to protect white families. The same Confederate captains and their sons, it seems, struggled once again alongside the loyal old black retainers and their offspring to rescue the South through the triumph of the Populist Party. Moreover, white Populists had to realize that if they did not talk candidly and openly to blacks, "Carpetbaggers, Scalawags and demagogues" would hold sinister negotiations behind closed doors.[20]

When Georgia Democrats accused Watson of endangering white supremacy by "splitting the vote" he replied by insisting that the only serious menace to "Southern customs" came from national politicians of "the old party" such as Grover Cleveland. Presumably Cleveland had demonstrated his attachment to "race mixing" as governor of New York by signing a "social equality law" in 1884 which prohibited the assignment of children to any school solely on the basis of race. When Cleveland overrode Governor Altgeld's protests to break an Illinois strike with Federal troops Watson objected as a reformer, but he also bitterly complained that the President had "violated states rights" and opened the door to a dangerous "centralism" which might be used at any time to "disrupt"

---

[19] On Watson's remarks about "wiping out the color line," see the *Atlanta Constitution*, August 25, 1892; and for other similar incidents, see the A. S. Van de Graff, "Unaided Solution of the Southern Racial Problem," *Forum*, 21 (1896), 332–35.

[20] For these and other remarks by Watson, see the *People's Party Paper*, September 16, 1892; May 25, July 13, August 24, 1893: and the *Atlanta Journal*, May 17, 1894.

Southern society. If Watson himself felt compelled to call for national legislation he was careful to demand the protection of "Southern rights" and to clothe his proposal in a neo-Jeffersonian states rights and anti-national rhetoric. Well aware of the fact that he had been charged with "fostering social equality on trains" for discussing Federal regulation of railroads, he generally salted his speeches with protestations of loyalty to Jim Crow transportation and opposition to new patterns of "race mixing."

The only obstacle to the "solution" of the "race problem," according to Watson, was the spectre of "Federal interference"; and since the national government had long ceased to "intervene" in school and transportation problems, elections provided the only area of possible danger. He agreed with his critics about the evil nature of the Lodge Federal Elections Bill ("Force Act") but he assured his followers that the bill failed twice and had no prospects of passage. With the Federal government out of the picture and with Negroes devoted to the pursuit of economic gain rather than "social equality," white Georgians could afford to ignore Democratic demands for white unity and forge the new party which would take in all those whites who would not vote Republican as well as those blacks who could not bring themselves to vote the Democratic ticket. The triumph of the People's Party would in the end bring about economic and social changes of great benefit to the lives of blacks as well as of whites. Thus, Watson firmly enunciated the principles of a partial and largely passive black presence in politics, general acceptance of the racial status quo, and black concentration on economic gains.[21] Limited as these goals may sound today, Watson and most white leaders began to denounce them as intolerable at the turn of the century.

The history of reform in the South during the Populist-Progressive era suggests very forcefully that the gap between white reformers and conservatives was small in comparison to that great chasm of race. In fact, white reform often meant black repression. Populists and Progressives frequently went so far as to equip their demands for more repression and Jim Crow laws with reform credentials calling for "better race relations" or "the prevention of friction between the races." Many black voters, who apparently grasped the fact that they had little or nothing to gain from the reformers, voted conservative as the lesser of two evils. It would be absurd to paint the conservatives in glowing colors since they believed as passionately in white supremacy, but it is important to note that they were inclined to accept the status quo and to doubt any urgent need for new repressive measures.[22]

If anyone wishes to insist that an element of mystery remains when

---

[21] For Watson's efforts to answer charges that he was an enemy of white supremacy (made in the *Atlanta Journal,* April 7, 1892), see the *People's Party Paper,* April 28, September 16, 1892. On Watson's efforts to help Speaker Reed stop the mass distribution of copies of the Lodge Bill, see the *Atlanta Constitution,* August 27, 1892.

[22] On Jim Crow practices and laws as "racial reform," see Crowe, "Atlanta Race Riot," *Journal of Negro History* (1968, 1969), Note 4, 234; Ray Stannard Baker, *Following the Color Line,* 243–246; Arthur Link, *Wilson: The New Freedom* (1956), 251; E. David Cronon, ed., *The Cabinet Diaries of Josephus Daniels, 1913–1921* (1963), 53; and Kathleen L. Wolgemuth, "Woodrow Wilson's Appointment Policy and the Negro," *Journal of Southern History,* 24 (1958), 457–71.

all of these factors have been taken into account, it still seems reasonably safe to say that only an extremely precise and thorough modern biographer could hope to provide the proper answers. Meanwhile, it is necessary to recognize the fact that Watson and his movement had little to do with radicalism or with the fate and aspirations of black people.[23]

The Supreme Court Defers to Southern Caste[*]

Barton J. Bernstein

> The felt necessities of the time, the prevalent moral and political theories, intuitions of public policy, avowed or unconscious, even the prejudices which judges share with their fellow-men, have had a good deal more to do than the syllogism in determining the rules by which men should be governed.
>
> OLIVER WENDELL HOLMES,
> *The Common Law*

For 58 years *Plessy* v. *Ferguson*,[1] the federal source of the "separate but equal" doctrine, had escaped judicial challenge. When the 1954 Supreme Court in effect overruled the *Plessy* doctrine in the *Segregation Cases*,[2] the Warren tribunal's decision was attacked as sociological juris-

---

[23] For comments by Watson on Debs and Berger, see the *Columbia Sentinel*, September 12, 1912; January 2, February 3, 1920. For examples of Watson's hostility to Wilson and his policies, see Watson, *Life and Times of Thomas Jefferson* (1903), 47, 86, 218, 356; *Tom Watson's Magazine*, 3 (1905), 154; *Watson's Jeffersonian Weekly*, January 25, April 11, 25, August 15, October 24, December 21, 1912, September 24, 1916, April 20, July 13, 1916; the *Atlanta Constitution*, May 12, 1912, April 18, 21, May 2, 1920; *Columbia Sentinel*, January 2, April 19, May 10, 1920; and Watson to W. J. Jelks, December 21, 1912, Watson Papers, University of North Carolina at Chapel Hill. For other examples of eccentric radicalism late in Watson's career, see the *Atlanta Journal*, September 3, 1920; the *Atlanta Georgian*, September 3, 1920; and the *Congressional Record*, 67th Cong., 1st Sess., 1921, pp. 162, 5580, 6780, 7903.

[*] Barton J. Bernstein, "*Plessy* v. *Ferguson*: Conservative Sociological Jurisprudence," *Journal of Negro History*, 7 (1963). By permission of the journal.

[1] 163 U.S. 537 (1896).

[2] *Brown et al.* v. *Board of Education et al.*, 347 U.S. 483, has since been called the *Segregation Cases*. Since only in a case identical in material facts to *Plessy* v. *Ferguson*, a transportation case, could the Supreme Court overrule *Plessy*. The overruling did not occur until such a transportation case came before the Warren court. *Gayle* v. *Browder*, 352 U.S. 903 (1956).

prudence.[3] Implicit in this criticism was an assumption that *Plessy* was free of social theory and allegedly based upon the more solid grounds of precedent and constitutional law.

However, recent studies of the tangled history of the Fourteenth Amendment establish that the Amendment did not require the Supreme Court's decision in *Plessy*.[4] And a careful examination of the case law cited by the *Plessy* court reveals that only through distortion could these cases have been used to support the court's holding.[5] In view of this research the court's opinion merits analysis to determine whether social theories shaped the "separate but equal" position.

Homer Plessy, part Negro, had been arrested in Louisiana where he had violated the state law requiring separate accommodations for the races in intrastate travel. Plessy's contention that the Louisiana statute was unconstitutional was rejected by the state court and appealed to the United States Supreme Court. With only Justice John Marshall Harlan dissenting, the Supreme Court held that the state law was a reasonable exercise of the state police power and therefore constitutional.

Before the Supreme Court, counsel for Plessy had attacked the segregation provision as unreasonable. In an argument which Harlan adopted in his dissent, the counsel had argued that a decision against Plessy and for segregation would authorize the states to require separate cars for people with different colors of hair, aliens, or Catholics or Protestants, or to require colored people to walk on one side of the street and white people on the other side, or to demand that white men's homes be painted white and black men's homes black. These analogies were close enough to the case at bar to compel the court to distinguish these fact situations and justify its reasoning in *Plessy*.[6]

---

3 In *Brown* the court had announced that "we cannot turn the clock back to 1868 when the Amendment [Fourteenth] was adopted, or even to 1896 when *Plessy* v. *Ferguson* was written. We must consider public education in the light of its full development and its present place in the American life throughout the nation." The court did not seek to erect an impressive legal argument, buttressed by case law, to overturn *Plessy*. Case law was deemed inapplicable, and the history of the original meaning of the Fourteenth Amendment was judged "inconclusive." The high court cited sociological and psychological studies to establish that separate educational facilities cannot be equal; the "separate but equal" doctrine was self-contradictory.

Criticism of the *Segregation Cases* as sociological jurisprudence has been based on three propositions: the Fourteenth Amendment was not intended to prohibit Jim Crow education and the framers' intent should be followed; the court should have followed the precedent, *Plessy*, and later segregation cases whose broad holdings could be interpreted as Supreme Court approval of "separate but equal"; and social theories should not be the basis for a legal decision.

4 John Frank and Robert Munro, "The Original Understanding of 'Equal Protection of the Laws,'" *Columbia Law Review*, 50, No. 1 (January 1950), 131; Jacobus Ten Brock, *The Antislavery Origins of the Fourteenth Amendment* (Cal., 1951); Howard Graham, "The Anti-Slavery Backgrounds of the Fourteenth Amendment," *Wisconsin Law Review*, 1950, No. 3 (May 1950), No. 4 (July 1950), 479, 610; Alfred Kelly, "The Fourteenth Amendment Reconsidered," *Michigan Law Review*, 54, No. 8 (June 1956), 1049; Robert Harris, *The Quest for Equality* (Louisiana State University, 1960); and Jack Greenberg, *Race Relations and American Law* (Columbia, 1959).

5 Bernstein, "Case Law in *Plessy* v. *Ferguson*," *Jour. of Negro Hist.*, 47, No. 3 (July 1962), 192–98.

6 S. F. Phillips and F. D. McKenney, *Brief for Plaintiff in Error in Plessy* v. *Ferguson*, 13.

Judge Henry Billings Brown, writing the court's opinion, replied that "every exercise of the police power must be reasonable, and extend only to such laws as are enacted in good faith for the promotion of the public good, and not for the annoyance or oppression of a particular class." He relied upon two arguments to establish the contention that the Louisiana statute was a reasonable exercise of the state police power. Each revealed that sociological and psychological theories controlled the court's decision.

First, Brown maintained that the Louisiana act was not designed as an "annoyance or oppression" and should not have been so considered. He contended that the laws requiring racial segregation did not "necessarily imply the inferiority of one race to the other." The underlying fallacy of the plaintiff's argument was "the assumption that enforced separation of the two races stamps the colored race with a badge of inferiority." Such reasoning, Brown explained, would mean that if a Negro legislature separated whites, the whites would feel inferior. He concluded that they would not.[7]

Harlan might have attacked Brown's analogy. Or the dissent might have noted that the court avoided relevant facts: the white race outnumbered the Negro in the nation; Negroes had only recently been freed from servitude and awarded legal equality; their alleged inferiority was attested to by a host of pseudo-scientific theories. Harlan, however, simply asserted that candor demanded recognition "that the statute in question had its origin in the purpose . . . to exclude colored people from the coaches" of white people. The Louisiana statute, he maintained, was designed as an annoyance and intended as oppression. "The brand of servitude and degradation" was placed upon a large class of fellow citizens. Harlan concluded: "The thin disguise of equal accommodation for passengers . . . will not mislead anyone, nor atone for the wrong this day done."[8] Harlan's statement about the law's purpose leads to the conclusion that the Louisiana act was unreasonable—by Brown's criteria.

Brown's second argument wrote conservative theory and the prevailing social science "truths" into law. The court explained that the standard of reasonableness is determined "with reference to the established usages, customs, and traditions of the people." This is the underlying social doctrine upon which the case is erected. Law is reasonable when it follows custom. The court implied that law is unreasonable when it violates custom or tradition or seeks to change the folkways of the people. Judge Brown denied that "social prejudices may be overcome by legislation. . . . 'This end can neither be accomplished nor promoted by laws which conflict with the general sentiment of the community upon whom they are designed to operate.'" Brown concluded that "legislation is powerless to eradicate racial instincts. . . . If one race be inferior to the other socially, the Constitution of the United States cannot put them upon the same plane."[9]

---

7 163 U.S. 537 at 551.

8 163 U.S. 537 at 562, 3.

9 163 U.S. 537 at 550, 1. The quote within the quote is persuasive authority from *People* v. *Gallagher*, 93 N.Y. 438 at 448 (1883). Earlier in the *Plessy* opinion the

The court believed that it was only within the duty and capacity of government to guarantee the races equal civil and political rights, and that state laws requiring racial segregation did not constitute a violation of these rights. Brown considered Jim Crow laws an abridgement of social equality.[10] Social equality could not be legislated, and the court approved that it should not be legislated. "If the two races are to meet upon terms of social equality," the court concluded, "it must be the result of natural affinities, a mutual appreciation of each other's merits and a voluntary consent of individuals."[11]

At least four questionable factual allegations or dubious legal and scientific theories were employed by the court to justify the legislation of prejudice: racial segregation is a custom or tradition; law is reasonable when it follows custom and unreasonable when it does not adhere to custom; a contrary decision in *Plessy* would have meant the enforcement of social equality; and law cannot "eradicate [the] racial instincts." Each of these reflects the underlying theories and prejudices upon which the decision rests.

Contrary to the *Plessy* court's contention, segregation in transportation was not consistent with custom or tradition. Racial segregation in the Old South had been unknown.[12] The system of slavery would have been virtually inoperative had Jim Crow prevailed.[13] Nor did Jim Crow spontaneously arise after the war. Negroes and whites frequently shared the same coaches; although sometimes the freedmen were barred from the first-class cars, the races did share the same second-class coaches. A South Carolinian remarked in 1877 that Negroes in his state "were permitted to, and frequently do ride in first-class railway and street cars." At first this had caused trouble, but it was then "so common as hardly to provoke remarks."[14] One reporter observed that Negroes rode "exactly as white people . . . and in the same cars" in Virginia.[15] When the *Plessy*

Supreme Court had recognized that Negroes were considered inferior. Brown had written: "the reputation of belonging to the dominant race, in this instance the white race, is property, in the same sense that a right of action, or of inheritance is property. . . . If he be a white man assigned to a colored coach he may have his action for damages against the company for being deprived of his so-called property. Upon the other hand, if he be called a colored man [and he is] . . . , he has been deprived of no property since he is not lawfully entitled to the reputation of being a white man." 163 U.S. 537 at 545.

10 John Marshall Harlan contended that the issue was a violation of a civil right, not a social right. A railroad, he reasoned, was a public highway, and all rights pertaining to its use were consequently civil rights.

11 163 U.S. 537 at 551.

12 Speaking about the Old South, W. E. B. DuBois later noted, the two races sometimes "lived in the same house, shared in the family life, often attended the same church, and talked and conversed with each other." *The Souls of Black Folks* (McClure, 1903), 184.

13 Three southern states—Florida and Mississippi in 1865, and Texas in 1866—did enact Jim Crow transportation laws. The last of these was repealed in 1873. Franklin Johnson, *The Development of State Legislation Concerning the Free Negro* (Arbor, 1918), 13–16.

14 Belton O'Neall Townsend, "South Carolina Society," *Atlantic Monthly,* 39 (June, 1877), 676.

15 George Cable, *Silent South* (New York, 1885), 85–86, quoted by C. Vann Woodward, *Origins of the New South, 1877–1913* (Vol. 9, *A History of the South,* Louisiana State University, 1951), 210.

court judged it custom, Jim Crow transportation was but a recent Southern creation. By 1896 only eight Southern states had such laws, and seven of the statutes were less than eight years old.[16] These regulations were frequently the enactment of codes of recent practice. The caste system was not yet a custom or tradition; it was a new pattern. Institutionalized prejudice had not hardened; that was the promise of *Plessy* v. *Ferguson*. By its decision the Supreme Court constitutionalized the state enactment of race prejudice.

Laws severely violating custom and tradition are usually unenforceable and may therefore be judged unreasonable. This proposition does not, however, mean that custom must be reflected in law. Customs can exist independently of law, and custom is not violated if it is not enacted in law. If the *Plessy* court had declared the Louisiana statute unconstitutional, custom would not have been violated. The court was right in stating that social equality cannot be enforced, because social relations constitute an area of free selection, and when human relations are legislated by government, they cease to be social and are transformed into political relations.

But if the court had decided that the law was unconstitutional, it would not have been enforcing social equality. The court's illogical predictions to the contrary, enforced commingling of the races would not have occurred. The practices of railroads and the social habits of passengers would not have been immediately affected. The prevailing policy would have been maintained: where informal segregation existed, it would have remained; where commingling occurred, it would have continued. However, the court's decision that "separate but equal" facilities were constitutional did enforce political inequality. Those of each race who were in the habit of mingling with members of the other were denied this right by law.

The court argued that social attitudes cannot be shaped by law.[17] While this was poor history, it was consistent with the popular sociology which emerged after the Civil War. All good Spencerians—most sociologists—agreed that society, the organism of evolution, could not be refashioned by legislation. William Graham Sumner explained that "legislation cannot make mores" and stateways cannot change folkways. Franklin Henry Giddings, Columbia University's counterpart of Sumner, had emphasized "consciousness of kind," a new guise for the "racial instincts" concept, to explain segregation. The implication in *Plessy* was that this social custom, the desire for racially segregated facilities, was grounded in "race instincts." These instincts were unchangeable before man-made law.[18]

---

16 See Johnson, *Development of State Legislation Concerning Free Negro*, 15, 54, 62–207, and Gilbert Stephenson, *Race Discrimination in American Law* (New York, 1910), 216–17.

17 The Massachusetts high court in *Roberts* v. *City of Boston*, 59 Mass. (5 Cush) 198 (1849), the source of the "separate but equal" doctrine, had stated that race prejudice "is not created by law, and probably cannot be changed by law."

18 It is to be noted that the court did not tilt against anti-miscegenation laws. Obviously if a "racial instinct" required segregation, such laws were unnecessary; by instinct everyone would refrain from interracial marriage.

The vague theory of "racial instincts," requiring the separation of the races, provided the "scientific" means for justifying the Southern system of white superiority which had been threatened by the abolition of slavery. One Southerner succinctly stated the new ideology as scientific fact: "there is an instinct, ineradicable and positive, that will keep the races apart."[19] Inferiority of the Negro was an article of Southern faith to which many clung. To yield their position of superiority and accept the Negro as an equal would have overturned the habits nurtured by many decades of slavery. However, only some Southern whites felt threatened by the rising status of Negroes. It was the lower class white who demanded Jim Crow laws when the Negro competed with him for subsistence wages.[20] White superiority could be guaranteed by this new enforced relationship between whites and blacks. For the poor white, caste would protect class. Jim Crow was designed as an "annoying oppression," contrary to the *Plessy* opinion. Separation of the two races would constitute a constant and visible affirmation of the continuing inferiority of blacks to whites.

Out of earlier American doubts and theories a new doctrine had arisen to justify segregation. It merged the discoveries of older thought and the contemporary science.[21] "Racial instinct" and white supremacy were intertwined theories promoted by the Frenchman, Joseph Gobineau,[22] who had not awaited the appearance of Darwinism. Shortly after Gobineau, "survival of the fittest," the popular catchword summary of Darwin's theory of organic evolution, was invoked to establish white superiority over the Negro. Biologists and anthropologists readily confirmed Negro inferiority. The Negro's skull was weighed and his brain measured.

---

19 Quoted by Paul Buck, *The Road to Reunion, 1865–1900* (Vintage, 1959), 299, from Joel Chandler Harris, *Life, Writings, and Speeches of Henry W. Grady* (New York, 1890), 299 ff.

20 Woodward speaks of this process as "one of the paradoxes of Southern history that political democracy for the white man and racial discrimination for the black were often products of the same dynamics." Negroes understood that economic pressures were creating the pressures for Jim Crow. "It took a lot of ritual and Jim Crow to bolster the creed of white supremacy in the bosom of a white man working for black man's wages. . . . A North Carolina Negro wrote: 'The best people in the South do not demand this separate car business . . . and, when they do, it is only to cater to those of their race who, in order to get a big man's smile, will elevate them to place and power.' " Quoted by Woodward, *Origins of the New South, 1877–1913*, 211, from Editorial, *Southland* (Salisbury, N.C.), 1 (1890), 166–67.

21 See William Stanton, *The Leopard's Spots* (University of Chicago, 1960); Oscar Handlin, *Race and Nationality in American Life* (Little, Brown, 1957), c. 1–4; William Jenkins, *Pro-Slavery Thought* (University of North Carolina, 1935); Charles Wesley, "Negro Inferiority in American Thought," *Journal of Negro History*, 25, No. 4 (October 1940), 540; and Leon Litwack, *North of Slavery* (University of Chicago, 1961).

22 In his *Essai sur l'inegalité des races humaines* (1853), he had demonstrated the alleged superiority of the white race over the other races, and Aryans over other whites. A translation of his work appeared in America in 1856, with some notes by an admirer, *Moral and Intellectual Diversity of the Races . . . with an Analytic Introduction and Copious Historical Notes, by H. Hotz to which is Added an Appeal Concerning a Summary of the Latest Scientific Facts Bearing Upon the Question of Unity or Plurality of Species*, by J. C. Nott (1856). For a brief discussion of Gobineau, see . . . Jacques Barzun, *Race: A Study in Modern Superstition* (Meuten, 1938).

Elaborate scientific studies were said to demonstrate that in brain size, pelvic expanse, and a great variety of physiological and psychological traits Negroes were inferior to whites. Comparative disease rates and criminality percentages, always favorable to the whites, "scientifically" established this superiority. It was demonstrated that the Negro's intelligence did not control his actions.[23] Studies showed that he was "light-hearted and carefree," seldom allowing "responsibility to weigh on his mind."[24] Obviously whites were more mature and civilized; they had advanced higher on the evolutionary scale. The Negro's inferiority made him a child while the white was an adult. Some racists sought to modify this bastard offspring of Darwinism by accenting the supremacy of the Anglo-Saxon or Aryan, terms more specific in the categories they excluded than those included. A German strain of racism, born in Romanticism and carried to America by German seminar-trained students, advanced this theory.[25] Either explicitly or implicitly, the Negro was always relegated to hopeless inferiority by the scientific "truths."

The influence of these ideas was apparent in *Plessy* v. *Ferguson*, and probably reflected the dominant thoughts and fears of an uneasy American society. At the same time sectional tensions were being eliminated at the price of abandoning the Negro. The Negro was sacrificed "on the altar of reconciliation, peace, and prosperity." The Supreme Court had anticipated this movement in earlier decisions. Southern writers had contributed their efforts. Thomas Nelson Page, Joel Chandler Harris, and their associates in the South, with the aid of Northern editors and publishing houses, had created an image of a friendly South where the childlike Negroes loved the white folks."[26] Northerners seeking sectional reconciliation with the South put the "bloody shirt" in their trunks and were mouthing the shibboleths of white supremacy and Negro inferiority.[27] Most Northerners who advocated Negro rights embraced a philosophy of segregation and wanted to improve the black man's status within this framework. The aggressive Negro leadership of Frederick Douglass

---

[23] Tests measuring the speed of mental reactions showed that the Negro reacted more rapidly than the white. From this it was concluded that intelligence did not control the black man's actions; actually he was close to the savage. R. M. Burke, "Reaction Time with Reference to Race," *Psychological Review,* 11 (1895), 474.

[24] Charles Johnson and Horace Bond, "Investigation of Racial Differences Prior to 1910," *Journal Negro Education,* 111, No. 3 (July, 1934), 337.

[25] The late nineteenth century germ theory of politics, promoted by Herbert Baxter Adams and John Burgess, the dominant intellectual figures at Johns Hopkins and Columbia, respectively, provided respectable garb for racism. Richard Hofstadter, *Social Darwinism in American Thought* (Boston, 1959), c. 9.

[26] See Buck, *Road to Reunion,* for a discussion of sectional reconciliation, particularly the literature of the period.

[27] C. Vann Woodward, *The Strange Career of Jim Crow* (Oxford, 1955), 52–53. Such expressions frequently appeared in *Nation, Harper's Weekly, North American Review,* and *Atlantic Monthly* of the period. Illustrative of the change in Northern attitudes is the case of Thomas Wentworth Higginson. As a young man he had led a mob to free a fugitive slave from jail, and in the Civil War he had commanded a regiment of Negro troops. Thirty years after Appomattox he shed tears as he read of the death of a slaveowner in a popular story. Buck, *Road to Reunion,* 244. See also Vincent De Santis, *Republicans Face the Southern Question* (Johns Hopkins, 1959), and Stanley Hirshson, *Farewell to the Bloody Shirt* (University of Indiana, 1962).

had been replaced by a new movement more concerned about Negro advancement than integration. The year before the *Plessy* decision became the law of the land, Douglass had died and Booker T. Washington, the spearhead of the new order, delivered the famous Atlanta address calling for a program of racial coexistence grounded in racial separation: "The opportunity to earn a dollar in a factory just now is worth infinitely more than an opportunity to spend a dollar in an opera-house."[28] Social advancement, it was hoped, would occur within the context of segregation.

While the most respected Negro leader was counseling patience and gradual progress through economic advancement, the Supreme Court, in constitutionalizing racial separation, had condemned the Negro to an inferiority confirmed by the legal recogntion of contemporary biological and social science "truths." By not acknowledging that social attitudes could be shaped by law, the court assured that Jim Crow would become custom and treatment of Negroes as second-class citizens habit.[29] The seeds of race hatred were sown. It was Harlan, the constant champion of Negro rights, who predicted that the decision would stimulate "aggressions, more or less brutal or irritating, upon the admitted rights of colored citizens." "What," he added, "can more certainly arouse race hatred?"[30]

---

[28] In the same address he explained, "The wisest among my race understand that the agitation of questions of social equality is the extremist folly. . . ." *Up From Slavery* (Doubleday, 1901), 223–24.

[29] A half century later the brief submitted for the Negro children in *Brown* v. *Board of Education* surveyed the success of the *Plessy* decision: "Without the 'constitutional' sanction which *Plessy* v. *Ferguson* affords, racial segregation could not have become entrenched in the South. . . . The doctrine of *Plessy* v. *Ferguson* was essential to the successful maintenance of a racial caste system in the United States." Herbert Hill et al., *Brief for Appellants in Brown v. Board of Education et al.,* 62.

[30] Harlan concluded: "State enactments, regulating the enjoyment of civil rights, upon the basis of race, and cunningly devised to defeat legitimate results of war, under the pretense of recognizing equality or rights, can have no other result than to render permanent peace impossible, and to keep alive the conflict of the races, the continuance of which must do harm to all concerned." 163 U.S. 537 at 560–61.

*Racist Responses in the North**

Rayford W. Logan

Three of the leading literary magazines—*Harper's New Monthly Magazine, Scribner's* (*Century* after 1881), and the *Atlantic Monthly*—mirrored the refined tastes of the upper classes. . . . [but] Readers had to go to magazines like the *North American Review* and to *Forum*, established in 1886, for regular discussion of the vital issues of the day. . . .

Harper's, Scribner's, Century, and to a less degree the *Atlantic*, regularly employed derisive terms that are rarely used today except in local color fiction, in private conversation, and by the most rabid of "wool-hat" politicians. Many stories, anecdotes, poems, and cartoons referred to Negroes as nigger, niggah, darkey, coon, pickaninny, mammy, aunt, uncle, buck, light-complected-yaller man, yaller hussy. Pralines were "nigger candy." Thomas Nelson Page had an article in the Editor's Drawer of *Harper's* entitled "All the Geography a Nigger Needs to Know." . . .

Negroes were described as being black, ebony, midnight black, black as a crow, or black as a total eclipse. A little white girl asked her mother whether God had made an "ebony" little boy. When her mother replied in the affirmative, the girl queried: "Mama, do you suppose God thought he was *pretty*?" Negroes were thick-lipped; they had flat noses, big ears and feet, kinky or woolly hair. An anonymous traveler in the "great black" regions of the South pictured "the uncouth, strangely shaped animal-looking Negro or mulatto, who seems mentally, even more than by his physical characteristics, to belong to a race entirely distinct from that of the white race around them." The writer of the article understood why white women were afraid of Negroes, since they were "a race alien, animal, half savage, easily made sullen or aroused to fury."[1]

Negroes were made ludicrous by the bestowal of titles, names of famous men or of folk expressions. Among the choice ones were Colonel, Senator, Sheriff, Apollo Belvedere, George Washington, Webster, Abraham Lincum, Napoleon Boneyfidey Waterloo, Venus Milo Clevins, Columbus, Pomp, Caesar, Lady Adeliza Chimpanzee, Prince Orang Outan, Hieronymous, Ananias, Solomon Crow, Piddlekins, Sosrus Dismal, Asmodeus, Bella Donna Mississippi Idaho, Violetta Marie Evaline Rose Christian, Nuttin 'Tal, Had-a-Plenty, and Wanna-Mo. The ultimate was achieved in Henri Ritter Demi Ritter Emmi Ritter Sweet-potato Cream Tartar Caroline Bostwick.

---

* Rayford W. Logan, *The Negro in American Life and Thought* (New York: Dial Press, 1954). By permission of the publisher.

1 Editor's Drawer, *Harper's*, 74 (May 1887), 993 (italics as in the original); Unsigned, "Studies in the South," *Atlantic Monthly*, 49 (February 1882), 183.

Virtually every derogatory stereotype was affixed upon the Negro. Sometimes several appeared in one passage or the same story. Thus, one colored woman was described as being a "typical Negro," since she was improvident, emotional, gossipy, kindhearted, high-tempered, vain, dishonest, idle, working only two or three days a week, and " 'res'n' " up the rest of the week, with always a hearty appetite and " 'miz'ry in de bres'.' " The Negro of Barbados was *sui generis,* for

> There is nothing like him on earth, above it, or under it. He will lie, cheat, and steal beyond all comprehension. He is impudent to a degree hardly to be understood by an American. They are outwardly very devout, but it never enters their heads to practice what they preach. As an English clergyman living among them once said, "They will go to communion, and steal yams on the way home."[2]

In various articles, stories, anecdotes, poems, and cartoons, the Negro was made at appear superstitious, dull and stupid, imitative and hence not creative, ignorant, suspicious, happy-go-lucky, improvident, lazy, immoral, criminal; he was a liar, a thief, and a drunkard. He used big words which he did not understand. He liked fine clothes and trinkets, chickens, " 'watermillions,' " " 'Sweet-'tators,' " and " ' 'possum.' " The inevitable razor-totin' Negro made his appearance. Preachers, and to a less degree lawyers, were the frequent butt of jokes. The Negro was portrayed in the plantation tradition as a faithful slave and servant. But he could not adapt to freedom. Occasionally he was revealed as the "tragic mulatto." While some articles and other contributions treated Chinese, Indians, Irish, Germans, and other immigrants in general in an unfavorable light, these aliens and the oldest Americans fared better than did the Negro. Jews, partly because articles about them were written by Jews, received more kindly treatment than did other minorities. . . .

The emigration of Negroes, which had been frequently advocated during the 1880s, again became a favorite theme in the 1890s. Page saw no need in 1892 for deportation since the Negro race in the United States would soon die out. Blyden opposed large-scale emigration until a new generation of both whites and blacks developed different ideas. At the turn of the century, John Roach Straton of Macon, Georgia, argued that conditions elsewhere should be made so inviting that Negroes would want to emigrate.[3]

Toward the latter part of the century, however, all other topics were submerged by the plethora of articles on American expansion. Social Darwinists[4] enjoyed the advantage of a generally accepted American belief in the inherent inferiority of the Negro when they justified that expansion on racial grounds. Reciprocally the failure of Negroes and

---

[2] A. Van Cleef, "Barbadoes," *Harper's,* 54 (February 1877), 387.

[3] Thomas Nelson Page, *A Southerner on the Negro Question,* pp. 411–12; Edward W. Blyden, "The African Problem," *North American Review,* 161 (September 1895), 327–39; John Roach Straton, "Will Education Solve the Race Problem?," ibid., 170 (June 1900), 800–801.

[4] Richard Hofstadter, *Social Darwinism in American Thought, 1860–1915* (Philadelphia and London, 1944); Josiah Strong, *Our Country* (New York, 1885).

other dark peoples in distant lands to match strides with Europeans and Americans was invoked to justify the inability of the American Negro to exercise rights which the Constitution conferred upon him. . . . Brazil was also cited in 1879 as "proof" that "the mixed races are invariably bad; they seem to combine all the worst characteristics of the two parent stocks. . . . A light mulatto or an almost black one may be a very decent sort of fellow; but the brown half-and-half is nearly always lazy, and stupid and vain." But shortly before this, another writer had offered Haiti as a "discouraging commentary on the theories of those humanitarians who believe in the ultimate elevation of the negro to the level of the Caucasian race. There is a backward tendency of which barbarism seems to be the inevitable goal unless a new people take possession of the soil."[5] . . .

Several articles in the *Atlantic* during this early period also revealed evidence of belief in the superiority of the Anglo-Saxon. But the *North American Review* surpassed all others in publishing articles which presented similar views. Typical of these was the prediction of Gayarré in 1877 that, "if contrary to the teachings of history and science, the negro should rise to an equality of intelligence and energy with the Caucasian," there would be a final struggle between the two races from which the Caucasian would emerge victorious.[6]

The revived creed of racial superiority was nurtured in the 1880s by agitation for Chinese exclusion, the wiping out of the Indian frontier, and the growing momentum for the scramble for Africa. A review in the *Atlantic* of Francis Galton's *Inquiries into Human Faculty and Its Development* agreed, 1883, that Chinese, Indians, and Negroes should be excluded from the earth and the sooner the better. But Social Darwinism continued to find a sturdy rationale in the growing deterioration of the Negro's status in the United States. A writer in the *Review*, 1881, asserted that "in no time or clime have the Caucasian race ever consented to live with inferior ones *save as rulers.*" Numerous articles supporting the concept of the inherent inferiority of the American Negro appeared in the *Review* and *Century*. John Fiske's famous lecture, "Manifest Destiny," which glorified the progress made by the Teutonic and "Aryan" races and praised English imperialism was published in *Harper's* in 1885.[7]

The refrain continued in the 1890s, reenforced undoubtedly by some of the speeches by Southerners who opposed the Lodge bill. Bryce argued that the Negro had not been able to protect himself in the exercise of suffrage because he was naturally inferior to the white man. Thomas Nelson Page contended: "The Negro has not progressed, not because he was a slave, but because he does not possess the faculties to raise himself above slavery. He has not yet exhibited the qualities of any race which has advanced." He also cited Liberia, Haiti, and the Dominican

5 R. W. Wright, "Richmond Since the War," *Scribner's*, 14 (July 1877), 311–12; Herbert H. Smith, "The Metropolis of the Amazons," ibid., 18 (May 1879), 65–77; Edmund Clarence Stedman, "Christophe," *Century*, 23 (November 1881), 34–35.

6 Charles Gayarré, "The Southern Question," *North American Review*, 125 (November 1877), 494–97.

7 W. Henry Holland, "Heredity," *Atlantic Monthly*, 52 (October 1883), 452; H. H. Chalmers, "The Effects of Negro Suffrage," *North American Review*, 122 (March 1881), 239–48. Italics as in the original; Hofstadter, *Social Darwinism*, p. 153.

Republic in order to establish the "fact" that the Negro did not possess the qualifications to conduct his own government. Theodore Roosevelt affirmed in 1895: "A perfectly stupid race can never rise to a very high plane; the negro, for instance, has been kept down as much by lack of intellectual development as anything else." Marion L. Dawson, former Judge Advocate-General of Virginia, explained in 1897 that the South was influenced by the same ruling spirit which had characterized the Anglo-Saxon from the beginning of his history to that time. He believed that the whole problem of the South was "whether the negro or the white man should occupy the seat of power; whether the inferior should dominate the superior, and whether ignorance should rule intelligence." Straton in 1900 declared that the Negro showed all the defects of a degenerate race —lessened fertility, prevalence of venereal and other diseases caused by immorality and resulting in a large infant mortality. The Negro would not, therefore, be able to adapt to Anglo-Saxon civilization.[8] . . .

A natural consequence of the acceptance of the concept of the inherent inferiority of the Negro was advocacy of the "White Man's Burden." Bryce, however, wanted it clearly understood that assumption of the burden did not involve mixing of the races. . . . Harper's ran in serial form "A White Man's Africa" by Poultney Bigelow, a well-known New York journalist and lawyer, which also gave the assurance that the English in South Africa were not mixing their blood with that of the natives. But the "degeneracy" of the Portuguese in Africa stemmed from the fact that since the fifteenth century they had intermarried with Negroes. The North American Review, as usual, presented articles praising and condemning European imperialism in India, China, and Africa, but the majority extolled the blessings of civilization that were being carried to the benighted heathen. . . . Most readers . . . probably agreed with the Reverend W. Garden Blaikie that European imperialism would "issue in great good to the Dark Continent." Even conditions in the Belgian Congo found favor in the eyes of a contributor to Century in 1896 and 1897. Stanley urged in 1896 that European partitioning of Africa should be looked upon as "civilization" rather than as "colonization." Another writer endorsed Rudyard Kipling's well-known views. There were, finally, undertones and overtones of racism in the "Anglo-Saxon mystique" which led Captain Alfred T. Mahan, Andrew Carnegie, Sir Charles Beresford, and others to favor an alliance between the United States and Great Britain and their eventual unification.[9]

---

[8] Bryce, "Thoughts on the Negro Problem," North American Review, 153 (December 1891), 641–60; Thomas Nelson Page, A Southerner on the Negro Question, pp. 411–13; Theodore Roosevelt, "Kidd's 'Social Evolution,'" 161 (July 1895), 94–109; Dawson, "Will the South Be Solid Again?," ibid., 164 (February 1897), 193–98; John Roach Straton, "Will Education Solve the Race Problem?" North American Review, 170 (June 1900), pp. 784–801; Washington, A Reply, pp. 221–32.

[9] Poultney Bigelow, "White Man's Africa," Harper's, 94 (January 1897), 775–89; Marquis of Lorne, "The Partition of Africa," North American Review, 151 (December 1890), 701–12; W. Garden Blaikie, "Central Africa Since the Death of Livingstone," ibid., 165 (September 1897), 318–32; E. J. Glave, "Glave in the Heart of Africa," Century 52 (October 1896), 918–33; Glave, "New Conditions in Central Africa," ibid., 53 (April 1897), 900–15; Henry M. Stanley, "The Story of the Development of Africa," ibid., 51 (February 1896), 500–09; Henry Rutgers Marshall, "Rudyard Kipling and Racial Instincts," ibid., 58 (July 1899), 375–77.

The way had thus been prepared for the acceptance of American imperialism on racial and moral grounds. One writer, reversing a position that he had taken in 1896, urged in 1898 permanent American intervention in Cuba in order to prevent the domination of the whites by the blacks. . . . Several articles supported the annexation of Hawaii and the Philippines by the plea that it was the duty of the United States to assume the obligation of civilizing backward peoples. An article in the *Atlantic* described most Cuban Negroes as ignorant, boastful, untruthful, ungrateful, fond of trinkets; "docility, except under abuse, is their most marked trait." Several editorials in *Century* emphasized the "purity" of the motives of the United States and endorsed the assumption of responsibility toward backward races.[10]

But opposition to American expansion also stemmed from racial considerations. Senator Vest (Democrat) condemned the idea of conferring citizenship upon the "half-civilized, piratical, muck-running inhabitants of two thousand islands, seven thousand miles distant." A less well-known author added that American expansion would bring vexing problems similar to those in the South. "Pitchfork" Ben Tillman naturally expressed opposition to annexation on racial grounds in the most extreme language. There would always be racial antagonism, he contended, because the Anglo-Saxon walked on the necks of every race with which he came in contact and resistance to his will meant destruction to the weaker race. Since the United States had its own race problem, it would be foolhardy to incorporate 9 million more brown men under the flag. How could the Republicans, he inquired, defend their abandonment of the Negroes at home, and at the same time defend McKinley's policy of subjugating the Filipinos with greater hardships than Southern Negroes had to endure. Probably more in triumph than in sorrow, Tillman concluded: "And no Republican leader . . . will now dare to wave the bloody shirt and preach a crusade against the South's treatment of the negro. The North has a bloody shirt of its own. Many thousands of them have been made into shrouds for murdered Filipinos, done to death because they were fighting for liberty." Even Carl Schurz, whom Du Bois has called "the finest type of immigrant American," and who had written a report shortly after the Civil War castigating the South, wrote in 1898:

> We are vexed by a very troublesome race problem in the United States now. That race problem is still unsolved, and it would be very sanguine to say that there is a satisfactory solution in near prospect. Cool-headed men think that we have enough of that. What will be the consequence if we indefinitely add to it by bringing under this republican government big lots of other incompatible races—races far more intractable, too, than those with which we have so far had to deal?[11]

---

[10] Leonard Wood, "The Existing Conditions and Needs in Cuba," *North American Review*, 168 (May 1899), 593–601; see other articles listed in Betty R. Jordan, "The Negro as Portrayed in the *North American Review*, 1877–1900" (M.A. thesis, Howard University). See also Herbert Pelham Williams, "The Outlook in Cuba," *Atlantic Monthly*, 83 (June 1899), 827–36 and Queen C. Green "The Negro as Portrayed in *Scribner's Monthly* and *Century*, 1877–1901" (M.A. thesis, Howard University).

[11] G. G. Vest, "Objections to Annexing the Philippines," *North American Review*,

Two of the best-known advocates of the Social Gospel revealed their astigmatism on the plight of the American Negro. Walter Rauschenbusch, who was born of German parents in Rochester, New York, on April 15, 1861, was equally unconcerned during the period under investigation about the political condition of Negroes in the South. Purvis M. Carter, who made a detailed study of his writings, including *For the Right* in the Yale University Library, *Dawn* and *Independent*, found that the great Baptist leader devoted practically no attention prior to 1901 to this subject. In May, 1890, Rauschenbusch urged that a petition be circulated in behalf of the downtrodden people of Russia. But in September of the same year, when Mississippi was revising its constitution and the fate of the Lodge bill hung in the balance, he wrote in *For the Right*, the organ of the Brotherhood of the Kingdom:

> Our institutions are the admiration and the inspirational beaconlight of noblemen from the Straits of Gibraltar to the bleak huts of Siberian exiles. Whenever a hand seeks to rear the banner of liberty, it is nerved by the thought of a great nation beyond the sea, in which men are free and equal.

He recognized that social equality had not been achieved: "Political liberty is ours, now let us use it to secure social equality."[12]

Lyman Abbott went further than did Gladden or Rauschenbusch, for he explicitly endorsed some Southern viewpoints. This endorsement is all the more significant because of his previous views and activities. He had publicly favored emancipation before Lincoln issued his preliminary Emancipation Proclamation. He had opposed granting Negroes immediate political responsibility because he would confine the administration of government "always to the moral and the intelligent." Since the South possessed neither the free schools nor the free churches necessary to develop these qualities, he believed as early as 1864 that the North should supply them. As corresponding secretary of the American Union Commission and as general secretary of the American Freedmen's Union Commission from 1865 to July 1, 1869, he had "performed a useful service in co-ordinating the efforts of the non-denominational benevolent societies, in acting as an intermediary between them and the Freedmen's Bureau, and in general stimulating interest in moral reconstruction." While he believed that children in the South might choose to attend school with companions of their own race, he insisted that no child should be barred from any Commission school because of his color. He was a gradualist as far as the abolition of segregation was concerned, but he was convinced that, once segregation was accepted, it could not be abolished. But in the 1880s Abbott began to be an apostle of the "New South." It is probable that his "conversion" was prompted by Henry W. Grady's speech which he heard in 1886. The *Christian Union*, which became the

---

167 (January 1899), 112–20; B. R. Tillman, "Causes of Southern Opposition to Imperialism," ibid., 171 (October 1900), 439–46; Carl Schurz, "Thoughts on American Imperialism," *Century*, 56 (September 1898), 781–88.

12 Purvis M. Carter, "The Astigmatism of the Social Gospel, 1877–1901," (M.A. thesis, Howard University).

Outlook in 1891, and which frequently reflected Abbott's views, supported the Blair bill in 1884 and 1888, but it took a positive stand against the Lodge bill. By 1890 Abbott had come to believe that the wisest policy was to allow the South to administer her own future. "The negro problem," averred an editorial in the *Christian Union* on June 12, 1890, "must be worked out by the negroes and the white men of the South with the aid of the North, not by the North or the Federal government over the heads of the negroes and the white men."[13] His conversion is also apparent in an article in the *North American Review* in 1898 in which he discussed the Indian problem in the United States. He advocated the abolition of reservations and urged that the Indian be treated as a man. He then added:

> Treat them [the Indians] as we have treated the negro. As a race the African is less competent than the Indian, but we do not shut the negroes up in reservations and put them in charge of politically appointed parents called agents. The lazy grow hungry; the criminal are punished; the industrious get on. And though the sporadic cases of injustice are often tragic, they are the gradually disappearing relics of a slavery that is past, and the negro is finding his place in American life gradually, both as a race and as an individual.

Three years later, after touring South Atlantic schools and attending the conference of the Southern Educational Board at Winston-Salem, North Carolina, he again gave explicit endorsement of Southern points of view. He approved the Southern suffrage amendments. The Southerner, he found, had less prejudice against the Negro and more interest in his welfare than did the Northerner. The South desired education for the Negro but felt, realistically, that it should be industrial rather than literary. Attempts to force political or social equality would inflict "uncalculable" injury on the Negro and on the nation.[14] Professor William Warren Sweet, perhaps the most authoritative historian of the church in the United States, has concluded that "no religious leader in modern times has exercised a more abiding influence than has Lyman Abbott."[15] Professor Sweet was not, of course, endorsing the contributions, positive and negative—not one of some 100 magazine articles by Abbott between 1890 and 1900 bore a title referring specifically to the Negro—that Abbott made to the development of the concept of the "New South" that religious and other intellectual molders of American thought were implanting in the minds of the American people. . . .

---

13 Ira V. Brown, "Lyman Abbott and Freedmen's Aid, 1865–1869," *Journal of Southern History*, 15 (February 1949), 22–38. Professor Brown generously permitted the author to use relevant parts of his manuscript which is now being published by the Harvard University Press.

14 Lyman Abbott, "Our Indian Problem," *North American Review*, 167 (December 1898), 719–28; *Outlook*, 67 (April 1901), 948.

15 William Warren Sweet, *Makers of Christianity* (New York, 1937), 3, 320.